A

HANDBOOK FOR TRAVELLERS

IN

CENTRAL ITALY.

PART I.

The Editor of the HANDBOOK for CENTRAL ITALY is very solicitous to be favoured with corrections of any mistakes and omissions which may be discovered by persons who have made use of the book. Those communications especially will be welcomed which are founded upon personal knowledge, and accompanied by the name of the writer to authenticate them. Travellers willing to make such communications are requested to have the kindness to address them to the Editor of the HANDBOOK, care of Mr. Murray, Albemarle Street.

CAUTION TO INNKEEPERS AND OTHERS.—The Editor of the Handbooks has learned from various quarters that a person or persons have of late been extorting money from innkeepers, tradespeople, artists, and others, on the Continent, under pretext of procuring recommendations and favourable notices of them and their establishments in the Handbooks for Travellers. The Editor therefore thinks proper to warn all whom it may concern, that recommendations in the Handbooks are not to be obtained by purchase, and that the persons alluded to are not only unauthorised by him, but are totally unknown to him. All those, therefore, who put confidence in such promises, may rest assured that they will be defrauded of their money without attaining their object.—1853.

** No attention can be paid to letters from Hotel-keepers in praise of their own inns; and the postage of them is so onerous, that they cannot be received.

A.

HANDBOOK FOR TRAVELLERS

IN

CENTRAL ITALY.

PART I.

SOUTHERN TUSCANY AND PAPAL STATES.

𝔚𝔦𝔱𝔥 𝔞 𝔗𝔯𝔞𝔟𝔢𝔩𝔩𝔦𝔫𝔤 𝔐𝔞𝔭.

THIRD EDITION,

CAREFULLY REVISED AND AUGMENTED.

LONDON:

JOHN MURRAY, ALBEMARLE STREET.

PARIS: A. & W. GALIGNANI AND CO.; STASSIN AND XAVIER.

FLORENCE: MOLINI, AND GOODBAN.

1853.

PREFACE TO THE THIRD EDITION.

In the former editions of the Handbook for Central Italy the description of Rome and its Environs was included: but the Publisher having good reason to believe that it would be more convenient for the traveller that it should be separate, the part containing Rome and its neighbourhood will hereafter form a volume apart.

The Publisher thinks proper to state, that the author of the former editions of this Handbook (Mr. Octavian Blewitt) has been prevented superintending the present, and is therefore not responsible for the additions, alterations, and omissions made in it: the greater part of the original work, however, has been retained; the changes now made are the results of personal observation made by the Editor during a recent residence in Italy, and travels of considerable duration and extent.

INTRODUCTION.

1. *General Topography.* — 2. *Government.* — 3. *Justice.* — 4. *Revenue.* —
5. *Ecclesiastical Establishment.* — 6. *Army and Navy.* — 7. *Education.* —
8. *Commerce and Manufactures.* — 9. *Agriculture.* — 10. *Characteristics of
the Country.* — 11. *Pelasgic Architecture.* — 12. *Cyclopean Architecture.*
— 13. *The Etruscans.* — 14. *The Romans.* — 15. *Christian Architecture.* —
16. *Christian Sculpture.* — 17. *Schools of Painting.* — 18. *Books.* — 19. *Maps.*
— 20. *Chronological Tables.*

1. GENERAL TOPOGRAPHY.

The Papal States are bounded on the north by the Po, which separates
them from the Lombardo-Venetian kingdom, on the north-east and
east by the Adriatic, on the south-east by the kingdom of Naples, on
the west and south-west by the Mediterranean, and on the west and
north-west by Tuscany and Modena. The superficial extent of the
Roman States, by the most accurate computation, is 12,152 geographical square miles, of 60 to a degree. No census having been taken
for some years, the population is not very accurately known ; in 1844 it
amounted to 2,907,355, and, allowing for the ordinary annual increase,
it cannot now fall much short of 3,063,000 ; from these data it results
that the average population does not exceed 245 for every square mile.
It is calculated, however, that only a third part of the surface is cultivated, and a considerable portion of the country, being mountainous
or desolated by malaria, is very thinly inhabited. Of its numerous
rivers, the Tiber alone is navigable to any distance from its mouth ;
the Fiora is the next river in size on the side of the Mediterranean ; on
the coast of the Adriatic the Tronto and the Metauro are the most important. The two principal seaports are Civita Vecchia and Ancona ;
the ancient harbours of Terracina, Porto d'Anzio, and Ostia have
been rendered useless to vessels of large burden by immense accumula-
tions of sand, and in the latter case by the rapid extension of the Delta
of the Tiber. The largest lakes are those of Thrasimene or Perugia,
Bolsena, and Bracciano.

The territories comprised in the Papal States have been acquired at
various periods, by inheritance, by cession, and by conquest. In the
eighth century the duchy of Rome, which constituted the first temporal possession of the Holy See, was conferred by Pepin and Charlemagne on Stephen II., with a large portion of the exarchate of Ravenna,
which they had conquered from the Lombards. The duchy extended
along the sea-coast, from Terracina to the mouth of the Tiber, and
included the southern Campagna, the Pontine marshes, and the Sabine
and Volscian mountains. In the eleventh century the duchy of
Benevento became the property of the Holy See, by cession to Leo IX.
of the emperor Henry II., in exchange for the revenues of the city
of Bamberg. In the twelfth century the allodial possessions of the
Countess Matilda passed by inheritance to the Church ; they included what is now known as the Patrimony of St. Peter, extending
from Rome to Bolsena, the coast-line from the mouth of the Tiber
to the Tuscan frontier, the March of Ancona, and the duchy of

Spoleto. On the return of the Popes from Avignon, and on the subsequent subjection of the petty princes of Romagna and Umbria, other important possessions gradually fell into their hands. In 1463 they obtained the principality of Pontecorvo, in the kingdom of Naples; and about the same period Perugia, Orvieto, Città di Castello, and several other towns acknowledged the sovereignty of the successors of St. Peter; and the conquests of Julius II. added to the dominions of the Holy See the important provinces of Bologna and Romagna. Ancona was occupied by the Papal troops in 1532; Ferrara was seized in 1597; the Duke of Urbino abdicated in favour of the Church in 1626; and a few years later the Papal territory received its last addition in the fiefs of Castro and Ronciglione, wrested by Innocent X. from the Farnese family. Such were the temporal possessions of the Popes when the wars arising out of the French revolution upset nearly all the governments of Italy. Into the changes which resulted in the States of the Church it is unnecessary to enter in detail; suffice it to say that the Popes, after a lengthened exile and spoliation, were reinstated on the throne of St. Peter at the close of the war in 1814, and that the temporal possessions of the Holy See have, from that time, remained as they were settled by the Treaty of Vienna; which restored to Rome the Marches, with Camerino, the duchy of Benevento, the principality of Pontecorvo, the legations of Ravenna, Bologna, and Ferrara, save, however, that part of the latter province situated on the left bank of the Po, which Austria retained, together with the right of occupying the *places* of Ferrara and Commacchio. The protest made by Cardinal Consalvi at the Congress of Vienna, against the latter measures, has hitherto remained a dead letter; but the occupation of the city as well as the citadel of Ferrara by Austria in 1847, on the ground that the word *place* in the treaty applied to the entire city, roused a spirit of nationality throughout Italy, and a feeling of sympathy throughout Europe, which momentarily restored it and its fortress to the Pope, to be subsequently occupied, as well as the greater part of the territories of the Church, by an Austrian army.

The States are divided into twenty provinces. The first is the Comarca of Rome, including within its jurisdiction the capital and the Agro Romano. The other nineteen are divided into two classes, Legations and Delegations. The Legations are governed by Cardinals, and the Delegations, for the most part, by Prelates, with the title of *Monsignore*. There are six *Legations*—Bologna, Ferrara, Forli, Ravenna, Urbino (with Pesaro), and Velletri. There are thirteen *Delegations* or Provinces—Ancona, Macerata, Camerino, Fermo, Ascoli, Perugia, Spoleto, Rieti, Viterbo, Orvieto, Civita Vecchia, Frosinone (with Pontecorvo), and Benevento. The Legations and Delegations are divided into Districts, the latter into Governorships, and these again into Communes.

2. GOVERNMENT.

An unlimited elective hierarchy, the head of which is the Pope, who is chosen by the College of Cardinals out of their own body. The number of the Cardinals was limited to seventy by Sixtus V., in allusion to the number of disciples whom our Saviour commissioned to spread the Gospel throughout the world; but, until the present year, the Sacred College, as it is designated, has been rarely complete. All vacancies in their body are filled up by the Pope, whose power in this respect is absolute. The Cardinals constitute the Sacred College, and are the Princes of the Church. They rank in three classes:—1. The six Cardinal Bishops, who hold the suburban dioceses of Ostia and Velletri, Porto and Civita Vecchia, Sabina, Palestrina, Albano, and Frascati; 2. Fifty Cardinal Priests; 3. Fourteen Cardinal Deacons. On the death of the Pope the supreme power is exercised by the Cardinal Chamberlain (Camerlengo) for nine days, and during that time he has the privilege of coining money bearing his own name and arms. On the ninth day the funeral of the deceased Pontiff takes place, and on the following the Cardinals meet in secret conclave to elect his successor. They are shut up till they agree: the voting is secret, and the election is determined by a majority of two-thirds, subject to the privilege possessed by Austria, France, and Spain, to impose each a veto on one candidate. The conditions of the election of late have required that the Pope be a Cardinal, and an Italian by birth. The government is administered by a Council of Ministers, of whom the Cardinal Secretary of State is the chief and most influential member, he holding at the same time the Portfolio of Foreign Affairs. The other ministers are, of the Interior, of Grace and Justice, of Finance, of War, and of Commerce, Agriculture and the Fine Arts. All may be laymen except the Cardinal Secretary of State, but at present one half are Prelates or Ecclesiastics: the old system, or Hierarchy of Congregazioni, has been abolished since the events of 1849, except for purely ecclesiastical purposes.

The municipal government of Rome is intrusted to the Senator, an officer of high antiquity; and generally one of the great patrician families; and the Conservatori, with a municipal body of forty Counsellors, who, having in the first instance been appointed by the Pope, now re-elect themselves, one half of the number being selected from amongst the nobility or large proprietors, the other from the middle classes and tradespeople. Their functions are purely municipal in the most contracted sense, neither exercising magisterial duties nor interfering with the police. The revenues of the city amount to about 800,000 scudi (160,000l.) annually, of which two-thirds are seized upon by the government, leaving the municipality with very inadequate means; hence it is that there are few capitals in Europe in so bad a state as Rome as regards cleansing, lighting, paving, &c.

The Auditor of the Camera, the Auditor of the Pope (Uditore Santissimo), and the Major-Domo or Steward of the Household, are prelates of high rank. The Pope's Auditor examines the titles of candidates for bishoprics, and decides all cases of appeal to the Pope on ecclesiastical questions; the Major-Domo is an officer who has the management of the Pope's household, and is entitled to a cardinal's hat on quitting office; the Maestro di Camera, also a prelate, and generally a personal friend of the reigning Pontiff, is charged with everything relative to ceremonial, presentations to the Pope, &c.

3. JUSTICE.

Justice is administered throughout the States of the Church according to the laws of the " Corpus Juris," and the Canon Law. The Judges are appointed by the Pope. They must be above thirty years of age, of unblemished character, of legitimate birth, doctors of law, and have practised at the bar as advocates for at least five years. The administration of justice in the Papal States is of a rather complicated machinery. In *civil cases* there is in the chief town of every province, delegation, and legation a judicial functionary bearing the title of Governatore, Guidice Conciliatore or Assessore, who takes cognizance of all affairs where the amount in litigation does not exceed 200 scudi. In the capital of every province there is a tribunal of 1ᵐ· Istanza, to which there is an appeal from the decisions of the local governors ; this court takes cognizance of all suits where the sum exceeds 200 scudi ; in Rome the Tribunale di 1ᵐ· Istanza is known by the name of the Tribunale del Senatore.

There are three Courts of Appeal—at Bologna, Macerata, and Rome— to revise the decisions of the Tribunale di 1ᵐ· Istanza; should there be a diversity of opinion, *i. e.* should the decision of the inferior court and of that of appeal be different, there is a second appeal to all the chambers of the Ruota united. The foregoing courts are courts of law and equity, but there is still a superior jurisdiction, corresponding in some measure to the French Cour de Cassation—the Corte della Segnatura, sitting at Rome, which can annul the decrees of the two inferior courts for errors of procedure, in which case the parties are sent before another tribunal for a new trial.

In *criminal cases* the governors have jurisdiction as far as inflicting one year's imprisonment or hard labour ; beyond this the tribunals of 1ᵐ· Istanza, sitting as a criminal court, alone have jurisdiction, even in cases carrying with them capital punishment. They also act as Courts of Appeal from the decisions of the local governors. The Criminal Court in Rome, however, is differently constituted : it is there called the Tribunale del Governatore, and composed of the Governor of Rome and four assessors. As in civil cases, the three Courts of Appeal take cognizance of the decisions of the Tribunals of 1ᵐ· Istanza in criminal matters, except in Rome, where a special court, the *Sacra Consulta*, acts as a Court of Appeal from the Tribunale del Governatore of the capital. All the courts in civil cases are open to the public, whilst in criminal the whole of the proceedings are conducted with closed doors. There are Tribunals of Commerce in all the chief towns ; in case of appeal the decisions attacked are carried before the Tribunale di Commercio at Ancona.

Such is the jurisdiction in all cases where laymen only are concerned, but should an ecclesiastic, or any one in the *remotest degree* connected with the Church, be mixed up in the litigation, then the cause, be it civil or criminal, must be carried before the Bishop's Court, which has alone jurisdiction. There is a Bishop's Court in every diocese, that in Rome being the Tribunale del Vicario. From the Bishops there is an appeal to the Court of the Metropolitan. This system is fraught with evils, and to such an extent that there are many persons who refuse to hold any kind of monetary transactions with ecclesiastics. In the provinces, the bishops, not being themselves lawyers, and little conversant with even the Canon Law, generally appoint needy lawyers of the locality to act for them. Whilst in the lay courts justice in civil cases is considered as being very impartially although slowly administered, it is quite different in the ecclesiastical, where venality is unhappily the rule instead of being the exception.

But perhaps the greatest stigma on the impartial administration of the law in the Papal States is as regards political offences, which are deferred to a secret tribunal, called the Consulta, and of late years in the greater number of cases to that of Rome. Here the prisoner is only permitted to employ the sworn advocate of this exceptional tribunal. He is never allowed to see the witnesses, nor to know the nature of the evidence adduced against him, and his paid advocate is not even permitted to divulge to him what may take place, or the nature of the accusation against him. Except at Rome, where there are four advocates to this Inquisitorial Court, he has no choice for his defence. The sentences are only communicated, if capital, a few hours before being carried into execution. The Vicario's Court at Rome, and the Bishops' Courts in the provinces, have the power of imprisoning summarily all persons, and especially females, on grounds of immorality, a power which leads to most crying injustice in a country where the immorality of the clergy is not uncommon, and where denunciations are often made, not from the purest motives.

In criminal proceedings there are no limits to imprisonment on suspicion, and the trial is often indefinitely delayed, the accused having no power to bring his case before the judges. This dilatory system, the rare infliction of fines, the absence of liberation on bail, and the universal practice of imprisonment for all kinds of offences, tend to keep the prisons constantly full, and constitute one of the great reproaches against the Papal Government. It is calculated that the average number of persons actually in confinement is about 6000. There are nine prisons for convicted criminals—Civita Vecchia, Ancona, Porto d'Anzio, Spoleto, Narni, St. Leo, the Castle of St. Angelo, Civita Castellana, and Palliano, the latter chiefly for political prisoners.

4. REVENUE.

According to the last published (1853) statement of the Finance Minister, the income of the Papal States is estimated at 11,110,569 *scudi* (2,364,000*l.*), and the expenditure at 12,906,419 (2,745,900*l.*), leaving a deficit of 1,795,850 *scudi* (381,900*l.*). The expense of collecting the revenue amounts to 25 per cent. on the gross receipts. More than one-half of the net revenue (4½ millions) goes to pay the interest on the public debt; 600,000 *scudi* (125,000*l.*) to defray the expenses of the Court, the College of Cardinals, diplomatic agents, the Pope's private household, &c.; 1,504,000 (313,330*l.*) for the expenses of the army; the private expenditure of the sovereign amounts to about 60,000 *scudi* (12,000*l.*).

The following are some of the items of which the revenue is made up: customs and excise (*dazi di consume*), 5,022,900 *scudi*; direct taxes, 2,736,400; post-office, 339,800; stamps, 842,100; mint, 906,370; lottery, 796,050: the latter demoralising impost scarcely yields 300,000 dollars profit to the State, after paying the expenses of collection; the number of tickets issued in the city of Rome alone is 55 millions annually. The land-tax forms the principal item of the direct taxation, 2,286,830 *scudi* (486,500*l.*), and is calculated at from 20 to 25 per cent. on the gross rental.

5. ECCLESIASTICAL ESTABLISHMENT.

Exclusive of Rome, the Papal States comprise 9 archbishoprics and 52 bishoprics : the archbishoprics are those of Bologna, Benevento, Camerino (with Treja), Ferrara, Fermo, Ravenna, Spoleto, Bevagna (with Trevi), and Urbino. The secular clergy are supposed to amount to about 35,000, the monks to upwards of 10,000, and the nuns to more than 8000. The number of monasteries, as far as we have been able to ascertain, is about 1800, and the convents 600. The office of *Prelate* is peculiar to the Papal States ; this dignitary is not, as is generally supposed, a bishop or necessarily an Ecclesiastic, although bound to celibacy as long as he retains his office, but a high official servant of the Government, either civil or ecclesiastical, with the title of Monsignore. Not being in many instances in holy orders, and unless he has been ordained, he becomes a layman on retiring from office, and may even marry. It is, however, essential to the candidate for the *prelatura* that he possess the degree of Doctor of Laws, and enjoy a small independent income. From 200 to 250 of these officers are employed in various departments of the State ; some are attached to the court of the Pope, and others act as secretaries or members of congregations or Government boards. It is the stepping-stone to preferment in most of the higher offices of state : the Prelate looks forward to become a Nuncio, a Delegate, a member of the Ruota, Governor of Rome, Treasurer of the Hospital of Santo Spirito, or one of the Ministers under the New Organization ; and he frequently obtains a seat in the Sacred College by promotion from one or other of these offices. He wears a distinguishing costume, and is recognised in Rome by his violet stockings, and by being followed in the streets by a servant in livery.

The Jews in the Papal States amount to about 12,000, and have 8 synagogues. Of this number there are 4000 in Rome, 1800 in Ferrara, and 1600 in Ancona.

6. ARMY AND NAVY.

The States of the Church are divided into three military divisions— those of Rome, Bologna, and Ancona. The Army is under the direction of the Minister of War, of late years a military man. The Swiss Body Guard of the Pope, commanded by a Captain and Lieutenant, comprises 126 foot soldiers, who carry the ancient halberd, and wear the singular costume said to have been designed by Michael Angelo. The Pope's Noble Guard (Guardia Nobile), a mounted corps of 80 noblemen, is commanded by one of the Roman princes. It is their province to attend the Pope on all public occasions and ceremonies of the Church ; and they constitute, both by their equipments and their rank, the most distinguished military body in the capital. In addition to the corps above mentioned, there is a Swiss regiment, 2 regiments of Italian Infantry, 2 battalions of *Chasseurs de Vincennes*, a regiment of Dragoons, one of Artillery, and a corps of Military Engineers. The whole Papal military force, at the commencement of 1853, amounted to 14,600 men and 1630 horses, exclusive of the *Gendarmeria*—a very fine body of men—placed under the direction of the police or civil authorities. The principal military strongholds are Ancona, Ferrara, and Comacchio, now held by the Austrians; Civita Castellana, Civita Vecchia, and the Castle of St. Angelo in Rome, garrisoned by the French. The Papal Navy consists of a solitary gun-brig, some small craft, and two or three small steamers.

7. EDUCATION.

The whole system of education is still very imperfect in the Roman States, where the instruction of the lower classes is less attended to than in any other country of Italy, except Naples. There are three classes of educational institutions—the Universities, the Bishops' Schools, and the Communal or Parish Schools. I. There are 8 Universities, divided into two classes, primary and secondary. The two primary Universities are that of the Sapienza at Rome, founded A.D. 1244; and that of Bologna, founded 1119. The six secondary are those of Ferrara (1264), Perugia (1307-20), Macerata (1548), Fermo (1589), Camerino (1727), the Gregoriana or Collegio Romano, in the capital. About 2650 young men receive an academical education at these eight universities. II. The Bishops' Schools are established in all the communes which are rich enough to support them. The masters are appointed by the communal councils, after an open competition before the Gonfaloniere, and must then be approved by the Bishop. III. The Communal Schools answer in some measure to the parish schools of England, but the state of education is generally very low, and entirely in the hands of ecclesiastics.

In Rome it is said that at least three-fourths of the children of the poor are gratuitously educated. The elementary schools, instituted in the middle of the last century, still exist, and include three classes: —1. Those in which a small sum is paid; 2. The gratuitous schools; 3. The infant schools—an admirable class of institutions, which have been attended with the best results to the lower orders of late years. The gratuitous schools are under the superintendence of the parish priests. The masters are publicly examined before election; the schools are periodically visited by ecclesiastical inspectors. In regard to female education, there are no private schools either for the aristocracy or the middle classes: the instruction of females of this rank is entirely confined to the convents, and those of the class below them are boarded and taught in the different *conservatori*.

8. COMMERCE AND MANUFACTURES.

There are few countries in Europe which enjoy more natural advantages of soil and climate than the States of the Church; and yet their great resources are very imperfectly brought into play. The enormous forests which cover the uncultivated tracts for miles together are almost entirely neglected; the excellent wines which are produced, almost without effort, in many of the provincial towns, are little known beyond the frontier; and the mineral wealth of the country has never been thoroughly explored. The provincial population are rather agricultural than manufacturing, and articles of natural produce are exported to a limited extent. The manufactures, on the other hand, though making creditable progress, are chiefly for home consumption, and are insufficient for the demands of the population, who derive their main supplies from foreign countries. The principal agricultural exports are the following:—corn from Romagna; oil from the southern provinces; hemp from Romagna, from the Bolognese, and the Polesina of Ferrara; wool from Rieti, Città di Castello, Spoleto, Matelica, and Camerino; tobacco from all parts of the States; pine-kernels from Ravenna to Austria; cork-bark, to the amount of 550,000 lbs., from Civita Vecchia to England; silk in large quantities to France and England; potash from Rome, Corneto, and Porto d'Anzio; oxen from Perugia, Foligno, and Romagna to Tuscany; and rags, to the large amount of 3,000,000 lbs., from all the great towns. The alum manufactured at La Tolfa near Civita Vecchia was formerly very celebrated, and was exported in considerable quantities, but this trade is nearly extinct. The works of La Tolfa belong to the Government, and are worked for the profit of the treasury. In the districts of Cesena, Pesaro, and Rimini, sulphur-mines are now worked to some extent, yielding an annual produce of 4,000,000 lbs. The salt-works of Cervia, Comacchio, and Corneto give an annual produce of 76,000,000 lbs.

Manufacturing industry is very generally diffused over all parts of the States: woollen cloths are produced at Rome, Spoleto, Foligno, Terni, Matelica, Perugia, Gubbio, Fossombrone, S. Angelo in Vado, Narni, Alatri, and other places of less importance. Silks, damasks, and velvets are manufactured at Rome, Bologna, Perugia, Camerino, and Fossombrone, where the late Duke de Leuchtenberg gave to the works the impulse of the steam-engine. Ribbons of good quality are manufactured at Bologna, Forlì, Fano, and Pesaro; and silk stockings are made at the same places, and at Ancona and Ascoli. The silk veils and crape of Bologna were formerly celebrated throughout Europe; and though the trade has declined, they are still esteemed in France and other countries. The carpets of Pergola were once exported in quantities to the Lombardo-Venetian kingdom, where they had a ready sale as a good imitation of the English patterns. The hats of Rome, which are manufactured to the value of 200,000 scudi annually, are in great demand in all parts of the States, and even in Naples and Tuscany. Wax candles, to the amount of 250,000 scudi, are made at Rome, Bologna, Perugia, Ancona, and Foligno: at the latter place the trade is particularly flourishing. The ropes and cordage produced in the asylums, public schools, and private rope-yards are of superior quality, and are exported to the Ionian Islands and to Greece. The paper manufactories of Fabriano, established as early as 1564, still keep up their reputation: the quantity of paper of different kinds manufactured annually in the Papal States is 3,600,000 lbs., of which the greater part is derived from Fabriano. The latter paper surpasses in its quality that of the great Neapolitan establishment on the Fibreno, especially that for copper-plate printing, which in some respects is even superior to that of England and France.

9. AGRICULTURE.

The agriculture of the Papal States, with the exception of the system which prevails in the Roman Campagna, differs very little from that of Tuscany. The leading peculiarity of the Papal system is the prevalence of very large farms in the least cultivated districts. The Campagna immediately around Rome, more commonly known under the name of the "Agro Romano;" the vast tract of Maremma, which spreads along the coast from the Tuscan frontier to that of Naples; and the marshy land in the neighbourhood of Ferrara and Ravenna, are all cultivated upon the system of large farms, and are consequently in the hands of a few wealthy agriculturists. The Maremma district is divided among 150 farmers. The Agro Romano, containing about 550,000 English acres, is divided into farms varying from 1200 to 3000 acres. This immense tract is in the hands of a class of farmers who are called "Mercanti di Campagna." Each Mercante rents several farms, paying a fixed annual rent as in England, and upon leases generally of 9 years: most of them are men of large capital and great enterprise; they generally reside at Rome, where they have counting-houses and clerks to transact the business of their farms. The farms of the Agro Romano require a capital of from 2000*l*. to 10,000*l*.; the *mezzeria* system is, however, the most common mode of tenure, and dates from the earliest times of Italian history. It is founded on a division of profits between the landlord and tenant: it necessarily implies a mutual good faith between the parties, and an entire reliance on the integrity of the cultivator. In Tuscany the system exists in great perfection. The *mezzeria* may be defined as a contract or partnership between the landlord and tenant. The landlord supplies capital, the land, oxen, and seed, keeps the farm-buildings in repair, and generally pays a considerable part of all permanent improvements, embanking, planting, reclaiming waste lands, &c., and the whole of the produce is divided between him and the tenant in equal parts. The tenant finds labour and the implements required in ordinary cultivation, and pays one-half of all casualties among the domestic animals confided to his charge. Grazing and cattle-feeding have of late years proved most profitable in the environs of Rome, from the large quantity of butter produced, which finds a ready and advantageous sale in the markets of the capital. The system of farming in the Roman Campagna is in many respects peculiar. In the first place, the farmer seldom lives on his estate, the solitary *casale* being tenanted by the *fattore*, or steward, and by the herdsmen. In the winter the farm is covered with cattle: the number of sheep collected on the Campagna at that season is said to amount to 600,000; and the large grey oxen, which are bred for the Roman market, cannot be much less than half that number. The herdsmen are seen riding over the plain wrapped in a sheepskin cloak, and carrying a long pole armed with an iron spike: the horses they ride are almost wild, and are turned loose in summer among the woods and morasses of the coast, where they mingle with the buffaloes and herds of swine which people that desolate tract. As the summer draws on, the climate becomes too unhealthy for the cattle: the sheep and oxen are then driven from the plain to the cool pastures on the Sabine hills, to the high ground in the neighbourhood of Rieti, and even to the mountains of the Abruzzi. At harvest-time the heat becomes excessive, and the malaria assumes its most virulent form. The peasants from the Volscian hills and from beyond the Neapolitan frontier come down into the plain to earn a few crowns for the ensuing winter: they work in the harvest-field all day under a scorching sun, and at night sleep out of doors. Even the strongest and healthiest are often struck down in a single week; before the harvest is gathered in, hundreds of hardy mountaineers are seized with intermittent fever, and either die, or on their return home bear the mark of the pestilence for life. As soon as the harvest is over, the immense Campagna is utterly deserted; the herdsmen are absent with their cattle, the *fattori* take refuge in Rome, and the labourers retire to the few scattered villages on the outskirts of the plain, where they are less exposed to the effects of its then pestilential climate. After each harvest the land, in some parts of the Maremma more especially, is generally left to pasture for an indefinite time, the farmer seldom allowing more than one wheat-crop in four years. In all parts of the States the agricultural implements are of the rudest kind; the native manufacture never deviates from the primitive style which has prevailed for ages, and the heavy duties on articles of foreign manufacture have proved great drawbacks to the introduction of the improvements of more advanced countries.

10. CHARACTERISTICS OF THE COUNTRY.

It is impossible to travel over Italy without observing the striking difference between its northern and southern provinces. The traveller will discover, on crossing the frontier of the Papal States, that he has entered on a country very different from that which he has left. That portion of Italy which forms the subject of the present volume includes within its limits a field of study and observation almost inexhaustible. Though described for centuries by all classes of writers, there is still no part of Europe which the traveller will find so richly stored with intellectual treasure. From the North it differs mainly in this, that it is pre-eminently the Italy of classical times. It carries the mind back through the history of twenty centuries to the events which laid the foundation of Roman greatness. It presents us with the monuments of nations which either ceased to exist before the origin of Rome, or gradually sunk under her power. Every province is full of associations; every step we take is on ground hallowed by the spirits of the poets, the historians, and the philosophers of Rome. These, however, are not the only objects which command attention. In the darkness which succeeded the fall of Rome, Italy was the first country which burst the trammels in which the world had so long been bound. Political freedom first arose amidst the contests of the popes with the German emperors; and in the republics of Middle Italy the human mind was developed to an extent which Rome, in the plenitude of her power, had never equalled. The light of modern civilization was first kindled on the soil which had witnessed the rise and fall of the Roman empire; and Europe is indebted to the Italy of the middle ages for its first lessons, not only in political wisdom, but in law, in literature, and in art. The history of the Italian republics is not a mere record of party, or of the struggles of petty princes and rival factions; it is the record of an era in which modern civilization received its earliest impulses. Amidst the extraordinary energy of their citizens, conquest was not the exclusive object, as in the dark ages which had preceded them. Before the end of the thirteenth century the universities of the free cities had opened a new path for literature and science, and sent forth their philosophers and jurists to spread a knowledge of their advancement. The constitutional liberties of Europe derived useful lessons from the municipal institutions of Italy, and the courts of the Italian princes afforded asylums to that genius which has survived the liberties in which it had its origin. The mediæval history of Central Italy has hitherto been less regarded by the traveller, although in many respects it is not less interesting than the history of classical times. The intimate connection of her early institutions with those of England, and the part which many of our countrymen played in the great drama of Italian history, associate us more immediately with this period than with any other in her annals. We may perhaps recognise, in the energy and originality of the Italian character during the middle ages, a prototype of that prodigious activity which our own country has acquired under the influence of the lessons which Italy taught her. We must at least regard with admiration and respect a people who have done so much in the great cause of human amelioration, and admit that the period in which Italy started from her slumber and led the way in the march of European improvement is one of the most brilliant in the history of the world.

The physical characters of Central Italy are not less interesting than her historical associations. To apply our remarks more particularly to the Papal States, we may say that their resources have hitherto been very imperfectly appreciated. Few countries in Europe have been less understood. The traveller who hurries from Bologna to Florence, and from Florence to Rome, neither stopping to explore the objects which present themselves on the road, nor turning aside into less beaten tracts, will form no idea of the treasures of art abundantly placed within his reach. He can have had no opportunity of becoming acquainted with the true character of the people, or of knowing the charms of the provincial cities. In regard to art, it is a mistake to suppose that it can be only studied in the galleries of the great capitals. The filiations of the different schools, the links of the chain which connect together the leading epochs, not merely in painting, but in architecture and sculpture, are to be traced, not in the museums and palaces of Rome, but in the smaller cities, where every branch of art, under the patronage of the local sovereigns or the republics, has left some of its important works.

The scenery of Central Italy is another charm which will appeal probably to a larger class. Whatever may be the beauties of particular districts traversed by the high road, the finest characters of Italian scenery must be sought, like the people, beyond the beaten track. The fertility of the March of Ancona, the rich cultivation of Romagna, the beautiful country intersected by the Velino, the Metauro, the Anio, and the Sacco, have each an interest of a different character. Nothing can be grander than the forms of the Sabine and Umbrian mountains, or more picturesque than the valleys which descend from them. Nature there appears in a richness of colouring to which the eye has not been before accustomed. In the southern provinces the purity of atmosphere is combined with an harmonious repose of nature, the costumes of the people are in the highest degree picturesque, and the buildings have the rare merit of being perfectly in keeping with the scenery by which they are surrounded.

Among the first objects which will be presented to the traveller, the monuments of antiquity are the most important. We shall therefore state, as concisely as possible, such general facts in reference to their archæological characters, as may be necessary to prepare the traveller for their study.

11, PELASGIC ARCHITECTURE.

No circumstance is so much calculated to mislead the stranger who travels into Italy as the frequent misapplication of the terms Pelasgic, Cyclopean, and Etruscan. Every specimen of ancient architecture in Central Italy has been called by one or other of these names, merely because the style is colossal compared to the later works of Roman construction.

The Pelasgic remains, of which the Papal States contain so many specimens, confirm the history of the migrations of that ancient people. Whether the Pelasgi were originally a people from Thrace, or from a country still more northward, as some authors contend, there can be no doubt that they were the great original colonists of Southern Europe. They may be traced from Thessaly to Asia Minor, through the greater part of Greece, and through many islands of the Ægean. We know that they united with the Hellenes to form the Greek nation, that they built Argos and Lycosura (B. C. 1820), which Pausanias calls "the most ancient, and the model from which all other cities were built." According to history, two distinct colonies emigrated to Central Italy, then occupied by the Umbri, a race probably of Celtic origin. The first came direct from Lycosura and settled in Umbria. The second Pelasgic colony invaded Italy from Dodona, and brought with them many arts unknown to their predecessors. They settled in the upper valley of the Velinus, near Rieti. The first, or Umbrian colony, seems to have lost its Greek language at an early period, if we may judge from one of the most ancient written monuments, the Eugubian tables. It is not the least interesting circumstance arising out of the history of this colony, that the Latin language, in its present form, is considered to derive its Greek element from the Pelasgi, and its Latin from the Umbrians. The Pelasgi were subdued in their turn by a race called Tyrrheni by the Greeks, and Etrusci by the Romans, about fifty years before the Trojan war ; and in the time of Tarquinius Priscus the whole race seems to have disappeared as one of the leading nations of Italy.

This historical sketch is confirmed by the ruins the Pelasgi have left behind them. The first colony does not appear to have founded any cities for themselves, but to have occupied those already inhabited by the Umbri ; the second settled in the valley of the Velinus, and thence spread over a large portion of the country to the south of it. Accordingly, in the neighbourhood of Rieti, we find a large cluster of ancient towns, many of which are still to be identified by the descriptions and distances handed down to us by the Greek and Roman historians. We find, in the precise locality indicated by Dionysius, the walls of Pala-tium, from which Evander and his Arcadian colonists emigrated to Rome forty years before the Trojan war. We recognise the sites of other cities of equal interest, and in some instances discover that their names have undergone but little change. We trace the Pelasgi from this spot in their course southwards, along the western slopes of the Sabine mountains, and mark their progress in civilization by the more massive construc-tions which they adopted. Their cities were now generally placed upon hills, and fortified by walls of such colossal structure, that they still astonish us by their solidity. The progressive improvement of their military architecture becomes more apparent as we approach their southern limits. Hence the very finest specimens of Pelasgic construc-tion in Europe are to be found between the Sabine and Volscian chains, at Alatri, Arpino, Segni, and other towns in the valleys of the Sacco and Liris, and which are described in the Handbook for Southern Italy.

The style of their construction was in most instances polygonal, con-sisting of enormous blocks of stone, the angles of one exactly corre-sponding with those of the adjoining masses. They were put together without cement, and so accurately as to leave no interstices whatever. This style may be traced throughout Greece, Asia Minor, and all the countries which history describes as colonised by the Pelasgic tribes. The exceptions to the polygonal style are where the geological formation of the country presented rocks, such as sandstones, occurring naturally in parallel strata, which obviously suggested the horizontal mode of con-struction, and afforded naturally masses more of a parallelipipedal than of a polygonal shape to the builder. Another variety was produced by local circumstances in the neighbourhood of Rome, where tufa is the pre-vailing stone. At Tusculum, for example, the softness and quality of the rock pointed out the horizontal style; and thus, in the instances in which the Pelasgi were compelled to adopt tufa as their material, the blocks in-cline to parallelograms. Even here, however, where the style was evi-dently controlled by circumstances, the taste for the national custom may still be recognised; and we often find that the blocks have been shaped so as to deviate in many places from regular squares. In the ruins of Am-piglione, near Tivoli, the supposed site of Empulum, we have a very ancient example of the Pelasgic style in tufa. It is entirely polygonal, but the blocks were apparently found broken into irregular masses by their fall from the mountains, and therefore afforded peculiar facilities for this construction. Instances of this are not wanting farther south. In the wild mountain-pass leading from the valley of Sulmona to the Piano di Cinquemiglia, in the second province of Abruzzo Ultra, the precipitous ravines present frequent examples of limestone so fissured and broken that they might almost be called natural Pelasgic walls. We may therefore assume as a general rule, that, whenever the materials which the Pelasgi employed were of hard rock, such as limestone, breaking naturally into polygonal masses, the polygonal construction was adopted in its utmost purity; and whenever the geo-logical formation of the country presented volcanic tufa or sandstone, occurring in horizontal strata, their style was parallelipipedal. The Romans imitated the polygonal style in all cases under similar circumstances, and hence we find polygonal walls in many towns of Latium which are known to date from the kingly and even republican period.

12. CYCLOPEAN ARCHITECTURE.

The difference of style between the Pelasgic and Cyclopean is difficult to define with accuracy. We have already seen that the Pelasgi built the walls of Lycosura eighteen centuries before Christ, and that Pausanias describes it as the most ancient of all such cities. The walls of Tiryns and Mycenæ were built about four centuries later, and, according to the same authority, by a different people, the Cyclopes. As these two cities, though upwards of 3000 years old, are nearly as perfect as when Pausanias visited them sixteen centuries ago, we may regard them as the type of all similar structures which we shall meet with either in Greece or Italy. That the Cyclopean style is really the work of a people different from the Pelasgi is probable from numerous circumstances. Euripides describes the walls of Mycenæ as built in the Phœnician method; and Pausanias found the style so peculiar that he thought it necessary to describe it. His description, from personal observation, applies at this day, not only to the Greek cities, but to every other example of the style which we shall meet with elsewhere. "The walls," he says, "the only portion which remains, are built of rough stones (λίθων ἀργῶν), so large that the smallest of them could not be moved from their position by a pair of mules. Smaller stones have been inserted between them, in order that the larger blocks might be more firmly held together." Homer, in the second book of the Iliad, characterises Tiryns as the walled city (Τίρυνθα τε τειχιόεσσαν), and mentions Mycenæ as remarkable for the excellence of its buildings (Μυκήνας εὐκτίμενον πτολίεθρον). To these facts we shall only add, that the Cyclopean style, wherever it is found, is composed, as stated by Pausanias, of irregular polygonal masses, with small stones filling up the interstices. It occurs very rarely in Italy; the constructions that approach nearest to it are the massive walls on Monte St. Angelo, the probable site of the ancient Corniculum, and at Artena, the modern Monte Fortino. It is remarkable that the extraordinary Cyclopean work, the great gallery of Tiryns, formed by cutting away the superincumbent blocks in the form of an arched roof, has its counterpart in the triangular gateway of the Pelasgic fortress of Arpino.

13. THE ETRUSCANS.

The inhabitants of Etruria were a people altogether distinct from the Pelasgic colonists, though probably descended from the same great family. The Greek historians, as we have already remarked, invariably called them Tyrrheni, while the Romans call them Etrusci. Herodotus, Strabo, Cicero, and Plutarch say that they were of Lydian origin, that they left their native land on account of a protracted famine, sailed from Smyrna, and settled in Umbria. Dionysius of Halicarnassus dissents altogether from this statement, and regards them as an indigenous race of Italy; but in spite of the objections of so weighty an authority, it is impossible, with our extended knowledge of the domestic life and habits of the Etruscans as developed in their tombs, not to come to the conclusion that their national customs, their religious rites, and their domestic manners must have been derived from an Asiatic source. The Etruscans subdued the Umbri and Pelasgi, who finally disappeared as distinct people by incorporation with their conquerors. They spread in time over the whole of central Italy, and as far south as the Campania, where they founded Capua. They had no doubt acquired much knowledge from the Pelasgi, but by encouraging Greek artists to settle among them they derived nearly all their more important arts directly from Greece. We know that Demaratus of Corinth brought with him to Tarquinii the plastic art and the manufacture of brass or bronze, which afterwards obtained much celebrity in all the cities of Etruria. The names of artists which occur on the vases of Magna Græcia are seen on many of those found among the cities of Etruria : in general these vases of Greek origin are superior in workmanship to those found at Clusium and other places where Etruscan characters are combined with a coarser material. The connection of Etruria with Egypt, either directly by commerce, or indirectly through Greece, is shown by vases of Egyptian form ; by scarabæi imitating the forms of Egypt, and frequently inscribed with subjects taken from the Egyptian mythology. It would carry us far beyond our limits to pursue this branch of the inquiry. It may, however, be said, that by far the largest proportion of the arts and civilization of Etruria came from Greece. In architecture the Etruscan walls are generally built of parallelograms of soft calcareous stone or of tufa, laid together with more or less regularity, in horizontal courses without cement. The architecture of their tombs has a subterranean character, being sometimes excavated in rocks above ground, as at Castel d'Asso; and at others sunk beneath the surface, and covered with tumuli or cones of masonry. When excavated in the form of cavern sepulchres they are decorated with architectural ornaments, which again show the influence of Grecian art. The mouldings of their façades, and the rude imitations of triglyphs, are but a corruption of Doric. The doors, contracting towards the top, differ little from the style still visible in Greece, and of which the great door of the Treasury of Atreus at Mycenæ is the finest example. The architecture of their temples, as preserved in the style adopted as Tuscan by the Romans, also shows an identity of principles with the oldest form of Doric. Their paintings are Grecian in mythology, in costumes, and in the ceremonies they represent. Their bronzes are also in the Greek style, and the excellence of the manufacture may probably be attributed to the Corinthian colonists already mentioned. Their sculpture is peculiar to themselves. It has neither the boldness of the Æginetan marbles, nor the repose of the Egyptian. With just proportions, the forms of the human figure are undefined, the position of the limbs is constrained and studied, the drapery is arranged with a minute attention to regularity approaching to stiffness, and the countenances are often wanting in character and expression. Of their language, as preserved to us in inscriptions, we know absolutely nothing ; and of the words which have been handed down to us by the Romans as examples of the Etruscan tongue, the two most commonly met with in inscriptions are LAR, king, and LASNE, the name of Etruria itself. The only expression satisfactorily made out is the very common one of

RUL AVIL, *vixit annos* ; beyond this all is mere conjecture. In fact, it is one of the most extraordinary phenomena connected with this wonderful people, that their alphabet is almost entirely deciphered, and yet their language remains unintelligible. It is unexplained by Hebrew, Greek, Latin, or Celtic. Nearly every letter is proved to be Greek, or rather that oldest form of it which is termed Pelasgic. It was written generally from right to left, like the inscriptions of the Eugubian tables, in which the Pelasgic letter is also recognised. The Etruscan words, however, have no affinity with the Umbrian of those celebrated monuments. The bilingual inscriptions hitherto discovered have been very few, and have not been of a character to throw much light on this difficult subject. It will require the discovery of some Rosetta Stone to afford the long-lost key to the language and literature of this mysterious people.

14. THE ROMANS.

There is no doubt that Rome derived her earliest ideas of art and civilization from Etruria. The Tuscan style was adopted by the Romans for their earliest temples, and the massive forms of Etruscan architecture were employed in their greatest public works. They derived their religious ceremonies from the priestly aristocracy of Etruria, and adopted the Etruscan arts without improving them. We must not therefore look for much originality in Roman works. From the period of the Kings to the conquest of Greece, art, so far from improving under the Romans, gradually declined. Even after that event had opened a new field of observation, and created a desire for works of art, the artists of the conquered nations were the only persons who were capable of supplying them. So long as the architecture of Etruria maintained its influence at Rome, the public works were characterised by great durability and grandeur. The bridges, the public roads, and the colossal aqueducts, were all probably suggested by the Etruscans, and Rome excelled more in these works of public utility than in any other branch of art. As the Tuscan style was imported for the earliest works of Rome, so the new conquests led to the introduction of Doric, Ionic, and Corinthian from Greece. But the beauty of Greek art, founded upon undeviating principles subservient to one main idea, was speedily corrupted : the Romans retained nothing but its forms; they rejected its principles, and at length corrupted what remained with devices of their own. Of all the works which the Romans have left to us, the most faultless in its proportions and the most beautiful in its general effect is the Pantheon. The circular tombs, and possibly the circular temples, were adopted from the Etruscans, but with such modifications and improvements as have made them rank among the most interesting monuments of Rome. About the time of Augustus, the Composite, or Roman order, seems to have been invented. The Arch of Titus is an example of this style. There, as in the later works of the Empire, in the Coliseum, the baths, the theatres, &c., we have, as the leading characteristics, a combination of the arch with the Grecian orders, in which for the first time columns are employed, not as essentials to the stability of the structure, but as mere ornaments. This nnovation naturally led to the employment of the column for other purposes, and hence we find an isolated pillar used either as a funeral or triumphal monument. The allegiance of the Romans to Greek art became gradually weaker, and was at last completely thrown off in the Basilicas. The Roman domestic architecture is only to be studied with advantage at Pompeii : it would be out of place therefore to enter into details in the present volume, more particularly as the subject is examined in detail in the Handbook for Southern Italy. In painting, the best specimens we have of Roman art are the fragments discovered in tombs, in the Baths of Titus, &c. The Nozze Aldobrandini is one of the finest examples of this kind. In the greater number of examples found at Pompeii and Herculaneum the subjects are either illustrative of some tale of classical mythology, or represent some single figure, as a dancer, thrown out in fine relief on a dark ground. All these, however, are mere house decorations, and we have no work which the ancients themselves described with praise. In sculpture, the Romans showed as little originality and as little native talent as in other branches of art. Most of the works which have survived to our time, if not imported from Greece as the spoils of conquest, were executed in Italy by Greek artists, down to the latest period of the empire. Of the leading works of this class we may mention that the Laocoon is referred by the best authorities to the time of Titus, the Apollo Belvedere to that of Nero, the Antinous to that of Hadrian, and the Torso Belvedere is probably still later. Even most of the imperial statues are supposed to be the work of Greek sculptors, resident at Rome ; and the statues of the Grecian divinities perhaps owe their excellence to the devotional feeling with which a Greek would have entered on his task. Under Hadrian, we have a striking proof of the imitation of foreign examples in the numerous copies of Egyptian architecture and art. The chamber of the Canopus in the Capitol, and the Egyptian Hall in the Vatican, are filled with statues of this class, all highly finished, but bearing ample evidence of Greek art applied to Egyptian subjects. The bas-reliefs of the Sarcophagi form an important class of sculptures, which might well be treated at greater length than our limits will allow. In them we read the metaphysical religion of the time expressed by such fables of mythology as have reference to death. The Cupid and Psyche, the story of Endymion, the battle-scenes from the poets, are all sufficiently explicit ; but in the later examples the symbolical meaning becomes more obscure, until we have the last example of foreign imitation in the introduction of the Mithratic mysteries. Many of these works are of the highest class of sculpture, and are full of materials of study both to the artist and mythologist.

15. CHRISTIAN ARCHITECTURE.

The early Christian architecture, avoiding the forms of the pagan temples, chose for its models the ancient Basilicas, which had served during the latter portion of the empire as the seats of the public tribunals. If the buildings themselves were not actually used for Christian worship, their form and general arrangement were so well adapted to the purpose that they were imitated with little change. The form of the central avenue allowed it to be easily converted into the *nave* or ship of St. Peter, the great characteristic of a Christian church. Even the raised tribune, which was peculiarly the seat of justice, was so well fitted for the seat of the bishop, who might thence, like a true *Episcopus*, look down on the congregation, that the form and title are still preserved in churches which have none of the distinctive characters of the basilica. The most important trace of the heathen temple which remained in the Roman basilica, was the continuous architrave. This was speedily abandoned, and the columns were united together by a series of arches. The basilica thus modified and adapted for Christian worship, was perhaps deficient in symmetry and proportion, but the simple grandeur of its style contained the germ of the ecclesiastical architecture of all Christendom. The form. was oblong, consisting of the nave and two side aisles, separated by lines of columns. From these columns sprang a series of arches supporting a high wall pierced with windows, and sustaining the bare wooden roof. At the extremity was the semicircular tribune, or absis, elevated above the rest of the interior for the bishop's seat. In front, between the tribune and the body of the nave, was the choir, with its two ambones or stone pulpits, from which the Epistle and Gospel were read. The nave beyond it was divided into two portions,—the *aula* or open space where the congregation was assembled, the men on one side and the women on the other, and the *narthex* for the catechumens and the lesser penitents. One of the lateral aisles, as in the courts of justice, was also set apart for the males, and the other for the females; and after this ancient division of the *aula* and *narthex* was abandoned, an upper row of columns was introduced into the nave, where galleries were constructed for the women. In front of the building was the *Quadriporticus* or fore-court, for the lowest class of penitents, surrounded on the inner side by a covered cloister, and having a fountain in the middle at which the people might wash their hands before they entered the building. The traveller who is desirous of studying Christian architecture, and the successive transformations of the temples for Christian worship, will do well to proceed in the first place to Ravenna, where, surrounded by the monuments of three kingdoms, he will be enabled to examine a collection of Christian antiquities which have undergone no change since the time of Justinian. In the church of St. Apollinare in Classe he will find the earliest specimen of a Christian basilica that now exists, and in the mosaics profusely scattered over the various churches of the city of the Exarchs he will see the first attempts of Christian art to embody the inspirations of religion. At Rome the finest example of a basilica is the venerable church of San Clemente, in which we still find the choir with its *ambones*, the tribunes, and the *quadriporticus*. In S. Agnese, and S. Lorenzo, we see the upper row of columns for the female gallery ; in S. Lorenzo and other churches we recognise the ancient portico, though the rest of the atrium has disappeared. At Ravenna the traveller will also have an opportunity of studying the Byzantine period of art. Under the Eastern Emperors the city was enriched with the finest examples of religious architecture which the world had then seen beyond the walls of Constantinople. The church of S. Vitale, built on the plan of S. Sophia, was the first edifice in Italy constructed with a dome, which was previously the peculiar feature of the Eastern church. We may therefore examine in the Byzantine dome of S. Vitale, and in the basilica of S. Apollinare, the two objects which still continue, after innumerable vicissitudes, the elements of Christian architecture throughout Europe. We shall not dwell on the Lombard architecture to be met with in the Papal States, and shall touch very lightly on the examples of Italian Gothic, all of which are noticed in detail in the body of the work. If the introduction of the dome, and the religious antiquities of Ravenna generally, are to be attributed to the patronage of the Eastern Emperors, the introduction of the Gothic style into Italy must be ascribed to the connection of the leading towns with the emperors of Germany. In some of the very few examples in which (as at Assisi, and perhaps at Subiaco) the origin of the style can be traced directly to the German artists, we have the Gothic rivalling the purity of transalpine churches; but in others of a later date, designed probably by native artists who had seen only the works of the foreign architects in Italy, the influence of classical examples was never wholly thrown off. We see it forming the well-known beautiful style now called the Italian Gothic, in the cathedrals and churches of Siena, Orvieto, Bologna, Arezzo, Cortona. Professor Willis has shown that the Italian Gothic is capable of a much more extended generalization than is commonly supposed; and the traveller will look in vain for finer examples than those presented by the cathedrals of Orvieto and Siena. In the fifteenth century Italian architecture in its modern sense was developed by the revival of the classical orders. In the previous century the public buildings and churches had shown a disposition to return to the ancient models; and in many of the ecclesiastical edifices of that period, the transition from the Gothic to the Roman orders is distinctly traceable. The new style was thoroughly developed by Brunelleschi in the middle of the 15th century: his cupola of the Duomo at Florence, the churches of San Lorenzo and Santo Spirito in the same city, show how the principles of his school had triumphed in so very short a period. His great follower Leon Battista Alberti gave a fresh impulse to the revival by his noble churches of S. Andrea and S. Sebastiano at Mantua, and by his extraordinary devices to conceal the pointed Gothic of S. Francesco at Rimini. Baccio Pintelli introduced it at Rome in S. Agostino and S. Maria del Popolo; and, lastly, it was established as the model of Italian ecclesiastical architecture by Bramante and Michael Angelo.

16. CHRISTIAN SCULPTURE.

Whoever would study the condition of Christian sculpture in the early ages of the Church will find many monuments at Ravenna of peculiar interest. The marble urn of St. Barbatian, the ivory pastoral chair of St. Maximian, the tomb of the exarch Isaac, the pulpit of the Arian bishops in the church of Santo Spirito, the sculptured crucifixes, and other objects described in our account of that imperial city, are precious specimens of art of the sixth and seventh centuries. At Rome the most remarkable are the sarcophagi of Junius Bassus and of Anicius Probus, in the vaults of St. Peter's. They are covered with bas-reliefs from the Old and New Testaments, of the highest interest as examples of art of the fourth century. Though stiff in attitude and drapery, these sculptures are far superior to any heathen works of the two preceding centuries: that of Junius Bassus is supposed to have been executed at Constantinople, and is one of the most remarkable Christian monuments in existence. The traveller who may desire to trace the progress of sculpture, from the period of its revival in the thirteenth century to that of its decline in the school of Bernini, will find abundant materials in the Papal States. At Bologna, he will see in the tomb of S. Domenico, executed in 1225, the first work of Niccola da Pisa, who there laid the foundation of the Christian department of sculpture. The pulpit at Pisa was not executed till thirty years later; but that of Siena, which dates only one year after the tomb of S. Domenico, is not inferior as a work of art, and is justly regarded as one of the finest productions of this great master. The tomb of Benedict XI. at Perugia, the fountain in the great square of the same city, the sculptures on the façade of the Duomo of Orvieto, the marble screen of S. Donato in the cathedral of Arezzo, all by his son Giovanni, may be classed as the next steps of the revival. The great work of his scholar Giovanni di Balducci, the shrine of St. Peter Martyr in the church of St. Eustorgio at Milan, is another important monument. At Arezzo he will meet with a specimen of equal interest in the tomb of its warrior-bishop, Guido Tarlati, executed between 1328 and 1330 by Agnolo and Agostino da Siena. Another work of the same period, in the cathedral of Arezzo, is the tomb of Gregory X., by Margaritone. Of another class, intermediate between the first masters of the revival and the period of the decline, are the bas-reliefs of the bronze doors, of which Florence, Pisa, Bologna, and other cities offer such interesting examples. We might dwell longer on the details and enter more fully into the characteristics of the several schools; but anything like a complete catalogue would be out of place in our brief summary, and would extend it beyond our object, which is to direct attention to the leading monuments of the art.

17. SCHOOLS OF PAINTING.

The mosaics of the early Christian Church are the true representatives of painting before its revival in the schools of Cimabue and Giotto. Nowhere are they so remarkable as at Ravenna, where they are still as fresh as in the days of Justinian. These early mosaics, though generally rude in execution, are astonishing specimens of expression: many of them breathe a spirit of pure devotion, and are invaluable to the Christian antiquary as giving him a perfect epitome of the religious ideas and symbols of the time. We shall not enter into a critical examination of the Schools of Art, as those which come within our province are noticed in the descriptions of their different localities; and it would be difficult to present any general arrangement of them without including details which would carry us into other schools, beyond the scope of the present volume. We shall merely mention, in illustration of the remark already made respecting the true mode of seeing Italy, that it is only by deviating from the high roads that the traveller can appreciate the works of many of the early masters. At Orvieto, for example, he will have an opportunity of studying the beautiful works of Gentile da Fabriano, of Angelico da Fiesole, of Benozzo

Gozzoli, and of Luca Signorelli. At Assisi he will find himself amidst those triumphs of Giotto to which Dante has given immortality. He will there be able to contrast them with the works of his great master and predecessor Cimabue. At Bologna he will be surrounded by the greatest works of the Eclectic school, founded by the Caracci and their pupils—a school which modern German critics are too much disposed to undervalue, and to judge more harshly than it deserves. Whatever may be its demerits on the score of originality, the English traveller will not forget how differently it was judged by one equally competent to appreciate works of art with any modern traveller—Sir Joshua Reynolds, who recommended the student to devote more time to Bologna than it had hitherto been the custom to bestow. The works of Francesco Francia, the most illustrious name in the history of the Bolognese school, are not liable to the objections urged against the school of the Caracci by the ultramontane Manierists. The works of this great master have been little known until of late years in England; and the traveller will recollect that there is no place where they can be studied to so much advantage as at Bologna. Among the cities on the shores of the Adriatic there is scarcely one which does not contain some work which is an episode in the general history of painting—a link in the chain which connects one school with another, and shows the means by which their filiation was accomplished. The little towns of Borgo San Sepolcro and Città di Castello may well bear the titles of cities of painters. Borgo San Sepolcro was the birthplace of Pietro della Francesca, the master of Melozzo da Forlì, Luca Signorelli, Santi di Tito, and other eminent painters. From the works of Pietro della Francesca at Arezzo Raphael derived his idea for the design of Constantine's Vision and Victory, in the Vatican; and was probably indebted to him for those effects of light and shade for which the Deliverance of St. Peter, in the Stanza of the Heliodorus, is so remarkable. Città di Castello is still rich in interesting and almost unknown works of Luca Signorelli, Beato Angelico, and other masters, whose style exercised an important influence on the genius of Raphael. It was in this town that Raphael found his earliest patrons, and no less than four of his most celebrated works were painted for its churches. Siena and Perugia are also remarkable as the centre of two schools of painting, whose influence on the great masters of the fifteenth century is confirmed generally by their works. The School of Siena is at least equal in antiquity to that of Florence, and presents us with the names of Guido da Siena, Simone and Lippo Memmi, Taddeo Bartolo, Sodoma, Beccafumi, and Baldassare Peruzzi. The School of Umbria, of which Perugia was the centre, may be regarded as the transition from the classical style prevalent at Florence to that deep religious feeling and spiritual tendency of the art which attained its maturity under Raphael. Its early masters were Niccolò Alunno and Benedetto Bonfigli, the immediate predecessors of Pietro Perugino, under whose instructions in that city the genius of Raphael was first developed. Giovanni Santi of Urbino, the father of Raphael, is generally referred to this school; and Perugia still contains some interesting works by Raphael himself, in which the traveller may trace the influence exercised upon his style by the early Umbrian masters.

To those travellers who are interested in the arabesque paintings of the 15th and 16th centuries it may be interesting to learn that this beautiful class of art has found an able illustrator, in England, in Mr. Gruner, whose burin has been so successfully employed in diffusing a knowledge of this class of works by Raphael and his coadjutors. Mr. Gruner's ' Architectural Decorations of Rome during the Fifteenth and Sixteenth Centuries' contain a selection from the works of Raphael, Giulio Romano, Baldassare Peruzzi, Perino del Vaga, Giovanni da Udine, and other painters, existing in the Vatican, the Farnesina Palace, the Villa Madama, and other edifices in and about Rome. These arabesques and medallions are full of interest, and *chef-d'œuvres* of decorative art; and travellers will be glad to have the power of studying their beautiful details on their return home after the completion of their journey.

18. BOOKS.

In the Introduction to the Handbook for Northern Italy will be found a list of works, most of which will be equally useful to the traveller in the countries described in the present volume.

Connected with the Fine Arts—on Painting, the most convenient and instructive work in our language is undoubtedly " Kügler's Handbook of Painting," in 2 vols., translated from the German by Sir C. Eastlake, whose valuable notes, and the numerous illustrations which accompany it, render it greatly superior to the original edition. The Lives of the Painters, by Vasari, will not be less indispensable to the traveller in Central Italy than in the other parts of the Peninsula. A very portable and cheap edition of this classical work on art, edited by a society of Tuscan *literati*, has been recently published at Florence by Lemonnier. What adds very considerably to the value of this edition, when compared with all those that preceded it, are the copious notes, in which the several works of art mentioned in Vasari's text are traced to their present resting-places; so that the traveller can ascertain at once where the great *chef-d'œuvres* of Italian art, if still in existence, are now to be found.[*]

Another very interesting work has been recently published by the same editor—' The Lives of the Painters of the Order of St. Dominic,' including Beato Angelico, Fra Bartolommeo, &c., by Padre Marchese.

On Architecture—the " Illustrated Handbook on Architecture," by Mr. Fergusson, will supply a very great desideratum in our literature of the fine arts; and must prove a valuable companion to travellers who take interest in the arts of construction, the history of which it embraces at every period, and for every country.

For those who may desire to enter more deeply into the study of the ancient classical architecture in Central Italy, the works of the celebrated Commander Canina will prove the surest guides, especially his splendid publication entitled ' L'Antica Architettura descritta e dimostrata coi Monumenti.' Roma, folio, 1851.

On Christian architecture, Mr. Gally Knight's ' Ecclesiastical Architecture of Italy,' with its beautiful lithographic illustrations, and Canina's ' Architettura dei Tempi Cristiani,' will be the best works to

---

[*] Vasari, Vite dei Pittori, Scultori, ed Architetti. 10 vols. 12mo. Firenze, 1850-53. Lemonnier.

accompany the descriptions of the early ecclesiastical edifices contained in this Handbook.

On Etruscan history and art, Mrs. Hamilton Gray's work, 'Sepulchres of Etruria,' which has done so much in directing the attention of the English public to that interesting class of ancient monuments, will be very useful to the traveller. Since its publication Mr. Dennis has supplied all that was wanting connected with the existing monuments of Etruria, in his most valuable volumes on the " Cities and Cemeteries of Etruria,"—a work which cannot be too highly praised and recommended as a Guide: it forms of itself an indispensable Handbook to all that remains of Etruscan art and civilization. The elaborate work of Canina, ' L'Antica Etruria Maritima nella Dizione Pontificia,' in the three folio volumes, embraces all the Etruscan sites within the Papal territory, and may be said to have exhausted the subject by representing almost every existing fragment of the edifices and tombs of the portion of that extraordinary people, with whose history we are best acquainted from their early connection and rivalry with Rome, accompanied by very learned and accurate descriptions.

For general criticism on architecture, Forsyth's 'Italy' is unsurpassed, perhaps, in our own or any other language. There is no work to which the traveller will recur with greater pleasure, or none from which, in so limited a space, he will derive more solid information.

For information generally on Italy, the work of Mr. Spalding, 'Italy and the Italians,' forming a part of the ' Edinburgh Cabinet Library,' contains, in a condensed shape, the leading facts of its ancient and modern history, and a good epitome of its arts and literature from the earliest times. Mr. Whiteside's ' Italy ' contains much information on the present condition of its people, institutions, &c. ; and his translation of Canina's ' Indicazione Topografica di Roma,' under the somewhat far-fetched title of the ' Vicissitudes of the Eternal City,' will interest the archæologist who may not be able to consult the original work, with its interesting illustrations.

Connected with Italian general literature, we may mention that the spirited editor of Vasari, above mentioned, has published very beautiful, cheap, and, what is scarcely less important to the traveller, compact editions of Dante, Petrarca, Ariosto, Tasso, Alfieri and Monti, &c., amongst the poets ; of Machiavelli, Cellini, Verri, Amari, &c., amongst the historians and biographers ; and of Manzoni, Guerazzi, Rossini, and Azeglio, amongst the more modern writers on historical romance.

19. MAPS.

Until very recently the best maps of the countries described in this volume were very inferior to those of Northern Italy.

Perhaps there are no better general maps of Italy than those accompanying the Handbooks. We have endeavoured to render them as accurate as possible, from the most recent authorities, and as far as the limited scale upon which they are constructed would permit of.

The Austrian Government has rendered a most important service to the traveller, and to geographical science generally, by extending its surveys into Central Italy. Already the great *Carta Topografica dello Stato Pontificio è del Gran Ducato di Toscana* is far advanced, and will

embrace the whole of Tuscany and the Papal States, on a scale of ₁/₅ₒₒ.
A great part of it has been already published, and the whole will be
completed in 1854 : it will then form by far the best Map of Middle Italy.

Count Litta's Map of the Southern Provinces of the Papal Territory,
in six sheets, was the most correct before the publication of the Austrian
survey, and until the latter is completed, will be best to guide the tourist.

Several maps of the environs of Rome have been published at different
times. The best is that of the Censo, in two sheets, published in 1839,
by the Government, but it only extends to a distance of five miles from
the City gates; the maps of the Campagna by Sir W. Gell and Mr.
Westphal do the greatest credit to their authors, when it is considered that they have been the result of their individual and unaided
exertions; but they are far from presenting the accuracy in their topographical details necessary to guide the archæological or the geological
tourist in his excursions. Baron Moltke has published at Berlin, in
1852, a map in two sheets, of the environs of Rome, taking in the
country within a distance of about 8 miles from the Capitol (*Carta
Topografica di Roma e de suoi contorni*), on a scale of ₁/₅ₒₒₒₒ.

But all these partial surveys of the classical ground round the Eternal
City must yield to that on the eve of publication by the French
Government, whose military engineers have completed an elaborate
trigonometrical survey of the Province of the *Comarca*, and which
will in a very few months be given to the public, in four large sheets,
by the Paris Dépôt de la Guerre.

Commander Canina's *Pianta Topografica della Campagna di Roma*,
in six sheets, is by far the best ever published as regards the determi-
nation of the several classical localities of this most classical region.
Nibby's map is an ill-engraved copy of Sir W. Gell's; Shickler's old
Pianta Topografica is, now-a-days, almost unworthy of notice.

It would be unjust in a detail of the recent topographical works on
Central Italy to omit mentioning the beautiful surveys of the coasts of
Tuscany and the Papal States published by the French Dépôt de la
Marine, accompanied by detailed plans of the principal ports, many of
which are of classical interest.

20. CHRONOLOGICAL TABLES.

ROMAN KINGS, B.C. 753–510.	ROMAN EMPIRE, B.C. 30—A.D. 476.
B.C.	*1. Heathen Emperors.*
753–714 Romulus.	
715–673 Numa Pompilius.	B.C. A.D.
673–641 Tullus Hostilius.	30– 14 Augustus.
641–616 Ancus Martius.	A.D.
616–578 Tarquinius Priscus.	14– 37 Tiberius.
578–534 Servius Tullius.	37– 41 Caligula.
534–510 Tarquinius Superbus.	41– 54 Claudius.
	54– 68 Nero.
ROMAN REPUBLIC, B.C. 510–30.	68– 69 Galba.
1st Period — From the Expulsion of	69 Otho.
Tarquin to the Dictatorship of Sylla,	69– 70 Vitellius.
B.C. 510–82.	70– 79 Vespasian.
2nd Period — Sylla to Augustus, B.C.	79– 81 Titus.
81–30.	81– 96 Domitian.

A.D.
96– 98 Nerva.
98–117 Trajan.
117–138 Hadrian,
138–161 Antoninus Pius.
161–180 Marcus Aurelius Antoninus and Lucius Verus.
180–192 Commodus.
193 Pertinax.
193 Didius Julianus.
193 Pescemius Niger.
193–211 Septimius Severus.
211–217 Caracalla.
217 Macrinus.
218–222 Heliogabalus.
222–235 Alexander Severus.
235 Maximinus.
238 Gordian I. & II., Pupienus.
238 Maximus Balbinus.
238 Gordian III.
244 Philippus the Arab.
249 Decius.
251 Trebonianus Gallus, Hostilianus, and Volusianus.
253 Æmilian.
253–260 Valerian and Gallienus.
261–268 Gallienus (Macrianus, Valens, Calpurnius, Piso, Aureolus, Odenathus).
268–270 Claudius II., surnamed Gothicus.
270–275 Aurelian.
275–276 Tacitus.
276 Florian.
276–282 Probus.
282–284 Carus (Carinus and Numeranus).
284–286 Diocletian.
286–305 Maximian.
305–306 Galerius and Constantius Chlorus.

2. Christian Emperors.

306–337 Constantine the Great (Maximinus II., Maxentius, Maximianus, &c.) transfers the seat of government to Constantinople, A.D. 330.
337–361 Constantine II., Constantius, Constans, co-emperors.
361–363 Julian the Apostate.
363–364 Jovian.
364–367 Valentinian I., Valens, co-emperors. (Formal division of the Empire into the Eastern and Western.)

3. Western Empire, to its Fall.

A.D.
364–375 Valentinian I. and Gratian.
375–383 Gratian and Valentinian II.
383–395 Valentinian II.
395–423 Honorius.
424–455 Valentinian III.
455 Petronius Maximus.
455–456 Flavius Cæcilius Avitus.
457–461 Julius Majorianus.
461–465 Libius Severus, or Serpentinus.
467-472 Procopius Anthemius.
472 Anicius Olybrius.
473–474 Flavius Glycerius.
474–475 Julius Nepos.
475 Romulus Augustulus.
476 Italy seized by Odoacer, and retained until 493.

4. Eastern Empire to Nicephorus.
A.D. 367–800.

364–378 Valens.
379–395 Theodosius the Great and Arcadius, from A.D. 383, as co-emperors.
395–408 Arcadius.
408–450 Theodosius II.
450–457 Pulcheria and Marcian.
457–474 Flavius Leo I.
474 Flavius Leo II.
474–491 Zeno.
491–518 Anastasius I.
518–527 Justinus I.
527–565 Justinian.
[Belisarius, Narses, and Longinus, Exarch of Ravenna.]
565–578 Justinus II.
578–582 Tiberius II.
582–602 Maurice the Cappadocian.
602–610 Phocas.
610–641 Heraclius.
641 Heraclius Constantinus.
641 Heracleonas.
641–668 Constans II.
668–685 Constantine III.
685–711 Justinian II.
711–713 Philippicus Bardanes.
713–716 Anastasius II.
716–717 Theodosius III.
718–741 Leo III. the Isaurian.
741–775 Constantine IV. Copronymus.
775–780 Leo IV.
780–797 Constantine V.
797–802 Irene.

A.D.
802 Nicephorus.
802 The Popes separate themselves
from the Eastern Emperors
about this time.

EAST GOTHIC KINGS OF ITALY.
A.D. 489–554.

493–526 Theodoric.
526–534 Athalaric.
534–536 Theodatus and Amalasontha.
536–540 Vitiges.
540–541 Hildebad or Theodebald.
541 Eraric.
541–552 Totila.
552–554 Teja, or Theias.

EXARCHS OF RAVENNA.

553–568 Narses.
569–584 Smaragdus.
590–597 Romanus.
597–602 Callinicus.
602–611 Smaragdus.
611–616 Lemigius.
616–619 Eleutherius.
619–638 Isaac.
638–648 Plato.
648 Calliopas.
649–652 Olympius.
652–666 Calliopas.
666–678 Gregorius.
978–687 Theodorius.
687–702 Platinus.
702–710 Theophylactes.
710 Rizocopus.
711–713 Eutychius.
713–727 Scholasticus.
727–728 Paul.
728–751 Eutychius. (Astolphus takes
possession of Ravenna.)

LOMBARD KINGS OF ITALY.
A.D. 568–769.

568 Alboin.
573 Clephis.
584 Authar.
591 Agilulf.
615 Adelwald.
625 Ariwald.
636 Rothar.
652 Rodwald.
653 Aribert I.
661 Pertharit and Godibert.
662 Grimoald.

A.D.
671 Pertharit.
686 Cunibert.
700 Leutbert.
701 Ragimbert and Aribert II.
712 Ansprand.
712 Luitprand.
736 Hildebrand.
744 Ratchis.
749 Astolphus.
757 Desiderius.
769 Adelchis.

FRANKISH EMPERORS OF ITALY.
A.D. 774–887.

774 Charlemagne (conquers Italy).
781 Pepin or Carloman.
814 Louis le Débonnaire.
820 Lothaire.
844 Louis II.
875 Charles the Bald.
881 Charles the Fat.

Interregnum, A.D. 887–962.

891 Guy, Duke of Spoleto, crowned.
895 Arnulfus, crowned.
898 Lambert of Spoleto.
900 Louis of Provence.
916 Berengarius, Duke of Friuli,
crowned.

GERMAN EMPERORS OF ITALY.
1. *Saxon Line*, A.D. 962–1002.

962 Otho the Great.
973 Otho II.
983 Otho III. (Theophania Empress
Regent).
1002 (Henry II. of Bavaria).

2. *Franconian Line*, A.D. 1024–1125.

1024 Conrad II. (the Salic).
1039 Henry III.
1056 Henry IV.
1106 Henry V.
1125 Lothaire II.

3. *Suabian Line*, A.D. 1138–1250.

1138 Conrad III.
1152 Frederic I. (Barbarossa).
1190 Henry VI.
1198 Otho IV.
1212 Frederic II.
1250 (Manfred).

Interregnum, 1250-1273.

EMPERORS OF GERMANY.
A.D. 1273-1848.

A.D.
1273 Rudolph of Hapsburg.
1292 Adolph of Nassau.
1298 Albert I. of Austria.
1308 Henry VII. of Luxemburg.
1314 Louis of Bavaria, and Frederic of Austria.
1346 Charles IV. of Luxemburg.
1378 Wenceslaus.
1400 Robert of Bavaria.
1410 Sigismund.
1438 Albert II.
1440 Frederic III.
1493 Maximilian I.
1520 Charles V.
1558 Ferdinand I.
1564 Maximilian II.
1576 Rudolph II.
1612 Matthias.
1619 Ferdinand II.
1637 Ferdinand III.
1658 Leopold I.
1705 Joseph I.
1711 Charles VI.
1742 Charles VII. of Bavaria.
1745 Francis I. (Grand Duke of Tuscany).
1765 Joseph II.
1790 Leopold II. (Grand Duke of Tuscany).
1792 Francis II. (Francis I. of Austria). Renounced, in 1806, the title of Emperor of Germany; from which date his successors have assumed the imperial dignity in Austria only.
1835 Ferdinand I. (Emperor of Austria).
1848 Francis Joseph (Emperor of Austria).

BISHOPS AND POPES OF ROME.

1. *Under the Heathen Emperors,*
A.D. 54-308.
Years of their Creation.
42 St. Peter.
66 St. Linus of Volterra.
67 St. Clement, Rome.
78 St. Anacletus, Athens.
100 St. Evaristus, Bethlehem.

A.D.
109 St. Alexander I., Rome.
119 St. Sixtus I., Rome.
127 St. Telesphorus, Greece.
139 St. Higinus, Athens.
142 St. Pius, Aquileja.
157 St. Anicetus, Syria.
168 St. Soter, Fondi.
177 St. Eleutherius, Nicopolis.
193 St. Victor I., Africa.
202 St. Zephyrinus, Rome.
219 St. Calixtus I., Rome.
223 St. Urban I., Rome.
230 St. Pontianus, Rome.
235 St. Anterus, Greece.
236 St. Fabian, Rome.
251 St. Cornelius, Rome.
252 *Novatian (Antipope),* Rome.
252 St. Lucius, Lucca.
253 St. Stephen I., Rome.
257 St. Sixtus II., Athens.
259 St. Dionysius, Greece.
269 St. Felix I., Rome.
275 St. Eutichianus, Tuscany.
283 St. Caius, Salona.
296 St. Marcellinus, Rome.

2. *Under the Christian Emperors, to the Division of the Empire,* A.D. 308-366.

308 St. Marcellus, Rome.
310 St. Eusebius, Greece.
311 St. Melchiades, Africa.
314 St. Sylvester, Rome.
336 St. Mark I., Rome.
337 St. Julius I., Rome.
352 St. Liberius, Rome.
355 *Felix II. (Antipope),* Rome.

3. *Under the Eastern and Western Empire,* A.D. 366-480.

366 St. Damasus I., Spain.
384 St. Siricius, Rome.
397 St. Anastasius I., Rome.
401 St. Innocent I., Albano.
417 St. Zosimus, Greece.
418 St. Boniface I., Rome.
420 *Eulalius (Antipope),* Rome.
422 St. Celestin I., Rome.
432 St. Sixtus III., Rome.
440 St. Leo I. (the Great), Tuscany.
461 St. Hilary, Sardinia.
467 St. Simplicius, Tibur.

4. Under the East Gothic Kings,
A.D. 489–554.

A.D.
482 St. Felix II. (called III.), Rome.
492 St. Gelasius, Africa.
496 St. Anastasius II., Rome.
498 St. Symmachus, Sardinia.
514 *Laurentius (Antipope)*, Rome.
514 St. Hormisdas, Frosinone.
523 John I., Tuscany.
526 St. Felix IV., Samnium.
530 Boniface II., Rome.
530 *Dioscurus (Antipope)*, Rome.
532 John II., Rome.
535 St. Agapetus I., Rome.
536 St. Sylverius, Frosinone.
538 Vigilius, Rome.
555 Pelagius I., Rome.

5. Under the Lombard Kings,
A.D. 568–769.

560 St. John III., Rome.
574 St. Benedict I., Rome.
578 St. Pelagius II., Rome.
590 St. Gregory I. (the Great), Rome.
604 Sabinian, Bieda.
607 Boniface III., Rome.
608 Boniface IV., Abruzzi.
615 Deusdedit, Rome.
619 Boniface V., Naples.
625 Honorius I., Frosinone.
640 Severinus, Rome.
640 John IV., Dalmatia.
642 Theodore I., Jerusalem.
649 St. Martin I., Todi.
654 Eugenius I., Rome.
657 Vitalian, Segni.
672 Adeodatus, Rome.
675 Domnus I., Rome.
678 Agatho, Sicily.
682 St. Leo II., Sicily.
684 Benedict II., Rome.
685 John V., Antioch.
686 *Peter (Antipope)*, Rome.
686 *Theodore (Antipope)*, Rome.
687 Conon, Sicily.
686 *Paschal (Antipope)*.
687 Sergius I., Antioch.
701 John VI., Greece.
705 John VII., Greece.
708 Sisinius, Syria.
708 Constantine, Syria.
715 Gregory II., Rome.
731 Gregory III., Syria.
741 Zacharias, Magna Grecia.

A.D.
752 Stephen II. or III., Rome.
752 Stephen III., Rome.
757 Paul I., Rome.
768 *Theophilactus (Antipope)*.
768 *Constantine II. (Antipope)*, Nepi.
769 *Philip (Antipope)*, Rome.
768 Stephen IV., Reggio.

6. Under the Frankish Emperors,
A.D. 774–887.

772 Adrian I. (Colonna), Rome.
795 St. Leo III., Rome.
816 Stephen V., Rome.
817 Paschal I., Rome.
824 Eugenius II., Rome.
826 *Zinzinius (Antipope)*, Rome.
827 Valentine, Rome.
827 Gregory IV., Rome.
844 Sergius II., Rome.
845 Leo IV., Rome.
　　　(*Fable of Pope Joan.*)
857 St. Benedict III., Rome.
858 *Anastasius (Antipope)*, Rome.
858 Nicholas I., Rome.
867 Adrian II., Rome.
872 John VIII., Rome.
882 Martin II., Gallese.
884 Adrian III., Rome.

7. Under the Interregnum,
A.D. 887–962.

885 Stephen VI., Rome.
891 Formosus, Ostia.
891 *Sergius III. (Antipope)*.
896 Boniface VI., Tuscany.
896 Stephen VII., Rome.
897 Romanus I., Gallese.
897 Theodore II., Rome.
898 John IX., Tivoli.
900 Benedict IV., Rome.
903 Leo V., Ardea.
903 Christopher, Rome.
904 Sergius III., Rome.
911 Anastasius III., Rome.
913 Landonius, Sabina.
913 John X., Ravenna.
928 Leo VI., Rome.
929 Stephen VIII., Rome.
931 John XI., Rome.
936 Leo VII., Rome.
939 Stephen IX., Germany.
943 Martin III., Rome.
946 Agapetus II., Rome.
956 John XII. (Prince Alberic), Rome.

8. *Under the German Emperors (Saxon line),* A.D. 962–1002.

A.D.
964 *Leo (Antipope),* Rome.
964 *Benedict V.,* Rome.
965 John XIII., Narni.
972 Benedict VI., Rome.
974 Domnus II., Rome.
975 Benedict VII., Rome.
980 *Boniface VII. (Francone), Antipope.*
983 John XIV., Pavia.
985 John XV., Rome.
996 Gregory V. (Bruno), Saxony.
998 *John XVII. (Antipope).*
999 Sylvester II. (Gerbert), Auvergne.

9. *Under the Franconian line of German Emperors,* A.D. 1024–1125.

1003 John XVI., Rome.
1003 John XVII., Rome.
1009 Sergius IV., Rome.
1012 Benedict VIII., Tusculum.
1024 John XVIII., Tusculum.
1033 Benedict VIII., Tusculum.
1043 *Sylvester III. (Antipope).*
1046 Gregory VI., Rome.
1047 Clement II. (Suidger), Saxony.
1048 Damasus II., Bavaria.
1049 St. Leo IX., Alsace.
1055 Victor II., Bavaria.
1057 Stephen X., Lorraine.
1058 *Benedict X. (Antipope),* Rome.
1058 Nicholas II. (Gherardus), Burgundy.
1061 Alexander II. (Badazio), Milan.
1061 *Honorius II. (Cadalous of Parma), Antipope.*
1073 St. Gregory VII. (Hildebrand, or Aldrobrandeschi), Soana in Tuscany.
1080 *Clement II. (Guibert of Ravenna), Antipope.*
1086 Victor III. (Epifani), Beneventum.
1088 Urban II., Rheims.
1099 Paschal II., Bieda.
1100 *Albert (Antipope),* Atella.
1102 *Theodoric (Antipope),* Rome.
1102 *Sylvester III. (Antipope),* Rome.
1118 Gelasius II. (Giov. Caetano), Gaeta.
1118 *Gregory VIII. (Antipope),* Spain.
1119 Calixtus II., Burgundy.
1124 Honorius II. (Fagnani), Bologna.

A.D.
1124 *Theobald ("Bocca di Pecore") Antipope.*
1130 Innocent II. (Papareschi), Rome.
1130 *Anacletus II. (Antipope).*

10. *Under the Suabian line of Emperors,* A.D. 1138–1250.

1138 *Victor IV. (Antipope).*
1143 Celestin II. (Città di Castello).
1144 Lucius II., Bologna.
1145 Eugenius III. (Paganelli), Pisa.
1150 Anastasius IV., Rome.
1154 Adrian IV. (Nicholas Breakspeare), Langley, England.
1159 Alexander III. (Bandinelli), Siena.
1159 *Victor IV. (Cardinal Octavian), Antipope,* Rome.
1164 *Paschal III. (Antipope),* Cremona.
1169 *Calixtus III. (Antipope),* Hungary.
1178 *Innocent III. (Antipope),* Rome.
1181 Lucius III., Lucca.
1185 Urban III. (Crivelli), Milan.
1187 Gregory VIII. (di Morra), Beneventum.
1187 Clement III. (Scolari), Rome.
1191 Celestin III. (Buboni), Rome.
1198 Innocent III. (Conti), Anagni.
1216 Honorius III. (Savelli), Rome.
1227 Gregory IX. (Conti), Anagni.
1241 Celestin IV. (Castiglioni), Milan.
1243 Innocent IV. (Fieschi), Genoa.
1254 Alexander IV. (Conti), Anagni.
1261 Urban IV., Troyes.
1264 Clement IV. (Foucauld), Narbonne.
1271 Gregory X. (Visconti), Piacenza.
1276 Innocent V., Savoy.
1276 Adrian V. (Fieschi), Genoa.
1276 John XIX. or XX. or XXI., Lisbon.

11. *Rome under the Popes.*

1st *Period.* *The Popes at Rome,* A.D. 1277–1305.

1277 Nicholas III. (Orsini), Rome.
1281 Martin IV., Champaign.
1285 Honorius IV. (Savelli), Rome.
1287 Nicholas IV. (Masci), Ascoli.
1292 Celestin V. (Pietro da Murrone), Sernia.

A.D.

1294 Boniface VIII. (Benedetto Caetani), Anagni.

1303 Benedict XI. (Boccasini), Treviso.

2nd Period. *The Papal See at Avignon,* A D. 1305-1378.

1305 Clement V. (de Couth), Bordeaux.

1316 John XXII. (Jacques d'Euse), Cahors.

1334 *Nicholas V. (Antipope at Rome),* Rieti.

1334 Benedict XII. (Jacques Fournier), Foix.

1342 Clement VI. (Pierre Roger), Limoges.

1352 Innocent VI. (Etienne Aubert), Limoges.

1362 Urban V. (Guillaume Grimoard), Mende.

1370 Gregory XI. (Pierre Roger), Limoges.

3rd Period. *Rome, after the return from Avignon,* A.D. 1378, *to the present time.*

1378 Urban VI. (Bartolommeo Prignano), Naples.

1387 *Clement VII. (Robert of Geneva), Antipope at Avignon.*

1389 Boniface IX. (Pietro Tomacelli), Naples.

1394 *Benedict XIII. (Pedro de Luna, a Spaniard), Antipope at Avignon.*

1404 Innocent VII. (Cosmato de' Meliorati), Sulmona.

1406 Gregory XII. (Angelo Corrario), Venice.

1409 Alexander V. (Petrus Phylargyrius), Candia.

1410 John XXIII. (Baldassare Cossa), Naples.

1417 Martin V. (Oddone Colonna), Rome.

1424 *Clement VIII. (a Spaniard), Antipope at Avignon.*

1431 Eugenius IV. (Gabriele Condolmeri), Venice.

1439 *Felix V, (Antipope).* [End of the Western Schism.]

1447 Nicholas V. (Tommaso Parentucelli, or Tomasso di Sarzana), Sarzana.

A.D.

1455 Calixtus III. (Alfonso Borgia), Valencia.

1458 Pius II. (Æneas Sylvius Piccolomini), Pienza.

1464 Paul II. (Pietro Barbo), Venice.

1471 Sixtus IV. (Francesco della Rovere), Savona.

1484 Innocent VIII. (Gio-Battista Cibo), Genoa.

1492 Alexander VI. (Rodrigo Lenzoli Borgia), Spain.

1503 Pius III. (Antonio Todeschini Piccolomini), Siena.

1503 Julius II. (Giuliano della Rovere), Savona.

1513 Leo X. (Giovanni de' Medici), Florence.

1522 Adrian VI. (Adrian Florent), Utrecht).

1523 Clement VII. (Giulio de' Medici), Florence.

1534 Paul III. (Alessandro Farnese), Rome.

1550 Julius III. (Gio. Maria Ciocchi del Monte), Monte San Savino.

1555 Marcellus II. (Marcello Cervini), Montepulciano.

1555 Paul IV. (Gio. Pietro Caraffa), Naples.

1559 Pius IV. (Giovan-Angelo de' Medici), Milan.

1566 St. Pius V. (Michele Ghislieri), Tortona.

1572 Gregory XIII. (Ugo Buoncompagni), Bologna.

1585 Sixtus V. (Felice Peretti), of Montalto, born at Grottamare.

1590 Urban VII. (Gio-Battista Castagna), Rome.

1590 Gregory VXI. (Nicolo Sfrondati), Cremona.

1591 Innocent IX. (Giov. Antonio Facchinetti), Bologna.

1592 Clement VIII. (Ippolito Aldobrandini), of a Florentine family, but born at Fano.

1605 Leo XI. (Alessandro Ottaviano de' Medici), Florence.

1605 Paul V. (Camillo Borghese), Rome.

1621 Gregory XV. (Alessandro Ludovisi), Bologna.

1623 Urban VIII. (Matteo Barberini), Florence.

A.D.
1644 Innocent X. (Gio-Battista Pamfili), Rome.
1655 Alexander VII. (Fabio Chigi),
Siena.
1667 Clement IX. (Giulio Rospigliosi),
Pistoja.
1670 Clement X. (Gio-Battista Altieri),
Rome.
1676 Innocent XI. (Benedetto Odes-
calchi), Como.
1689 Alexander VIII. (Pietro Ottoboni), Venice.
1691 Innocent XII. (Antonio Pigna-
telli), Naples.
1700 Clement XI. (Gio. Francesco Albani), Urbino.
1721 Innocent XIII. (Michelangelo
Conti), Rome.
1724 Benedict XIII. (Pietro Francesco
Orsini), Rome.
1730 Clement XII. (Lorenzo Corsini),
Florence.
1740 Benedict XIV. (Prospero Lambertini), Bologna.
1758 Clement XIII. (Carlo Rezzonico),
Venice.
1769 Clement XIV. (Antonio Ganganelli), St. Angelo in Vado.
1775 Pius VI. (Giov. Angelo Braschi),
Cesena.
1800 Pius VII. (Gregorio Barnaba
Chiaramonti), Cesena.
1823 Leo XII. (Annibale della Genga),
Spoleto.
1829 Pius VIII. (Francesco Xaviere
Castiglione), Cingoli.
1831 Gregory XVI. (Mauro Cappel-
lari), Belluno.
1846 Pius IX. (Giovanni Maria Mas-
tai-Ferretti), born at Sinigallia,
May 13, 1792; created Cardinal
December 23, 1839, elected
Pope June 16, 1846.

LORDS, THEN MARQUISES, AFTERWARDS
DUKES OF FERRARA.

1067 Frederic I.
1118 Guy Salinguerra.
1150 Taurello.
1196 Salinguerra II.
1196 Azzo VI., Marquis d'Este : to the
ascendency of whose house the
Torrelli afterwards gave way.
1212 Aldrovandino.

A.D.
1215 Azzo VII. d'Este.
1264 Obizzo II.
1293 Azzo VIII.
1308 Folco d'Este.
1317 Obizzo III. and Rinaldo d'Este.
1352 Aldrovandino III.
1361 Niccolò II.
1388 Alberto.
1393 Niccolò III.
1441 Lionello.
1450 Borso, first Duke of Ferrara and
Modena in 1452.
1471 Ercole I.
1505 Alfonso I.
1534 Ercole II.
1559 Alfonso II.
1597 Cesare I. declared illegitimate by
Clement VIII., and forced to
relinquish in 1598 Ferrara to
the Church; retires to Modena.
From him are descended the
Dukes of Modena, until the
extinction of the male branch
of the House of Este, in the
person of Duke Ercole Rinaldo
in 1803.

DUKES OF URBINO.

1474 Federigo di Montefeltro, Count
of Urbino from 1444, created
Duke by Sixtus IV. in 1474.
1482 Guid' Ubaldo I. di Montefeltro.
1508 Francesco Maria della Rovere.
1538 Guid' Ubaldo II. della Rovere.
1574 Francesco Maria II. della Rovere,
abdicated in 1626.

GRAND-DUKES OF TUSCANY.

1. *House of Medici.*

1537 Cosmo I. (1569).
1574 Francesco I.
1587 Ferdinando I.
1609 Cosmo II.
1621 Ferdinando II.
1670 Cosmo III.
1723 Giov. Gastone.

2. *House of Lorraine.*

1737 Francis (emperor of Germany in
1745).
1765 Leopold II. (id., 1790).
1790 Ferdinand III.
1824 Leopold II.

HANDBOOK

FOR

TRAVELLERS IN CENTRAL ITALY.

THE PAPAL STATES.

PRELIMINARY INFORMATION.

§ 1. Passports.—§ 2. Lascia-passare.—§ 3. Frontier and Custom-Houses.—§ 4. Money.—§ 5. Roads.—§ 6. Railroads.—§ 7. Posting.—§ 8. Vetturini.—§ 9. Inns.

ROUTES.

To facilitate reference, the names are printed in *italics* in those Routes under which they are fully described.

ROUTE	PAGE
1. Mantua to Ferrara	10
2. Modena to Ferrara	10
3. Padua to *Ferrara*	10
4. Ferrara to Bologna, by *Malalbergo*	23
5. Ferrara to Bologna, by *Cento*	23
6. Modena to *Bologna*	25
7. Bologna to Florence, by *Pietramala* and the *Pass of la Futa*	65
7A. Bologna to Florence, by *La Poretta*, the *Pass of la Collina*, and Pistoia	68
7B. Faenza to Florence, by *Marradi* and *Borgo S. Lorenzo*	71
8. Florence to Forli, by *Dicomano* and the *Pass of S. Benedetto*	72
9. Forli to Ravenna	73
10. Faenza to Ravenna	73
11. Venice to Ravenna, by the *Canals* and *Comacchio*	73

ROUTE	PAGE
12. Bologna to *Ravenna*, by Imola and *Lugo*	76
12B. Bologna to Ravenna, by *Medicina* and Lugo	95
13. Ravenna to Rimini	95
14. Bologna to Ancona, by *Forli, Cesena, Rimini, San Marino, Pesaro, Fano*, and *Sinigallia*	96
15. Ancona to Foligno, by *Loreto, Macerata, Tolentino*, and the *Pass of Colfiorito*	116
16. Fano to Foligno, by the Strada del *Furlo, Cagli*, and *Nocera*	126
17. Fano to *Urbino*, by *Fossombrone*	130
18. Urbino to *Città di Castello*, by *San Giustino*	134
19. San Giustino to *Borgo San Sepolero* and Arezzo	142
20. Città di Castello to *Gubbio*	144

Cent. It.

B

ROUTES—continued.

ROUTE	PAGE	ROUTE	PAGE
21. Città di Castello to Perugia . 147		26A. Florence to Siena, by the Post-road . . . 204	
22. Perugia to Rome, by *Todi*, Narni, *Pontefelice*, and the Tiber 147		26B. Siena to Arezzo, by Monte S. Savino 205	
22A. Perugia to *Città della Pieve* 148		26C. *Chiusi* and the Val di Chiana to Siena . . . 205	
23. Montefiascone to Orvieto, Città della Pieve, and Chiusi . 149		26D. Siena to *Grosseto* . . 206	
24. Rieti to Rome, by the Via Salara 160		26E. Florence to *Volterra*, the *Boracic Acid Lagoni*, and *Massa Maritima* . . 207	
25. Leghorn to *Civita Vecchia*, by the *Sea-coast* . . 163		27. Florence to Rome, by the *Val d'Arno di Sopra*, Arezzo, *Cortona*, *Perugia*, *Assisi*, *Foligno*, *Spoleto*, and *Civita Castellana* . . 221	
25A. Civita Vecchia to Rome . 170			
26. Florence to Rome, by *Siena* and *Viterbo* . . . 172			

§ 1.—PASSPORTS.

BEFORE the traveller enters the Papal States, it is indispensably necessary that his passport bear the *visa* either of the Nuncio residing in the last capital he has visited, or of a Papal Consul at the nearest seaport. It will be useful, in the event of his passing through France at the outset of his tour, to obtain the *visa* of the Nuncio at Paris; although this will not dispense with the *visa* of the Papal agent at the nearest town to the frontier. But if circumstances deprive him of the opportunity of applying to a Minister, the signature of the Consul in some important town will be sufficient. The Austrian *visa* is also desirable, not merely for the Papal States, but for all parts of Italy. On arriving at the frontier, the passport is examined and countersigned as usual; and in seaports, as Ancona and Civita Vecchia, where a British Consular Agent resides, his signature is likewise necessary.

On entering the principal towns of the Papal States, with few exceptions, the passport is demanded at the gates, in order to be signed; but to save delay, the traveller is allowed to name the inn at which he proposes to stop, so that the passport may be sent after him. A fee of one or two pauls is required for each *visa*; and in garrison towns this process is repeated on leaving them.

Before the traveller quits Rome on his return to England, it is desirable that his passport be signed by the Ministers of all the Sovereigns through whose dominions it is intended to pass: those of Austria, Tuscany, and France should on no account be omitted.

§ 2.—LASCIA-PASSARE.

Persons travelling in their own carriage should write a week beforehand to their correspondent or banker at Rome, or to the British Consul, requesting that a *lascia-passare* may be forwarded to the frontier, and another left at the gates of Rome, in order to avoid the formalities of the custom-house. The lascia-passare is never granted to persons travelling in public carriages.

§ 3.—FRONTIER AND CUSTOM-HOUSES.

The Papal frontier-stations and custom-houses (Dogana) are marked by the arms of the reigning Pontiff, surmounted by the triple crown and crossed keys.

The custom-house visit is less severe than in many other States of Italy, and a timely fee will save the traveller much inconvenience. It is by far the best plan to propitiate the officer by administering this fee at once; for the saving of time and trouble amply compensates the outlay of 2 or 3 pauls. Books are an especial object of inquiry; but on the whole they are less rigidly examined in these States than in the Lombardo-Venetian kingdom and in Naples.

§ 4.—MONEY.

Letters of Credit, or the circular notes of Herries or Coutts, are usually carried by travellers; the latter are in many respects the most convenient. Letters of credit are useful in the large capitals in securing the good offices of the banker. Travellers will find it very convenient to take a certain sum in French gold napoleons, which pass currently in the Papal States, as throughout Italy, and generally bear a premium. English bank-notes and sovereigns can only be exchanged in the larger towns, and then with difficulty and at a loss.

The Roman coinage, which is arranged on the decimal system, consists of scudi, pauls, baiocchi, and quattrini; each scudo consists of 10 pauls; the paul of 10 baiocchi; and the baiocco of 5 quattrini. The principal coinage is in silver and copper; of gold there is very little, although, from the present lower price of that metal, some gold coins have been recently issued from the mint. In consequence of the premium which they bear in Tuscany, nearly the whole of the smaller silver coins have disappeared, and have been replaced by a most inconvenient copper coinage, to the extent of several millions of dollars.

During the last 5 years the principal circulating medium at Rome has been paper, in notes varying from 1 to 100 scudi: this paper, although a legal tender, has been at all times at a discount, varying from 35 per cent. in 1850, to 5 per cent. in 1853; that is, to obtain 100 dollars in silver, it is necessary to pay 105 in paper, whilst the agio between the paper and copper money did not exceed 1 per cent. In consequence of the increasing prosperity of the Roman finances, and the issue of a metallic coinage in 1853, the discount on paper-money has fallen of late; still the traveller, in all his pecuniary transactions at Rome, should be on his guard, and, especially with tradespeople and hotel-keepers, specify in what currency his bills are to be paid; many of the latter gentry especially, having taken a very unfair advantage of foreigners by insisting on all payments being made in silver—an imposition as regards them, at least, which ought to be resisted, considering the very high prices charged, and that such a pretension is raised principally by the masters of the most expensive hotels.

The following table will show the value of Roman money, in the currency of England, France, and the other Italian States, at the ordinary rate of exchange, always supposing the Roman scudo, or fractions of it, to be in gold or silver.

	English.	French Francs, or Italian Lire.	Tuscan Lire, Soldi, and Denari.	Tuscan Florins and Cents.	Austrian Lire and Cents.
GOLD.					
Doppia nuova of Pius VII. (pistole) = 32 pauls 1 baj.	s. d. 13 8¼	17 27 0	20 11 2	12 33	19 83
Zecchino (sequin) = 20 „ 5 „	9 4½	11 80 0	14 1 0	8 43	13 55
The new piece of 5 scudi . . = 50 „ . .	21 4½	26 86 0	31 19 6	19 18	30 87
Ditto of 2½ scudi . = 25 „ . .	10 8⅛	13 44 0	16 0 0	9 60	15 44
SILVER.					
The scudo (Roman dollar) . . = 10 „ . .	4 3¼	5 37 0	6 6 8	3 80	6 17
Mezzo scudo . . = 5 „ . .	2 1½	2 69 0	3 3 4	1 90	3 09
Testone . . . = 3 „ . .	1 3¼	1 61 0	1 18 0	1 14	1 85
Papetto . . . = 2 „ . .	0 10¼	1 07 0	1 5 4	0 76	1 23
Paolo (paul) . . = . 10 baj.	0 5¼	0 0 54	0 12 8	0 38	0 61
Grosso (½ paul) . = . 5 „	0 2½	0 0 27	0 6 4	0 19	0 30
COPPER.					
Bajoccho . . = . 5 quat.	about ½	0 0 5	0 1 3	. .	0 6
Mezzo bajoccho . = . 2½ „					
Quattrino . . = . 2 den.					

By a decree issued in March 1848, it was ordered that the 5-franc piece of silver coinage, and the napoleon or 20-franc piece of gold coinage, current in the Republic of France, the Kingdom of Sardinia, and the Grand Duchy of Parma, shall circulate in the States of the Church—the first at the rate of 93 baj., and the second at the rate of 3 scudi 72 baj., and their multiples in gold in the same ratio. Before this decree the napoleon was generally worth 37 pauls. The Spanish dollar is worth 10 pauls; the Tuscan francescone 10½ pauls; the Neapolitan piastre 9 pauls 4 baj. The exchange with England may be generally calculated at 47 pauls in silver money for the pound sterling; but as accounts have been of late years kept in the depreciated paper currency, the exchange has been computed according to the discount on it, so that, in the official weekly table of the Roman bankers, the exchange has frequently been set down as high as at 48 and 49 pauls. In Bologna the Roman scudo is divided into 5 lire, and the bajoccho is called a soldo: this lira is equal to 1 fr. 07 cents. The accounts throughout the Papal States are kept in scudi and pauls.

Weights and Measures.

There can scarcely be said to be any general system of weights and measures in the Papal States, each locality having its particular units of each, which it has preserved from time immemorial. The following is a table of the weights and measures more generally in use, and especially in the capital.

Measures of Length.

Roman foot	English inches	. $11\frac{73}{100}$
„ palm	„	. $8\frac{79}{100}$
„ braccio of 4 palms	„	. $33\frac{7}{10}$
„ „ used in measuring silk goods .	„	. 27
„ canna of 8 palms	„	. $78\frac{1}{3}$

Measures of Distance.

Roman mile	English yards .	1629
„ post	„ miles .	7$\frac{1}{10}$

Ancient Measures of Length according to Canina.

Roman foot	English inches .	11$\frac{45}{100}$
Passus of 5 feet	„ feet .	4$\frac{84}{100}$
Roman mile, 1481$\frac{3}{4}$ metres	„ yards .	1600$\frac{1}{2}$

Land Measure.

Rubbio	Imperial acres .	4$\frac{9}{10}$

Measures of Capacity.

Barile, 32 bocale, wine measure	English gallon .	12$\frac{64}{100}$
Bocale	„ quarts .	1$\frac{6}{10}$
Barile for oil	„ gallons	12$\frac{84}{100}$
Rubbio for grain	Imperial bushels	8$\frac{7}{10}$

Weights.

Ordinary Roman pound	avoirdupois oz.	13
Pound used in weighing gold and silver, of 12 ounces, or 288 denari . . . . . }	grains troy	5187
Ounce	„	432$\frac{1}{4}$
Denaro	„	18

§ 5.—ROADS.

The roads in the Papal States have undergone great improvement of late years; although still inferior to those of Tuscany, they are generally well kept.

The roads are divided into three classes: the consular, provincial, and communal. They are under the direction of the minister of Public Works, aided by a council of engineers, and fixed taxes are levied for their construction and repair. The consular roads are maintained by the levy of a tenth of the land-tax; the provincial by a variable tax upon the provinces; and the communal by a similar tax on the parishes. The expenses of the roads form a considerable item in the disbursements of the treasury. The Papal Government deserves great credit for the liberality with which improvements in this respect have been promoted; there are few countries in which the establishment of new lines of communication has been more encouraged, in proportion to the limited means at its disposal.

§ 6.—RAILROADS.

It is hoped that in a few years the principal towns of Southern Italy will be brought into communication by means of railroads. The only railroad yet opened in the countries described in this volume is the branch of the Tuscan Leopolda railway between Empoli and Siena, and which traverses the beautiful Val d'Elsa from the Val d'Arno to Poggibonsi, rising by a rapid incline from thence to Siena.

Of projected railways, which are likely to be executed in a few years, the most important will be the branch of the great Centro-Italian line, cor nécting the valleys of the Po and Arno, and traversing the Apennines between Bologna and Pistoja by the valley of the Reno. The surveys for this line have been completed, and a treaty concluded between the Governments of Austria, Modena, Parma, Tuscany, and the Holy See, whose territories it will traverse, for its execution, each state guaranteeing a minimum rate of interest to the shareholders. The Centro-Italian Railroad will connect Piacenza, Parma, Modena, and Bologna, and the latter with Florence, Leghorn, and Siena, by the Tuscan railways now in operation; and by branches from Piacenza to Milan, and from Modena to Mantua, the Austrian possessions in Lombardy with the countries south of the Po. South of the Apennines the Tuscan Government has given its sanction to a railway between Florence and Arezzo, from whence, at some future day, it is expected that a branch will be extended to the upper valley of the Tiber, and from thence to the shores of the Adriatic.

A line of railway (Pia Latina) to connect Rome with Naples, by the valley of the Sacco, Ceprano, and San Germano, &c., has been long decreed by the Papal Government, but want of funds has hitherto prevented its execution. During the present year, a company having come forward with the necessary capital, the section extending from Rome to Frascati· and Albano has been resumed, and, as the greater part of the earthworks are completed, it is expected this short branch will be opened in 1854.·

§ 7.—POSTING.

The Post-houses in the Papal States are distinguished by the arms of the reigning Pontiff. The service is under the control of Government. Fixed charges are made for posting, postilions, &c. The postmasters must be approved by Government, and be furnished with a licence granted by the postmaster-general at Rome. There are no turnpikes, and the general arrangements are very nearly like those of France.

The postmasters are supplied with a printed book of instructions, in which all particulars of their duties are noted. The most important items, so far as the convenience of the traveller is concerned, are the following:—Horses and postilions are to be always ready for service; but the postmaster is bound only to keep the precise number of each specified in his agreement, or by the order of the director-general. One open and two covered carriages are to be kept for travellers who require them. Postmasters are forbidden to supply horses without a written licence from the authorities of the place of departure, or a passport from the secretary of state. Postmasters are not allowed to supply horses to travellers, unless they have a sufficient number remaining to fulfil the duties of the post; nor are they allowed to send horses forward to change on the road, nor to transfer horses from one station to another. They are bound to keep two postilions ready for service night and day, and to have written over the principal door of the post-house the length of the post, price of the course, and a statement of the right of a third or fourth horse. The third or fourth horse can only be enforced where the tariff specially allows it. They are bound to keep a book, with pages numbered and signed by the director-general or his deputy, in which a regular entry of the daily journeys may be kept, and travellers may enter any complaint against postilions. Travellers by post cannot relinquish this mode of travelling in less than three days from the time of departure, nor change their carriage, without permission from the secretary of state or the provincial authorities. Travellers who order post-horses, and afterwards alter their plans, are bound to pay half a post if they come to their lodgings before they are countermanded. When there are no horses, postmasters are bound to give travellers a declaration in writing to that effect (la fede); after which they may provide themselves with horses elsewhere, but only to carry them to the next post; and if there are no horses at that post, then the postilions are bound to go on without stopping to the third post, where they may stop an hour to bait: this rule applies to all the successive posts, until regular post-horses are procured. The time allowed for the passage of government messengers from one post to another is two hours ; for ordinary or extraordinary estafettes, carrying despatches on horseback, one hour and a half. Postmasters and postilions are forbidden to demand more than the price allowed by the tariff.

The following are the regulations in force as to carriages. Three classes are recognized, and the following rules adopted in regard to each :—

1. For cabriolets or covered carriages with one seat, whatever their number of wheels, carrying a small trunk and travelling bag (or a small imperial only), two horses if travellers be not more than three ; three horses if there are four passengers, with power to charge for four horses, which the travellers may have attached to the carriage on paying for a second postilion.

2. For covered carriages, with two seats and leather curtains by the side, like the common vetturino, and for regular calèches having only one seat, both descriptions carrying a trunk, a travelling bag, and a small portmanteau, three horses if there be two or three persons ; if four persons, then a fourth horse is charged, which the travellers may have, as before, on paying a second postilion. If these carriages contain five or six persons, they are considered carriages of the third class.

3. For berlines and carriages of four seats, with an imperial, a trunk, travelling bag, &c., four horses if carrying two or three persons; if four, then a fifth horse is charged; if five or six persons, six horses; if seven, the number of horses is the same, but seven are charged.

Where carriages contain a greater number than is mentioned above under each class, no greater number of horses is required, but a charge of four pauls per post is fixed for each person above the number. A child under seven years is not reckoned, but two of that age are counted as one person.

When the quantity of luggage is evidently greater than the usual weight, a tax of three pauls per post is allowed to be imposed. Travellers may obtain, on starting, a *bolletta di viaggio,* specifying in separate columns all particulars relating to the number of horses, baggage, charges, &c. exclusive of postilions and ostlers. In this case one is given to the traveller, the other to the postilion, who is bound to pass it to the next, until it is finally lodged in the post-office of the town at which the journey ends. All complaints may be noted on this document, as well as any expression of *ben servito* on the part of the postilions. Travellers should obtain this *bolletta* at the post-office of the first post-town ; it will protect them from imposition, and costs only one paul.

In case of dispute between travellers and postmaster or postilions, it is provided by the general order of the Cardinal Secretary, that an appeal be made to the local director (*direttore locale*), who has power to put both postmaster and his men under arrest for three days, or to suspend them for ten days, reporting the fact to the director-general in Rome, to whom it belongs to take ulterior measures. In places where the post-house is an inn, travellers are sometimes told that there are no horses in order to induce them to stop. If there be reason to suspect that this statement is made from interested motives, application should at once be made to the local director.

However precise and clear the postal regulations may appear on paper, in practice they are so much open to being differently interpreted, especially as regards the classification of carriages, that travellers are subject to most gross imposition from postmasters by insisting to put on a larger number of extra horses than the law warrants their doing. This generally occurs in remote situations, where the traveller, having no redress, must submit stoically to such imposition and annoyance. To avoid this the Bureau of the Pontifical Diligences at the Roman post-office undertakes to furnish post-horses, and to pay th·

Postmasters on depositing a fixed sum, the amount of which is settled after the carriage and its luggage have been inspected by one of their *employés*, the traveller having only to pay the barriers, bridge tolls, and extra *buonamano* to the postilions. This arrangement may be now (1853) made for the roads from Rome to Naples by Terracina, from Rome to Florence by Siena, and thence to Bologna and Padua, and will probably be extended to all the other post-roads in the Pontifical States. The adoption of this mode of payment, whilst it assures to the postmaster what he is entitled to by the post regulations, will save the parties adopting it a vast deal of annoyance and quarrelling.

The following is the Tariff for Ordinary Posts:—

Each horse	5 pauls per post.
Postilion, each	3½ ditto ditto
Stable-boy, for every pair	½ ditto ditto
Saddlehorse, or courier	4 ditto ditto
Two-wheel carriage, furnished by postmaster	3 ditto ditto
A carriage with four places inside, and four wheels, also furnished by postmaster .	6 ditto ditto

The postilion's *buonamano*, although fixed by the preceding tariff at 3½ pauls, is generally 5½ or 6 pauls, or more, according to good conduct. A separate postilion is required for each pair of horses. The following will therefore be the expense of posting, giving each postilion 5½ pauls per post:—

Post.	2 horses.	3 horses.	4 horses and 2 postilions.
1 . . .	16 pauls . . .	21 pauls . . .	32 pauls.
1¼ . . .	20 ,, . . .	26·2 ,, . . .	40 ,,
1½ . . .	24 ,, . . .	21·4 ,, . . .	48 ,,
1¾ . . .	28 ,, . . .	36·6 ,, . . .	56 ,,

The length of the Roman post is 8 miles, equal to 7¼ English miles nearly. The length of the modern Roman mile is 1629 English yards, a little more than nine-tenths of an English mile. The length of the Tuscan mile is 1808, and of the Neapolitan 2436 yards. The Italian or geographical mile, of 60 to the degree, is 2025·4 English yards.

§ 8.—VETTURINI.

Families who do not travel in their own carriage must in a great measure be dependent on the vetturino: indeed there are many parts where it is the only available mode of communication. A duplicate agreement should be drawn up before starting, and attested by some person in authority. Before making the agreement, when the exclusive use of the carriage is required, it is necessary to see both carriage and horses in order to ascertain that they are what they ought to be, and take such note of them as to be able to declare that any others which may be substituted at the moment of starting are not those agreed for: it is also desirable to specify in the agreement that the journey is to be performed with the particular carriage and horses already seen and approved. The vetturino generally undertakes to provide breakfast, dinner, supper, and bed; but the experienced traveller knows well that he is worse off by this arrangement, although more economical, than he is when he provides for himself at the inns. The charge for one person varies, but it ought not to be more than 2 scudi a-day; from Bologna to Rome, a journey occupying 7 or 8 days, the charge for one person is from 12 to 18 scudi; from Bologna to Florence 3 to 4 scudi; and from Florence to Rome 10 to 15 scudi in 5 to 6 days, the price and time employed varying with the season of the year. When a single traveller or a party of friends engage a carriage for their own use, the agreement should expressly stipulate that no other person is to be taken up on any pretence whatever; otherwise occasions will soon be found for forcing other persons into it. 10 scudi a-day should cover all expenses of a private vetturino carriage with 2 or 3 horses, including the fee to the driver and *chevaux di renfort* when necessary. All tolls should be made payable by the vetturino. It sometimes happens that the vetturino sells his engagements, in which case a traveller may be exposed to two or three changes of vehicle: this should also be distinctly provided against in the agreement, as well as any particular stages into which he may wish to divide the journey. The *buonamano* or *mancia,* i. e. fee to the driver, is usually ⅓ scudo a-day if " ben servito," or more if the journey be a short one: it is desirable that this be not included in the contract, but made conditional on good behaviour. When a vetturino is required to stop on the road for the convenience of travellers, he expects them to pay one or two scudi a night for each horse's expenses. The sum to be paid in this case should be stated in the agreement; one scudo per horse nightly is enough. In this respect posting has the advantage of permitting travellers to stop when they please, and visit places on the road, without this additional cost.

§ 9.—INNS.

These are given in detail under the description of the different towns: in the capitals and provincial cities they are generally good throughout Central Italy; but at the intermediate post-stations they are often very bad, and, like all the Italian inns, out of the largest towns, they are dirty and infested with vermin to an extent of which those who travel only in winter can have no idea. The prices vary in different towns, and particularly according to the circumstances in which the traveller makes his appearance; the charges for those who travel in their own carriages being notoriously higher, frequently by 100 per cent., than for those who travel by vetturino. Those who wish tea and coffee in the evening in preference to supper should carry milk with them from the place where they have slept on the previous night, as it is often not to be had in the evening at the inns on the road. The tea to be found at the smaller inns is generally so bad that travellers in Italy will do well to carry their own supply, and, what is equally necessary, a small metal teapot. In regard to prices, in the country and smaller towns 3 pauls a head is a proper price for dinner, 3 pauls for a bed, and 2 to 2½ pauls for breakfast, and 1 paul per night for servants; but the English in general are charged much higher, unless their previous experience enables them to resist the overcharge; as a general rule, it will save trouble and annoyance to fix beforehand the prices to be paid. In many places the inns at the post-houses are often built near the stables. The second floor of these houses is preferable to the first. In the smaller towns it would be absurd to carry English habits and prejudices so far as to expect the comforts and conveniences of great cities: travellers never gain anything by exacting or requiring more than the people can supply; and if they have sufficient philosophy to keep their temper, they will generally find that they are treated with civility.

ROUTES.

ROUTE 1.

MANTUA TO FERRARA.—52½ m.[1]

	Posts.
Mantua to Governolo	1½
Governolo to Sermide	1½
Sermide to Bondeno	1¾
Bondeno to Ferrara	1¾
	—
	6½

The old post-road from Mantua to Ferrara followed that to Padua as far as Nogara (1 post), whence it turned southward to Ostiglia, crossing the Po at Revere.

The present route follows the l. bank of the Mincio to Governolo, near which that river falls into the Po.

1½ Governolo. Leaving this place, the road skirts the l. bank of the Po as far as Ostiglia, whence it crosses to Revere. It then follows the rt. bank as far as

1½ Sermide, a post station. 8 m. farther, the frontier of the Lombardo-Venetian kingdom is passed at Quatrelle; and a little farther on is *Stellata*, the Papal Custom-house, where passports and baggage are examined; from hence the road follows the l. bank of the Panaro to

1¾ *Bondeno*, a small town on the l. bank of the Panaro, formerly a fief of the house of Este. The road hence to Ferrara lies through a flat, well-irrigated country, through Vigarano, Cassana, and Mizzana, to

1¾ FERRARA, described in Rte. 3.

ROUTE 2.

MODENA TO FERRARA.—49 m.

	Posts.
Modena to Bomporto	1
Bomporto to Finale	2
Finale to Bondeno	1½
Bondeno to Ferrara	1¾
	—
	6

[1] All miles not otherwise designated are English.

The road follows the banks of the Panaro for the first 3 posts.

1 Bomporto. From here it proceeds through Campo Santo, Cà de' Coppi, and Passo di Cà Bianca, to

2 Finale, situated on either side of the Panaro, which is here crossed. 3 m. farther on, at Serragliolo, the Modenese frontier is reached, and soon after the Papal Custom-house at *Santa Bianca*, from which the road soon reaches Bondeno, where it falls into the high post-road from Mantua. (Rte. 1.)

1½ Bondeno.

1¾ FERRARA (Rte. 3).

ROUTE 3.

PADUA TO FERRARA.—51¾ m.

	Posts.
Padua to Monselice	1½
Monselice to Rovigo	1½
Rovigo to Polesella	1
Polesella to Ferrara	2
	—
	6

The road between Padua and Rovigo follows the course of the canal, and in its interesting character contrasts strongly with the dull and wearisome plains which extend southward as far as Bologna. Before arriving at Rovigo, the Adige is crossed by a ferry-boat; and between it and Ferrara the Po is passed in a similar manner. The height of the embankments necessary to restrain the inundations of the Po will convince the traveller how much Ferrara and its plains are at the mercy of that river, the level of which is higher than the roofs of many of the houses in that city. The Papal frontier station and Dogana are at *Ponte Lagoscuro*, on the S. side of the river, called the "Port of the Po," from the considerable commerce it maintains with Lombardy in corn and wine, which are brought here for shipment. The Panfilio Canal leads direct from Ponte Lagoscuro to the Porta S. Benedetto at Ferrara, distant 3 m.

[FERRARA, *Forum Allieni* of Tacitus. —*Inns:* Albergo dell' Europa, kept by Bottazzi, opposite the Post and Diligence offices, is now the best in Ferrara, and highly spoken of: the Tre Mori, an old inn, is also much frequented, and not unreasonable: le Tre Corone.] Few cities ranking among the ancient Italian capitals are so much neglected by travellers as Ferrara, and yet few are more associated with interesting recollections. It is situated in a fertile but unhealthy plain, at a level of only 6½ ft. above the sea, and at a short distance from the Po, which forms here the boundary of the Lombardo-Venetian kingdom. The dreary plain of the Polesina, intersected only by the dikes of the river, presents an uniform and unbroken horizon, and extends, with little variation, up to the walls of Ferrara.

The aspect of the city, once the residence of a court celebrated throughout Europe, still retains many traces of its ancient grandeur. The broad, regular, and ample streets appear like those of a deserted capital; grass grows on the pavement, the magnificent palaces are falling into decay, and the walls, 7 miles in circuit, which once contained nearly 100,000 souls, now enclose scarcely one-third of that number. The population is collected together in the centre of the city, and thinly scattered over the remaining portion. Ravenna itself is hardly more fallen than Ferrara, although it was the great commercial emporium of Italy during the middle ages, the *città bene avventurosa* of Ariosto, and the *gran donna del Pò* of Tassoni.

The modern city is supposed to have been founded in the 5th century, when the invasion of the Huns and the destruction of Aquileja drove the inhabitants into the marshes for security. Its walls were built in the 6th century by the Exarchs of Ravenna, and it was raised to the rank of a city in 661, when the bishopric of Vigovenza was transferred to it. But the chief interest of Ferrara arises from its connection with the house of Este. As far back as the 10th century we find Ferrara connected with this family; first as supreme magistrates, and afterwards as hereditary princes (1240), holding generally of the Pope, though sometimes asserting their independence. It remained under their sway until the extinction of the legitimate branch in 1597, in the person of Alfonso II.; and in the following year it was attached to the Church by Clement VIII., on the pretext that Cæsar D'Este, the representative of the family by a collateral line, was disqualified by illegitimacy. During the 16th century the Court of Ferrara was unsurpassed by any other in Europe for its refinement and intelligence; its University was renowned throughout Christendom, and so many English students were collected within its walls as to form, as they did in Bologna, a distinct nation in that learned body. But there are greater names associated with the history of Ferrara at this period than those of its princely sovereigns. "Melancholy as the city looks now, every lover of Italian poetry," says Forsyth, "must view with affection the retreat of an Ariosto, a Tasso, a Guarini. Such is the ascent of wealth over genius, that one or two princes could create an Athens in the midst of this Bœotia. The little courts of Ferrara and Urbino seemed to emulate those of Alexandria and Pergamos, contending for pre-eminence only in literature and elegance."

The School of Ferrara, founded and patronised by the D'Este family, deserves especial notice in connection with this tribute to the intellectual history of the city. It is observed by Lanzi that "Ferrara boasts of a series of excellent painters, far superior to its fortunes and population; a circumstance which will not excite surprise when we consider the series of poets which it cherished, from Bojardo and Ariosto down to our own times, a sure criterion of accomplished and refined minds more than ordinarily disposed towards the fine arts." To this circumstance, and to the good taste of the inhabitants in their patronage of art, may be added the favourable position of the city, in its contiguity to Venice, Parma, and Bologna, and its convenient distance from Florence and Rome; so that its students were enabled to select from the different schools of Italy what was most congenial to the tastes of each, and to profit by their several excellences. So great, indeed, was the influence of this latter circumstance, that Zanetti considered it doubtful whether, after the 5 great schools, Ferrara did not claim precedence over all others. The first fact recorded in connection with the fine arts at Ferrara is the commission given by Azzo D'Este, in 1242, to the Venetian painter Gelasio di Niccolò, a pupil of the Greek artist Teofane of Constantinople, for a picture of the Fall of Phaëton. In the 14th century, when Giotto passed through Ferrara, on his way from Verona to Florence, he was employed by the Duke to paint some frescoes in his palace and in the church of St. Agostino, which were still extant in the time of Vasari. After the lapse of some years, during which several names are mentioned which have survived their works, Galasso Galassi appeared early in the 15th century; his works are chiefly confined to Bologna, and none are now found in his native city. He was followed by Antonio da Ferrara, known by his works at Urbino and Città di Castello, who painted some chambers in the palace of Alberto D'Este in 1438, at the time when the General Council was held there for the union of the Greek and Latin churches, and which is supposed to have supplied him with his subject. But the most celebrated of the early painters was Cosimo Tura or Cosmè, the pupil of Galassi, employed at the court of Borso D'Este: his minute and elaborate workmanship is admirably seen in the miniatures of the choir-books preserved in the cathedral. Among the painters of this period may be mentioned Lorenzo Costa, the reputed pupil of Francia, and Francesco Cossa, both known by their works at Bologna. Costa, indeed, may be regarded as the

true father of the school; for the series of painters from his time may be clearly traced; and Lanzi classes him among the first masters of Italy. His most eminent pupil was Ercole Grandi, called by Vasari Ercole da Ferrara, whose great work, painted for the Garganelli chapel, is now preserved in the Academy of Fine Arts at Bologna. Lodovico Mazzolino, better known as Mazzolino da Ferrara, another pupil of Costa, is known by his works in various galleries; and Domenico Panetti, the master of Garofalo, is remarkable for having become the pupil of his own scholar, and for the works he produced after his style had been remodelled on the example of Garofalo. The school of Ferrara was at its prime under the latter painter and the two Dossi, in the early part of the sixteenth century, when Alfonso D'Este was the patron of literature and art. This prince had invited Titian to adorn his palace; and, among other celebrated paintings, the "Cristo della Moneta," of the Dresden Gallery, was painted during his stay at Ferrara. Dosso Dossi, and his brother Giobattista, born at Dosso, in the vicinity of Ferrara, were among the earliest protégés of Alfonso and his successor Ercole II.; and their merit is sufficiently attested by the fact that Ariosto has immortalized them among the best painters of Italy. Ortolano is another painter of this school, whose works are often confounded with those of Garofalo; he is known as a successful imitator of Raphael, and some of his works are yet seen in his native city. Benvenuto Tisio, better known by the name of Garofalo, from the pink which he introduced into his paintings, stands at the head of the Ferrarese school, and is justly called the Raphael of Ferrara: some of his most celebrated works are still found here. His pupil, Girolamo de' Carpi, recommended to Ercole II. by Titian himself, and whose oil paintings were of extreme rarity in the time of Lanzi, may also be studied at Ferrara. While these two artists excelled in the graces of the art, Bastianino, or Bastiano Filippi, was introducing the style of Michael Angelo, as seen in the grand picture of the Last Judgment in the cathedral. Another painter of this school, Scarsellino, who was called the Paul Veronese of Ferrara, and who studied under that master, has left some works in his native place; he is, however, better known by those to be found in the galleries at Rome, where the name of his pupil, Camillo Ricci, a successful follower of the Venetian school, also occurs. Giuseppe Mazzuoli, known by the surname of Bastaruolo, and the contemporary of Bastianino, was called the Titian of Ferrara : we shall hereafter see that he has left behind him several works by which his claim to that title may be appreciated. Ferrara likewise contains some interesting examples of Domenico Mona, and of his able pupil Giulio Cromer, or Croma, who was selected to copy the principal paintings in the city, when the originals were transferred to Rome, after Clement VIII. had seized upon Ferrara and attached it to the Church. After this event the school rapidly declined for want of patronage and judicious management. Some Bolognese masters endeavoured, with little success, to introduce the style of the Caracci; Carlo Bonone, the scholar of Bastaruolo, was perhaps the most celebrated follower of this new method; his works in Sta. Maria in Vado are highly praised by Lanzi for their complete knowledge of that kind of foreshortening called *di sotto in su*, where figures are supposed to be seen above the eye. Another artist, worthy of mention as a follower of Bonone, is Chenda, or Alfonso Rivarola, who was employed, at the recommendation of Guido, to finish some of Bonone's works, but was better known by his decorations for public spectacles and tournaments. It is unnecessary to enumerate any of the painters whose names appear in the subsequent history of this school, for Ferrara never recovered the change of masters; and its school gradually declined, until, at length, in spite of the establishment of an academy, it became completely extinct: Notwithstanding, however, this decline and the loss of its political influence, Ferrara still retains many interesting examples of the school,

which will be noticed in the subsequent description of the city.

In addition to the brilliancy of its court and the celebrity of its school of art, Ferrara is remarkable for the impulse which it gave to the Reformation. The names of Ariosto and Tasso have almost eclipsed the recollection of that event, and of the asylum given to Calvin and to Marot by the Duchess Renée, the high-minded daughter of Louis XII., and the wife of Ercole II. At an early period Ferrara afforded protection to numerous friends of the reformed faith who fled from other parts of Italy, and even from countries beyond the Alps. Dr. M'Crie ascribes this circumstance to the influence of the accomplished princess just mentioned, who had become acquainted with the reformed doctrine previous to her departure from France in 1527, by means of some of those learned persons who frequented the court of Margaret Queen of Navarre. "The first persons to whom she extended her protection and hospitality were her own countrymen, whom the violence of persecution had driven out of France. Madame de Soubise, the governess of the duchess, had introduced several men of letters into the court of France during the late reign. She now resided at the court of Ferrara, along with her son, Jean de Parthenai, sieur de Soubise, afterwards a principal leader of the Protestant party in France; her daughter, Anne de Parthenai, distinguished for her elegant taste; and the future husband of this young lady, Antoine de Pons, Count de Marennes, who adhered to the reformed cause until the death of his wife. In the year 1534 the celebrated French poet Clement Marot fled from his native country, in consequence of the persecution excited by the affair of the *placards*; and, after residing for a short time at the court of the Queen of Navarre, in Bearn, came to Ferrara. He was recommended by Madame de Soubise to the duchess, who made him her secretary; and his friend Lyon Jamet, finding it necessary soon after to join him, met with a reception equally gracious. About the same time, the celebrated reformer John Calvin visited Ferrara, where he spent some months, under the assumed name of Charles Heppeville. He received the most distinguished attention from the duchess, who was confirmed in the Protestant faith by his instructions, and ever after retained the highest respect for his character and talents." Among the other learned personages assembled here at this time was Fulvio Peregrino Morata, who had been tutor to the two younger brothers of the duke, and who became still more celebrated as the father of Olympia Morata, the most enlightened female of her age; who first "acquired during her residence in the ducal palace that knowledge of the gospel which supported her mind under the privations and hardships which she afterwards had to endure."

The description of Ariosto, and the testimony of numerous contemporary authorities, proves that, under the sway of the house of Este, Ferrara was one of the great commercial cities of Italy. Its trade began to decline in the 16th century, and, although it has been much reduced even since that period, the city still carries on a considerable trade in agricultural produce. A great deal of business was formerly done here in hemp, of which large quantities found their way into the English dockyards, the Ferrara growth being considered the best for cordage; but, from the heavy export duties and other circumstances, the trade has considerably declined. The high duties on manufactured articles have thrown the foreign trade into the hands of the Swiss and the merchants of Lombardy, and all the circulating capital is in the hands of the Jews, who are in Ferrara a very opulent body; their number is about 3000. They inhabit, as in all the other Papal cities, a distinct quarter of the town called a *ghetto*; it was formerly usual at Rome and other places to lock them in at night; here, however, their importance has exempted them from the rigid observance of that rule. At the present time Ferrara is the capital of a Legation, comprehending 220,000 inhabitants, and 1278 square miles of territory; the population of the city and suburbs is 25,586.[1] In spite of their deserted appearance, the effect of its broad and handsome streets is particularly imposing; that of San Benedetto is 1¼ m. in length; and its palaces, though many of them are dilapidated have an air of grandeur in accordance with the former celebrity of the city.

The Cathedral, dedicated to St. Paul, was consecrated in 1135; its Gothic exterior, with few exceptions, belongs to that period, but the interior has been altered and spoiled by modern renovations. The front is divided by small towers, crowned with pinnacles, into 3 equal portions, each surmounted with a gable containing a wheel window, and ornamented with a range of pointed arches. The porch is composed of a semicircular arch supported by columns; the flanks have also semicircular arches. The bas-reliefs with which this part is covered are in a fine state of preservation; they represent the Last Judgment, various events in the life of Christ, the seven Mortal Sins, with numerous sacred, profane, and grotesque emblems. Over the left-hand door is a colossal bust of the Virgin, in Greek marble, long venerated as the miraculous Madonna of Ferrara. On the same side is a statue of Alberto d'Este, in the pilgrim's dress in which he returned from Rome, with bulls and indulgences, in 1390. The interior, in the form of a Greek cross, had been modernised at various times; the semicircular choir was first added in 1499, by Rosette, a native architect, known as one of the earliest restorers of Italian architecture; the portion beyond the transept dates from 1637; and the remainder from between 1712 and 1735. There are several interesting paintings to be noticed; the Assumption, the St. Peter and St. Paul, and the superb picture of the Virgin throned with Saints, are by *Garofalo.* The chapel of the SS. Sacramento contains some remarkable sculptures of

1 These numbers, as all others respecting population, &c., given in this volume, are taken from the last official returns published by the Papal Government. Whenever square miles are mentioned, they are understood to be Geographical.

angels, saints, &c., by *Andrea Ferreri,* a sculptor of the last century; the altar-piece is by *Parolini,* a native painter (1733), whom Lanzi describes as " l'ultimo nel cui sepolcro si sia inciso elogio di buon pittore; con lui fu sepolta per allora la gloria della pittura Ferrarese." In the choir is the Last Judgment by *Bastianino* (Filippo Bastiano), one of the favourite pupils and the best copyist of Michael Angelo. Lanzi says that it occupied 3 years in painting, and describes it as " so near to that of Michael Angelo in the Sistine Chapel, that the whole Florentine school has nothing to compare with it. It is characterised," he says, "by grandeur of design, a great variety of figures, a good disposition of the groups, and by the pleasing repose which it presents to the eye of the spectator. It seems impossible that in a subject already occupied by Buonarroti, Filippo should have had the power of showing himself so original and so grand. We see that, like all true imitators, he copied not the figures, but the spirit and the genius of his example." Like Dante and Michael Angelo, Bastianino availed himself of this opportunity to put his friends among the elect, and his enemies among the damned; and the picture consequently contains numerous portraits of both. Among these are pointed out the young woman who refused his hand, placed by the artist among the latter; while the one whom he married is classed among the blessed, and is seen maliciously gazing at her early rival. It is much to be regretted that recent attempts to restore this fine work have injured the effect of the original colouring. The fifth chapel contains another painting by this master, the St. Catherine, called by Lanzi "la gran tavola di S. Caterina." The Annunciation and the St. George are by *Cosimo Tura* or *Cosmè,* the painter of the 23 choirbooks presented by Bishop Bartolommeo di Rovere, the execution of which has been so highly prized as to be preferred by many to that of the famous miniatures in the Library of Siena. On an adjoining altar are 5 bronze statues representing the Saviour on the Cross, the Virgin, St. John, and St. George, by *Bindelli* and *Marescotti,* much admired by Donatello. The cathedral contains the sepulchral monument of Urban III., who died of grief on hearing of the reverses of the second crusade, previous to the loss of Jerusalem; that of Lilió Gregorio Giraldi, the celebrated mythologist, has been removed to the Campo Santo; the inscription on the tablet, dated 1550, and written by himself, records the poverty which excited the compassion of Montaigne,

" Nihil
Opus ferente Apolline; "

but, in spite of his complaints, it appears from Tiraboschi that he was assisted by the Duchess Renée, and that he left at his death a sum of 10,000 crowns.

Ch. of S. Francesco, founded by the Duke Ercole I., is one of the most interesting in Ferrara. Among its pictures are the following, by *Garofalo:* the Betrayal of the Saviour, unfortunately much injured; the Virgin and Child, with St. John and St. Jerome, a charming picture; a beautiful Holy Family; the Raising of Lazarus, one of his best works; and the Massacre of the Innocents, one of the most touching representations of the subject. The Flight out of Egypt is by *Scarsellino;* there are 3 fine works by *Mona,* the Deposition, the Resurrection, and the Ascension; and a Holy Family, a very interesting work, by *Ortolano.* The church contains also the monument of the Marchese di Villa of Ferrara, celebrated for his defence of Candia against the Turks in 1676; several tombs of the princes of the house of Este; and that of Giambattista Pigna, the historian of the family, and the secretary of Duke Alfonso. Not the least remarkable curiosity of the church is the famous *echo,* said to reverberate 16 times, from every part of the edifice.

"The nave seems to have been intended to present a series of cupolas, as the side aisles actually do on a smaller scale: but in its present state, at the point where the square is reduced to a circle, a flat ceiling is introduced instead of a cupola. Standing under any one of these, the slightest footstep is repeated a great many times, but so rapidly that it is difficult to count the reverberations. I counted sixteen; but the effect is a continued clatter, rather than a succession of distinct sounds."—*Woods.*

The Ch. of Sta. Maria del Vado, one of the oldest in the city, is celebrated for a miracle resembling that of Bolsena, which the genius of Raphael has immortalized. The Church tradition relates that, the faith of the prior having failed at the moment of consecration on Easter Sunday 1171, the host poured forth blood, and converted him from his disbelief. This church is also celebrated for its magnificent paintings by *Carlo Bonone,* whose talent can only, in Lanzi's opinion, be appreciated here. He relates that Guercino, when he removed from Cento to Ferrara, spent hours in studying these works. Among them are the Marriage of Cana ; the Visit of the Virgin to Elizabeth ; the Crowning of the Virgin ; the Paradise ; the Miracle of the Host ; the Sposalizio, left unfinished at his death, and completed at the suggestion of Guido by *Chenda ;* the Ascension, copied from Garofalo, and the half figures on the pillars, one of which represents, under the form of St. Guarini, the portrait of the author of 'Il Pastor Fido.' The splendid painting of St. John in Patmos contemplating the harlot of Babylon is by *Dosso Dossi :* the head of St. John was considered by Lanzi a "prodigy of expression," but the picture has been disfigured by the green drapery added by some Bolognese artist to satisfy the fastidious scruples of the clergy. The Tribute Money, a graceful work in the Varano Chapel, is by *Palma Vecchio.* Opposite is the painting of Justice and Power, containing the celebrated Latin enigma of Alessandro Guarini, which has not yet been explained. The Visitation is by *Panetti,* the master of Garofalo; the Miracle of St. Antony is one of the best works of Garofalo's pupil, *Carpi ;* and the Death of the Virgin is by *Vittore Carpaccio.* the Venetian painter. In the sacristy are the Annunciation by

Panetti, and a Flight out of Egypt, another work of the Venetian School. Sta. Maria del Vado contains the tombs of some of the most remarkable artists of Ferarra, and of Tito Vespasiano Strozzi, and his celebrated son Ercole, classed by Ariosto himself among the first of poets. The painters whose ashes repose here are Ortolano, Garofalo, Bonone, Bastianino, and Dielai. The elder Strozzi is known also as the President of the Grand Council of Twelve, but he acquired a less enviable notoriety as a minister than as a poet, for it is recorded by Muratori that in his official capacity he was hated "più del diavolo."

The Ch. and Monastery of San Benedetto, classed among the finest buildings of Ferrara, have suffered more vicissitudes than perhaps any other edifice in the city. The monastery was occupied as barracks by Austrian, Russian, and French troops, and was afterwards converted into a military hospital ; the church, during the political troubles of Italy, was shut up, and was only reopened for divine service in 1812. It was formerly celebrated for the tomb of Ariosto, transferred to the public library by the French in 1801 ; and for the fine paintings of the school of Ferrara which it still retains. The most remarkable of these are Christ on the Cross, with St. John and other Saints, by *Dosso Dossi ;* the Martyrdom of St. Catherine, by *Scarsellino,* one of his finest works; and a Circumcision, by *Luca Longhi,* of Ravenna. The four Doctors of the Church, by *Giuseppe Cremonesi* (G. Caletti), are much praised by Lanzi, who applies the epithet "maraviglioso" to his grand and expressive figure of St. Mark, and extols the execution of the books, whose truth and nature gained for the artist the title of the "Painter of Books." On the ceiling of the vestibule of the refectory is the celebrated painting of Paradise, with the choir of angels, by *Dosso Dossi.* Ariosto was so enamoured of this work, that he requested Dossi to introduce his portrait, being desirous, he said, of securing a place in that paradise, since he was not very sure of reaching the other. The poet was accordingly introduced, and his portrait is seen between the figures of St. Sebastian and St. Catherine. About the middle of the last century, the bust which surmounted the tomb of Ariosto was struck by lightning, and a crown of iron laurels which surrounded it was melted away; an incident which Lord Byron has happily embodied in his well-known stanza:—

" The lightning rent from Ariosto's bust
   The iron crown of laurel's mimick'd leaves;
   Nor was the ominous element unjust,
   For the true laurel-wreath which Glory
        weaves
   Is of the tree no bolt of thunder cleaves,
   And the false semblance but disgraced his
        brow;
   Yet still, if fondly Superstition grieves,
   Know, that the lightning sanctifies below
   Whate'er it strikes;—yon head is doubly sa-
        cred now."

The *Ch. of S. Paolo*, the last public building in Ferrara which contained a work by the rare master *Ercole Grandi*, is remarkable for one of the master-pieces of *Scarsellino*, the Descent of the Holy Ghost. A Nativity, and the ceiling of one of the side chapels, are by the same master. The choir was painted by *Scarsellino* and *Bonone*. The Resurrection is by *Bastianino*. 2 painters of this school are buried here, Giambattista Dossi, and Bastaruolo, who perished while bathing in the Po. Another tomb in this church records the name of Antonio Montecatino, the friend and minister of Duke Alfonso, better known as a professor of Peripatetic philosophy. His bust, which is much admired, is by *Alessandro Vicentini.*

The *Ch. of San Domenico* is remarkable for the statues on its façade by *Andrea Ferreri*, and for some interesting works of Garofalo and Carlo Bonone. The dead man raised by a piece of the true cross, and the Martyrdom of S. Pietro di Rosini, are by *Garofalo*; the S. Domenico and S. Thomas Aquinas are by *Carlo Bonone*. The adjoining convent was once celebrated for its Library, bequeathed to it by the celebrated Celio Calcagnini, "a poet, scholar, antiquarian, moralist, professor, ambassador, wit, and astronomer; one of the first who maintained the earth's movement round the sun; whose praises have been sung by Ariosto, his fellow traveller in Hungary, in the suite of Cardinal Ippolito d'Este. The number of volumes amounted to 3584, but most of them are now dispersed. Calcagnini also bequeathed fifty golden crowns for the repairs of the library, and to furnish the chairs, benches, and desks then in use."—*Valery.* Over the door of the library is the bust and dilapidated tomb of this eminent philosopher; the inscription is a remarkable testimony to the insufficiency of human learning:—*Ex diuturno studio in primis hoc didicit : mortalia omnia contemnere et ignorantiam suam non ignorare.* Ariosto, in the Orlando, records his astronomical discoveries in a beautiful passage:—

" Il dotto Cello Calcagnin lontana
   Farà la gloria, e 'l bel nome di quella
   Nel regno di Monese, in quel di Juba,
   In India e Spagna udir con chiara tuba."
                        Or. Fur. xlii. 90, 5

The *Ch. of S. Andrea* contains several good pictures: the Virgin Throned, with saints, by *Garofalo*, is supposed by some to have been executed with the assistance of Raphael; the Guardian Angel is by *Carlo Bonone;* the Resurrection is attributed by some to *Titian*, by others to *Garofalo*; the St. Andrew is by *Panetti;* and there is a fine statue of St. Nicholas of Tolentino, by *Alfonso Lombardo*. In the refectory is a grand allegorical picture by *Garofalo*, representing the victory of the New Testament over the Old, the ceremonies of the Mosaic being contrasted with the sacraments of the New Law.

The *Ch. of the Theatines* (de' *Teatini*) contains a large painting of the Presentation in the Temple by *Guercino;* and a Resurrection, and a S. Gaetano, by *Chenda.*

The *Ch. of the Capuchin Convent* has some fine paintings: the Virgin Throned, with saints; a similar subject, with Capuchin nuns, both by *Scarsellino;* S. Christopher and S. Antonio Abate, S. Domenico, and S. Francis, in the sacristy, by *Bonone.* The small statue of the Conception is by *Ferreri.*

The Ch. of S. Giorgio is celebrated as the scene of the General Council held at Ferrara by Pope Eugenius IV., in 1438, for the purpose of effecting a union between the Greek and Latin Churches, and at which the Emperor John Paleologus was present. Even at that period the atmosphere of Ferrara was tainted by malaria, for it is recorded that the council was removed to Florence, in consequence of the unhealthy climate of this city.

The Ch. of the Campo Santo, whose fine architecture is attributed to Sansovino, is decorated internally with the finest sculptures of that celebrated artist. The twelve chapels are remarkable for as many paintings of the Mysteries by Niccolò Rosselli, classed, doubtfully, among the Ferrarese school by Lanzi, who mentions these works as imitations of the style of Garofalo, Bagnacavallo, and others. The Nativity is by Dielai; S. Bruno praying, and the Marriage of Cana, are by Carlo Bonone; the S. Christopher, by Bastianino, is mentioned with the highest praise by Lanzi; the Descent of the Holy Ghost, and the Deposition from the Cross, are by Bastaruolo; the S. Bruno is by Scarsellino; the Last Supper, by Cignaroli; and the Beheading of John the Baptist, by Parolini. The Campo Santo was formerly the Certosa Convent. The cloisters are now covered with statues, bas-reliefs, and sepulchral monuments. Among the tombs are those of Borso d'Este, first Duke of Ferrara, the founder of the convent; of Duke Venanziano Varano and his wife, by Rinaldini; of Lilio Giraldi, the mythologist, removed from the cathedral; of the wife of Count Leopoldo Cicognara, and of the Bernardino Barbulejo, or Barbojo, said to have been the preceptor of Ariosto; &c.

The Ch. of Gesù has a picture of the 3 Japanese Martyrs, by Parolini; and a ceiling painted by Dielai. In the choir is the mausoleum of the Duchess Barbara of Austria, wife of Alfonso II., so well known by the eloquent eulogies of Tasso.

The Ch. of the Convent of the Corpus Domini contains several tombs of the D'Este family; that of Lucrezia Borgia is said to be among them, but there is no authority for the statement.

The Castle, formerly the Ducal Palace, surrounded by its ample moat, and furnished with towers and bridges, carries the imagination back to the fortunes of Ferrara during the middle ages. "It stands," says Forsyth, "moated and flanked with towers, in the heart of the subjugated town, like a tyrant intrenched among slaves, and recalls to a stranger that gloomy period described by Dante:—

> " Che le terre d'Italia tutte piene
>   Son di tiranni; ed un Marcel diventa
>   Ogni villan che parteggiando viene."
>   *Purg.* vi. 124.

It is a huge, square building, defended at the angles by 4 large towers; it retains few traces of the ducal family, and wears an air of melancholy, in accordance with the deserted aspect of the city. Its apartments were formerly decorated by the first masters of the Ferrarese school, but the paintings have entirely disappeared, excepting on the ceilings of the antechamber and the Saloon of Aurora, where some by Dosso Dossi still remain. In the dungeons of this castle Parisina and her guilty lover were put to death. The outlines of that dreadful tragedy have been made familiar to the English reader by the beautiful poem of Lord Byron, to whom the subject was suggested by a passage in Gibbon. A more complete account, however, is found in the learned Dr. Frizzi's History of Ferrara, from which the following is an extract descriptive of the closing catastrophe:—"It was, then, in the prisons of the castle, and exactly in those frightful dungeons which are seen at this day beneath the chamber called the Aurora, at the foot of the Lion's tower, at the top of the street of the Giovecca, that, on the night of the 21st of May, were beheaded, first Ugo, and afterwards Parisina. Zoese, he that accused her, conducted the latter under his arm to the place of punishment. She, all along, fancied that she was to be thrown into a pit, and asked at every step whether she was yet come to the spot? She was told that her punishment was to be by the axe. She inquired what was become of Ugo, and received for answer that he was already dead; at which, sighing grievously, she exclaimed, ' Now, then, I wish not myself to live;' and, being come to the block, she stripped herself with her own hands of all her ornaments, and, wrapping a cloth round her head, submitted to the fatal blow,· which terminated the cruel scene. The same was done with Rangoni, who, together with the others, according to two records in the library of St. Francesco, was buried in the cemetery of that convent."

Gallery of Pictures. This gallery, formerly in the Palazzo del Magistrato, has recently been transferred to the "Pinacotheca" in one of the most beautiful palaces of Ferrara, purchased to receive it. It contains many excellent works by the leading painters of the school of Ferrara. Among them are the following:— *Garofalo*, the Agony in the Garden, the Resurrection, the Descent of the Holy Ghost, the Twelve Apostles ; *Dosso Dossi*, Noah's Ark; *Bastianino*, the Nativity, Birth of the Virgin, the Assumption; *Cosmè (Cosimo Tura)*, Martyrdom of St. Maurelius ; *Ortolano*, the Nativity; *Guercino*, S. Bruno; *Agostino Caracci*, the Fall of Manna. Many of the finest pictures which formerly existed in the Churches of San Francesco, San Andrea, &c., have been removed here, and copies substituted in their place.

Palazzo del Magistrato. In a hall of this palace the Ariostean Academy, *Accademia degli Ariostei*, holds its sittings; it has succeeded to the *Accademia degli Intrepidi*, one of the first poetical societies of Italy, but it has now become more generally useful as a literary and scientific institution. Near its hall of assembly some small rooms are shown which were occupied by Calvin, when he found an asylum at the Court of the Duchess Renée, under the assumed name of Charles Heppeville. It is impossible to visit them without carrying one's thoughts back to the meetings at which the stern reformer secretly expounded his doctrines to the small band of disciples whom the favour of his

patroness had collected together. Among these were Anne de Parthenai, Olympia Morata, Marot, Francesco Porto Centese, and other Protestants whom persecution had driven from beyond the Alps, and who assembled in these apartments to derive instruction from the great teacher of Geneva.

The Studio Pubblico enjoys some celebrity as a school of medicine and jurisprudence. It contains a rich cabinet of medals, and a collection of Greek and Roman inscriptions and antiquities ; among which is the colossal sarcophagus of Aurelia Eutychia, wife of P. Pubius. But its chief interest is the *Public Library*, containing 80,000 volumes and 900 MSS., among which are the Greek Palimpsests of Gregory the Nazianzien, St. Chrysostom, &c. The most remarkable, however, and the most valuable of all its treasures, are the manuscripts of Ariosto and Tasso. The former are preserved in an apartment where the poet's arm-chair of walnut-wood, the beautifully executed medal bearing his profile, which was found in his tomb, and his bronze inkstand surmounted by a Cupid enjoining silence, which he is said to have designed himself, are deposited. These manuscripts comprise a copy of some cantos of the *Orlando Furioso*, covered with corrections, and remarkable also for the following memorandum which Alfieri begged permission to inscribe, " Vittorio Alfieri vide e venerò 18 Giugno, 1783 ;" one of the Satires ; the comedy of La Scolastica; and some highly interesting letters, among which is one from Titian to Ariosto. The manuscript of the *Gerusalemme* is one of the most touching records in Ferrara; it was corrected by Tasso during his captivity, and has the words *Laus Deo* at the end. Like the Orlando, this is also remarkable for its corrections and cancelled passages, many of which are extremely curious, and worthy of being published. There are likewise nine letters of Tasso, written while confined in the hospital of St. Anna; and a small collection of *Rime*. Another manuscript, which seems to lose its interest by the side of the two great Epic poets, is that of the *Pastor Fido* of Guarini.

A valuable treasure, but of a different character, is the series of *Choir Books,* in 18 volumes, filled with beautiful miniatures, which formerly belonged to the Certosa. There is also a *Bible,* in one large volume, illustrated with miniatures of the same kind, and apparently by the same hand.

Of the printed books in the library, we may mention 52 early editions of Ariosto, a fine collection of cinquecento editions, and a very perfect series of books printed at Ferrara, which was one of the first cities in which the printing press was established. Signor Antonelli, one of the curators of this library, in his work on the Ferrarese printers of the 15th century, states that during the first 30 years of the 15th century upwards of 100 editions were issued from the press of 9 printers in Ferrara. Among the most famous of these printers was Giambattista Guarini, from whom Aldus, before settling at Venice, received instructions in printing Greek. The medical traveller will find here the exceedingly rare work of Giambattista Canani, "Musculorum humani corporis picturata dissectio," without date, but evidently referable to the middle of the 16th century.

In one of the rooms of this library is a very interesting collection of *Portraits of Ferrarese Authors,* from the earliest period down to Cicognara and Monti; and in another, 18 *Portraits of Ferrarese Cardinals,* the most interesting of which, from his connection with Ariosto, is that of Cardinal Ippolito d'Este, in whose service the great poet had spent so many painful and unprofitable years;

" Aggiungi che dal giogo
Del Cardinal da Este oppresso fui."

In a third room, called the Sala d'Ariosto, is his *Tomb,* brought here by the French from the ch. of S. Benedetto, on the 6th of June, 1801, the anniversary of the poet's death. The inscriptions, recording the merits of Ariosto as a statesman as well as a poet, were written by Guarini. The library, is open to the public from 8 to 12, and from 3 to 4.

The Casa d' Ariosto is marked by an inscription composed by the great poet himself:—

" Parva sed apta mihi, sed nulli obnoxia, sed
non
Sordida, parta meo sed tamen sere domus."

Above it is the following, placed there by his favourite son and biographer, Virgilio:—

" Sic domus bsec Ariosta
Propitios habeat deos, olim ut Pindarica."

Ariosto is said to have inhabited this house during the latter years of his life, and, when some visitor expressed surprise that one who had described so many palaces had not a finer house for himself, he replied that the palaces he built in verse cost him nothing. After his death nearly all the well-known characteristics of the house, described with so much interest by Ariosto himself, were destroyed by its subsequent proprietors. In 1811 Count Girolamo Cicognara, when Podestà, induced the town council to purchase it, as one of those national monuments which ought to be beyond the caprice of individuals. The chamber of the poet was then carefully restored, and the circumstance was recorded in the following inscription placed under his bust:—*Lodovico Ariosto in questa camera scrisse e questa casa da lui abitata edificò, la quale CCLXXX anni dopo la morte del divino poeta, fu dal Conte Girolamo Cicognara Podestà co danari del comune comprata e ristaurata, perchè alla venerazione delle genti durasse.*

The Casa degli Ariosti, in which the poet was educated, is still preserved, and is situated near the ch. of Sta. Maria di Bocche. He lived there for the purpose of pursuing his legal studies under the superintendence of his paternal uncles; but he soon gave up law for the more congenial study of poetry and romance. It was in one of the chambers of this residence that Ariosto, with his brothers and sisters, performed the Fable of Thisbe, and other comic pieces of his own composition. The apartment is still shown, and is well adapted for such representations. On the death of his father, the poet removed from this house to the one already described.

The Casa Guarini, still inhabited by the Marquises of that name, recalls the name of the author of the *Pastor Fido*, whose bust decorates the hall. On the corner of the house is this inscription: *Herculis et Musarum commercio favete linguis et animis.*

The Piazza Grande, now the *Piazza di Ariosto*, formerly contained a statue of Pope Alexander VII.; but this was removed by the republicans of 1796 to make room for one of Napoleon, whose name the Piazza bore until the peace of 1814, when both the statue and the title gave way to those of the "Italian Homer."

One of the greatest objects of interest in Ferrara is the cell in the hospital of St. Anna, shown as *the prison of Tasso*. Over the door is the following inscription, placed there by General Miollis: *Rispettate, o Posteri, la celebrità di questa stanza, dove Torquato Tasso infermo più di tristezza che delirio, ditenuto dimorò anni* vii. *mesi* ii. *scrisse verse e prose, e fu rimesso in libertà ad istanza della città di Bergamo, nel giorno* vi. *Luglio*, 1586. It is below the ground floor, and is lighted by a grated window from the yard; its size is about 9 paces by 6 and about 7 feet high. "The bedstead, so they tell, has been carried off piecemeal, and the door half cut away, by the devotion of those whom 'the verse and prose' of the prisoner have brought to Ferrara. The poet was confined in this room from the middle of March 1579, to December 1580, when he was removed to a contiguous apartment, much larger, in which, to use his own expressions, he could philosophise and walk about. The inscription is incorrect as to the immediate cause of his enlargement, which was promised to the city of Bergamo, but was carried into effect at the intercession of Don Vincenzo Gonzaga, Prince of Mantua."—*Hobhouse.* Few questions have been more debated than the cause of the great poet's imprisonment, some believing that it was actual insanity, others that it was mere detention in a *Maison de Santé*, combined with vexatious annoyances of the police;

while by far the greater number coincide in regarding Tasso as neither more nor less than a prisoner of state, whose sufferings were aggravated by the capricious tyranny of Alfonso. His biographer, the Abate Serassi, has shown that the first cause of the poet's punishment was his desire to be occasionally, or altogether, free from his servitude at the court of Alfonso. In 1575 Tasso resolved to visit Rome, and enjoy the indulgences of the jubilee; "and this error," says the Abate, "increasing the suspicion already entertained that he was in search of another service, was the origin of his misfortunes. On his return to Ferrara, the Duke refused to admit him to an audience, and he was repulsed from the houses of all the dependants of the court; and not one of the promises which the Cardinal Albano had obtained for him were carried into effect. Then it was that Tasso—after having suffered these hardships for some time, seeing himself constantly discountenanced by the Duke and the princesses, abandoned by his friends, and derided by his enemies—could no longer contain himself within the hounds of moderation, but, giving vent to his choler, publicly broke forth into the most injurious expressions imaginable, both against the Duke and all the house of Este, cursing his past service, and retracting all the praises he had ever given in his verses to those princes, or to any individual connected with them, declaring that they were all a gang of poltroons, ingrates, and scoundrels (poltroni, ingrati, e ribaldi). For this offence he was arrested, conducted to the hospital of St. Anna, and confined in a solitary cell as a madman." His own correspondence furnishes the best evidence of the treatment he experienced;—for almost the first year of his imprisonment he endured nearly all the horrors of a solitary cell, and received from his gaoler, Agostino Mosti, although himself a poet, every kind of cruelty—"ogni sorte di rigore ed inumanità."

"On the walls of Tasso's prison are the names of Lord Byron, Casimir Delavigne, and Lamartine's verses on Tasso, written in pencil. Notwithstanding these poetical authorities, with the inscription *Ingresso alla prigione di Torquato Tasso* at the entrance, another inside, and the repairs of this pretended prison, in 1812, by the prefect of the department, it is impossible to recognize the real prison of Tasso in the kind of hole that is shown as such. How can any one for a moment suppose that Tasso could live in such a place for seven years and two months, revise his poem there, and compose his different philosophical dialogues in imitation of Plato? I had an opportunity of consulting several well-informed gentlemen of Ferrara on this subject, and I ascertained that not one of them believed this tradition, which is equally contradicted by historical facts and local appearances. There was enough in Tasso's fate to excite our compassion, without the extreme sufferings he must have experienced in this dungeon. Alfonso's ingratitude was sufficiently painful: a slight on the part of Louis XIV. hastened the death of Racine; and with such spirits mental afflictions are much more keenly felt than bodily pains. Madame de Staël, who was ever inclined to commiserate the misfortunes of genius, was not misled by the legend of the prison of Ferrara; Goethe, according to the statement of a sagacious traveller, maintains that the prison of Tasso is an idle tale, and that he had made extensive researches on the subject."— *Valery.*

Sir John Hobhouse, in reference to the inscription on the cell, says that "Common tradition had long before assigned the cell to Tasso: it was assuredly one of the prisons of the hospital; and in one of those prisons we know that Tasso was confined. Those," he adds, "who indulge in the dreams of earthly retribution will observe that the cruelty of Alfonso was not left without its recompence, even in his own person. He survived the affection of his subjects and of his dependants, who deserted him at his death, and suffered his body to be interred without princely or decent honours. His last wishes were neglected; his testament cancelled. His kinsman, Don Cæsar, shrank from the excommunication of the Vatican, and, after a short struggle, or rather suspense, Ferrara passed away for ever from the dominion of the house of Este."

" Ferrara! in thy wide and grass-grown streets,
    Whose symmetry was not for solitude,
There seems as 'twere a curse upon the seats
Of former sovereigns, and the antique brood
Of Este, which for many an age made good
Its strength within thy walls, and was of yore
Patron or tyrant, as the changing mood
Of petty power impell'd, of those who wore
The wreath which Dante's brow alone had worn
    before.

And Tasso is their glory and their shame;
Hark to his strain! and then survey his cell!
And see how dearly earn'd Torquato's fame,
And where Alfonso bade his poet dwell:
The miserable despot could not quell
The insulted mind he sought to quench and
    blend
With the surrounding maniacs, in the hell
Where he had plunged it. Glory without end
Scatter'd the clouds away—and on that name
    attend

The tears and praises of all time; while thine
Would rot in its oblivion—in the sink
Of worthless dust, which from thy boasted
    line
Is shaken into nothing; but the link
Thou formest in his fortunes bids us think
Of thy poor malice, naming thee with scorn—
Alfonso! how thy ducal pageants shrink
From thee! if in another station born,
Scarce fit to be the slave of him thou mad'st to
    mourn."   *Childe Harold.*

The Theatre of Ferrara is reputed to be one of the finest in the States of the Church. The first in Italy is said to have been opened here.

The Citadel was founded in 1211. After Clement VIII. had seized the principality as a fief which had lapsed to the Church for want of heirs, it was entirely rebuilt; an expedient so successfully adopted at Perugia and Ancona, to resist the malcontents likely to rebel against the usurpations of the Holy See. It was completed by Paul V. By the treaty of Vienna, Austria acquired the right of occupying this citadel and the small neighbouring fortress of Comacchio; since which time it has been occupied by an Austrian garrison, at present amounting to 2500 men.

Ferrara is one of the 8 archbishoprics of the Papal States: the bishopric dates from A.D. 661; its archbishopric was founded by Clement XII. in 1735.

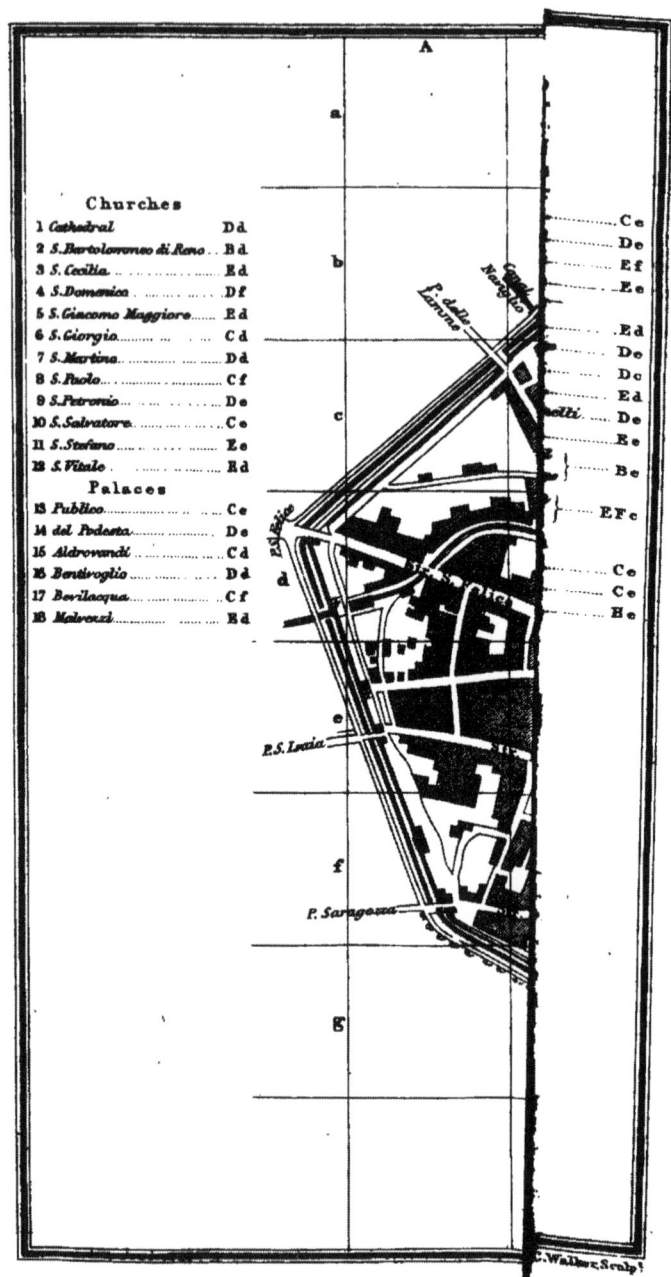

Churches

1 Cathedral .... **D d**
2 S. Bartolomeo di Reno .. **B d**
3 S. Cecilia .... **E d**
4 S. Domenico .... **D f**
5 S. Giacomo Maggiore ...... **E d**
6 S. Giorgio .... **C d**
7 S. Martino .... **D d**
8 S. Paolo .... **C f**
9 S. Petronio ...... **D e**
10 S. Salvatore ...... **C e**
11 S. Stefano .... **E e**
12 S. Vitale .... **R d**

Palaces

13 Publico .... **C e**
14 del Podesta ...... **D e**
15 Aldrovandi ...... **C d**
16 Bentivoglio ...... **D d**
17 Bevilacqua ...... **C f**
18 Malvezzi .... **E d**

A

a

b

c

d

e

f

g

.... C e
.... D e
.... E f
.... E e

.... E d
.... D e
.... D c
.... E d
.... D e
.... E e

.... B e

.... E F c

.... C e
.... C e
.... H e

P. della Lamme
Canale Naviglio

P. S. Isaia

P. Saragozza

C. Walker Sculp

[Boats may be hired at Ferrara for Venice, a voyage of 20 hours. There is a procaccio twice a week to Bologna, by water. Travellers may also proceed by the canals to Ravenna. The canals from Ferrara are the following (these communicate with many others, by which a constant intercourse is maintained with the central towns of Northern Italy):—The canal called the *Pò di Volàno* leads from the Porta Romana to the Adriatic, by a course of 56 m., skirting the northern district of Comacchio: it is navigable all the year, and has some valuable fisheries. The *Cavo Tassone* and *Canale di Cento*, 28 m. in length, keeps up a communication between Cento and Ferrara. From the Porta di S. Benedetto the *Cavo Panfilio* proceeds to Ponte di Lagoscuro, a course of 3 miles. From the Porta di S. Giorgio the *Pò di Primaro* leads to S. Alberto and the Adriatic: it is navigable all the year by boats of considerable burden.]

tute of interest. From the walls of Ferrara to the gates of Bologna it is covered with hemp, corn, rice-grounds, and meadow lands. At Santa Catarina, a short distance N. of the Reno, the line of separation between the Legations of Ferrara and Bologna is passed; and about a mile before arriving at Malalbergo the Reno enclosed between high embankments, is crossed by a bridge.

1½ *Malalbergo (Inn: La Posta)* is a place of considerable activity; and as the traveller approaches Bologna he cannot fail to be struck with the improved aspect of the country—the corn-fields, the maize-plantations, and the hemp-grounds denote the extreme fertility of the soil, and bespeak a careful and better system of husbandry. The cottages are neat, and the general appearance of the people indicates prosperity and industry. Travellers by vetturino from Ferrara to Bologna usually make the inn at Altedo the halting-place on the road.

1 Capo d'Argine.
1 BOLOGNA, described in Rte. 6.

ROUTE 4.

FERRARA TO BOLOGNA, BY MALALBERGO.—26 m.

	Posts.
Ferrara to Malalbergo	1½
Malalbergo to Capo d'Argine	1
Capo d'Argine to Bologna	1
	3½

This is the high post-road, which has superseded the old route through Cento. Close to the walls of Ferrara the canal, called the Cavo Tassone, communicating with the Pò di Primaro, is crossed, and the road proceeds along a dead flat, remarkable for its fertility and cultivation, but otherwise desti-

ROUTE 5.

FERRARA TO BOLOGNA, BY CENTO.

About 32 Eng. m.

This was formerly the principal line of communication between Ferrara and Bologna, and it is still interesting on account of its passing through the birthplace of Guercino, which all lovers of art will consider worthy of a pilgrimage. At a short distance from Ferrara it leaves the post-road to Mantua at Cassana, and proceeds by Vigarano, Mirabella, S. Agostino, and along the Reno, by Dosso, to Cento.

Cento.—This interesting and pretty town is situated in a fertile plain not far from the Reno. It is said to have derived its name from an ancient settlement of fishermen, who were led to fix upon this spot by the great number of craw-fish for which the neighbouring waters were celebrated. They are said to have built a hundred cottages (*cento capannucce*), which they surrounded with a deep fosse; and the number of their cottages thus became the appellation of the town which subsequently arose upon their site. The population of Cento is 4572. The town was formerly celebrated for the college of S. Biagio, which was suppressed on the establishment of the kingdom of Italy; but its great interest arises from its being the birth-place of *Guercino*. The ch. is full of the works of this great artist; and his house, which it was his delight to cover with his paintings, is still preserved without any alteration or change, save what has been produced by time. The *Casa di Guercino* has been correctly termed a real domestic museum. "In the little chapel is an admirable picture of *two pilgrims praying to the Virgin*. The extreme destitution, no less than the fervour of these pilgrims, is painted with great minuteness of detail (even to the patches of the least noble part of their habiliments), without in any way weakening the general effect of this pathetic composition. The ceiling of one room presents a series of horses of various breeds; there is one superb group of two horses; another horse at grass, nothing but skin and bone, is a living skeleton of this poor animal. A *Venus* suckling Cupid is less pleasing than the rest, despite its celebrity and the merit of the colouring.

"Guercino had for Cento that love of locality, if we may so say, of which Italian painters and sculptors have in all ages offered numerous examples: he preferred residing in his native town to the titles and offices of first painter to the kings of France and England; he had his school there, and remained in the town till driven away by the war between Odoardo Farnese, Duke of Parma, and ·Pope Urban VIII., when

Taddeo Barberini, nephew of the latter, general of the Pontifical troops, determined on fortifying Cento. The campaign and operations of these two combatants seem but mean at the present day beside the glory of the fugitive Guercino. The house of Guercino, in its present state, attests a simple, modest, laborious life, which inspires a kind of respect. This great artist, really born a painter, *the magician of painting* as he has been surnamed, was also a pious, moderate, disinterested, and charitable man; an excellent kinsman, whose comrade and first pupils were his brother and nephews: beloved by his master Gennari, praised and recommended by Lodovico Caracci, he seems to have escaped the enmity too frequent among such rivals. The house of Guercino is not, however, devoid of magnificence: it is easy to conceive that he might there receive and regale, *ad uno squisito banchetto*, those two cardinals who had come to the fair, when his most distinguished pupils served at table, and in the evening performed *una bella commedia*, an extemporised proverb, with which their eminences were enraptured. Christina of Sweden also visited Guercino at Cento; and after admiring his works, that queen wished to touch the hand that had produced such *chefs d'œuvre*.

"The *Chiesa del Rosario* is called at Cento the *Galerie*, a profane title, partially justified by its appearance and the arrangement of the paintings. Guercino is not less resplendent there than at home. The ch. is full of his paintings: he is said to have given the design of the front and steeple, and to have worked at the wooden statue of the Virgin; he is consequently to be seen there as a painter, sculptor, and architect, but especially as a Christian. A chapel founded by him bears his name: he bequeathed a legacy for the celebration of mass there, and left a gold chain of great value to the image of the Virgin of the Rosary. This pious offering was stolen about the middle of the last century by a custode of the ch.; a double sacrilege in the town where his memory is still popular and venerated."
— *Valery.*

The fair of Cento, above alluded to, formerly celebrated throughout the province, still takes place on the 7th of September; but it has much fallen off of late years.

On leaving Cento, the road crosses the Reno. A little distance beyond the river is *Pieve di Cento*, a town of 4000 souls, surrounded with walls, and formerly celebrated for its miraculous crucifix and the College of Sta. Maria Assunta, suppressed at the establishment of the Kingdom of Italy. It possesses a fine Assumption by *Guido*, forming the altar-piece in the ch. This noble picture was under sentence of removal at the French invasion in 1797; but the people rose against the intended robbery, and effectually prevented it. Close to Pieve the boundary of the Legation of Ferrara is passed, and we enter that of Bologna.

The road now proceeds through S. Giorgio and Castagnol Maggiore to BOLOGNA, Rte. 6.

ROUTE 6.

MODENA TO BOLOGNA.—24 m.

	Posts.
Modena to Samoggia	1½
Samoggia to Bologna	1½
	—
	3

An excellent road, perfectly straight and level throughout: it follows the course of the ancient *Via Æmilia.*

3 m. after leaving Modena the road crosses the Panaro by a fine modern bridge at Ponte *S. Ambrogio*, the Modenese frontier station. The Panaro here separates the duchy from the States of the Church; the Papal frontier station and custom-house are at *Castelfranco*, 3 m. farther on, where *Cent. It.*

a small fee to the officials will prevent annoyance and delay. Castelfranco is considered by Dr. Cramer to agree with the position of *Forum Gallorum*, the scene of several important actions during the siege of Modena, and particularly of the defeat of Antony by Hirtius and Octavian, after the rout of Pansa. Near it is Forte Urbano, a fortress built by Urban VIII., in a commanding position: it is now of little importance, and is falling fast into ruin.

1½ Samoggia (*Inn*, La Posta), a village situated on the river of the same name, about midway between Modena and Bologna; considered to occupy the site of *Ad Medias*, one of the stations of the Æmilian Way. Beyond Anzola the road crosses the Lavino; and 2 m. before reaching Bologna the Reno is passed by a long stone bridge. Between La Crocetta and Trebbo, 2 m. on the l., is an island in the Reno, which Dr. Cramer, Calindri, and other antiquaries regard as the scene of the meeting of the second Triumvirate, A. U. C. 709.

Monte Guardia, crowned by the well-known ch. of the *Madonna di San Luca*, is a conspicuous object from the road on approaching Bologna; on the rt. is the Certosa, now the Campo Santo. The entrance to the city is highly picturesque; the road passes through an open and finely-wooded country, diversified by meadows and rich pasture-grounds, beyond which the hills which bound the prospect are clothed with vegetation, sprinkled with handsome villas, and cultivated to their summits.

1½ BOLOGNA [*Inns:* the San Marco, the oldest and most comfortable; the staircase is covered with coats of arms recording the visits of emperors, kings, and princes, and the Traveller's book contains the names of most of our own nobility, who express satisfaction at the excellence and comfort of the establishment: Grande Albergo Svizzero, with a good table-d'hôte, now much frequented by Austrian officers, to the neglect of less favoured guests; the charges are generally high considering the accommodation. Il Pellegrino, very good, and not so dear as the Svizzero:

c

La Pace, and I Tre Mori, both fair vetturino inns. The Albergo Svizzero, which is not far from the diligence office, was formerly the palace of the Company of the Drapers (Stracciaiuoli), and was built, according to tradition, from the designs of *Francesco Francia*.

Bologna, the second capital of the States of the Church, and one of the most ancient cities of Italy, is picturesquely situated at the foot of the lower slopes of the Apennines in a beautiful and fertile plain; it is surrounded by a high brick wall without fortifications from 5 to 6 miles in extent; the Savena washes its walls, and a canal from the Reno passes through the city. It is the capital of the most important Legation of the Holy See, embracing a population of 350,600 souls, and a superficial extent of 1581 sq. m. The city is about 2 m. long by 1½ broad, divided into 4 quarters; it has 12 gates, and a population of 74,500 Inhab. It is the residence of the Governor of the Province; the seat of an archbishopric, and one of the 3 Courts of Appeal of the Roman States, comprising within its jurisdiction all the northern Delegations. It is one of those interesting provincial capitals which no country but Italy possesses in such abundance. With its rich and varied colonnades, affording a pleasant shelter from the sun and rain, with well-paved streets, noble institutions, and a flourishing, intelligent, and learned population, it rivals Rome in all except classical and religious interest, and the extent of its museums. It would do honour to any country in Europe as its metropolis; and the inhabitants still cherish in their love of freedom the recollections inspired by its ancient motto, "Libertas." Bologna has always been the most flourishing and the most advanced in an intellectual point of view of all the cities of the Papal States, although it has never been the residence of a court nor the seat of a Sovereign; and there can be no doubt that this prosperity is attributable to the long continuance of its privileges, and to the freedom of manners and opinions for which its people are remarkable.

On entering its principal streets the attention of the stranger is at once attracted by the covered porticoes, like those of Padua and Modena. The older quarters of Bologna, however, wear a heavy and antique aspect; their arcades are low and gloomy, and the streets are irregular and narrow; but these only serve as a contrast to the broad thoroughfares and noble arcades of the modern city.

The early history of Bologna carries us back to the time of the Etruscans. Its ancient name of *Felsina* is supposed to have been derived from the Etruscan king of that name, to whom its foundation as the capital of the 12 Etruscan cities, in 984 B.C., is attributed. His successor, Bono, is said to have given it the name of Bononia, although some antiquaries refer it to the Boii, who occupied the city in the time of Tarquinius Priscus.

In the middle ages Bologna had become independent of the German Emperors during their contests with the Popes; and had obtained from Henry V., in 1112, not only an acknowledgment of its independence, but a charter granting to its citizens the choice of the consuls, judges, and other magistrates. It subsequently appeared among the foremost cities of the Guelphic league; and, after the Emperor Frederick II. had left the war in Lombardy to the management of his illegitimate son Hensius King of Sardinia, it "undertook to make the Guelph party triumph throughout the Cispidine region. Bologna first attacked Romagna, and forced the towns of Imola, Faenza, Forlì, and Cervia to expel the Ghibelines, and declare for the Church. The Bolognese next turned their arms against Modena. The Modenese cavalry, entering Bologna one day by surprise, carried off from a public fountain a bucket, which henceforth was preserved in the tower of Modena as a glorious trophy. The war which followed furnished Tassoni with the subject of his mock-heroic poem entitled ' La Secchia Rapita.' The vengeance of the Bolognese was, however, anything but burlesque; after several bloody battles, the 2 armies finally met at Fossalta, on the 26th of May, 1249. Filippio Ugoni of Brescia, who was this year podestà of Bologna, commanded the Guelph army, consisting chiefly of detachments from all the cities of the Lombard league. The Ghibelines were led by King Hensius: each army consisted of from 15,000 to 20,000 combatants. The battle was long and bloody; but ended with the complete defeat of the Ghibeline party: King Hensius himself fell into the hands of the conquerors; he was immediately taken to Bologna, and confined in the palace of the Podestà. The senate of that city rejected all offers of ransom, and all intercession in his favour. He was entertained in a splendid manner, but kept a prisoner during the rest of his life, which lasted for 22 years."—*Sismondi.* In the latter part of the 13th century the city became a prey to family feuds, arising out of the tragical death of the lovers, Imelda Lambertazzi and Bonifazio Gieremei; and for many years it was harassed by the fierce contests for supremacy among these and other noble families. The Gieremei were the leaders of the Guelph party, and the Lambertazzi were the leaders of the Ghibelines; but their mutual hatred was kept in check by the authorities until the occurrence of this domestic tragedy, which bears, in some respects, a strong similarity to the history of Edward of England and his devoted Eleanor. The Guelph party at length appealed to the Pope, then Nicholas III., whose mediation was so successful that the city acknowledged him as Suzerain; but the tyranny of his legate brought on a revolution in 1334, which ended in the supreme power being seized by the captain of the people, the celebrated Taddeo Pepoli, who subsequently sold it to the Visconti. For upwards of a century after that event Bologna was subject either to the tyranny of the Visconti and of the Popes, or to popular anarchy: the family of Bentivoglio, taking advantage of these feuds, seized and maintained the government in the Pope's name; but their power was too independent to be acceptable to the warlike Julius II., who dispossessed them; and, after a long struggle, established, by military force, the absolute supremacy of the Holy See.

Bologna is one of the few cities of Italy which have been occupied by British troops. During the last struggle of Napoleon in Italy, in 1814, the Austrian army was supported in its operations on the Adige by a body of English troops, under General Nugent, who landed at the mouth of the Po and occupied Bologna in February of that year.

In 1848 an unjustifiable attempt of the Austrian General Welden to take possession of Bologna was repulsed with great bravery by the Bolognese, and the invading force obliged to retreat on Ferrara. During the following year the Austrians were more successful. Having determined to seize on the capital of the Romagna, to counterbalance the occupation of Rome by the French, they attacked the city, posting themselves on the heights above with a force of 15,000 men. The Italian party within the walls resisted bravely for 10 days, when they were obliged to surrender after an heroic defence. Since that period Bologna has been occupied by the Austrians; an occupation subsequently legalized by a treaty with the Pontifical Government.

Bologna has been the seat of a bishopric since A.D. 270. It was raised to the rank of an archbishopric by Gregory XIII. It has had the honour of contributing more prelates to the sacred college perhaps than any other city of Italy except Rome; among the natives who have been raised to the pontificate are Honorius II., Lucius II., Gregory XIII., Innocent IX., Gregory XV., and Benedict XIV.

The School of Bologna in the history of art occupies so prominent a place, and numbers among its masters so many great names, that it would be impossible in the limits of this work to enter into anything like a detailed account of its history; and the publication of an English translation of *Kugler's Handbook of Painting* will now render this less required. But while the traveller is referred to that learned work for the details of the school, it may be

c 2

useful, as an introduction to a description of the public institutions of the city, to give a brief general outline of its progress.

The first name of any eminence among the early followers of Giotto at Bologna is that of *Franco Bolognese*, supposed to have been the pupil of Oderigi di Gubbio, the missal painter, immortalised by Dante. He opened the first academy of art in Bologna in 1313, and is termed by Lanzi the Giotto of the Bolognese school. Among his successors were *Vitale da Bologna* (1320), *Jacopo Paolo* or *Avanzi* (1404), *Pietro* and *Orazio di Jacopo, Lippo di Dalmasio, Maso da Bologna, Marco Zoppo*, scholar of Lippo, and afterwards of Squarcione, at Padua (1471), who founded an academy of great celebrity at Bologna, and *Jacopo Forti*, the friend and imitator of Zoppo (1483). But the most celebrated name which occurs in the early history of the school is that of *Francesco Francia* (1535), who may perhaps be considered as its true founder. Of the style of this great master, whose works are now fully appreciated in England, Lanzi says, "It is, as it were, a middle course between Perugino and Bellini, partaking of them both;" and Raphael, in a letter given by Malvasia, says that he had seen no Madonnas better designed, more beautiful, or characterised by a greater appearance of devotion, than those of Francia. Among the scholars of Francia, whose works may yet be studied at Bologna, were his son *Giacomo* (1575), *Lorenzo Costa* (1530), *Girolamo Marchesi da Cotignola* (1520), and *Amico* and *Guido Aspertini* (1552). From the time of Francia to that of the Caracci various styles were introduced by Bagnacavallo, 1551; Innocenzio da Imola, a pupil of Francia, 1542; Francesco Primaticcio, 1570; Niccolò Abate, 1571; and Pellegrino Tibaldi, 1591. The style introduced into the Bolognese school by *Bagnacavallo*, and adopted by *Innocenzio da Imola*, was that of Raphael; while that of Michael Angelo was adopted by *Pellegrino Tibaldi*. Their contemporaries, *Primaticcio* and *Niccolò Abate*, left Bologna to study under Giulio Ro-

mano, at Mantua, and subsequently settled in France. The school was for a time supported by *Lavinia Fontana, Lorenzino* (Lorenzo Sabbatini), *Orazio Samacchini*, and *Passerotti;* but it gradually declined until the third and greatest epoch of the Bolognese School, which produced the Caracci and their pupils.

Before the close of the 16th century we find a new style created by the Caracci, which superseded the ancient maxims, and finally supplanted those of every other master. This revolution in art originated with *Lodovico Caracci*, "a young man," says Lanzi, "who, during his earlier years, appeared to be slow of understanding, and fitter to grind colours than to harmonise and apply them." After visiting the works of his predecessors in the different cities of Italy, he returned to Bologna, and, with the co-operation of his cousins, *Agostino* and *Annibale*, established an academy. By their judgment and kindliness of feeling, and by their mild conduct, in spite of opposition and ridicule from the artists who then monopolised public favour at Bologna, they succeeded in attracting a crowd of pupils.

The most distinguished scholar of the Caracci was *Domenichino (Domenico Zampieri)*, considered by Poussin as the greatest painter next to Raphael. His friend *Albani* is another name imperishably associated with the school of the Caracci, and the traveller will not fail to recognise his powers in all the great galleries of Italy. But *Guido*, another disciple of this school, is frequently considered as its greatest genius; and it is well known that no pupil of the Caracci excited so much as he did the jealousy of his masters. Among the names which figure in the history of the Bolognese school at this period are those of *Guido Cagnacci, Simone Cantarini*, and *Francesco Gessi* (the best pupils of Guido), *Guercino*, and *Lanfranco*. Among the scholars of the Caracci who remained in Bologna after this time are *Sisto Badalocchi, Alessandro Tiarini, Lionello Spada, Lorenzo Garbieri, Giacomo Cavedone, Pietro Fucini, Lucio Massari*, &c., all artists of considerable reputation, and *Gobbo de' Caracci*, so famous as a painter of fruit. The school of Bologna declined with that of the Caracci; the attempt of *Michael Angelo Colonna* arrested its downfall for a period, but was wholly inadequate to restore it to its ancient celebrity. The fourth and last period of the school boasts the names of *Pasinelli* and *Carlo Cignani*; the former aimed at uniting the design of Raphael with the colouring of Paolo Veronese, and the latter the grace of Correggio with the varied knowledge and correctness of the Caracci.

After this general sketch of the Bolognese school, which will be found necessary to a correct appreciation of the treasures of art profusely scattered over the city, we proceed at once to the *Accademia delle Belle Arte.*—This noble institution, formerly the Jesuits' College, is truly a national establishment. It contains a rich gallery of pictures, mostly of the native school, which have been here preserved from the collections of suppressed convents and churches. By an excellent arrangement the older works are placed at the entrance of the gallery; and thus the student has an opportunity of following the progress of art. The great charm of the collection is its nationality, and no city in Italy has, in this respect, a higher or more lasting interest. Some beautiful modern paintings and good specimens of recent sculpture have lately been added. Sir Joshua Reynolds, in recommending Lodovico Caracci to the young student, as the model for style in painting, pointed out the peculiar advantages of Bologna as a place of study. "It is our misfortune," he says, "that those works of the Caracci which I would recommend to the student are not often found out of Bologna, * * * and I think those who travel would do well to allot a much greater portion of their time to that city than it has been hitherto the custom to bestow."—*Disc. II.* At the entrance of the gallery is a large collection of altar-pieces, of the 14th and 15th centuries, mostly of Bolognese origin. The following may be specified as the most remarkable works :—

Giotto. The side wings of the small altar-piece preserved in the Brera Gallery at Milan, brought hither from the ch. of Santa Maria degli Angeli.

Bolognese School.— *Vitale da Bologna* (1320). Madonna and Child. *Simone da Bologna* (1404). Coronation of the Virgin. *Jacopo Paolo.* The Crucifixion. *Santa Caterina Vigri.* St. Ursula. *Francesco Francia.* This great master may be studied here with advantage. 78, Madonna and Child, with SS. Augustin, Francis, Proclus, Monica, John the Baptist, and Sebastian, painted, according to the date inscribed on it, in 1494, for Sta. Maria della Misericordia, and celebrated for the beauty of the St. Sebastian. 79, The Annunciation. *Giacomo Francia.* 84, Holy Family. *Girolamo Marchesi da Cotignola.* 108, The Sposalizio. *Guido Aspertini.* 9, Adoration of the Magi. *Lorenzo Costa.* St. Petronius throned, with two saints, an altar-piece, dated 1502, and characterised by its exceeding gracefulness. *Bagnacavallo.* 133, Holy Family and Saints. *Innocenzio da Imola.* 89, Madonna in glory, with SS. Michael, Peter, and Benedict. 90, Holy Family, one of the finest known; copied for the late King of Prussia, on account, it is said, of the resemblance of the Virgin to his young and beautiful queen. *Pellegrino Tibaldi.* Marriage of St. Catherine,—very graceful. *Prospero Fontana.* 74, The Deposition. *Lavinia Fontana.* 75, The Queen of France presenting her infant to St. Francis. *Lorenzo Sabbatini.* 146, The Assumption of the Virgin, with various angels and saints in adoration, much praised by the Caracci. *Orazio Samacchini.* The Virgin in a glory of angels, crowned by the Trinity, and worshipped by John the Baptist, the Magdalen, St. Catherine, SS. Francis, Clare, Nabor, and Felix; also much admired and praised by the Caracci.

The Caracci and their School.—The gallery contains some of the finest works of this interesting period of art, and nowhere, perhaps, can the genius of the Caracci, Domenichino, and Guido, be so well studied and appreciated. *Lodovico Caracci.* 42, The Madonna and Child throned, with 4 Saints.

43, The Transfiguration; a grand picture, praised by Sir Joshua Reynolds, as worthy the attention of the student. 44, The Calling of St. Matthew; 45, Nativity of St. John Baptist, both praised by Sir Joshua Reynolds. 46, Preaching of St. John. 47, Conversion of St. Paul. 48, Madonna and Child, standing on the half-moon, in a glory of angels, with St. Jerome and St. Francis; "an inimitable painting, in which the artist has displayed the richest stores of genius. The countenance of the Virgin is exquisitely beautiful; a veil, touched with great skill, covers her head, falling in light folds over the bosom and shoulders, and the child, presenting all the animated graces of infantine loveliness, is full of life and nature. St. Francis in adoration, and kissing the child's hand, is painted in a dark tone not to interfere with the principal figures, and is yet finely made out, as are the angels and the other accompaniments of the picture; the colouring soft and sweetly tinted, the whole being, with wonderful art and keeping, entirely subordinate to the great object of the composition." —*Bell.* 49, The Flagellation of our Saviour: a "wild and savage production, portraying a scene totally unsuitable to the dignity of the Saviour of mankind. The drawing is good, and the foreshortening of the figures finely managed."—*Bell.* 50, The Crowning with Thorns. 51, Three Monks, 53, St. Roch. Several of these pictures have a view of Bologna in the background. *Agostino Caracci.* 34, The Communion of St. Jerome; a masterpiece. 35, Assumption of the Virgin. *Annibale Caracci,* a few of his best works. 36, Madonna and Child in glory, with St. John Baptist, the Evangelist, and St. Catherine. 37, Madonna throned with Saints. 38, Assumption of the Virgin. 201, Justice.

Scholars of the Caracci.—Alessandro Tiarini. 182, Deposition from the Cross, attributed to the Caracci by some, and by others to Cignani. "The figures are considerably smaller than life, which might be supposed to hurt the general effect, but the composition is so perfect as to leave no feeling in the mind but that of admiration. The drawing and colouring of our Saviour's body are in such a style of excellence as to give the most affecting expression to a representation generally so painful; his figure, forming the great central light of this touching picture, is sketched out with the finest truth of nature. It is the silent, motionless rigidity of death, yet bearing a character full of interest, having nothing of the tame flat drawing and cadaverous colouring so frequently seen in this subject. The head and left hand are supported; while the right, which is drawn with exquisite skill, hangs down lifeless and stiff."—*Bell.* 183, Marriage of St. Catherine. *Giacomo Cavedone.* 55, Madonna and Child, in glory with Saints. 56, Martyrdom of St. Peter, the Domenican; the saint is represented writing with his blood upon the ground the words " *Credo in Deum,*" while the robber repeats his blow. *Domenichino.* 206, Martyrdom of St. Agnes, a masterpiece, formerly belonging to the church of the same name. "A deeptoned, grand, and richly painted picture crowded with figures, and a background of fine action. The serene and beautiful countenance of the saint is irradiated by an expression of rapt holiness and heavenly resignation, infinitely touching, and finely contrasting with the terror and amazement described with admirable skill and effect in the attitudes of the surrounding multitude. The episode of the 2 women forming the foreground of one corner of the picture, who are represented as hiding the face and stilling the screams of a terrified child, affords a scene of fine action very admirably delineated. But yet the act of the martyrdom is too deliberate. The murderer plunging the dagger into her bosom should turn off with something of horror from a deed committed in cold blood, unexcited by any principle of fury or revenge."—*Bell.* 207, Madonna del Rosario, another grand masterpiece, ranked by many above the St. Jerome of this master. It is a double composition; the lower part representing the persecutions and martyrdoms of the Church, while, in the upper, St. Gregory is interceding for the faithful with the Madonna, who sits with the infant Saviour on the throne showering flowers on the saint. 208, The martyrdom of St. Peter Martyr the Domenican, treated in a different way from the celebrated picture of Titian at Venice, and from the same subject by his imitator Cavedone, already noticed. " The elevated and exalted resignation painted on the features of a noble countenance, the effect of the black drapery cast around the kneeling figure, and held in one large majestic fold by the left hand, has a combined effect of grandeur and chaste simplicity, which is inexpressibly fine."— *Bell. Francesco Albani.* 1, Madonna throned with St. Catherine and the Magdalen. 2, Baptism of the Saviour; a finely treated picture. 3, Madonna and Child, in glory. *Guido.* 134, Madonna della Pietà; in the upper part the dead body of the Saviour, with the Madonna and 2 weeping angels by the side; a view of Bologna in the landscape, and the patrons of the city, SS. Petronio, Domenico, Carlo Borromeo, Francesco d'Assisi, and Proclus. A superb and touching picture. 135, The Massacre of the Innocents, a celebrated picture, full of deep feeling and beauty of expression. " A most powerful piece, and composed with wonderful effect and skill. The figures are of the full size of life; the terror, dismay, and wildness of the different groups are admirably portrayed, and, notwithstanding the violence of the action, each head is beautiful as that of an angel; the naked ruffians, with their uplifted daggers and sacrilegious hands stained with blood, are drawn in the finest style, and with all the energy of pitiless soldiers inured to such deeds. The outcry of one mother, dragged by her scarf and hair, and held by one of these men till he reaches her child; the pale dishevelled aspect of another, breathless with terror, fainting, and delayed in her flight from agitation; the despair and agony of a third beyond these, who sits wringing her hands over her slaughtered babes; the touch of madness pictured on the fine countenance, which is uplifted with an indescribable expression of the utmost

agony; the murdered babes filling the lower corner of the picture, lying on the blood-stained marble, so pale, so huddled together, so lifeless, yet so lovely and innocent in death, present an historical picture, perhaps the most domestic and touching that ever was painted. The broad shadows, the correctness, roundness, and simplicity of drawing in the whole, are inconceivably striking, the colours consistent and harmonious, no one point overlaboured, yet no effect neglected."—*Bell.* 136, The Crucifixion, a grand and solemn composition, from the suppressed Church of the Capuchins. "The agony of our Saviour, the gentle love and adoration of St. John, the fervour with which Mary Magdalene, kneeling, embraces the lower part of the cross, the last drooping of Mary, the mournful solemnity, the sombre tint of the landscape are very striking. It is, perhaps, the finest and most finished picture in existence. The magnificent size of the figures, the fulness without heaviness of the drapery, the deep fine tones of the colouring, with the impression excited from the awful stillness of the scene, are wonderful."—*Bell.* 137, The Victory of Samson over the Philistines. "The grandeur and noble elevation of mind delineated in the form, contour, and action of the conqueror, thus represented alone in the midst of death; the admirable drawing and foreshortening of the bodies heaped on each other; and the deep solitude and silence that seems to pervade the whole, are inexpressibly fine. Nothing barbarous or brutal is represented; no blood is seen. It is one great simple epic story. A fine and solemn scene, forming a very inestimable picture." 138, Madonna and Child, in glory; painted on silk, and formerly used as the banner of the ch. of S. Domenico in solemn processions. 139, Portrait of San Andrea Corsini, in pontifical robes. 140, St. Sebastian; a sketch, but full of expression. " A wonderful sketch, in a very simple style. The head of the young enthusiast, passionately turned up to heaven, is exquisitely foreshortened, and shaded with black hair, curling almost in a circle round his fine open forehead. The rounding and display of the shoulder and its parts, the expansion of the flat wide chest, the Apollo-like slenderness yet manliness of the limbs, the negligent flow of the slight drapery thrown around the middle, the effect of the light falling down almost perpendicularly on the head and shoulders, the just proportion of the figure to the canvas, with the low unfinished tint of the distant landscape, render this the finest sketch perhaps in existence." 141, Coronation of the Virgin. 142, The Agony of Christ. 199, Lucrezia, very beautiful. *Guercino.* 17, God the Father; a grand impromptu painting, done in a single night, and put up in the morning; formerly belonging to the Church di Gesù e Maria. 12, Duke William of Aquitaine kneeling before St. Felix, bishop; very fine. 13, St. Bruno, a beautiful picture, one of Guercino's most powerful works. 14, St. Peter the Domenican. 15, St. John the Baptist. 19, The Magdalen. *Elisabetta Sirani.* 175, The infant Saviour appearing to St. Antony. *Simone da Pesaro.* 39, The Assumption; a masterpiece. 30, Portrait of Guido in his old age, very spirited and lifelike.

Other Schools—Roman School.—Perugino. 197, Madonna in glory, with angels and saints; very beautiful: John, Michael, Catherine, and Apollonia. *Raphael.* 152. The Santa Cecilia; originally painted for the Bentivoglio Chapel in the Church of S. Giovanni in Monte. This immortal work is without doubt the great treasure of the gallery. "Santa Cecilia is represented with a lyre, held by both hands, carelessly dropped; the head, turned up towards heaven, with a beautiful pensive countenance, having an expression of concentrated and exalted feeling, as if devoting the best faculties and gifts of God to God, is deeply and touchingly impressive; her drapery is of finely enriched yellow, thrown over a close-drawn tunic; St. Paul, a superb dignified figure, fills one corner; St. John, drawn with a greater expression of simplicity and delicacy of form, is next to him; St. Augustine, another grand figure, and Mary Magdalene, like sister

of the heaven-devoted Cecilia, stands close by her. All the figures are in a line, but so finely composed, and the disposition of the lights and shades such, as to produce the effect of a beautiful central group, consisting of Santa Cecilia, Mary Magdalene, and St. Peter. Musical instruments, scattered on the foreground, fill it up, but without attracting the eye; a pure blue element forms the horizon, while high in the heavens a choir of angels, touched with the softest tints, is indistinctly seen." — *Bell.* The effect produced by this picture on Francia is well known by the account of Vasari, who says that the great painter died of mortification and surprise shortly after the Sta. Cecilia arrived in Bologna. *G. Romano.* 210, A copy of the St. John, of Raphael, in the Desert. *Timoteo delle Vite.* 204, The Magdalen in the Desert, painted for the Cathedral of Urbino; very pleasing and expressive.

Florentine School. — *Vasari.* 189. St. Gregory the Great entertaining 12 poor pilgrims; painted for the Convent of S. Michele in Bosco. This work is a series of portraits of the artist's friends and patrons; Gregory is represented by Pope Clement VII.; Duke Alessandro de' Medici, and even the butler of the convent, are introduced.

School of Parma.—Parmegiano. 116, Madonna and Child, with saints in adoration. "The colouring is fresh, beautiful, and deep-toned, and the shades of the drapery and dark sides of the figures finely wrought, but the composition is in a stiff elementary style, which, though admired by connoisseurs, is, in my opinion, wanting in grace and expression. The heads of the angels around the Virgin are as regular as a circle of a Gothic fringe above an arched door, and the figures below painted in the same spirit of strict uniformity."—*Bell.*

School of Milan.— Bolognese Masters. —*Camillo Procaccini.* 131, The Nativity.

Venetian School.—Tintoretto. 143, The Visitation. *Cima da Conegliano,* a Virgin and Child.

The University of Bologna, celebrated as the oldest in Italy, and as the first in which academical degrees were conferred, was long the glory of its citizens. It was founded in 1119 by Irnerius, or Wernerus, a learned civilian, who taught the law with such reputation in his native city, that he acquired the title of "Lucerna Juris." During the troubled period of the 12th century the fame of this university attracted students from all parts of Europe; no less than 10,000 are said to have assembled there in 1262, and it became necessary to appoint regents and professors to the students of each country. Irnerius succeeded in introducing the Justinian code; his disciples were called Glossators, who, treading in the footsteps of their master for nearly 2 centuries, spread the study of the Roman law over Europe, and sent to England Vacarius, one of the ablest of their body. At this period civil and canon law formed almost the exclusive study at Bologna; the faculties of medicine and arts were added before the commencement of the 14th century; and Innocent VI. instituted a theological faculty some years later. In the 14th century, also, it acquired celebrity as the first school where dissection of the human body was practised; and in more recent times it became renowned for the discovery of Galvanism within its walls. The University of Bologna has also been remarkable for an honour peculiarly its own—the large number of its learned female professors. In the 14th century, Novella d'Andrea, daughter of the celebrated canonist, frequently occupied her father's chair; and it is recorded by Christina de Pisan, that her beauty was so striking that a curtain was drawn before her in order not to distract the attention of the students.

"Drawn before her,
Lest, if her charms were seen, the students
Should let their young eyes wander o'er her,
And quite forget their jurisprudence."—*Moore.*

The name of Laura Bassi, professor of Mathematics and Natural Philosophy, is of more recent date; she had the degree of Doctor of Laws, and her lectures were regularly attended by many learned ladies of France and Germany, who were members of the University. Another, and, as our English travellers may consider, more surprising instance, is that of Madonna Manzolina, who graduated in surgery and was Professor of Anatomy; and even in our own times, the Greek chair was filled by the learned Matilda Tambroni, the friend and immediate predecessor, we believe, of Cardinal Mezzofanti. At the present time the university has lost its high legal reputation, and the traveller who is interested in the early history of the Glossators will be disappointed in his researches at Bologna. Medical studies appear to have the superiority, and the name of Tommasini has given a reputation to it as a clinical school, which has been well maintained by other professors since his removal to Parma.

The noble Palace in the Strada S. Donato, which includes the University, the Institute, and other similar establishments, was formerly the Palazzo Cellesi. It was built by Cardinal Poggi, the front being designed by Pellegrino Tibaldi, and the fine and imposing court by Bartolommeo Triachini, a native architect of the 16th century. It was purchased in 1714 by the Senate of Bologna, to receive the library and the collections of natural history and scientific instruments presented to the city, as the foundation of a national institute, by Count Marsigli, the friend of Sir Isaac Newton, and a fellow of the Royal Society of London.

The Palace at first included the Academy of Sciences, or the Instituto delle Scienze di Bologna, founded in the 17th century, by a noble youth named Manfredi, at the age of 16, who formed a literary society at his house, and assembled there all the men of talent in the city. In 1803 the university was transferred here, under the general name of the "Pontificia Universita."

The halls of the loggiato and the adjoining chambers are remarkable for their frescoes, by *Pellegrino Tibaldi.* In the court, by Triachini, is the statue of Hercules at rest, a singular work in grey stone, by Angelo Pio, a sculptor of some repute in the 17th century. On the staircase are several memorials, erected in honour of celebrated professors and others, natives of the city.

1 The Cabinet of Natural Philosophy contains some paintings by Niccolò dell' Abate, engraved at Venice in 1756. The Anatomical Museum is rich; and the various branches of pathological, general, and obstetrical anatomy are well illustrated by preparations and wax figures. The Museum of Natural History has been considerably augmented of late years, and the rooms in which it is contained, newly fitted up at the expense of the present Archbishop of Bologna, Cardinal Oppizzoni; it is well arranged, and contains a good geological collection of the provinces around. The Museum of Antiquities is small, but possesses some curious and interesting fragments. The first apartment contains the inscriptions, among which is that belonging to the sacred well, which gave rise to the commentary of Paciaudi on the "Puteus Sacer;" 2 milestones from the Via Æmilia, numbered CC., and CCXXCVI.; 2 fragments of latercoli, or military registers, and a large number of sepulchral tablets. The second chamber contains some Egyptian and Etruscan antiquities; among the latter is the celebrated fragment of the engraved plate, or, according to Chev. Inghirami, of the mystic mirror, called, from the name of its first possessor, the Cospiana Patera. It represents the birth of Minerva, who issues armed from the head of Jupiter, while Venus is caressing him. The names of the figures are in Etruscan characters. Another mirror represents, but in relief, Philoctetes healed by Machaon, the names of which are also in Etruscan characters. The following are worthy of examination. A bronze foot, larger than natural, and a Bacchic vase in marble, both found in the island of Capri; a series of Roman weights in black stone, and some metal weights of the middle ages; among which is one of the time of Charlemagne, with the inscription "Pondus Caroli." In the third chamber are some architectural remains, with 2 fragments of marble torsi, the one of a Venus coming out of the bath, the other

of the same goddess standing; a male torso, attributed to Augustus, found in the Via di S. Mamolo; an Isiac table of black basalt, found on the Aventine in 1709, and an elliptical vase of porphyry. In the next chamber are works after the revival, among which is a bronze statue of Boniface VIII., by Manno, a native sculptor, erected by the Bolognese in 1301; it is remarkable only as showing the state of art at that early period. Some carved ivories and Majolica plates are worthy of notice. The Chamber of Medals contains some ancient Roman coins, Greek pieces from Sicily, a collection of Italian and foreign money, and a good series of modern medals of sovereigns and illustrious men. There is also a small collection of gems, among which is the Maffei agate, highly prized by archæologists, representing Achilles and Ulysses. It would be an omission in an account of the antiquities of Bologna not to mention the celebrated Latin inscription discovered in some excavations of the city. This famous riddle, which gave rise to so much learned controversy in the 17th century, is as follows:—

" D. M. ÆLIA LÆLIA CRISPIS, nec vir, nec mvlier, nec androgyna, nec pvella, nec jvvenis, nec anvs, nec casta, nec meretrix, nec pvdica, sed omnia; svblata neqve fame, neqve ferro, neqve veneno, sed omnibvs; nec cœlo, nec aqvis, nec terris, sed vbiqve jacet. Lvcivs Agatho Priscivs, nec maritvs, nec amator, nec necessarivs, neqve mœrens, neqve gavdens, neqve fiens, hanc nec molem, nec pyramidem, nec sepvlchrvm, sed omnia, scit et nescit cvi posverit." At the top of the building of the University is the Observatory, containing some good astronomical instruments. The view from the terrace of its tower is most extensive, and no traveller should leave Bologna without ascending to it, which is easily done on application to the Custode of the University.

The *University Library* occupies a building constructed by Carlo Dotti, and added to the Institute by Benedict XIV. (Lambertini). It contains about 140,000 volumes and 9000 manuscripts; of these, not less, it is said, than 20,000 volumes were presented by that Pope, who also induced Cardinal Monti, another native of Bologna, to follow his patriotic example. Among the printed books are the following: the first edition of Henry VIII.'s famous book against Luther, *Assertio Septem Sacramentorum adversus Martinum Lutherum, Lond. in Œdibus Pynsonianis,* 1512, dedicated to Leo X., with the autograph signature "Henricus Rex:" a *Lactantius,* printed at Subiaco, 1465. Among the MSS. may be mentioned a *Lactantius,* of the 5th, or, according to Montfancon, of the 6th or 7th century; the *Four Evangelists* in Armenian, of the 12th century, given to Pope Benedict XIV. by Abraham Neger, an Armenian Catholic; the *Images of Philostrates,* in the handwriting of Michael Apostolius, a Greek exile, and protégé of Cardinal Bessarion; and about 200 volumes of scientific MSS. by Ulisse Aldrovandi.

It is scarcely possible to consider any record of this library complete which fails to commemorate its connexion with one of the most extraordinary men of our time, the late Cardinal Mezzofanti, who commenced his early career as its librarian. He was the son of an humble tradesman of Bologna, and had become celebrated throughout Europe for his knowledge of languages, even while he filled the chair of professor of Greek and Oriental literature in this university; but it remained for the late pope (Gregory XVI.) to raise him from the humble dignity of an abbé to the highest honours which it was in his power to confer. At the age of 36 Mezzofanti is said to have read 20, and to have conversed fluently in 18 languages; at the time of his death in 1849 he spoke 42. Mezzofanti was called to Rome by the late pope, and appointed to a post in the Vatican, under Maï; and when that illustrious scholar was created a cardinal, Mezzofanti was raised to the same dignity, under circumstances which will ever remain an honour to Gregory XVI. Perhaps the English traveller may desire no higher evidence of the unequalled powers of Cardinal Mezzofanti than the following extract from the 'Detached Thoughts' of Lord Byron:— "I do not recollect," he says, "a single foreign literary character that I wished to see twice, except, perhaps, Mezzofanti, who is a prodigy of language, a Briareus of the parts of speech, a walking library, who ought to have lived at the time of the tower of Babel, as universal interpreter; a real miracle, and without pretension too. I tried him in all the languages of which I knew only an oath or adjuration of the gods against postilions, savages, pirates, boatmen, sailors, pilots, gondoliers, muleteers, camel-drivers, vetturini, postmasters, horses, and houses, and everything in post; and, by Heaven! he puzzled me in my own idiom."

In connexion with the University, there remain to be noticed the Botanical and Agrario Gardens, and the Public Hospitals. The *Botanical Garden* was formed in 1804, on the site of the ancient Collegio Ferrerio de' Piemontesi. The Agrario Garden, *Orto Agrario,* one of the results of the French invasion, was commenced in 1805 under the direction of Professor Re, and was intended as a practical school for agricultural students, for whom a course of theoretical and experimental lectures on agriculture are delivered. The lecture room is the ancient Palazzino della Viola, formerly the villa of Giovanni II., Bentivoglió, and celebrated for its frescoes by *Innocenzio da Imola.* These fine works represent Diana and Endymion; Acteon metamorphosed into a stag; Marsyas, Apollo, and Cybele. There were originally other frescoes by Costa, Chiodarolo, Aspertino, Prospero Fontana, and Niccolò dell'Abate, but they have all been destroyed for the purpose of building additional apartments. The *Ospedale Grande* was founded in 1667, and opened in 1725; the clinical cases are received in a separate building, near the university, called the *Ospedale Azzolini,* from the Senator Francesco Azzolini, by whom it was founded, in 1706, for the sick and infirm poor of the parish of S. M. Maddalena. In the Borgo di S. Giuseppe is the *Ospedale de' Settuagenari*, for the aged poor ; and in the ancient Benedictine Monastery of S. Procolo is the *Ospedale degli Esposti*, or *Bastardini*, recently enlarged. Dr. Fraser gives us the following note of the Ospedale Grande:—" A good hospital and a separate building for clinical cases. There are at present 500 students. There is a large collection of anatomical figures, but it is inferior to that at Florence. The average number of cases of ' stabbing' admitted annually into the hospital is 500 ! "

Churches. — Among the hundred churches of Bologna there are few which do not contain some painting, which, if not itself a masterpiece, supplies an episode in the history of art. In the following pages we have given such details as will enable the traveller to select and judge for himself, amidst the multiplicity of riches ; at the same time, the student must bear in mind that there are none from which he will fail to derive instruction.

The most ancient church in Bologna, and one of the oldest and most characteristic in Italy, is that of *San Stefano*, quite a labyrinth, formed by the union of 7 churches or chapels. It is, moreover, remarkable, not only for its Greek frescoes of the 12th and 13th centuries, but for its ancient tombs and madonnas, its miraculous well, its Lombard architecture, Gothic inscriptions, and other relics which carry the imagination vividly back to the early ages of the church. In what is called the first church (del Crocifisso) is a painting by *Teresa Muratori* and her master *Giuseppe Dal Sole*, representing a father supplicating St. Benedict to intercede for his dying son. The Banzi chapel in which is the marble sarcophagus containing the body of the Beata Giuliana de Banzi is called the second church. The third, del Santo Sepolcro, is a round building, supposed to have been the ancient Lombard Baptistery. The marble columns are said to have been derived from a neighbouring temple of Isis. The upper gallery has long been

closed ; but the well for immersion sufficiently proves its original destination. The marble sepulchre, with its ancient symbols, was erected to receive the body of S. Petronio, who is said to have given miraculous qualities to the water of the well. The ancient Greek paintings on the walls will not fail to attract the attention of the traveller ; they are full of nature and expression, but many of them have unfortunately perished or been injured in recent years. The fourth church, dedicated to SS. Peter and Paul, is supposed to have been the old Cathedral, founded by S. Faustiniano, A.D. 330. It contains a remarkable Crucifixion, by *Simone da Bologna*, known also as Simone dai Crocifissi, from the excellence with which he treated this subject ; it bears his name, "Simon fecit hoc opus." There are some arabesques and an Ionic capital in this ch., apparently antique. The Madonna and Child, with St. Nicholas and St. John, is by *Sabbatini*. The St. James, St. John, and St. Francis, is referred to *Lippo di Dalmasio*. This ch. has small round windows in the nave, and has some general resemblance to our old Norman architecture. The 5th is formed of the cloister, called the Atrio di Pilato. Another cloister has 2 rows of galleries : the upper one is very elegant, and composed of antique columns derived from the Temple of Isis, which are coupled with fanciful capitals, composed of monsters supporting small circular arches, over which is a frieze with other whimsical ornaments of the same kind. The ancient Greek frescoes of this ch. have suffered greatly ; an ex-voto Madonna, left here by a company of English pilgrims about A. D. 1400, may interest the English traveller. The S. Girolamo adoring the Crucifix, with the Magdalen and S. Francis, is attributed to *Fr. Francia*. In the small cortile is a large marble vase or font, bearing an inscription, recording the names of Luitprand and Ilprand, kings of the Lombards, and of Barbato, bishop of Bologna. An adjoining Hall constructed by Benedict XIV. recalls the ancient " Compagnia de'

Lombardi," founded in 1170, and numbering in its annals almost all the illustrious names in the history of Bologna. The keys of the gates of Imola, captured a second time by the Bolognese in 1222, are preserved there. The 6th church (I Confessi) is a kind of crypt, and is remarkable only for its ancient bas-reliefs, and as containing the bodies of 2 native saints and martyrs, Vitale and Agricola. The Madonna in the wall is said to have been placed here, in 488, by S. Giocondo, bishop of the diocese. One of the pillars professes to give the exact height of our Saviour. The 7th church, called la SS. Trinità, also contains some interesting works of ancient art, a few of which are regarded as contemporaneous with S. Petronio. The St. Martin, bishop, praying for the restoration of a dead child to life is by *Tiarini*, a repetition of the same subject painted for the ch. of S. Rocco. The S. Ursula, on the wall, is by *Simone da Bologna*; and the Holy Trinity is by *Samacchini*. This ch. is celebrated for its relics, among which are the bodies of 40 martyrs, brought by S. Petronio from Jerusalem. Outside these churches are two marble sarcophagi, appropriated in former times by the Orsi and Bertuccini families; one of them at least is an ancient Christian sarcophagus, and is an interesting relic. In an adjacent portico is an inscription recording the existence of the Temple of Isis, already mentioned as occupying this site.

The Cathedral, dedicated to St. Peter, is a very ancient foundation, but it has been several times rebuilt. The present edifice was begun in 1605; the front and some of the chapels were added in 1748 by Benedict XIV., from the designs of Torreggiani. The interior is in the Corinthian style, well arranged and imposing in its effect. In the 2nd chapel on the left is preserved among the relics the skull of St. Anna, presented in 1435 by King Henry VI. of England to the Blessed Niccolò Albergati. In the 3rd chapel is the fine work of *Graziani*, a native painter of the 17th century, representing St. Peter consecrating St. Apol-

linaris. Cardinal Giovanetti, archbishop of Bologna in 1788, is buried here. In the 4th chapel is the St. Peter commanding Pope Celestin to elect S. Petronius bishop of Bologna, by *Bigari*; and the Holy Family, and the frescoes of S. Pancras and S. Petronius, by *Franceschini*, painted in his 80th year. The 5th chapel contains the urn of bronze gilt adorned with lapis lazuli, containing the body of the martyr S. Proclus, presented by Benedict XIV., in 1745. The *Sacristy* contains, among other works of more or less merit, the Crucifixion, by *Bagnacavallo*; paintings by the *Zanotti*; and the St. Peter, in the fisherman's dress, mourning with the Virgin for the death of the Saviour, a strange invention of *Lodovico Caracci*. The 6th chapel, designed by *Domenico Tibaldi*, contains a fine picture designed by *Fiorini* and coloured by *Aretusi*, representing our Saviour giving the keys to St. Peter in the presence of the 12 apostles; and on the arch above the high altar the celebrated painting of the Annunciation, the last work of *Lodovico Caracci*. The foot of the angel bending before the Virgin was a little crooked, and it is related that when the aged artist made the discovery, he offered to defray the expense of re-erecting the scaffold in order that he might re-touch it, but the request was refused, and Lodovico died of grief and chagrin a few days after. In 1830 the error was corrected by Prof. Fancelli, who was employed to clean and restore the paintings in this chapel and in the Sacristy. Returning towards the entrance, the chapels of the opposite side remain to be examined. The first of these is worthy of observation, as it was here, and not in S. Petronio, as Vasari believed, that the ancient Garganelli chapel, painted by Ercole Grande of Ferrara, existed; some remains of these pictures were presented by the Tanari family to the academy, and have been for some years in England. The chapel of the SS. Sacramento contains a work by *Donati Creti* which has been much admired: it represents the Virgin in the clouds with the infant Saviour, S. Ignatius, and angels. The gilt bronze ornaments were designed by Torriggiani at the cost of Benedict XIV., then Cardinal Lambertini, and archbishop of this his native city. In the Baptistery is a finely composed and beautifully coloured painting of the Baptism of our Saviour, by *Ercole Grazini*. On St. Peter's day some fine tapestries are exhibited in this church, executed at Rome from the designs of Raphael Mengs, and presented by the same pontiff. The Subterranean Ch. below the choir is curious: it contains numerous relics, and some works of art, among which is that by *Alfonso Lombardo* representing the two Marys weeping over the dead body of Christ. Behind the cathedral is the archbishop's palace, a fine and spacious modern edifice.

The Ch. of San Petronio, the largest in Bologna, and, though unfinished, one of the most interesting and remarkable, is a fine monument of the religious munificence which characterised the period of Italian freedom. It was founded in 1390, while Bologna was a republic, the architect being Antonio Vicenza or Vincenzi, celebrated as one of the 16 *Riformatori*, and as the ambassador of the Bolognese to the Venetian Republic in 1396. The original plan was a Latin cross, and if the building had been completed, it would have been more than 600 ft. long, or upwards of 100 more than St. Peter's at Rome. Of the exterior, a small portion of its front alone is finished, and of the interior little more than the nave has been completed. In spite of these drawbacks, San Petronio is one of the finest specimens of the Italian Gothic of the 14th century. It is almost a museum of sculpture, and its rich pointed windows, although sadly mutilated and transformed, still retain their rich mouldings in perfect preservation. The 3 canopied doorways of the unfinished façade are pure and interesting examples of the late Italian Gothic; they are covered with bas-reliefs representing various events of Scripture history from the creation to the time of the apostles, and are ornamented with busts of prophets and sibyls which recal

the taste and design of Raphael. The *central doorway* and its bas-reliefs were justly considered the master-piece of Jacopo dalla Quercia, and were entirely completed by his own hand. They must be carefully studied to appreciate their details; there are no less than 32 half figures of patriarchs and prophets, with the Almighty in the midst; 5 subjects from the New Testament in the architrave, and 5 from the Old Testament, from the creation to the deluge, on each pilaster. Over the architrave are 3 statues as large as life, the Virgin and Child, San Petronio, and St. Ambrose. It is recorded that the artist was commissioned to execute this door for the sum of 3600 golden florins, the Reverenda Fabbrica providing the stone; Vasari says that he devoted 12 years to the work, and that its completion filled the Bolognese with astonishment. *The l. doorway* is remarkable for the angels and sibyls on the arch, by Tribolo, well known as the friend of Benvenuto Cellini, who has left an amusing record of him in his most entertaining of biographies. Of the 4 subjects on the l. pilaster, the 1st, 3rd, and 4th, are by Tribolo, as well as the 4th on the rt. pilaster, supposing the spectator to be looking at the door. Tribolo was assisted in these works by Seccadenari, Propersia de' Rossi, the Bolognese Sappho; and by Cioli and Solosmeo, pupils of Sansovino. The 3 other subjects on the rt. pilaster are by Alfonso Lombardo, and represent different events of the Old Testament. The second subject of the l. pilaster, representing Jacob giving his blessing to Isaac, is by an unknown artist. Under the arch is the superb sculpture of the Resurrection, by Alfonso Lombardo, praised by Vasari, and admirable for its simple dignity and truth. *The right doorway* is another monument of the taste and purity of Tribolo. The angels of the arch, the sibyls, and the 8 subjects from the Old Testament on the pilasters, are by this master. Under the arch is the group of Nicodemus with the dead body of Christ, by Amico; the Virgin is by Tribolo; and the St. John the Evangelist by Ercole Seccadenari.

The interior of San Petronio is particularly imposing, and never fails to excite regret that it has not been completed on its original extensive plan. Some fault might be found with the proportion of the edifice ; but the size and peculiar simplicity of the design produce an effect which reminds the English traveller of the purer Gothic of the north. " It possesses in a high degree the various peculiarities which characterise the arrangements of the Italian Gothic, such as the wide and low pier arches whose span equals the breadth of the nave, the absence of the triforium and of the clerestory string, the great empty circles which occupy the space of the clerestory, the extensive doming of the vaults, the shallowness of the side aisles, the heavy capitals which surround the piers and half piers like a band of leaves, and the squareness of the piers with their nook shafts; all these serve to make a wide distinction between this example and those of the genuine Gothic ; and they are rarely found so completely united even in Italian churches. Each compartment of the side aisle has two arches, which open into shallow chapels."—*Willis.*

On entering the ch., the ornaments in relief round the great doorway are by Francesco and Petronio Tadolini. Over the side doors are the fine bas-reliefs by Lombardo, one representing the Annunciation, the other Adam and Eve in Paradise, formerly attributed to Tribolo. In the chapels on the rt., there are several objects to engage attention. The 2nd is the chapel of the Pepoli, so celebrated in the history of Bologna; and some of the pictures contain portraits, it is said, of different members of that illustrious family. The painting of the Almighty has been attributed to *Guido;* but it was more probably retouched by him. The paintings on the lateral walls, with their Gothic ornaments and inscriptions, are curious; one of the female figures praying on the right wall bears the inscription, *Sofia de Inghiltera fe fa.* 4th chapel—the ancient Crucifixion, repainted, it is said, by *Francia;* the Madonna underneath is referred to *Tiarini.* The railing is a good specimen of the iron-work of the 15th century. 6th—St. Jerome, by *Lorenzo Costa,* the pupil of Francia, spoiled by retouching. 8th—the marble ornaments of this chapel were designed by *Vignola,* and are said to have cost him the loss of his situation as architect to the ch. through the jealousy of his rival Ranuccio. The St. Francis is by *Mastelletta;* and the St. Antony raising the dead man to liberate the father, who is unjustly condemned, is by *Lorenzo Pasinelli.* 9th —Chapel of St. Antony of Padua. The marble statue of the Saint is by *Sansovino.* The miracles of the Saint painted in chiaro-scuro are fine works, by *Girolamo da Treviso.* The windows of painted glass are celebrated as having been coloured from the designs of *Michael Angelo.* 10th—the large painting of the Coronation of the Madonna del Borgo S. Pietro and the beautiful fresco opposite it are by *Francesco Brizzi,* a favourite pupil of the Caracci: he commenced life as a journeyman shoemaker, and became the principal assistant of Lodovico. 11th—The superb bas-relief of the Assumption, in marble, by *Tribolo,* formerly at the high altar of the Madonna di Galliera. The two angels by the side are by *Properzia de' Rossi.* The walls of this chapel support the entire weight of the Campanile. At the high altar the two marble statues of St. Francis and St. Antony of Padua are by *Girolamo Campagna,* and were formerly in the ch. of S. Francesco. 14th—Chapel (l.). Sta. Barbara beheaded by her father, considered the best work of *Tiarini.* 15th—the Archangel Michael, by *Calvart* (Fiammingo), which explains the celebrated picture by his pupil Guido in the Capuchins at Rome. 16th—St. Roch, larger than life, a portrait of Fabrizio da Milano, by *Parmegiano,* one of his best works ; copied as a study by Lod. Caracci. 17th—the Chapel of the Baciocchi family, containing the Tombs of the Princess Eliza Baciocchi, the sister of Napoleon, of her husband, and 3 of her children, with a beautiful altar-piece by *Costa,* Madonna and

Saints; and a fine painted glass window. 19th—the Annunciation, and the 12 Apostles, among the finest works of *Costa*, and the martyrdom of St. Sebastian in his earlier manner. The Magdalen by *Filippo Brizzi.* The pavement of earthenware dates from the earliest times of its manufacture. On the pilaster of this chapel is a statue of S. Petronius, generally believed to be the most ancient likeness of that saint extant, but it has been so altered by frequent restorations that little probably of the original countenance now remains. 20—the paintings of the Magi, and of the Paradiso and Inferno on the opposite wall, formerly attributed to Giotto, and subsequently by Vasari to Buffalmacco, are now generally considered to have been painted by Simone da Bologna, early in the 15th century. The head of S. Petronius, removed by order of Benedict XIV. from the other relics of that saint in S. Stefano, is preserved in this chapel, which is also that in which divine service was first performed in 1392.

On the floor of the ch. is traced the celebrated meridian of Gian Domenico Cassini, 178 Bolognese feet $6\frac{1}{2}$ inches long: it was substituted in 1653 for that of P. Ignazio Danti, and corrected in 1778 by Eustachio Zanotti. It was in this church that the Emperor Charles V. was crowned by Pope Clement VII. The halls of the *Reverendu Fabbrica*, adjoining the ch., contain a highly interesting series 'of original designs for the still unfinished façade, by the first architects of the period. 3 of these are by Palladio; another bears the following inscription in his own hand, "Laudo il presente disegno," and has, no doubt erroneously, been attributed to him. There are 2 by Vignola, 1 by Giacomo Ranuccio, his great rival; 1 by Domenico Tibaldi; 3 by Baldassare Peruzzi; 1 by Giulio Romano and Cristoforo Lombardo; 1 by Girolamo Rainaldi; 1 by Francesco Terribilia, which received the approbation of the senate in 1580, and was published by Cicognara in the plates to his History of Sculpture; 1 by Varignano; 1 by Giacomo di Andrea

da Formigine; 1 by Alberto Alberti, of Borgo San Sepolcro; and 3 by unknown artists. Over the entrance door is the noble marble bust of Count Guido Pepoli, by *Properzia de' Rossi*, supposed to be that ordered by his son Alessandro, to prove the powers of that extraordinary woman, as mentioned by Vasari. In the 2nd chamber is her masterpiece, the bas-relief of the Temptation of Joseph, in which it is believed she recorded the history of her own misfortunes. The life of this celebrated and accomplished woman, at once a painter, sculptor, engraver, and musician, is one of the most tragical episodes in the annals of art; "Finalmente," says Vasari, in a passage which will hardly bear translating, "alla povera inamorata giovane ogni cosa riuscì perfettissimamente, eccetto il suo infelicissimo amore." She died of love at the very moment when Clement VII., after performing the coronation of Charles V. in this church, where he had seen and appreciated her genius, expressed his desire to take her with him to Rome. Vasari records the touching answer given to his Holiness: *Sta in chiesa, e gli si fa il funerale!* Her death was made the subject of a tragic representation in the theatre of Bologna, by Professor Costa, in 1828.

The *Sacristy* contains a series of 22 pictures, representing various events in the history of S. Petronius from his baptism to his death, by Ferrari, Francesco Colonna, Mazzoni, and others. The inside of the Ch. of San Petronio is now undergoing a thorough repair, during which some early frescoes of the 15th century have been discovered under the whitewash on the columns of the nave.

Immediately before the great door of this ch. stood that famous colossal bronze statue of Julius II., executed by Michael Angelo after the reconciliation of their quarrel on the subject of the Moses. The Pope at his own request was represented with a sword in his left hand, and in the act of reprimanding the Bolognese with his right. But this great masterpiece lasted only 5 years. In 1511, on the return of Bentivoglio, it was destroyed by the people, and the bronze, said to have weighed 17,300 lbs., was sold to the Duke of Ferrara, who converted it into a piece of ordnance, under the appropriate name of the *Julian*. It is recorded of this statue, the loss of which will ever be deplored by the lovers of art, that when Michael Angelo asked the warlike pontiff whether he should put a book in his left hand, he replied, "A book! no: let me grasp a sword; I know nothing of letters."

The *Piazza* surrounding the *Ch. of San Domenico* is remarkable for some interesting monuments, which deserve examination before proceeding to the still greater treasures in the ch. itself. These are the statue of S. Domenico, in copper gilt, cast at Milan in 1623, standing on a red brick column; the Madonna del Rosario, by Giulio Cesare Conventi; and two sepulchral monuments, one the tomb of the learned jurist Rolandino Passaggeri, who, while holding the office of town-clerk, was selected to write the answer of the Republic to the haughty letter of the Emperor Frederick II., demanding the release of his son, King Enzius. The other is the tomb of the noble family of Foscherari, now extinct, and was built by Egidio Foscherari, in 1289. Its rude bas-reliefs appear to be more ancient than this date. Both tombs stand under canopies, supported by columns, and were restored in 1833.

The *Ch.*, celebrated as containing the tombs of St. Dominick, the founder of the order of Preaching Friars which bears his name, and of the Inquisition, of King Enzius, of Taddeo Pepoli, and of Guido, is as rich in works of art as it is in illustrious names. The *Tomb of San Domenico*, the early triumph of the genius of *Niccolò di Pisa*, forms in itself an epoch in the history of art, which ought to be closely studied by every one who desires to trace the progress of sculpture from the 13th century. This great master, who has been justly called the precursor of the revival of the art of sculpture, did not complete the pulpit at Pisa until 35 years later than the date of the present work (1225),

and consequently we may regard this as the foundation of a new era in art. The bas-reliefs by Niccolò di Pisa represent various events in the life of the saint and the miracles performed by him; they are full of character and truth. The knight thrown from his horse and brought to life by St. Dominick in the presence of his family, who are deploring his death, and the St. Peter and St. Paul in heaven, presenting the saint with the constitutions and baton of the order, are among the most remarkable of these graceful compositions. Below them is another interesting series by *Alfonso Lombardo*, executed 3 centuries later, and not superior in delicacy or feeling. The statue of S. Petronio, on the tomb, is a work of *Michael Angelo* in his youth, as is likewise the exquisitely beautiful angel on the left, now made to hold a very indifferent candlestick. It is recorded in the city annals, that the great artist received 12 ducats for the angel, and 18 ducats for the statue of S. Petronio! The other angel and the saints Francesco and Procolo are, according to Vasari, by Niccolò dell' Arca: the St. John Baptist is said to be by Girolamo Cortellini. The architecture of this (the 6th) chapel is by Terribilia; the 1st picture on the rt. hand, the Child brought to life, is one of the masterpieces of *Tiarini*, and was much admired by Lodovico Caracci. The great picture, representing the Storm at Sea, in which St. Dominick is rescuing the sailors praying to the Virgin; the knight thrown from his horse, and brought to life by the saint; the stories in the lunettes, and the graceful figures representing his virtues, are by *Mastelletta*. The fresco on the roof, representing the glory of Paradise, with the Saviour and the Virgin receiving the soul of the saint, amidst the music of the angels, is by *Guido*. "In the highest circle of the dome, a soft radiance, emanating from the Holy Spirit, illuminates the picture, touching, with partial lights, the heads of our Saviour, of Mary, and the saint, who are placed at equal distances, while a choir of angels, exquisitely designed, and finely coloured, fills the

space below. The composition of the
whole rises in a fine pyramidical form,
harmonising at once with the subject
and the proportions of the dome."—
Bell. The saint burning the books of
the converted heretics, a fine and expressive picture, is esteemed the masterpiece of *Lionello Spada.*

The other chapels of this church
present additional objects of interest:
1st, the Madonna, called "Del Vel-
luto," by *Lippo Dalmasio.* 3rd, St.
Antoninus with the Saviour and the
Virgin appearing to St. Francis, by
Facini, the pupil of Annibale Caracci,
who praised his skill in painting
flesh; below it is a Virgin, attributed
to *Francia.* 4th, St. Andrew the
Apostle preparing for his martyrdom,
by *Antonio Rossi.* 9th, St. Catherine
of Siena, by *Francesco Brizzi.* 10th,
St. Thomas Aquinas writing on the
subject of the eucharist, with 2 inspir-
ing angels, by *Guercino.* Near the
entrance of the Sacristy is the monument erected by the Clementine Academy to the memory of General Count
Marsigli, the founder of the Institute,
whose patriotic zeal for the welfare of
Bologna, and whose connexion with
the science of England, have been
noticed in a previous page. The high
altar has the fine picture by *Bartolommeo Cesi,* the Adoration of the Magi.
The stalls of the choir present an interesting example of *tarsia,* of the 15th
century, by Fra Damiano da Bergamo,
assisted by Fra Antonio Asinelli, both
Domenican monks; the subjects are
taken from the Old and New Testaments. The 13th chapel is remarkable
for the tomb of King Enzius, the unfortunate son of the great Emperor
Frederick II., made prisoner by the
Bolognese in 1249, and retained here
in captivity for 22 years, until his death
in 1272. It bears the following inscription, in which the haughty republic
makes the record of its royal captive
the source of a much higher compliment to itself:

"Felsina Sardiniæ regem sibi vincla minantem
   Victrix captivum consule ovante trahit;
Nec patris imperio credit, nec capitur auro;
   Sic cane non magno sæpe tenetur aper."

in singular and striking contrast to

this tomb, the adjoining chapel (14th)
contains the marble sarcophagus of
Taddeo Pepoli, the celebrated republican ruler of Bologna, by the Venetian
artist Jacopo Lanfrani, dated 1337, with
black and white squares on the front like
a chess-board. The sculptures on its
front represent Pepoli rendering justice
to his fellow-citizens. The altar-piece,
with St. Michael, S. Domenico, and
other saints, said to be by *Francia.*
15th, the Chapel of the Relics: among
the other relics here preserved is the
head of S. Domenic, in a silver case of
114 lbs. weight, made in 1383, at the
joint expense of the city, of Benedict
XI., and Cardinal Matteo Orsini. The
body of the Beato Giacomo da Ulma,
the painter, whose portrait by Bellini is
in front of the adjoining chapel, is also
preserved here. On the wall opposite
the monument of King Enzius is the portrait of St. Thomas Aquinas, by *Simone
da Bologna,* proved by the annals of the
Order to be an authentic likeness, and
preserved here, as the inscription under
it conveys, during the last 400 years;
near to it is the disgusting mummy of the
Venerabile Serafino Capponi. 17th, the
Annunciation, by *Calvart* (Fiammingo).
19th. This magnificent chapel, dedicated to the Madonna del Rosario, contains 2 tombs which inspire very different feelings from that of the founder
of the Inquisition, or those of King
Enzius and the Pepoli: they are those
of Guido and of Elisabetta Sirani, who
died of poison in her 26th year. The
chapel contains a series of small paintings representing the 15 mysteries of
the Rosary; the Presentation in the
Temple is by *Calvart* (Fiammingo);
the Descent of the Holy Spirit, by *Cesi;*
the Visitation, and the Flagellation of
the Saviour, are by *Lod. Caracci;* the
Assumption is by *Guido.* The statues
over the altar are by *Angelo Piò;* the
painting of St. John the Evangelist is
by *Giuseppe Marchesi.* The ceiling,
painted in 1656, is an able work of
Michael Angelo Colonna and *Agostino
Mitelli;* the Assumption of the Virgin,
in the middle, is particularly fine. In
the vestibule of one of the side doors is
the fine tomb of the celebrated jurisconsult, Alessandro Tartagni, surnamed

l'Imolese, by the Florentine sculptor Francesco di Simone; and opposite is that of the Volta family, with a marble statue of S. Procolo, by Lazzaro Casario. 22nd Chapel, St. Raymon crossing the sea on his mantle, by *Lod. Caracci*, another fine work, which serves to prove the originality and invention of this remarkable painter. 23rd. This chapel contains a bust of S. Filippo Neri, from a cast taken after death.

The *Sacristy* has also some pictures and other objects of interest: the Birth of the Saviour, or "La Notte," by *Luca Cangiasi*, is considered by many as a repetition of the smaller painting preserved in the academy, while others regard it as a copy. The Paschal Lamb is attributed to *Vasari*. The S. Girolamo is by *Lionello Spada*. The *tarsie* of the closets and of the entrance door are by the artists who executed those of the choir. The large statues of the Virgin and of San Domenico are of cypress wood, and, according to the verses inscribed underneath, were carved out of a tree which S. Domenico himself had planted —one of those, perhaps, which Evelyn saw growing at the period of his visit, in the quadrangle of the convent.

The Cloisters of the adjoining convent of San Domenico, the first of which is supposed to be that built in 1281 by Niccolò di Pisa, are remarkable for their inscriptions and ancient tombs. Among these are to be noticed that of Gio. d'Andrea Calderini, the work of the Venetian Jacopo Lanfrani, in 1238; and that of Bartolommeo Salicetti, by Andrea da Fiesole, in 1412. There is still preserved here a portion of a painting by *Lippo Dalmasio*, representing the Magdalen at the feet of Christ, which Malvasia describes as his earliest public work; in one corner is a fragment of an inscription *...lmasi f.* Near it is a Crucifixion, with S. Lorenzo presenting a Doctor kneeling; it bears the inscription *Petrus Johanis* (Pietro di Giovanni Lianori?), and is a very beautiful specimen of art of the 14th century. On leaving the convent, under the portico built by Niccola Barella,

leading up the Via di S. Domenico, on the l. hand, is a picture of the Virgin and Child, with St. John, by *Bagnacavallo.*

In connexion with the Domenican Convent, the *Biblioteca Comunale*, or Magnani Library, remains to be noticed. This library consists chiefly of the collections bequeathed to the city by the learned ecclesiastic Antonio Magnani, formerly librarian of the Scientific Institute; who has by will especially provided that this library shall be available on those holidays and *festas* when every other is closed: the number of books is said to be upwards of 90,000, and it is continually increasing by the munificence of the city authorities. Besides its literary treasures, the lover of art will not fail to appreciate and admire the unfinished Deposition from the Cross, by *Baroccio*, said to be his last work: it is hardly surpassed in effect and composition by any production of that great painter.

The elegant *Ch. of S. Bartolommeo di Porta Ravegnana* was commenced in 1653, on the site of a more ancient building erected in 1530, from the designs of Andrea da Formigine, at the cost of the Prior Gozzadini. The original site was occupied by an ancient ch. built in the 5th century by S. Petronio on the foundations of one of the early Christians. The portico of Formigine is still preserved; and the bas-reliefs of its pilasters, the work, it is said, of Lombard sculptors, are well worthy of observation. The ch. contains some interesting paintings: in the 2nd chapel is S. Carlo Borromeo kneeling at the tomb of Varallo, by *Lod. Caracci.* 4th, the Annunciation, significantly called "del bell' Angelo," a beautiful and expressive work of *Albani;* by whom also are the lateral pictures representing the Birth of the Saviour and the Angel warning Joseph to fly out of Egypt. 7th, "The altarpiece, by *Franceschini*, on the Martyrdom of St. Bartholomew, a grand but horrible picture, yet less savage than the statue of Milan on the same subject, as here at least the actual representation of torture is spared. The saint is tied and drawn up high on a tree for sacrifice; two ferocious figures are seen tightening the ropes, while a third is deliberately preparing to excoriate one of his legs, where a little blood appears, but there only."—*Bell.* 9th, the Madonna and Child, a small oval, by *Guido*, an exquisite and touching picture. 12th, S. Antony of Padua, by *Tiarini.* 13th, the St. Bartholomew, the altarpiece of the old church, is by *Aretusi*, from the designs of *Sabbatini.* The frescoes, representing the events in the life of S. Gaetano, are by the pupils of *Cignani.* The roof of the ch. was painted by *Colonna*, who is said to have received in payment the 3rd chapel, which he also decorated with his frescoes.

The *Ch. of S. Bartolommeo di Reno* is remarkable for some fine works of the Caracci. In the 6th chapel is the Nativity, by *Agostino Caracci*, painted at the age of 27. The two Prophets on the vault of the chapel are by the same master. The two admirable pictures of the Circumcision and the Adoration of the Magi are by *Lod. Caracci*; the last of these has been engraved by Annibale. The marble ornaments are by *Gabriele Fiorini*, the son of the painter. The 4th chapel (Capella Maggiore) contains a miraculous image of the Virgin, of very high antiquity, called "La Madonna della Pioggia." On the wall opposite the stairs leading to the oratory is a large landscape in oil, the only example in painting of the copperplate engraver *Mattioli.* The oratory contains the St. Bartholomew, a good work of *Alfonso Lombardo.*

The *Ch. of S. Benedetto* has, in the 1st chapel, the Marriage of St. Catherine in the presence of John the Baptist, SS. Jerome, Mauro, and Placido, by *Lucio Massari*, a pupil of the Caracci and the friend and favourite companion of Albani. In the 2nd, the 4 Prophets are by *Giacomo Cavedone.* In the 4th, S. Antonio Abate, beaten by demons and consoled by Christ; the beautiful "Charity," on the ceiling, and the Virtues of God the Father, are also by *Cavedone.* 5th, S. Francesco di Paolá, by *Gabriele Ferrantini*, called also G. dagli Occhiali, one of the mas-

ters of Guido. 7th, S. Antonio, by *Cavedone.* 11th, the Virgin holding the crown of thorns, and conversing with the Magdalen on her son's death, a touching and expressive work of *Tiarini*; by whom are also the Prophets and the Angels on the side walls. In the Sacristy is the beautiful picture of the Crucifixion, with the Virgin, the Archangel Michael, and St. Catherine, by *Andrea Sirani*, the father of Elisabetta, retouched by his master Guido, formerly in the suppressed Ch. of San Marino.

The *Ch. della Carità*, belonging to a convent of Franciscans suppressed in 1798, and converted into a military hospital, contains, in the 1st chapel, the celebrated Visitation by *Galanino*, so much extolled by Malvasia. Galanino was one of the ablest pupils and a relative of the Caracci; but his fortune, says Lanzi, was not equal to his merit, and he was obliged to become a portrait-painter, like many artists of our own day, from lack of encouragement in the higher branches of the art. He retired to Rome, and was long at the head of portrait-painters in that capital. The 3rd chapel contains the picture of St. Elizabeth, queen of Hungary, in a swoon at the Saviour's appearing to her, an able work by *Franceschini.* At the high altar is the Virgin and Child, Charity and St. Francis, another joint work of *Fiorini* and *Aretusi.* 5th, the Virgin and Child, St. Joseph and St. Antony of Padua, by *Felice*, son of *Carlo Cignani.* 6th, Sta. Anna, by *Bibiena* the Elder (Gio. Maria Galli).

The ancient *Ch. of Sta. Cecilia*, once celebrated for its frescoes by Francia, Costa, and other early painters of Bologna, was ruined by the French; but it still exhibits many interesting fragments for study. The following enumeration of the subjects, commencing on the l. hand, may be useful:—1, The Marriage of Valerian (or, as Malvasia says, of Tiburtius) with Sta. Cecilia, by *Francia.* 2, Valerian instructed in the faith by St. Urban, by *Lor. Costa.* 3, The Baptism of Valerian, by *Giacomo Francia* (?). 4, The Angel crowning the betrothed

Saints with garlands of roses, by *Chiodarolo.* 5, The brothers Valerian and Tiburtius beheaded in the presence of the Prefect. 6, Their Funeral. 7, Sta. Cecilia and the Prefect: these three subjects are by *Amico Aspertini.* 8, Sta. Cecilia placed in the boiling bath, by *Giacomo Francia.* 9, The wealth distributed by the Saint, by *Costa.* 10, Her Funeral, a very graceful composition, by *Francesco Francia.*

The *Ch. of the Celestini,* with a façade from the designs of Francesco Tadolini, has in its 1st chapel one of the best works of *Lucio Massari*—the Saviour appearing to the Magdalen in the form of a dove. The painting at the high altar, representing the Virgin and Child, with John the Baptist, St. Luke, and S. Pietro Celestino, is by *Franceschini.* The sacristy and the cloisters of the convent were designed by the Tadolini.

The *Ch. of the Corpus Domini,* called also *Della Santa* from Sta. Caterina Vigri of Bologna, is attached to the vast Franciscan nunnery of the same name. The frescoes of the cupola, the roof and the walls, are able works by *Marcantonio Franceschini,* assisted by *Luigi Quaini.* 1st chapel, St. Francis, with a fine landscape, by *Calvart.* 4th, the Saviour appearing to the Virgin, with the Patriarchs; and the Apostles engaged in the burial of the Virgin, described by Malvasia as "la prima di maniera delicata, la seconda terribile," are fine and interesting works by *Lodovico Caracci.* The Virgin and Child, the mysteries of the Rosary which surround them, and the two large Angels, are by *Giuseppe Mazza,* by whom are also the bas-reliefs of the high altar. The high altar-piece, representing the Last Supper, is a celebrated work by *Marcantonio Franceschini.* 6th, the Resurrection is a copy of the famous picture by *Annibale Caracci,* which was carried off by the French and never returned. Through a window in this chapel may be seen the blackened body of Sta. Caterina Vigri, sitting in all the pomp of dress, and decorated with a crown upon her head. 8th, The Annunciation, by *Franceschini,* whose

masterpiece, the Death of St. Joseph, is in the next (9th) chapel, the ceiling of which is painted in fresco by the same hand.

The *Ch. of S. Cristina,* attached to the Augustine Convent, is decorated with paintings executed almost entirely at the expense of different nuns. The Ascension, at the high altar, is by *Lodovico Caracci;* the Nativity and the Journey of the 3 Magi, in the 1st chapel, are by *Giacomo Francia.* The St. Peter and St. Paul, in the niches between the pilasters, are the production of *Guido* in his early youth.

The *Ch. of S. Giacomo Maggiore,* belonging to the Augustine hermits, was founded in 1267, enlarged and vaulted in 1497, but never completed. Some of its existing details, however, are interesting, as illustrations of early Italian Gothic. The doorway, said to have been erected at the expense of the Bentivoglio family, has a canopy in which the shafts supporting it rest on lion bases, and the lateral compartments have each a large painted window, with tracery, which lights the side aisles. Its immense vaulted roof has been much praised for the boldness of its structure. The paintings in the different chapels are the chief objects of attraction. In the 1st chapel, the small fresco of the Virgin, "della Cintura," is by *Francia.* 4th. The fall of St. Paul, by *Ercole Procaccini.* 5th. Christ appearing to S. Gio. da S. Facondo, by *Cavedone,* who also painted the side walls. 6th. The Virgin throned, surrounded by John the Baptist, St. Stephen, St. Augustin, St. Anthony, and St. Nicholas; a fine work, by *Bartolommeo Passerotti,* much praised by the Caracci. 7th. St. Alexis bestowing charity on the poor, and the frescoes of the arch, by *Prospero Fontana.* 8th. The Marriage of St. Catherine, in the presence of Joseph, John the Baptist, and John the Evangelist, by *Innocenzio da Imola,* justly called an "opera Raffaelesca," for it is almost worthy of that great master. The small Nativity, on the gradino underneath, is another beautiful work of Innocenzio da Imola. 10th. St. Roch struck with the plague, and comforted by an angel, by *Lodo-*

vico Caracci : the glory of angels above, and the saints by the side, are by *Francesco Brizzi.* 11th. The four Evangelists and the four Doctors of the Church are by *Lorenzo Sabbatini.* The celebrated Angel Michael, by his scholar *Calvart,* is said to have been retouched by Sabbatini. Its merit was so much appreciated by Agostino Caracci, that he engraved it. 12th. The chapel of the Poggi family, designed by Pellegrino Tibaldi. The altar-piece, representing the Baptism of our Lord, was finished by *Prospero Fontana,* by desire of Tibaldi. The compartments of the roof are also fine works of Fontana. The grand picture of St. John baptizing, and that in illustration of "Many are called, but few are chosen," are by *Pellegrino Tibaldi :* they are characterised by great power of composition and expression, and are said to have been much studied by the Caracci and their school. 13th. The Virgin, with St. Catherine and St. Lucy, and the Beato Riniero below, is by *Calvart.* 14th. The Virgin and Child in the air, with SS. Cosmo and Damiano below, and the portrait of one of the Calcina Family, patrons of this chapel, are by *Lavinia Fontana.* 15th, said to contain a relic of the true cross. Among the 1300 figures of this chapel, the Coronation of the Virgin is worthy of observation, as bearing the name of *Jacopo Avanzi.* The Crucifixion bears the name of *Simone* (da Bologna), with the date 1370. 18th. The celebrated chapel of the Bentivoglio family, the ancient lords of Bologna in her high and palmy days, is, on many accounts, the most interesting in this ch. The Virgin and Child, with 4 angels and 4 saints, is one of the most celebrated works of *Francesco Francia,* "painter to Giovanni II., a Bentivoglio." The signature of this fine old master is "Franciscus Francia aurifex," a proof that he had not then (1490) abandoned his early profession of a goldsmith. The *pietà* above is also attributed to this master. In the lunette, one of the visions of the Apocalypse is by *Lorenzo Costa,* retouched by *Felice Cignani,* who painted the Annunciation. The fresco of the Virgin throned,

with Gio. II., Bentivoglio, and his numerous family in adoration, interesting as a study of costume and character, is by *Lorenzo Costa,* Francia's able scholar (1488). The alto-relievo of Annibale Bentivoglio on horseback is by *Niccolò dell'Arca.* The two triumphs in fresco opposite are supposed by some to be by *Francia,* while others attribute them to *Lorenzo Costa.* The marble bas-relief of Giovanni II., seen on one of the pilasters of this chapel, is said to have been sculptured by *Francesco Francia.* 19th. The Christ in the Garden, and in the 20th chapel the St. Peter, St. Paul, and King Sigismund, are by *Ercole Procaccini.* 21st. The Virgin, with John the Baptist, S. Francis, and S. Benedict, by *Cesi,* one of his most pleasing works, is now much spoilt; Guido is said to have spent hours when a student in the contemplation of this picture. Opposite are the marble monuments of Antonio Bentivoglio, the eminent jurisconsult, father of Annibale I., and that of Niccolò Fava, Doctor of Philosophy and Medicine, with the date 1433. 27th. The Martyrdom of St. Catherine, by *Tiburzio Passerotti,* is said to have been painted under the direction of his father, Bartolommeo, of whose style it bears, indeed, abundant evidence. 29th. The Presentation in the Temple is the masterpiece of *Orazio Samacchini ;* it was engraved by Agostino Caracci. The lateral figures are also by Samacchini. 32nd. The monument to Cardinal Agucchi, with the statues and bas-reliefs, are by *Gabriele Fiorini,* from the design, it is said, of Domenichino. 35th. The Last Supper is supposed to be a repetition of the celebrated picture by *Baroccio,* in the Ch. di S. M. sopra Minerva, at Rome, by the painter himself. The frescoes of Melchisedek and Elijah, and the Angels of the ceiling, are good works of *Cavedone.* In the 37th chapel is a miraculous crucifix of wood, the history of which can be traced as far back as the year 980.

The Ch. of San Giorgio, built by the Servite Fathers, contains a few interesting pictures. In the 4th chapel, S. Filippo Benizio, kneeling before the

Virgin and Child in the midst of Angels, was begun by *Simone Cantarini*, and finished in the lower part by *Albani*. The St. George, at the high altar, is by *Camillo Procaccini*. In the 7th chapel, the Annunciation is by *Lodovico Caracci*, and the graceful paintings underneath are by *Camillo Procaccini*. 8th. The Probatica Piscina in this chapel is also by *Lodovico Caracci*. 11th. The Flight out of Egypt, by *Tiarini*.

The *Ch. of S. Giovanni in Monte*, one of the most ancient in Bologna, founded by St. Petronius, in 433, and rebuilt in 1221, was completely modernised in 1824. Some of its antique paintings contrast strangely with these recent changes and decorations. 1st chapel. The Saviour appearing to the Magdalen, by *Giacomo Francia*. 2nd. The Crucifixion by *Cesi*. 3rd. The St. Joseph and St. Jerome, in the ovals on the side walls, are by *Guercino*. 6th. The Madonna, placed below Mazzoni's picture of the Liberation of St. Peter, is by *Lippo Dalmasio*. 7th. The Virgin throned with Saints is a fine work of *Lorenzo Costa*. 8th. The miraculous figure of the Virgin, originally in the very ancient ch. of S. Eutropio, was formerly celebrated for its powers in curing the sick: it is of high antiquity. 9th. The S. Ubaldo Vescovo is a fine work of *Gio. Battista Bolognini*: the frescoes of the ceiling, and the lunettes, are either by Samacchini or Sabbatini. The picture at the high altar, representing the Virgin, with the Almighty and the Saviour; and John the Evangelist, St. Augustin, St. Victor, and other saints below, is by *Lorenzo Costa*. The busts of the 12 Apostles and the 2 Evangelists are by *Alfonso Lombardo;* the *tarsia* of the stalls in the choir are by *Paolo Sacca*, 1523. The ancient Madonna, on the pilaster, a fresco detached from some suppressed ch., is known from authentic documents to be anterior to the year 1000. 12th. The picture of Sta. Cecilia, by *Raphael*, now in the gallery, was the altar-piece of this chapel until 1796. Beneath the altar is buried the Beata Elena Duglioli dall' Olio, at whose expense the Sta. Cecilia was painted. 13th. The figure of the Saviour, carved out of a single block

of a fig-tree, is attributed to *Alfonso Lombardo*. 17th. The St. Francis, with arms crossed upon his breast, adoring the crucifix, here represented lying upon the ground, is a powerfully expressive work by *Guercino*. The adjoining convent, whose cloisters were designed by *Terribilia*, in 1548, has been converted into a prison.

The Ch. of *St. Gregorio*, almost entirely rebuilt after the earthquake of 1779, contains, in the 6th chapel, one of the first oil paintings of *Annibale Caracci*: it represents the Baptism of the Saviour. In the 8th chapel, the St. George delivering the Queen from the Dragon, with the Archangel Michael above pursuing the demons, and likewise the grand picture of God the Father, are by *Lodovico Caracci*. The picture over the high altar, representing St. Gregory's miracle of the Corporale, is by *Calvart*.

The Ch. of *S. Leonardo* contains, in its 1st chapel, the fine Annunciation, by *Tiarini*, in which the Almighty, holding a dove as the symbol of the Holy Spirit, is represented as awaiting the answer of the Virgin to the announcement of the Angel. The altarpiece, the Martyrdom of St. Ursula, and the St. Catherine in prison, converting the wife of Maximian and Porphyrus to Christianity, are both excellent and interesting works by *Lodovico Caracci*.

The Ch. of *Sta. Lucia* is, perhaps, more remarkable for a curious literary relic preserved there—a long letter written by St. Francis Xavier, in Portuguese, which is exposed with singular homage on the festival of that saint—than for its works of art, although there are several pictures which deserve notice, among which may be specified the Sta. Lucia and Sta. Anna, with the Virgin and Child, at the high altar, by *Ercole Procaccini;* the Death of St. Francis Xavier, considered the best work of *Carlo Antonio Rambaldi*, in the 6th chapel; the Virgin and Child, with John the Baptist, S. Carlo, and Sta. Teresa, by *Carlo Cignani*, in the 7th chapel ; and in the Sacristy, the Crucifixion by *Lavinia Fontana;* and the Immaculate Conception, one of the first

works of *Calvart* while yet a pupil of
Sabbatini: In the adjoining college
of the Barnabite friars, a chamber, now
converted into a chapel, is shown as that
in which St. Francis Xavier was
lodged, in 1531, by D. Girolamo Casa-
lini, the then rector of this ch.

The Ch. of the *Madonna del Baraccano* was so called from a Confraternità, established in 1403, in honour
of the miracles performed by a picture
of the Virgin painted on a bastion of
the city walls, called " Il Baraccano
di Strada Santo Stefano." Over the fine
portico, constructed from the designs
of Agostino Barella, is a statue of the
Virgin by *Alfonso Lombardo*. At the
high altar, the miraculous picture of
the Virgin bears the name of *Francesco
Cossa*, of Ferrara, who repainted it in
1450, with the addition of 2 portraits,
of Gio. I. Bentivoglio, and of Maria
Vinciguerra. The frieze of flowers
which adorns this altar, and other
sculptures of the chapel, are graceful
works by *Properzia de' Rossi*. The Virgin
and Child, with SS. Joseph and Joachim,
in the 4th chapel, is by *Lavinia Fontana;*
and the St. Catherine, in the 5th, is by
Prospero Fontana.

The *Madonna di S. Colombano* is remarkable for being covered internally
by frescoes, painted by various pupils
of Lodovico Caracci. The St. Francis
on the rt. wall is by *Antonio*, son of
Agostino Caracci; the Virgin and Child,
with Joseph gathering dates, is by
Spada; the Sibyl over the side door,
and the Coronation of St. Catherine,
are by *Lorenzo Garbieri;* the Sta. Marta
conversing with the Saviour, before
whom the Magdalen is kneeling, is by
Lucio Massari; by whom are also the
Sibyl over the other door, and the
angel bearing the palm of martyrdom
to Sta. Ursula; the infant Saviour
playing with St. John in the presence
of little angels is by *Paolo*, brother of
Lodovico Caracci, who gave the design.
In the upper oratory, the frescoes representing the Passion were all, it is
said, the result of a trial of skill among
the younger pupils of the Caracci;
among them, the fine picture of St.
Peter going out weeping from Pilate's
house, by *Albani*, may be particularly

noticed. The Virgin, over the altar of
this ch., is by *Lippo Dalmasio*.

The Ch. of the *Madonna di Galliera*
contains some interesting paintings.
In the 1st chapel (del Crocifisso) the
frescoes on the ceiling, representing the
Death of Abel, and the Sacrifice of
Abraham, are the last works of *M.
Angelo Colonna*. In the 2nd, the St.
Antony' of Padua is by *Girolamo
Donnini*, the pupil of Cignani. In
the 3rd, the Virgin and Child, with
Joseph. S. Francesco di Sales, and
S. Francesco d' Assisi, is by *Franceschini*, who painted the frescoes of this
chapel with the assistance of *Luigi
Quaini*. The 4th, or Capella Maggiore,
contains a miraculous and very ancient
painting of the Virgin and Child; the
figures of the angels adoring this
painting are by *Giuseppe Mazza*, a
clever sculptor and painter of the last
century. In the 5th, the Incredulity of
St. Thomas is by *Teresa Muratori*, celebrated as much for her talent in music
as in painting; the angels in the sky of
the picture, frequently praised for their
delicacy and grace, are said to have
been added by her master, Gio. Giuseppe Dal Sole. The 6th chapel contains the infant Saviour in the midst of
his kindred, showing to the Almighty
the instruments of the Passion, which
are borne by angels, by *Albani;* the
Adam and Eve in oil, the Cherubim, and
the Virtues, in fresco, are by the
same master. In the 7th is S. Filippo
Neri in ecstacy, by *Guercino*. In
the Sacristy, St. Philip, the 2 Beati
Ghislieri, the Conception, and the S.
Francesco di Sales, are by *Elisabetta
Sirani*. The Celestial Love, and the
St. Elizabeth Queen of Hungary, are
by *G. Andrea Sirani*. The Assumption
is by *Albani*. The adjoining oratory,
built from the designs of Torreggiani,
has over the entrance door a fresco of
a dead Christ by *Lodovico Caracci*.

The *Madonna del Soccorso* contains
the famous picture of Christ shown to
the people, by *Bartolommeo Passerotti*,
the eminent master who improved, if
not instructed, Agostino Caracci in the
art of engraving, whose portraits were
considered by Guido as second only to
those of Titian, and are said by Lanzi

to be often shown in galleries under the name of the Caracci. The frescoes of this ch. and oratory were painted by *Gioacchino Pizzoli,* a painter of the 17th century, and a member of the order to which the ch. belonged. In the 5th chapel is shown a miraculous crucifix, formerly in the suppressed ch. of St. Francis, which is said to have spoken to Padre Giovanni Peciani, in 1242!

Sta. Maria Maddalena contains, at the first altar, the Madonna, S. Onofrio, and S. Vitale, by *Tiburzio Passerotti;* and at the 3rd, the St. Francis, and St. James, by the same. The Virgin, with S. Sebastian and S. Roch, is by *Bagnacavallo.* The oratory contains an altar-piece by *Ercole Procaccini,* cleverly restored by Giovannini; the Archangel Gabriel and the Virgin by *Giuseppe Crespi,* and other works by his two sons.

Another ch., called also *La Maddalena,* contains, among other paintings by Bolognese masters, the St. Catherine, one of the earliest works of *Bartolommeo Passerotti.*

Sta. Maria Maggiore, one of the ancient churches of the city, contains some fine works by *Tiarini.* At the 1st altar, the St. John the Evangelist dictating to St. Jerome is, in spite of the anachronism, a pleasing example of this master. The 11th altar has one of his latest works, the Sta. Agata, Sta. Apollonia, and St. Antony of Padua. The 3rd altar has a very ancient wooden crucifix. The 5th has a Madonna and Child, with St. James and St. Antony, by *Orazio Samacchini.* The 7th was decorated by *Carlo Francesco Dotti,* at the expense of Benedict XIV. The 9th has a Virgin, Child, and St. John, painted, in 1570, by *Ercole Procaccini.*

The Ch. of *Sta. Maria della Vita,* founded in 1260, by the Beato Riniero of Perugia, who devoted himself on this spot to the relief of the sick, was entirely remodelled in the last century. In the 2nd chapel are preserved the bones of the Beato Buonaparte Ghisilieri, brought here, in 1718, from the suppressed ch. of S. Eligio. The picture representing the Beato Buonaparte and

St. Jerome is by *Aureliano Milani;* the Angels, in stucco, are by *Angelo Più.* The 3rd chapel contains an Annunciation, with S. Lorenzo underneath, painted by *Tamburini* from the design of *Guido,* who is said to have retouched it. At the high altar, a miraculous fresco of the Virgin and Child is by *Simone da Bologna;* the marble ornaments are by *Angelo Venturoli,* from the designs of Fancelli and Bianconi. The two marble statues by the side are by *Petronio Tadolini;* and those in plaster by *Giacomo Rossi.* The most curious object, however, at this altar, is the medallion portrait of Louis XIV., painted by Petitot, and set in diamonds: it was given by the king to Count Malvasia, in return for his presentation copy of the "Felsina pittrice," and bequeathed to this ch. by that learned scholar. In the 5th chapel is another gift of Count Malvasia, the bust of S. Carlo Borromeo, the head of which is silver. In the Sacristy is a picture of S. Eligio, attributed to *Annibale Caracci* (?), and in the oratory is the masterpiece of *Alfonso Lombardo,* a bas-relief, representing the death of the Virgin in the presence of the apostles, whose heads are said to have inspired many painters of the Bolognese school. The Beato Riniero healing the sick during the plague is by *Cavedone,* whose history is scarcely less affecting than that of Properzia de' Rossi. Cavedone, at the death of his son, was so much oppressed with grief that he lost his talent, and with it his employment: his old age was passed in beggary, and, after having contributed so much in early life to the decoration of the churches and palaces of his native city, he was allowed to die in a stable.

The splendid ch. of *S. Martino Maggiore* belonged to the Carmelite Friars from the 13th century up to the period of the French invasion. The Adoration of the Magi, in the 1st chapel, is one of the most graceful works of *Girolamo de' Carpi;* the Annunciation, over the side door, is by *Bartolommeo Passerotti.* In the 4th chapel is a picture of St. Joachim and St. Anna, with the date 1558, and the inscription TAR, supposed to refer to Giovanni

Cent. It.   D

Taraschi, the Modenese painter. In the 5th is the picture of the Virgin and Child, with a sainted bishop on one side, and Sta. Lucia on the other, with St. Nicholas below, giving their dowry to 3 young girls, by *Mastro Amico Aspertini*, the pupil of Francia, called "dai due pennelle," because he worked with both hands, holding at the same time one for light and another for dark tints. The 7th chapel contains the only work in Bologna by *Girolamo Sicciolante*, the well-known imitator of Raphael: it represents the Virgin and Child, with St. Martin, St. Jerome, &c., and contains a portrait of Matteo Malvezzi, for whom it was painted. Near the door of the Sacristy is the monument and bust of the eloquent Filippo Beroaldi the elder, by *Vincenzo Onofrio*. Above it is the Ascension, by *Cavedone*. In the 8th chapel is an Assumption, attributed to *Perugino*, although others regard it as one of the best works of *Lorenzo Costa*. In the 9th is the grand picture of St. Jerome imploring the Divine assistance in the explanation of the Scriptures, by *Lodovico Caracci*; "quel S. Girolamo," says Lanzi, "che sospesa la penna volgesi al cielo in atto sì grave e sì dignitoso." In the 10th is the Crucifixion, with St. Bartholomew, St. Andrew, and the Beato Pietro Toma, by *Cesi*. The 11th (the chapel of the Holy Sacrament) was entirely painted by *Mauro Tesi*, an eminent artist of the last century, and the friend of Algarotti. In the 12th chapel is the Madonna and Child, with several saints, by *Francia*. The St. Roch in the painted glass of the window over the altar is by the Beato *Giacomo da Ulma*. The oratory, formerly the conventual library, was painted by *Dentone*; the Dispute of St. Cyril is by *Lucio Massari*. The altarpiece, representing the Incredulity of St. Thomas, is a fine work of *Giampietro Zanotti*, painted for the suppressed ch. of S. Tommaso del Mercato. In the cloister are several sepulchral monuments, among which we may particularly notice the fine tomb of the 2 Saliceti, by *Andrea da Fiesole*, in 1403.

The Ch. of *S. Mattéa*, formerly belonging to the Domenican Nuns, contains 3 interesting paintings; an

Annunciation, by *Tintoretto*, at the third altar; the Virgin, with Saints, God the Father above, and a gradino containing 5 small compositions, by *Innocenzio da Imola;* and the Virgin appearing to S. Giacinto, with 2 angels, by *Guido*, painted in his 23rd year.

The celebrated Ch. of Sta. Maria della Pietà, better known as *I Mendicanti*, which the great masters of the Bolognese school had enriched with some of their finest works, was strippe of its most valuable treasures at the first invasion by the French; the Madonna della Pietà by Guido, the St. Matthew by Lodovico Caracci, the S. Alò and S. Petronio of Cavedone, are in the gallery; and the Job of Guido, which accompanied them to France, has never been restored. Among the most interesting paintings which remain are the following: at the 1st altar, the Sta. Ursula, by *Bartolommeo Passerotti*. 2nd, Christ feeding the Multitude, by *Lavinia Fontana.* 3rd, St. Francis, with S. Luigi Gonzaga and S. Francesco Borgia, by *Ercole Graziani*. 4th, the 2 miracles of S. Alò, by *Cavedone;* one representing the saint seizing the devil by the nose in the disguise of an old woman; the other, the saint bringing back a horse's foot which he had carried to the forge in order to have it shod with more convenience. 7th, entirely painted by *Tiarini.* 8th, the Flight out of Egypt, with a fine landscape, and the paintings on the side walls, by *Mastelletta*, much admired by Guido and Annibale Caracci. 10th, the St. Anna adoring the Virgin in a vision, by *Bartolommeo Cesi*. 11th, the Crucifixion, with the Virgin, St. John, and other saints, by the same estimable master.

The Ch. of *S. Michele de' Leprosetti* is remarkable for the masterpiece of *Francesco Gessi*, the picture at the high altar representing the Virgin and Child throned, crowned by angels, with the Archangel Michael, who commends to her protection the city of Bologna, then suffering from the plague. The St. Sebastian, at the 5th altar, is by *Sementi*.

S. Niccolò di S. Felice, modernised in the last century, has a fine painting by *Annibale Caracci*, the Crucifixion, with the Madonna, S. Petronius, S. Francis, S. John, and S. Bernardino. Over the entrance door is a head by *Alfonso Lombardo*.

The magnificent Ch. of *S. Paolo*, built by the Barnabite fathers in 1611, was restored in 1819 from the designs of Venturoli. The marble statues of St. Peter and St. Paul on the façade are by *Domenico Mirandola*, much praised by Agostino Caracci. At the 1st altar, the Christ in the Garden, and the Christ bearing the Cross, are by *Mastelletta*. At the 2nd is the fine painting of Paradise, by *Lodovico Caracci*, one of those enumerated by Lanzi as a proof that Annibale himself could not have given more gracefulness to the figures of maidens and boys. The small Madonna underneath is by *Lippo Dalmasio*. In the 3rd are the Nativity, and the Adoration of the Magi, by *Cavedone*, which the testimony of his contemporary artists and the judgment of modern critics have agreed in regarding as his masterpiece. The frescoes of the ceiling, representing the Circumcision, the Flight out of Egypt, and the Dispute with the Doctors, are also by the same painter. At the 4th altar is the Purgatory of *Guercino*, in which St. Gregory is represented as showing to the souls the Almighty, the Saviour, and the Virgin in heaven. At the high altar the 2 statues of St. Paul and the Executioner are by *Alessandro Algardi*, who is said to have given Facchetti the design of the Tribune, and to have sculptured the ivory Crucifix with the symbols of the Evangelists. At the 7th, the S. Carlo Borromeo carrying the cross through Milan during the plague, and the other pictures of the same saint on the side walls, are by *Lorenzo Garbieri*. At the 8th, the Communion of St. Jerome, and the other paintings of this chapel, are by *Massari*. At the 9th, the Baptism of the Saviour, and the Birth and Burial of St. John the Baptist, are by *Cavedone*.

The Ch. of *S. Procolo* belonged previously to the French invasion to the Benedictine monks of Monte Cassino; its foundation is of very ancient date,

but the present ch. was built in 1536. Over the principal entrance door is a Virgin and Child with S. Sisto and S. Benedict, a beautiful example of *Lippo Dalmasio*, painted in *oil*, and therefore adduced by Malvasia and Tiarini as a proof of the much higher antiquity of oil-painting than Vasari had supposed. Beneath the organ is the Almighty surrounded by a glory of Angels over the Magi, in relief, copied by *Cesi* from a design of Baldassare Peruzzi, formerly in the Bentivoglio palace. In the 2nd chapel, the St. Benedict in ecstasy is also by *Cesi*, who is buried in this ch. In the 6th, the Virgin in glory, with some Benedictine saints, is one of the last works of *Ercole Graziani* the younger. In the 8th chapel, designed by Torreggiani, is the marble mausoleum in which are preserved the bodies of the 2 martyrs who gave their names to this ch.—S. Procolo Soldato, and S. Procolo Vescovo, found in the ancient subterranean ch. in 1380. In the 9th chapel, the S. Mauro is by *Ercole Graziani*. On a wall adjoining the ch., the following inscription to the memory of a person called Procolo, buried in the ch., who was killed by one of the bells falling on him as he was passing under the campanile, was much admired in the last century, when this kind of play upon words was more in fashion than it is now:—

" Si procul a Proculo Proculi campana fuisset,
  Jam procul a Proculo Proculus ipse foret."

The Ch. of *S. Rocco*, converted in 1801 into a "Camera Mortuaria," is remarkable for one of those agreeable examples of generous and patriotic rivalry for which the school of Bologna was particularly distinguished. The oratory is covered with the frescoes of the young artists of the period, who, for no greater sum than two pistoles each, adorned its walls with paintings illustrating the life of S. Roch, and other suitable subjects. Their zealous emulation has been justly described as a "tournament of painting." Beginning with the first subject opposite the entrance door, is the mother of S. Roch praying for offspring, by *Francesco Ca-*

mullo ; S. Roch giving to the poor, by *Alessandro Provaglia ;* the Saint healing the Sick of the Plague, by *Valesio ;* the Cure of Card. Britanno, by *Pietro Desani ;* Saint Roch wounded, by *Sebastiano Razzali ;* his Flight, by *Paolo Caracci ;* his Discovery in the Wood, by *Cavedone ;* his Liberation by the Angel, by *Massari ;* his Apprehension as a Spy, by *Guercino ;* the Angel comforting him, by *Francesco Caracci ;* and his Death in Prison, by *Gessi.* The 18 compartments of the ceiling are also filled with interesting works. Of the 4 protectors of the city, St. Petronius and St. Francis are by *Gessi ;* the St. Proclus by *Colonna.* Of the 4 doctors of the ch., St. Ambrose and St. Augustin are by *Colonna ;* and are so beautiful that they have been considered worthy of Domenichino. Of the Evangelists, St. Luke, St. Matthew, and St. Mark, are by *Massari.* Of the 6 Virtues, Faith and Charity are by *Colonna,* Hope and Divine Love by *Gessi,* Patience by *Cavedone,* and Heavenly Glory by *Valesio.* These frescoes were published in 1831, by Gaetano Canuti, an ingenious engraver of Bologna.

The Ch. of the *Santissimo Salvatore* has some interesting paintings. In the 1st chapel is the Beato Arcangelo Canetoli refusing the Archbishopric of Florence, by *Ercole Graziani.* In the 2nd is a Resurrection, by *Mastelletta.* In the 3rd, the Magi, by *Prospero Fontana.* The Miracle of the Crucifix bears the inscription, "*Jacobi Coppi,* civis Florentini, opus, 1579," and is mentioned by Lanzi as one of the best pictures in Bologna prior to the time of the Caracci. Near the Sacristy is a picture of the Virgin and St. Thomas à Becket, "S. Tommaso di Cantuaria," by *Girolamo da Treviso,* formerly at the altar "de' Scolari Inglesi" in the old ch. The Judith going to meet the Hebrew Damsels with the Head of Holofernes is by *Mastelletta.* The Virgin holding the Infant Saviour to St. Catherine, with St. Sebastian and St. Roch, is a fine work of *Girolamo de' Carpi.* The finely-preserved painting of the Virgin crowned, underneath this picture, is of the 14th century. In the choir, the Saviour bearing his cross,

was designed by *Guido,* who painted the head, and retouched the whole picture, after it was finished by *Gessi.* Of the 4 Prophets, the David is by *Cavedone.* The subjects illustrating the miraculous crucifix, are by *Brizzi,* and the St. Jerome is by *Carlo Bonone.* In the 6th chapel is a striking Nativity by *Tiarini ;* in the 7th, a fine Crucifixion surrounded by Saints, by *Innocenzio da Imola ;* in the 8th, the Ascension, by *Carlo Bonone ;* in the 9th, St. John kneeling before the aged Zacharias, by *Garofalo.* The 4 doctors of the Church, painted over the 4 small chapels, are by *Cavedone.* The large picture over the door, representing the Marriage in Cana of Galilee, is a fine work, by *Gaetano Gandolfi,* a modern painter of Bologna. In the Sacristy, the frescoes of the roof are by *Cavedone ;* the S. Domencio is attributed to *Guercino ;* and the St. John the Baptist, with the Lamb, to *Simone Cantarini ;* the Madonna is by *Mastelletta.* Paolo Antonio Barbieri, the beloved brother of Guercino, is buried in this ch. ; the affectionate wish of the great painter to be buried in the same grave, although unfulfilled, deserves to be commemorated by an inscription.

The grand *Portico de' Servi,* built upon marble columns, in 1392, by Fra Andrea Manfredi of Faenza, General of the Servites, presents a series of interesting frescoes in the lunettes, illustrating various events in the life of S. Filippo Benizzi. Of these 20 subjects, the principal are by *Cignani Giovanni Viani, Peruzzini, Giuseppe Mitelli, Lorenzo Borgonzoni,* &c.

The Ch. of the *Servi,* also built by Fra Andrea Manfredi, is remarkable for some fine paintings. In the 2nd chapel, the Virgin giving the conventual dress to the 7 founders of the order, is one of the last works of *Franceschini,* painted by him when nearly 85 years of age. 4th, the death of Sta. Giuliana Falconieri, and the St. Anthony above, are by *Ercole Graziani.* 5th, the Paradise, a large and elaborate work, by *Calvart.* 7th, the Madonna del Mondovì, with angels, John the Baptist, S. James, and S. Francesco di Paolo, by *Tiarini.* In the 10th chapel is preserved a marble pitcher, said to have been used at the marriage of Cana, presented by Fra Vitale Bacilieri, General of the Servites, who had been ambassador to the Sultan of Egypt in 1359. At the cloister-door is the monument of the senator Gian-Giacomo Grati, with a marble bust by *Teodosio.* The monument at the door of the Sacristy is that of Lodovico Fronti, by *Giacomo Ranuccio.* In the 12th chapel, the miracle of S. Gregory at mass is by *Aretusi;* the 12,000 crucified near this is by *Elisabetta Sirani.* In the 14th, the Virgin and Child painted on the wall, and 2 saints by the side, are by *Lippo Dalmasio;* opposite, the Beato Gioacchino Piccolomini fainting during the celebration of mass is by *Ercole Graziani;* the Madonna above it is another work of *Lippo Dalmasio.* 15th, St. Joachim and St. Anna, by *Tiarini.* On the front of the adjoining door is a sepulchral tablet to Fra Andrea Manfredi of Faenza, the eminent architect and general of the order, by whom the ch. was founded. 16th, S. Onofrio, by *Calvart.* 17th, on one of the pilasters is a memorial of this artist, erected by Fantuzzi. The stalls of the choir were designed by Manfredi. In the 20th chapel, the fresco representing the soul of S. Carlo in heaven was painted by *Guido,* gratuitously, in one day. 22nd, the Annunciation, a fine work by *Innocenzio da Imola.* The frescoes of the roof and side walls are by *Bagnacavallo.* 24th, the St. Andrew adoring the Cross prepared for his martyrdom, a fine picture by *Albani.* The monument of the Cardinal Ulisse Gozzadini has a fine portrait of that prelate in Roman mosaic. 26th, the Noli-me-tangere is another fine work of *Albani.* The large painting of the Nativity of the Virgin, with numerous figures over the door, was the last work of *Tiarini.* In the Sacristy, the Nativity of John the Baptist, his Preaching, and the Baptism of the Saviour, are by *Mastelletta.* In the adjoining convent is the grand staircase designed by *Terribilia,* and a fine perspective by *Dentone.*

The Ch. of the *SS. Trinità* has, at the 2nd altar, the Birth of the Virgin, by *Lavinia Fontana.* At the high altar is the S. Roch supplicating the Virgin,

by *Guercino.* At the 7th altar is the Madonna in glory, with SS. Girolamo, Francesco, Donino, and Apollonia, and some children playing with the cardinal's hat, by *Gio. Battista Gennari,* of Cento, painted in 1606 for the ch. of S. Biago.

The very ancient ch. of *St. Vitale ed Agricola,* consecrated in 428 by St. Petronius and St. Ambrose, has a graceful painting of *Francia,* covering the ancient image of the Madonna in the 8th chapel. Beside it are 2 fine pictures, one representing the Nativity, by *Giacomo Francia,* his son, and the other the Visitation, by *Bagnacavallo.* Opposite is an inscription recording the consecration of the ch.: the column, with a cross of the early Christians, brought here in 1832, formerly stood on the spot in the adjoining street where S. Vitale and S. Agricola suffered martyrdom. The 2nd chapel has a picture by *Tiarini,* the Virgin mounting the ass, in the flight out of Egypt. The Nativity, in the 7th chapel, with St. Roch and St. Sebastian, has been attributed to *Perugino* (?).

The PIAZZA MAGGIORE, called also the Piazza del Gigante, was the Forum of Bologna in the middle ages: it is still surrounded by remarkable edifices rich in historical associations, the relics of the once formidable republic. It was considered by Evelyn, in his time, as the most stately piazza in Italy, with the single exception of San Marco at Venice. The ch. of San Petronio has been already described; the other buildings which give an interest to this spot are the Palazzo del Pubblico, the Palazzo del Podestà, and the Portico de' Banchi. On entering the Piazza, the attention of the traveller is arrested by the magnificent fountain called

The *Fontana Pubblica,* or the Fontana del Gigante, constructed in 1564, while Cardinal (since S. Carlo) Borromeo was legate: the general design is by *Lauretti;* the pedestal and the vase are by *Antonio Lupi;* and the Neptune, with the other figures and bronze ornaments, are by *Giovanni di Bologna.* The Neptune, one of the most celebrated works of that great master, is 8 ft.

high, and the weight of the bronze employed in the figures is said to be 20,012 Bolognese pounds. The cost of the fountain, with its pipes and aqueducts, amounted to 70,000 golden scudi. The merits of the Neptune have been very differently estimated by different critics. Forsyth says he "saw nothing so grand in sculpture" at Bologna: "the Neptune is admired for the style, anatomy, and technical details: his air and expression are truly noble, powerful, commanding—perhaps too commanding for his situation." Bell, on the other hand (a high authority on such a subject), says, "Neptune, who presides over the fountain, is a colossal heavy figure, in the act of preaching and wondering at, rather than commanding, the waves of the ocean; boys in the 4 corners are represented as having bathed small dolphins, which they are holding by the tail to make them spout water; while 4 female Tritons fill the space beneath; these fold their marine extremities between their limbs, and press their bosom with their hands, to cause the water to flow. The whole composition and manner is quaint, somewhat in the French style, and such as I should have been less surprised to find at Versailles than at Bologna."

The *Palazzo Maggiore del Pubblico*, begun at the end of the 13th century, is one of the great public monuments of the city. Prior to 1848 it was the residence of the Legate and of the Senator, as it is now of the Prolegate or Civil Governor. Its façade still exhibits some traces of the pointed style, but the building has been so altered at various periods, that little uniformity remains. In the upper part of the façade is a Madonna in relief, by *Niccolò dell' Arco*, in terra cotta gilt, erroneously described by Vasari as bronze. The ornaments of the clock are by *Tadolini*. The entrance doorway is by *Galeazzo Alessi* of Perugia (1570): the bronze statue of Gregory XIII. (Buoncompagni), in the niche above, was erected at the cost of his fellow-citizens; it is by *Alessandro Menganti*, called by Agostino Caracci the "unknown Michael Angelo." At the revolution of 1796 the tiara was changed into a mitre, and a pastoral staff inserted into the right hand, with the inscription "Divus Petronius Protector et Pater." The pastoral staff placed in the saint's hand in 1796 is quite out of proportion with the dimensions of the statue. On entering the building and proceeding to the 3rd court, formerly a garden, we find the beautiful cistern constructed by *Terribilia*, at the cost of 6000 scudi.

A grand staircase *à cordoni*, 85 ft. in length, by *Bramante*, conducts us to the upper halls. The bronze bust of Benedict XIV., and the ornaments over the door where it is placed, are by *Giobattista Bolognini*. The great Hall of Hercules takes its name from his colossal statue by *Alfonso Lombardo.* On the rt. is a hall, covered with frescoes, the architectural portions of which are by *Antonio Bibiena;* the figures on the ceiling are by *Angelo Bigari;* and those on the walls by *Scarabelli.* In the adjoining chapel is a fresco of the Madonna, called the Madonna del Terremoto, supposed to have been painted by the school of Francia in 1505. The gallery leading out of the Hall of Hercules is covered with frescoes illustrating the glories of Bologna by *Colonna* and *Pizzoli.* The Sala Farnese, so called from a bronze statue of Paul III., is perhaps the most magnificent. Its roof and walls are covered with fine paintings representing the history of the city, by *Cignani, Francesco Quaini, Scaramuccia, Pasinelli,* the elder *Bibiena,* and other eminent artists.

The *Palazzo del Podestà,* begun in 1201, with a façade added in 1485 by Bartolommeo Fioravanti, although still an unfinished building, has an air of grandeur which accords with its character as the ancient seat of municipal authority. Its greatest interest, however, is derived from its having been the prison of King Enzius, son of the Emperor Frederick II., who was captured by the Bolognese in 1249, and kept here a prisoner until his death in 1272. The history of this unfortunate monarch, whose tomb we have already noticed in the account of S. Domenico, offers a singular illustration of the manners of the middle ages. The haughty republic rejected all the overtures of the emperor for the restitution of his son, and his threats and money were equally lost in the attempt to obtain his liberty. During his long imprisonment, Enzius employed his time in poetical compositions: some of these poems have been published, and are marked by considerable taste. The young king moreover was beloved in his captivity by a fair damsel of Bologna, Lucia Vendagoli, who succeeded in visiting him under various disguises; and the Bentivoglio family are believed to derive their origin from these mysterious meetings. The great hall is still called *Sala del Re Enzio*, although there is no proof that it was occupied by him; indeed its size, 170 feet by 74, would almost seem conclusive against such a belief. This hall has likewise had its vicissitudes of fortune: in 1410 the conclave for the election of Pope John XXII. was held there; in the last century it was converted into a theatre; it was afterwards used for the game of *pallone;* and was latterly degraded into a workshop. In other parts of the building are the Sala de' Notari, and the public Archives. The latter are rich in rare and inedited materials for the history of Bologna, and indeed of Italy during the middle ages; among them is pointed out the Bull called "Dello Spirito Santo," published at Florence, July 6, 1439, by Eugenius IV., for the union of the Greek and Latin Churches. A picture of the Annunciation preserved here is by *Jacopo Paolo Avanzi.* The lofty tower, called *Torrazzo dell' Aringo*, built upon arcades, is a massive and imposing pile: it was erected in 1264, for the purpose, it is said, of watching Enzius. The statues of the 4 protectors of the city, on the columns which support its arcades, are in terra cotta, by *Alfonso Lombardo.*

The *Portico de' Banchi,* occupying one side of the Piazza, 300 ft. in length, was designed and executed by *Vignola,* who had to adapt it to the irregularities of the old building.

Adjoining St. Petronio is the building called *Il Registro,* formerly the College of Notaries, presented to that body in 1283 by the learned jurisconsult and chief magistrate Rolandino Passaggeri. The hall, now converted into a chapel, is remarkable for little, except a Madonna by *Passerotti;* the Sacristy contains, among other documents, a Diploma of the Emperor Frederick III., dated Jan. 3, 1462, and confirmed by a Bull of Julius II., dated Feb. 15, 1505, granting to the Correttore de' Notari the power of creating apostolical and imperial notaries, and the singular privilege of legitimatising natural children.

Private Palaces.—The Palaces of Bologna are extremely numerous, but they are with few exceptions most unsatisfactory to visit; the works which formerly gave them celebrity are gradually disappearing; so that it would be difficult to give any description of their moveable contents. Their frescoes, however, like their architecture, cannot be exported; and in both these branches of art there is much to engage the attention of the traveller.

Palazzo Albergati, agreeably placed in the Strada Saragozza, is a fine example of the architecture of *Baldassare Peruzzi* (1540). The ceilings of the rooms on the ground floor are by *Gessi;* and in the upper halls are some wainscots by the scholars of the Caracci. Under this palace some foundations of ancient Roman Baths have been discovered.

Palazzo Aldrovandi, a name in itself full of interesting recollections, was almost entirely rebuilt in 1748, by Card. Pompeo Aldrovandi, on a scale of grandeur worthy the fame of that illustrious scholar. The façade is ornamented with Istrian marble. The noble library and the gallery of pictures collected by the Cardinal, and augmented by his successors, have been nearly all dispersed.

Palazzo Arcivescovile, the residence of the archbishop, was built in 1577 by Tibaldi, and has been recently restored and decorated with considerable taste at the cost of Cardinal Oppizzoni, the present Archbishop of Bologna. The apartments are painted by the most eminent modern artists of Bologna, Professor Frulli Pedrini, Fancelli, Fantuzzi, Zanotti, &c.

The *Palazzo Baciocchi,* formerly *Ranuzzi,* is one of the most imposing specimens of domestic architecture in Bologna : its principal façade is by *Palladio,* by whom some of the other details were probably designed. The grand hall is by *Bibiena ;* the handsome staircase has been attributed to Giuseppe Antonio Torri, and to Giobattista Piacentini.

The fine *Bentivoglio Palace* has been frequently the residence of sovereign princes during their visits to Bologna ; it recalls the magnificence of the ancient palace of the Bentivoglios, destroyed by the populace at the instigation of Julius II., who adopted this mode of revenging himself on his great rival Annibale Bentivoglio. In the reprisals which followed, the vengeance of the populace and their chief fell, as we have already stated, on the statue of the Pope, the masterpiece of Michael Angelo.

Palazzo Bevilacqua, whose grand architecture is attributed to *Bramantino da Milano,* yields to few in the magnificence of its courts, staircases, and halls. In one of the chambers is an inscription recording that the Council of Trent assembled there in 1547, having been removed to Bologna by order of their celebrated physician *Girolamo* Fracastorio, under the pretext of contagion.

Palazzo Biagi, formerly *Odorici,* in the Strada San Stefano, was built by Ambrosini ; it is remarkable for 2 ceilings painted by *Guido* and his school.

Palazzo de' Bianchi, in the same street, has a fine ceiling by *Guido,* representing the Harpies infesting the table of Æneas.

Palazzo Fava, opposite the Ch. of the Madonna di Galliera, is rich in frescoes by the *Caracci.* The great hall contains the first fresco painted by *Agostino* and *Annibale,* under the direction of Lodovico, after their return from Parma and Venice : it represents, in a series of 18 pictures, the Expedition of Jason, and is one of the most interesting examples of the Eclec-

tic School. The small chamber adjoining is painted by *Lodovico,* who has represented the Voyage of Æneas in 12 pictures ; 2 of them, the Polyphemus and the Harpies, were coloured by Annibale. The next chamber is painted by *Albani,* with the assistance of Lodovico Caracci : it presents 16 subjects, also taken from the Æneid. The next chamber is painted by *Lucio Massari,* with the assistance of the same great master. The decorations of the other chambers are by his other pupils, the last room being by *Cesi ;* the subject of the Æneid prevails throughout the whole. The paintings of a cabinet representing the Rape of Europa are by *Annibale Caracci.*

Palazzo Grassi has the magnificent fresco by *Lodovico Caracci,* respresenting Hercules armed with a flambeau treading on the Hydra ; and some curious cameos by *Propersia de' Rossi,* engraved on peach-stones, and illustrating different events of Scripture history. A description of these delicate works, with engravings, was published in 1829, by Canuti.

Palazzo Guidotti, formerly *Magnani,* is an imposing design of *Domenico Tibaldi.* It is celebrated for the frescoes of the *Caracci,* representing the history of Romulus and Remus, and not inferior either in composition or in colour to those in the Farnese palace. They are called by Lanzi " the miracle of Caraccescan art."

Palazzo Hercolani, restored at the close of the last century from the designs of *Venturoli,* was famous throughout Europe for its pictures, sculptures, and library, rich in MSS. and printed books ; but they have nearly all disappeared.

Palazzo Malvezzi Bonfioli has in its second court an interesting series of frescoes illustrating the Gerusalemme Liberata, by *Lionello Spada, Lucio Massari,* and *Francesco Brizzi.* In the gallery is a portrait by *Domenichino,* a Sibyl by *Guido* in his early youth, and some other fine works of the Bolognese school.

Palazzo Malvezzi Campeggi, designed by the Formigini, is remarkable for some tapestries from the design of

Luca von Leyden, presented to Cardinal Campeggi by Henry VIII. of England.

Palazzo Marescalchi, formerly so famous for its pictures by Correggio, the St. Peter of Guido, the St. Cecilia of Domenchino, and other masterpieces, has been despoiled of its principal treasures. The façade is attributed to *Tibaldi ;* the vestibule at the top of the stairs is painted in chiaroscuro by *Brizzi;* and so profusely has art lavished her resources at Bologna, that even the chimney-pieces are painted by the *Caracci, Guido,* and *Tibaldi.*

Palazzo Pallavicini, formerly the *Fibbia,* has a noble hall painted by *Domenico Santi* and *Canuti.* The interior of the chapel, and the vestibule leading to it, are painted by *Michael Angelo Colonna.* 12 busts of illustrious ladies of Bologna are mostly the work of *Algardi ;* the rest are copied from *Alfonso Lombardo.*

Palazzo Pepoli, built from the designs of *Torri,* in the beginning of the last century, occupies the site of the ancient palace of the great captain Taddeo Pepoli. It is a fine building, with frescoes of *Colonna* and *Canuti,* illustrating the history of Taddeo Pepoli : its halls and chambers are also painted in fresco by *Donato Creti, Ercole Graziani,* and other artists.

Palazzo Piella, formerly the *Bocchi* Palace, was built by *Vignola* for the learned Achille Bocchi, who is said to have had some share in its design. The hall on the ground floor has a ceiling painted by *Prospero Fontana ;* its chief interest consists in its connexion with Bocchi, the historiographer of Bologna and founder of the Academy.

Palazzo Ranuzzi, formerly *Lambertini,* built from the designs of Bartolommeo Triachini, is interesting for its paintings by Bolognese masters prior to the Caracci. The most remarkable of these works are the ceiling of the upper hall by *Tommaso Lauretti,* the Virtues by *Lorenzo Sabbatini,* the Fall of Icarus by *Orazio Samacchini,* and the Death of Hercules by *Tibaldi.*

Palazzo Sampieri, once so celebrated for the treasures of its gallery; its famous pictures have been sold; the greater part have been transferred to the Brera Gallery at Milan. But its fine ceilings and chimney-pieces, by the Caracci and Guercino, are well preserved and will amply repay a visit.—I. In the 1st hall, the ceiling, painted by *Lodovico Caracci,* represents Jupiter with the Eagle and Hercules ; "in form, dignity of feature, and magnificence of character," says Mr. Bell, "finely suited to harmonise as a group. The muscular figure and gigantic bulk of Hercules is imposing without extravagance ; a perfect acquaintance with the human figure is displayed with admirable foreshortening and great skill and boldness in composition and execution. The artist's knowledge of anatomy is discoverable from his correct proportions and fine bendings, but is not obtruded on the eye by caricatured or forced lines." The chimney-piece of the same apartment has a painting by *Agostino Caracci,* representing Ceres with her torch in search of Proserpine, and, in the background, the Rape of the Goddess.—II. The 2nd hall has a ceiling by *Annibale Caracci,* representing the Apotheosis of Hercules, conducted by Virtue.—III. The ceiling of the 3rd hall, by *Agostino Caracci,* represents Hercules and Atlas supporting the Globe. The chimney-piece of this hall, by the same master, represents Hercules holding down Cacus, preparing to pierce him with the sharp end of his club.—IV. In the 4th hall, the ceiling, representing Hercules strangling Antæus, is by *Guercino.* "A superb piece, with fine deep-toned colouring, and wonderful power of chiaroscuro. The figure of Hercules is very grand, but seems to have occupied rather too much of the artist's care. Antæus is wanting in vigour ; the resisting arm is not drawn with force or bulk corresponding to the action ; neither are the figures sufficiently connected. But the whole piece, although liable to these criticisms, is a work of great vigour and unquestionable merit. In one of the accompanying ornaments of the ceiling of the next rooms there is a beautiful little painting by *Guercino,* of Love (I think it should have been Ganymede) carrying off the spoils of Hercules, the skin of the

Nemean lion, and the club. The motto under it is 'Iter ad superos gloria pandet.'"—*Bell.*

Palazzo Sedazzi, formerly *Leoni,* has a façade designed by Girolamo da Treviso. Under this portico is the fine Nativity by *Niccolò dell' Abate,* well known by the engraving of Gaetano Gandolfi : it was damaged, however, by restoration in 1819. In the great hall and the adjoining chamber is a series of very beautiful paintings by the same master, illustrating the history of Æneas.

Palazzo Tanara has several interesting paintings; the Bath of Diana, the Toilet of Venus, St. Paul shaking off the Viper, and the Last Supper, are by *Agostino Caracci;* the Kiss of Judas, and the Birth of Alexander, are by *Lodovico;* the Assumption of the Virgin, and the Cumæan Sibyl, are by *Guercino;* a Madonna by *Guido;* the portrait of *Albani* is by himself; the portrait of S. Carlo Borromeo by *Carlo Dolci;* the portrait of a Cardinal by *Tintoretto.*

Palazzo Zambeccari da S. Paolo has a fine gallery, rich in works of the Caracci and other masters. Among these may be noticed Jacob's Ladder, and Abraham at table with the Angels, by *Lodovico Caracci;* the Dead Christ, by *Agostino;* the Sibyl, the Elijah, and the Madonna and Child, by *Guercino;* the Marriage of St. Catherine, by *Albani;* portrait of Cardinal de' Medici, by *Domenichino;* his own portrait, by *Baroccio;* St. John, by *Caravaggio;* a St. Sebastian, and the portrait of Charles V., by *Titian;* a fine Landscape by *Salvator Rosa;* the Marriage of Anne Boleyn, by *Giulio Romano;* and the 6 Mistresses of Charles II., by *Sir Peter Lely.* Besides these works, there is a Crucifixion, in silver, a very beautiful work of *Benvenuto Cellini.* On the entrance-door are 2 bronze Lion-knockers by *Giovanni di Bologna.*

An interesting modern residence is the *Casa Rossini,* built in 1825 for the great "Maestro," who resided here until the Austrian occupation, when he returned to Florence. It is covered with Latin inscriptions in large gold letters, taken chiefly from classic writers. In the front is the following from Cicero :—

"Non domo dominus, sed domino domus."

On the side is an inscription from the Æneid :—

"Obliquitur numeris septem discrimina vocum Inter odoratum lauri nemus."

Another interesting house is that of Guercino, in which the great painter lived during his residence at Bologna: it is in the small piazza behind the Ch. of St. Niccolò degli Albári, No. 1647. The house of Gido has a fresco of 2 angels holding a crown, painted by him, on the exterior.

Of the other public buildings and institutions of Bologna, one of the most interesting to the architectural antiquary is the *Foro de' Mercanti,* or Palazzo della Mercanzia, the best preserved example of Italian Gothic in the city. It was built in 1294 of moulded brick-work, and restored by the Bentivoglio during their political ascendency. It is the seat of a Chamber of Commerce; but it has nothing beyond its exterior architectural details to interest the traveller.

Near the Foro de' Mercanti are the 2 celebrated leaning towers, called the Torre Asinelli and the Torre Garisenda, the most remarkable edifices in Bologna, but so destitute of architectural attractions, that Mr. Matthews likens them to the "chimney of a steam-engine, blown a little out of the perpendicular." The *Torre Asinelli,* begun in 1109 by Gherardo Asinelli, was proved, by the investigations of Tadolini, to have been finished at different periods. It is a square and massive brick tower, divided into 3 portions: the lowest has a projecting battlement, which is occupied by shops; the others contract as they ascend; and the whole is surmounted by a cupola. The height from the street to the apex of the cupola is 256 Bolognese feet 7 inches, according to Bianconi and other local authorities. Of English travellers, Mr. Woods gives it as 256 feet. The inclination of the tower was ascertained by careful measurements, in 1706, to be 3 feet 2 inches, as is recorded by an inscription under the statue of St. Michael the Archangel, in the niche of the western wall. After the earthquake of 1779, it was again measured, but no alteration was discovered. In 1813, the Abbatè Bacelli, professor of physics in the University, assisted by Professor Antolini, again measured the inclination, and found that it had slightly increased. A flight of 447 steps conducts to the summit by a winding staircase, which is one of the rudest and most impracticable in Italy. The view is fine, extending to the hills about Verona, the Euganean hills, and the more distant Alps; embracing, in the plain, Modena, Ferrara, and Imola; and bounded on the S. by the lower slopes of the Apennines, studded with villages and beautifully wooded.

The other tower, the *Torre Garisenda,* built by the brothers Filippo and Oddo Garisenda, in 1110, is 130 feet high, according to the same authorities. Its inclination, measured in 1792, was 8 feet to the E., and 3 to the S.; but the experiments of Professors Bacelli and Antolini, in 1813, showed an increase of an inch and a half over the former observations. Alidosi and other writers have endeavoured to maintain that the inclination of the Garisenda is the effect of art; as if Italy did not present an abundance of such examples in situations where the ground is liable to gradual sinking, and earthquakes are of common occurrence. The best answer to this absurd idea is the simple fact that the courses of brick and the holes to receive the timbers of the floors are also inclined, which they certainly would not have been if the tower had been built in its present inclined form. The Garisenda, however, has a higher interest than that derived from this question, since it supplied Dante with a fine simile, in which he compares the giant Antæus, stooping to seize him and his guide, to this tower, as it is seen from beneath when the clouds are flying over it:—

" Qual pare a riguardar la Carisenda
  Sotto il chinato, quando un nuvol vada,
  Sovra essa sì, ch' ella in contrario penda,
  Tal parve Anteo a me, che stava a vada
  Di vederlo chinare, e fu tal ora
  Che io avrei voluto ir per altra strada."
                                    Inf. xxxi.

The noble building called the *Scuole Pie,* the ancient seat of the university before it was transferred to the Institute, is one of the finest edifices in Bologna. It was designed in 1562, by *Terribilia,* and has often been erroneously attributed to Vignola. The Scuole Pie were established here in 1808; and as a proof that the great Italian cities are not backward in their education of the poor, they afford gratuitous instruction to the poor children of the town, under the direction of able teachers, partly laymen and partly ecclesiastics. The course of teaching embraces writing, arithmetic, the Latin language, singing, and drawing; and to these the munificent legacy of Professor Aldini has added chemistry and physics as applicable to the arts. The apartments appropriated to the schools have some good paintings by *Samacchini, Sabbatini,* and their scholars. In the loggie above are several interesting memorials of deceased professors : that of the physician Muratori is by his accomplished daughter Teresa, with the assistance of Gio. Giuseppe dal Sole ; that of the Canonico Pier Francesco Peggi, the philosopher, erected by his pupils, is by Giuseppe Terzi ; that of the celebrated anatomist Malpighi is by Franceschini ; that of Mariani is by Carlo Cignani; and that of the philosopher Sbaraglia is by Donato Creti. In the adjoining chapel of Sta. Maria de' Bulgari are some paintings which deserve a visit : the Annunciation at the high altar is by *Calvart,* and the tasteful frescoes on the walls, representing the history of the Virgin, sibyls, and prophets, are by *Cesi ;* they are well preserved, and have been engraved by Canuti, the able artist who has done so much to perpetuate and diffuse the knowledge of the treasures which art has so prodigally scattered over his native city.

The *Collegio Jacobs,* or *de' Fiamminghi,* the Flemish College, was founded in 1650, by Johann Jacobs, a Flemish goldsmith, for the education of young men of Brussels, belonging to the parish of Notre Dame de la Chapelle, and elected by the Goldsmiths' Company of that city. The portrait of the founder, preserved here, was painted by his friend *Guido*.

The Spanish college with the high-sounding title of *Almo Collegio Reale della Illustrissima Nazione Spagnuola*, was founded in 1364, by Cardinal Albornoz. It was formerly remarkable for the frescoes of its portico by *Annibale Caracci*, in his youth, but they have mostly disappeared. In the upper loggia is the fine fresco by *Bagnacavallo*, representing the Virgin and Child, St. Elizabeth, St. John, and St. Joseph, with an angel above scattering flowers, and the Cardinal founder kneeling in veneration. But the great fresco of Bagnacavallo, representing Charles V. crowned in S. Petronio by Clement VII., although much injured, is by far the most interesting work, because it is a contemporary record. From this circumstance we may regard the picture as a series of authentic portraits, in the precise costume of the period.

The *Collegio di S. Luigi*, founded in 1645 by Count Carlo Zani, occupies a palace built by Torreggiani in the beginning of the last century. It has a small theatre, remarkable for its scenes by Bibiena, Scandellari, and Gaetano Alemani.

The *Collegio Venturoli*, so called from the eminent architect of Bologna, who founded it for architectural studies in 1825, occupies the building formerly used as the Hungarian College. The pupils are educated here until their 20th year. The establishment is well managed, and tends to keep alive the arts of design among the young students of Bologna. The marble bust of Venturoli is by Professor *Demaria*.

The *Dogana*, or Custom-house, occupies the ancient ch. of S. Francesco, formerly remarkable for its Gothic architecture, for the riches of its altars and convent: it was appropriated to its present profane use after the revolution of 1798. It contains some interesting tombs, among which are that of Vianisio Albergati the younger, by *Lazzaro Casario;* and that of the learned doctor Boccaferri, from the design of *Giulio Romano;* with a bust by Girolamo Cortellini. In the lunettes of the adjacent

portico are painted the miracles of St. Anthony of Padua; the greater part of them are by *Gio. Maria Tamburini*, a favourite pupil of Guido; 3 are by *Gessi;* 3 by *Tiarini;* 2 by *Pietro Desani;* and one, representing the Saint preaching, by *Michael Angelo Colonna*.

The Mint, *La Zecca*, built, it is said, from the designs of *Terribilia* in 1578, is tolerably well provided with modern machinery.

The *Teatro Comunale* was built in 1756, on the site of the ancient palace of Giovanni II. Bentivoglio, which was destroyed by the populace at the instigation of Pope Julius II. The design of the theatre is by *Bibiena*, but it has been frequently altered and adapted to the purposes of the modern opera. The curtain, representing the marriage of Alexander and Roxana, is considered the masterpiece of Signor Pietro Fancelli, a living painter of Bologna, and the worthy coadjutor of Signor Ferri in the decorations of the stage.

The *Teatro Contavalli* was built in 1814, in a part of the suppressed Carmelite convent of S. Martino Maggiore. The old convent stairs serve for the approach to the modern theatre—another of those strange contrasts so frequently met with in Italy.

The *Teatro del Corso* was built in 1805, from the designs of Santini, and is one of the most popular places of amusement in the city.

In the Palazzo Bolognini, near the Strada S. Stefano, a *Casino*, supplied with literary and political journals, was formed a few years ago for the convenience of the upper classes, with the addition of musical parties, conversazioni, and balls.

The *Accademia de' Filarmonici*, and the *Liceo Filarmonico*, institutions peculiarly appropriate to a city which boasts of being the most musical in Italy, have acquired a European reputation. The academy was founded by Vincenzo Carrati, in 1666, and has numbered among its members the most eminent professors of the 2 last centuries. The Lyceum, founded in 1805, by the common council of the city as a school of music, is enriched with the unrivalled musical library and collections of the celebrated Padre Martini. The library contains no less than 17,000 volumes of printed music, and the finest collection of ancient manuscript music in existence. There is an interesting collection of portraits of professors and dilettanti, another of antique instruments, and a fine series of choir-books with miniatures.

The Montagnuola, a slight elevation at the N. extremity of the town, was converted, during the occupation of the French, into a handsome promenade, the only one within the walls.

Environs of Bologna.—A short distance beyond the Porta Castiglione is the ch. of the *Misericordia*, ruined in the wars of the 15th century, and partly rebuilt with like regard to the uniformity of the original plan. It contains some pictures of interest. The Annunciation, on the wall of the small nave, is by *Passerotti;* the Virgin, at the 2nd altar, is by *Lippo Dalmasio;* at the 5th, is the Descent of the Holy Spirit, by *Cesi;* at the 6th, the Virgin, Child, and St. John, attributed to *Innocenzio da Imola;* at the high altar, the Annunciation and the Resurrection are by *Francia;* 8th, the Tabernacle, supported by 4 Doctors of the Church, is carved in cypress wood by *Marco Tedesco* of Cremona, an able sculptor in wood, who also carved the ornaments of the organ and singing gallery.

Outside the Porta di S. Mamolo is the fine ch. of the *Annunziata*, belonging to the Francescan convent. It has some interesting paintings, particularly by *Francia.* In the 2nd chapel is the Madonna and Child, with St. John, St. Paul, and St. Francis, by this celebrated master. In the 3rd is the Crucifixion, with the Magdalen, the Virgin, St. Jerome, and St. Francis, by the same, with the ordinary inscription "Francia Aurifex." 4th, the Sposalizio, by *Costa.* 5th, St. Francis in ecstasy, by *Gessi*, a superb painting worthy of Guido. 8th, the Madonna del Monte, supposed by Massini to be a Greek painting, had the inscription on the back " *Opus Lippi Dalmasii;"*

but it was unfortunately cut away a few years back. 10th, the Annunciation, with St. Francis and St. George, another beautiful work of *Francia.* 12th, the Adoration of the Magi, by *Massari.* 17th, the St. John the Evangelist is from the design of Lodovico Caracci by *Antonia Pinelli*, who has added her name and the date, 1614. Outside the church is a long and beautiful portico, painted in fresco by *Giacomo Lippi' da Budrio* and other pupils of the Caracci. The Shepherds worshipping the newly-born Saviour is by *Paolo Caracci*, from a design by his brother Lodovico.

The ancient little church of the *Madonna di Mezzaratta*, built in 1106, was formerly one of the chief museums of sacred Italian art. Malvasia and Lanzi both regarded its frescoes as invaluable illustrations of the first epoch of the Bolognese school. Lanzi indeed says, "This church is, with respect to the Bolognese school, what the Campo Santo of Pisa is with regard to the Florentine—an arena where the best artists of the 14th century, who flourished in those parts, wrought in competition with each other. They have not the simplicity, the elegance, the grouping, which constitute the merit of the *Giotteschi;* but they evince a degree of fancy, a fire, a method of colouring, which Michael Angelo and the Caracci, considering the time in which they lived, thought by no means contemptible. On the contrary, when these pictures began to exhibit symptoms of decay, they advised and promoted their restoration. Hence in this church there were painted at various times historical pictures from the Old and New Testament, not only by the scholars of Franco Bolognese, but by Galasso of Ferrara, and an unknown imitator of Giotto's style, who Lamo in his MS. maintains to be Giotto himself." The names of these early fresco painters, given by Lanzi as the scholars of Franco Bolognese, and by whom this ch. was painted, are *Vitale da Bologna, Lorenzo, Simone da Bologna, Jacopo Avanzi*, and *Cristoforo*, recorded only as " Cristoforo pittore." But their frescoes have suffered much from the effects of time, and more particularly from repairs and alterations for the convenience of the adjoining building. Of those which remain, the following may be enumerated. A Nativity, with a multitude of angels, over the great door, attributed by Malvasia to *Vitale.* On the rt. wall are 2 series of subjects from the Old Testament; 1 illustrating the Creation; Adam and Eve, with Cain and Abel, Eve represented as spinning, Adam at work, and the 2 children gracefully at play; Noah building the ark. In 6 other compartments is given the history of Moses: 4 of these are fortunately well preserved: the 1st represents Moses exhibiting the Tables of the Law; the 2nd, the Punishment of the Rebels, believed to be by *Giotto;* the 3rd, the Slaughter of the Idolaters; and the 4th, the Worship of the Golden Calf. On the left wall are 2 series of subjects from the New Testament; the upper begins with the Circumcision, but they have been spoiled by retouching. Of the other series only 2 remain, the 1st of which represents Christ healing the Sick; and the 2nd, the Probatica Piscina, with the inscription *Simon fecit.*

On the summit of the Strada del Monte are the church and convent of *S. Paolo in Monte,* recently constructed from the designs of Dr. Vannini. The ch. has some paintings by Passerotti, Cavedone, Elisabetta Sirani, Carlo Cignani, &c.

Not far from this are the *Bagni di Mario,* an octagonal building, constructed in 1564, by Tommaso Lauretti, for the purpose of collecting and purifying the water for the fountain of Neptune. It derives its name from the ruins of the ancient aqueduct, built, it is said, by Marius, and restored by Hadrian and Antoninus Pius, as proved by inscriptions in the Museum.

On the hill above Bologna, beautifully situated, stands the ch. of *San Michele in Bosco,* attached to the suppressed monastery of the Olivetans. This great establishment, in the time of Bishop Burnet one of the finest examples of monastic splendour in Italy, was suppressed at the French invasion; its magnificent halls were converted into barracks and prisons for condemned criminals, and its best pictures were carried to Paris. The walls and ceilings, painted by the Caracci and their school, are gradually falling into ruin, and the famous court, which was entirely decorated by these great artists, is now a melancholy wreck. Many of the paintings have entirely disappeared, and of those which remain the subjects are hardly to be distinguished. They represented the history of St. Benedict and St. Cecilia; those by Guido were retouched only a few years before his death.

The library of the convent, built from the designs of Giovanni Giacomo Monti, had in its several compartments paintings illustrating the subjects of the works contained in them; they were executed by *Canuti,* a pupil of Guido, at the suggestion of the Abbate Pepoli, but they have shared in the general ruin. In the splendid dormitory, 427 ft. in length, is preserved the dial of the clock painted by *Innocenzio da Imola* with figures and festoons of fruit.

Outside the gate called La Porta di Saragozza, is the fine arch designed by Monti in 1675 as a propylæum or entrance to the celebrated *Portico* leading to the *Madonna di S. Luca.* This extraordinary example of public spirit and devotion, which we regret to say sustained damage from the Austrian soldiery in 1849, was projected by the Canonico Zeneroli of Pieve di Cento, who presented to the senate his memorial on the subject in 1672. On the 28th June, 1674, the first stone was laid between what are now the 130th and 131st arches. The portico is 12ft. broad and 15ft. high, and consists of 2 portions, one called the Portico della Pianura, the other the P. della Salita; it is not in a straight line, but has several angles or turnings in consequence of the irregularity of the ground. In 1676, the whole portico of the plain, consisting of 306 arches, was completed at the cost of 90,900 scudi. Here the Portico della Salita begins, and is united to the 1st portico by the grand arch, called, from the neighbouring torrent, the "Arco di Meloncello," built at the cost of the Monti family, from the designs of Bibiena. The difficulties of the ascent were skilfully overcome; and the money was raised by the voluntary contributions of the inhabitants, aided by the donations of the corporation and religious communities, as is shown by the inscriptions recording their benefactions. The theatres even promoted the work by presenting the proceeds of different performances given for the purpose. From 1676 to 1730, 329 arches of the ascent were finished, with the 15 chapels of the Rosary, at the cost of 170,300 scudi ; and in 1739 the entire portico was completed, including, from the Porta di Saragozza to the ch., no less than 635 arches, occupying a space little short of 3 m. in length.

The magnificent ch., occupying the summit of the Monte della Guardia, derives its name of the *Madonna di S. Luca*, from one of those numerous black images of the Virgin, traditionally attributed to St. Luke. It is said to have been brought to this spot in 1160, by a hermit from Constantinople; and is still regarded with so much veneration, that its annual visit to the city is the scene of one of the greatest public festivals of the Bolognese. The church was built in the last century from the designs of Dotti, but not in the purest taste. It contains numerous paintings by modern artists, but none of the great Bolognese masters, excepting a Madonna with S. Domenico, and the 15 Mysteries of the Rosary, in the 3rd chapel on the rt., by *Guido*, one of his earliest productions. The miraculous image of the Virgin is preserved in a recess above the high altar, in a case of marble and bronze gilt, the donation of Cardinal Pallavicini, and is still the object of many pilgrimages. The view from Monte della Guardia is alone sufficient to repay a visit to the ch. The rich and glowing plains, from the Adriatic to the Alps and Apennines are seen spread out like a map in the foreground, studded with villages, churches, convents, and cities, among which Ferrara, Modena, and Imola may be distinctly recognised. Towards the E. the prospect is bounded by the Gulf of Venice, and on the W. and S. the eye ranges along the picturesque and broken line of Apennines. It is impossible to imagine a scene more charming or more beautiful.

In returning to the city, the ancient *Certosa*, built in 1335 by the Carthusian monks, and suppressed in 1797, deserves a visit. It was consecrated in 1802 as the public cemetery, and has been much praised as one of the finest models for an extensive modern Campo Santo. It was the first result of the government of Napoleon, who forbad the burial of the dead within the city ; and its regulations are remarkable as establishing no exclusion of sect, although a separate enclosure is set apart for Protestants and Jews. The ch. still retains many remarkable paintings : in the 1st chapel on the rt. hand, the Last Judgment, and the 2 saints by the side, are by *Canuti ;* the S. Bruno, at the altar, is by *Cesi.* The other large picture, representing the Ascension, is by *Bibiena*, the founder of the eminent Bolognese family of that name, and the pupil of Albani, whose style is evident in this work. In another chapel is the Supper in the House of the Pharisee, and the Magdalen at the feet of Christ, by *Gio. Andrea Sirani.* The Baptism of Christ is a large and powerful composition, by his celebrated daughter *Elisabetta Sirani*, painted in her 20th year, and inscribed with her name. The Miraculous Draught of Fishes, Christ driving the money-changers from the Temple, and the 4 Carthusian Saints were the last works of *Gessi.* The 2 pictures representing Christ entering Jerusalem, and Christ appearing to the Virgin with the host of patriarchs after the resurrection, are by *Lorenzo Pasinelli.* At the high altar, the Crucifixion, the Christ praying in the garden, and the Deposition, are by *Cesi.* In the inner chapel are the Annunciation, by *Cesi ;* Christ bearing the Cross, a half-length in fresco, by *Lodovico Caracci ;* S. Bernardino in fresco, by *Amico Aspertini ;* and Christ bearing the Cross, by *Massari.*

The *Cemetery* occupies the spacious corridors and cloisters of the convent, in which niches in the walls have been built to receive the dead, on the plan of the ancient catacombs. The general effect is very fine, and some of the tombs and monuments are remarkable not only for the names they record, but for the character of their design. Three collections of engravings from these monuments have been published, as well as two volumes of inscriptions, composed by Professor Schiassi, and much admired for their pure Latinity.

The ancient ch. of the *Capuccini* contains a fresco of the Virgin and Child, said to be one of the earliest productions of *Annibale Caracci*. At the 1st altar, the S. Giuseppe da Leonessa is by *Ercole Graziani;* the portrait of the Beata Imelda Lambertini in fresco, is a contemporaneous work (1833), and is therefore regarded as authentic. In the 3rd chapel, the Virgin and Child, with St. Francis and St. Jerome, half figures, are by *Innocenzio di Imola;* the Sposalizio, at the high altar, is by *Orazio Samacchini;* in the 8th chapel, the Crucifixion is by *Passerotti;* and in the 9th, the Beato Lorenzo da Brindisi is by *Ercole Graziani.* The Madonna and Child, in fresco, on the side wall, is by *Lippo Dalmasio,* and was brought here from the ruins of some other ch. The singular series of heads of saints is regarded as the work of the thirteenth or fourteenth century, as are also the symbolical paintings of the roof.

Leaving the city in the opposite direction, at the Porta Maggiore, is the *Portico degli Scalzi,* consisting of 167 arches, and 1700 feet in length, leading to the ch. called *Gli Scalzi,* or the Madonna di Strada Maggiore. The ch. has some good paintings, among which may be remarked a very beautiful Holy Family by *Pasinelli;* the Sta. Teresa praying, by *Canuti;* the Assumption of the Virgin, by *Sabbatini,* and other works of the Bolognese school.

The epithet of *Grassa,* given to Bologna by the historian Paul Van Merle, of Leyden, in the 15th century, applies as much to the *living* and culinary delicacies of the inhabitants as to the productions of its fertile territory. The wines of its neighbourhood are very tolerable, and the fruits, particularly the grapes, are much esteemed. The *mortadella,* everywhere known as the Bologna sausage, still keeps up its reputation: and the *cervellato,* or pudding of raisins and fine kernels, is claimed as peculiar to the city. It is only made in the winter.

Mr. Beckford has designated Bologna as "a city of puppy dogs and sausages." The dogs of Bologna, so celebrated in the middle ages, which still figure in the city arms, and are alluded to in the epitaph on King Enzius in the ch. of S. Domenico, were worthy of more respect than is implied in this flippant remark; they have unfortunately disappeared, and no trace of their pure breed can scarcely now be discovered.

In a University town, so celebrated for its medical professors, the invalid can never be at a loss for good advice; the ordinary fee, either for physicians or surgeons, is 5 pauls, and for simple consultation 2 scudi.

The climate is considered healthy, but in winter Bologna is reputed to be cold and in summer the hottest city in Italy. In other respects Bologna, from its beautiful situation, amply provided with the necessaries and luxuries of life, with a learned and intellectual society, to say nothing of its works of art, is peculiarly calculated to be an agreeable and economical residence.

The Bolognese dialect, of all the forms of unwritten speech which the traveller will meet with in the provinces of Italy, is the most puzzling and corrupt. It was aptly described by the learned grammarian of the 16th century, Aulus Gellius Parrhasius, as the *raucida Bononensium loquacitas.* Forsyth says, "with all the learning in its bosom, Bologna has suffered its dialect, that dialect which Dante admired as the purest of Italy, to degenerate into a coarse, thick, truncated jargon, full of apocope, and unintelligible to strangers."

In regard to the character of the Bolognese, we may refer to the well-known description by Tassoni :

" Il Bolognese e un popol del demonio
 Che non si puo frenar con alcun freno."

This character, at first sight so formidable, would seem to refer to the independent spirit, and to the love of political freedom imbibed from their ancient republican institutions. It has been a fashion with many passing tourists of our own time to depreciate the Bolognese; but the calumny, if there ever were any foundation for it, applies no longer; and in education, in character, and in the arts of civilisation, Bologna stands prominently forward in the first ranks of European cities.

Diligences.—Diligences run twice a-week between Bologna and Rome, performing the journey in 84 hours, fare 14 scudi; the Post Office Courrier with 3 passengers daily by way of Ancona and the Furlo road alternately, fares 24 and 22 scudi; to Florence a diligence 3 times a-week by Covigliajo and daily by La Porretta and Pistoia, performing the whole trajet in 16 and 14 hours, fares 35 and 32 pauls. A diligence daily by Ferrara between Bologna and Padua, and thence to Venice by rly. in 15 hours, fare 20 fr.; and to Milan daily through Modena, Parma, and Piacenza, fare 40 francs. A diligence 3 times a-week to Ravenna in 10 hours, returning on the alternate days.

The Mail Courrier passes daily by Bologna on its way to Florence, and places may be obtained either for Florence or Mantua, fares 35 fr.

Travellers who are desirous of proceeding from Bologna to Rome, without passing through Florence, may follow the interesting road through Forlì, and along the Adriatic to Ancona (Rte. 14), from whence, or from Fano (Rte. 16), a post-road falls into the high Roman road at Foligno.

ROUTE 7.

BOLOGNA TO FLORENCE, BY PIETRA-MALA AND THE PASS OF LA FUTA. 71 m.

	Posts.
Bologna to Pianoro	1½
Pianoro to Lojano	1½
Lojano to Filigare	1
Filigare to Covigliajo	1
Covigliajo to Monte Carelli	1
Monte Carelli to Cafaggiolo	1
Cafaggiolo to Fontebuona	1
Fontebuona to Florence	1
	9

There is a very good diligence 3 times a week to Florence, performing the journey in 16 hours; and as the mail from Mantua to Florence passes through Bologna, places may also be secured in this more rapid conveyance.

The road from Bologna to Florence crosses the central chain of the Apennines. It is in general in good repair, but in many places the ascents are so rapid that, in addition to the ordinary extra horses, oxen are required. The time occupied in performing the journey is from 12 to 15 hours by post, and from 15 to 18 by vetturino. The scenery of this part of the Apennines is often picturesque, but it wants the grandeur and boldness of the Alps.

Leaving Bologna, the road soon enters the valley of the Savena, which it crosses at S. Rufillo, rising very gradually along the rt. bank of the river, through a fertile district, and passing by the villages of Rastigniano and Musiano to

1½ Pianoro, situated close to the Savena, which the post-road quits here, and from whence the ascent of the Apennines may be said to commence. From hence to Lojano an additional horse is required for every pair, with oxen for the very steep ascents. The price of the extra horse is 6 pauls. During the ascent between this and the next post, the road offers several fine points of view over the plains of Bologna and the valley of the Po.

1½ Lojano. A post station with

poor inn. From this elevated spot the view is very striking and extensive; the eye ranges along the chain of distant Alps, embracing the vast basin of the Po to the Adriatic, Mantua, Verona, Padua, Bologna. The papal frontier is! at *La Cà*, where there is a clean inn.

1 Filigare, the first station in Tuscany, is 1 mile beyond the custom-house, where passports are examined and viséed, and luggage generally plumbed, an operation for which a small fee is paid, but which will save trouble and delay on passing the gate at Florence. There is a tolerable inn at Pietramala, 3 m further on. This upper portion of the Pass is much exposed to storms, and is bitterly cold in winter. About 1½ m. E. of Pietramala is a singular phenomenon, called the "i Fuochi," which deserves a visit. It occurs at the base of the Monte di Fo, in a very limited space, and consists of emanations of inflammable gas, which being ignited present at first something of a volcanic appearance. The flames rise about a foot from the ground, and to be seen to advantage must be visited by night: they burn most brightly, and rise to a greater elevation in rainy or stormy weather, owing probably to the diminished atmospheric pressure. Round the orifices from which the gas issues, a carbonaceous deposit like soot is formed, as occurs in the ordinary gas-burners of our houses. Volta, who was the first to investigate these phenomena, very properly attributed these flames to emanations of carburetted hydrogen (coal-gas) from the subjacent Arenaceous Rock, which here, as elsewhere, contains vegetable remains, from the decomposition of which this gas is probably derived. Similar phenomena are met with in other parts of the Apennines, and from the same causes—at Barigazzo, La Porretta, &c. (see Rte. 7A). The flames vary in colour, from blue to yellow, according to the light in which, and the time of the day when they are seen, and emit an odour of burning spirits of wine. The Acqua Buja, 1 m. to the W. of Pietramala, is a similar phenomenon, but here the in-

flammable gas, passing through water, only becomes ignited on the approach of a light to the bubbles as they reach the surface.

From Pietramala, an ascent of 3 m., at the base of the Peaks of Monte Beni and Sasso di Castro, leads to Covigliajo. The geologist will find much to interest him in this part of the route—the above named mountains, which attain respectively elevations of 4080 and 4135 English feet above the sea, being formed of serpentine, which has broken through the subjacent stratified rocks of the cretaceous formation.

1 Covigliajo, at the foot of Monte Beni, a solitary post-house, which had in former days a bad reputation, but which is now a very comfortable inn, much more so indeed than the traveller has a right to expect in such a situation; from its great elevation the climate is very cold, and warm clothing is at all seasons advisable on this journey. A further ascent of 4 m. brings us to the summit of the Pass of la Futa, the highest point of the road between Bologna and Florence, 2987 feet above the sea. From this Pass, which in the winter season is at times impassable from the accumulation of snow, a rapid but well-managed descent leads to

1 Monte Carelli. From this post-station to Covigliajo, a third horse, or oxen, are required by the tariff. The road from this place runs on the summit of a spur of the Apennines, before descending into the beautiful valley of the Sieve, which is so celebrated in the history of the middle ages and in Italian poetry, under the general name of Val di Mugello. Here a road on the rt. leads to Barberino, and thence to Prato and Pistoja. On approaching the valley of the Sieve, about 3 m. from Cafaggiolo is *Le Maschere*, formerly a nobleman's country-seat, now converted into an inn, and so picturesquely placed that many travellers, desirous of seeing more of the beauties of this part of the Apennines, make it their halting-place. "It overlooks the brow of a mountain which, although covered with trees, is almost perpendicular; while on the plain far below lies

the beautiful vale of Arno, bounded by a circle of magnificent hills, sometimes rising in acclivities, sometimes in polished knolls or bold promontories, cultivated to the very summit with the vine and olive, interspersed with fruit and forest trees, and thickly studded with villas, convents, and churches, presenting an aspect of extraordinary animation and beauty. Turning from the contemplation of this rich, lively, and cultivated landscape, to the bold country spread abroad among the Apennines behind the Maschere, you behold a prospect finely contrasting nature in all its most polished splendour with the wild and majestic grandeur of mountain scenery."—*John Bell.*

1 Cafaggiolo, a post station on the rt. bank of the Sieve. A short distance beyond it the old road from Bologna to Florence through Firenzuola and Scarperia falls into this route. About midway between this and the next station we pass the village of Vaglia, on the Carza torrent, whose left bank the road follows to Fontebuona. On an eminence on the l., surrounded by cypress plantations, is seen the picturesque convent of Monte Senario, belonging to the Servites, which forms so remarkable an object in the landscape N. of Florence.

1 Fontebuona. A third horse is necessary from Florence to this station, and there is a very steep ascent on leaving this post-house. A short distance beyond Fontebuona on the l. is *Pratolino*, once the favourite seat of the Grand Dukes of Tuscany, situated on the southern slopes of a hill embosomed in fine trees. The beautiful villa, designed by the great architect Bernardo Buontalenti, for Francesco de' Medici, son of Cosmo I., to receive his mistress Bianca Capello, has long been demolished. The money lavished upon its decorations, its *giuochi d'acqua*, &c., amounted to no less a sum than 782,000 crowns, an expenditure upon which the Grand Duke Ferdinand II. gave an expressive commentary when he said that the money there wasted would have built a hundred hospitals. Besides the grottoes, fountains, and labyrinths of Pratolino, there is a

colossal monster, called the Statue of the Apennines, 60 feet in height. The artist's name is unknown. The beauties of Pratolino and of Bianca are frequently celebrated by Tasso :—

" Dianzi all' ombra di fama occulta e bruna,
  Quasi giacesti, Pratolino, ascoso ;
  Or la tua donna tanto onor t' aggiunge,
  Che piega alla seconda alta fortuna
  Gli antichi gioghi l' Apennin nevoso ;
  Ed Atlante, ed Olimpo, ancor si lungo,
  Nè confin la tua gloria asconde e serra ;
  Ma del tuo picciol nome empì la terra."
                              Rime, 360.

The rapid descent hence to Florence, along an excellent road, is one of the most interesting drives in Europe. Every eminence is studded with villas ; the country, rich in vineyards and olive-groves, seems literally "a land of oil and wine ;" cultivation appears in its highest perfection ; the Etruscan fortress of Fiesole, consecrated by the genius of Milton, with its Arx now occupied by the Franciscan Convent, rises magnificently over the opposite bank of the Mugnone ; and Florence, with its domes, and campaniles, and battlemented towers, bursts upon the view. This approach recalls the remark of Ariosto, that if all the villas which are scattered as if the soil produced them over the hills of the Val d'Arno were collected within one wall, two Romes could not vie with Florence.

" A veder pien di tante ville i colli,
  Per che'l terren vele germogli, come
  Vermene germogliar suole, e rampolli.
  Se dentro un mur, sotto un medesmo nome
  Fosser raccolti i tuoi palazzi sparsi,
  Non ti sarian da pareggiar due Rome."
                              Rime, cap. xvi.

Florence is entered by the Porta San Gallo, where passports are demanded, and a receipt given. If the traveller has taken the precaution to have his luggage *plombed* at the frontier, he will meet no detention here.

1 FLORENCE ; described in ' Handbook for Northern Italy.'

ROUTE 7 A.

BOLOGNA TO FLORENCE, BY LA POR-
RETTA, THE PASS OF LA COLLINA,
AND PISTOJA.—70 m.

This route, which has been only
opened of late years, now forms the most
direct line of communication between
Bologna and Florence: it is certainly
more agreeable and picturesque than
that by Pietramala and the Pass of La
Futa; and by it travellers can easily
reach Florence in one day. There
are as yet no post-stations on it, but
persons travelling in their own carriages
can make arrangements at the diligence
office to have the use of their horses at
the ordinary posting rates; by this
means, and starting early from Bologna,
they will reach Pistoja in time for the
last railway train, which arrives at
Florence at 6¼ P.M.

An excellent diligence starts daily
at 4 A.M., performing the journey to
Pistoja in 12 or 14 hours, and arriving
in time for the last train to Florence
by the Maria Antonia Railway. Vetturini perform the same journey in 2
days, including the transit by railway.

The road follows the bank of the
Reno nearly to its source; it is kept in
tolerable repair in the Papal portion,
where the nature of the soil renders this
difficult; whereas, as soon as it enters
the Tuscan territory, it is excellent.

The diligence-stations are, reckoning
the distance from Bologna,—

Castel del Vescovo	9 m.
Vergato	22
La Porretta	34
La Collina Pass	43
Pistoja	52

Leaving Bologna by the Porta di
Modena, the road skirts the walls of
the town, and afterwards (on the l.)
the beautiful hills on which the ch. of
Santa Lucia is so picturesquely situated,
surrounded by numerous villas of
the Bolognese nobility. 3 m. further it
crosses the Reno, over a handsome 4-
arched bridge, at the village of Casalecchio, where the mountain-valley in
which the Reno runs may be said to
commence.

Casalecchio was the scene of the

battle in which Giovanni Bentivóglio
was overthrown by the army of Gian
Galeazzo, on June 26, 1402. The
allied army of Florence and Bologna,
under Bentivoglio and Bernardo de
Serres, had encamped at Casalecchio,
contrary to the judgment of the latter
general, who was anxious to have retired within the walls of the city.
While they were awaiting reinforcements from Florence, the Milanese,
under Alberigo da Barbiano, gave them
battle. The Bolognese troops, weary of
the tyranny of Bentivoglio, refused to
fight; Bernardo de Serres was taken
prisoner; the inhabitants, encouraged
by the faithless promises made by Gian
Galeazzo that he would restore their republic, opened the gates to the Milanese,
and 2 days afterwards Bentivoglio was
massacred by order of Barbiano. In
1511 Casalecchio was the scene of the
victory gained by the Sieur de Chau-
mont, general of Louis XII., over the
troops of Julius II., commanded by the
Duke of Urbino. It was fought on
the 21st of May, and was called the
" day of the ass-drivers," because the
French knights returned driving asses
laden with their booty.

From Casalecchio the road runs along
the base of the low hills that border the
valley of the Reno on the W. to Castel
del Vescovo, a small village (where the
only accommodation is a poor café),
situated above the river. The road, on
leaving it, runs through the narrow defile of Il Sasso, along a deep cliff over-
hanging the torrent. This part of the
road is not without danger in the rainy
season, being in some parts ill-protected.
on the edge of the precipice, the ravine
only allowing sufficient room for the
river to pass. Immediately above it the
valley widens; a wide torrent, the Setta,
here equal in size to the Reno, joins it
from the S. From the summit of the
Pass of Il Sasso the view up the valley
of the Setta is very fine. Following the l.
bank of the Reno, the road crosses several
ravines, which, being excavated in the
tertiary marls, offer some disagreeable
passes in the rainy season; passing
through the hamlet of Marzabotto, above
which is a large villa belonging to the
Ario family.

Vergato, an inconsiderable village near the Reno; on leaving it, a rapid, and in the winter season a dangerous, torrent, the Vergatello, is forded, as there is no bridge, the bed being so extensive, and the rolled masses of rock so large and numerous, as to render the construction of one very difficult; indeed, all along this road from Il Sasso to La Porretta, one of the great drawbacks · is the want of bridges. On leaving Vergato the appearance of the country changes; the valley of the Reno, hitherto enclosed between bare, precipitous mountains, now widens; the hills on either side becoming rounded and covered with vegetation—a circumstance arising from the change in the geological nature of the soil, from the tertiary marls and sandstones to the calcareous rocks of the cretaceous or eocenic period. Nearly opposite to Vergato rise the rugged peaks of Morte Ovolo and Monte Vigese; at the foot of the latter the village of Vigo was overwhelmed, in 1851, by a terrific landslip. Continuing along the l. bank of the Reno, the ruined castle of Savignano on the l. forms a picturesque object in the landscape, near to which the Limentra, descending from the S., empties itself into it; from thence, crossing a spur of hills, the traveller discovers another reach of the Reno, at the head of which the village of Porretta is seen in the distance. This part of the valley forms a picturesque amphitheatre surrounded by verdant hills, on the summit of which are seen, on the rt., ruins of square mediæval towers. 2 m. before reaching Porretta the Sella torrent is crossed on a new and handsome bridge, one of the finest works of art upon the entire extent of this road within the Papal territory.

La Porretta, or Le Porrette, a very neat village, of upwards of 2000 Inhab., celebrated for its mineral waters and baths, which are much frequented in the summer months. There are several inns and lodging-houses; that which appears to be most convenient for travellers is the Locanda Nova, near the road; for persons travelling in their own carriage it may be made the breakfast-station, as it forms the sleeping-place for those employing vetturino horses between Bologna and Pistoja, and *vice versâ*.

The waters of Le Porrette have long been celebrated for their medicinal qualities, and are much resorted to from July to September; they issue from the sandstone-rock of the cretaceous period, and reach the surface at a temperature varying, according to the springs, from 89° to 101° Fahr.; they contain a variable portion of sulphuretted hydrogen and carbonic acid gases, and in some localities so large a quantity of carburetted hydrogen as to make its collection profitable for lighting purposes. Strange to say, in this remote district of the Apennines, this application of natural gas was first made by an ingenious shoemaker, named Spiga; since which a part of the village is lighted by it. Besides these gaseous contents, the waters of Porretta contain muriate, bromate, and carbonate of soda, and a peculiar pseudo-organic matter; they are used both in the form of baths and internally, and are considered to be very efficacious in chronic glandular obstructions, in rheumatism, paralysis, and nervous affections generally.

During the heats of summer, La Porretta, from its elevation above the sea (1130 English feet), is cool; the situation is considered healthy; fevers, which exist lower down the valley of the Reno, are unknown here.

The Monte Cardo, which rises behind the village, offers several emanations of carburetted hydrogen from the fissures in the sandstone, which ignite on the approach of a light. They are entirely similar to those of Pietramala and Barigazzo. (See Rte. 7.)

Leaving Porretta, the road passes through a narrow limestone defile, barely affording room for the Reno to pass: the road is necessarily cut along the side of the precipice. The mineral spring, called La Porretta Vecchia, is situated in this defile, and is principally resorted to by drinkers, the temperature being 89°. Having passed this defile, the valley expands; thick woods of oaks clothe the sides of the hills. The road ascends more than it has hitherto done, and the Papal Dogana of Le Capanne is soon reached, where passports are *vised.* The river Reno, which is crossed by a bridge, forms here the boundary between Tuscany and the States of the Church; from this point the road leaves it, the river running to the S.S.W. The Tuscan Dogana is about ¼ a mile further on; here the traveller, who will experience much civility from the officials, will do well to have his luggage *plombed,* as it will save much trouble, and avoid all examination, on reaching the Rly. Stat., Florence; a very small charge is made for this operation; another, more objectionable one, is preferred, of 2 grazie for each parcel for porterage, which forms strictly one of the duties of the diligence employés.

The ascent of the Apennines may be said to commence from this point, although, for the first 2 m., it is very gradual along the Limentra; here the road enters a deep, narrow ravine, and for the next 5 m. ascends continually, but so excellently constructed is it, and in such good repair, that it is easily surmounted. About 7 m. from La Porretta the torrent divides into 2 branches; at the point of junction is seen, far below, Lo Spedaleto, formerly an *hospice* for the travellers crossing this part of the Apennines. An extremely well-managed ascent of about 2 m. leads from this point to the Collina Pass, a low saddleback over the central chain of the Apennines. On the summit of the pass is a large inn, but in general badly supplied with comforts. The most elevated point of the Via Leopolda, at the Collina pass, is 3350 English feet above the sea.

The view from the Collina Pass, or, better still, from a point a few hundred yards lower down, is perhaps as fine as from any place in the Apennines, and will well repay a short delay on the part of the traveller. Looking towards the S. and Pistoja, you have on the rt. the highest peaks of the Modenese and Lucca mountains, generally covered with snow; the serrated pinnacles about the 'Cisa and Abetone Passes (see 'Northern Italy,' Rte. 37); the mountains of La Pania; to the S.W. the Lakes of Fucecchio and Bientina, with the upper Valley of the Ombrone in

the fore, the Valley of the Arno beyond, and the distant hills beyond the Arno in the background. The whole Valley of the Ombrone, with Pistoja in the centre, and the chain of hills which separate it from the Val d'Arno Inferiore and the plains of Pisa on one side, whilst the Val d'Arno, extending to Florence, and the Apennines of Valombrosa, close to the E. the distant horizon. "I seldom have witnessed a grander panorama of Italian scenery than from the Collina Pass in a fine clear November's evening." —J. B. P.

A rapid and well-managed descent of 6 m., by a series of zigzags, leads into the Valley of the Ombrone, passing rapidly through every zone of Italian vegetation, from pasturage and pines, through woods of oaks to chesnut-trees, and thence through vineyards to olive-groves, which are here first seen by the traveller arriving from Northern Italy. From the foot of the descent, a level road of 2 m., through neat farm-houses and villas, leads to the gates of Pistoja; ½ m. before reaching which, are seen on the l. the beautiful villa and grounds of Count Puccini.

Instead of passing through the town of Pistoja, to avoid the annoying visit at the gates, travellers generally drive round the walls to the railway-station, situated near the Florentine gate, near which the Hôtel de Londres, with clean beds, and civil landlord, and moderate charges, is by far the best in the place, and where persons desirous of visiting this interesting city will do well to take up their quarters.

Railway trains from Pistoja to Florence start 4 times a day, by the Maria Antonia Railway, performing the journey in an hour. The stations are, reckoning the distances from Pistoja—

San Piero . .	4¼	Tuscan m.
Prato . . .	9¼	,,
Sesto . . .	15¼	,,
Castello . .	17	,,
Riffredi . .	18¼	,,
Florence . .	20	,,

For a description of this part of the route see 'Handbook for Northern Italy,' Rte. 41.

ROUTE 7B.

FAENZA TO FLORENCE, BY MARRADI AND
BORGO SAN LORENZO.—69 m.

This road, which was opened in 1844, establishes a very convenient communication between Florence and Ravenna. Except for the eastern portion of the Romagna, it has, perhaps, little advantage over that to Forlì (Rte. 8), the distance being nearly the same. It passes through a good and picturesque country.

Leaving Faenza, it soon reaches the foot of the first sub-Apennine hills at San Prospero, from whence it follows the l. bank of the Lamone by San Ruffillo to Brisighella, a picturesque village overlooking the plain of the Lamone, to

12 m. Fognano, an inconsiderable village on the l. bank of the river, with a wretched inn. The views of the Apennines, in their lower elevations, covered with woods of chesnut-trees, are very pleasing. The Lamone, here nearly dry during the summer months, is an impetuous and dangerous torrent in the rainy season. Following its l. bank, the road crosses it at S. Eufemia, 4 m. higher up the Tuscan frontier is passed, and 3 m. still farther we arrive at

18 m. Marradi. Marradi is one of those strange Italian villages often met with out of the high roads. It contains 2200 Inhab. The Hôtel del Lamone is indifferent. The valley here becomes very narrow; the precipices on each side merely allowing room for the passage of the river and the road.

1 m. beyond Marradi, at a hamlet called La Biforca, the Limone receives the Campigno torrent on the l.; the road continues along the Limone for 5 or 6 m., until it reaches Crespino, formerly the seat of a suppressed Vallombrosian monastery. Not far from it is the picturesque cascade of Valbura. From Casaglia commences the ascent of the central chain, which is crossed at Casa di Alpe or Colla di Casaglia,

2980 English feet above the level of the sea. On ascending from Marradi the chesnut woods gradually disappear, the mountains become nearly bare. It requires 3½ hours to reach the highest part of the pass, as it does 2 more to descend to Borgo San Lorenzo. From the Pass of Casaglia the road descends rapidly along the Razotta torrent to Puliciano on the Elsa, and from thence to 20 m. Borgo San Lorenzo. *Inns:* Locanda della Rivola, clean and civil; Locanda del Sole. Borgo San Lorenzo, situated near the l. bank of the river, is the principal town in the upper part of the valley of the Sieve, generally called the Mugello. It is in a fertile plain, and contains a population of 3500 souls. Its ch., dedicated to San Lorenzo, is an edifice of the 13th century, as appears from an inscription bearing the date of 1263; the campanile is nearly a century later. 2 roads lead from Borgo San Lorenzo to Florence: the first and most direct, 15 m. up the valley of the Fistona to near its source, and from thence descending along the Mugnone to the gates of the city. 5 m. from Borgo San Lorenzo the monastery and mountain of Monte Senario are passed 3 m. on the rt. Before reaching Florence the Mugnone cuts through a deep glen, bounded by the hill on which the Etruscan arx of the ancient Fesulæ stood on the l., and the Monte Rinaldi, celebrated amongst the Tuscan architects for its quarries of building-stone, on the rt. Emerging from this ravine, we cross the Ponte della Badia, so called from the neighbouring convent, founded by Cosmo de Medicis (see 'Handbook for Northern Italy' p. 553), from which the road is bordered by lines of farm-houses and villas to the Porta di San Gallo, where it is joined by the high road from Bologna by Covigliajo. (Rte. 7.)

The second route, from Borgo San Lorenzo, although longer by 3 m., is to be preferred, the road being less hilly and more suited for heavy carriages, following the l. bank of the Sieve to San Piero, a large village in one of the most fertile districts of the Mugello, near the junction of the Carza and Sieve, and, a mile farther, joins the high road from Bologna to Florence (Rte. 7), not far from Caffagiolo.

ROUTE 8.

FLORENCE TO FORLI, BY DICOMANO AND THE PASS OF S. BENEDETTO.

	Miles.
Florence to Dicomano	20
Dicomano to S. Benedetto	18
Benedetto to Rocca S. Casciano	12
Rocca San Casciano to Forlì	20
	—
	70

This road, opened of late years by the Tuscan government, for the purpose of establishing a direct communication across the Apennines between Florence and the Romagna, is in good order, and constructed on the best principles of modern engineering.

A diligence, or rather a large vetturino carriage, leaves Florence 3 times a week for Forlì, at least during a part of the year, changing horses at Dicomano and Rocca San Casciano, employing about 18 hours on the road. The fare is 25 pauls. The time occupied in the journey would be perhaps less in a private carriage or a hired vetturino, and different resting-places would probably be chosen according to the convenience of the parties. The journey, however, would be too long and too fatiguing for many travellers if performed in a single day, and in that case San Benedetto would be the best halting-place for the first night. These matters should be arranged with the vetturino before leaving Florence. A party of 2 or 3 would find it more agreeable to hire a carriage for the journey than to travel by the diligence; and not much more expensive.

Leaving Florence, we proceed along the banks of the Arno as far as Pontassieve, the first post-station on the road to Rome by Arezzo, where the Forlì road strikes off to the N.E., and ascends the valley of the Sieve as far as Dicomano. The scenery is very fine in many parts, but it becomes wild and rugged as we approach the lofty chain of Apennines over which the road is carried. Like many other by-roads of Italy, this route would enable the pedestrian to fill his sketch-book with picturesque scenes, which have never yet been illustrated by the artist.

20 m. *Dicomano*, the first stage. *Inns:* Locanda Passerine, and the Leone d'Oro. It is an old town, prettily situated at the junction of the Sieve and Dicomano torrents, but has little beyond its position to attract the attention of a passing traveller. On leaving it the road proceeds up the valley of San Godenzo. At Carbonile extra horses are put on, in order to master the ascent, which is extremely steep. The village of *San Godenzo*, through which the road passes, is situated at the southern base of the central chain, among richly wooded scenery. Here the ascent of the Apennines, properly speaking, commences, but the road is admirably constructed, although it appears dangerous in parts from being insufficiently protected above the deep ravines. The descent is gradual and well managed; the Osteria Nuova, 2 m. below the pass, is soon reached, and the road shortly attains the banks of the Montone, which it follows the course of to Forlì.

18 m. *San Benedetto.* This place is about half-way between Florence and Forlì; it has a very fair inn, the Leone d'Oro, the best on the road, and, although the diligence does not stop there, it would be the most eligible resting-place for travellers in a private carriage. If the journey be divided into 2 days, San Benedetto would be the proper sleeping-place. Between this village and Rocca San Casciano the road passes through Portico, an old fortified town. There are some emanations of inflammable gas, similar to those at Pietramala, near the hamlet of Querciolano on the l. of the road.

12 m. Rocca San Casciano (*Inn:* the Locanda del Giglio, very tolerable), a village of 1600 Inhab., on the l. bank of the Montone. It is the most important town of the Tuscan Romagna;

but contains little to detain the traveller. A very fair road has of late years been opened from it across the pass of Le Forche to Galeata and Santa Sofia, in the upper valley of the Ronco. Leaving San Casciano, the road continues along the l. bank of the Montone, between Monte Grosso on the rt., and Monte Torcella on the l. Before arriving at Dovadola a good road of 10 m. on the l. leads to Modigliana, a very ancient town of 3000 Inhab., probably the Castrum Mutilum of Livy. Across the pass of Monte Trebbio, between Dovadola and Terra del Solo, is the village of Castro Caro (the ancient Salsubium), celebrated for its mineral waters, which contain a considerable portion of iodine, and have proved very efficacious in glandular and scrofulous affections.

Terra del Sole, the frontier station of Tuscany, is a walled town on the l. bank of the Montone. Here passports are examined. 1¼ m. farther we come to Rovere, the Papal Dogana, where a small fee to the custom-house officials will save delay and trouble; from this a pleasant drive of about 2 m. across the plain through Varano brings us to 20 m. FORLI (described in Rte. 14).

ROUTE 9.

FORLI TO RAVENNA.

20 m.

A diligence runs from Forlì to Ravenna 3 times a week.

A good country road of about 20 m., lying along the l. bank of the Ronco, which from here to the sea is confined in its narrow channel by high banks. Like the following, this route presents a succession of farm-houses thickly scattered over a country which is surpassed by no district of Italy in fertility or cultivation. About 2 m. before reaching Ravenna, the ch. of San Apollinare *in Classe* is seen on the rt.; a little farther on, the canal formed by the united waters of the Montone and Ronco is passed by

Cent. It.

the Ponte dell Asse, and the city is entered by the Porta Sisi.

20 m. RAVENNA (Rte. 12).

ROUTE 10.

FAENZA TO RAVENNA.

A cross-road of 2½ posts = 19 m.

An agreeable drive of about 3 hours through a country of extraordinary fertility. To the English traveller, the neat appearance of the farm-houses with their gardens and poultry-yards will recall many recollections of home. 4 m. after leaving Faenza the road crosses the Lamone at the Ponte della Castellina. Between Russi and Godo, which lie on the rt. of the road, the present route falls into the high road from Bologna to Ravenna through Lugo and Bagnacavallo.

2½ RAVENNA (Rte. 12).

ROUTE 11.

VENICE TO RAVENNA, BY THE CANALS AND COMACCHIO.

About 90 m.

Venice to Chioggia,	20 m.
Chioggia to Cavanella,	2 posts.
Cavanella to Mesola,	2 —
Mesola to Pomposa,	2 —
Pomposa to Magnavacca,	2 —
Magnavacca to Primaro,	1 —
Primaro to Ravenna,	2 —
	11 posts.

The traveller who is desirous of proceeding from Venice to Ravenna by the shortest route may do so by means of the canals which intersect the vast lagunes between the 2 cities. Although only a short portion of the route can be performed in a carriage, there is a series of post stations from Chioggia to Ravenna, the route being estimated at 11 posts.

A person having his own carriage must be prepared to run all risks of trans-shipment from the ferry-boats; but a traveller not so encumbered will do well to rely on the canal-boats and on the carriages of the country, which

E

he will find at Mesola to convey him to Ravenna.

It may be useful to premise, that persons proceeding by this route will have the best possible opportunity of visiting the famous *Murazze*, or great Sea wall of Venice, during their progress; as the boat must pass along it, whether it follows the canal inside the island of Malamocco, or takes the outer or seaward route.

The ordinary course is to proceed down the Malamocco canal, and from thence, inside the long narrow island which lies beyond it, to

Chioggia or *Chiozza*. This would be the best resting-place for the first night. The time occupied in rowing the distance in a 6-oared boat is about 6 hours; it would, of course, be much shorter in a sailing-boat, with a fair wind. *Chioggia* is a fine, well-built town, with a convenient port, much frequented by the coasting vessels of the Adriatic. Its history and association with the naval achievements of Venice, recalling "the Doria's menace," so beautifully sung in 'Childe Harold,' belong to the description of that city, and need not be particularised here. Leaving the town, we proceed to Brondolo, on the Brenta, and from thence by the Canal di Valle, which connects the latter river and the Adige, to Cavanella, and ascend the Adige for 2 m., and then follow the Canal di Loreo to *Cavanella di Pò*, on the l. bank of that branch of the Po called the Pò Grande, or della Maestra. The other branch farther S. is the Pò di Goro, and between the point of separation at Sta. Maria and the sea these two arms of the river inclose an island, called *Isola d' Ariano*, frequently subject to the destructive inundations of both its branches. On the northern shore of this island, and about 3 m. lower down, is *Taglio del Pò*, to which, if the island be passable, the traveller should proceed, and there leave his boat; otherwise he must ascend the northern branch of the Po, and make a tedious *détour* round the western angle of the island at Sta. Maria, near the town of Ariano: in either case he will land at *Mesola*, the frontier town of the Papal States. The difference of time occupied by these two

modes is considerable: from Chioggia to Taglio the voyage by canal, *direct*, occupies about 8 hours; from Taglio to Mesola, across the island, is little more than 1 hour; whereas the route from Chioggia to Mesola, going round by the Po, requires at least 14 hours.

Mesola, on the rt. bank of the Pò di Goro. This should be made the sleeping-place on the second day; there is a tolerable inn here; and a country carriage, quite good enough for the roads, may be hired for the next day's journey. Mesola has a population of 4000 souls: it appears to have been considered important as a frontier town, since it is recorded that it has been twice purchased of the House of Austria by the Church—by Pius VI., for a million of scudi, and by Leo XII., in 1822, for 467,000. The difficulty and expenses of keeping up the embankments of the canals and rivers in this part of Italy, which are admirably constructed and managed, as the traveller will not fail to observe during his journey, are said by the inhabitants to have made the acquisition a dear one to the Papal government.

Leaving Mesola, the road proceeds along the flat sandy tract to *Pomposa*, near the Pò de Volano, which it crosses by a ferry, traverses the eastern line of the *Valle di Comacchio*, to *Magnavacca*. W. of Magnavacca is the fortified town of *Comacchio*, with 5500 souls, situated in the midst of the unhealthy salt marshes, and garrisoned by Austria, under the treaty of Vienna. The traveller appears to be constantly approaching the town without getting near it. These marshes, called the "Valleys of Comacchio," although unhealthy and desolate from humidity and fever, are still celebrated for their fisheries as in the time of Ariosto and Tasso, who describe the contrivances for securing the fish which have come up from the sea, in order to prevent their return.

"Come il pesce colà, dove impaluda
Ne' seni di Comacchio il nostro mare,
Fugge dall' onde impetuosa e cruda,
Cercando in placide acque, ove ripare.
E vien, che da sè stesso ei si rinchiuda
In palustre prigion, nè può tornare;
Chè quel serraglio è con mirabil uso
Sempre all' entrar aperto, all' uscir chiuso."
Gerus. Lib. vii. 16.

Ariosto calls *Comacchio*

" La città, che in mezzo alle piscose
Paludi del Pò teme ambe le foci."
Orl. Bur. iii. 41. 3.

About 7 m. S. of Magnavacca the road crosses the southern branch of the Po, called the Pò di Primaro, the *Spineticum Ostium* of the ancients, at Il Passo, leaving on the l. the town of Primaro and its small port, defended by the Torre Gregoriana.

The ancient name of the Pò di Primaro recalls the celebrated Greek city of *Spina,* situated on the l. bank of the river, a few miles from the Adriatic. The high antiquity of Spina has been the subject of much controversy; some writers, on the authority of Dionysius of Halicarnassus, referring it to the Pelasgi, who arrived on this coast from Epirus long before the Trojan war; while others, who dispute its foundation by the Pelasgi, admit that it was of Greek origin, and that it had acquired much celebrity in the age of Crœsus. There are no remains by which its ancient site can be identified; but it is generally supposed that it stood near the village of Argenta, on the l. bank of the Pò di Primaro, about 12 m. inland.

1 m. beyond Primaro the Lamone is crossed, and we soon enter the northern extremity of the *Pineta,* described in the account of Ravenna, in the succeeding Route. After a drive of a few miles along the turf through this venerable forest, we fall into the road near the tomb of Theodoric, and enter Ravenna by the Porta Serrata. The journey from Mesola to Ravenna occupies about 10 hours, and is a fair day's work.

RAVENNA, described in the next Route.

[A recent traveller, Dr. Fraser, who performed the journey from Ravenna to Venice, gives the following account of his progress:—" This route is not devoid of interest, although it is seldom followed. On leaving Ravenna, the road passes by the tomb of Theodoric, and soon after enters the Pineta. The deep silence of the forest is unbroken by the noise of the carriage, which now passes over the green turf, scarcely marked, and in some places not at all, by any track; and the traveller soon feels that

without the aid of a guide, or. the instinct of the North American, his path would soon be lost. We were told that wild boars abound in the recesses of the forest; but we saw no game, nor indeed any other living thing. After threading its mazes for 2 hours, we observed with regret a thinning of the trees, and gradually entered on the open country. An uninteresting drive brought us to Magnavacca, where, in addition to our own stock of provisions (for every person taking this route ought to carry a supply), we found the means of making a tolerable breakfast. We changed horses and carriage at this place, by which we neither improved our vehicle nor the quality of the horses. We were now given to understand that no one would take a good carriage by this road, so that we had been deceived by the innkeeper at Ravenna, who had agreed to convey us to Mesola in his snug barouche; whereas the one to which we were now transferred was somewhat ruder in construction than a tax-cart. We had, however, no alternative, and were given to understand that next day we should obtain a better carriage at Mesola, which we reached at sunset. We slept there, although our original intention was to make Ariano our resting-place for the first night; but the usual road was cut up by the late floods, and that which we were to follow so increased the distance, that the landlord would not furnish us with horses that evening. As he had everything in his own hands, we submitted with as good grace as possible. Mesola is the frontier town of the Papal States, and consists of a large building, the residence of the governor, apparently constructed so as to be turned into a fort if necessary, and a few straggling houses, all lying below the level of the river, which is here magnificently embanked. During this day's journey we crossed five streams by means of ferry-boats; but the steepness of their banks, and the bad arrangements of the boats, convinced us that no English carriage could be safely transported without improved means. On one occasion, indeed, our carriage, from its impetus in descending, was nearly thrown into the river, dragging

E 2

the men and everything after it. If this accident had happened, we should have had our baggage destroyed, if not lost, and should have been compelled to proceed for some distance on foot. We started from Mesola the next morning at daybreak, and drove along the S. bank of the Pò di Goro, or Pò Piccolo, to the point opposite Vicolo, where we found numerous boatmen, and soon made an arrangement for our conveyance to Chioggia. We were now dragged, as in a canal boat, by two men, up the Po to Sta. Maria in Ponto, without landing at Ariano. Before arriving at Sta. Maria we left the boat in order to avoid the tiresome navigation round the western point of the island. We reached Sta. Maria in this way, after a walk of a mile, while the boat did not arrive for 3 hours. Sta. Maria is the Austrian frontier station: we found the officers extremely civil and obliging, and were subjected to far less inconvenience than we had met with in many petty towns of the Papal States. The effects of the floods on this island of Ariano were still visible in the broken banks, and in the vast masses of shingle thrown up on various parts of the surface. The inhabitants were unable to leave their houses for 15 days during the great flood of November, 1839. On the arrival of our boat we proceeded on our voyage, passing through numerous canals, and seldom encountering a lock, in consequence of the level character of the country. We crossed the branch of the Po called Pò Maestra, the Adige, and the Brenta, during the day; but the only towns we passed were Cavanella di Pò and Loreo. We arrived at Chioggia at 8 in the evening, and our anxiety to reach Venice was so great that we immediately hired a boat, and landed in that city at 2 in the morning. We ought to have slept at Chioggia, as we suffered much from cold in passing the lagunes, and had but an imperfect view of the great wall, which is so well seen on this passage. Our route altogether, in spite of the drawbacks mentioned, was far from being uninteresting; the swamps, canals, and rivers were so unike anything we had seen before, that we were amused by the novelty of the scene; the time passed away pleasantly under the awning of the boat, or in walking along the banks of the canals, which the slow movement of our boat permitted; we were struck by the simple manners of the peasantry, and still more by the extreme beauty of the women; we were not annoyed by beggars; we enjoyed a freedom unknown to travellers in a diligence; and at the close of our journey we almost regretted that it was the only one, and the last of the kind."]

Travellers will perceive from this that it is desirable to divide the journey into 3 days, sleeping at Mesola or Ariano on the first night, and at Chioggia on the second. They would thus reach Venice early on the third day.

ROUTE 12.

BOLOGNA TO RAVENNA, BY IMOLA AND LUGO.

55 m.

	Posts.
Bologna to S. Niccolò . . .	1¼
S. Niccolò to Imola . . .	1¼
Imola to Lugo	2
Lugo to Ravenna	3
	7½

The first 2 stages of this route, between Bologna and Imola, are described in Rte. 14, where an account of Imola is also given. The route from Imola to Ravenna is somewhat longer than that from Faenza; but the roads are excellent, and the country through which it passes is interesting on account of its high state of cultivation.

Leaving Imola, the road proceeds along the l. bank of the Santerno as far as Mordano. After crossing the Santerno it turns towards Lugo. 3 m. N.W. from this is the walled town of *Massa Lombarda*, generally supposed to have been so called from the Mantuan and Brescian emigrants who fled from the persecutions of Frederick Barbarossa, and settled here in 1232. There is no doubt that the establishment of this colony contributed to the prosperity of the district; and it is recorded that Francesco d'Este, one of the generals of the Emperor Charles V., on his deathbed at Ferrara in 1573, directed that the Lombards of Massa should carry his body from Ferrara to this town, where, in accordance with his wishes, it was buried. The present population is about 4000. On the l. bank of the Santerno, a branch road from Ferrara through the marshes of Argenta falls into this route.

2 *Lugo* (*Inn :* Albergo di San Marco, tolerable), situated in the plain, nearly midway between the Santerno and the Senio rivers, supposed to occupy the site of *Lucus Diana*, whose temple was in the neighbourhood. Lugo, now an important provincial town of 9300 souls, was raised to municipal rank by Julius II., and was confirmed in its privileges by Pius VII. It was sacked by the French in 1796, and contains nothing to detain the traveller, unless indeed he happen to visit it at the period of its fair, which commences September 1st, and lasts till the 19th of the month. This fair is said to date from the time of Marcus Æmilius, proconsul of Ravenna. It was confirmed by Pope John IV., in 640; by Clement VIII., in 1598; and by Pius VII. During its continuance, the porticoes of the fine piazza are converted into shops. In the vicinity of Lugo are 2 small towns, each of which is interesting as the birthplace of personages whose name occupy a distinguished place in Italian history. The first of these, *Colignola*, lies 3 m. to the S.E. of Lugo, on the banks of the Senio, is the birthplace of Attendolo Sforza, the founder of that illustrious house which subsequently played so important a part. It was in this village that he threw his pickaxe into the branches of an oak, in order that it might decide by its fall, or by remaining fixed, whether he should remain a tiller of the ground, or join a company of adventurers. The other town is *Fusignano*, about 4 m. N., also on the l. bank of the Senio, memorable as the birthplace of Vincenzo Monti the poet, and of Angelo Corelli the composer. The castle of Cunio, so celebrated in the middle ages as one of the strongholds

of Romagna, was in the immediate neighbourhood of Cotignola : its ruins may yet be traced.

A short distance from Lugo the road crosses the Senio, and passes through *Bagnacavallo,* a small town of 3500 souls, originally called Tiberiacum, in honour of Tiberius. Several Roman inscriptions, and other antiquities of the time of the Empire, discovered there in 1605, prove its existence at that period as a Roman city. The present town is walled, and was formerly famous for its strong castle. It has a cathedral dedicated to St. Michael the Archangel, and a circus for the game of pallone, but it contains little to interest the stranger. 2 m. beyond Bagnacavallo the road crosses the Lamone, and proceeds across the plain to Ravenna. Near Godo that from Faenza falls into this route.

3 RAVENNA.—(*Inn :* La Spada Nova, or Spada d'Oro, very good, a large and new Hotel recently opened in the Palazzo Raize — charges reasonable; the original Spada is much decayed. Passports are demanded on entering the city.) Ravenna, the capital of the Western Empire, the seat of the Gothic and Longobardic kings, and the metropolis of the Grecian exarchs, is one of those historical cities which are best illustrated by their own monuments. Within its walls repose the remains of the children of Theodosius, and amidst the tombs of exarchs and patriarchs rests all that was mortal of Dante. A short distance beyond the gates is the sepulchre of Theodoric, king of the Goths: the city ramparts still retain the breaches of the barbarians, and the deserted streets are filled with Christian antiquities which have known no change since the time of Justinian. As the traveller wanders through the streets, once traversed by the pomp and pageantry of the exarchs, their unbroken solitude recalls the feelings with which he may have rode round the walls of Constantinople; but Ravenna has preserved more memorials of her imperial masters, and possesses a far higher interest for the Christian antiquary, than even that celebrated seat of empire. "Whoever loves early

Christian monuments, whoever desires to see them in greater perfection than the lapse of 14 centuries could warrant us in expecting, whoever desires to study them unaided by the remains of heathen antiquity, should make every effort to spend some days at least in this noble and imperial city. From Rome it differs mainly in this—that your meditations on its ornaments are not disturbed by the constant recurrence of pagan remains, nor your researches perplexed by the necessity of inquiring what was built and what was borrowed by the faithful. Ravenna has only one antiquity, and that is Christian. Seated like Rome in the midst of an unhealthy, desolate plain, except when its unrivalled pine-forests cast a shade of deeper solitude and melancholy over it; quiet and lonely, without the sound of wheels upon its grass-grown pavement; it has not merely to lament over the decay of ancient magnificence, but upon its total destruction—except what Religion has erected for herself. She was not in time to apply her saving as well as purifying unction to the basilicas and temples of preceding ages; or rather, she seemed to occupy what she could replace, and therefore, in the strength of imperial favour, raised new buildings for the Christian worship, such as no other city but Rome could boast of."— *Cardinal Wiseman, Dublin Rev.*

The history of Ravenna embraces a considerable portion of the history not only of Italy during the middle ages, but also of the Eastern and Western Empires. Without entering into these details, it will be absolutely necessary for the appreciation of its antiquities to give a rapid sketch of its magnificence under its ancient masters.

The accounts of the classical writers prove that the ancient city was built on wooden piles in the midst of a vast lagune, and so intersected with marshes that communication was kept up by numerous bridges, not only throughout the adjacent country, but even in the city itself. The sea, which is now from 3 to 4 m. distant, then flowed up to its walls. Ravenna became early a Roman colony, and, judging from an expression in Cicero, was an important naval station in the time of Pompey the Great. Cæsar occupied it previous to his invasion of Italy. Under Augustus its consequence was increased by the construction of an ample port at the mouth of the Candianus, capable of affording shelter to 250 ships, and which superseded the old harbour at the mouth of the Ronco. He connected the new port with the Po by means of a canal, and carried a causeway to it from the city, which he made his frequent residence, and embellished with magnificent buildings. The new harbour was called *Portus Classis*, a name still retained in the distinctive title of the noble basilica of S. Apollinare; and the intermediate settlement which arose from the establishment of the port was called *Cæsarea*, whose name also is still perpetuated by the ruined basilica of S. Lorenzo in Cesarea. Subsequent emperors added to the natural strength of Ravenna by fortifying its walls and maintaining its fame as a naval station. But its true interest does not commence until after the classical times. On the decline of the Roman empire, Honorius chose Ravenna as the seat of the Western Empire, A.D. 404. As early as this period the alluvial deposits of the Po had begun to accumulate on the coast; the port of Augustus had been gradually filled up, and the forest of pines which supplied the Roman fleet with timber had usurped the site where that fleet had before anchored; and spread far along the shore, now becoming more and more distant from the city. These and other circumstances combined to make Ravenna a place of security; and Honorius, afraid of remaining defenceless at Milan, chose Ravenna as his residence, where his personal safety was secure amidst the canals and morasses, which were then too shallow to admit the large vessels of the enemy. He availed himself of these changes to strengthen the city with additional fortifications, and so far succeeded that its impregnable position saved it from the inroads of the northmen under Radagaldus and Alaric. Without entering into details of the administration of Ravenna under Placidia, the sister of Honorius, during the minority of Valentinian, it may suffice to state that under her feeble successors even the natural advantages of the city were unable to offer an effectual resistance to the wild tribes of Odoacer, who, in little more than 70 years after the arrival of Honorius, made himself master of Ravenna, and extinguished the Empire of the West. His rule, however, had lasted but 15 years when Theodoric, king of the Eastern Goths, crossed the Alps with a powerful army, and after several gallant struggles overthrew Odoacer, and made Ravenna the capital of the Gothic kingdom. Theodoric was succeeded in the sovereignty of Italy by two of his descendants, and they in turn by a series of elective kings, from the last of whom Justinian endeavoured to reconquer the lost provinces, aided by the military genius of Belisarius. The campaign of that great general, and his siege and capture of Ravenna, are well known to every reader of Gibbon.

It is unnecessary to dwell upon the circumstances attending the recall of Belisarius, and the appointment of Narses, the new general of Justinian, who drove the Goths out of Italy, and was intrusted with the administration of the Italian kingdom by the title of EXARCH of Ravenna. The title thus conferred upon the favourite lieutenant of the emperor was extended to his successors during the continuance of the Greek sovereigns: the functions of the exarchs corresponded in some measure to those of the ancient prætorian prefects, and the imperial delegates who filled that office acquired a place in the chronology of princes. Their government comprised the entire kingdom of Italy, including the city of Rome, and the pope or bishop of the Christian capital was regarded as subject to their authority, possessing merely a temporal barony in Rome dependent on the exarchate. The territory understood to be comprised in the *Exarchate* included modern Romagna, the districts of Ferrara and Comacchio, the maritime Pentapolis or the line of towns extending from Rimini to Ancona, and a second or inland Pentapolis, including several towns on the eastern side of the Apennines. The exarchate lasted 185 years: the people of Rome erected a kind of republic under their bishop; and Astolphus, king of the Lombards, seeing that Ravenna would be an easy prey, drove out Eutichius, the last exarch, made himself master of the city, and created it the metropolis of the Longobardic kingdom, A.D. 754. The attempt of the Lombards to seize Rome also, as a dependency of the exarchate, brought to the aid of the Church the powerful army of the Franks under Pepin and Charlemagne, by whom the Lombards were expelled, and Ravenna with the exarchate given to the Holy See as a temporal possession; "and the world beheld for the first time a Christian bishop invested with the prerogatives of a temporal prince, the choice of magistrates, the exercise of justice, the imposition of taxes, and the wealth of the palace of Ravenna."

This rapid sketch of Ravenna during the days of its prosperity as the seat of sovereignty will hardly be complete with tracing its history through its subsequent decline; since many memorials of the events which occurred during this period will be found hereafter in the particular description of the city. After the transfer of the exarchate to Rome by the Carlovingian princes, the fortunes of Ravenna began rapidly to decline; its archbishops frequently seized the government, and it was the scene of repeated commotions among its own citizens. In the 13th century the constitution of Ravenna strongly tended to aristocracy; the 'Monumenti Ravennatis,' a most valuable collection of statutes illustrative of the manners and state of society of the time, show that its general council was composed of 250, and its special council of 70 persons. In the contests of the Guelphs and Ghibelines, Pietro Traversari, an ally of the former faction, declared himself Duke of Ravenna (1218), without changing the civil institutions of the city. His son and successor quarrelled with the emperor Frederick

II., who reduced Ravenna to obedience, and despoiled it of many of its treasures. The city was taken shortly after by Cardinal Ubaldini, legate of Innocent IV., and reduced again to the authority of the Roman pontiffs, who governed it by vicars. In 1275 it was ruled by the family of Polenta, whose connection with it is commemorated by Dante under the image of an eagle which figured in their coat of arms:—

" Ravenna sta com' è stata molti anni:
  L'aquila da Polenta là si cova,
  Sì che Cervia ricopre coi suoi vanni."
               Inf. xxvii.

After some subsequent changes the inhabitants were induced by civil tumults, arising from the ambition or cupidity of its powerful citizens, to throw themselves under the protection of Venice, by which the government was seized in 1441. Ravenna flourished under the republic; its public buildings were restored, its fortress was strengthened, and the laws were administered with justice and wisdom. After retaining it for 68 years, the Venetians finally ceded it to the Church in 1509 under Julius II.; and it then became the capital of Romagna, and was governed by the papal legates. In less than 3 years after this event the general Italian war which followed the league of Cambray brought into Italy the army of Louis XII. under Gaston de Foix, who began his campaign of Romagna by the siege of Ravenna. After a vain attempt to carry it by assault, in which he was bravely repulsed by the inhabitants, the arrival of the papal and Spanish troops induced him to give battle, on Easter Sunday, April 11, 1512. Italy had never seen so bloody a combat; little short of 20,000 men are said to have lain dead upon the field, when the Spanish infantry, yet unbroken, slowly retreated. Gaston de Foix, furious at seeing them escape, rushed upon the formidable host in the vain hope of throwing them into disorder, and perished in the attempt about 3 m. from the walls of Ravenna. The French gained the victory, but it was dearly purchased by the loss of their chivalrous commander.

At the French invasion of 1796 Ravenna was deprived of its rank as the capital of Romagna, which was given to Forlì; but it was restored by Austria in 1799, only to be again transferred by the French in the following year. On the fall of the Kingdom of Italy, Ravenna was again made the chief city of the province, but its ancient glory was gone for ever, and only 3 towns and a few castles were left subject to its authority.

Ravenna, at the present time, is the chief city of a legation, comprehending a pop. of 172,595 Inhab., including the suburbs, and a surface of 816 square m.; the city is inhabited by 20,160 persons, and its immediate territory irrigated by 7 rivers and numerous torrents. It is the seat of an archbishop, always a cardinal, to whom all the bishops of Romagna are suffragans. Its bishopric, one of the most ancient in the Christian world, was founded A.D. 44, by S. Apollinaris, a disciple of Peter; and it obtained the dignity of an archiepiscopal see as early as 439, under Sixtus III. The circuit of the city is about 3 m. Besides its churches and other objects of antiquarian interest, it contains a college, a museum, public schools, and an academy of the fine arts. Its port, communicating with the Adriatic by a canal, is still considered one of the great outlets of Romagna, and carries on an extensive commerce with the Lombardo-Venetian kingdom.

The *Cathedral*, once a remarkable example of the ancient Basilica, has lost all traces of its original character. It was built by S. Orso, archbishop of the see, in the 4th century, and called from him "Basilica Orsiana." It was rebuilt in the last century, and completely spoilt; the cylindrical campanile, whose form recalls the minarets of Constantinople, alone remains of the original building. The chief interest of the present ch. is the celebrated painting by *Guido* in the chapel of the SS. Sacramento representing the fall of the manna, and the lunette above representing the meeting of Melchizedek and Abraham; these are classed by Lanzi among Guido's best works. Among the other pictures which deserve notice are the grand Banquet of Ahasuerus by *Carlo Bonone*, well known by the minute description of Lanzi, and the modern painting by *Camuccini* of the Consecration of the ch. by St. Orso. The high altar contains an urn of Greek marble, in which are deposited the remains of 9 early bishops of the see. The silver crucifix is covered with sculptures of the 6th century. The chapel of the Madonna del Sudore contains a large marble urn covered with bas-reliefs, in which, as related by the inscription, are the ashes of St. Barbatian, confessor of Galla Placidia. Behind the choir are 2 slabs of Grecian marble, with symbolical representations of animals, which formed part of the ancient pulpit, the work of the 6th century. In the vestibule of the sacristy is a *Paschal calendar* on marble, much prized by antiquaries as a remarkable monument of astronomical knowledge in the early times of Christianity. It was calculated for 95 years, beginning with 532, and ending in 626. Here is also a fine picture by *Guido*, the Angel offering Bread and Wine to Elijah. The *Sacristy* contains the *pastoral chair of St. Maximian*, formed entirely of ivory, with the monogram in front of "Maximianus Episcopus." The bas-reliefs below the monogram represent the Saviour in the character of a shepherd and priest in the midst of the 4 evangelists: on the 2 exterior sides is the history of Joseph, and those which remain on the back represent various events in the life of the Saviour. It is precious as a specimen of art in the 6th century, but it has evidently suffered from injudicious cleaning. Behind the grand door of the cathedral are still preserved some fragments of its celebrated *Door of vine-wood*, which has been superseded by one of modern construction. The original planks are said to have been 13 feet long and nearly 1¼ wide—a proof that the ancients were correct in stating that the vine attains a great size, and that we may rely on the assertion that the statue of Diana of Ephesus was made of the vine-wood of Cyprus. It is probable that the wood of the Ravenna doors was imported from Constantinople.

The *ancient Baptistery*, called also "S. Giovanni in Fonte," now separated from the cathedral by a street, is supposed to have been likewise founded by S. Orso: it was repaired in 451 by archbishop Neo, and dedicated to St. John the Baptist. It is, like many baptisteries of the early Christians, an octagonal building; the interior has 2 circles, each of 8 arcades, the lower resting on 8 columns with different capitals, placed in each angle of the building: the upper are 24 in number, dissimilar in form as well as in the capitals. The lower columns are considerably sunk, and both these and the upper series are supposed to have belonged to some ancient temple. The cupola is adorned with well-preserved mosaics of the 5th century, representing in the centre Christ baptized in the Jordan, and in the circumference the 12 apostles, with other ornaments. The grand vase, which was formerly used for baptism by immersion, is composed of Greek marble and porphyry. There are 2 chapels in the building: that on the rt. contains a sculptured marble of the 6th century, which formerly belonged to the ciborium of the old cathedral; that on the l. has a beautiful urn of Parian marble covered with symbols supposed to relate to the ancient nuptial purifications; it was found in the temple of Jupiter at Cæsarea. The ancient metal cross of the summit of the baptistery merits notice on account of its antiquity: it bears an inscription recording that it was erected in 688 by Archbishop Theodorus. It has recently been removed, and now stands in front of the church.

The magnificent *Basilica of San Vitale*, in the pure Byzantine style, exhibits the octagonal form with all the accessories of Eastern splendour. As one of the earliest Christian temples, it is of the highest interest in the history of art. It was built in the reign of Justinian by S. Ecclesius, the archbishop of the see, on the spot where St. Vitalis suffered martyrdom, and was consecrated by St. Maximian in 547. It was an imitation of Sts.

Sophia at Constantinople, and was adopted by Charlemagne as the model of his church at Aix-la-Chapelle. The original pavement is considerably below the present floor, and is now covered with water. The architecture of the interior exhibits 8 arches resting on as many piers, between which are semicircular recesses of 2 stories, each divided into 3 small arches by 2 columns between the principal piers. The spaces between the lower columns open into the side aisles, and those between the upper into a gallery. Above, the building becomes circular. The fourteen columns of the upper story have Gothic capitals, some of which bear an anchor, supposed to indicate that they belonged to a temple of Neptune. The 14 columns of the lower story have also Gothic capitals; and on the imposts of the arches are 28 monograms. The pilasters and the walls are covered with large plates of Grecian marble, on which are still to be traced some fragments of a frieze. The colossal dome was painted, in the early part of the 18th century, with frescoes representing the fathers of the Old and New Testaments, with various decorations, such as festoons of roses hanging from the roof; all in the worst taste, and at variance with the architectural character of the building. The dome is constructed of earthen pots, and is perhaps the most perfect specimen known of this kind of work. They are small twisted vessels, having the point of one inserted in the mouth of the other in a continued spiral, and placed horizontally. The spandrils are partially filled with others of larger size, twisted only at the point, and arranged vertically. The upper walls and vault of the choir are covered with mosaics of the time of Justinian, as beautiful and as fresh as on the day when they were first finished; invaluable as specimens of art during the middle ages, no less than as studies of costume. The most elaborate of these mosaics is that of the tribune, representing on the right the Emperor Justinian with a vase containing con-

secration offerings in his hand, surrounded by courtiers and soldiers, and accompanied by St. Maximian and two priests. On the left the Empress Theodora with a similar vase, attended by the ladies of her court. In the vault above is the Saviour throned on the globe between the archangels; on the right hand is S. Vitalis receiving the crown of martyrdom; and on the left S. Eutichius in the act of offering a model of the church. The vault is decorated with arabesques, urns, and other ornamental devices. The other mosaics represent the Saviour with the 12 apostles; St. Gervasius, and S. Protasius, sons of S. Vitalis; the Offering of Abel, and of Melchizedek; Moses, with the sheep of Madan; Moses on Mount Horeb; Moses in the act of taking off his sandals at the command of the Almighty, represented by a hand in the heavens; the Sacrifice of Isaac; the three Angels foretelling the birth of a child to Abraham, while Sarah stands in the doorway ridiculing the prediction; Moses on Mount Sinai; the prophets Isaiah and Jeremiah; and the four Evangelists with their emblems. The preservation of these extraordinary mosaics, still retaining the freshness of their colours amidst all the revolutions of Ravenna, is truly wonderful; they have been the admiration of every writer, and they cannot fail to afford the highest interest not merely to the Christian antiquary, but to all travellers of taste. The splendid marble columns are mostly of Greek marble, and others are considered unique. On the imposts of the arches of the right columns of this choir are two monograms of Julianus, written in one of them in the reverse. Near the high altar, on the right, are the celebrated bas-reliefs, in Greek marble, called the "Throne of Neptune," compared for their execution and design to the works of Phidias and Praxiteles. In them are seen the throne of the god, with a sea-monster extended in front of it; a winged genius holds a trident on the right, and on the left two other genii are seen bearing a large shell. The ornaments of these sculptures are pilasters of the Corinthian order, a cornice with tridents, dolphins, shells, and two sea-horses. It is recorded by M. Valery that these beautiful sculptures were mutilated "by a too scrupulous priest, who narrowly escaped under the French administration being punished for his strange crime." The *Chapel of the SS. Sacramento* contains a gilded ciborium attributed to *Michael Angelo*, and a picture of St. Benedict by *Francesco Gessi*, a pupil of Guido. The Assumption of St. Gertrude is by *Andrea Barbiani*. In the *vestibule of the Sacristy* is a superb bas-relief of Greek marble, supposed to be of the time of Claudius, representing the "Apotheosis of Augustus." It is divided into two portions: in the first is the goddess Rome, with Claudius and Julius Cæsar bearing a star on the forehead as an emblem of divinity. Livia is represented under the figure of Juno, and Augustus under that of Jupiter. The second represents a sacrifice. This precious sculpture is supposed to have been one of the decorations of a temple dedicated to Augustus. The pictures in the Sacristy are the Virgin and Child throned, with St. Sebastian and other saints, mentioned by Lanzi among the best works of *Luca Longhi*, a native artist; the Sta. Agata is by his daughter *Barbara*, and the Annunciation by his son *Francesco*; the Martyrdom of S. Erasmus is by another native painter, *Giambattista Barbiani*; the Martyrdom of St. James and St. Philip is by *Camillo Procaccini.* The *Tomb of the Exarch Isaac*, "the great ornament of Armenia," remains to be noticed. It was erected to his memory by his wife Susanna, and bears a Greek inscription recording the glory he acquired in the east and in the west, and comparing her widowhood to that of the turtle dove. The urn containing his ashes is of Greek marble, with bas-reliefs of the Adoration of the Magi, the Raising of Lazarus, and Daniel in the Lions' Den. Isaac was the 8th exarch of Ravenna, and died in the city according to Muratori, A.D. 644.

The *Basilica of S. Giovanni Evangelista* was founded in 425 by the Empress Galla Placidia, in fulfilment of a vow made in a tempest during her voyage from Constantinople to Ravenna with her children. Like the cathedral it has lost much of its ancient character by restorations, and most of its mosaics have disappeared. The church tradition relates, that not knowing with what relic to enrich the church, the empress was praying on the subject when St. John appeared to her in a vision; she threw herself at his feet for the purpose of embracing them, but the evangelist disappeared, leaving one of his sandals as a relic. This vision is represented in a bas-relief over the transom of its pointed doorway, the work probably of the twelfth century. The bas-relief is in Greek marble; the lower part shows St. John incensing the altar, with the empress embracing his feet; in the upper part she appears offering the sandal to the Saviour and St. John, while S. Barbatian and his attendants are seen on the other side. The doorway, especially in the small niches, is richly sculptured with figures of saints, and is an interesting example of the Gothic architecture of the period. The interior of the church, consisting of 3 naves supported by 24 ancient columns, contains the high altar, beneath which repose the remains of SS. Canzio, Canziano, and Canzianilla, martyrs; the ancient altar of the confessional, constructed of Greek marble, porphyry, and serpentine, the work of the fifth century; and some fragments of a mosaic, representing the storm and the vow of Galla Placidia. The vault of the second chapel is painted by *Giotto*, representing the four Evangelists with their symbols, and St. Gregory, St. Ambrose, St. Augustin, and St. Jerome. The other paintings in this ch. do not merit any particular attention; but the ancient quadrangular *Campanile*, the articulations of which are ornamented with white and green mosaics, is remarkable for its 2 bells cast by Robert of Saxony in 1208.

The *Ch. of S. Giovanni Battista*, built by Galla Placidia for her confessor St. Barbatian in 438, was consecrated by St. Peter Chrysologus, but it was almost entirely rebuilt in 1683. On the rt. of the entrance are 3 sepulchral urns or sarcophagi, the largest of which contains the ashes of Pietro Traversari, already mentioned as lord of Ravenna, who died in 1225. The marble and other columns of the interior are chiefly adapted from the ancient building; some of them, however, were found in the neighbourhood of the ch. on the supposed site of the imperial palace in which Galla Placidia resided. The ch. contains 2 paintings by *Francesco Longhi*, one representing the Virgin and Child with St. Clement and St. Jerome; the other the Virgin and Child with St. Matthew and St. Francis of Assisi.

The ancient *Ch. of San Vittore* contains a painting of St. Joseph and the infant Saviour, with S. Victor and S. Eustachius by *Filippo Pasquali* of Forlì, mentioned with praise by Lanzi.

The *Ch. of San Domenico*, a restoration of an ancient basilica founded by the exarchs, contains some fine works by *Nicolò Rondinello*, of Ravenna, a pupil of Bellini. The Virgin and Child with S. Jerome, S. Domenico, S. Joseph, and S. Francis of Assisi, the two paintings of the Annunciation, the S. Domenico and St. Peter in the choir, and the Virgin and Child, with the Magdalen and other saints, are by this master. In the chapel of the Crucifix is an ancient wooden crucifix curiously covered with fine linen in imitation of human skin, which is said to have sweated blood during the battle of Ravenna under Gaston de Foix. The 2nd chapel on the l. contains the Fifteen Mysteries of the Rosary, by *Luca Longhi:* and the 3rd chapel on the rt. has a fine picture by the same artist representing the Invention of the Cross.

The *Ch. of S. Apollinare Nuovo*, built by Theodoric in the beginning of the sixth century as the cathedral of his Arian bishops, was consecrated for Catholic worship by S. Agnello archbishop, at the close of the Gothic kingdom, under the name of *S. Martino*. It was also called *Chiesa di Cielo Aureo*, on account of its magnificent decorations. It assumed its present name in the 9th century, from the belief that the archbishops had buried the body of S. Apollinaris within its walls, in order to secure it from the attacks of the Saracens. The 24 columns of Greek marble with Gothic capitals dividing the nave from the aisles were brought from Constantinople. The walls of the nave are covered with superb mosaics, executed under the archbishop Agnello in the 6th century. On the l. is represented the city of Classe, with the sea and ships ; in the foreground 22 virgins, each holding in her hand a crown, and accompanied by the magi, in the act of presenting their offerings to the Virgin and Child sitting on a throne between angels. "This superb mosaic, the finest in the whole of Ravenna, may deserve attention on another account: the earliest monuments of Christian art give little or no countenance to Mariolatry, or the peculiar veneration to the Virgin, which has so long distinguished the Greek and Roman churches. In this mosaic, however, though the presence of the magi with offerings may seem to denote some relation to the Nativity as an historical fact, the 22 Virgins in their company, the 4 Angels as it were guard the Mother and Child, and especially the Glory round her head, exclude all but an allegorical or symbolical meaning, and lead to the conclusion that this great corruption of Christianity was established in the Church before the end of the 10th century, while the absence of similar representations in earlier works leads to an opposite inference."—*H. H.*

On the opposite side of the nave, the mosaic presents us with a picture of Ravenna at that period, in which we distinguish the Basilica of S. Vitale, and the palace of Theodoric bearing the word *Palatium* on the façade : 25 saints holding crowns and receiving the benediction of the Saviour sitting on a throne between 4 angels. The rest of these walls, as high as the gilded roof, are covered with mosaics representing the fathers of the Old and New Testaments, and various miracles of the Saviour. It is said that another mosaic, representing the emperor Justinian, exists in tolerable preservation behind the organ. In the nave is the ancient pulpit of Greek marble covered with Gothic ornaments, supported by a mass of grey granite. The altars of this ch. are rich in rare marbles and verde antique. In the last lateral chapel is preserved the ancient marble chair of the Benedictine abbots, to whom the ch. formerly belonged : it is supposed to be a work of the 10th century.

The *Ch. of S. Francesco*, supposed to have been erected in the middle of the 5th century, by St. Peter Chrysologus on the site of a temple of Neptune, has suffered from modern restorations. It has a nave and 2 aisles divided by 22 columns of white marble. In the rt. aisle is the urn containing the remains of S. Liberius, archbishop of the see, a fine work, referred to the 4th or 5th century. The chapel of the Crucifix contains 2 beautiful columns of Greek marble, decorated with capitals sculptured by *Pietro Lombardo*, by whom likewise are the rich arabesques of the frieze and pilasters. In the l. aisle is the tomb of Luffo Numai, of Forlì, secretary of Pino Ordelaffi, lord of that city, the work of *Tommaso Flamberti*. On the rt. wall of the entrance door is a sepulchral tablet with the figure in bas-relief of Ostasio da Polenta, lord of Ravenna, clothed in the robes of a Franciscan monk, and bearing the following inscription in Lombard characters : " Hic jacet magnificus Dominus Hostasius de Polenta qui ante diem felix obiens occubuit MCCCLXXXVI die xiv mensis Martii, cujus anima requiescat in pace." The Polenta family, so celebrated for their hospitality to Dante and for the fate of Francesca da Rimini, are all buried in this ch. On the l. wall of the doorway is a similar sepulchral stone, on which is sculptured the figure of Enrico Alfieri, general of the Franciscan order, who died at the age of 92, in 1405, as recorded by the inscription. He was of the Asti family, and was therefore an ancestor of the illustrious tragic poet who has given immortality to the name. We may here mention the monument called *Braccio-forte*, outside this ch., representing a dead warrior, whose name and history have not been preserved : it was highly praised by Canova.

The *Ch. of Sta. Agata*, another ancient edifice dating from the 5th century, has a nave and 2 aisles divided by 20 columns partly of granite, partly of cipolino, with others of Greek marble. The choir contains a painting of the Crucifixion, by *Francesco da Cotignola* ; and in one of the chapels of the right nave is one of *Luca Longhi's* best works, representing S. Agata, St. Catherine, and St. Cecilia. The altar of this chapel contains the bodies of S. Sergius martyr, and S. Agnello archbishop, and bears the two monograms of *Sergius Diuconus*. The very ancient pulpit is worthy of notice.

The ruined *Ch. of S. Michele in Affricisco*, built in the 6th century, now profaned by a fish market, still retains the mosaics of its tribune and its ancient campanile. The ancient mosaics, contemporaneous with the foundation of the ch., have been sold, and are now in Berlin.

The *Ch. of the Santo Spirito*, called also the ch. of *S. Teodoro*, was built in the 6th century by Theodoric, for the Arian bishops ; it assumed the name of S. Theodore after its consecration to the Catholic worship by Archbishop S. Agnello, and afterwards took the present name. Besides its rich marbles, it contains the ancient pulpit of the 6th century with Gothic sculptures.

The *Ch.*, or *Oratory of Santa Maria in Cosmedin*, near it, was the ancient Arian baptistery : its vault was decorated with mosaics in the 6th century, after it had passed to the Catholic worship. It is an octagonal building. The mosaics of the roof represent the Baptism of the Saviour in the Jordan ; the Twelve Apostles, each bearing a crown in his hand, with the exception of St. Peter, who carries the keys, and St. Paul, who bears 2 books. The large round block of Oriental granite in the centre of the floor is supposed to be the remains of the ancient baptismal vase.

The *Ch. of Santa Croce*, built by Galla Placidia in the 5th century, and consecrated by St. Peter Chrysologus, has been sadly ruined.

The *Ch. of S. Niccolò*, built by Archbishop Sergius, in 768, in fulfilment of a vow, contains numerous paintings by *Padre Cesare Pronti*, an Augustinian monk, sometimes called *P. Cesare di Ravenna*. Among these may be mentioned the St. Thomas of Villanova; the St. Nicholas; the St. Augustin, and the frescoes of the chapel; the Virgin, with St. Nicholas of Tolentino, St. Thomas of Villanova, and other saints: Sta. Monica, considered his masterpiece; and the San Francesco di Paola. The large painting of the Nativity over the entrance door, the St. Sebastian on the l. wall, and the St. Catherine on the rt., are by *Francesco da Cotignola*; the archangel Raphael is by *Girolamo Genga* of Urbino.

The *Ch. of S. Romualdo*, or *Classe*, originally belonging to the Carthusians, has become the chapel of the college of Ravenna. The cupola is painted in fresco by *Giambattista Barbiani*, who was also the painter of the S. Romualdo in the choir, and of the frescoes in the 1st chapel on the l. of the entrance. The 2nd chapel contains a picture of S. Romualdo, by *Guercino*. The 1st chapel on the rt. has a painting of S. Bartholomew and S. Severus, by *Franceschini*; and the 2nd a picture of S. Benedict, by *Carlo Cignani*. The sacristy contains 2 fine columns of oriental porphyry, found near St. Apollinare in Classe; and the celebrated picture of the Raising of Lazarus, by *Francesco da Cotignola*, highly praised by Lanzi. The frescoes of the roof are by *P. Cesare Pronti*. In the refectory is a fine fresco of the marriage at Cana, by *Luca Longhi* and his son *Francesco*; the veil thrown over the woman on the l. of the Saviour was added by his daughter *Barbara*, to satisfy the scruples, it is said, of Cardinal S. Carlo Borromeo, then legate of Ravenna. The altars of this ch. almost surpass in brilliancy and riches all the others in the city.

The *Ch. of Sta. Maria in Porto*, built of the remains of the Basilica of S. Lorenzo in Cesarea, in 1553, with a façade erected in the last century, is perhaps the finest ch. of recent date in Ravenna. It is celebrated for an image of the Virgin, sculptured in marble, in oriental costume, and in the act of praying—a very early specimen of Christian art, originally placed in the ch. of Sta. Maria in Porto Fuori, and transferred here in the sixteenth century. The 3rd chapel contains the masterpiece of *Palma Giovane*, the Martyrdom of St. Mark. The 6th chapel of the opposite aisle has a painting by *Luca Longhi*, representing the Virgin, with St. Augustin and other saints. The sacristy contains an ancient porphyry vase, beautifully worked, supposed to have been a Roman sepulchral urn. Near this ch. is

The suppressed Convent of Sta. Chiara, founded in 1250 by Chiara da Polenta, and now almost entirely ruined. In the interior, however, may still be seen some of the frescoes of *Giotto*, by whom it was originally decorated.

Mausoleum of Galla Placidia, called also the Ch. of SS. Nazario e Celso. This once magnificent sepulchre was built by the Empress Galla Placidia, the daughter of Theodosius the Great, and the mother of Valentinian, third emperor of the West, towards the end of the 5th century. It is in the form of a Latin cross, 55 Roman palms in length and 44 in breadth, and is paved with rich marbles, among which giallo antico predominates. The cupola is entirely covered with mosaics of the time of the empress, in which we see the four evangelists with their symbols, and on each wall two full-length figures of prophets. The arch over the door has a representation of the Saviour as the Good Shepherd; over the tomb of the empress is the Saviour with the gospels in his hand: and in each of the lateral arches are two stags at a fountain, surrounded by arabesques and other ornaments. The high altar in the centre of the mausoleum, composed of three grand plates of Oriental alabaster, was formerly in the ch. of St. Vitale, and is referred to the sixth century. The great attraction however is the massive sarcophagus of Greek marble, resembling a large coffer with a convex lid, which contains the ashes of Galla Placidia. It was formerly covered with silver plates; but these have disappeared, together with the other ornaments with which it was originally enriched. In the side next the wall was formerly a small aperture, through which the body of the empress was seen, sitting in a chair of cypress wood, clothed in her imperial robes. Some children having introduced a lighted candle, in 1577, the robes took fire, and the body was reduced to ashes; since that time the aperture has remained closed. On the right is another sarcophagus of Greek marble covered with Christian symbols, which contains the ashes of the Emperor Honorius, the brother of Galla Placidia. On the l. is the sarcophagus of Constantius, the Roman general, the second husband of Galla Placidia, and the father of Valentinian. On each side of the entrance door is a small sarcophagus, one containing the remains of the tutors of Valentinian, the other those of Honoria, his sister. "The subterranean mausoleum of Galla Placidia is as a monument of the dreadful catastrophes of the Lower Empire. This daughter of Theodosius, sister of Honorius, mother of Valentinian III., who was born at Constantinople, and died at Rome, was a slave twice, a queen, an empress; first the wife of the King of the Goths, Alaric's brother-in-law, who fell in love with his captive, and afterwards of one of her brother's generals, whom she was equally successful in subjecting to her will: a talented woman, but without generosity or greatness, who hastened the fall of the empire—whose ambition and vices have obscured and, as it were, polluted her misfortunes."—*Valery.*

Palace of Theodoric.—Of this magnificent palace of the Gothic king, which served as the residence of his successors, of the exarchs, and of the king of the Lombards, the only portion remaining is a high wall, in the upper part of which are encrusted eight small marble columns. At its base is a porphyry basin of large size, on which an inscription was placed in 1564, stating that it formerly contained the ashes of Theodoric, and that it was originally situated on the top of his mausoleum. Many antiquaries, however, now consider that it was a bath; and that the only argument in favour of its having been the sarcophagus of Theodoric is the inconclusive fact that it was found near his mausoleum. They urge the difficulty of placing so great a mass on the roof of the mausoleum, and contend that the late date of the inscription must be received as an additional ground for suspicion. In regard, however, to one of these objections, the size and weight of the vase, it must not be forgotten that the same machinery which raised the solid roof, calculated to weigh at least 200 tons, would be equally efficient in elevating the porphyry vase. There is a flat projection on the summit of the roof, on which tradition relates that a vase or urn containing the royal ashes originally stood. Mr. Hope, however, observes that "The porphyry receptacle, now immured in the front of the building at Ravenna, called Theodoric's palace, but more probably that of the late exarchs, supposed to have contained, on the top of Theodoric's monument, the body of that king, likewise in its form proclaims itself a *bath*." The palace was chiefly ruined by Charlemagne, who, with the consent of the Pope, carried away its ornaments and mosaics, and removed to France the equestrian statue of the king which stood in the adjoining piazza.

The Tomb of Dante.—Of all the monuments of Ravenna, there is none which excites so profound an interest as the tomb of DANTE. In spite of the bad taste of the building in which it is placed, it is impossible to approach the last resting-place of the great poet without feeling that it is one of the first monuments of Italy.

"Ungrateful Florence! Dante sleeps afar,
Like Scipio, buried by the upbraiding shore;
Thy factions, in their worse than civil war,
Proscribed the bard, whose name for evermore
Their children's children would in vain adore
With the remorse of ages; and the crown
Which Petrarch's laureate brow supremely wore,
Upon a far and foreign soil had grown,
His life, his fame, his grave, though rifled—not thine own."   *Byron.*

The remains of the poet were originally interred in the ch. of San Francisco; but on the expulsion of his patron Guido da Polenta from Ravenna, they were with difficulty protected from the persecutions of the Florentines, and from the excommunication of the Pope. Cardinal Beltramo del Poggetto ordered his bones to be burnt with his tract on "Monarchy," and they narrowly escaped the profanation of a disinterment. After the lapse of a century and a half, Bernardo Bembo, Podestà of Ravenna for the republic of Venice in 1482, and father of the cardinal, did honour to his memory by erecting a mausoleum on the present site, from the designs of Pietro Lombardo. In 1692 this building was repaired and restored at the public expense by the cardinal legate, Domenico Corsi of Florence, and rebuilt in its present form in 1780, at the cost of Cardinal Gonzaga. It is a square building, internally decorated with stucco ornaments little worthy of such a sepulchre. On the ceiling of the cupola are four medallions of Virgil, Brunetto Latini (the master of the poet), Can Grande della Scala, and Guido da Polenta, his patron. On the walls are two Latin inscriptions, one in verse, recording the foundation of Bembo, the other the dedication of Cardinal Gonzaga to the "Poetæ sui temporis primo restitutori." The sarcophagus of Greek marble which contains the ashes of the poet bears his portrait, and is surmounted by a crown of laurel with the motto *Virtuti et honori.* The inscription is said to have been written by himself. Below it, in a marble case, is a long Latin history of the tomb, to which it is not necessary to refer more particularly, as all the leading facts it records have been given above.

The feelings with which this sepulchre was visited by three of the greatest names in modern literature deserve to be mentioned. Chateaubriand is said to have knelt bareheaded at the door before he entered; Byron deposited on the tomb a copy of his works; and Alfieri prostrated himself before it, and embodied his emotions in one of the finest sonnets in the Italian language.

"O gran padre Alighier, se dal ciel miri
Me tuo discepol non indegno starmi,
Dal cor triendo profondi sospiri,
Prostrato innanzi a' tuoi funerei marmi," &c.

Lord Byron's lines commemorating the tomb of the poet and the monumental column of Gaston de Foix will scarcely fail to suggest themselves to the reader:—

"I canter by the spot each afternoon
    Where perished in his fame the hero-boy
Who lived too long for men, but died too soon
    For human vanity, the young De Foix!
A broken pillar, not uncouthly hewn,
    But which neglect is hastening to destroy,
Records Ravenna's carnage on its face,
While weeds and ordure rankle round the base.

"I pass each day where Dante's bones are laid:
    A little cupola, more neat than solemn,
Protects his dust, but reverence here is paid
    To the bard's tomb, and not the warrior's column:
The time must come, when both alike decay'd,
    The chieftain's trophy, and the poet's volume,
Will sink where lie the songs and wars of earth,
Before Pelides' death, or Homer's birth.

"With human blood that column was cemented,
    With human filth that column is defiled,
As if the peasant's coarse contempt were vented
    To show his loathing of the spot he soil'd:
Thus is the trophy used, and thus lamented
    Should ever be those blood-hounds, from whose wild
Instinct of gore and glory earth has known
Those sufferings Dante saw in hell alone."

Near the tomb of Dante is the house occupied by *Lord Byron,* whose name and memory are almost as much associated with Ravenna, as those of the great "Poet-Sire of Italy." He declared himself more attached to Ravenna than to any other place, except Greece; he praised "its delightful climate," and says he was never tired of his rides in the pine-forest; he liked Ravenna, moreover, because it was out of the beaten track of travellers, and because he found the higher classes of its society well educated and liberal beyond what was usually the case in other continental cities. He resided in it rather more than two years, "and quitted it," says the Countess Guiccioli, "with the deepest regret, and with a presentiment that his departure would be the forerunner of a thousand evils. He was continually performing generous actions: many families owed to him the few prosperous days they ever enjoyed: his arrival was spoken of as a piece of public good fortune, and his departure as a public calamity." The "Prophecy of Dante" was composed there, at the suggestion of the Countess Guiccioli; and the translation of the tale of "Francesca da Rimini" was "executed at Ravenna, where just five centuries before, and in the very house in which the unfortunate lady was born," Dante's poem had been composed." The "Morgante Maggiore," "Marino Faliero," the fifth canto of "Don Juan," "The Blues," "Sardanapalus," "The Two Foscari," "Cain," "Heaven and Earth," and the "Vision of Judgment," were also composed during his residence at

" that place
Of old renown, once in the Adrian sea,
Ravenna ! where from Dante's sacred tomb
He had so oft,'as'many a verse declares,
Drawn inspiration."   *Rogers.*

Palaces. — The *Archbishop's Palace,* near the cathedral, is one of the most interesting edifices in Ravenna to the Christian antiquary. The chapel, still used by the archbishops, is the one which was built and used by St. Peter Chrysologus in the 5th century, without the slightest alteration or change: no profaning hand has yet been laid on its altar or mosaics. The walls are covered with large plates of Greek marble, and the ceiling still retains its mosaics as fresh as when they were first made. In the middle they represent the symbols of the evangelists; and below, arranged in circles, the Saviour, the apostles, and various saints. The altar has some mosaics which belonged to the tribune of the cathedral previous to its re-erection. In one of the halls of the palace is a collection of ancient Roman and Christian inscriptions, with other fragments of antiquity. In the hall called the "Appartamento Nobile" is a bust of Cardinal Capponi by Bernini, and one of S. Apollinaris by Thorwaldsen. On the 3rd floor is the small *Archiepiscopal library,* formerly famous for its records; but most of these disappeared during

the political calamities of the city. It still, however, retains the celebrated MS. whose extraordinary size and preservation have made it known to most literary antiquaries: it is a brief of the 12th century, by which Pope Pascal II. confirmed the privileges of the archbishops. The most ancient parchments preserved in these archives date from the 5th century.

Palazzo del Governo, a building of the 17th century, recently restored, contains nothing to interest the stranger. The portico is supported by 8 granite columns, with Gothic capitals, on 4 of which is the monogram of THEODORICUS.

Palazzo Comunale has marble busts of 7 cardinal legates, and a portion of the gates of Pavia, captured from that city by the inhab. of Ravenna. The public archives formerly contained a large collection of historical documents, but most of them have disappeared.

Palazzo Cavalli, the *P. Lovatelli,* the *P. Rasponi,* the *P. Spreti,* &c., had all of them small galleries of paintings; but with few exceptions the patriotism of their noble owners induced them to transfer their collections to the Public Academy of the Fine Arts. The fine ceiling of the Pal. Giulio Rasponi, representing the death of Camilla, queen of the Volsci, by *Agricola,* is interesting because the figure of the queen is the portrait of Madame Murat, whose daughter married into the family.

The Library, Biblioteca Comunale, founded by the Abate D. Pietro Caneti of Cremona, in 1714, and subsequently enriched by private munificence and by the libraries of suppressed convents, contains upwards of 40,000 volumes, 700 manuscripts, and a large collection of first editions of the 15th century. Among its MS. collections, the most precious is the celebrated *Aristophanes* of the 10th century, long known as unique, and used by Bekker for the Invernizi edition, published at Leipzig in 1794. It is recorded of this MS. that Eugene Beauharnois wished to purchase it; but the inhab. being resolved not to lose so great a treasure, concealed the volume. A MS. of *Dante,* on vellum, with beautifu miniatures of the 14th century, is preserved here: its version is little-known. Among the *princeps* editions, which range from 1465 to 1500, are *the Decretals of Boniface VIII., on vellum, Mayence, Faust and Schoeffer,* 1465; the *Pliny the Younger, on vellum,* 2 vols. *Venice, Gio. Spira,* 1468; *The Bible, with miniatures, on kid, Venice, Janson,* 1478; the *St. Augustin, De Civitate Dei,* 1468; the *Dante of Lodovico and Alberto Piemontesi, Milan,* 1478. Among the miscellaneous collection may be noticed, the *History of the Old and New Testament, in Chinese, printed on silk,* and a series of upwards of 4000 parchments, beginning with the 11th and ending with the last century, chiefly relating to the order of the Canons Regular of the Lateran.

The *Museum,* besides a good miscellaneous collection of vases, idols, bronzes, and carved work in ivory, contains a rich cabinet of *medals,* ancient and modern. The ancient are arranged in 3 classes: 1. Medals of the free cities; 2. Consular; and 3. Imperial. In the 2nd class is one of Cicero, struck by the town of Magnesia, in Lydia: it bears on one side his profile and name in Greek characters, and on the other a hand holding a crown with a branch of laurel, an ear of corn, a bough of the vine bearing a bunch of grapes, with the inscription in Greek "Theodore of the Magnesians, near Mount Sipylus." It is supposed to be an unique example. The modern collection is also arranged in 3 classes: 1. Medals of the Popes from Gregory III.; 2. Medals of illustrious personages and of royal dynasties; 3. Coins of various Italian cities. In the 1st class is a fine medal of Benedict III., interesting because it is considered conclusive as to the fable of Pope Joan. In the 2nd class is a complete series of bronze medals of the House of Medici, 84 in number, and of the same size.

The *Academy of the Fine Arts,* an admirable institution of recent date, does honour to the patriotic and enlightened feelings of the citizens. It contains a Pinacotheca or museum of pictures, and a good collection of plaster casts of celebrated masterpieces of ancient and modern sculpture. Many of the

resident nobility, desirous of promoting the design, have removed their family collections from their palaces and deposited them in this public museum, to which all classes of students have free access. The Municipality likewise contributed the pictures in their possession; and the Archbishop Cardinal Falconieri has encouraged the institution by similar liberality and patronage. Among the works it contains may be mentioned the St. John Baptist and the St. Francis, by *Leonardo da Vinci*; head of St. Anna, *Correggio* (?); sketch of a Fury, *Michael Angelo*; the Crucifixion, *Daniele da Volterra*; St. John, *Guercino*; the Deposition, and a Portrait, *Baroccio*; the Deposition, the Nativity, *Guido*; the Virgin throned, *Sassoferrato*; Adam and Eve, the Magdalen, *Albani*; two portraits, *Tintoretto*; the Holy Family, Portrait of Charles V., the Deposition, the Nativity, Virgin and Child throned, *Luca Longhi*; a Nun, *Barbara Longhi*; the Deposition, *Vasari*; the Flight out of Egypt, *Luca Giordano*; the Virgin throned, *Francesco da Cotignola*; Descent of the Holy Spirit, *Innocenzio da Imola*; St. Jerome, *Albert Durer*; two battles, *Rubens*; the Chemist, *Gerard Dow*; a banquet, *Teniers*; landscapes, by *Vandervelde* and *Berghem.*

The *Hospital,* formerly a convent, was founded by Archbishop Codronchi at his own expense, in order to supersede the old hospital in the Via del Girotto. In the court is a cistern supposed to have been designed by Michael Angelo.

The *Theatre* was erected in 1724, by Cardinal Bentivoglio: it has 4 tiers of boxes.

The *Piazza Maggiore,* supposed to correspond with the ancient Forum Senatorium, has 2 granite columns erected by the Venetians, one of which bears the statue of S. Apollinaris by Pietro Lombardo; the other a statue of S. Vitalis by Clemente Molli, which replaced one of St. Mark by Lombardo, in 1509, when Ravenna was restored to the church. Between them is the sitting statue of Clement XII., with an inscription recording that it was erected by the "S. P. Q." of Ravenna, in gratitude for the service rendered by that pontiff in diverting the channel of the Ronco and Montone, by which the city was threatened.

The *Piazza dell' Aquila* is so called from the Tuscan column of grey granite surmounted by an eagle, bearing the arms of Cardinal Gaetani, to whose memory it was erected in 1609.

The *Piazza del Duomo* has a similar column of grey granite, surmounted with a statue of the Virgin, placed there in 1659.

The *Torre del Pubblico*, a large square leaning tower, cannot fail to attract the notice of the stranger, but nothing is known of its history or origin.

The *Five Gates* of Ravenna merit notice; the *Porta Adriana*, a handsome gateway of the Doric order, was built in 1585 by Cardinal Ferrerio, on the supposed site of the famous Porta Aurea built by Claudian and ruined by the Emperor Frederick II. The *Porta Alberoni*, formerly called P. Corsini in honour of Clement XII., was built by Cardinal Alberoni in 1739. The *Porta S. Mamante*, of the Tuscan order, so called from a neighbouring monastery dedicated to S. Mama, was built in 1612, and called P. Borghesia, in honour of Paul V. Near this, the French army of 1512 effected the breach in the walls by which they entered and sacked the city. The *Porta Nuova*, supposed to have been designed by Bernini, in the Corinthian order, occupies the site of the P. San Lorenzo, rebuilt in 1653 by Cardinal Donghi, under the name of P. Panfilia, in honour of Innocent X.; but the common name still remains. The *Porta Serrata*, so called because it was closed by the Venetians during their government of Ravenna, was re-opened by Julius II. under the name of P. Giulia, and restored in the 17th century by Cardinal Cibo under his own name; but the old title commemorative of the Venetians has survived the names both of the pope and of the legate. The *Porta Sisi*, in the Doric style, formerly called P. Ursisina, and P. di Sarsina, was rebuilt in its present form in 1568, on the site of an ancient gateway, the origin of which is unknown.

The *Fortress* of Ravenna, built by the Venetians in 1457, and then esteemed one of the strongest in Italy, supplies us in its present state of ruin with a commentary on the fall of the imperial city: it was partly demolished in 1785 to furnish materials for the Ponte Nuovo over the united stream of the Ronco and Montone, and little now remains but the foundations.

The *Port of Ravenna* is still much frequented by the trading barges of the Adriatic. The old Porto Candiano being rendered useless by the diversion of the Ronco and Montone, the *Canale Naviglio* was opened in 1737, for the purpose of effecting a direct communication with the sea at the new *Porto Corsini*. The length of this canal is about 5 miles, and a broad road has been made along its r. bank, which contributes much to the accommodation of the city. Convenient boats may always be hired here for the passage by the canals to Venice or Chioggia. (See the last Route.)

About a mile beyond the Porta Serrata is the *Mausoleum of Theodoric, king of the Goths*, now the ch. of Sta. Maria Rotonda: it was built by Theodoric himself, in the beginning of the 6th century. On the expulsion of the Arians, the zeal of the Church in promoting the Catholic worship ejected the ashes of the king as an Arian heretic, and despoiled his sepulchre of its ornaments. It is a rotunda, built of square blocks of marble, resting on a decagonal basement, each side of which has a deep recess covered with a semicircular arch formed of 11 blocks of stone notched into each other. An oblique flight of steps on each side of the front leads to the upper story; they were added to the building in 1780. The lower part of the upper story, though circular within, is decagonal externally. In one of these sides is the door: in each of the other nine is a small square recess, said to have been formerly filled with a range of columns (?). Over these is a broad circular band, above which all the rest is also circular. The vault stones of the doorway are curiously notched into each other, forming a straight arch. Above the circular band is a row of small windows, over which is a massive cornice. The roof is a solid dome of marble, 30 feet in its internal diameter, hollowed out to the depth of 10 feet; the thickness of the centre is about 4 feet, and of the edges about 2 feet 9 inches. The weight of this enormous mass is estimated at above 200 tons. On the outside are 12 large pointed projections perforated as if designed for handles: they bear the names of the 12 apostles, but it is difficult to conceive how any statues could have stood on them. The summit is flat, and upon it is supposed to have rested the porphyry vase containing the ashes of the king (?). It is now divided into two unequal portions by a large crack, produced, it is said, by lightning. The basement is filled with water, and the lower story is buried to the top of the arcades, in consequence of the raising of the soil. The interior of the building is circular, with a niche opposite the door, apparently intended for an altar.

About 3 m. from the city is the *Ch. of Sta. Maria in Porto Fuori,* built towards the end of the 11th century by B. Pietro Onesti, called *Il Peccatore,* in fulfilment of a vow to the Virgin made during a storm at sea in 1096. The l. nave on entering the ch. contains the ancient sarcophagus in which the body of the founder was deposited in 1119. The chief interest of this ch. arises from its frescoes by *Giotto,* in noticing which Lanzi justly alludes to the honour conferred upon Ravenna by the family of Polenta, in leaving behind them at their fall the memory of two such names as Dante and Giotto. It is believed that the entire ch. was covered with the frescoes of that great master; and the lateral chapels, part of the l. wall of the middle aisle, and other parts of the ch., still retain sufficient to give weight to this belief. The *Choir* is completely covered with his works; on the l. wall are the Nativity, and the Presentation of the Virgin; the rt. wall contains the Death, Assumption, and Coronation of the Virgin, and the Massacre of the Innocents. The frescoes of the tribune represent various events in the life of the Saviour; under the arches are different Fathers and Martyrs; and on the ceiling are the four Evangelists with their symbols, and four Doctors of the Church, all undoubted works of *Giotto.* The altarpiece, of the Conception, is by *Francesco Longhi.* The quadrangular tower, which is the base of the *Campanile,* is considered by local antiquaries to be the remains of the ancient *Faro* of the port, which is supposed to have been situated on this spot; from this circumstance the ch. derives the name of "*di Porto* without the walls."

Basilica of S. Apollinare in Classe.— No traveller should leave Ravenna without visiting this magnificent basilica, which is a purer specimen of Christian art than any which can be found even in Rome. It lies on the road to Rimini, and may therefore be visited in passing by persons proceeding S.; but the distance from the city (about 2 m.) will not deter the traveller interested in early Christian antiquities from devoting an hour or two to it, as a separate excursion. About ¼ m. beyond the gates of the city a Greek cross on a small fluted marble column marks the site of the splendid Basilica of S. Laurenzo in *Cesarea,* founded by Lauritius, chamberlain of the Emperor Honorius, and destroyed in 1553 to supply materials for the Ch. of Sta. Maria in Porto within the city. This act of spoliation was opposed by the citizens; but the monks to whom the basilica belonged had obtained the consent of the Pope, and the cardinal legate, Capo di Ferro, completed the work of destruction by sending all its columns excepting two, together with its precious marbles, to Rome. The ancient basilica was the last relic of the city of *Cesarea.* A short distance beyond, the united stream of the Ronco and Montone is crossed by the *Ponte Nuovo,* a bridge of 5 arches, erected while Cardinal Alberoni was legate of Romagna. The road crosses the marshy plain for about 2 m.; and about 1 m. from the pine-forest is *S. Apollinare in Classe.* This grand basilica, whose antiquities carry us back to the early ages of Christianity, was built in 534, by Julian Argentarius, on the site of a temple of Apollo, and was consecrated by the archbishop, St. Maximian, in 549. It was formerly surrounded by a quadriporticus, but the lateral portions have been destroyed. It is built of thin bricks or tiles, in the manner of some ancient Roman edifices. The architrave of the door still retains the bronze nails, used to sustain the awning on solemn festivals. The interior is divided by 24 elegant columns of green Cipolino marble into a nave and two aisles of lofty and imposing proportions. These columns, surmounted by capitals in imitation of the Corinthian order, support round-headed arches and a wall, with double semicircular windows. From the nave 12 steps lead to the altar, placed above a crypt, and to the absis, which is circular internally, and polygonal on the exterior, like that of St. John Lateran. The floor is green with damp, and many times in the year the subterranean chapel of the saint is full of water. The walls of the nave, and part of those of the aisles, are decorated with a chronological series of portraits of the bishops and archbishops of Ravenna, beginning with St. Apollinaris of Antioch, a follower of St. Peter, who suffered martyrdom under Vespasian, A.D. 74. The portraits in the nave are in mosaic, those in the aisles are painted; they come down in unbroken succession to the present archbishop, Cardinal Falconieri, who is the 126th prelate from the commencement, giving an average of 14 years to each. These mosaic portraits have a common character, and do not seem to have been executed for the archbishops successively; the earlier, of course, cannot be real portraits. The other mosaics of the nave have disappeared, and the marbles which once covered the walls of the side aisles were carried off by Sigismund Malatesta, to adorn his ch. of S. Francesco, at Rimini. In the middle of the nave is a small marble altar, dedicated to the Virgin by St. Maximian, in the 6th century. *In the l. aisle* are 4 marble sarcophagi, covered with bas-reliefs and Christian symbols, in which are buried 4 of the archbishops of Ravenna. On the wall between there is an inscription, which seems not to be older than the 18th century, beginning, OTHO III. ROM.

IMP., recording, as a proof of his remorse for the murder of Crescentius, that, "ob patrata crimina," he walked barefooted from Rome to Monte Gargano, and passed 40 days in penance in this basilica, "expiating his sins with sackcloth and voluntary scourging." *In the rt. aisle* are 4 sarcophagi, similar to those just described, and likewise containing the remains of early archbishops of the diocese. All these tombs were placed in the early ages of the Church, under the external portico, and were removed to their present places as a measure of security. A long inscription in the wall of this aisle records that the body of St. Apollinaris was formerly buried there. On each side of the grand doorway is a sarcophagus of Greek marble, larger than the preceding, but covered with similar ornaments and symbols. The high altar, beneath which rests the body of the saint, is rich in marbles and other ornaments; the baldacchino is supported by 4 columns of Oriental "bianco" and "nero antico." The *tribune* or absis, and the arch immediately in front of it, are covered with *mosaics* of the 6th century, in a fine state of preservation. The upper part represents the Transfiguration; the hand of the Almighty is seen pointing to a small figure of the Saviour introduced into the centre of a large cross, surrounded by a blue circle studded with stars. On the top of the cross are the 5 Greek letters expressing, "Jesus Christ, the Saviour, the Son of God." On the arms are the Alpha and Omega; and at the foot the words, "Salus Mundi." Outside the circle are Moses and Elijah; and below are 3 sheep, indicating the 3 apostles — Peter, James, and John. In the middle mosaic is St. Apollinaris, in archiepiscopal robes, preaching to a flock of sheep, a common symbol of a Christian congregation. Between the windows are the portraits of S. Ecclesius, S. Severus, S. Ursus, and S. Ursicinus, in pontifical robes, in the act of blessing the people. On the l. wall is represented the consecration of the ch. by St. Maximian; on his l. stand 2 priests; and on his rt. the Emperor Justinian, with his attendants, one of whom is supposed to be the founder of the ch. On the rt. wall are represented the sacrifices of Abel, Melchizedek, and Abraham. On the arch is a series of 5 mosaics; that in the middle represents the Saviour, and the symbols of the 4 evangelists; in the second are seen the cities of Bethlehem and Jerusalem, from which a number of the faithful, under the form of sheep, are issuing; in the third is a palm, as a symbol of victory; the fourth contains the archangels Michael and Gabriel; and the fifth, St. Matthew and St. Luke. Under the high altar is the ancient tomb of St. Apollinaris, now damp and green from frequent inundations. The stone book by the side of the altar is called the breviary of Gregory the Great.

The ancient town of *Classis*, of which this noble basilica is the representative, was one of the 3 districts of Ravenna in the time of Augustus. It was, as its name imports, close to the sea, now 4 m. distant, and was the station of the Roman fleet. With the exception of the present ch., the town was totally destroyed by Luitprand, king of the Lombards, in 728.

The celebrated *Pineta*, or *Pine Forest*, is approached not far beyond the basilica, and the road to Rimini skirts it as far as Cervia. This venerable forest, the most ancient perhaps in Italy, extends along the shores of the Adriatic for a distance of 25 m., from the Lamone N. of Ravenna, to Cervia on the S., and covers a flat sandy tract, varying in breadth from 1 to 3 m. It affords abundant sporting; and the produce of its cones, said to average 2000 rubbii annually, and esteemed the best in Italy, yields a considerable revenue. No forest in the world is more renowned in classical and poetical interest: it is celebrated by Dante, Boccaccio, Dryden, and Byron; it supplied Rome with timber for her fleets; and upon the masts which it produced the banner of Venice floated in the days of her supremacy. One part of the forest still retains the name of the *Vicolo de' Poeti*, from a tradition that it is the spot where Dante loved to meditate:—

" Tai, qual di ramo in ramo si raccoglie,
  Per la pineta in sul lito di Chiassi,
  Quando Eolo scirocco for disicioglie."
                          Purg. xxviii. 20.

Boccaccio made the Pineta the scene of his singular tale *Nastagio degli Onesti*; the incidents of which, ending in the amorous conversion of the ladies of Ravenna, have been made familiar to the English reader by Dryden's adoption of them in his *Theodore and Honoria*. Count Gamba relates that the first time he had a conversation with Lord Byron on the subject of religion was while riding through this forest, in 1820. "The scene," he says, "invited to religious meditation; it was a fine day in spring. 'How,' said Byron, 'raising our eyes to heaven, or directing them to the earth, can we doubt of the existence of God?—or how, turning them to what is within us, can we doubt that there is something more noble and durable than the clay of which we are formed?'" The Pineta inspired also those beautiful lines in the 3rd canto of Don Juan:—

" Sweet hour of twilight!—in the solitude
    Of the pine-forest, and the silent shore
  Which bounds Ravenna's immemorial wood,
    Rooted where once the Adrian wave flow'd
    o'er,
  To where the last Cæsarean fortress stood,
    Evergreen forest! which Boccaccio's lore
  And Dryden's lay made haunted ground to me,
  How have I loved the twilight hour and thee!

  The shrill cicalas, people of the pine,
    Making their summer lives one ceaseless
    song,
  Were the sole echoes, save my steed's and
    mine,
    And vesper bells that rose the boughs along:
  The spectre huntsman of Onesti's line,
    His hell-dogs, and their chase, and the fair
    throng
  Which learn'd from his example not to fly
  From a true lover,—shadow'd my mind's eye."

Colonna de' Francesi. About 2 m. from Ravenna, on the banks of the Ronco, is the square column or pilaster, erected in 1557 by Pietro Donato Cesi, president of Romagna, as a memorial of the battle gained by the combined army of Louis XII. and the Duke of Ferrara, over the troops of Julius II. and the King of Spain, April 11, 1512. Four inscriptions on the medallions of the pilaster, and an equal number on the 4 sides of the pedestal, record the events of that memorable day. We have already alluded to this sanguinary battle in a preceding page. Lord Byron mentions the engagement and the column in a passage quoted in the description of the tomb of Dante, and commemorates the untimely fate of the heroic Gaston de Foix, who fell in the very moment of victory. "The monument of such a terrible engagement, which left 20,000 men dead on the field, and made the Chevalier Bayard write from the spot, 'If the king has gained the battle, the poor gentlemen have truly lost it,' is little funereal or military; it is ornamented with elegant arabesques of vases, fruit, festoons, dolphins, and loaded with 8 long tautological inscriptions, and one of them is a rather ridiculous *jeu de mots.* The speech that Guicciardini makes Gaston address to the soldiers on the banks of the Ronco is one of the most lauded of those pieces, diffuse imitations of the harangues of ancient historians. Besides the illustrious captains present at this battle, such as Vittorio and Fabrizio, Colonna, the Marquis della Pallude, the celebrated engineer Pedro Navarra, taken prisoners by the French, and Anne de Montmorency, yet a youth, afterwards constable of France under 4 kings, who began his long military career amid this triumph, several persons eminent in letters were there; Leo X., then Cardinal de' Medici as papal legate to the Spaniards, was taken prisoner; Castiglione and Ariosto were present. The bard of Orlando, who has alluded to the horrible carnage he witnessed there, must have been powerfully impressed by it, to paint his battles with so much fire. In several passages of his poem Ariosto attributes the victory on this occasion to the skill and courage of the Duke of Ferrara. It has been stated that Alfonso, in reply to an observation that part of the French army was as much exposed to his artillery as the army of the allies, said to his gunners, in the heat of the conflict, 'Fire away! fear no mistake —they are all our enemies!' Leo X. redeemed the Turkish horse which he rode on that day, and used it in the ceremony of his *possesso* (taking possession of the tiara at St. John Lateran), celebrated April 11, 1513, the anniversary of the battle. He had this horse carefully tended till it died, and permitted no one to mount it."— *Valery.*

ROUTE 12 B.

BOLOGNA TO RAVENNA, BY MEDICINA AND LUGO.

A diligence runs 3 times a week from Bologna to Ravenna, returning on the alternate days; it employs 10 hours, and starts early in the morning from Bologna. Fare 16 pauls. This conveyance offers the most convenient means of visiting Ravenna.

The distance from Bologna to Medicina is about 18 English m.; the road passing through one of the richest agricultural districts of La Romagna, crossing successively the Idice, Quaderna, and Gajana streams, running towards the Po; about 10 m. beyond Medicina it passes Massa Lombarda, and, after crossing the river Santerno, falls into the road from Imola to Ravenna at Lugo (see Rte. 12).

ROUTE 13.

RAVENNA TO RIMINI.

35 m.

This is a good road, although not supplied with post-horses. It follows the coast of the Adriatic, but presents few objects of picturesque beauty, and the sea is generally concealed by banks of sand.

The first portion of the route, as far as S. Apollinare in Classe and the Pineta, has been described in the account of that magnificent basilica. After passing through the Pineta for several m., the road crosses the Savio at S. Saverio, and passes through *Cervia*, an episcopal town of 2800 souls on the Adriatic, in an unhealthy situation close to very extensive salt-works, upon which its prosperity depends. Farther S. is the town of *Cesenatico*, partly surrounded with walls, but presenting no object of any interest to detain the traveller. It is about half way between Ravenna and Rimini, and is therefore the usual resting-place of the vetturini, although the only inn in the place is detestable.

Beyond this we pass some small torrents which have been erroneously supposed to be the Rubicon. Farther on, at the distance of 9 m. from Rimini, near San Martino, we cross a wooden bridge spanning the Uso, a considerable and rapid stream descending to the sea from Sant' Arcangelo, and called by the country people on the spot *Il Rubicone.* The reasons for regarding this as the Rubicon, to the exclusion of the numerous streams whose pretensions to that honour have been advocated by former travellers, are stated at length in the next Route.

The present rte. falls into the high post-road at Celle shortly before it reaches the Marecchia, and Rimini is entered by the Bridge of Augustus.

35 m. RIMINI (Rte. 14).

ROUTE 14.

BOLOGNA TO ANCONA, BY FORLI, CESENA, RIMINI, SAN MARINO, PESARO, FANO, AND SINIGALLIA.

115 m.

	Posts.
Bologna to S. Niccolò . . .	1¼
S. Niccolò to Imola	1¼
Imola to Faenza	1
Faenza to Forlì	1
Forli to Cesena	1½
Cesena to Savignano . . .	1
Savignano to Rimini . . .	1
Rimini to La Cattolica . . .	1½
La Cattolica to Pesaro . . .	1
Pesaro to Fano	1
Fano to La Marotta . . .	1
La Marotta to Sinigallia . .	1
Sinigallia to Case Bruciate . .	1
Case Bruciate to Ancona . . .	1
	——
	15¼

The road from Bologna to Forlì follows the ancient *Via Æmilia*, which extended from Piacenza to Rimini.

It is the high post-road, and is not only perfectly level, but pursues a straight line through Imola and Faenza to the walls of Forlì. The country through which it passes is rich and highly cultivated, and is one of the most productive districts in the States of the Church.

Leaving Bologna, the road crosses the Savena and the Idice (*Idex*), and proceeds through the village of S. Lazzaro, to

1¼ S. Niccolò, a small village and post station. Between this and Imola we pass through *Castel S. Pietro,* on the Silaro (*Silarus*), a fortified town of the middle ages, whose castle was built by the Bolognese in the 13th century. It now contains, with Poggio, 5000 Inhab.

1¼ *Imola* (*Inns:* S. Marco, good: La Posta, dirty.) This ancient town occupies the site of Forum Cornelii, and is situated on the Santerno, the ancient Vatrenus. It is generally considered to have been founded by the Lombards after the decline of the Roman empire. In the middle ages its position between Bologna and Romagna made it an important acquisition in the contests for power. and it was successively held by the different chiefs who exercised such important sway in the cities of central Italy. It was united to the Church under Julius II. As Forum Cornelii, and one of the stations of the Emilian Way, it was a city of some importance; it is mentioned by Cicero, and by Martial in the following lines (iii. Ep. 3):—

> " Si veneris unde requiret,
> Æmiliæ dicos de regione viæ.
> Si quibus in terris, qua simus in urbe rogabit,
> Corneli referas me, licet, esse Foro."

The present town, which has a pop. of 15,200 souls, contains little to detain the traveller. Among its public establishments are the *Hospital,* a *Theatre,* and a small *Public Library,* containing the celebrated MS. Hebrew Bible on parchment, of the 13th century, so highly praised by Cardinal Mezzofanti, and an Arabic MS. on legislation, of the 17th century, taken by Count Sassatelli of Imola from the Turks.

The *Cathedral,* dedicated to S. Casciano, martyr, contains the bodies of that saint, and of St. Peter Chrysologus, the eloquent archbishop of Ravenna, who was born here about A.D. 400. Vassalva, the celebrated anatomist, was also born at Imola in 1666. The bishopric dates from 422, in the pontificate of Celestin I.; S. Cornelius was its first bishop. Pius VII. was bishop of Imola at the period of his elevation to the pontificate in 1800, and the reigning pontiff, Pius IX., in 1847.

The works of Innocenzio da Imola must not be looked for in this his native town; the Palazzo Publico contained 2 of his paintings, but, as Lanzi remarks, he lived almost entirely in Bologna, and probably found little patronage in the city of his birth.

[A road leads from Imola to Ravenna, through Lugo, 5 posts (Rte. 12); but travellers not desirous of visiting *Lugo* will find a shorter and excellent road from Faenza to the city of the exarchs, and through a most interesting country. See Rte. 10.]

Leaving Imola, we pass the Santerno by a handsome bridge of recent construction. Midway between it and Faenza is . *Castel Bolognese*, so called from the strong fortress built there by the Bolognese in 1380. It was surrounded with walls in 1425, and in 1434 was the scene of a decisive battle between the Florentines and the army of the Duke of Milan, which took place on the 28th of August, the Milanese being commanded by Piccinino, and the Florentines by Niccolò di Tolentino and Gattamelata. The army of the Florentines, amounting to 9000 men, was completely overthrown; Tolentino, Orsini, and Astorre Manfredi lord of Faenza, were made prisoners, together with the entire army, with the exception of 1000 horse; and what is more remarkable, only 4 were left dead on the field, and 30 wounded. Beyond Castel Bolognese, the Senio (*Sinuus*) is crossed.

1. FAENZA (*Inns:* Il Leone d'Oro, good; La Corona). This city occupies the site of the ancient *Faventia*, famous in the history of the civil wars for the victory of Sylla over the party of Carbo. It is situated on the Lamone (*Anemo*), and contains a population of 20,400 souls. It has several handsome

Cent. It.

edifices, and is built in the form of a square, divided by 4 principal streets which meet in the Piazza: it is entirely surrounded by walls. Faenza is memorable in Italian history for its capture and sack by the celebrated English condottiere, Sir John Hawkwood, of Sible Hedingham, in Essex, then in the service of the pope (Gregory XI.): he entered the town March 29, 1376, and delivered it up to a frightful military execution; 4000 persons, says Sismondi, were put to death, and their property pillaged. Among the masters under whose sovereignty Faenza figures in the middle ages, the Pagani will not fail to suggest themselves to the reader of Dante. The poet, in the beautiful passage figuring Machinardo Pagano under his armorial bearings, a lion azure on a field argent, says, in reply to the inquiry of Guido da Montefeltro,

" La città di Lamone e di Santerno
    Conduce il leoncel dal nido bianco,
    Che muta parte dalla state al verno."
                              Inf. xxvii.

The old tradition that Faenza takes its name from Phaëton is thus alluded to by an elegant modern poet:

        " Ecco l'eccelsa
    Città che prese nome di colui
    Chi si mal carreggiò la via del sole
    E cadde in Val di Po."
        Count Carlo Pepoli's Eremo, canto ii.

Faenza is supposed to have been the first Italian city in modern times where the manufacture of earthenware was introduced; whence the adoption of the name *faïence* for such pottery into the French language. The manufacture still flourishes, although it has been long surpassed by the productions of the north. Another branch of industry inherited by the inhabitants from their ancestors, and still in operation, is the spinning and weaving of silk: the art is said to have been introduced into Faenza by 2 monks on their return from India, who erected their largest spinning machine here in 1559. The enterprising citizens have added to these manufactories a large paper-mill situated about 3 m. beyond the walls.

The *Liceo*, or College, contains some

F

examples of Jacomone of Faenza; an imitator of Raphael, and the supposed painter of the cupola of S. Vitale at Ravenna.

The Cathedral, dedicated to S. Costanzo, the first bishop of the see, A.D. 313, is remarkable for the picture of the Holy Family by Innocenzio da Imola. The Capuchin Convent outside the town has a fine picture of the Virgin and St. John by Guido, which was despatched by the French to the Louvre, but was subsequently restored. Faenza has produced many native painters, whose names and works are interesting rather as supplying connecting links in the history of the Italian schools, than for any remarkable eminence as followers of the school of Raphael. Among these Lanzi mentions Jacomone, mentioned above, whom he identifies with Giacomo Bertucci. Faenza also claims the honour of being the birth-place of Torricelli, the celebrated philosopher and mathematician, and inventor of the barometer.

Among the public establishments of Faenza, the Hospital and Lunatic Asylum may engage the attention of, at least, the professional tourist.

The Palazzo Comunale was formerly the palace of the Manfredi family, lords of Faenza. Its middle window, covered with iron grating, is pointed out as the scene of one of those domestic atrocities which figure so conspicuously in the annals of Italian families during the middle ages. It recalls the fate of "Galeotto Manfredi, killed by his wife Francesca Bentivoglio, a jealous and injured Italian, who, seeing that he was getting the advantage of the 4 assassins she had concealed, leaped out of her bed, snatched up a sword and despatched him. Monti has written a fine tragedy on Galeotto Manfredi. The window of the chamber that witnessed the murder may still be seen; the marks of the blood are said to have disappeared within these few years under the Italian whitewashing. Lorenzo de' Medici subsequently interested himself in the fate of Francesca; kept imprisoned by the inhabitants of Faenza, and obtained her release."

The Zanelli Canal, so called from Signor Scipione Zanelli, by whom it was opened in 1782, connects Faenza with the Adriatic. It commences at the Porta Pia, and, after traversing Romagna for 34 m., falls into the Pò di Primaro at S. Alberto.

The country around Faenza is not to be surpassed in richness and fertility: it was praised by Pliny, Varro, and Columella, and is still the theme of every traveller.

[An excellent road leads from Faenza to Ravenna distant about 24m.; (Rte. 10), and another across the Apennines to Florence, by Marradi and Borgo San Lorenzo. Rte. 7B.]

Leaving Faenza, the Lamone is crossed, and the road proceeds along the plain, passing the Montone (Utens). This stream divides the Legation of Ravenna from that of Forlì, and after uniting with the Ronco (Bedesis) near Ravenna falls into the Adriatic soon afterwards.

1 FORLI (Inn, La Posta, good). This city, situated at the foot of the Apennines, in a pleasant and fertile plain, watered by the Ronco and Montone, is the capital of a legation comprehending 836 sq. m., and 202,500 Inhab. The city itself, by the last census, contains a population of 18,050; and, prior to 1848, was the residence of the cardinal legate. It occupies the site of Forum Livii, founded by Livius Salinator after the defeat of Asdrubal. During the middle ages it was a place of some importance as a free city, but it at length fell into the power of the Malatesta and the Ordelaffi. This illustrious family, whose name was so well known in the 14th and 15th centuries as princes of Forlì, became extinct in the person of Luigi Ordelaffi, who died in exile at Venice about 1504, after having in vain offered to sell the principality to that republic. Forlì was attached to the Church almost immediately after that event by Julius II. The Ordelaffi are mentioned by Dante, under the figure of the green lion borne on their coats of arms, in a fine passage containing an allusion to the defeat of the French army at Forlì by Guido da Montefeltro:

" La terra, che fe' già la lunga prova,
  E di Franceschi sanguinoso mucchio,
  Sotto le branche verdi si ritrova."
                        Inf. xxvii.

Forlì is a handsome and well-built city; its architecture, particularly in many of the private palaces, is imposing: the Guerini Palazzo, built after the designs of Michael Angelo, the Palazzo Comunale, and the Monte di Pietà may be especially mentioned among its best public edifices. It has a circus for the game of *pallone*, and a public garden.

The Cathedral of Santa Croce is celebrated for the chapel of the Madonna del Fuoco, the cupola of which was painted by *Carlo Cignani* after 20 years' labour. "He passed," says Lanzi, "the last years of his long life at Forlì, where he established his family, and left the grandest monument of his genius in that fine cupola, which is perhaps the most remarkable work of art which the 18th century produced. The subject, like that in the cathedral of Parma, is the Assumption of the Virgin; and here, as there, is painted a *true paradise,* which is loved the more it is contemplated. He spent 20 years on his work, visiting Ravenna from time to time to study the cupola of Guido, from which he borrowed the fine St. Michael and some other ideas. They say that they removed the scaffolding against his will, as he never made an end of retouching and finishing his work in his accustomed style of excellence." A *ciborium* in this cathedral is shown as the design of Michael Angelo, with a *reliquiary* of carved and enamelled work of the 14th century, supposed to be the work of German artists. The magnificent door of the grand entrance is ornamented in the same style as that of Rimini, with sculptures and bas-reliefs of the 15th century.

The Ch. of S. Filippo Neri contains a picture of S. Francesco di Sales, by *Carlo Maratta,* considered by Lanzi to be one of his most carefully studied works; a S. Giuseppe, by *Cignani,* and 2 fine works by *Guercino*—the Christ, and the Annunciation, in which the angel is represented as receiving the commands of the Almighty.

The *Ch. of S. Girolamo* contains the superb picture of the Conception, one of the masterpieces of *Guido;* it represents the Madonna surrounded by a cloud of angels. This ch. contains the tomb of Morgagni, the celebrated anatomist, a native of Forlì, and the mausoleum of Barbara Ordelaffi (1466). The chapel adjoining is said to be by Mantegna.

The *Ch. of S. Mercuriale,* dedicated to the first bishop of Forlì, and belonging to the monks of Vallombrosa, contains the Capella de' Ferri, which has a beautiful painting by *Innocenzio da Imola,* and is decorated with fine sculptures of 1536. The campanile is remarkable for its architecture and great height. There are also several good pictures by *Marco Palmegiani,* a native master.

The house adjoining the *Spezeria Morandi* still exhibits some traces of the extraordinary frescoes with which its exterior was adorned by the famous Melozzo da Forlì. This celebrated painter and mathematician was, as his name imports, a native of the city; and is supposed by many writers to have been a pupil of Pietro della Francesca, from whom probably his mathematical knowledge was derived. Lanzi, describing these frescoes, says he covered "the front of a *spezeria* with arabesques of the best style, and over the entrance a half-figure remarkably well painted, in the act of pounding drugs." It is much to be regretted that these remains of so interesting a master have not been more carefully preserved: they are now nearly destroyed.

Forlì has a very fine piazza, an university, and numerous wealthy palaces. On the *Palazzo Comunale* there is a fine bust by Desiderio da Settignano; and in the Casa Manzoni is a repetition of the Danzatrice of Canova. Cornelius Gallus the poet, Flavio Biondi the historian, and Morgagni the anatomist, were natives of this town.

The Citadel was founded by Cardinal Albornoz in 1361, and enlarged by the Ordelaffi and Riarii under Innocent VI.; it is now used as a prison. The ruined *Ramparts* recall many historical associations of the middle ages. In the 15th century the sovereignty of Forlì and Rimini was vested in Girolamo Riario, the nephew, or as some suspect the son, of Sixtus IV. He was one of the chief actors in the conspiracy of the Pazzi, and had married Catherine Sforza, the natural daughter of Gian Galeazzo, an alliance by which he secured the powerful protection of the house of Sforza. His enemies did not venture·to attack openly a prince so protected; but at the instigation, it is said, of Lorenzo de' Medici, the captain of his guard and 2 of his own officers stabbed him while at dinner in his palace of Forlì. The conspirators threw the body out of the window, and the populace dragged it round the walls. The insurgents, having seized his wife and children, and thrown them into prison, proceeded to demand the keys of the citadel; but the commander refused to surrender unless ordered to do so by Catherine Sforza herself. The conspirators accordingly allowed her to enter the gates, retaining her children as hostages for her return; but she had no sooner passed within the walls, than she gave orders to fire on the besiegers. When they threatened to resent this by inflicting summary vengeance on her children, she mounted the ramparts and exclaimed, "If you kill them, I have a son at Imola; I am pregnant of another, who will grow up to avenge such an execrable act." The populace, intimidated by her courage, did not execute their threat, and the house of Sforza shortly afterwards avenged the indignities she had suffered. In 1499 Catherine again defended Forlì against the combined forces of France and the Church under Cesar Borgia and Ives d'Allegre; but after an heroic struggle, in which she is described as contesting every inch of ground, retreating before her assailants from tower to tower, she was captured and sent a prisoner to the castle of St. Angelo. Machiavelli, although the counseller of the alliance with Borgia, celebrates the "magnanimous resolution" of this remarkable woman,

and her conduct is recorded with admiration by most of the contemporary historians.

[A road leads from Forlì along the l. bank of the Ronco to Ravenna, about 20 m. distant (Rte. 9); and there is an excellent road across the Apennines to Florence, Rte. 8, which is traversed by a diligence 3 times a week during the summer months.]

The road to Rimini crosses the Ronco soon after leaving Forlì, and is generally in excellent order.

Beyond Forlì is the small town of *Forlimpopoli*, with a pop. of 4900, which almost retains its ancient name of Forum Populi. It was ruined by Grimoaldo, king of the Lombards, in 700. In the neighbourhood is Bertinoro, a town of 2000 Inhab., situated on a hill, whose slopes are famous for their wines. It was one of the ancient fiefs of the Malatesta, by whom it was given to the Church. Under Alexander VI. it became the property of Cesar Borgia. At the village of *Polenta*, 3 m. farther S., originated the eminent family of Polenta at Rimini.

After passing the Adusa and Bevano torrents, the river Savio (*Sapis*) is crossed under the walls of Cesena by a fine bridge constructed of Istrian marble by Clement VIII., and lately restored.

1½ Cesena (*Inn*, Posta, called also Leone Bianco; civil people, but dirty), still retaining the name of the last town of Cisalpine Gaul on the Æmilian Way. It is a neat town of 14,500 Inhab., prettily situated in an agreeable and fertile country, on the slopes of a hill overlooking the plain, and washed by the Savio. This description of its position will not fail to recall to the Italian scholar the lines of Dante:—

" E quella, a cui il Savio bagna il fianco,
Così com' ella sie' tra il piano e il monte,
Tra tirannia si vive e stato franco "
Inf. xxvii.

The *Palazzo Pubblico* in the great piazza is a fine building, and is ornamented with a statue of Pius VI., who was a native of the town, as was also his successor Pius VII. In the interior of the palace is a remarkable picture of the Virgin and Saints, by

Francesco Francia. The *Capuchin Ch.* contains a fine work of *Guercino.* The principal object of interest in Cesena is the Library, founded by Domenico Malatesta Novello, brother of Sigismund lord of Rimini, in 1452, and composed of 4000 MSS., which, like those of the Laurentian at Florence, are chained to the desks. Many of them were executed by order of Malatesta himself. The oldest and most curious MSS. in the collection are the Etymologies of S. Isidore, of the 8th or 9th century. It was in this library that PaulusManutius shut himself up for a considerable time to collect materials for his editions. The establishment was founded by Malatesta, when that illustrious warrior returned to Cesena, severely wounded, and was bequeathed by him to the Franciscans with an annuity of 200 golden ducats.

Cesena is one of the earliest Italian bishoprics, the first bishop was St. Philemon, A.D. 92; under St. Clement I. In the turbulent pontificate of Gregory XI. the town was ferociously pillaged by the infamous cardinal legate Robert of Geneva, whom the pope sent into Italy from Avignon with a company of Breton adventurers. He entered Cesena, February 1, 1377, and ordered all the inhabitants to be massacred. Sismondi says that he was heard to call out during the fearful scene, "I will have more blood! Kill all! Blood! blood!"

About a mile from Cesena, on a commanding hill, is the handsome ch. of Santa Maria del Monte, the reputed work of Bramante, where many urns and other relics have been found. Pius VII. took the vows as a Benedictine monk in the adjoining monastery, and was long known there as the Padre Chiaramonte.

A few m. south of Cesena are the sulphur-mines. which in a great measure supply the sulphuric acid works of Bologna, and the sulphur refinery at Rimini. The sulphur is beautifully crystallised, and is imbedded in the tertiary marine marls. The mines of the whole district between Cesena and Pesaro are so rich that double the quantity now produced might easily be obtained.

2 m. after leaving Cesena, the little river Pisciatello, supposed by many to be the Rubicon, is crossed, and farther on the Rigossa; and between Cesena and Savignano by the roadside stands a column inscribed with a *Senatus-Consultum*, denouncing as sacrilegious any one who should presume to cross the Rubicon with a legion, army, or cohort. It was considered authentic by Montesquieu, but no doubt is now entertained that it is apocryphal. Beyond it the road crosses the Fiumicino, by the bridge of Savignano, a remarkable Roman work of the Consular period, built of travertine, and little noticed by travellers. The small stream which flows under it, the Fiumicino, has had almost as many believers as the Pisciatello that it is the true representative of the Rubicon, the celebrated line of separation between ancient Italy and Cisalpine Gaul. It unites with the Rugone and Pisciatello, and falls into the Adriatic about 6 m. lower down. Dr. Cramer thought that these united streams, which are here known as the Fiumicino, must be identified with the Rubicon; but we shall presently arrive at one which has much more claim than either of them to the name of Rubicon.

1 *Savignano,* a fine country town of 4000 Inhab. (*Inn,* Posta.) Savignano has been considered to mark the site of *Competum Viæ Æmiliæ;* but many antiquaries are disposed to place that ancient town at Longiano, a village a few m. farther inland, where there are ruins among which several relics confirming this opinion have been found. Some years ago Savignano was the residence of Cavaliere Borghese, the removal of whose collection of ancient coins to San Marino was considered a public loss. The town was fortified in 1361, during the pontificate of Innocent VI.

A few miles beyond this place, before arriving at the town of Sant' Arcangelo, the road crosses, by a Roman bridge, the Uso, a stream of considerable magnitude. which is called by the country people to this day *Il Rubicone.* It flows directly into the Adriatic, after a course of about 25 m. from its source between

Monte Tiffi and Sarsina, rising about midway between the Savio and the Marecchia, and running parallel to the latter river for several miles. At its mouth it is a copious stream, and, if its course be carefully examined, the traveller can hardly avoid arriving at the conclusion that it is more likely to have formed a boundary than any of the others he has passed. A further confirmatory proof is the fact that the peasantry, who can have no interest in upholding the theories of travellers, to this day give it the name of Il Rubicone. From these circumstances, and from an attentive examination of the ground, we cannot but consider this stream to be the Rubicon, and our surprise is that its claims have been so much overlooked by former tourists, who were probably misled by the inscriptions, which Gruter detected to be a fabrication of the local antiquaries. It will, perhaps, be useful to give a summary of the several streams between Cesena and Rimini which have been considered the Rubicon, in order that travellers may prosecute the investigation for themselves:—1st, the Pisciatello, rising near Monte Farnetto; 2nd, the Ragossa, near Roncofreddo; 3rd, the Fiumicino, or River of Savignano, near Sogliano; all 3 uniting into a single channel before entering the sea, where it is crossed by the road from Ravenna to Rimini; and 4th, the Uso, rising close to the Monte Tiffi, near to the Tuscan frontier, and flowing direct to the Adriatic, receiving some minor torrents in its course, and becoming an ample stream at the embouchure—course about 25 m.

We enter Rimini on this side by the noble *Bridge of Augustus,* erected over the Marecchia, the ancient Ariminus, more than 18 centuries ago, and still one of the best preserved Roman monuments in Italy. It was begun by Augustus, and finished by Tiberius; it has 5 arches, and is constructed entirely of white marble. The principal arches have a span of 27 feet, and the thickness of the piers is nearly 13 feet. The inscriptions on it and the lituus are scarcely to be traced, but a copy is preserved on a tablet under the Porta

S. Giuliano. The river at this point separates Romagna from the ancient province of Pentapolis; and the Via Æmilia from Piacenza and Bologna here joins the Via Flaminia.

1 RIMINI (*Inns:* Posta, dear, dirty, but otherwise fair; Tre Re), an interesting episcopal city of 16,600 souls, situated in a rich plain between the Marecchia and the Ausa. It occupies the site of the ancient Umbrian city of Ariminum. It became early a Roman colony, and was patronized and embellished by Cæsar, Augustus, and many of their successors. During the Lower Empire it was the most northern of the 5 cities which gave to a lieutenant of the Emperor of Constantinople the title of "Exarch of the Pentapolis." The cities governed by this exarch were Rimini, Pesaro, Fano, Sinigallia, and Ancona: his jurisdiction comprised nearly all that portion of the shores of the Adriatic embraced by the modern provinces of La Romagna and La Marca. There was another and more inland Pentapolis, from which this was often distinguished by the epithet "maritima." In 1200, when Rimini belonged to the German Empire, Otho III. sent into the Marca as his viceroy Malatesta, the ancestor of that illustrious family to which Rimini is indebted for its subsequent importance. His descendant Galeotto was made lord of Rimini by Clement VI. It passed from the Malatesta family to the Venetians by sale, and became the property of the pope after the battle of Gera d'Adda. The Malatestas often endeavoured to regain it, but the treaties of Tolentino and of Vienna confirmed it to the Church. The name of Malatesta recalls the fine passage of the Inferno, in which Dante describes the lord of Rimini as "the old mastiff:"—

"E il mastin vecchio, e il nuovo da Verucchio,
Che fecer di Montagna il mal governo,
Là dove soglion, fan dei denti succhio."
Inf. xxvii.

The famous council of 359, between the Arians and Athanasians, was held here.

The principal object of classical interest at Rimini, after the bridge, is the *Triumphal Arch of Augustus,* now the

Porta Romana, through which the post-road to Rome passes. It is one of the most remarkable monuments on the eastern coast of Italy, and, like the bridge, is built of white marble. It was erected in honour of Augustus, and commemorates the gratitude of the inhabitants for the repairing of their roads. Its architecture is simple and massive, with 2 Corinthian columns on each side; between the arch and the columns are medallions, with the heads of Neptune and Venus on one side, and of Jupiter and Minerva on the other. The pediment is proportionately small, being scarcely larger than the breadth of the arch: a great part, however, of the superstructure is evidently later than the age of Augustus; which must not be charged with these deformities.

The great attraction of the town is the *Ch. of S. Francesco,* now the cathedral. This noble edifice, originally built in the 14th century in the Italian-Gothic style, was remodelled into its present form by Sigismundo Pandolfo Malatesta, from the designs of Leon Battista Alberti, about the middle of the 15th century. It is the masterpiece of the great Florentine, and is one of the most interesting links in the history of art, since the effort here made by Alberti to conceal the Gothic, formed one of the first steps towards the revival of the classical style. The front, consisting of 4 columns and 3 arches, is unfinished, but the side is masked by a series of 7 grand and simple arches on panelled piers detached from the wall of the ch., elevated on a continued basement, and concealing without altering the Gothic windows. The whole building is covered with coats of arms of the Malatestas and their alliances; but the most striking and frequent of these ornaments are the rose and elephant, and the united ciphers of Sigismund and his wife Isotta. Under the arches above mentioned, on the side of the building, are 7 large sarcophagi in the ancient style, wherein are deposited the ashes of the great men whom Malatesta had collected around him, poets, orators, philosophers, and captains. The effect produced by these tombs is as grand as the idea of

making them an ornament to his ch. was generous and noble. The interior retains nothing more of its original architecture than the pointed arches of the nave, but it is full of interesting memorials of the Malatesta family.

The chapels are rich in bas-reliefs, many of which are of great beauty: as works of art they deserve an attentive study. The elephants of the first chapel which support the elaborately worked arch give an Oriental character to the building. Among the sarcophagi, those of Sigismund himself, of his favourite wife Isotta (dated 1450), of his brother "olim principi nunc protectori," his stepson (1468), and the illustrious females of the house "Malatestorum domûs heroidum sepulcrum," are the most remarkable; that of Sigismund is dated 1468, and is perhaps the finest in taste and execution. The bronze fruits and flowers on the columns of the chapel of the SS. Sacramento are supposed to be by Lorenzo Ghiberti (?); the 3 bas-reliefs are erroneously considered by some to be of Greek workmanship.

Many of the other churches of Rimini deserve a visit; the *Ch. of S. Giuliano* contains a fine altarpiece, representing the martyrdom of St. Julian, by *Paolo Veronese,* and a curious early picture of the life of that saint in compartments by *Lattanzio della Marca,* dated 1357. The ch. of *S. Girolamo* has a good painting of the Saint by *Guercino;* the chapel is painted by *Pronti;* and round the choir are small pictures in bistre representing the history of the Saviour. Rimini was made a bishopric A.D. 260; its first prelate is supposed to have been S. Gaudenzio. At the *Capuccini* are the reputed ruins of the amphitheatre of Publius Sempronius, but there are no good grounds for the belief.

The *Palazzo del Comune* contains a beautiful altarpiece by *Domenico Ghirlandaio,* a good picture by *Simone Cantarini,* and a most interesting early *Pieta* of *Bellini,* in distemper, painted about 1470. The *Palace of the Marchese Diottolevi* also contains several good pictures.

In the market-place is a pedestal with the following inscription, recording that it served as the *suggestum* from which Cæsar harangued his army after the passage of the Rubicon:— C. CAESAR DICT. RUBICONE SUPERATO CIVILI BEL. COMMILIT. SUOS HIC IN FORO AR. ADLOCUT. This is probably as apocryphal as the Senatus Consultum on the column at Savignano. Near this is pointed out the spot where St. Anthony preached to the people, and near the canal is a chapel where the saint is said to have preached to the fishes because the people would not listen to him. In the square of the Palazzo Pubblico may be noticed a handsome fountain and a bronze statue of Pope Paul V. (Borghese.) The ancient port of Rimini, situated at the mouth of the Marecchia, has been gradually destroyed by the sands brought down by that stream; and the marbles of the Roman harbour were appropriated by Sigismund Malatesta to the construction of his cathedral. Theodoric is said to have embarked his army in this port for the siege of Ravenna. It is now the resort of an immense number of vessels exclusively occupied in the fisheries; half the population of Rimini are said to be fishermen.

The *Castel Malatesta*, or the fortress, now mutilated and disfigured by unsightly barracks, bears the name of its founder: the rose and elephant are still traceable upon its walls.

The *Library* was founded in 1617, by Gambalunga the jurist. It contains about 23,000 volumes. With the exception of a few classical MSS., and a papyrus known by Marrini's commentary, the interest of its manuscript collection is chiefly local.

The house of *Francesca da Rimini* is identified with that occupied by Count Cisterni, formerly the Palazzo Ruffi; or rather, it is supposed to have occupied the site of the existing building. There is, perhaps, no part of the Divina Commedia so full of touching pathos and tenderness as the tale of guilty love in which Francesca reveals to Dante the secret of her soul, and of her soul's master. Its interest is increased by the recollection that Francesca was the daughter of Guido da Polenta, Lord of Ravenna, who was the friend and generous protector of

Dante in his old age. The delicacy with which she conveys in a single sentence the story of her crime is surpassed only by the passage where the poet represents the bitter weeping of the condemned shades as so far overcoming his feelings that he faints with compassion for their misery:—

" Noi leggiavamo un giorno per diletto
    Di Lancilotto, come amor lo strinse :
    Soli eravamo, e senz' alcun sospetto.
Per più fiate li occhi ci sospinse
    Quella lettura, e scolorocci 'l viso :
    Ma solo un punto fu quel, che ci vinse.
Quando leggemmo il disiato riso
    Esser basiato da cotanto amante,
    Questi, che mai da me non fia diviso,
La bocca, mi basiò tutto tremante :
    Galeotto fu il libro, e chi lo scrisse :
    Quel giorno più non vi leggemmo avante.
Mentre che lo uno spirto questo disse,
    Lo altro piangeva sì, che di pietade
    Io venni men così come io morisse,
E caddi, come corpo morto cade."

The *Villa Zollio*, 7 m. S.E., of the town, is celebrated for 15 or 16 fine works of Guercino, painted by him during frequent visits to the family of that name.

The *Castel di S. Leo*, to the westward of Rimini, is remarkable as the place where Cagliostro, the celebrated impostor, died in exile and disgrace, in 1794.

There is a bridle-road to S. Leo, and from thence by the great sanctuaries of Tuscany, Camaldoli and Vallombrosa, to Florence, by which the fishermen at times supply the Tuscan capital with the produce of the Adriatic. The mountains over which it passes are highly picturesque, and command a view of both seas.

EXCURSION TO SAN MARINO.

About 13 m. from Rimini, isolated in the heart of the Papal States, like the rock on which it stands, is SAN MARINO, the last surviving representative of the Italian republics. This miniature State, the smallest which the world has seen since the days of ancient Greece, and whose unwritten constitution has lasted for 14 centuries, has retained its independence while all the rest of the peninsula, from the spurs of the Alps to the gulf of Taranto, has been convulsed by political change. Yet, with all this, the republic, until the year 1847, made but little progress, rather studying to preserve itself unaltered by communication with its neighbours, than keeping pace with the improvements of the time. The printing press had not then found its way into its territory, mendicity was common, and a gaming table had very recently contributed its share to the public revenues. The constitution of this singular republic underwent an important change in 1847 amidst the general agitation of the Italian States. The general council, which had hitherto been composed promiscuously of 60 nobles and plebeians, elected by the people, was then transformed into a chamber of representatives. Every citizen was declared an elector, and the sittings of the chamber were ordered to be public. This chamber constitutes the legislative body. The voting is by ballot, and two-thirds are necessary to confirm all official acts. A council of 12, two-thirds of whom are changed every year, communicate between the legislative body and 2 captains — 1 appointed for the town, the other for the country—who are charged with the executive power, and are elected every 6 months. The judicial office is not confided to any citizen of the republic, but a stranger, possessing a diploma of doctor of laws, is appointed to discharge its functions, and is elected for 3 years; a physician and surgeon are also chosen from persons who are not citizens, and are elected only for 3 years. In a state so constituted, it might be expected that great simplicity of manners would prevail; hence the chief magistrate will often be found farming his own land, and the senators pruning their own vines. The territory of the republic is 17 sq. m., its population is under 7000, and its miniature army does not number more than 40 men. It has 3 castles, 4 convents, and 5 churches, 1 very recently built of hewn stone, with a handsome portico.

The city occupies the crest of the rocky mountain which forms so conspicuous an object from the high road, and contains about 700 Inhab. Only one road, that from Rimini, leads to it; although steep and rugged, it is broad and practicable for carriages.

The hamlet of *Borgo*, at the foot of the mountain, is the place where the principal inhab. reside; it contains about 500 souls. The soil of the lower grounds is fertile, and the little town of Serravalle, 9 m. from Rimini, is said to have a thriving trade with several towns in the plain. S. Marino itself, from its high situation, is exposed to a cold and variable climate, and snow frequently lies there when the lowlands enjoy a comparatively summer temperature.

The origin of the republic is as romantic as its position. According to the legend, a mason of Dalmatia, called Marino, who had embraced Christianity, after working 30 years at Rimini, withdrew to this mountain to escape the persecutions of Diocletian. Leading the life of an austere anchorite, his fame soon spread, and he obtained disciples, as well as a reputation for sanctity. The princess to whom the mountain belonged presented it to him, and instead of founding a convent, after the example of the time, he established a republic. During the middle ages the independence of the state was often threatened by the dangerous vicinity of the Malatesta. In the last century Cardinal Alberoni, then legate of Romagna, intrigued against it, and on the pretence that the government had become an oligarchy, invaded and took possession of its territory in the name of the Church. An appeal to Pope Clement XII. obtained an order that the citizens should determine their own fate; at a general assembly they unanimously voted against submission to the Church, and the papal troops were withdrawn. But the events which subsequently convulsed Europe threatened the republic more than the intrigues of the Church; and it would doubtless have long since ceased to exist except in history, if it had not been saved by the magnanimous conduct of Antonio Onofri, who deserved the title of "Father of his country," inscribed by his fellow-citizens upon his tomb. This remarkable man spent his life in its service, and by his bold and decided patriotism induced Napoleon to rescind his decree for the suppression of the republic. When summoned before the emperor, he said, "Sire, the only thing you can do for us is to leave us just where we are." In spite of all subsequent overtures, Onofri maintained so perfect a neutrality, that he was enabled to vindicate his country before the Congress of Vienna, and obtain the recognition of its independence. Unlike other republics, San Marino did not forget its debt of gratitude to the preserver of its liberties, for, besides the inscription on Onofri's tomb, a marble bust in the council chamber records his services, and their acknowledgment by the state.

There are few objects of interest to be found in San Marino, if we except the picture of the Holy Family in the council chamber, attributed to *Giulio Romano*. At Borgo there is a singular cavern, into which a strong and dangerous current of cold air perpetually rushes from the crevices of the mountain. The view from the summit of the mountain, and from various points of its declivities, is sufficient to repay a visit; on a clear day, the deep gulf of the Adriatic is traced as far as the coast of Dalmatia, and a wide prospect of the chain of Apennines is commanded, singularly in contrast with the sea view. But the great interest of San Marino in our own time, independently of its historical associations, has been derived from the Cavaliere Borghese, one of the first scholars of modern Italy, whose superb cabinet of medals, rich in consular and imperial examples, has obtained a European celebrity. This learned man is an adopted citizen, and his archæological acquirements have made a pilgrimage to San Marino a labour of love to the most eminent antiquarian travellers. His collection amounts to upwards of 40,000, and, besides the interest he finds in its arrangement, he has profited by his retirement to compose an elaborate work on the consular annals. The house in which Melchiore Delfico composed his historical memoir of San Marino is marked by an inscription expressive of the author's gratitude for the hospitality he experienced there during his exile.

———

The road from Rimini to La Cattolica runs at a short distance from the coast, and is perfectly flat. Before reaching the hamlet of S. Lorenzo it crosses the Morano, and 1 m. before la Cattolica, the Conca (the *Crustumius rapax* of Lucan).

1¼ La Cattolica, a small village of 1300 Inhab., so called from the shelter it afforded to the orthodox prelates who separated themselves from the Arian bishops at the Council of Rimini. The country between La Cattolica and Pesaro becomes more hilly—the hills being formed of tertiary marls and sandstones, is rich and scattered with numerous villas. 1 m. after leaving La Cattolica the river Tavollo is crossed near its embouchure in the Adriatic, from which the road rises in La Saligata at the base of Monte Trebbio. On a hill about 2 m. from the road on the rt. is the village of Gradara, where, in its principal ch., Santa Sofia, there is an altarpiece by Giovanni Santi, the father of Raphael. A gradual descent of 3 m. brings us to the Foglia, which is crossed close to the gates of

1 *Pesaro* (Pisaurum). *Inns*, Posta, or Villa di Parma, civil; La Pace, clean. This ancient town is pleasantly situated 1 m. from the mouth of the Foglia, the ancient Isaurus. It was one of the cities of Pentapolis, and was celebrated during many centuries for its intellectual character, and for the distinguished persons it produced. It passed to the Church in the pontificate of Urban VIII., and it shares with Urbino the honour of being the capital of a legation comprising a population of 235,400 souls, and a superficies of 1649 sq. m. Until of late years it was the residence of a legate. The population of the town amounts to 12,350 souls. It is an episcopal town, surrounded by walls and bastions, and has a small port. In the 16th century, Pesaro, as the court of the dukes della Rovere, became the rallying point of the literary men, poets, and painters of the time.

It is described in the Cortegiano of Castiglione, and is celebrated by Ariosto as the refuge of poets:—

" La feltresca corte
Ove col formator del Cortigiano
Col Bembo e gli altri sacri al divo Apollo
Facea l' esilio suo men duro e strano."
Sat. 3.

The Princess of Urbino, Lucrezia d'Este, induced Bernardo Tasso and his son to settle at Pesaro. Behind the Lunatic Asylum near the Rimini gate is the casino they inhabited, and in which Bernardo composed his Amadis. Among the eminent men whom Pesaro has produced in modern times are Perticari and Rossini. Pesaro was formerly famous for its paintings; many of these were removed to Paris, and nearly all those which were restored were taken to Rome, whence few have found their way back to their original sites.

The Cathedral contains little to interest the stranger. The ch. of *S. Fran-cesco* has a good work of *Giovanni Bellini*, the Coronation of the Virgin; on the predella and the pilasters are some beautiful little pictures by the same artist. In the ch. of *S. Domenico*, the first altar on the left has a Madonna and Saints by *Presciutti* of Fano; in the sacristy a Madonna and Child, by *Della Robbia*. In the sacristy of S. Antonio, a fine Gothic altarpiece by *Antonio da Murano*, 1464; and in that of the Annunziata an Annunciation, by some attributed to *Vittorio Carpaccio*. The ch. of the *SS. Sacramento* has a Last Supper by *Niccolò da Pesaro*. *S. Cassiano* has a fine picture of Sta. Barbara, by *Simone Cantarini. S. Giovanni de' Riformati* was built by Bartolommeo Genga, the engineer and architect to the Duke of Urbino; the altarpiece, by *Guercino*, has suffered from the carelessness of restorers.

The *Biblioteca Olivieri*, founded and bequeathed to his native town by the learned antiquary and abbé of that name, contains about 13,000 volumes, besides 600 MSS. The latter are exceedingly rich in memorials of Pesaro and of the duchy, for the most part inedited. Among other interesting MSS. may be mentioned an inedited canzone by Pandolfo Collenuccio, strangled here

in prison by Giovanni Sforza, on account of his connection with Cesar Borgia; an eclogue by Serafino d'Aquila, and various readings of the Stanze of Politian. Of Tasso some inedited letters, and also a valuable commentary on his great poem by Malatesta della Porta. His annotations on Dante, originally in the Giordani Library, were given to the poet Monti, before it was added to this library. Annexed to the library is a small museum of antiquities and coins, chiefly Roman, collected and partially illustrated by the Abbé Olivieri.

The ancient palace of the Dukes of Urbino is now the residence of the chief Pontifical authority; its grand saloon is on a scale of princely magnificence, perfectly in character with the pomp of their court. The large building opposite the palace, now converted into shops, was occupied by the pages.

Close to Pesaro is Monte S. Bartolo, the ancient Accius, so called from the Latin tragedian L. Accius, who was a native of the town, and was buried on the mountain. Near its summit, at the distance of about 2 m. from the town, is the *Imperiale*, once the favourite villa of the Dukes of Urbino, built by the Duchess Leonora Gonzaga, wife of Francesco Maria I., in order to surprise him on his return from his campaigns. It was decorated by Raffaele del Colle with frescoes now nearly ruined; on the walls of one of the courts are verses in honour of the Duke's return written by Bembo, whose residence here is celebrated by Tasso, Rime ii. 36. This once beautiful villa is described by Bernardo Tasso, who represents it as one of the most delightful spots in Italy; but it fell into decay in the last century, when it became the refuge for the Portuguese Jesuits expelled by the Marquis de Pombal. Its rich staircases and galleries, and its broad terrace, from which there is a fine view of the valley of the Foglia to its junction with the sea, shows that there was much truth in the poet's description.

In the neighbouring church of the Gerolamiti is a picture of St. Jerome attributed to *Giovanni Santi*, and from the point behind the convent may be enjoyed one of the most beautiful views in the neighbourhood.

On the road to Rimini is *La Vittoria*, another villa, which has acquired notoriety as the residence of Queen Caroline of England, while Princess of Wales; in the garden may still be seen a small monument she erected to the memory of the Princess Charlotte, and another to her brother the Duke of Brunswick, who fell at Waterloo.

The fortress of Pesaro was begun in 1474 by Costanzo Sforza, from the designs of Lauranna Dalmatino, and finished by Giovanni Sforza.

The port is formed by the *embouchure* of the Foglia: it was enlarged by Francesco Maria II. della Rovere, but has subsequently become shallow; it can contain 200 small vessels, the greatest burthen of which is 70 tons; Pius VII. contributed to its safety by the addition of a fort and small light-house in 1821. The manufacture of pottery which existed at Pesaro since the time of the Roman Emperors was revived in 1300 under Boniface VIII., and attained great perfection under the Sforzas and the Dukes of Urbino, and especially Guidobaldo II., in the middle of the 17th century.

Pesaro is famous for its figs, which have been celebrated by Tasso, Bembo, and Castiglione.

The promenade of the Belvedere San Benedetto is in a fine situation, and worthy of a visit.

[There is a direct road from Pesaro to Urbino, ascending the Foglia and the Apsa, and passing under the villages of Montecchio, Colbordolo, and Ricece. A diligence runs between the 2 towns 3 times a week. For *Urbino*, see Rte. 17.]

Leaving Pesaro, a beautiful drive, partly along the coast, brings us to

1 FANO (Pop. 9000), the ancient Fanum Fortunæ, and one of the cities of Pentapolis. (*Inns* Il Moro, clean and civil, with moderate charges; Tre Re.) Fano is a well built and agreeable town, surrounded by walls, no longer necessary for the purposes of defence, but still recalling the remembrance of its once celebrated fortress. Its situation in a fertile plain ensures it an abundant supply of fresh air; the climate is said to be extremely healthy, but cold in the winter and spring. The scenery of the neighbourhood is beautiful, and numerous excellent roads ensure facilities of communication with all the great towns. The high road passes round the walls without entering the town, so that unless the traveller be aware beforehand how many objects of interest it contains, it is very probable that he would be driven on without having an opportunity of discovering them himself.

The ancient name of the town is commemorated by a modern statue of Fortune in the middle of the graceful public fountain, which is probably the representative of one more ancient. The principal object of classical interest in Fano is the *Triumphal Arch* of white marble, erected in honour of Augustus, upon which Constantine built an attic with columns, 2 of which are still standing. On the adjoining chapel, by the side of its arabesque door-post, is carved a representation of the arch as it originally stood with the 2 inscriptions on the arch and attic. This interesting monument is the last representative of the riches and magnificence of Fano under its Roman rulers, who adorned the city with sumptuous baths and with a basilica designed by Vitruvius. The town walls were erected by Augustus, and restored by the sons of Constantine.

The *Cathedral*, dedicated to S. Fortunato, is still an interesting building, though it has suffered from modern innovations. The first object which attracts attention on its exterior are four recumbent lions, on which the columns of the Gothic portico evidently rested. On entering the church, on the lt. hand is the chapel of S. Girolamo, containing the monument of a member of the Rainalducci family, with his portrait painted on stone, said to be by *Vandyke* (?). The altar-piece of this chapel is a picture of the Crucifixion by an unknown artist. Nearly opposite to this is a chapel containing 16 frescoes by *Domenichino*: they were once among his most beautiful and expressive works; but they have been almost wholly ruined by injudicious attempts at restoration. The Annunciation, the Salutation, the Marriage of the Virgin, the Nativity, and the Presentation in the Temple, are among the finest conceptions of this master. In the chapel of the Sacristy, on the same side, is a Madonna with 2 saints in adoration by *Lodovico Caracci.* The corresponding chapel in the opposite aisle has a painting of the Fall of the Manna by an unknown artist.

The *Ch. of Sta. Maria Nuova* contains 2 excellent works by *Perugino ;* one a very beautiful picture of the Annunciation, the other in a chapel opposite to it representing the Virgin and Child —a still finer work. Above and below this painting are small pictures once ascribed to *Raphael ;* the lunette above represents a Pietà, with the Madonna, St. John, St. Nicodemus and Joseph of Arimathea; the gradino underneath has 5 compartments illustrating the life of the Virgin; both of these paintings have been erroneously attributed to Raphael; many consider the latter to be the work of *Genga.* Behind the altar is a small Madonna by *Sassoferrato,* and in the first chapel on the left on entering the ch., is the Visitation of St. Elizabeth, by the father of Raphael, *Giovanni Santi.*

The *Ch. of S. Paterniano,* dedicated to the first bishop of Fano (elected A. D. 300), is a noble edifice ; it contains the Sposalizio of *Guercino,* well known by the engraving of Volpato. In a chapel opposite to this is the Death of S. Joseph by the *Cav. d'Arpino,* and the Virgin and Child, with S. Carlo Borromeo, and S. Sebastian, by *Claudio Ridolfi,* the pupil of Baroccio. The altarpiece is by *Alessandro Viarini,* the friend of Guido; the chapel of the saint has some frescoes by *Viviani,* and three others representing events in the life of S. Paterniano by *Carlo Bonone.*

The small ch. of *S. Tommaso* has an altarpiece of the saint by *Pompeo* and *Bartolommeo Presciutti,* two native artists, in the dry style of the 14th century.

The *Ch. of S. Pietro,* another splendid building, rich in marbles, frescoes, and paintings, contains a good picture by *Guido.* It is in the Gabrielli chapel, and represents the Annunciation. On one side of the altar is a picture considered fine, representing a miracle of S. Peter by *Cantarini.* The frescoes of *Viviani* are also regarded as masterpieces of that artist.

The Ch. of *S. Agostino* contains an exquisite Guardian Angel by *Guercino.* The Ch. of *S. Filippo* has a Magdalen by the same master. In the Ch. of *S. Domenico* is a picture of St. Thomas by *Palma Vecchio. Sta. Croce,* now the hospital, has an interesting altarpiece, representing the Virgin and Child, with several saints, by *Giovanni Santi.* In the *Chiesa del Suffragio* is a St. Francis by *Muziani.* In *Sta. Teresa* there is a fine altarpiece by *Albani.* In *S. Michele,* adjoining the Arch of Augustus, is another characteristic work of the *Presciutti.* The *Capuccini* contains 2 works regarded as the masterpieces of *Mancini* and *Ceccarini.*

In the *Folfi College* is preserved the celebrated painting of David with the head of Goliath, by *Domenichino,* with copies of his frescoes in the cathedral, " His David," says Lanzi, " is an object of curiosity to all foreigners of any pretensions to taste ; it is a figure as large as life, and would alone suffice to render an artist's name immortal."

The Ch. of *S. Francesco* presents us with an interesting example of sculpture, as an addition to the catalogue of works of art already described, in the tombs of Pandolfo Malatesta and his wife. These remarkable monuments are placed under the portico of the ch. The door in the centre is extremely rich, and has a round-headed arch and pilasters, covered with arabesques and foliage. On the right of this is the tomb erected by Sigismund Pandolfo to his father Pandolfo Malatesta, in 1460. On the left is the superb sarcophagus of the wife, erected in 1398: it is ornamented with busts of saints on the front, and is placed under a rich Gothic canopy divided into three compartments, and elaborately carved. It is interesting no less as an example of art, than as a memorial of the illustrious family whose name and works are so much associated with the eastern coast of Italy.

The Theatre of Fano, recently rebuilt, was one of the most famous in Italy; it was built by a native artist, *Torelli*, and ornamented with curious paintings. The scenes were so arranged as to be really what they appeared, and not mere painted representations. They were the work of *Bibiena*.

The Port was once a well-known resort of the traders of the Adriatic: it was repaired by Paul V., in 1616, under the direction of Rinaldi, and derived from that pope the name of Porto Borghese. The commerce of the town however has declined, and the harbour is now choked up.

Clement VIII. was a native of this town. It will ever remain an honour to Fano that the first printing-press known in Europe with Arabic types was established here, in 1514, at the expense of Julius II.

[An excellent road leads from Fano to Urbino (Rte. 17), and from thence to Florence by Arezzo, or to Rome by Perugia (Rtes. 18, 21). There is also a post-road from Fano to Foligno, by the Strada del Furlo (Rte. 16)].

The road from Fano to Sinigallia, follows the shores of the Adriatic, and forms an agreeable drive.

On leaving Fano, the road crosses the celebrated Metaurus, now the Metauro or Metro, a broad and rapid stream, recalling the fate of Asdrubal:

" Quid debeas o! Roma Neronibus
    Testis Metaurum flumen, et Asdrubal
    Devictus."   *Hor.* iv. 4.

From which it follows for 8 m. the flat shore of the Adriatic to

La Marotta, a post station, close to the sea, 2 m. beyond it the Cesano, the Sena of Lucan, is crossed, near which is a road on the rt., which ascends the stream to Pergola, a town of 3000 Inhab. 10 m. distant.

1 Sinigallia (*Inn*, Locanda della Formica), the ancient Sena, known by the appellative of Gallica to distinguish it from the Etruscan Sena. It is an important episcopal town, containing a population of about 11,700 Inhab., placed in a situation peculiarly favourable to commerce at the mouth of the Misa, which nearly retains its classic name of Misus. The port, enlarged and improved by Sigismund Malatesta, affords convenient accommodation to numerous fishing and trading vessels. This ancient town of the Galli Senones was sacked by Pompey in the wars of Marius and Sylla: it became in later ages one of the cities of Pentapolis; but it suffered so much from fire and sword during the troubles of the middle ages, that the present town is almost entirely modern.

Sinigallia has acquired an infamous celebrity in history from the massacre of the confederate chiefs, or condottieri, by their ally Cesar Borgia, December 31st, 1502. Borgia, through whose services his father Alexander VI. had reduced nearly all his rebellious vassals of Romagna, found himself unexpectedly deserted by a large body of his French troops, and determined, in order to counteract the influence of this defection, to attack Sinigallia. This little principality was then governed by a daughter of Federigo duke of Urbino, brother of Guido Ubaldo, the reigning duke. On the approach of the hostile force the princess retired to Venice, leaving the town in command of the confederate captains, who refused to surrender unless Borgia invested it in person. In order to allay suspicions, Borgia dismissed a large portion of his forces, and requested the confederates to disperse their troops in the neighbouring villages, in order that his own might find quarters in the city. On the 21st December he left Fano, and arrived at Sinigallia the same night, with 2000 horse and 10,000 foot. Three of the captains, Vitellozzo Vitelli, Paolo and Francesco Orsini, went out unarmed to meet him as an ally; they were received by Borgia with courtesy, but were placed under the *surveillance* of 2 gentlemen of his suite. The fourth captain, Oliverotto, the only one who had not dispersed his troops, met Borgia near the town, and, like his companions, was also placed under surveillance. They all alighted together at the palace, and the 4 captains had no oner entered than they were arrested. Borgia immediately gave orders to attack the barracks in which the company of Oliverotto was quartered, and every man was massacred. The same evening he had Vitellozzo and Oliverotto strangled; and on the 18th of January following Paolo Orsini and his brother underwent the same fate. This atrocious perfidy, although it did not excite the wrath of a people already weary of the military tyranny of their late masters, has scarcely a parallel even in that depraved chapter of Italian history in which Alexander VI. and his family were the chief actors. It has been attributed, by Roscoe and others, to the instigation or connivance of Machiavelli; but the great Florentine has been defended by Sismondi, on the evidence which his own letters afford against such a suspicion. He considers that Roscoe's strongest argument, that Machiavelli does not indulge in any reflections on the crime, is not admissible, since he was only bound to state facts, and a diplomatic despatch is not expected to convey the expression of private feelings.

Sinigallia contains few objects of interest, and most of its pictures have disappeared. The convent appropriated to the Padri Riformati, 2 m. to the W. of the town, was built by Giovanni della Rovere and Giovanna di Montefeltro his wife, who are both buried within its church, with only a simple lapidary inscription. A small picture preserves their portraits on either side of the Madonna. A fine picture of the Madonna and 6 saints by *Perugino*, in the choir, has been lately badly injured by cleaning. Sinigallia became a bishopric in the 4th century. Its cathedral is dedicated to St. Peter. It may be considered a proof of the commercial character of the town that it contains a Jewish synagogue. Many of the houses and public edifices are well built, and the town wears an air of general neatness, expressive of life and energy on the part of its inhabitants. It is the birthplace of the present Pope, Pius IX., and of the late distinguished lady Madame Catalani.

The great modern interest of Sini-

gallia is the celebrated *Fair of St. Mary Magdalen,* tracing its remote antiquity for more than 600 years, and still preserving its freedom from customs and tribute. It was established by Sergius Count of Sinigallia in 1200, and was made free by Paul II. in 1464, a privilege which the political and domestic changes of successive ages have not affected. It commences on the 20th July, and lasts to the 8th August; during these 20 days the town is crowded with visitors from all parts of Italy, with merchants from countries beyond the Alps and from the Levant, mingling the manufactures of the N. with the rich produce of the E. There is scarcely a language of Europe which may not be heard on this occasion. The city wears the aspect of a bazaar, and as every house is converted into a shop, and every street is covered with awnings, the eastern traveller may almost imagine himself in Constantinople. It is beyond all comparison the richest and best attended fair in Italy. As the merchandise pays duty on passing out of the town, every art and device are practised to elude the vigilance of the officers of customs; and yet, in spite of much smuggling, the revenue it affords to the State is of large amount. " Every article, from costly jewellery for the noble to the coarsest wares for the peasantry, may be met in this universal emporium. Tradesmen from Venice, Geneva, Trieste, France, Germany, and the Levant display their various merchandise, not in small parcels to tempt the casual stroller, but in bales and cases, for the supply of the inland dealers. Every dialect of the Italian language, cut into by the rougher tones of the transalpine or the guttural jargon of transmarine languages, is heard, generating a Babel of sounds. On all sides are greetings of *dear friends,* who only meet once a year at the fair, yet are as loud and hearty in their salutations as though they were sworn brothers. From a semicircle of 50 miles radius (the city being upon the sea) the population pours in, with serious intentions of laying out their money to some purpose; while crowds of Roman, Tuscan, and other idlers, come to enjoy a lounge through this bazaar-city, or partake of its amusements. In the thoughts of the former the custom-house officers have a considerable place; for as all the merchandise comes in free and pays its duty upon passing the gates to enter into the country, many are the schemes and devices for escaping the vigilance of these most inconvenient and inconsiderate officials. Much that is bought is concealed in the town, so as to evade the minute domiciliary visit which closes the fair, and then is gradually conveyed home. What is in use passes of course free; hence troops of countrymen, tanned to colour of bronze, as they go out of the gates shade their delicate complexions from the sun with their new umbrellas; and young men protect themselves against the chill of Italian dog-days with well-lined and fur-collared cloaks wrapped close around them. Dropsies too look very common, and pocket handkerchiefs seem vastly like shawls. A sudden fashion seems to have come in of wearing double apparel, and many can no longer tell the time without at least 3 watches in their pockets. Yet great is the squabbling, the entreating, the bullying at the gates; and many faint just at that particular moment, and cannot recover unless they drive outside and feel the country air. In fact, it is an epoch in the year to which everything is referred: a person is said to have died or to have gone abroad before or after the last fair of Senigallia; many know only those two periods in the year."—*Cardinal Wiseman*.

The English traveller, who so often seeks in vain for fresh objects of excitement, will do well to visit the town at this period of general enjoyment: it is a scene where national character and costume may be studied more effectually than in any other place perhaps in Italy.

Leaving Sinigallia, the line of road follows close to the sea-shore as far as

1 Case Bruciate, a post station, a mile before reaching the river Esino, where it begins to turn inland.

[Before crossing the Esino, a road leading westward ascends the l. bank

of the river to *Jesi*, 21 m. from Ancona, one of the most important towns of the delegation of Ancona. It is the ancient Œsium, the Œsis of Ptolemy, a Pelasgic city, dating 15 centuries before the foundation of Rome. The great emperor Frederick II. was born here, on which account it was designated by the title of a " royal city." Its cathedral is dedicated to St. Septimius Martyr, its first bishop on the creation of the see, A.D. 308. Jesi has of late years become a manufacturing town, for which its vicinity to Ancona and its position near the Esino render it well adapted. A road leading S. through Filotrano, and crosing the Esino and Musone, falls into the high post-road from Ancona to Foligno, on the banks of the Potenza, below Macerata.] After crossing the Esino, the road passes through Torretta, the traveller having constantly in view the Promontory on which Ancona is built.

A custom-house is encountered on entering the gate of Ancona (the Porta Pia), where passports are viséed both on entering and leaving the town.

1½ ANCONA. (*Inns:* Albergo Reale; La Pace or the Posta, extremely filthy; cooking wretched; Gran Bretagna, badly situated, with dirty entrance, but clean rooms.) This ancient city still retains its Greek name, descriptive of the angular form of the Monte Comero, the Cumerium promontorium, on which the town is placed. It has the best harbour on the Italian shores of the Adriatic, and is the most important naval station in the States of the Church. The city is beautifully situated on the slopes of a natural amphitheatre, spreading between the two promontories of Monte Ciriaco and Monte Comero, the latter of which is also known by the name of Monte Guasco.

Ancona is supposed to have been founded by a Doric colony, or by the Syracusans who fled from the tyranny of Dionysius. It was a celebrated port in the time of the Romans, and was occupied by Cæsar after the passage of the Rubicon. Its importance in the time of Trajan is proved by the magnificent works undertaken by that emperor, and still remaining with scarcely any change. It was one of the cities of the Pentapolis, and during the middle ages sustained more vicissitudes than almost any other town on the coast. In 550 it was besieged by Totila, and was plundered in the same century by the Lombards, who placed over it an officer whose title (marchese) gave rise to the general name of the *March*, which the territory of Ancona still retains. After having recovered from the sack of the Saracens, it became a free city, and, in the 12th century, was one of the most important cities of the league of Lombardy. When Frederick Barbarossa, in 1173, sent Christian, archbishop of Mentz, into Italy as his representative, the warlike prelate succeeded in inducing the Ghibeline cities of Tuscany and Romagna to second the attack upon Ancona, which he commenced during the following spring. It was during the famine occasioned by this siege that the young mother, called the "heroine of Ancona," gained immortality. The detailed account of the transaction will be found at length in Sismondi, who says that, observing one day a soldier summoned to battle, but too much exhausted to proceed, this young and beautiful woman refused her breast to the child she suckled, offered it to the warrior, and sent him forth thus refreshed to shed his blood for his country. Ancona enjoyed its privileges until 1532, when it was surprised by Gonzaga, general of Clement VII., who, under the pretence of defending it against the incursions of the Turks, erected a fort and filled the city with papal troops. The first result of this measure was the overthrow of the aristocratic constitution which had prevailed for about 2 centuries; the senators or Anziani were expelled, the principal nobles were banished, and the absolute dominion of the Holy See was established beyond the power of the inhabitants to resist the encroachment. From that time it has remained attached to the States of the Church, excepting during those periods when political convulsions filled Italy with the armies of the north. In 1798 it was seized by the French, and in the following year it sustained under General Meunier the memorable siege which terminated in its surrender to the Allies, after a long and gallant resistance. Under the rule of Napoleon it was the capital of the department of the Metauro; but in 1814 it was made over to the Church by the Congress of Vienna. In 1832 it was again occupied by the French to counterbalance the Austrians in the N., and was not evacuated by them until 1838. During the revolutionary outbreak of 1849 it was besieged and bombarded for 9 or 10 days by the Austrians under Marshal Wimpffen, to whom it capitulated on the 18th June, and on the following day the forts and the port were occupied by the imperial troops in the name of the Pope, since which they have retained possession of it.

Ancona is now the capital of the Marca, and the chief city of a Delegation comprehending in extent 514 sq. m., and a population of 167,000 souls. The population of the city and its suburbs amounts to 28,000. It is divided into two portions, the Città Vecchia and the Città Nuova; the former occupies the highest ground and is inhabited by the poorer classes; the latter is situated on the lower slopes and alongside the sea. The city contains some fine buildings, but it is badly arranged, and the narrow and irregular streets have a dreary aspect; almost the only exception being the new line of houses on the Marina, begun by Pius VI.

The famous *Port*, begun by Trajan after that of Civita Vecchia, is one of the best in Italy: it was enlarged by Clement XII., who made it a free port as an encouragement to its commerce, which had declined considerably after the discovery of the passage to India by the Cape. It has 2 moles, one erected by Trajan, the other by Clement XII. The *Triumphal Arch of Trajan*, which has been pronounced the finest marble arch in the world, stands on the old mole, in singular and striking contrast to everything around it. It was formerly the entrance to the old harbour, but subsequent alterations have left it elevated above the quay, and consequently it is not now used for its original purpose. This superb monument is constructed entirely of white Grecian marble, and is a fine specimen of the Corinthian order. It was erected in honour of Trajan, A.D. 112, by Plotina his wife and Marciana his sister; it was ornamented by bronze statues, trophies, and bas-reliefs, but all these have disappeared, and its marble bas-reliefs alone remain to attest the magnificence of its decorations. The sides have two Corinthian columns elevated on their pedestals, and the attic bears an inscription recording the motives of its erection. The remarkable whiteness of the marble, the elegant proportions of the arch, and its elevated position, combine to make it one of the most imposing monuments of Roman grandeur which Italy now retains.

The *new Mole* is also decorated with a triumphal arch erected by Clement XII., from the designs of Vanvitelli, the well-known architect of the palace of Caserta. It is a fine example of the great Roman architect, but its effect, contrasted with that of the arch of Trajan, is somewhat heavy. Forsyth criticises these arches in the following passage:—"The ancient part of the mole is crowned by Trajan's arch, and the modern by a pope's. But what business has a priest with triumphal arches? And what business has any arch on a mole? Arches like these suppose a triumph, a procession, a road, the entry into a city. The mole of Trajan called for a different monument. Here an historical column like his own might have risen into a Pharos, at once to record his naval merits, to illuminate his harbour, and realise the compliment which the senate inscribed on this arch, by making the access to Italy safer for sailors."

The harbour is defended by several *forts*; one was built by Clement VII. in 1532, from the designs of Antonio Sangallo, enlarged by Gregory XIII. in 1575, and improved by the Germans and the French in later years. Near the Capuccini is another fort, restored by the French in 1832; and other strong fortifications occupy the heights of Monte Pelago and Monte Cardeto. Within the harbour, in a convenient position on its shores, is the *Lazzaretto*, built in the form of a pentagon by Clement XII. in 1732, and completed by Vanvitelli. Its domestic and sanatory arrangements are still far inferior to those of Malta, but great improvements have taken place since the establishment of the Austrian steamers between Trieste and the Levant.

The *Cathedral*, dedicated to S. Ciriaco, the first bishop of Ancona, stands on an eminence overlooking the town and harbour, and occupies the site of the ancient temple of Venus, round which the original town is supposed to have been built. This temple is mentioned by Juvenal, Sat. iv., in a passage expressive of the Greek origin of the city. The present Cathedral is an edifice of the 10th century, with the exception of the façade, which is said to be the work of Margaritone of Arezzo in the 13th century. The columns of the ancient temple have contributed to the embellishment of the Christian church; and independently of the fine prospect which its elevated position commands, its architectural and other relics will repay the trouble of the ascent. The exterior of the edifice was once ornamented with a wheel window, which is now closed up, but the Gothic doorway still remains, and is a superb example of its kind. It has 9 columns and a pointed arch, the first frieze of which has 31 busts of saints; the second has grotesque animals and other similar devices. The projecting porch is supported by 4 columns, the 2 outer resting on colossal lions of red marble; on one side of the inner vault of the porch are an angel and a winged lion, and on the other an eagle with a book and a winged bull; on the left of the porch are several bas-reliefs of saints. The interior exhibits the fine columns of the temple of Venus; the 2 naves or side aisles are ascended by steps. The cupola is octangular, and is considered by D'Agincourt as the oldest in Italy. In one of the subterranean churches is a splendid sarcophagus of Titus Gorgonius, prator of Ancona. In the other are the tombs of St. Ciriacus and 2 other saints, a copy of the Pietà of Genoa, and portraits of Pius VI. and VII. In a chapel above is a painting by *Podesti*, representing the martyrdom of S. Lorenzo; and in another, over the monument of the Villa family, is a fine portrait of a child by *Tibaldi*. The Giannelli monument is an interesting specimen of the cinque cento style: that of Lucio Basso is also worthy of examination. In addition to these objects, the ch. contains a fine repetition of the Madonna of *Sassoferrato*.

The *Ch. of S. Francescone*, now a hospital, has a very rich Gothic doorway, with a pointed arch and a projecting transom covered with heads of saints. The canopy is very elaborate, containing statues of saints in niches, surmounted by fretwork pinnacles; the arch is an imitation of an escalop shell.

S. Agostino has another rich doorway, in which Corinthian columns are introduced, exhibiting an interesting example of the transition from the Gothic to the classic style. It is the only vestige of its Gothic architecture, for the interior was entirely rebuilt by Vanvitelli. The fine picture of St. John baptizing, by *Tibaldi*, was painted for Giorgio Morato, the Armenian merchant, who first brought the artist to the city. But the principal works in the ch. are by Lilio, known as *Andrea di Ancona*, a painter of the Roman school in the last century, a pupil and imitator of Baroccio; his best production is the Madonna crowning St. Nicholas of Tolentino. The sacristy contains 14 small pictures illustrating the history of the saint by the same hand. The St. Francis praying is mentioned by Lanzi as one of the best works of *Ronoalli*.

Sta. Maria della Piazza exhibits the most curious prodigality of Gothic ornament. Its small façade has 3 parallel rows of round-headed arches, with enriched mouldings resting on low columns in imitation of the Corinthian order; the door has likewise a round-headed arch, with knotted columns. The frieze is full of birds, animals, grotesque figures and leaves; the side door is pointed and has a porch. The interior contains a picture of the Madonna going to the temple in childhood, a fine example of the Roman painter *Marco Benefial*; and a Virgin throned by Lorenzo Lotto, the Venetian painter of the 16th century.

S. Domenico was rebuilt in 1788: it contains a Crucifixion by *Titian*, and the grave of Rinaldo degli Albizzi, the rival of Cosmo de' Medici, who died here in exile in 1425. A simple inscription recording his name and the year of his death is the only monument of the great Florentine. The ch. contains also the tombs of Tarcagnota the historian, and of Marullo the poet.

S. Francesco contains 3 interesting paintings: a Madonna by *Titian*, painted in 1520; an Annunciation by *Guido*; and a Crucifixion by *Bellini*.

Sta. Pelagia contains a fine picture by *Guercino*, representing the saint and an angel; the ch. of the *Vergine della Misericordia* has a curious door, ornamented with fruits, and presenting another example of the transition period.

The *Loggia de' Mercanti*, or Exchange, is another remarkable adaptation of Gothic architecture, designed by *Tibaldi*, who covered the interior with productions of his pencil. The ornaments of its façade are most elaborate, and the arches have a Saracenic character. The bas-reliefs are said by Vasari to be the work of Mocrio. The roof is covered with the superb frescoes of *Tibaldi*, representing Hercules taming the monsters.

Near the cathedral are some remains of an ancient *Amphitheatre*, supposed to be more ancient than that of Verona.

The *Palazzo del Governo* contains a small gallery of pictures, and is the residence of the governor. The *Palazzo Ferretti* affords a fine example of the twofold powers of Tibaldi, as an architect and painter. The *Piazza di S. Domenico* has a marble statue of Clement XII., less remarkable as a work of art than as a memorial of the benefits conferred upon the city by that pontiff. The fountain called *del Calamo* is the work of *Tibaldi*.

The *Prisons* are surpassed in size only by those of Civita Vecchia and Spoleto. They will hold 450 criminals;

the number actually confined generally exceeds 400.

The Jews settled at Ancona are said to number 5000; they have a synagogue and their separate quarter, called the *ghetto*, but they are not subject to such restrictions as the Jews of Rome. It is one of the characteristics of Ancona that all religious sects enjoy complete toleration.

Ancona is the birthplace of many eminent men, among whom may be mentioned Carlo Maratta; the poets Cavallo (praised by Ariosto), Leoni, and Ferretti; the philosopher Scacchi; and Rinardini the mathematician.

"It would be ungallant," says Forsyth, "to pass through Ancona without paying homage to the multitude of fine women whom you meet there. Wherever there is wealth or even comfort in Italy, the sex runs naturally into beauty; and where should beauty be found if not here?—

"'Ante domum Veneris quam Dorica sustinet Ancon?'"

The steamers belonging to the *Lloyd's Austriaco* leave Ancona for Corfu, Patras, Syra, Athens, Smyrna, and the Levant generally every Wednesday during the summer months; and for Trieste also 4 times a month, in the afternoon, on their return from the Levant, arriving at day-break on the following morning. In winter the departures are less frequent; the outward-bound steamers touch at Molfetta, Brindisi, Corfu, and the other Ionian Islands.

The diligence from Bologna, on its way to Rome, passes through Ancona twice a week (on Mon. and Thurs.) and takes up passengers, performing the journey in 56 hours, and to Bologna in 30 hours (on Tues. and Sat.), by way of Pesaro, Rimini, and Forlì.

The mail from Ancona to Rome starts 3 times a week, performing the journey, including a halt at Foligno, in 30 hours: fare, 19¼ scudi—it takes 2 passengers only.

The traveller may proceed from Ancona direct to Naples, without passing through Rome. This route is described in the Handbook for Southern Italy. (Rte. 40.)

ROUTE 15.

ANCONA TO FOLIGNO, BY LORETO, MACERATA, TOLENTINO, AND THE PASS OF COLFIORITO.—85 m.

	Posts.
Ancona to Osimo	1½
Osimo to Loreto	1
Loreto to Recanati	0¾
Recanati to Sambucheto . . .	0¼
Sambucheto to Macerata . . .	1
Macerata to Tolentino . . .	1½
Tolentino to Valcimara . . .	1
Valcimara to Ponte della Trave .	1
Ponte della Trave to Serravalle .	1
Serravalle to Case Nuove . . .	1
Case Nuove to Foligno . . .	1
	11½

There are 2 roads from Ancona as far as Loreto: that most direct but more hilly runs nearer to the sea-coast through Camerano and Crocette; the country through which it passes is highly cultivated and pretty; it is generally followed by the vetturini. The post-road runs farther inland, and is more circuitous, passing through Osimo; on leaving Ancona it ascends the hills of Monteago, and from thence running above and parallel to the Baracola and Aspio torrents, at the end of 11 m. reaches

1½ Osimo (*Inn*, La Posta). An additional horse is required from Ancona to Osimo, but not *vice versâ*. Osimo is a small city of high antiquity, and is considered by many to have been the capital of Picenum. We easily recognise the classical Auximum in the modern name. Lucan mentions it as

"Admotæ pulsarunt Auximon alæ."

Belisarius nearly lost his life in the siege of Osimo; the arrow from its walls must have transpierced him "if the mortal stroke had not been intercepted by one of his guards, who lost in that pious office the use of his hand."— *See Gibbon*, xli. The modern town, containing 6850 Inhab., is situated in the midst of a fertile and beautiful country, and, from its great elevation

(805 ft.), in a position of considerable strength. The cathedral is dedicated to St. Tecla: it is a place of some sanctity as containing the body of S. Giuseppe di Copertino. In the Casa Galli, *Roncalli* painted a fresco of the Judgment of Solomon, considered by Lanzi to be his best performance of that class; and in the Church of Sta. Palazia a picture of that saint, also pronounced by the same authority to be one of his finest works. The Palazzo Pubblico has a small museum of ancient statues and inscriptions found among the ruins of the Roman city. Leaving Osimo, the road turns again towards the coast along a ridge of hills on the l. side of the Musone, and passing by Castelfidardo, soon after which that river is crossed, and a steep ascent leads to

1 LORETO (*Inns*, La Campana; La Posta; Gemelli's Hotel is said to be very clean and reasonable, with a civil landlord). This small city, whose entire circuit may be made in less than half an hour, has obtained a high celebrity as a religious sanctuary. For upwards of 5 centuries Loreto has been the great place of pilgrimage of the Roman Catholic Church, and the most pious pontiffs and the most ambitious monarchs have swelled the crowd of votaries whom its fame and sanctity have drawn together from the remotest parts of the Christian world. The original name of the town was the Villa di Sta. Maria; it was afterwards called the Castello di Sta. Maria; and the present name is derived either from a grove of laurels in which the Santa Casa is said to have rested, or from the person to whom the grove belonged. The foundation dates from the 10th December, 1294, in the pontificate of Celestin V., when the Santa Casa arrived from Nazareth. The tradition of the Church relates that this sacred house was the birthplace of the Virgin, the scene of the Annunciation and Incarnation, as well as the place where the Holy Family found shelter after the flight out of Egypt. The house was held in extraordinary veneration throughout Palestine after the pilgrimage of the Empress Helena, who built over it a magnificent temple

bearing the inscription " Hæc est ara, in qua primo jactum est humanæ salutis fundamentum." The fame of the sanctuary drew many of the early fathers of the Church into Palestine; among other celebrated pilgrims was St. Louis of France. The subsequent inroads of the Saracens into the Holy Land led to the destruction of the basilica which Helena had erected; and the legend goes on to state that by a miracle the house was conveyed by angels from Nazareth to the coast of Dalmatia, where it was deposited at a place called Kaunizza, between Tersatto and Fiume. This occurrence is placed by the tradition in 1291, during the pontificate of Nicholas IV. In 1294 it is said to have been suddenly transported in the night to a grove near Loreto; and according to the legend the Virgin appeared in a vision to St. Nicholas of Tolentino, to announce its arrival to the faithful. After 3 times changing its position, the Santa Casa at length fixed itself, in 1295, on the spot it now occupies. The concourse of pilgrims soon created the necessity for means of accommodation, and by the pious zeal of the inhabitants of Recanati the foundations of the present town were speedily laid. Loreto became a city in 1586, when Sixtus V. surrounded it with walls, to resist the attacks of Turkish pirates, who were tempted by the known riches of the sanctuary to make frequent descents upon the coast.

The city, containing a population of 9700, is built on a hill, about 3 m. from the sea, commanding an extensive prospect over the surrounding country, and visible to the mariner for a distance of many leagues from the coast. It may be said to be composed of one long and narrow street, filled with shops for the sale of crowns, medals, and pictures of the "Madonna di Loreto;" a trade which is said to produce an annual return of from 80,000 to 100,000 scudi. On first entering the town the traveller is almost led to imagine that it is peopled with beggars, for he is at once beset with appeals to his charity and piety,— a singular contrast to a shrine rich in gold and diamonds: but it is remarkable that there is no poverty so apparent as that met with in the great sanctuaries of Italy.

The piazza in which the church is situated is occupied on one side by the convent of Jesuits, and on the other by the noble palace of the governor, erected from the designs of Bramante. In the middle is the fine bronze statue of Sixtus V., representing him seated and giving his benediction: it is the work of *Calcagni* of Recanati, pupil of Girolamo Lombardo of Siena (1589).

The *Ch.* called the *Chiesa della Santa Casa* occupies the 3rd side of the square. Its façade was built by Sixtus V. Over the grand door is the full length bronze statue of the Virgin and Child by *Girolamo Lombardo*. The principal ornaments of the exterior are the 3 superb bronze doors, inferior only to those of John of Bologna in the Duomo of Pisa. The central one was cast by the four sons of Girolamo Lombardo, in the 16th century. It is divided into compartments, containing bas-reliefs illustrating events in the history of the Old Testament, from the creation to the flight of Cain, with symbolical representations of the progress and triumphs of the Church. The left-hand door was cast by *Tiburzio Verzelli*, of Camerino, also a pupil of the elder Lombardo. It represents, amidst the richest arabesques and figures of prophets and sibyls, various events in the Old and New Testaments, so arranged as to make every symbol of the old law a figure of the new. The door on the rt. is the work of *Calcagni*, assisted by Jacometti and Sebastiani, also natives of Recanati. It represents, in the same manner as the preceding, different events of both Testaments. These fine works were finished during the pontificate of Paul V. The campanile was designed by Vanvitelli, and finished in that of Benedict XIV. It is of great height, and exhibits a combination of the four orders. It is surmounted by an octagonal pyramid, and contains a bell said to weigh 22,000 lbs., cast by Bernardino da Rimini in 1516, at the expense of Leo X.

On entering the ch., the vault of the middle aisle presents various paintings of the prophets in chiaroscuro by *Luca*

Signorelli; the last 3 towards the arch above the high altar are the work of *Cristofano Roncalli*.

The great attraction of the ch. is the *Santa Casa*, and the marble casing in which it is enclosed. The Santa Casa is a small brick house, 13½ Eng. feet in height, 27½ in length, and 12½ in breadth. It has a door in the N. side, and a window on the W.; its construction is of the rudest kind, and its general form is that of the humblest dwelling. Over the window is pointed out the ancient cross, and from the vault of the outer case are suspended the 2 bells said to have belonged to the house itself. The original floor is entirely wanting, having been lost, it is said, during the miraculous passage from Nazareth; the present floor is composed of squares of white and red marble. In a niche above the fireplace is the celebrated statue of the Virgin, reputed to be sculptured by St. Luke. It is said to be of the cedar wood of Lebanon, and is quite black with age. The height of the Virgin is 33½ inches, that of the Child is 14. The figures both of the Virgin and Child are literally resplendent with jewels, the effect of which is increased by the light of the silver lamps which are constantly burning before the shrine. It would be tedious to attempt the enumeration of the various relics and treasures contained in the Santa Casa; among the former are 2 pots of terra cotta, said to have belonged to the Holy Family: they were covered with gold plates previous to the French invasion, but only one now retains them. On the southern wall, fixed with iron cramps, is a stone of the Santa Casa, taken away by the Bishop of Coimbra in the time of Paul III., and restored in consequence of the loss of health he suffered while it remained in his possession. On the same wall is another singular offering, a cannon-ball consecrated to the Virgin by the warlike Julius II., in remembrance of his preservation at the siege of Mirandola, in 1505. Hompesch, the grand master of the Knights of Malta, and the family of Plater of Wilna, so well known in the history of the Polish struggle for independence, are also remarkable for their presents. In less than a year after the short-lived peace of Tolentino the French took Loreto, sacked the town and sanctuary, and carried the statue of the Virgin to Paris. It is recorded that the conquerors deposited the statue in the cabinet of medals in the great library of Paris, where it was placed immediately over a mummy and exhibited to the public as one of the curiosities of that scientific collection! On its restoration in 1801, the papal commissioner refused to have it invoiced, lest it might derogate from the peculiar sanctity which had marked its previous wanderings.

The *Marble Casing* which encloses the Santa Casa is one of the most remarkable monuments of the best times of art. The design was by Bramante, and the sculptures by Sansovino, Girolamo Lombardo, Bandinelli, Giovanni da Bologna, Guglielmo della Porta, Raffaele da Montelupo Sangallo, Tribolo, Cioli, and other eminent artists of the period. The materials for this great work were prepared in 1510 under Julius II., the work was begun under Leo X., continued under Clement VII, and finished in the pontificate of Paul III. It has 4 fronts of white marble covered with sculptures in relief.

1. *The Western front* presents us with the Annunciation by *Sansovino*, in which the Angel Gabriel, kneeling in the air, surrounded by a crowd of angels, announces to the Virgin the object of his mission. The details of this wonderful work, called by Vasari an *opera divina*, are beyond description: the figure of Gabriel seems perfectly celestial, and the expression of the angels is of extraordinary delicacy and beauty. The vase of flowers introduced in the foreground is much admired. The smaller tablets, representing the Visitation, and St. Joseph and the Virgin in Bethlehem, are by *Sangallo*. At the angles are figures of the prophets Jeremiah and Ezekiel; the former is an expressive work of *Sansovino*, the latter is by his pupil *Girolamo Lombardo*. In the niches above are the Libian and Persian sibyls by *Guglielmo della Porta*.

2. *The Southern front* has another grand production of *Sansovino*, the Nativity, in which the shepherds, the angels and the other figures are represented with extraordinary minuteness and truth. The David with the head of Goliath at his feet, and the prophet Malachi, are by *Girolamo Lombardo*; the Cumæan and Delphic sibyls are by *Guglielmo della Porta*. The Adoration of the Magi was begun by *Sansovino*, and finished by *Raffaele da Montelupo* and *Girolamo Lombardo*. The figures of boys over the first door are attributed to *Simone Mosca*, and those over the Porta del Santo Camino are by *Simone Cioli*.

3. *The Eastern front* has the fine bas-relief by *Niccolò Tribolo*, representing the arrival of the Santa Casa at Loreto, and the effect of its sudden appearance on the people. The attack of the robbers in the wood, the surprise of the countryman, and the peasant whistling to his loaded horse, are marvellous examples of the powers of art. The bas-relief above represents the death of the Virgin and her burial by the apostles. The 4 angels in the clouds and the party of Jews endeavouring to steal the body are full of expression. It was begun by *Tribolo* and finished by *Varignano* of Bologna. The prophet Balaam is supposed to be the work of *Fra Aurelio*, brother of Girolamo Lombardo, The Moses is by *Della Porta*, as are also the Samian and Cumæan sibyls.

4. *The Northern front* is ornamented with a bas-relief representing the Nativity of the Virgin, begun by *Sansovino*, continued by *Baccio Bandinelli*, and finished by *Raffaele da Montelupo*. The figures introduced into the composition express the 7 virtues of the Virgin,—innocence, fidelity, humility, charity, obedience, modesty, and love of retirement. The fine bas-relief of the Sposalizio, begun by *Sansovino* and continued by *Raffaele da Montelupo*, has a remarkable group of figures introduced by *Niccolò Tribolo*; the most striking of these figures is the man in a passion breaking a withered bough. The prophet Daniel is by *Fra Aurelio Lombardo*; the prophet Amos, with the shepherd's staff in his hand and his dog at his feet,

is by *Girolamo Lombardo*, his brother. The Phrygian sibyl and the sibyl of Tivoli are by *Guglielmo della Porta*. The boys over the door are attributed to *Simone Mosca* and *Simone Cioli*. These sculptures, with the ornaments on the frieze and the festoons between the columns by *Mosca*, complete the catalogue of bas-reliefs which piety and art have lavished on the external casing of the Santa Casa.

This magnificent work, which is a perfect museum of sculpture, is said to have cost 50,000 Roman scudi, independently of the statues, the cost of the marble, and the wages of the workmen, which amounted to 10,000 scudi more. This expense would have been greater if many of the artists and workmen had not given their services gratuitously.

The next object which attracts attention is the *Baptistery*, a superb work in bronze, cast by *Tiburzio Verzelli* and *Giobattista Vitali*. It is covered with bas-reliefs relating to the sacrament of baptism, and is surmounted by the figure of St. John baptising the Saviour. Among these bas-reliefs may be mentioned St. John baptising in the Jordan, the Circumcision, Naaman cured of his leprosy, Christ curing the blind, St. Philip and the Eunuch, &c. The 4 female figures at the angles of the vase illustrate the history of the Santa Casa, under the symbols of Faith, Hope, Charity, and Perseverance.

The *chapels* of this nave are mostly ornamented with mosaics from the paintings of the great masters. Among these are the S. Francesco d'Assisi of Domenichino, and the Archangel Michael of Guido, from the celebrated picture in the Capuccini at Rome. In the last chapel is a mosaic copy of the Last Supper, by Simon Vouet, the original of which is in the palace of the governor.

In the opposite nave, the 1st chapel contains the fine bas-relief of the Deposition in bronze, called also the Pietà, by *Calcagni*, and 4 bronze female portraits of the families of Massilla and Rogati, to whom the chapel belongs, by the same artist. Several of the other chapels, like those of the opposite side, are ornamented with mosaics, among which are the Conception and the Sposalizio, by Carlo Maratta; in the chapel containing these are 2 frescoes representing the Sposalizio, and the Presentation at the Temple by *Lombardelli*.

In the 1st chapel of the *left cross aisle* is the copy in mosaic of a painting by Angelica Kauffmann; the 2nd has some paintings by *Lorenzo Lotto*; and the 3rd, called the Annunziata del Duca, from having been erected by Francesco Maria II. duke of Urbino, contains a mosaic of the Annunciation of Baroccio, copied from the picture in the Vatican. The frescoes of the chapel were painted by *Federigo Zuccari* in 1583. The rich arabesques, illustrative of the origin of the house of Rovere, are fine specimens of art. The *Sagrestia della Cura* is painted in fresco by *Luca Signorelli*; the arabesques and other sculptures of the presses or *Armadj*, and the intaglio of the *lavamano*, are believed to be the work of *Benedetto da Majano*, the celebrated Florentine sculptor of the 16th century. The large oil painting of St. Louis of France is by *Charles le Brun*. The bronze kneeling figure of Cardinal Gaetani is the work of *Calcagni*, assisted by Jacometti. In the upper part of this cross aisle the 1st chapel contains the mosaic copy of the Nativity of the Virgin by Annibale Caracci, reputed the finest work of its class in the ch. The 2nd, called the chapel della Marca, contains a fresco supposed to be by *Pietro da Cortona*, representing Godfrey in arms and Tancred wounded at the siege of Jerusalem: it has also the tomb of Cardinal Visconti. The 3rd chapel is ornamented with a mosaic copy of the celebrated picture of the Assumption of the Virgin by Fra Bartolommeo. The paintings on the vault representing the Nativity, the Circumcision, the Transfiguration, the Preaching of St. John the Baptist, and his Martyrdom, are by *Pellegrino Tibaldi*. Over the door of the *Sacristy of the Chapter* is the figure of St. Luke in glazed terra cotta; and over that of the other sacristy is the figure of St. Matthew in the same material, both interesting works of *Luca della Robbia.*

In the *right side aisle*, the 1st chapel has a mosaic copy of the Visitation by Baroccio; its paintings are by *Muziano.* The 2nd, called the Rosario, is painted by *Gasparini* of Macerata; and the 3rd, originally called the chapel of the Conception, is said to be the work of *Lombardelli.* Passing onwards, we reach the *Treasury and its Chapel.* The beautiful picture above the *lavamano* in the hall, representing a pious lady instructing female children, is by *Guido.* The chiaroscuro on the right of the entrance, protected by a glass covering, is attributed to *Tintoretto;* the Madonna and Child, also protected by glass, is a copy of Raphael, probably by *Garofalo;* there is also another Madonna and Child, by *Andrea del Sarto;* and a Holy Family on wood, variously attributed to *Schidone* or *Correggio.* The Christ at the column is supposed by some to be by Tiarini, and by others by *Gherardo della Notte.* The *Chapel* of the Treasury is remarkable for the frescoes of its roof, representing the history of the Virgin, interspersed with full-length figures of prophets and sibyls by *Cristofano Roncalli.* The Treasury, previous to the French invasion, contained the richest collection of costly offerings which the piety, the policy, and the vanity of the world had ever brought together. Sovereign princes, pontiffs, prelates of the church, and the rank and beauty of Christendom had munificently contributed to swell its treasures; but the calamities which the Papal States sustained in their unequal struggle with France compelled Pius VI. to despoil it of its riches, in order to pay the sum demanded by the provisions of the treaty of Tolentino in 1797. At the restoration of peace, the zeal of the faithful endeavoured to compensate for these losses, and the Treasury is now well filled with the results of their devotion. The catalogue of offerings exhibits a curious collection of names; those of Murat, Eugène Beauharnois, and the queen of Joseph Buonaparte, are read side by side with the titles of the dynastic princes of Austria and

Cent. It.

Sardinia; many are those of illustrious and noble houses in Italy, France, Poland, Russia, and Spain: and among the multifarious assemblage of offerings may be found the wedding dress of the King of Saxony! The chalice presented by Pius VII., and used by that pontiff in the celebration of the mass, records his gratitude for his restoration to the Holy See after his long detention in France.

The octagonal cupola of the ch., begun by Giuliano da Majano, was strengthened at its base and nearly rebuilt by Antonio Sangallo. The skill and judgment with which he accomplished this difficult task have received the praises of Vasari. The interior is painted throughout by *Roncalli*, assisted by *Jacometti* and *Pietro Lombardo.* It is considered the masterpiece of Roncalli, and it is recorded that his success so exasperated Caravaggio that he employed a Sicilian bravo to disfigure his face.

The magnificent Palace of the Governor, or the *Palazzo Apostolico*, an edifice worthy of the capital, was begun in 1510 by Julius II., from the designs of Bramante. It forms 2 wings composing the half of a parallelogram, and is constructed with 2 grand loggie with round-headed arches, the lower of which is of the Doric, and the upper of the Ionic order. The former of these loggie affords accommodation to the canons of the Ch.; the latter is inhabited by the bishop and governor, and contains the noble room called the "Apartment of the Princes," now used as a picture gallery. The most remarkable works in this collection are the Woman taken in Adultery, by *Titian*, treated in a very different manner from his other celebrated picture of the same subject in St. Afra at Brescia; the Last Supper by *Simon Vouet*, the original of the mosaic in the ch.; the Sta. Chiara of *Schidone;* the Deposition by *Guercino;* and the fine painting of the Nativity of the Virgin by *Annibale Caracci.* In the bedchamber adjoining is a small Nativity painted on slate by *Gherardo della Notte*, and another of the same

G

subject on copper by *Correggio.* In another apartment are 9 tapestries presented to the Santa Casa by Cardinal Sforza Pallavicini, representing various subjects of the Gospel history, and erroneously supposed to be after designs by Raphael.

The *Spezieria* is celebrated for its 380 apothecary's pots, painted after the designs of Raphael, Michael Angelo, Giulio Romano, and other great masters. They were executed, according to Lanzi, by *Orazio Fontana* of Urbino, who acquired considerable fame by his imitations of the great painters on earthenware. They represent different events of Scripture history, the history of Rome and Greece, and ancient mythology, and were presented by Francesco Maria II., duke of Urbino, for whose father they were originally painted. It is related by Bartoli, a local chronicler, that one of the grand dukes of Florence offered to purchase them by a similar number of silver vases of equal weight.

Loreto contains little beyond its ch. to engage the attention of the stranger. The Piazza della Madonna contains a bronze fountain ornamented with armorial bearings, eagles, dragons, and tritons, the work of the pupils of Calcagni. The Piazza de' Galli also contains a fountain from which it derives its name, being ornamented with a dragon and 4 cocks by Jacometti. The Capuchin Hospital was founded in 1740 by Cardinal Barberini; near it is the hospital maintained at the sole expense of the chapter for the reception of poor pilgrims.

We cannot better conclude this account of Loreto than by recalling to the Italian scholar the offering made at its shrine by TASSO. Religious feeling never perhaps inspired more devotion than that which breathes through the magnificent *canzone* composed in honour of the Virgin by that illustrious pilgrim. No translation can convey any idea of the original, and our space allows but a small extract:

" Ecco fra le tempeste, e i fieri venti
   Di questo grande e spazioso mare,
   O santa Stella, il tuo splendor m' hà scorto,
   Ch' illustra, e scalda pur l' umane mente,

Ove il tuo lume scintillando appare,
E porge al dubbio cor dolce conforto
In terribil procella, ov 'altri è morto :
E dimostra co' raggi
I sicuri viaggi
E questo lido, e quello, e 'l polo, e 'l porto
De la vita mortal, ch' a pena varca
Anzi sovente affonda
In mezzo l' onda alma gravosa, e carca."

Leaving Loreto, on the road to Recanati we pass at a short distance from the town the fine aqueduct, stretching across the valley from hill to hill, and communicating with the subterranean canal by which Loreto is supplied with water. It was undertaken and completed by Paul V. at an expense of 186,000 scudi.

A good but hilly road, parallel to the valley of the Musone, leads to

⅜ Recanati (*Inn*, Locanda di Raffaele, called La Corona, a small tavern with indifferent accommodation). A third horse is required from Loreto to Recanati, but not *vice versâ.*

This small but ancient town is placed on a lofty and commanding eminence overlooking the rich plains of the Marca. Its population is 4500. It has been supposed by many antiquaries that Recanati occupies the site of Helvia Ricina, founded by Septimius Severus, and destroyed by Alaric in 408 ; but although it may have sprung from its ruins, the proper position of that city of the Piceni is more inland, and on the banks of the Potenza. In the 11th century Recanati was a powerful military position ; in 1229 the Emperor Frederick II. took it under his especial protection, and conferred upon it many privileges, among which was the permission to build a port, granting to the inhab. for that purpose the whole line of coast between the Potenza and Musone. The Cathedral, dedicated to St. Flavian Martyr, which contains the monument of Gregory XII. (1417), has a Gothic doorway, and many of its Gothic windows, now closed up and concealed by modern alterations, may still be traced. The roof is richly carved, and dates from the beginning of the 17th century. The churches of S. Domenico and S. Agostino have also Gothic doors with round-headed arches. The Palazzo Comunale has a bronze bas-relief by Jacometti, representing the arrival of the Santa Casa. In the great hall is preserved the original diploma of Frederick II., "Dei Gratia Romanorum Imperator," dated 1229, with his monogram and his golden seal, granting to the town the port of Recanati already mentioned.

Some of the palaces at Recanati may be worth looking at. The view from the balcony of the Caradori palace is truly beautiful: it commands Loreto, the hill of Ancona, the Adriatic, and the fine rich plain of the Marca, called by the natives "Il Giardino d' Italia."

The *Port* of Recanati is about 3 m. from Loreto: it is now a small fishing town, with a population of 3000 inhab. About 2 m. from it are the ruins of Potentia, close to the convent which preserves the name of the city in that of S. Maria di Potenza.

On leaving Recanati, the road descends rapidly into the valley of the Potenza, passing by the ch. of the Vergine di Loreto, from which it follows the l. bank of the river to

¾ *Sambuchetto*, a post station on the Potenza. A third horse is required from this place to Recanati, but not *vice versâ*. The country between Sambuchetto and Macerata is not surpassed by any in Europe for its fertility: situated on either side of the Potenza, its rich meadows interspersed with plantations of mulberry trees and irrigated by numerous canals, recall to the traveller some of the richest districts of Lombardy. 4 m. above Sambuchetto the road crosses the river, having left the picturesque village of Monte Cassiano on the rt. At the point where it crosses the Potenza, 3 branch roads from Osimo, Cingoli, and Jesi fall into the main line. There is a *dogana* at the junction, and close to it are the ruins of an amphitheatre and other buildings, marking the site of Helvia Ricina.

The post-road ascends to within a short distance of the gate of Macerata without entering the town.

1 MACERATA (*Inns*, La Pace (Post,) Albergo di Monachese), a fine provincial city prettily situated on a lofty eminence in the centre of the ridge of the hills that separate the valleys of Potenza and Chienti, about midway between the Apennines and the sea, and commanding views of both. It is the capital of a Delegation, comprehending a surface of 1041 sq. m., and a population of 233,000 souls, and is the seat of one of the 3 appeal courts of the Papal States, embracing in its jurisdiction the eastern provinces. The population of the city, with its suburbs, amounts to 9970. Its foundation dates from 1108.

At first sight Macerata may appear, to a stranger, a dull town, but it is in reality one of the most agreeable and intellectual of the numerous provincial cities with which the States of the Church abound. Its society is of a high order; the resident nobility yield to none in courtesy; it has a university, several handsome palaces, a theatre, and other public establishments. Many of the churches retain their Gothic porticoes, which serve to mark the passage from the old style to the new. In the *Cathedral* sacristy is a picture attributed to *Perugino* (?), representing the Madonna and Child with S. Francis and S. Julian, to whom the ch. is dedicated; and an altarpiece by *Allegretto Nucci*, representing the same subject with S. Benedict and S. Julian; the name of the painter is recorded underneath with the date 1368. The altar of the SS. Sacramento has a very good imitation in wood of the façade of St. Peter's at Rome. In the *Ch. of St. Giovanni* is a fine painting of the Assumption of the Virgin, by *Lanfranco*.

The *Palazzo Compagnoni* contains a small museum of Roman remains and inscriptions, found principally among the ruins of Helvia Ricina. There is a casino in the town supplied with modern works and journals; and in the same establishment is the *Biblioteca Comunale*, founded in 1824 by Leo XII. Outside the gate leading to Fermo is a fine building, erected for the national game of *pallone*, by the architect Alcandri: it is said to be the largest of the kind. About a m. beyond it is the beautiful Ch. of the Madonna della

Vergine, one of the best designs of Bramante.

Macerata is the birthplace of Crescimbeni, the founder of the Arcadian Society, and of Matteo Ricci, the well-known Chinese scholar and missionary. The walls of the city were built by Cardinal Albornoz. The triumphal arch, called the Porta Pia, is somewhat heavy in its effect, notwithstanding its accurate proportions.

[There is a road of 10½ m. from Macerata to Fermo, crossing the Chienti and the Tenna; it is a very agreeable drive. It passes beneath Mont' Olmo, the birthplace of Lanzi, the celebrated writer on Italian art.]

Leaving Macerata, the road descends to the left bank of the Chienti, which it reaches at Sforza Costa, and proceeds along it to Tolentino, through a rich and highly cultivated country. Between these towns is passed the deserted fortress of La Rancia. This position, and indeed the ground on both sides of the river, was the scene of the bloody and decisive battle between Murat and the Austrians in May, 1815. Previous to the battle the Imperial troops occupied the heights of Monte Milone on the rt. of the road; the Neapolitans had advanced within sight of Tolentino when they halted for the night, and subsequently took up a position under the heights of Montolmo and Petriola. On the 3rd, at daybreak, it was seen that the Austrians had received reinforcements during the night, increasing their strength to 16,000 men, the Neapolitans scarcely numbering 10,000. The battle was fought by Murat in person; the Austrians were commanded by Bianchi. At its commencement the Austrians had their rt., and the Neapolitans their l. wing covered by the Chienti. The attack was commenced by Murat, the Austrians acting on the defensive. The combat continued during the whole day, and when both armies drew off for the night 2000 men on both sides lay dead and dying on the field. The unexpected arrival of 2 couriers, one with the news of the defeat at Antrodoco, the other bringing despatches from Naples detailing the disturbances in Calabria and the Campania, induced Murat to retreat on the following morning. In the preliminary movements he was very nearly captured, and, by an injudicious manœuvre on the part of one of his generals, his best position fell into the hands of the Austrians, so that his entire army was thrown into confusion. Insubordination had long prevailed; the untoward events of the day rendered his own personal courage of no avail; his plans were frustrated by disobedience; and to use the language of Colletta, corruption spread from the highest to the lowest. He fell back on Macerata with much loss, and was obliged to retrace his steps to Naples with the remnant of an army which was never worthy of his heroic bravery. This battle sealed the fate of Murat; on the 22nd of the month he fled from Naples, and in the October following his brave career terminated in his inglorious and cruel execution at Pizzo.

1½ TOLENTINO (*Inn*, La Corona, very tolerable and clean). The Gothic gateway by which Tolentino is entered on this side is one of the most interesting and best preserved specimens of the castellated architecture of the middle ages. Tolentino nearly retains the ancient name of a considerable city of Picenum, from whose ruins it sprung. It was erected into a city by Sixtus V. in 1586. It was once strongly fortified. The present population is 6670 souls. It was the scene of the life, death, and miracles of St. Nicholas of Tolentino.

The *Cathedral* dedicated to this saint was originally a Gothic edifice, as may be seen by the closed arches of its windows in the side walls. The rich doorway of its façade remains untouched; the bands of the arch are formed of acanthus leaves, and in the canopy is the figure of one of the Visconti with the dragon: at first sight it might be taken for St. George. The interior of the ch. has a superb roof of carved wood richly gilt, with figures of the Virgin, Saviour, and numerous saints in bold relief. The *capellone* is interesting for the remarkable frescoes by *Lorenzo* and *Jacopo da San*

Severino, representing various subjects from the life of S. Nicholas. Though much injured by repainting, enough remains to afford materials of study; the heads are in general full of expression and feeling. In the chapel of the saint are 2 paintings, one representing the Fire of St. Mark at Venice, attributed to *Tintoretto,* and the other the Plague in Sicily, attributed perhaps on as slight authority to *Paul Veronese,* who is considered by some to have painted the former picture (?).

Tolentino was the birthplace of the learned Francesco Filelfo, whose bust has been erected over the door of the Palazzo Pubblico. In diplomatic history the town has acquired some celebrity for the treaty which bears its name, signed 19th February, 1797, between the commissioners of Pius VI. and General Buonaparte on the part of the French Republic. By this humiliating treaty the pope ceded the province of Romagna, in addition to the Legations of Bologna and Ferrara already surrendered to the Cispadane Republic. He left Ancona in possession of the French, and surrendered to them his territories at Avignon, besides engaging to pay a ransom for other provinces, and to deliver the manuscripts and works of art which had excited the cupidity of his conquerors.

Leaving Tolentino, the road continues along the left bank of the Chienti through very beautiful scenery, presenting in its immediate vicinity many characteristics of an English landscape. The country is very productive and rich in oaks, and the prospect is bounded by the chain of Apennines, covered with snow so late as the beginning of summer, and in some years never free from it. Soon after passing the village of *Belforte* the frontier of the province of Macerata is passed, and we enter the Delegation of Camerino. On the l. are seen the villages of Caldarola and Pieve Favera, picturesquely situated on the other side of the river.

. 1 Valcimara, a post station and hamlet of 400 souls. The road passes through Campolorzo, and, some distance further, a sudden bend opens on the picturesque Rocca di Varano, with an ancient castle

perched upon its summit. At this place a road branches off from the post-road to Camerino, 15 m. distant.

[CAMERINO, the capital of a Delegation of 372 square m. and 37,700 souls, and the seat of an archbishopric, is situated at the foot of the Apennines on a lofty hill, from whose base several tributaries of the Potenza take their rise. It retains the name of the ancient Camerinum, a border city of Umbria, which acquired some note from its alliance with Rome against the Etrurians. In 1545 Paul III. received it in exchange for the cession of Parma and Piacenza. The cathedral dedicated to S. Sansovino occupies the site of a temple of Jupiter. Camerino was made an archiepiscopal see by Pius VI. in 1787; the see of Treja was united to it by Pius VII. in 1817. Its bishopric dated from 252, under Lucius I., and S. Sansovino, the titular saint of the cathedral was its first bishop. The city has a university of some repute, and a small manufactory of silk. Its present population is 5240. Carlo Maratta was born here.]

1 Ponte della Trave, a post station. At *La Muccia,* the usual resting-place of the vetturini (*Inn,* Il Leone), the road which has crossed from the l. to the rt. bank of the Chienti returns again to the l. There is a branch road from this to Camerino, distant 6 m. The several villages which are passed between Valcimara and Serravalle are picturesquely placed on the lower slopes of the mountains. On the l. hand are Pieve-Bovigliano, S. Marco, Pieve-Torrina, Massadì, and Prefoglio; and on the rt. Colle, S. Marcello, and Gelagno. The road now begins to ascend.

1 Serravalle, a long straggling village in a steep and narrow defile, completely commanded by the ruins of an old castle, a stronghold of the middle ages. 2 m. higher up are the sources of the Chienti, which, after a course of 58 m., falls into the Adriatic at the port of Civitanuova. A gradual ascent by a fine wild mountain road brings us to the plain of Colfiorito, an extensive table-land. In severe winters the route, from its great elevation, is often impass-

able from snow. The plain has a local reputation for the excellence of its hay and pasturage. The country becomes more desolate as the village *Colfiorito* is approached, at nearly the highest point of the road 2716 ft. above the sea. There is a new inn at this village called the Locanda di Bonelli. After passing the Lake of Colfiorito, famous for its leeches, the road begins to descend, and a great change in the character of the country and its scenery is soon apparent; the land is rich and generally covered with oaks. In severe winters the ascent to the Colfiorito from Foligno is difficult, and in some parts dangerous, for an English carriage.

1 Case Nuove, a small hamlet of 130 souls, built under the ruins of an old castle near a rapid torrent. (In posting *from* Foligno by this road a third horse is required from Case Nuove to Serravalle, but not *vice versâ*.) Beyond it is the village of Pale, above which is a remarkable pointed peak, Il Sasso di Pale, among the last elevations of the Apennines; there is a curious cavern filled with stalactites, in the precipitous cliffs above the village. In the descent from hence the view looking down upon the city and fertile plain of Foligno is very beautiful; it commands a great extent of country stretching over the valley of the Clitumnus, and scarcely to be surpassed in richness of cultivation or picturesque beauty.

The road continues to follow the course of the torrent: about a m. before reaching Foligno it is joined by the Via Flaminia, the high post-road from Fano through Nocera by the Strada del Furlo.

1 FOLIGNO; described in Rte. 27.

ROUTE 16.

FANO TO FOLIGNO, BY THE STRADA DEL FURLO, CAGLI, AND NOCERA.

78 m.

	Posts.
Fano to Calcinelli	1
Calcinelli to Fossombrone . .	1
Fossombrone to Acqualagna . .	1
Acqualagna to Cagli	0¾
Cagli to Cantiano	0¾
Cantiano to La Schieggia . .	1
La Schieggia to Sigillo . .	1
Sigillo to Gualdo Tadino . .	1
Gualdo Tadino to Nocera . .	1
Nocera to Ponte Centesimo . .	1
Ponte Centesimo to Foligno . .	1
	10½

This route follows the line of the ancient Flaminian Way throughout its entire course from Fano to Foligno.

The early part of the road is extremely beautiful. Leaving Fano, we pass the public promenade, and soon enter upon the varied and beautiful country between it and the mountains, ascending along the base of the hills that bound on the N. the fertile valley of the Metauro. This classic stream, memorable for the defeat of Asdrubal, is apostrophised by Tasso in one of his most touching poems (Rime Eroiche, xxxiv.):—

"O del grand' Apennino
Figlio picciolo."

1 Calcinelli: here the road approaches the river, and the valley narrowing still continues beautiful.

1 m. before reaching Fossombrone it passes San Martino al Piano, where a torrent of the same name enters the Metauro. Near this spot stood the Roman station of Forum Sempronii, where there still exist some vestiges of a theatre.

1 *Fossombrone* (*Inns*, La Posta; Il Re, new, ill-kept, and very dear), a thriving episcopal town of 2890 Inhab. which rose from the ruins of the Forum Sempronii. The ancient city was ruined by the Goths and Lombards. The modern town is built along the l. bank of the Metauro, and was the property of the Malatesta family until the pontificate of Sixtus IV., when Galeazzo sold it to the Duke Federigo della Rovere for 13,000 golden florins. In more recent times it passed to Eugène Beauharnois, and has descended to his son the late Duke de Leüchtenberg, to whom it is indebted for much of its prosperity. Fossombrone is celebrated throughout Italy for the fine silk produced in its neighbourhood, for winding and spinning which it has several mills. It has

some manufactures of the finer descriptions of woollen cloths.

The cathedral, dedicated to S. Aldebrando, contains some Roman inscriptions from the ruins of the ancient city: its bishopric dates from the 5th century. The modern bridge over the Metauro, spanning that broad mountain stream by a single arch, is a striking work. The road over it leads to S. Ippolito, where there are the best marble quarries in the province,—to Sorbolungo,—to the ancient walled town of Mondavio,—to Pergola, with extensive carpet manufactories,—and to other places of less consequence between the valleys of the Metauro and the Cesano.

Leaving Fossombrone, the scenery becomes remarkably fine; the country is varied and picturesque, and rich in oaks which would be ornamental to any English park. The road to *Urbino* branches off from the main route 3 m. from Fossombrone, where the Metauro, descending from the former town, is joined by the Candigliano. (See next Route, 17.)

The Foligno road crosses the Metauro and at once strikes into the mountains, ascending the l. bank of the Candigliano, which rises in the Apennines under Valboscosa and San Benedetto. 3 m. from Fossombrone commences the pass of the Furlo, on one side of which is the hill of Pietralata, also called *Il Monte d' Asdrubale*, in which tradition has preserved the record of the memorable battle between the Carthaginian general and the Roman consuls Livius Salinator and Claudius Nero, B.C. 207. The battle is supposed, from the account of Livy, to have taken place on the l. bank of the river, where it begins to be contracted by high rocks; 56,000 men shared the fate of their commander, and 5400 were made prisoners. The loss of the Romans is admitted by their historians to have been 8000 killed and 3000 prisoners. The pathetic lamentation of Hannibal for the death of his brother is well known to every reader of Horace:—

> " Carthagini jam non ego nuntios
> Mittam superbos: occidit, occidit

> Spes omnis, et fortuna nostri
> Nominis, Asdrubale interempto."
> *Hor.* iv. od. 4.

In the caverns of the neighbouring mountains some fossil remains are found, which the inhabitants erroneously believe to be the relics of the army of Asdrubal.

The *Pass of the Furlo* upon which the road now enters affords one of those remarkable examples of Roman energy, which are no where more surprising than in the construction of their public roads. The traveller who is acquainted with the magnificent remains of the highway constructed by Trajan in the precipices of Servia along the Danube, will not fail to recognise in this pass the same skilful engineering and the same power of overcoming difficulties for which that wonderful work is celebrated. The high perpendicular precipices of the Passo del Furlo close in so narrowly on the very edge of the river, that it appears as if the mountains would allow nothing beyond the passage of the stream. The Roman engineers however cut through the rock, on its l. bank, carrying the road through a tunnel which gives name to the defile for about 116 feet, and thus formed a passage for the Flaminian Way, 18 ft. broad and 15 high. The whole length of the pass is about half a mile, and the scenery is exceedingly grand. An inscription cut in the rock records its construction by order of Vespasian. This interesting work is called *Petra Intercisa* in the Peutingerian and Hierosolymitan Itineraries, and *Petra Pertusa* by Procopius, who has accurately described it; it is also commemorated by Claudian in the beautiful passage—

> " Qua mons arte patens vivo se perforat arcu,
> Admittitque viam sectæ per viscera rupis."
> *VI. Cons. Hon.*, 500.

1 Acqualagna, a small village and post station at the junction of the Candigliano with the Burano. The neighbouring plain has been considered by some antiquaries to be the scene of the defeat and death of Totila, but we shall presently see that the true site of the battle must be placed at Gualdo. 3

m. farther is a new and apparently clean inn called the Aurora, which may be better than the wretched town inns along this road. Before entering Cagli, a stream which flows into the Burano is crossed by a fine Roman bridge called Ponte Manlio; the central arch, 39 feet in span, is composed of 19 large stones. The ascent is very steep to
¼ *Cagli* (*Inn*, La Posta, wretched), a small and industrious provincial town of nearly 3700 Inhab., constituting, in conjunction with Pergola, the seat of a bishopric. It occupies the site of *Callis*, a station of the Via Flaminia, built on the flanks of Monte Petrano. The present town dates from the 13th century. Several ancient remains, medals, and fragments of statues have been found in its vicinity. In the ch. of *S. Domenico* is one of the best works of *Giovanni Santi*, a fresco of the Madonna and Saints, with the Resurrection and other subjects, of great beauty. The angel to the rt. of the Madonna has been supposed to be the portrait of the young Raphael. It contains also a Pieta between 2 Saints, by *Giovanni Santi*, over the tomb of a lady of the family of Tiranni. Opposite is an Annunciation, probably by *Fra Carnevale*, a very rare early master. In *S. Francesco* are some fine frescoes of St. Antony, supposed to be by *Guido Palmerucci*, a fine picture by *Baroccio*, and a good Madonna by *Gaetano Lapis* of Cagli. In the Artieri chapel of *S. Angelo Minore* the altar-piece is an admirable " Noli me tangere," by *Timoteo Vite*. The *Ch. of the Capuchins*, above the town, has an excellent Pieta by *Fra Bernardo Catelani*. Cagli has some trade in tanned and dressed leathers. Beyond Cagli are 3 Roman conduits passing under the road for the purpose of carrying off the water of the torrents into the valley below; the road passes through a narrow defile, between the high peaks of Monte Petrano on the rt. and Monte Tenetra on the l. Between this and Cantiano the river is crossed by a stone bridge of Roman architecture, called the Ponte Grosso.
¼ *Cantiano* (*Inn*, La Posta, very poor), a small fortified town supposed to have sprung from the ruins of Luccolo, an episcopal city destroyed by Narses in his pursuit of Totila, the site of which is placed by Calindri at a short distance beyond the present town near the Ponte Ricioli. Leaving Cantiano, the road rapidly ascends the mountains until it attains the highest point, 2297 English ft. above the level of the sea. (A third horse is required to La Schieggia, but not *vice versâ*.)
1 *La Schieggia*, a walled village with an ancient Palazzo and cathedral. Its interest is derived from the ruins of the famous Temple of Jupiter Apenninus, still traceable on Monte Petrara, to which the confederated tribes of Umbria repaired to sacrifice, as the Etruscans did to the temple of Voltumna. Its oracle was consulted by the Emperor Claudius, and it is mentioned by Claudian in the following passage :—

" Exsuperant delubra Jovis, saxoque minantes Apenninigenis cultas pastoribus aris."

In the neighbourhood of the ruins several remains, as bronze idols, eagles, and Roman inscriptions, have been discovered, together with the vestiges of baths near the present town. The country around Schieggia is rich in oaks, and is in parts well cultivated. The bridge called the Ponte a Botte (or the barrel-shaped) was built by Fabri in 1805, by order of Pius VI. Its construction is peculiar. It spans the ravine by a single arch at the height of 230 feet from the bottom; above this arch the engineer has introduced a cylindrical aperture 65 ft. in diameter, which has given name to the bridge.
[A road strikes westward from Schieggia 8 m. across the mountains to Gubbio, from whence another of 13 m. by S. Marco falls into the present route at S. Facondino, near Gualdo Tadino, so that it is not necessary for the traveller desirous of visiting Gubbio to retrace his steps, and this detour adds but 4 m. to his journey. For a description of *Gubbio*, and of other roads leading from it to Perugia and Citta di Castello, see Rt. 20. Schieggia to Sassoferrato 13 m.]

E. of La Schieggia, and about mid-way between it and the Cesano, is an interesting classical locality, recording, in the modern name of *Sentina*, the site of ancient Sentinum, celebrated for the battle between the Romans and the combined forces of the Gauls and Samnites, B.C. 296, in which the younger Decius devoted himself for his country.

The road from La Schieggia to Sigillo runs along the valley or depression in the chain of the Apennines, whose lofty range here appears to separate into 2 portions. Between Costacciaro and Sigillo we leave the Legation of Urbino and Pesaro, and enter the Delegation of Perugia.

1 Sigillo, the *Svillum* of Pliny, another Umbrian city, now reduced to a wild mountain village of little more than 1000 souls. In the middle ages it was one of the dependencies of Perugia, and was strongly fortified; some portions of its walls and castle still remain. In the neighbourhood are 2 bridges at-tributed to Flaminius, and the pavement of the ancient road may still be traced. In the mountains of Sigillo is a re-markable cavern, which has not been sufficiently explored: it is only to be en-tered by means of a rope. The galle-ries in it are filled with stalactites; the 4th is said to be upwards of a m. in length, terminating in a deep lake. The floor of this cavern, we believe, has never been broken; and it would be interesting if some resident geologist would explore it with a view to the discovery of fossil remains.

3 m. farther on, at Fossato, a small place on the l. remarkable for its suc-cessful resistance to Francesco Sforza, and for having been sacked by Cesar Borgia, a road branches off to *Fabriano;* an important town of 6600 souls, whose celebrated paper manufactories, esta-blished so early as 1564, not only supply the States of the Church, but rival the great Neapolitan establishment on the Fibreno, at Isola. S. Facondino, the point where the road from Gubbio, 13 m., falls into the Flaminian Way, is passed 1 m. before arriving at

1 Gualdo Tadino, a walled town of about 2600 Inhab., 1½ m. from which was the ancient city of Tadinum mentioned by Pliny. The site was not discovered until 1750, when its ruins were found close to the church of Sta. Maria Tadina, and several interesting remains were brought to light. The neighbourhood is remark-able as the scene of the great battle in which Narses, the general of Justinian, overthrew Totila king of the Goths, who was mortally wounded. The march of the Romans and their allies from Ravenna by the pass of Furlo, and the particulars of the battle, are finely described by Gibbon, chap. xliii.

Leaving Gualdo, the road gradually descends, passing by Carbonara in the upper valley of the Topina, to

1 *Nocera,* the Nuceria of the Itine-raries, and Nuceria Camellaria of Pliny (*Inn,* La Posta). This Umbrian city, celebrated by Strabo for its manufac-tory of wooden vessels, has dwindled down to a poor village of 1150 souls. It is, however, the seat of a bishopric in conjunction with the town of *Sasso-ferrato.* In the neighbourhood of No-cera are some mineral springs which have enjoyed great local repute from the time of Bernardino da Spoleto, by whom they were first described in 1510. They are much resorted to by the country people, but an accurate analysis of them is yet wanting. The road now leaves the mountains, and rapidly descends into the valley of the Topina, whose banks it follows through-out the remainder of the route.

1 Ponte Centesimo, a post-station, on the rt. bank of the Topina. 1 m. lower down, the valley widens and be-comes more fertile; the river is crossed. Passing through the hamlet of Vescia, the village of San Giovanni pro Fiamma is seen on the opposite side of the river. It occupies the site of the ancient Forum Flaminii, which existed as an impor-tant city as late as 253, when it was destroyed by the Lombards, and Foligno rose from its ruins. It was one of the most ancient episcopal sees in Christen-dom, having been erected in A.D. 52 by St. Peter for his disciple Crispaldus. At S. Paolo the road from Ancona joins that by the Furlo, and a m. farther,

G 3

after a beautiful drive through a fertile country, brings us to

1 FOLIGNO (Rte. 27).

ROUTE 17.

FANO TO URBINO, BY FOSSOMBRONE.

28 m.

The road follows the Flaminian Way, described in the preceding route, as far as Fossombrone.

1 Calcinelli.
1 Fossombrone.

From the point where the Foligno road crosses the Metauro to strike into the Passo del Furlo the road to Urbino begins to ascend. It soon loses that rich character of cultivation so remarkable on the banks of the Lower Metauro, and forming so strong a contrast with the bare and barren hills by which Urbino is surrounded. As we approach the city the fine ducal palace on the rt. of the gate of entrance, and the old castle or citadel on the hill opposite, are conspicuous objects. About half way, at S. Andrea, the road leaves the valley of the Metauro on the l., and a very steep ascent of 5 m. brings us to

URBINO, 13 m. from Fossombrone (*Inns*, La Stella, bad and dear; Albergo dell' Italia, clean and homely). This interesting city, the birthplace of Raphael, and the seat of an hereditary sovereignty before the close of the 15th century, is situated on an isolated hill in the midst of bleak and desolate mountains, wearing more the aspect of a feudal fortress than that of an archiepiscopal city. It is one of the capitals of the delegation of Urbino and Pesaro, which comprehends a superficial extent of 1649 sq. m., and a population of 235,400 souls. The city itself, with its dependencies, has a population amounting to 7650.

The little State of Urbino was acquired by the house of Montefeltro in the 13th century, but it was not until the close of the 15th that it obtained celebrity as the centre of art and learning under the encouragement of Federigo and his successor Guid' Ubaldo.

These remarkable men converted their palace into an academy, and changed a school of military tactics into one of refinement and taste. The impulse thus given to the literature and arts of the period is best proved by the illustrious names associated with the history of their court, and by the fact that the social and political importance of Urbino under their sway exercised considerable influence on the larger states of Italy. It is remarkable that Romagna was celebrated at the same time for 3 of the most brilliant courts in Europe—that of Sigismund Malatesta at Rimini, that of Alessandro Sforza at Pesaro, and that of Federigo di Montefeltro at Urbino. The court of Urbino surpassed both the others in its influence and character. Federigo di Montefeltro, the founder of its greatness, who in early life was the counsellor and minister of Galeazzo Malatesta, bore a conspicuous part in the political events that agitated Italy during the 15th century. He was one of the commanders of the Milanese army at the bloody battle of S. Flaviano, in 1460; a few years later he was general of the army of Florence, and fought the battle of Molinella with Bartolommeo Coleoni in 1467. He defeated the army of the pope (Paul II.) at Rimini in 1469; in 1472 he reduced Volterra. 2 years afterwards (1474) he married his daughter Giovanna to Giovanni della Rovere, brother of Julius II., and was created Duke of Urbino in the same year by a papal rescript. In 1482, in spite of his great age, he was appointed general of the league between the Church and its allies against Ferrara; but he died Sept. 10th in that year, on the same day as his son-in-law Robert Malatesta, and was succeeded by his son Guid' Ubaldo I.

The military character of Federigo may suffice to show what an important part he played in the eventful drama of Italian politics. In the more pleasing character of an encourager of learning the name of *Itala Atene* bestowed upon Urbino in his time is perhaps the best evidence of his merits. Sismondi calls him the Mecaenas of the fine arts; his exploits and virtues are celebrated by

Giovanni Santi, the father of Raphael, in a MS. poem in *terza rima*, now preserved in the Vatican; but his highest eulogium is no doubt to be found in the unanimous language of respect and praise in which Italian writers have delighted to picture Urbino as the seat of science, literature, and the arts. His wife, the Countess Battista Sforza, was in no way inferior to himself: her character exercised an important influence in forming the mind of her son Guid' Ubaldo, and her virtues are recorded in glowing colours by Bernardo Tasso.

Guid' Ubaldo I., by his liberal patronage and by his own intellectual acquirements, contributed even more than his father to raise the character of Urbino as a school of art and taste. His wife, Elizabetta Gonzaga, was celebrated no less for her beauty than for her high mental accomplishments and domestic virtues: the 'Cortegiano' of Castiglione may be taken as a record of the refinement for which Urbino under her auspices was remarkable. Mr. Eastlake, in an able article in the 'Quarterly Review,' No. 131, on Passavant's Life of Raphael, observes that —" Perhaps no praises ever bestowed on woman can be compared, both for eloquence and sincerity, with those contained in Bembo's little volume (De Guido Ubaldo, &c., Romæ, 1548), composed, as the writer tells us, when the duchess had lost her beauty through sorrow and misfortune. That her fame was long remembered in England we can hardly doubt; and not improbably Shakspeare may have taken from Bembo's portraiture a hint for his Miranda, *e. g.* :—

> ————' for several virtues
> Have I liked several women ; never any
> With so full soul but some defect in her
> Did quarrel with the noblest grace she owed
> And put it to the foil ; but you, O you,
> So perfect and so peerless, are created
> Of every creature's best.'"

In 1497, Guid' Ubaldo, commanding the papal forces, was defeated at Soriano by Vitellozzo Vitelli, lord of Citta di Castello, and made prisoner. Alexander VI. was not ashamed to make him pay 40,000 ducats for his ransom, although he had lost his liberty in the papal cause ; a sum which was raised partly by the contributions of his subjects, and partly by his duchess, who sold her jewels for the purpose. The treachery of Cesar Borgia, after these reverses with the Vitelli, drove the duke from his capital to take refuge in the north of Italy ; but on the death of Alexander VI. the citizens rose, expelled the partisans of Borgia, and brought back Guid' Ubaldo in triumph. The accession of his relative Julius II. to the papal throne confirmed this restoration, and again established the duke in his possessions. In 1506 this celebrated pontiff, with 22 cardinals and a numerous suite, passed 3 days at Urbino on his way to Bologna. During this stay he is said to have become acquainted with Raphael.

Duke Guid' Ubaldo and his amiable duchess were well known in England ; the duke was made a knight of the garter by Henry VII., and Castiglione visited London as his proxy at the ceremony of installation. In return for this distinction, Guid' Ubaldo sent the king the picture of St. George and the Dragon, painted by *Raphael* expressly for the occasion, and now one of the greatest ornaments of the Hermitage at St. Petersburg.

In 1508 Francesco Maria della Rovere, nephew of the pope, succeeded to the dukedom of Urbino, on the death of Guid' Ubaldo ; and to his influence and recommendation the employment of Raphael at the Vatican is attributed by some of his biographers. Francesco Maria, like his illustrious predecessors, acquired laurels in the field no less than in the retirement of his polished court. He was one of the principal commanders of the papal army at the siege of Mirandola, where, among the *élite* of the gallant captains of France, he was brought into opposition with the " chevalier sans peur et sans reproche." But in the subsequent campaign of the same year he sustained a signal defeat at the memorable battle of Casalecchio, May 21, 1511. This battle, as already mentioned, was followed by the loss of Bologna; and so convinced was the Duke of Urbino that the panic which produced it was caused by the treachery of Alidosi, the cardinal legate, who had gone to Ravenna to justify his conduct to Julius II., that, when he met him in that city returning from his interview with the pope, surrounded by his guard and by all the pomp and circumstance of his station, the duke, unable to subdue his passion, rushed among the crowd and stabbed the legate to the heart, in the presence of his soldiers.

The house of La Rovere and the independence of Urbino, however, were not destined to survive the fate of other princes and states swallowed up in succession by the grasping power of the Church: and in little more than a century both had become extinct. In 1538 Francesco Maria was succeeded by Guid' Ubaldo II., and in 1574 Francesco Maria II. ascended a throne which he was incapable of retaining. In 1626 this last duke of Urbino, childless and old, and unable to cope with the necessities of the times, yielded to the entreaties of Urban VIII., and abdicated in favour of the Church. The latter period of the duchy presents few circumstances to arrest our attention, and the mind naturally recurs to the influence of the patronage bestowed on art and literature by Federigo and Guid' Ubaldo. The collections of ancient and modern art with which their palace was enriched, and the distinguished society brought together at their court, must have had an important effect on the early genius of Raphael; and his connexion with the court no doubt provided him with powerful friends, whose influence was subsequently available at Rome and Florence. Raphael spent his early years, to the age of 21, between Urbino and Perugia, and his works, in many instances, bear evidence of those precepts of taste which guided the social and domestic habits of the court of Montefeltro, as perpetuated in the 'Cortegiano.' "The resources and renown of this little dukedom, improved and upheld by Federigo da Montefeltro, remained ultimately un-

impaired in the hands of his successor Guid' Ubaldo; the state, in short, was represented, and its warlike population led to the field, by hereditary sovereigns, before Florence had learned to yield even to temporary sway. That a Tuscan writer on art should be silent on the past glories of a neighbouring state is quite natural; but it seems unaccountable that so many biographers in following Vasari should have overlooked the remarkable circumstances by which Raphael was surrounded in his youth—circumstances which must not only have had an influence on his taste, but which brought him in contact with the most celebrated men of his age, many of whom afterwards served him, at least with the communication of their learning, when he was employed at the court of Rome."—*Quart. Rev.* cxxxi.

It is, however, remarkable, that although Raphael is known to have painted several pictures at his native place, none now remain there; and the specimens shown as the productions of his boyish days are certainly not authentic. Raphael was born at Urbino on the 6th April (Good Friday), 1488. Among the other remarkable men to whom it gave birth may be mentioned Baroccio the painter; Timoteo della Vite, the pupil of Raphael; Polydore Vergil, celebrated in the history of the Reformation as the last collector of the Peter-pence in England; and Clement XI., the founder of the princely family of Albani. For an inquiry into the influence of the court of Urbino on the early genius of Raphael, the reader is referred to the admirable critique on Passavant's Life of Raphael, in the *Quarterly Review*, already quoted.

Urbino, independently of its historical and artistic associations, still contains much to interest and instruct the stranger.

The magnificent *Ducal Palace* built by Federigo di Montefeltro, from the designs of Luciano Lauranna, which was reputed at the time of its erection to be the finest edifice of its kind which Italy had then seen, is still, in many respects, without a rival as a specimen of the *cinque cento* style. The tasteful imitation of the antique for which this style is remarkable is here combined with lightness of proportions and extraordinary richness of decoration. The doors, windows, cornices, pilasters, and chimney-pieces are covered with arabesque carvings of foliage, trophies, and other ornaments of singular beauty. They were the work of Francesco di Giorgio of Siena, assisted by Ambrogio Baroccio, ancestor of the painter, whose execution of the architectural foliage is praised by Giovanni Santi in the MS. poem in *terza rima* to which we have already referred. The saloons and other apartments are well proportioned and handsome, although the frescoes with which many of them were painted have disappeared. The room adjoining the library was decorated with portraits representing the celebrated men of all ages. The inlaid ornaments or *tarsia* of the panelling were by Maestro Giacomo of Florence. In one of the saloons may still be seen a piece of tapestry worked in 1380, representing the duke and his party on a hawking excursion. The galleries have a valuable collection of ancient inscriptions, Roman as well as early Christian, found chiefly in the neighbourhood of the city—but only the wreck of the large collection of bronze and marble statues which Castiglione has described, and which it is supposed were transferred to the Vatican, where the ducal library was also removed.

The *Fortifications*, also considered a remarkable specimen of the military architecture of the period, were designed and probably executed by Francesco di Giorgio of Siena.

The *Cathedral* contains 2 fine paintings by *Baroccio*: one representing the martyrdom of S. Sebastian; and the other the Last Supper, a work remarkable for its richness of composition and colouring. The small pictures of the Apostles, painted for the sacristy by *Pietro della Francesca*, justify the praises of Lanzi by their beauty and the grand style of their drapery. The sacristy also contains one of the best collections of ch. plate and embroidery which Italy retained after the French invasion. It was almost wholly the gift of the Cardinal Annibale Albani, to whom,

more than to any other, Urbino is indebted for its modern prosperity.

The *Ch. of S. Francesco* has a fine picture by *Giovanni Santi*, representing the Virgin and Child, with St. John the Baptist, S. Sebastian, S. Jerome, and S. Francis in adoration. It was long supposed that the painter had introduced into this picture portraits of himself, his wife, and their child the infant Raphael; but it is now known that the 3 kneeling figures represent members of the Buffi family, at whose expense the picture was painted. There are at the entrance of the choir two smaller pictures by *G. Santi*, representing S. Roch and Tobias and the Angel.

The *Ch. of S. Francesco di Paola* contains 2 works by *Titian*, one representing the Resurrection, the other the Last Supper.

The sacristy of *S. Giuseppe* has a fine Madonna by *Timoteo della Vite*, the friend and pupil of Raphael.

The oratory of the *Confraternità di S. Giovanni* is covered with paintings by *Lorenzo da S. Severino* and his brother, followers of the school of Giotto, representing various scriptural events, and possessing great interest as studies of costume. The grand Crucifixion, covering the entire wall behind the altar, although injured by neglect, is full of expression.

The *Ch. of Sta. Chiara* has in the sacristy a painting by *Giorgio Andreoli*, formerly believed to be by Bramante; it represents a circular architectural building with Corinthian pilasters, like that in the Sposalizio and other pictures of Raphael and Perugino. The nuns of the Sta. Chiara convent have 2 pictures erroneously attributed to Raphael; one of them, by *Raffaelino del Garbo*, bears these inscriptions on the back: "Raffaele Sante," and "Fu compra di Isabella da Gobio, madre di Raffaelo Sante di Urbino, 14—."

The *Ch. of Sta. Agata* is remarkable for a proof of the liberality shown by Federigo di Montefeltro in the distribution of his patronage. It is an old picture by *Justus van Ghent*, pupil of Van Eyck, and is dated 1474. In the background he has introduced the duke with 2 attendants, one of whom is the painter himself, and the other the Venetian Caterino Zeno, then residing at the court of Urbino as the Persian ambassador.

The *Capuchin Convent*, situated a little beyond the walls, contains one of the finest works of *Baroccio*, the St. Francis in ecstacy.

The *House of Raphael*, in which he was born, will not fail to command the respect and veneration of the stranger. An inscription over the door records the event in the following terms:

NUNQUAM MORITURUS
EXIGUIS HISCE IN ÆDIBUS
EXIMIUS ILLE PICTOR RAPHAEL
NATUS EST,
OCT. 1 D. APRILIS. AN. M.CD.XXCIII.
VENERARE IGITUR HOSPES
NOMEN ET GENIUM LOCI.
NE MIRERE,
LUDIT IN HUMANIS DIVINA POTENTIA
REBUS,
ET SÆPE IN PARVIS CLAUDERE MAGNA
SOLET.

On one of the walls is a Madonna and sleeping child, long supposed to be one of the great painter's boyish attempts; but it is now known to be by his father *Giovanni Santi*. It is, however, very probable that the originals of this picture, now much injured by repainting, were Magia Ciarla and her infant son Raphael.

The *Theatre*, formerly celebrated for its decorations by *Girolamo Genga*, a pupil of Pietro Perugino, is also remarkable as the place where the first Italian comedy was represented, the 'Calandria' of Cardinal Bibiena.

In the 16th century Urbino was famous for its manufactory of earthenware, perfected in 1538, under Orazio Fontana. Giorgio Andreoli is said to have introduced it into Gubbio from this city in 1498; and so great was the celebrity of Urbino for the fabric, that Maestro Rovigo of Urbino in 1534 established a factory at Fermignano. In the beginning of the last century, under Clement XI., and his successor Innocent XIII., Urbino had a reputation for its manufactories of pins, needles, and firearms: its extensive pin manufactory,

formerly the property of the Albani family, still gives employment to hundreds, and supplies nearly all the Papal States.

The bishopric of Urbino dates from the year 313, S. Evando being the 1st bishop; it was created an archbishopric by Pius IV. in 1563. The college, under the direction of the Scolopie Fathers, contains nearly 100, who receive instruction in law, medicine, and theology. Urbino is not without classical associations; it is the Urbinum Hortense of Pliny, and was the place where Valens, the general of Vitellius, was put to death.

A diligence runs 3 times a week between Urbino and Pesaro, 23 m. The road descends northwards on leaving Urbino, and proceeds along the l. bank of the torrent which flows from Urbino into the Foglia below Montecchio. It passes on the l. Coldazzo and Colbordolo, and on the rt. Petriano and Serra di Genga.

ROUTE 18.

URBINO TO CITTA DI CASTELLO, BY SAN GIUSTINO.

48 English m.

	Rom. Miles.
Urbino to Urbania . . .	13
Urbania to S. Angelo in Vado .	7
S. Angelo to Mercatello . . .	4
Mercatello to Lamoli . . .	6
Lamoli to Summit of the Pass .	6
Summit to San Giustino . . .	10
San Giustino to Citta di Castello .	6
	—
	52

A diligence runs now (1853) once a week between Urbino and San Giustino; it leaves Urbino on Wednesday at 1 P.M., stops during the night at Sant' Angelo, and arrives next day at San Giustino at 10 A.M., when another sets out for Citta di Castello and Perugia. The same diligence leaves San Giustino on Tuesday at 1 P.M., and reaches Urbino at 10 A.M. in time for the coach to Pesaro and Ancona—fare 17 pauls.

This is a long day's journey for a vetturino, by an admirable mountain road, carried with great skill over the central chain of the Apennines by the

Pass of Bocca Trabaria, here called also the Alpe della Luna, and constructed at the joint expense of the Papal and Tuscan governments.

The ascent becomes steep after leaving Urbino, and oxen are required. On approaching Urbania it again descends, commanding beautiful views of that town and of the valley of the Metauro. The mountains which are so conspicuous between Urbino and Urbania, and which are such remarkable objects from the former city, are the Monte Cucco, whose height is 5140 feet above the sea; Monte Catria, celebrated for the convent of S. Albertino, 5586 feet; and Monte Nerone, 5011 feet. The road crosses the Metauro on entering *Urbania* (13 m.), a small town of 2400 souls, situated on the rt. bank of the river, near the site of the Urbinum Metaurense of Pliny. The present town was built from the ruins of Castel Ripense in the 13th century, and called Durante from its founder. In 1635 Urban VIII. created it a city, and changed its name to Urbania, making it also an episcopal see with S. Angelo in Vado. There is little to interest the traveller here. In the Ch. of S. Francesco there is a Madonna by Baroccio, and in the Confraternita of the Corpus Domini some good frescoes by Raffaelle del Colle. 2 m. distant is Stretta, the birthplace of Bramante.

The road for some distance, now nearly level, ascends the valley of the Metauro, crossing the river at S. Giovanni in Pietra, to *S. Angelo in Vado* (7 m.), a small town of 3300 Inhab. built upon the site of Tifernum Metaurense. (*Inn:* Locanda Faggioli, a poor place, but civil people.) The cathedral is dedicated to St. Michael the Archangel. The ch. of *Sta. Caterina* has a picture by *Federigo Zuccari*, with portraits of the painter and his family, which was once in Milan. This painter and Clement XIV. (Ganganelli) were born here.

The road proceeds along the rt. bank of the *Metauro* to *Mercatello* (4 m.), a dirty town of 1200 souls without an inn, but which the vetturini nevertheless frequently make their resting-place. Borgo Pace, 3 m. farther on, is situated in the angle formed by the junction of the Meta and Auro, whose united waters form the Metauro, which pursues, from hence to the sea, a course of nearly 60 m.; from Borgo Pace, the road ascends along the l. bank of the Meta to Lamoli (4 m.). Here commences the ascent of the central chain, properly speaking, and oxen are required to overcome the difficulty. The highest point of the road, called La Bocca Trabaria, is 3485 English feet above the level of the sea, and is seldom reached in less than 2½ hours from Lamoli. The western side of the mountain is by no means so steep as the eastern; and 2 hours more bring the traveller to San Giustino (10 m.). During the descent the view over the rich vale of the Tiber, with Città di Castello and Borgo San Sepolcro, is very fine. The road is carried down the mountain, as on the ascent, in a masterly manner, by series of well-contrived zigzags, and is in excellent order. At the foot of the descent we arrive at *San Giustino* (10 m.), formerly a place of strength, which gives the title of count to the Bufalini family. It has some reputation for its manufactory of straw hats, which are said to rival those of the Val d'Arno. The only object of interest in the town is the *Palazzo Bufalini*, some of the apartments in which were painted by *Doceno* in a style which has been praised by Vasari. The palace was much injured by the earthquake of 1789. San Giustino is just within the frontier of the Papal States: and travellers proceeding into Tuscany must have their passports *viséed* at the frontier village of Cospaja.

From San Giustino 2 roads branch off; that to the N. leading into Tuscany by Borgo San Sepolcro and Arezzo (Rte. 19), and that to the S. to Città di Castello and Perugia. The road from San Giustino to Città di Castello passes over a portion of the highly cultivated valley of the Tiber, presenting the appearance of a continued vineyard.

CITTA DI CASTELLO (6 m.) (*Inns:* Locanda Lorenzone, clean and tolerable; La Cannoniera). This agreeable and interesting city of 5430 souls is pleasantly situated near the l. bank of the Tiber. It is remarkable no less for the numerous works of art which it contains, than for the courtesy and intelligence of its inhabitants; and it is one of those towns so often met with in Central Italy, where a stranger, even unprovided with introductions, may calculate on finding friends. It occupies the site of Tifernum Tiberinum, celebrated by Pliny the younger, who was chosen at an early age to be its patron, and who built a temple there at his own cost. Tifernum was one of the fortified towns destroyed by Totila; the present city rose from its ruins under the auspices of S. Florido, its patron saint. In the 15th century Città di Castello was governed by the Vitelli family, whose military exploits hold so high a rank in the history of Italian warfare. Vitellozzo Vitelli was the conqueror of the duke of Urbino at Soriano, and he subsequently became one of the victims of Cæsar Borgia at the infamous massacre of Sinigallia. Giovanni Vitelli signalised himself at the siege of Mirandola under Julius II., and indeed there are few members of the family who do not figure in the political transactions of the 15th and 16th centuries. The Vitelli had also the more distinguished honour of being among the earliest patrons of *Raphael*, who, notwithstanding the defeat sustained by his sovereign, Guid' Ubaldo, became a resident at the court of Vitellozzo in the year succeeding that event. Many of his earliest works were painted here, and were preserved in the churches and private galleries for which they were executed, until dispersed by the French invasion. The well-known *Sposalizio*, or marriage of the Virgin, now in the Brera gallery, was formerly in the Albizzini chapel in the ch. of S. Francesco. The ch. of S. Agostino contained the *Coronation of St. Nicholas of Tolentino*, the first work which Raphael painted in the town: it was much damaged, and the upper portion of it had been sold to Pius VI., but it was taken from the Vatican by the French, and can no longer be traced. The chapel of the Gavari family in the ch. of S. Domenico contained the well-known picture of the *Crucifixion*, which was for some time the ornament of the gallery of Cardinal Fesch, and is now the property of Lord Ward. It was sold by the representatives of the family for whom it was painted, in 1809. The *Adoration of the Magi*, now in the Berlin Museum, and the *Coronation of the Virgin*, in the Vatican, are also believed to have been painted during Raphael's residence in Città di Castello. In spite of these losses, it will presently be seen that the city still retains 2 small pictures by this great master, besides the works of other painters, sufficient to form the museum of a capital.

The *Cathedral*, dedicated to S. Florido, a native of the city, appears, on the authority of an ancient inscription, to occupy the site of an earlier Christian edifice constructed on the ruins of the temple of Felicitas, erected by the 2nd Pliny. The present ch. was built in 1503 as it now appears, from the designs, according to some writers, of Bramante, and at the joint expense of the citizens and the Vitelli family. The edifice is in the form of a Latin cross. The principal façade, like so many others in Italian churches, was never completed: it was begun in 1631, and carried as far as the capitals of the columns, but no attempt has since been made to finish it. Before we enter into any details of the interior, its rich Gothic doorway, which belonged to the older ch., demands attention. This fine relic is a remarkable specimen of the most beautiful and elaborate Gothic carving. It has a pointed arch and a transom; on each side are 4 spiral columns with richly sculptured capitals, and every part of it is covered with foliage and other ornaments. The bas-reliefs upon it represent Justice with the sword overcoming Iniquity, Mercy with the lily, &c.; and in the open spaces between the tendrils of vines which rise between these figures are various subjects, either typical or descriptive of Scripture history—the Pelican feeding her young, the Death of Abel, St. Amantius, a native saint, and his serpent, the Annunciation, the Visitation, the Nativity, the Sacrifice of Isaac, &c.

The interior contains a number of paintings, chiefly by native artists. The 1st chapel on the rt. of the main entrance contains the picture by *Bernardino Gaglardi*. It represents the Martyrdom of St. Crescentian, a native of the town. The next chapel, dedicated to St. John the Baptist, contains a copy of Raphael's Baptism of the Saviour, in the Loggie of the Vatican. The chapel of the Angelo Custode contains the Guardian Angel, and the Virgin in the clouds sustained by angels, by *Pacetti*. In the tympanum of the altar is a head of the Almighty, by *Gagliardi:* the Angel Raphael, and the boy Tobias, in this chapel, are by the same painter. The 2 pictures representing the history of Tobias on the lateral walls are by *Virgilio Ducci*, a pupil of Albani. The adjoining chapel, belonging to the Ranucci family, and dedicated to the Archangel Michael, is entirely painted by *Squazzino*. The chapel of the Assunzione di Mɛria Vergine has a picture of S. Carlo Borromeo by *Giovanni Serodine*. The chapel of the Madonna del Soccorso contains a large oil painting of the Virgin and several saints, said to have been painted by *Gagliardi* in 24 hours. *The Cupola* was built by *Niccolò Barbioni*, an architect of this town, and painted by *Marco Benefial*; the St. Peter and St. Paul, and the Doctors of the Church, the fine Assumption of the Virgin, on the vault, and the paintings of the tribune, some representing events of the Old Testament, and others the life and actions of S. Crescentian and S. Florido, are among his best works. The inlaid work of the stalls of the choir is worthy of examination; the designs for the first 6 on each side have been attributed to Raphael, but they were more probably by Raffaelo del Colle: they represent subjects taken from the Old and New Testaments, while the remaining 22 are illustrative of the lives and actions of the saints who were natives of the city. The 2 singing-galleries of walnut-wood are remarkable for their carvings, supposed to have been executed by the artists of the stalls in the choir. The gallery on the side of the Sacristy has

a bas-relief of the Crucifixion; that on other side of the ch. has the Ecce Homo, with SS. Lorenzo and Amanzio; at the extremities are the 4 evangelists, with St. Jerome, St. Gregory the Great, St. Augustin, and St. Ambrose. The *Capellone*, or chapel of the SS. Sacramento, built by Barbioni, the architect of the cupola, contains a large picture of the Transfiguration, by *Rosso Fiorentino*. The *Sacristy* was famous for its riches prior to the French invasion of 1798; it now contains but a small portion of its former treasures. In the Record-room of the Chapter is preserved the ancient altarpiece of carved silver, which D'Agincourt has described in detail. It was presented to the cathedral of this his native town by Celestin II. in the 12th century; the sculptures represent subjects in the Life of Christ, the Nativity, the Adoration of the Magi, the Visitation, and various saints. It is considered by D'Agincourt, who calls it a "magnificent work," to be a specimen of the Greek school, either purchased in Greece, or executed in Italy by Greek artists. An adjoining chamber contains portraits of bishops of the see and of benefactors to the cathedral. The *Subterranean Church* is of vast size, supported by low and massive buttresses; it has an air of venerable grandeur, which is increased by the picturesque effect of its numerous columns and chapels. It contains the relics of S. Florido.

The Ch. of San Francesco, formerly a Gothic edifice, contains in the first chapel on the rt. of the entrance the Stoning of Stephen by *Niccolò Circignani*; the second contains a picture of San Bernardino di Siena, by *Tommaso Conca*, and a silver reliquiary of the 15th century, containing the relics of St. Andrew the apostle; the third has the Annunciation, by *Niccolò Circignani*, with the date 1575; the fourth contains the Assumption of the Virgin, with all the apostles below, a beautiful work of *Raffaelo del Colle*, whose genius can only be appreciated in this and the neighbouring city of Borgo S. Sepolcro. In the adjoining chapel is a fine picture of the Conception, by *Antonio*, the little-known son of the elder Circignani. On the l. hand, the first chapel belonging to the Vitelli family contains the Coronation of the Virgin, with St. Catharine, St. Jerome, St. Nicholas of Tolentino, and other saints, one of the finest works of *Vasari*. In this chapel are buried many illustrious members of the house of Vitelli. The stalls or seats are worked in *tarsia*, representing the life of St. Francis. In the adjoining chapel is St. Francis receiving the Stigmata, in terra-cotta, which has suffered great injury. It is attributed to *Luca della Robbia*, but is more probably the work of Agostino and Andrea, the brother and nephew of that artist.

The *Ch. of S. Agostino* formerly contained the celebrated picture of St. Nicholas of Tolentino, by Raphael; the Nativity and the Adoration of the Magi, by Luca Signorelli; the St. John Baptist, of Parmegiano; the Massacre of the Innocents, by N. Circignani; and the Ascension, in terra-cotta, by Luca della Robbia: but all these fine works were dispersed at the French invasion. The present ch. has little interest beyond a modern work by *Chialli*, representing S. François di Sales, S. Agostino, and S. Françoise di Cantal, and a good copy of the Sposalizio of Raphael.

The *Ch. of S. Bartolommeo* has a Martyrdom of the Apostle by *Squazzino*. In the wall by the side of the altar is a bas-relief of the 11th or 12th century, in peperino, which appears from the ciborium in the central compartment, to have belonged to the altar of the Holy Sacrament. The lateral figures represent St. Bartholomew and St. Benedict, above whom are Sta. Scolastica and another saint.

The *Ch. of Sta. Caterina* contains a painting of S. Francesco di Paola praying, by *Andrea Carlone*, whose works are found in so many palaces of Genoa, his native city. The fresco of the Almighty over the high altar is attributed to *Niccolò Circignani*. The 4 frescoes by the side, illustrative of the Life of the Madonna, are by *Gagliardi*. The Crucifixion is by *Squazzino*.

In the *Ch. of the Convent of Sta. Cecilia* is a fine altarpiece by *Luca Signorelli*, representing the Virgin in the heavens in the midst of saints, with St. Cecilia and others in the foreground. It was ordered to be removed to Paris at the French invasion, but it fortunately got no further than Perugia, and was restored. The picture of the Annunciation occupies the place of the grand painting of the Coronation of the Virgin, by Pietro della Francesca, now in the gallery of Cav. Mancini.

The *Ch. of S. Domenico* is a fine Gothic edifice of considerable size, with a wooden roof. On entering the ch., the first altar on the rt. has a fine Sposalizio of S. Catherine, by *Santi di Tito*. The next, richly ornamented, has a picture of the Virgin and Child, with several saints in adoration; an *ex voto* painted by *Gregorio Pagani* for Antonio Corvini of this city, who was one of the generals of the Duke of Burgundy. It is related, that, during the siege of some town, he was engaged in storming a gate over which was placed an image of the Madonna, and that, being seized with remorse, he made amends for the outrage by dedicating this chapel to her honour. The altar of the Madonna del Rosario was painted in fresco by *Cristoforo Gherardi*. The Gavari chapel contained the celebrated Crucifixion by Raphael, which has passed into Lord Ward's gallery. The high altar is imposing; it contains the body of B. Margherita, who flourished as a Dominican nun in the 14th century. On the other side of the ch. the Brozzi chapel has a picture by *Luca Signorelli*, in his first manner, representing S. Sebastian in the midst of the archers. The fresco near the last altar on this side, representing the Madonna and Saints, is a work of the 15th century, but the author is unknown. In the choir are a large Madonna, a remarkable work of the 13th century, and a fine picture of the Annunciation, by the native painter *Francesco da Castello*, dated 1524, which Lanzi considers his best work. The *Gothic Cloisters*, though not in the best taste, are worthy of a visit. The paintings in the lunettes are principally by *Salvi Castelluci*, pupil of Pietra da Cortona; a few are by *Squazzino*.

The Ch. of Sta. Maria Maggiore is a specimen of the Gothic architecture of the 15th century. It was begun by Niccolò Vitelli, after he had captured the city and destroyed the citadel of Sta. Maria, erected by Sixtus IV., and was finished early in the 16th century.

The Ch. of S. Michele Archangelo has an altarpiece by *Raffaello del Colle,* representing the Madonna and Child on a throne between St. Sebastian and St. Michael, who is trampling upon Satan,

The Ch. of the Servites contains the grand painting of the Deposition by *Raffaello del Colle.* The gradino represents the Resurrection, the Saviour releasing the Patriarchs, and his appearing to the Magdalen. One of the pedestals of the columns of the altar represents in miniature the Supper at Emmaus, the other the Saviour appearing to the Virgin. Opposite is the Annunciation, the finest work of *Raffaello del Colle* in the city. On the rt. of the high altar is the Presentation in the Temple, by the same great master, which had been carried to Rome, but restored after it had undergone some restorations by Camuccini.

The *Confraternità of the SS. Trinità* contains 2 Standards by *Raphael,* classed among his earliest works, and the only ones remaining in the public edifices of a city in which he produced so many of his grandest compositions. In the first of these is represented the Crucifixion, with the Almighty and the Holy Spirit in the act of sustaining the Cross, and S. Sebastian and S. Roch kneeling by its side. In the other is represented the Creation of Eve. The style and expression of these pictures are still admirable, although they have suffered much from neglect, and perhaps still more from recent attempts to restore them, and give an artificial brightness by means of varnish.

Besides these churches, there are some works of art, worthy of notice to a traveller who has plenty of time to dispose of, in the churches of S. Egidio, S. Giovanni Decollato (in the Sagrestia of which is a standard said to be painted by *Pinturicchio*), San Giovanni Battista, San Pietro, San Sebastiano, and of the Convent of Tutti Santi.

The *Hospital* occupies the site of one founded in 1257 by the Vitelli family, and is the representative of several similar charities formerly existing in the city. It is a modern building of great extent, but somewhat low in proportion to its length. Its elegant chapel contains the Descent of the Holy Spirit by *Santi di Tito;* it is perhaps the finest of his works in point of colouring.

The *Palazzo Comunale* was, previous to the 13th century, the episcopal palace; it is a massive building, constructed with large blocks of stone, which have resisted the earthquakes by which so many of the churches have suffered. It is in the Gothic style, with pointed windows and doors. The vault of its massive gateway is said to have been painted by *Luca Signorelli.* The grand saloon contains a collection of ancient marbles and Roman inscriptions, the interest of which is chiefly local. There is a collection of portraits in the council-chamber, representing many native celebrities and others who have been officially connected with the city and diocese.

The *Palazzo Vescovile,* an ancient building, remodelled, after the earthquake of 1789, in its present style, was formerly the Palazzo Comunale. The altar of its private chapel has a good modern painting of the Madonna and Child, by *Chialli.* The adjoining *Campanile,* called *Torre del Vescovo,* is a work of the 13th century, the only one now left of the many which the city formerly possessed. In 1474 the exterior was painted with a grand fresco, by *Luca Signorelli,* representing the Madonna with St. Jerome and St. Paul, but it is sadly injured.

The *Palazzo Apostolico,* the residence of the governor, begun, it is said, early in the 14th century by the lords of Pietramala, was considerably altered in later periods. The portico and Loggie del Grano were added in the 17th century, when the present façade was built by Niccolò Barbioni.

The *Vitelli Palaces:*—Città di Castello contains no less than 4 palaces

which formerly belonged to this family.
1. The *Palazzo Vitelli a S. Giacomo*, now the property of the Marchese del Monte, representative of the family, was built by Angela de' Rossi, mother of Alessandro Vitelli, the contemporary of Cosmo de' Medici.

2. Near the gate of S. Egidio is the *Palazzo di Paolo Vitelli*, so called from the celebrated architect of that name, by/whom it was designed and built about 1540. It forms a quadrangle of large proportions, the northern front looking out upon the extensive gardens which once constituted the pride and ornament of the city. The style and execution of this palace are equally magnificent, and the grand staircase is worthy of a royal palace. The staircase and its lofty vault were painted by *Doceno;* the upper part represents various mythological subjects, and the other portions are covered with grotesque figures, quadrupeds, fish, birds, &c., thrown together by the most extravagant and capricious fancy, the whole of which, as Lanzi observes, are by his own hand. The saloon was decorated by *Prospero Fontana* with the most brilliant achievements of the family; it has been barbarously divided into small chambers, to the serious injury of the paintings; indeed many of them are entirely ruined by neglect. They represent the history of several events in which the Vitelli bore a part: among which may be mentioned Pius V. creating Cardinal Vitellozzo Vitelli his chamberlain; the death of Giovanni Vitelli at the siege of Osimo; the reconciliation of Niccolò with Sixtus IV. after the Conquest of Città di Castello; the sons of Niccolò driving out the enemies of the city; Alessandro carrying back to Florence Strozzi, Cavalcanti, and other rebels against the authority of Cosmo de' Medici; Niccolò in full council, declared " Father of his Country;" Charles VIII. of France knighting Camillo in the presence of the army; the same sovereign creating him Duke of Gravina. The other walls record the bravery of Paolo, who drives the Venetian army from Casentino; the capture of Guid' Ubaldo, duke of Urbino, by Vitel-

lozzo; the league of the Orsini, Vitelli, &c., against Cæsar Borgia; the capture of Mirandola by Giovanni Vitelli, under Julius II.; the gallant resistance offered by Vitello Vitelli to the passage of the Adda by the French; and several exploits of Alessandro during his alliance with Cosmo de' Medici. These frescoes are stated, on the authority of Malvasia, to have been painted by Prospero Fontana in a few weeks, and Lanzi says that they bear evidence of the fact. In that part of the palace called " del Marchese Chiappino," from the famous general who added to the celebrity of the name in Flanders, are 2 painted chambers representing various mythological subjects, besides other events in the history of the family; part of these are supposed to be the work of *Prospero Fontana* and part of *Doceno.* Another large saloon has a roof painted by Doceno with mythological subjects remarkable for their colouring and execution. Another chamber is painted with events of the Old and New Testaments. Another has a rich roof of gold and bas-reliefs and grotesque figures, in the midst of which is the Banquet of the Gods, supposed to be by *Prospero Fontana.* The other portions of the palace are equally rich, but do not require minute description. Of *the Gardens* little remains of their former magnificence; the plane-trees, said to have been 3 centuries old, have been cut down, the fountains no longer play, and even the pipes which supplied them, although laid down at an immense cost, have been recently cut off. *The Loggia* at the extremity of the gardens is a fine example of the powers of *Doceno* as a fresco-painter; its walls are decorated with caryatides, animals, birds, fruits, and flowers, with a profusion almost unrivalled; few subjects are repeated, and there are said to be no less that 70 kinds of birds introduced in the composition. Although painted 3 centuries ago, and exposed to the inclemency of the weather, the colours are still fresh. Cav. Mancini describes it as entirely the work of Doceno; it is now deserted and falling into decay.

3. The noble *Palazzo di Alessandro Vitelli*, now belonging to the Bufalini family, situated near the ch. of S. Fortunato, occupies the original site of the first house of the family. It was erected by Alessandro on the foundations of a more ancient palace built in 1487 by Camillo, Giovanni, and Vitellozzo Vitelli.

4. The *Palazzo Vitelli alla Cannoniera* was so called from the foundry of cannon which adjoined it when the city flourished under the sovereignty of the family. The French seized, in 1798, several large cannons cast here with the arms of Vitelli, and the establishment was then suppressed. This palace was the habitation of Niccolò, "the father of his country."

The *Palazzo Bufalini* is said to have been designed by Vignola, during his mission to the city from Gregory XIII. for the settlement of the boundary line between Rome and Tuscany. Cardinal Bufalini, while bishop of Ancona, added a gallery which contained the St. John Baptist of Parmigiano, and other fine pictures, now mostly dispersed. Of those which remain, the Madonna and Child of *Simone Cantarini*, the fine portrait of Cardinal Ricci attributed to *Titian*, the Madonna and Child, with St. John, supposed to be by *Andrea del Sarto*, and a portrait by *Vandyke*, may be mentioned.

The *Palazzo Mancini*, the house of the learned Cav. Mancini, the historian of his native city, contains the following good works:—*Giotto*, a crucifix covered with miniature paintings. *Luca della Robbia*, a fragment of the Ascension, in terra-cotta, formerly in the ch. of S. Agostino. *Pietro della Francesca*, the Coronation of the Virgin, with S. Francis, S. Bernardin, and other saints in the lower part; 6 small pictures representing Saints. *Luca Signorelli*, the Nativity, one of the masterpieces of this great artist; the Madonna and Child, with St. Jerome, S. Niccolò di Bari, St. Sebastian, and a female saint; this fine painting was executed for the neighbouring village of Montone. *Raphael*, a small but very beautiful picture of the Annunciation, said to have been in the gradino belonging to the "Cru-

cifixion" of Cardinal Fesch's gallery. *Raffaello del Colle*, 8 small pictures, representing the Miracles of the Holy Sacrament; 2 other small pictures by the same hand. *N. Circignani*, a large picture of the Massacre of the Innocents. *Vasari*, portrait of Cosmo de' Medici on wood. *Annibale Caracci*, a boy and cat, perfect. *Cesare Maggieri* of *Urbino*, a large picture of the Virgin and Child, with saints in adoration (S. Jerome, S. Bernardin of Siena, S. Antony of Padua, and S. Antonio Abate), formerly in the ch. of S. Agostino. *Chev. Francesco di Mancini*, of St. Angelo in Vado, the Flagellation, the crowning with thorns, and the Saviour in chiaro-scuro. In an upper room is a collection illustrative of the geology of the Apennines, various antiquities, and a small cabinet of medals.

In the neighbourhood of Città di Castello is the Monte di Belvedere, supposed by some to be the site of *Tusci*, the favourite villa of the younger Pliny. Others have concluded, from various remains, and from traces of Roman foundations which have been discovered on the spot, that Palmolara is more probably the site; but all are agreed that it was in the immediate vicinity of Tifernum. Pliny, indeed, thus describes its situation: "Oppidum est prædiis nostris vicinum, nomine Tifernum." He says that it was placed among an amphitheatre of wooded mountains, on the slope of a hill gradually rising from the plain, whose fertile meadows were watered by the Tiber; the lower hills were clothed with vines and shrubs, and the breezes from the upper Apennines purified the air and rendered it salubrious. He preferred it to his other villas, and has left a minute description of it in his beautiful letter to Apollinaris (lib. v., Ep. 6). Città di Castello was made a bishopric A.D. 300, but the see was divided by Leo X., in 1520, in order to form the neighbouring diocese of Borgo S. Sepolcro. The *fair*, once much resorted to from all parts of Italy, has now declined to a second-rate gathering of provincial traders; it is held from the 23rd to the 31st August.

ROUTE 19.

**SAN GIUSTINO TO BORGO SAN SEPOLCRO
AND AREZZO.**

	Miles.
San Giustino to Cospaja (frontier) .	1
Cospaja to Borgo San Sepolcro . .	1
Borgo San Sepolcro to Arezzo . .	24
	26

It has been already mentioned in the previous route that, on descending the Apennines from Urbino to Città di Castello a road branches off at San Giustino to Borgo San Sepolcro, and, proceeding thence into Tuscany, falls into the great post-road between Rome and Florence at Arezzo. This enables travellers desirous of reaching Florence from the shores of the Adriatic to visit many interesting towns in their way, and indeed opens a tract of country hitherto but little known to tourists.

The papal frontier is passed at the village of *Cospaja*, and we enter Tuscany 1 m. before reaching the town of

1 m. *Borgo San Sepolcro* (*Inn*, Aquila Nera del Fiorentino, very tolerable). Borgo was formerly a fortified town, but nearly all its towers were destroyed by the earthquake in 1789, by which Città di Castello so severely suffered. Borgo San Sepolcro may be called a city of painters, for few provincial towns in Italy have produced so many. The names of Pietro della Francesca, Raffaello del Colle, Santi di Tito, Cristoforo Gherardi, and numerous others of more or less note, are sufficient to justify the partiality of local historians, who have called it a school of art: indeed Lanzi has remarked that Pietro della Francesca himself is one of those painters who form an era in art. This remarkable man, whom Mr. Eastlake (*Quart. Rev.* cxxxi.) has described as "one of the most accomplished painters of his time," was born about 1398. He was one of the first masters who successfully treated the effects of light, and made his designs subservient to principles of perspective. "Pietro was the guest of Giovanni Santi in Urbino

in 1469. His portraits of the duke (then Count Federigo) and his consort Battista Sforza, forming a dyptich, are now in the gallery at Florence. A single specimen only of his talents remains at Urbino; but in his native city, Borgo S. Sepolcro, many of his works are still extant. * * * Lastly, this master was skilled above all his contemporaries in perspective and geometry, and Vasari goes so far as to say, 'the most important information that exists on such subjects is derived from him.' His MSS. were deposited in the ducal library at Urbino, and some of them are now in the possession of the Marini family at Borgo S. Sepolcro. The most distinguished contemporary painters of Romagna and Umbria are said to have studied under Pietro della Francesca. Among these, Melozzo da Forli and Luca Signorelli confirm such a tradition by their works more than Pietro Perugino."—*Quarterly Review.*

Borgo San Sepolcro formerly belonged to the Holy See, but in 1440 Eugenius IV. transferred it to the Florentines. It was raised to municipal rank by Leo X. in 1515.

The Cathedral is a fine building with 3 aisles, and is said to date from the time of the Abbot Roderigo Bonizzo, in 1012. On entering the building by the principal door, the Graziani chapel, the first on the rt. hand, contains a fine work painted for the family by *Palma Giovane* (1602): it represents the Assumption, with the 12 apostles in the foreground. The Ventura chapel (the 4th) has a painting by *Santi di Tito*, representing the incredulity of St. Thomas. The chapel of the SS. Sacramento contains a fine modern work, the Anime purgante, by *Chialli*. In the Choir is the Resurrection by *Raffaello del Colle*, the Crucifixion by *Chialli*, and a repetition by *Pietro Perugino* of his great picture of the Ascension, now in the Ch. of St. Peter at Perugia. It is recorded by Cav. Mancini that this copy was painted at Florence, and brought hither on men's shoulders "con spesa gravissima." On the opposite side of the ch. is the Madonna del Rosario sustained by angels, by *Antonio Cavallucci*. Near it is the Holy Trinity, with St. Andrew,

Sta. Cristina, and the Magdalen, by *Cherubino Alberti*, a native painter, known also as an engraver of the works of Michael Angelo. Lower down, the Pichi chapel has a Nativity by another native artist, *Durante Alberti.* The Laudi chapel contains a picture of the Annunciation by *Giovanni de' Vecchi*, also a native painter. The last chapel has a Crucifixion by *Giovanni Alberti*, the painter of the Sala Clementina in the Vatican, and the brother of Cherubino already mentioned. Over the door of *the sacristy* is a grand painting representing the Almighty supported by angels, by *Raffaello del Colle.* The sacristy contains a very fine Baptism of the Saviour, by *Pietro della Francesca*, with a gradino representing various events in the life of St. John Baptist. The fragment in fresco of various saints is by *Gerino da Pistoja*, pupil of Pinturicchio.

The ancient *Ch. of S. Francesco*, with its rich Gothic doorway, whose choir was formerly remarkable for its paintings by Giotto, contains a St. Francis receiving the stigmata, by *Giovanni de' Vecchi;* and Christ disputing with the doctors, a fine work of *Domenico Passignano* (Cresti). The sacristy contains a picture of St. Andrew and St. Nicholas by *Durante Alberti.*

The Ch. of the *Madonna della Grazie* has a fine painting of the Madonna by *Raffaello del Colle*, which can only be seen by permission of the bishop, and a picture of S. Rocco and S. Sebastian by *Gio. Battista Cungi.*

The *Ch. of the Orphans* contains a good work of *Rosso Fiorentino*, representing the Deposition from the Cross; and an Annunciation attributed to *Raffaello Scaminossi*, another native painter.

The *Ch. of the Servites* contains a Madonna and Child with St. Luke and St. Francis d'Assisi, by *N. Circignani;* a Presentation in the Temple by *Giovanni de' Vecchi;* an Annunciation variously attributed to Matteo Roselli, Circignani, and Domenico Passignano; and a fine Assumption by an unknown Sienese master of the 15th century.

The *Ch. of S. Chiara* has at the high altar an Assumption of the Virgin, with St. Francis, Sta. Chiara, and 2 other saints, by *Pietro della Francesca;* cruelly mangled to suit the architecture of the ch.

The *Ch. of the P.P. Minori Osservanti* has the Adoration of the Magi, full of expression and colouring, by *Bassano;* the Nativity of the Virgin, by *Giovanni de' Vecchi;* a Crucifixion by *Passignano;* and in the choir a fine Assumption by *Raffaello del Colle.*

The *Ch. of S. Rocco* has a painting of the Resurrection by *Raffaello del Colle.*

The *Ch. of Sta. Maria della Misericordia*, now the chapel of the hospital erected as a memorial of the plague in 1348, contains a picture of the Virgin surrounded by figures, by *Pietro della Francesca*, with a beautiful gradino.

The ancient *Ch. of S. Antonio Abate*, built in 1345, has a remarkable Standard painted on both sides by *Luca Signorelli;* on one is the Crucifixion with the Virgin at the foot of the Cross, beautiful and touching in its effect, with a fine landscape and every figure full of expression; on the other is S. Antonio Abate and S. Eligio. This is one of the finest works in the city, and is in excellent condition.

The *Ch. of S. Agostino* contains the Nativity of the Saviour, by the school of *Caracci;* and a picture representing the Virgin subduing Satan, by *Gerino da Pistoja*, bearing his name and the date 1502.

The *Monte di Pietà* contains the fresco of the Resurrection, by *Pietro della Francesca*, which Vasari describes as the best of all his works.

An interesting but hilly road leads from Borgo San Sepolcro to Arezzo, traversing the group of hills that separate the upper valleys of the Arno and Tiber. It crosses the Tiber soon after leaving Borgo: traversing a range of low tertiary hills, it descends into the valley of the Sovara, from which another hilly road of 2 m. leads into that of the Cerfone. Here at the village of Villa the road from Borgo falls into the so-called Strada Anconitana, that from Arezzo to Urbino by Citta di Castello; 2 m. E. of Villa, and just within the papal territory, is the village of Citerna, the ch. of which, S. Francesso, contains some pictures worthy of a visit: Our Saviour surrounded by angels and saints, by *Raffaello del Colle*; a Crucifixion, by *Circignani*; a St. Francis and St. Jerome, erroneously attributed to Raphael; and in the choir a Madonna and Child with St. John, which, according to a modern inscription, is from the pencil of the same great artist. From Villa a gradual ascent of several miles along the Cerfone leads to Magano (San Donino), where the ascent up the ravine of the Fiumicello to S. Fiorenzo becomes more rapid. From this point the watershed between the Tiber and the Arno, a continuous and precipitous descent of less than 4 m., brings us to Arezzo.

Another, but less convenient, although shorter, road between Borgo San Sepolcro and Arezzo, passes by Anghiari. The Tiber is crossed about 1 m. higher than in the former route, and a straight and good road across the plain leads to the bottom of the hills on which Anghiari rises, 4 m. W. of Borgo. Anghiari, a town of 1600 Inhab., is celebrated for the battle fought there June 29, 1440, between Piccinino, the Milanese general, and the Florentine army under Giovanni Paolo Orsini. Piccinino previous to the battle occupied Borgo San Sepolcro; and so unprepared were the Florentines for an attack, that Michelotto Attendolo had barely time to occupy the bridge over the Tiber before the Milanese arrived. For 2 hours this bridge was the scene of a desperate struggle between the combatants; it was several times forced by the Milanese, who on one occasion made their way to the walls of Anghiari; but they were again and again repulsed, until at length the Florentines succeeded in passing the bridge and making good their ground on the other side of the river. By this manœuvre they divided the 2 wings of Piccinino's army, and threw the whole into confusion. Piccinino himself was compelled to retire on Borgo San Sepolcro, and half his army fell into the hands of the Florentines. The pillage is said to have been immense, no less than 400 officers and 3000 horses being captured by the conquerors. At Anghiari there is a large picture of the Last Supper by *Pietro della Francesca*.

About 10 m. N. of Anghiari, in the valley of the Singerna, one of the principal affluents of the Upper Tiber, is the small town of Caprese, the birthplace of Michael Angelo, in 1474.

From Anghiari to Arezzo the road is unfit for carriages, but easily performed on foot or on horseback, and very interesting in a geological point of view: following the valley of the Sovara, it passes near the base of Monte Acuto, a remarkable conical peak (formed of serpentine, which has been forced up through the limestone strata), to descend along the Chiassa torrent into the Piano di Arezzo.

24 m. AREZZO, described in Rte. 27.

ROUTE 20.

CITTÀ DI CASTELLO TO GUBBIO.

35 English m.

	Rom. Miles.
Città di Castello to Fratta . . .	12
Fratta to Gubbio	26
	——
	38
	——

The first part of this route carries us along the excellent road which leads S. from Città di Castello to Perugia. It follows the l. bank of the Tiber as far as Santa Maria Maddalena, where it crosses the river, and proceeds along the rt. bank until it recrosses it at Fratta.

15 m. *Fratta*, a small town, with a pop. of 4600 souls. It is supposed to occupy the site of *Pitulum*, and to have been founded by the remnant of the Roman army after their defeat by Hannibal. Situated in the narrowest part of the valley of the Tiber, where the hills on either side approach close to its banks, it occupied in the middle ages a place of some military importance. During the struggles between the republicans of Perugia and the popes, Fratta was frequently the scene of contests between their hostile armies, and from its attachment to the Church it acquired the titles of "Nobilis," "Insignis," and "Fidelissima," from successive pontiffs.

It was formerly famous for its ironworks and its earthenware. In the Ch. of Sta. Croce is a Deposition from the Cross, by *Luca Signorelli*; and Signor Domenico Mavarelli's Collection of Majolica is worth a visit.

A bridle-road of about 15 m., over a very hilly and uninteresting country, branches off from hence to Gubbio, passing by Civitella Ranieri, the Abbadia of Campo Riggiano, and San Cristoforo, where it enters the Plain of Gubbio, at its N.E. extremity, and thence through Morcia and Semonte ; but the most convenient, although making a detour of 11 m., is by the carriage-road to Perugia as far as Busco on the Tiber ; from this place a very good road of 21 m. leads to Gubbio, over a wild and hilly country, with fine woodland scenery ; leaving Busco, the road ascends the valley of the Primo torrent as far as Piccione, which is generally made the halting-place by the vetturini from Gubbio, from which the ascent is rapid, and oxen required for carriages : 5 m. farther is the village of *Scritto.* From this point there is a gradual descent to the Plain of Gubbio, passing through *Santa Maria di Colonnata* and Ponte de Tassi, where the road enters the plain, and from which a drive of 3 m. brings us to the city. The most convenient place for stopping on the way from Perugia is at the osteria of *Le Capenacce,* half-way between Piccione and Scritto.

26 m. GUBBIO. (*Inns :* Locanda del Giglio ; Locanda di Sperniche, very poor.) This interesting town, beautifully situated on the declivity and at the base of the Monte Calvo, occupies the site of the ancient Umbrian city of *Iguvium,* whose possession was considered of so much importance by Cæsar in his invasion. The present population amounts to 8000 souls. The town, which is well built, is entirely of the middle-age character. The ancient city extended further into the plain previous to its partial destruction by the Goths ; in 1155 it was besieged and threatened with ruin by Frederick Barbarossa, but it was preserved by the interposition of its patron saint and bishop, S. Ubaldo.

The *Palazzo del Comune* is a very *Cent. It.*

interesting relic of the times of the republic, as well as an imposing ornament of the town. It was built by Matteo di Giovenello of Gubbio, called Gattapone, between 1332 and 1340. It is now abandoned.

The *Ducal Palace* was built by Luciano Lauranna, architect of the palace at Urbino, and decorated in the same style as that remarkable edifice. Though containing fewer remains of its ancient magnificence, it is a good example of the architecture and sculpture of the 16th century. Among its inlaid ornaments may be traced the insignia of the Order of the Garter, conferred upon Duke Guid' Ubaldo by Henry VII.

In the *Palaces* of Conte Ranghiasci Brancaleoni and of Conte Beni are some good pictures, and the public library is rich in materials for local history.

The *Cathedral,* dedicated to St. Marian and St. James the Martyr, contains several good pictures well preserved. The first altar on the l. has a Madonna enthroned between S. Ubaldo and S. Sebastian, on a gold ground, by *Sinibaldo Ibi,* a rare master of the school of Perugino. The Magdalen is a fine specimen of *Timoteo Vite,* by whom also are the frescoes behind the episcopal chair. A *presepio* of the school of Perugino is probably by Giannicolo ; S. Thomas is by *Nucci,* a pupil of Raffaello del Colle. Behind the sacristy is preserved a very remarkable *priviale* or priest's robe, with various scenes of the Passion beautifully embroidered on a gold ground.

The ch. of *S. Maria Nuova* has the finest work of *Ottaviano Nello,* one of the most intensely devotional painters of the Umbrian school, and probably the master of Gentile da Fabriano. It is a fresco representing the Madonna and Child, with St. Paul, St. Anthony, a choir of Angels, and the donors. *S. Agostino* has in the roof of the choir very well preserved frescoes by *Giacomo Bedi,* another rare painter of Gubbio, representing 4 scenes in the life of St. Augustine, and the evangelists. Over the gate of S. Agostino is

H

a Madonna enthroned by *Martino Nello*. In *S. Pietro* is a Visitation by *Giannicola*, and some finely illuminated choral books by *Attavante* of Florence. *S. Francesco* has an excellent copy of Daniele da Volterra's deposition from the cross in the Trinità del Monte at Rome, and a Coronation of the Madonna signed by *Francesco Signorelli*. At *S. Domenico*, on the l., is a good fresco by *Raffaello del Colle* of the Madonna with a choir of angels, dated 1546; a statue in terra-cotta of St. Anthony is the work of *Maestro Giorgio Andreoli*, the celebrated painter on porcelain. The stalls of the choir are ornamented with arabesques in gold by *Nucci*. In the l. transept is a good Circumcision by *Damiano*, a native artist; it abounds in portraits, like most of his works in the other churches in this town.

There are some pictures of the 2 *Nucci* to be found in Gubbio, and frescoes of its early school, among which is a St. Anthony by *Palmerucci* under the arcade of the College of Painters.

An inscription marks the house erroneously supposed to have been occupied by Dante during his residence at Gubbio; the intimacy which he here formed with Oderigi, the missal-painter, and the merits of the latter as an artist, are immortalised by the great poet, *Par.*, xi. 100:—

Oh, diss' io lui, non sei tu Oderisi,
L'onor di Eugubio, e l'onor di quella arte
Che alluminare è chiamata in Parisi?

The chief interest of Gubbio is derived from the celebrated *Eugubian Tables*, which have excited the attention and curiosity of the learned men of Europe during the last 4 centuries. They were found in 1444 among the ruins of an ancient theatre near this town. These tables, now preserved at Gubbio, are of bronze, covered with inscriptions, 4 in Umbrian, 2 in Latin, and 1 in Etruscan and Latin characters. Among the numerous antiquaries who have written to illustrate them, it may be sufficient to mention that Buonarotti, by whom fac-similes were first published, in his Supplement to Dempster, considered them as

articles of treaties between the States of Umbria; Bourguet, Gori, and Bardetti thought that they were forms of prayer among the Pelasgi after the decline of their power; Maffei and Passeri, that they were statutes, or donations to the temple of Jupiter; while Lanzi conceived that they related solely to the sacrificial rites of the various towns of the Umbrian confederacy,—an opinion in which most subsequent antiquaries have been disposed to concur. Dr. Lepsius of Berlin, struck by the assertion of Lanzi that the language of the tables is full of archaisms, and bears great affinity to the Etruscan dialect, visited Gubbio for the purpose of examining them as philological illustrations of the formation of Latin, and has arrived at the conclusion that the Latin language, both among the people of Italy generally and among the Umbri, was much more recent than the Etruscan, and that the Etruscan literature was common to the Umbri. The tables present, moreover, many peculiarities to which we would desire to draw the attention of the tourist. The lines, like the Etruscan and other ancient languages, run from rt. to l.; the letters show that there is little difference between the Umbrian character and that form of ancient Greek which we call Pelasgic. The Umbrian inscriptions appear to be of various dates, for the spelling of several words which occur in the different plates is dissimilar. The connection of the Umbri with the Greeks is shown by the names of their deities in these tables, most of which are of Greek origin; and numerous other Greek words occur almost without change. In one of the inscriptions relating to the sacrifice of a dog, the words *katle* (catulus) and *hunte* occur; the last is curious as an argument in favour of the reputed origin of the Umbri from the Gauls, by which of course the Celtic nation generally is implied. The Latin inscriptions are highly interesting to the philological student; the letter O is used in place of V; G, a letter supposed to have been unknown before B.C. 353, is also to be recognised; *pir* (πυϱ) is used for fire, *puni* for bread, and *vinu* for wine. Gubbio was, perhaps, the most important of the Umbrian communities whose names are recorded in the tables, and it is supposed to answer to Juviscana.

There is a very fair mountain road, adapted for carriages, between Gubbio and La Schieggia, 8 m. on the high post-road from Fano to Foligno. (*See* Rte. 17.) The ascent for the first 4 m. is very rapid and requires the assistance of oxen, passing through the Madonna della Perzola and Troppola.

A road of about 13 m. leads from Gubbio to San Facundino, where it joins the Via Flamina. (*See* Rte. 17.) Near Gualdo, this route runs through a richly wooded country for the first 7 m. to Ponte della Branca, where it crosses the torrent of that name, one of the affluents of the Tiber, from which there is a considerable ascent to San Facundino, 2 m. before reaching Gualdo Tadino.

ROUTE 21.

CITTÀ DI CASTELLO TO PERUGIA.

30½ Eng. m.

	Roman miles.
Città di Castello to Fratta .	12
Fratta to Perugia	21
	—
	33

The first part of this route, as far as Fratta, is described in the preceding Route.

12 m. *Fratta.* A road, described in the preceding Route, branches off on the l. from this place to Gubbio, from whence there is another to Gualdo, where it joins the Flaminian Way from Fano to Foligno.

From Fratta this route follows the l. bank of the Tiber as far as Resina, whence a cross road leads direct to Perugia, passing the river at Ponte Patoli. The principal road follows the valley at the foot of the hills, through a well-cultivated country, and after crossing

the Primo at Ponte Busco, and the Tiber at Ponte Felcino, rises by a rapid ascent of nearly 4 m. to

15 m. Perugia (Rte. 27).

ROUTE 22.

PERUGIA TO ROME, BY TODI, NARNI, PONTEFELICE, AND THE TIBER.

60 Eng. m.

	Roman miles.
Perugia to Todi	27
Todi to Narni	24
Narni to Pontefelice . . .	14
	—
	65

As regards absolute distance this is the most direct road between Perugia and the capital, and may be now conveniently and economically performed since steam navigation has been established on the Tiber. There are no post-horses between Perugia and Narni, but gigs and light carriages of the country can be easily hired; a public conveyance goes from Perugia to Todi at 9 P.M. on Mondays and Thursdays, in correspondence with another from Todi to Narni; a coach leaves Narni at 5 P.M. on Tuesdays and Fridays for Pontefelice, near to Borghetto, where there is a fairly good locanda, and the steamer leaves Pontefelice at daybreak on Wednesdays and Saturdays, arriving at Rome in 8 to 10 hours: during the very dry season, when the boat cannot ascend so far, she sails from the Porto della Rosa, 12 m. lower down. The fares are as follows:—Perugia to Todi, 7½ pauls; to Narni, 22 pauls; to Pontefelice, 35 pauls; and to Rome, 42 pauls. As a diligence arrives on the corresponding mornings from Florence and Arezzo, the whole distance from Florence to Rome may be performed at an outlay of 8 scudi.

Leaving Perugia by the post-route to Foligno, our road soon strikes off to the rt., and by a steep descent reaches the plain; 8 m. from the city it crosses the Tiber at Ponte Novo, a little below the embouchure of the Chiascio, and from hence follows the l. bank of the river, close to the base of the hills which all along border its eastern bank, to Todi. 28 m. TODI (*Inn*, Corona, very tolerable). This ancient Umbrian city is situated on a hill commanding magnificent views of the surrounding country, and so high as to be a conspicuous object for a great distance.

    " excelso summi qua vertice montis
  Devexum lateri pendet Tuder."
                      Sil. Ital.

It is now a small episcopal town of 4500 Inhab.; remarkable chiefly for the remains of its ancient Etruscan walls. These present in many parts some specimens of regular masonry as perfect as any which are met with in the cities of ancient Etruria, perhaps even more so than Volterra; the stones are laid in horizontal courses. They generally alternate, one course being narrow and the next broad. Another interesting ruin is the extensive building which has given rise to so much controversy among antiquaries; some calling it a Temple of Mars, for whose worship the ancient city was celebrated, while others regard it as a basilica of the time of the early emperors.

The *Cathedral*, a Gothic building, contains some frescoes which deserve examination. The ch. of the *Madonna della Consolazione*, built in the form of a Greek cross, is remarkable for its cluster of cupolas, considered one of the masterpieces of Bramante. The ch. of *S. Fortunato* has a rich Gothic doorway. [From Todi there is a mountainous bridle-road of about 18 m. to Orvieto.]

On leaving Todi the road is one continued ascent over the high range of hills that separate the valley of the Tiber from that of the Nera; about half-way is Castel Todino, with a small *osteria*; beyond it and before reaching S. Gemini, is Carsoli, on the site of the ancient Umbrian city of Carsulæ; near this the road from Foligno to Narni, by Bevagna, joins. S. Gemini is a miserable town of 1500 souls, in a high situation; from it the road descends constantly to the Nera, which it crosses near the bridge of Augustus, before ascending the hill to Narni. Near to S. Gemini a road branches off, on the l. to Terni (9 m.),

passing by to Cesi, celebrated for a large natural cavern in the limestone cliffs.

Narni (*Inn*, La Corona), with the road to Pontefelice, by Otricoli, is described under Rte. 27.

ROUTE 22A.

PERUGIA TO CITTA DELLA PIEVE.

26 m.

This route, although a hilly one, is through a very beautiful country, crossing the region that separates the valley of the Tiber from that of the Chiana. Since the opening of the railway between Siena and Florence it affords, connected with the good diligence conveyance between Chiusi and Siena, a cheap and agreeable mode of transport between Perugia and the capital of Tuscany. A public conveyance leaves Perugia on the mornings of Tuesdays, Thursdays, and Saturdays (returning from Città della Pieve on the intermediate days), reaches Chiusi on the same evening; so that, by means of the coach which starts from the latter on the following morning, the traveller will arrive in Florence at 7 P.M. on the same evening.

The road to Città della Pieve leaves Perugia by the same gate as that to Florence; 2 m. beyond which, after a steep ascent, it reaches San Sisto; and 8 m. farther the Madonna del Giglio, an osteria below the town of San Martino in Colle. The S.E. part of the Lake of Thrasymene is about 4 m. distant from this point. A gradual descent from San Martino leads into the valley of the Nestore, the road running parallel to the northern bank of the river as far as Tavernelle, which is considered the half-way house by the vetturini. The route continues to rise with the stream; for 5 m.; to the village of Piegaro, where it commences to ascend the hills, which are here thickly wooded with chesnut-trees and oaks; having the Nestore in the ravine on the l. 1 m. before arriving at Città della Pieve this road joins that described in the following (Route 23) from Orvieto;

ROUTE 23.

MONTEFIASCONE TO ORVIETO, CITTA
DELLA PIEVE, AND CHIUSI.

51 m.

	Roman miles.
Montefiascone to Orvieto . .	20
Orvieto to C. della Pieve . .	28
C. della Pieve to Chiusi . .	7
	—
	55

1. This route offers a comparatively little frequented line of communication between Rome and Florence, and travellers who are already acquainted with the 2 great post-routes by Siena and Perugia will find in it an agreeable digression, both as regards the beauty of the scenery, and the interest of Orvieto and Città della Pieve in the history of the fine arts. Tourists may combine with this route a visit to the Etruscan towns of South-eastern Tuscany—Chiusi, Sarteano, and Cortona; an excursion through the rich agricultural district of the Val di Chiana; and proceed to Florence either by way of Siena or the Val d' Arno di Sopra. The road we are about here to describe, although very hilly, is in good repair; but the inns are indifferent, especially at Orvieto and Città della Pieve.

For the traveller not having his own carriage the best mode of proceeding will be by the diligence, which leaves Rome on the mornings of Tuesday, Thursday, and Saturday, and arrives at Viterbo early in the afternoon. At daybreak on the following morning, a carriage that conveys the mail, not the cleanest or most comfortable of vehicles, starts for Orvieto, and arrives there about 11 o'clock, giving him sufficient time to visit that interesting city on the same day. On the following morning a similar vehicle sets out for Città della Pieve, and reaches it also at an early hour, so as to permit his seeing everything of interest there, and reaching Chiusi, where there is a tolerable inn, by 4 o'clock on the same evening.

The coach from Viterbo to Orvieto starts at 4 A.M. on Mondays, Wednesdays, and Fridays; from Orvieto to Città della Pieve on Tuesdays, Thursdays, and Saturdays; and from Città della Pieve to Chiusi 3 hours after the arrival of that from Orvieto. A very good diligence leaves Chiusi every Monday, Wednesday, and Friday, for Siena, at 4 A.M.

Before reaching the gate of Montefiascone from Viterbo by the post-road between Rome and Siena, that to Orvieto turns off to the rt. near to the inn of the "Aquila Nera."

Soon afterwards the old ch. of San Flaviano, with a curious balcony and a pointed doorway, is passed on the l.; and, a little farther on, an interesting (to the geologist) current of black lava is seen on the rt. of the road; from here an uninteresting hilly country for 4 m. is travelled over, along the eastern declivities of the hills that enclose the Lake of Bolsena, peeps of which are had during this portion of the route. 5 m. from Montefiascone commences a long valley, bordered on the S. by an extensive current of lava, which tops the range of hills that enclose it in that direction. A road strikes off on the rt. to Bagnarea (Balneum Regis), 5 m. off, celebrated for its mineral hot-springs; and 5 m. still farther, the road from Bolsena to Orvieto joins from the l. that from Montefiascone. A bleak and ill-cultivated region extends from this to the Osteria Nova, 6 m. from Orvieto; here the road commences to ascend, by the chapel of Santa Trinita, to a table-land which borders the valley of the Paglia on the W. Arrived at its eastern extremity, the view over the valley below, and Orvieto, is very fine. From this point a rapid descent, by an excellent road of well-managed zigzags, leads to a depression that separates the hill on which Orvieto is situated from the escarpment extending from Castel Viscardo by Sugana to the junction of the Paglia and Tiber. A small river is crossed, from which a steep ascent, requiring nearly an hour to surmount, brings us to the gates of Orvieto, The first view of Orvieto is very fine; placed on the summit of an elongated ridge, surrounded on all sides by v

·cal escarpments, it presents all the appearance of an immense bastioned fortification: in the midst, and on its highest point, rises its magnificent cathedral. The position of the city derives much of its peculiar beauty from the escarped rock of volcanic tuffa on which it stands; the base of which is washed by the Paglia, which, rising on the eastern declivities of Mont' Amiata, joins the Tiber, 4 m. lower down, near Torre di Monte.

[The geologist will find much to interest him in the country between Montefiascone and Orvieto. The whole region between the Lake of Bolsena and the valley of the Paglia is volcanic. The town of Orvieto itself is on one of the last eminences towards the E. of the great igneous mass which constitutes the volcanic group of Bolsena and Monte Cimino. Very good sections of the superposition of the latter on the tertiary marine formation are seen all round the city. The elongated plateau of Orvieto is as it were an island of volcanic breccia, similar in age and composition to that of the Ciminian range, and of the Tarpeian rock at Rome. Under it, on every side, lie the sub-Apennine tertiary marls, extending across the Paglia as far as the foot of the central chain of the Umbrian Apennines; the volcanic tuffa of Orvieto being the most eastern point to which the volcanic rocks of Central Italy extend on this parallel of latitude; the valleys of the Paglia and Tiber cutting off the volcanic rocks in this direction—all beyond, to the shores of the Adriatic, being of stratified marine deposits. The height of the volcanic mass at Orvieto is about 150 English feet. The elevation of the plateau on which the town stands is 720 feet above the Paglia, and 1250 above the level of the sea.]

20 m. ORVIETO (*Inn*, Locanda dell' Acquila Bianca, the only one in the town, dirty and in every respect indifferent). The position of Orvieto, a modern corruption of Urbs Vetus, represents the Herbanum of Pliny, bespeaks a more ancient, probably an Etruscan origin. In the middle ages it was one of the strongholds of the Guelph party. The local chroniclers record the names of no less than 32 popes who resided at various periods within its walls, the greater part of whom were driven to seek the security of its impregnable position during the troubles of the 12th and 13th centuries.

Orvieto at the present time is the chief city of a delegation, and is the residence of a bishop. The population of the city itself is 6350.

The Cathedral, or *Duomo*, is one of the most interesting examples of Italian Gothic, and in many other respects is without a rival in the history of art. It is built of black and white stone, like the cathedrals of Siena and Florence; but it is in a great measure free from the bizarre effect produced by the strong contrast of colours in both of those celebrated structures. The façade, with its bright mosaics and marble sculptures, is hardly to be surpassed in richness of material or in beauty of effect. The interior presents the largest collection of sculpture belonging to the schools of the 16th century, and is enriched by those celebrated frescoes of Luca Signorelli, from which Michael Angelo did not disdain to borrow for his great work of the Last Judgment.

This remarkable building owes its origin to the miracle of Bolsena, which occurred, according to the Church history, in the middle of the 13th century. — (See Rte. 26.)   Urban IV., being then resident at Orvieto, the priest who had been convinced by the miracle proceeded to this place to obtain absolution for his doubts, and brought with him the linen and other relics of the altar upon which the blood had fallen. The pope, attended by several cardinals, met the relics at the bridge of Rio Chiaro, and resolved that an edifice should at once be erected to receive them. Lorenzo Maitani, the celebrated Sienese architect, gave the design, and the first stone was laid by Nicholas VI., in 1290. From that time to the end of the 16th century almost every artist of eminence in architecture, sculpture, and mosaic was employed upon the works; and P. della Valle, in his learned history of the cathedral, records the names of no less than 33 architects, 152 sculptors, 68 painters, 90 workers in mosaic, 28 workers in *tarsia*, and 15 *capi maestri*; making altogether no less than 386 artists whose talents were devoted to the embellishment of the edifice. The bases of the 4 pilasters of the façade are covered with bas-reliefs by Giovanni di Pisa, Arnolfo, and other able scholars of Niccolò di Pisa. The sculptures of the *first* pilaster on the l. hand are arranged in compartments formed by the branches of a large ivy. The subjects embrace the history of man from the Creation to the settlement of the children of Noah; in the fifth compartment, Tubal Cain is represented as making bells, and Seth has a compass in his hand to indicate his reputed skill in astronomy. In the *second* the arrangement is different: Abraham is the principal figure, and all the others serve as connecting links, illustrating the descent of the Virgin from the house of David; the 13 figures around the sleeping patriarch represent the judges who ruled over Israel after the death of Joshua; the pedigree of the Virgin is shown in a series of 8 ovals, on which are sculptured the principal personages and events which may be considered as the successive stages of the descent. The *third* pilaster, of which the principal figures are Jacob and the prophets, is entirely illustrative of the history of the Saviour from the Annunciation to the Resurrection. The *fourth*, in a series of surprising sculptures, represents the Last Judgment, the Inferno, and the Saints in Paradise. There is perhaps no work of the kind, whether we consider the early period of its execution, or the minute variety of its details, more deserving of attentive study than this remarkable composition. In the Inferno the imagination of Giovanni di Pisa seems to have been inexhaustible; the horrid monsters and the grotesque modes of punishment are entirely original, and the execution of the whole is characterised by an elaborate and careful workmanship. Above these pilasters are the 4 bronze emblems of the Evangelists. The spaces over the doors, and below the 3-

pointed gables of the front, are filled with modern mosaics on a gold ground, representing the Annunciation, the Sposalizio, the Baptism of Christ, the Coronation of the Virgin, &c. The 3 doorways are also richly worked, and present some fine examples of spiral columns covered with mosaic, foliage, and other ornaments.

The *interior* is of black basaltic lava and yellowish grey limestone, both found in the vicinity of Orvieto, and in the form of a Latin cross; the length from the choir to the great door is 278 Eng. feet, the width 103, the height 115. The windows are all lancet shaped, and many of those which are not closed up have finely painted glass in the upper portions, and diaphanous alabaster in the lower. The nave is divided from the aisles by six arches on each side, the columns supporting them are 62 feet high, and have capitals of different styles. A beautiful gallery, with an elaborately carved balustrade, runs all round the nave over the arches. The roof is modern, having been completed in 1828, without ornament; and, from its undecorated appearance, quite out of keeping with the magnificence of the edifice it covers. The floor is of red Apennine marble, decorated before the choir with inlaid fleurs-de-lis.

In front of these columns stand the statues of the 12 apostles in white marble; they are 9 feet 6 inches in height, and are placed on pedestals 5½ feet high, so that their colossal proportions produce an effect not less imposing than that of the guardian figures which surround the tomb of Maximilian at Innspruck. On the l. side are — St. Peter, by Francesco Mosca; St. Andrew, by Fabiano Toti, finished by Ippolito Scalza; St. John, by Ippolito Scalza; St. Philip, by Francesco Mochi; St. Matthew, by John of Bologna; St. Taddeus, by Francesco Mochi. On the rt. are—St. Simon, by Bernardino Cametti; St. James the Less, by the same; St. Bartholomew, by Ippolito Buzio; St. Thomas, by Scalza, said to be a representation of himself; St. James, by Giovanni Caccini; and St. Paul, by Francesco Mosca, a bad imitation of the Farnese Hercules. The most remarkable of these figures are the St. Matthew and the St. Thomas; the latter is full of dignity and life.

At the high altar are the celebrated figures of the Annunziata and the Archangel, by Mochi. The Virgin is represented as starting from her seat at the salutation of the archangel; her hand grasps the chair with almost convulsive energy, and her countenance wears a disagreeable expression of indignation, little in accordance with the feelings which inspired the great painters on the same subject. The *tarsia* of the choir was executed chiefly by artists of Siena in the 14th century; that of the pulpit is of later date, and is said to have been designed by Scalza. The 2 altars in the transepts, representing the Adoration of the Magi and the Visitation, are masterpieces of sculpture. The Visitation is composed of 9 figures, in almost whole relief, and nearly as large as life, with an abundance of arabesques and other ornaments; it was designed by San Micheli of Verona, and executed at the age of 15 by Moschino, son of Simone Mosca. By the side is a statue of Christ at the Column, by Gabriele Mercanti. The other altar, of the Adoration of the Magi, is by Mosca himself, and is praised by Vasari as a noble specimen of art. The statue of the Ecce Homo near it is by Scalza.

The Chapel of the *Santissimo Corporale* contains the splendid reliquiary of the *Corporale* of Bolsena, which cannot be seen without permission of the Bishop. On entering the chapel there are 2 statues in niches on either side, which deserve attention—that of the Saviour is by Raffaello da Montelupo, and that of the Virgin by Fabiano Toti. The magnificent reliquiary was executed in solid silver by Ugolino Veri of Siena, in 1338; it contains no less than 400 lbs. of metal. It represents the façade of the cathedral, and is covered with enamels of the most minute and delicate workmanship, and so brilliant in their colours, that it is almost difficult to consider them 5 centuries old. The subjects of the enamels are chiefly connected with the history of the Miracle, or illustrative of the Pas-

sion of our Saviour. In this same chapel is a picture of the Madonna, by Gentile da Fabriano.

The Chapel of the *Madonna di S. Brizio*, in the opposite transept, containing the miraculous image of the Virgin, is still more remarkable for its paintings, and for the group of the Pietà, the masterpiece of Scalza. At the entrance are 2 niches, with statues of Adam and Eve, by Fabiano Toti and Raffaello da Montelupo. The walls are entirely covered with the frescoes of *Luca Signorelli*, and the compartments of the roof are painted by the *Beato Angelico da Fiesole, Benozzo Gozzoli*, and other eminent artists of that period. The Christ sitting in Judgment, the Coronation of the Virgin, with the noble group of the Prophets and the army of Martyrs, are among the most characteristic works of *Fra Angelico;* the Christ in Judgment is believed to have suggested the well-known figure of the Saviour in the Sistine chapel. The subjects chosen by *Luca Signorelli* are, the History of Antichrist, the Resurrection, and the Last Judgment. They are so arranged as to furnish the successive chapters of one great epic; and the illustrious artist, then nearly 60 years of age, has given us, in these paintings, an explanation of many remarkable passages in the great work of Michael Angelo. The representation of the Fall of Antichrist comes first. He is seen preaching to the people, prompted by the Evil Spirit: at his feet are the gold, and jewels, and money, with which he tempts his followers; the crowd of listeners are in themselves a study of costume and character. In the next we have the descent of the Archangel, who hurls the Antichrist into the pit; in the corner of this compartment the Beato Angelico and Luca himself are introduced among the spectators. The Resurrection follows, and is worthy of long and careful examination; the anatomical knowledge it exhibits is combined with a truth of expression perfectly wonderful. The Inferno and the Paradiso complete the series, and in their contrasts of deformity and beauty constitute one of the most extraordinary pictures ever painted. In the

Inferno the invention of the artist seems to have been lavished in creating new forms of demons; while in the fine composition of the Paradiso the figures of the Seraphim are no less astonishing for their beauty. Besides these paintings there is a singular series of subjects taken from classical history and biography—the Descent of Æneas, Perseus and Andromeda, the Rape of Proserpine, Ino and Melicerte, and portraits of Virgil, Ovid, Claudian, Seneca, and Statius; forming a curious and rather startling mixture of sacred and profane inspirations. The lower parts of the wall were whitewashed till the year 1845, when they were cleaned and found to be also painted in fresco. The subjects are medallion portraits of the Italian poets, scenes from the Divina Commedia and mythological subjects. We have already stated that Michael Angelo did not disdain to borrow from these works of Luca Signorelli, if indeed he did not altogether form the design of his Last Judgment upon them.

The celebrated *Pietà*, executed in 1579, is the masterpiece of Ippolito Scalza. It is a group of 4 figures a 3rd larger than life, representing the Deposition from the Cross, and is sculptured out of a single block. It is perhaps the grandest production of the school of Michael Angelo.

In the chapels of the side aisles are several pictures: the graceful Madonna and St. Catherine, by *Gentile da Fabriano*; the Healing the Blind and the Resurrection of the Widow's Son, by *Taddeo Zuccari*; the Raising of Lazarus, by *Circignani*; and the Marriage of Cana, by the same, still retaining its singular freshness of colour. On the other side are the Christ in the Garden; the Flagellation; Calvary; and the Crowning with Thorns, &c., by *Muziano*.

The statue of St. Sebastian, by Scalza, at the W. end of the cathedral is the most perfectly beautiful of all the single figures in the building: it is said to have been executed in 4 months, for the sum of 10 golden crowns!

The *Ch. of S. Domenico* contains the fine monument of Cardinal G. di Brago, who died in 1282, by *Arnolfo*, and a picture, in 5 compartments, by Simone Memmi, representing the Virgin and 4 saints, signed and bearing the date of 1320.

After the cathedral, the most remarkable object in Orvieto is the Well called, in honour of the Apostle of Ireland, *Il Pozzo di San Patrizio*. It is situated near the fortress, at the eastern extremity of the town. It was designed and begun by Antonio Sangallo to relieve the garrison when Clement VII., after the sack of Rome in 1527, took refuge here with his whole court. It is a surprising proof of the versatile powers of that great architect, and is hardly inferior to the best works of ancient Rome. It bears a great resemblance to the celebrated 'Joseph's Well,' in the citadel of Cairo, and, although not so deep, it is broader and grander in appearance than that remarkable work of the Sultan Saladin. It is enclosed in a hollow circular tower with double walls, between which 2 spiral staircases are carried, one above the other, with separate entrances; so that we descend by the one, and ascend by the other. It is partly cut in the tufa rock, and partly built; the depth of the well is 179 Eng. feet, its diameter 46; the inner wall is perforated with 72 windows from top to bottom to admit light. The staircase has 248 steps arranged '*a cordoni,*' so that mules may be employed in bringing up the water. The upper part of the well, or rather all the buildings above ground, were finished by Simone Mosca, in the pontificate of Paul III. Between the 2 entrance doors is the inscription— '*Quod Natura munimento inviderat industria adjecit.*' Orvieto has long ceased to be a garrison town, its castle has long been dismantled, and the well is no longer used.

The *Palazzo Gualterio*—belonging to *Count Gualterio*, the talented historian of the recent political events in Italy—contains an interesting collection of Cartoons by Domenichino, Annibale Caracci, Franceschini, Albani, &c., which the owner liberally permits strangers to examine. In the 1st room are 2 battle-pieces by Franceschini, designed for Genoa. In the 2nd room are Temperance, by Domenichino, very fine; and other designs by Ann. Caracci, Albani, and Franceschini. In the 3rd are Mars, by Ann. Caracci; and Joseph's dream, by Carlo Cignani. In the 4th room are Fame and History, by Domenichino. In the chapel adjoining is a beautiful fresco of the Archangel Michael, removed from its original position, and attributed, perhaps with good reason, to Luca Signorelli. It has been restored in parts by Prof. Cornelius of Munich. In the 5th room are the Fame, History and Fidelity, by Domenichino; Love and Venus, and Love and Hymen, by Albani. In the 6th room is a series illustrating various events in the life of St. Catherine of Siena, by Ann. Caracci. On the roof of another room is a fresco of Endymion sleeping and surprised by Diana, said to be by Gherardo della Notte. In the gallery is a Deposition, by Baroccio, damaged; a good Gherardo della Notte; and 2 heads, said to be by Titian?

In the *Palazzo Petrangeli* there is also a collection of pictures. There is a small theatre in the town, where operas are occasionally performed. There are several other Palaces in Orvieto, some interesting from their architecture. The old town-hall in the Piazza del Popolo, until recently used as a Theatre, is an interesting specimen of the Domestic Architecture of the 15th century; its rounded windows, with their chequered ornaments, are almost Norman. The town is very dirty, and no place can appear duller to the casual visitor.

The road from Orvieto to Bolsena, about 12 m., follows that to Montefiascone, from which it branches off on the rt.; to persons travelling post and merely wishing to visit Orvieto, Bolsena will be the best place to start from. A bridle-road of 18 m. leads from Orvieto to Todi; it is very hilly, and offers little interest.

The distance from Orvieto to Citta della Pieve is about 26 m.; the miserable vehicle called a Diligence seldom performing it in less than 7 hours. On leaving the city the road descends along the northern slope of its hill for 4 m., to the Paglia, which it crosses at the Ponte dell' Adunata, ½ a m. below its

junction with the Chiana. Crossing the latter it ascends, for 7 m., high above the river, and through hills composed of tertiary sands, abounding in marine shells, to the village of Bagni, so called from some mineral springs in the neighbourhood. From Bagni the ascent becomes still more rapid through a country richly clothed with oak forests, until it reaches the culminating point at La Croce, about 1150 feet above the Chiana. Here an equally rapid descent commences to the village of Ficulle, about half way between Orvieto and Citta della Pieve, where there is a neat homely inn at the entrance of the town, which is situated on a rising on the rt. of the road: there is a Gothic ch. within the walls, with a crypt. Near the road are the remains of a Roman bridge, attributed to the reign of Nero, and in the wall of the ch. of Santa Maria, an ancient inscription, recording the erection of a Temple of the Sun, by Claudius. A rapid descent of 4 miles, through a lovely wooded country, during which the traveller will enjoy many fine views of the subjacent Val de Chiana, brings us to the plain; the Chiana is here crossed on a handsome bridge, the river taking a more easterly course—that along which it is proposed to carry the projected railroad between the valleys of the Arno and Tiber. From this point the road follows, for 3 m., the base of the hills which border on the E. the southern, or pontifical portion of the Val de Chiana, to Il Borgo, where the ascent to Citta della Pieve commences, still through a picturesquely wooded country by the villages of San Lorenzo and Monteleone, where it attains its greatest elevation, 900 feet, above the subjacent valley. From Monteleone to Citta della Pieve the road runs along the ridge that separates the torrents flowing into the Chiana on the W., and into the Nestore on the E. 1 m. before reaching the gate a good road down the valley of the latter river leads to Perugia. (Rte. 22A.)

28 m. CITTA DELLA PIEVE. (*Inn*, Giornella's, near the gate, where the diligences stop; indifferent, but tolerable as a resting-place for a few hours.

The town is clean, though poor. Its chief interest to the traveller is derived from its being the birthplace of Pietro Perugino—to many persons a sufficient inducement to make it the object of a pilgrimage. In the oratory of the *Disciplinati*, or of *Santa Maria de' Bianchi*, attached to the Chiesarella, is one of his finest frescoes. It represents the Adoration of the Magi; the Madonna and Child are sitting under a shed, receiving the offerings of the wise men. The Virgin is exquisitely beautiful; the grouping is varied and full of character; a rich landscape with horsemen and various figures forms the background; the heads are full of expression and elaborately finished. This picture, although injured by the damp of the adjoining sacristy, the floor of which was formerly much higher than the oratory, has suffered less than any other picture by Perugino in the town. In an *armoire* below the fresco are preserved 2 letters of Pietro relating to the picture, and some earthen pots which are supposed to have contained his paints. They were discovered by the Prior Bolletti under the floor of the sacristy in 1835. In the first letter Pietro states that the picture ought to cost at least 200 florins, but that he will be content with 100 as a townsman (*come paisano*); 25 to be paid at once (*scubeto*), and the rest in 3 years, 25 each year. It is signed, " *Io Piectro penctore mano propia*," and dated " *Peroscia vencte de Frebaio,* 1504." The second shows that he was obliged to lessen his terms to 75 florins; he requests the syndic to send a mule and guide, that he may come and paint, and says that he will abate 25 florins, "*e niente piu;*" it is signed as before, and dated "*Peroscia* 1 *de Marzo,* 1504." In the ch. of the Servites, outside the Orvieto gate, are the remains of his fresco of the Crucifixion, ruined by building the present belfry. In the Cathedral, the interior of which has been modernized, are his Baptism of the Saviour, in the first chapel on the l., and an altar piece in the choir representing the Madonna and Child, with St. Peter, St. Paul, and 2 other saints below. In the ch. of S. Antonio, at the bottom of the town, is another painting by Pietro, representing St. Paul and 2 saints. The view from the door of this ch. over the valley which separates the Papal States from Tuscany is very fine.

EXCURSION TO CHIUSI, 6 m.

An excellent road of 7 m. leads from Citta della Pieve to Chiusi; first, by a rapid descent of 4 m. into the Plain of the Chiana, in the centre of which is the frontier between the Papal and Tuscan states. Passports and baggage are not examined until arriving at *Chiusi.* The Tre Mori, a new inn, has been recently opened outside the Roman gate, where the accommodation is very fair, *but prices should be fixed beforehand.* The diligence from Citta della Pieve, as well as that to Siena and Perugia, stop here.

The most intelligent guide to the antiquities of Chiusi is Giambattista Zeppoloni, a civil and obliging shoemaker, who will save the traveller much delay and trouble by procuring the keys of the principal tombs from their respective *custodi.* Those travellers who are interested in Etruscan antiquities will hardly fail to find friends, particularly among the learned ecclesiastics and resident land-owners, who have done so much to preserve and illustrate the sepulchral and other monuments of the city.

Chiusi was one of the Twelve cities of the Etruscan league, and one of the Five which assisted the Latins against Tarquinius Priscus. Its antiquity is further proved by the fact that Virgil represents it as sending assistance to Æneas against Turnus. Its history during the reign of Porsena is familiar to every one. It will be sufficient for our purpose to say that its name seems to have preserved its name and its position through all the changes and vicissitudes of Rome. Even in the Middle Ages, though its population was thinned by malaria, the site was never deserted like that of other Etruscan cities. The traveller, therefore, finds Chiusi occupying its ancient site, which is agreeably placed on an eminence 500 feet above the level of the small but pretty lake to which it gives its name. It is an episcopal town of 2200 souls, but its vicinity to some of the marshy districts of the Val di Chiana renders it at times unhealthy. Of its ancient walls very few fragments can now be traced; those which are visible are generally capped by mediæval masonry, and in some cases by Roman work. They are invariably composed of rectangular blocks of travertine, of much smaller size than those of most other Etruscan cities, but are put together carefully, and without cement. Though there are so few remains of the fortifications, the town is literally undermined by subterranean passages, many of which have been called "labyrinths" by ancient and modern writers: it is now believed that some of them were connected with the sewerage of the ancient city; but there are others which were evidently destined for other purposes, although what those purposes may have been is still a mystery. Independently of these remains, the traveller will find that Chiusi is rich in interest and novelty, particularly in her museum and tombs. The great museum is that of Signor Casuccini, one of the wealthy proprietors of the city, whose entire collection was found, with few exceptions, on his own property. It is rich in vases of every known variety of Etruscan form, in tazze, in bronzes, specchj, focolari, cinerary urns, and square or round pedestals of cippi, which it would fill a volume to describe. Several of these urns and cippi are decorated with bas-reliefs illustrating the religious, civil, or domestic life of the country; many of these sculptures are of peculiar and touching interest, and some are altogether unique as representations of national manners. The collection of sepulchral monuments show that the Chiusans burned their dead, and very seldom buried the bodies entire. The sarcophagi are not more than 3 or 4 in number, while of cinerary urns or ash-chests there are upwards of 100 in

terracotta, about 50 in marble, and nearly the same number in travertine; the collection is daily increasing, and as a whole it forms one of the finest Etruscan museums ever formed. The pottery in this museum includes specimens from various Etruscan cities, but the most interesting is of course that which is peculiar to the city and its territory. This is a coarse unglazed black ware, rude rather than inelegant in form, and decorated with quaint and exaggerated figures of animals and monsters in low relief, the style and execution denoting a period of manufacture long anterior to the influence of Greek art. In the middle of the apartment containing the tombs is what may be called a statue-sarcophagus, the figure of a female in coarse limestone, sitting in a chair in white robes, with bas-reliefs on the pedestal. The head, arms, and feet are in separate pieces, attached by metal pins to the body, which is hollow, and when discovered contained the ashes of the deceased. It is sculptured in a stiff and archaic style, and the whole figure seems to have been coloured. The palace of Signor Casuccini contains several interesting objects. Among them is the celebrated black vase called by the Prussian antiquaries "the Anubis Vase," from the resemblance of the first figure in the group of mysterious personages who are represented upon it to the Egyptian deity of that name. Another vase, celebrated for its great beauty, represents the Judgment of Paris; it was found in the Poggio Gajella. The collection of Signor Paolozzi is also rich in urns, vases, medals, and bas-reliefs, which have been collected by successive generations of the Paolozzi family, and preserved as heir-looms by their descendants. Among the most remarkable objects in the collection we may mention the cinerary jars called Canopi, from their resemblance to those of Egypt, with lids in the form of human heads, the variety of which leaves no doubt that they are portraits of those whose ashes they contain. Another celebrated object is a bas-relief which has been illustrated by Inghirami and Micali, representing the death-bed of a lady surrounded by the mourners who were hired at funerals to tear their hair and lacerate their cheeks; the deep grief of her little son is a striking contrast to this hired sorrow, and is in itself as touching an episode as we shall find in the whole range of ancient sculpture. The Bishop of Chiusi has formed in his palace an interesting collection of vases found in the neighbourhood of the town; several of the Canons have collected Scarabæi and other relics, and Captain Sotzi keeps a variety for sale at moderate prices.

The *tombs* in the neighbourhood are very numerous, as we might anticipate in a place which was once the most important capital of Etruria. The one which the very name of the city will recall to every traveller—the mausoleum and labyrinth of Porsena, so well known by the descriptions of Pliny and Varro—has had no less than 4 representatives; in other words, 4 tumuli have disputed the honour of being the tomb of the conqueror of Rome. Although one of these contains the largest labyrinth yet opened, it is now generally believed that the tomb of Porsena has yet to be discovered. In regard to the description of that celebrated monument with 3 piles of pyramids, it is worth while to observe, that, although the description was doubtless written from tradition, and therefore probably exaggerated, the remains of the tomb of Aruns, the son of Porsena, at Albano, are sufficient to show that its main outlines were correct.

It would be useless to enter into a minute account of the various tombs which lie scattered over the hills around Chiusi. They do not occur in a necropolis, as in other Etruscan cities, but are found among the neighbouring heights, excavated mostly in the hill side, and entered by a level passage in the slope. They are often at some distance from each other; for which reason they are best visited on horseback. Without attempting to give a complete list of all that may be seen, we shall mention a few of the most remarkable to which the traveller can obtain access. As we have already stated, the principal tombs are kept locked, so that the cicerone must be instructed beforehand to make the necessary arrangements with their respective *custodi*. Of the 6 we shall notice, 3 lie on the N.E. of the town, viz. the Deposito del Poggio Gajella, the Deposito del Sovrano, and the Deposito della Scimia; one lies on the E. of the town, called the Deposito del Colle Casuccini; and 2 lie on the N.W., viz. the Deposito de' Dei, and the Deposito delle Monache.—1. *Deposito del Poggio Gajella*, so called from the hill of that name, 3 m. N.E. of the town. This tomb, or series of tombs, was discovered in 1840 by the Casuccini family, whose museum has been enriched by many of the treasures it contained. Its discovery, however, had a higher interest for the antiquary, in the peculiar labyrinths which have made the Poggio Gajella celebrated throughout Europe, and induced archæologists to compare its mysterious passages with the well-known description of the labyrinths of the tomb of Porsena. The Gajella is a conical hill of about 50 feet in height, originally surrounded at its base by a circular wall of masonry, composed of uncemented blocks, beyond which is a fosse, more than 900 feet in circumference. The hill is literally filled with tombs, which are excavated in 3 tiers, above each other, like the floors of a house, while the tombs of each tier or level are arranged like groups or streets of houses. Some of the tombs are painted, some have roofs carved, with beams and rafters, and many have rock-hewn couches for the dead. On the lower tier on the S. side, approached by an oblong vestibule, is a circular chamber, 25 feet in diameter, supported by a high circular column in the centre; in this chamber some beautiful vases were discovered, and from its N. side mysterious labyrinthine passages communicate with a more numerous group of square tombs on the W. side of the hill. These passages are just large enough to allow a man to enter on all fours; sometimes they wind like a circle, at others they throw off branches which terminate in a *cul de sac*. On the second tier, there are several groups of tombs both square and circular, in 2 of which are passages like those on the tier below. In one of the chambers of this tier the celebrated vase of the Judgment of Paris, now in the Casuccini museum, was discovered, together with several fragments of gold and jewellery. On the third tier there are similar groups of tombs, among which some jewellery and broken vases were found. This tomb has been illustrated by Dr. Braun, whose work, entitled 'Laberinto di Porsena, comparato coi Sepoleri di Poggio Gajella,' contains plans and drawings of it; and Dennis's Etruria contains a plan of the labyrinths copied from that work.— 2. *Deposito del Sovrano*, called also "del Gran Duca," 2 m. N.E. of the town, discovered on 1818 on a slope of the hill above the lake. It is a single chamber with an *arched* roof of solid masonry. It was entered by folding doors of travertine, of which only one remains. The benches which surround the chamber still retain without change 8 cinerary urns, inscribed with the name of the PERIS family.—3. *Deposito della Scimia*, discovered in 1846, in the hill called La Pellegrina, 1 m. N.E. of the town. It is a tomb of 4 chambers, the central of which is painted with representations of games performed in the presence of a female, whose high rank may be inferred from the fact that she is seated beneath an umbrella, the only known example of its occurrence in Etruscan paintings. The games include chariot races, wrestling, boxing, &c.; and among the various figures which compose the different groups are minstrels, a man in armour, a dwarf, and a monkey (Scimia) — the latter having the honour of giving its name to the tomb.—4. *Deposito del Colle Casuccini*, 1 m. E. of the town, discovered in 1833. The entrance is still closed by two folding doors of travertine more than 4 feet high, still working on their an-

cient pivots. The tomb contains 3 chambers, 2 of which are decorated with paintings now gradually perishing. Those in the first chamber represent funeral games, horse-races, dancing, tumbling, and a funeral symposium of 10 men attended by their slaves. Those in the second chamber represent a chorus of youths, with instruments of music for the dance.—5. *Deposito de' Dei*, 2 m. N.W. of the town, on the hill called Poggio al Moro, discovered in 1826 on the property of Signor Dei, from whom of course it derives its name. It is decorated internally with paintings representing a funeral banquet and funeral games, resembling in so remarkable a manner the paintings of the Dep. del Colle Casuccini, that there can be no doubt that they were designed by the same hand. The tomb contains several sarcophagi and other monuments, and a bilingual inscription. —6. *Deposito delle Monache*, so called because it was found in the grounds of the convent of San Stefano, 1½ m. N.W. of the town. It is a single vaulted chamber, remarkable as retaining, without change, nearly all the monuments which it contained when first discovered. There are 8 cinerary urns and 2 sarcophagi, most of which bear the name of UMRANA, though there is one inscribed with that of CAULE VIPINA, or Cæles Vibenna, a name which carries us back to the days of Romulus.—The *Tombs of the Early Christians* at Chiusi will interest travellers who have not seen those of Rome and Naples, from which, however, they present few points of difference.

The Cathedral has been evidently constructed with the ruined fragments of ancient edifices. Its nave is divided from the side aisles by 18 antique columns of unequal size, and even the tomb containing the ashes of St. Mustiola, to whom the building is dedicated, is formed out of an ancient column. On the walls of the arcade on the Piazza del Duomo numerous fragments of Roman as well as Etruscan workmanship occur, and in one of the oratories of the Confraternità della Misericordia is a beautifully worked column of African marble, which must have belonged to an edifice of imposing magnitude. These scattered fragments explain the disappearance of the ancient monuments of Clusium; its temples, like those of Rome, were no doubt destroyed to build the churches and other edifices of the modern city.

Travellers desirous of proceeding further into Tuscany may go from Chiusi to Montepulciano, another Etruscan town of high antiquity. The shortest road is that which leads northwards by the Granducal fattoria of Dolciano by Borgo Vecchio (16 m.). It passes the lake which bears the name of Chiaro di Montepulciano, although it is lower down in the valley and some m. distant from that town. A longer but more interesting road is that through Cetona, Sarteano, and Chianciano. The picturesque village of *Cetona*, with its castle of the middle ages, 7 m. distant from Chiusi, is an interesting point for the geologist and the antiquary. It is situated on an olive-clad height at the base of the lofty dolomite mountain of the same name, which rises above the valley watered by the Astrone, to an elevation of 3750 feet above the level of the sea. The ravines in the neighbourhood exhibit fine sections of the tertiary marine formations. Cetona has a small *inn* kept by Alessandro Davidi. The antiquarian interest of the place is derived from the choice collection of Etruscan antiquities discovered in the neighbourhood by the Cavaliere Terrosi, who liberally allows it to be seen by travellers. It contains numerous vases, and 2 cinerary urns of singular beauty and perfection, which have been illustrated by Micali. *Sarteano*, 4 m. distant, is situated at the extremity of an elevated plateau above the Val di Chiana, and with its mediæval walls presents a very picturesque object from all parts of the valley. It has a very tolerable inn kept by Signora Serafina. Sarteano is interesting to the antiquary as possessing 3 private collections of Etruscan antiquities. The 1st, that of Cavaliere Bargagli, containing merely cinerary urns, the 2nd that of Dr. Borselli consisting of vases and pottery, and the 3rd, that of Signor Lunghini containing vases and cinerary urns. All these objects were found in the Etruscan necropolis on the table-land west of Sarteano, where a vast number of Etruscan tombs have been opened since 1825, and from which the collection of black vases in the Florence Gallery was obtained. The tombs generally consist of single chambers, with a central pillar, and a ledge running round the unpainted walls, like those in the necropolis of Volterra. The whole range of hills which bound the valley on the W., from Cetona to Montepulciano, abound with Etruscan tombs. *Chianciano*, 7 m. from Sarteano, is one of the most popular bathing-places of Tuscany: its mineral waters and hot springs are in high repute in rheumatic and paralytic affections, and during the season it is much frequented by visitors. It has 2 *Inns*, kept by Faenzi and Sporazzini.

The position of *Montepulciano*, 4 m. distant from Chianciano, surrounded by mediæval walls, and perched upon a lofty height, is highly picturesque. The fine ch. of the Madonna di San Biagio, built from the designs of Sangallo, is considered one of his most successful works, and several of the palaces in the town are by the same great architect. The Palazzo Buccelli contains several Etruscan antiquities found in the neighbourhood, which confirm the opinion that the town occupies the site of an Etruscan city. The façade of this palace has built into it several bas-reliefs, and numerous fragments of Etruscan and Latin inscriptions. The wines of Montepulciano are celebrated throughout Italy, and especially that called Manna, the "d'ogni vino il re" of Redi.

A road from Montepulciano through Pienza (9 m.) leads into the Siena road at San Quirico (6 m.), as noticed in Rte. 26; or the traveller may cross to Arezzo by the Val di Chiana, which would give him an opportunity of seeing the hydraulic works which have rendered this valley, under the direction of the Tuscan government, one of the most fertile districts in Europe. To Fajano is 16 m. (Rte. 26 c.)

ROUTE 24.

RIETI TO ROME, BY THE VIA SALARIA.

39 m.

Rieti to Poggio San Lorenzo .	9
Poggio to Osteria di Correse .	19
Ost. di Correse to Rome .	14
Roman miles	42

This road is in very good condition, although not furnished with post relays. It follows for a part of its course the ancient Via Salaria, and is a much shorter route than that from Rieti to Rome through Terni. Although by no means so agreeable as that route, it is interesting to those who are disposed to examine the ancient cities which lie in its immediate vicinity.

There is a very fair coach that leaves Rieti 3 times a week for Rome, on Mondays, Wednesdays, and Fridays, at daybreak, performing the journey in 10 hours, returning from Rome on the intermediate days. Fares 22 pauls. There are also conveyances from Rieti at fixed periods for Antrodoco and Civita Ducale in connection with it.

After leaving Rieti the road crosses the Turano, and proceeds up the rich plain watered by that stream, gradually ascending the hills. The descent on the Roman side is extremely steep.

9 m. Poggio San Lorenzo, a miserable *osteria*. Between it and Nerola are two others, called the Osteria della Scaletta and Ost. del Olmo, near which are several ancient tombs. From the Ost. della Scaletta to Nerola the road skirts the base of Monte Carpignano, opposite to which is

Nerola, a small village of less than 400 souls, placed in a commanding and

picturesque position among the mountains, with an old feudal castle belonging to the Barberini family. It is supposed by many antiquaries to mark the site of Regillum, the place from which Appius Claudius migrated to Rome. A short distance beyond it the road crosses the Lignessa, and soon afterwards the ancient Via Nomentana falls into it.

Further on is the ruined ch. of *S. Pietro*, supposed to have been the cathedral of a bishopric in the early ages of the Church. A m. from it, on the rt. of the road, is the village of *Correse*, on the flanks of the hills which mark the site of the famous city of Cures, the capital of the Sabines, long anterior to the foundation of Rome. It was founded by the Umbrians, who were expelled from Reate by the Pelasgi, and assumed the name of Sabines on settling here. The war between Tatius the king of Cures and Romulus after the rape of the Sabine virgins, the famous compact by which the inhabitants of Cures were removed to Rome, where Tatius shared the throne with Romulus, and the still more interesting history of Numa, will no doubt suggest themselves to every traveller. On one of the hills occupied by the ancient city is the ch. of the Madonna dell' Arci, founded, it is believed, by the monks of the monastery of Farfa, which lies beyond the hills to the N.E. The ch. is surrounded by a square enclosure, whose walls are built of massive blocks, which would seem to indicate the ancient citadel. There are no further traces of walls, which may be regarded as another corroboration of the position, for we have the authority of Dionysius that it was not walled. The history of Tatius and of Numa are frequently noticed by the Roman poets :—

" Nec procul hinc Romam, et raptas sine more Sabinas
Consessu caveæ, magnis Circensibus actis,
Addiderat, subitoque novum consurgere bellum
Romulidis, Tatioque seni, Curibusque severis."
Virg. Æn. viii.

The neighbourhood of Correse has

been very little explored: a path leads down the valley from the ruins to the Ost. di Correse. The road twice crosses the little torrent Linguessa before it reaches the tavern.

19 m. *Osteria di Correse* or Barberini, a poor solitary tavern, close to where the road to Terni through Cantalupo branches off. The vetturini who spend a night on the road generally make this their half-way house. The village of Fiano, a fief of the ducal family of Ottobuoni, is seen from here on the opposite side of the Tiber.

On the l. of the road is the lofty range of hills which bound the Campagna on the N.E., conspicuous among which is the Monte Genaro, which may be ascended on this side from Palombara.

The road follows the l. bank of the Tiber, and crosses many of its tributary streams. After passing the little river Mosso, E. of the Osteria del Grillo, is the village of *Rimane*, on the l. hand, where some remains, chiefly of reticulated masonry, have been considered to mark the site of Eretum, mentioned by Virgil as one of the cities which sent assistance to Turnus. A few miles further on is the town of *Monte Rotondo*, on a conspicuous hill, considered by Gell to be the site of the Alban colony of Crustumerium, well known for its capture by Romulus, and which the older antiquaries had placed at Sette Bagni on the Allia. The present town is surmounted by the lofty tower of the old feudal castle now belonging to the Barberini family. The country for miles around it abounds in plantations of pear-trees, for which Crustumerium is celebrated by the classic writers, who notice the remarkable redness of one side, "ex parte rubentia," a peculiarity which distinctly marks the pears of Monte Rotondo to the present day.

The traveller who visits Monte Rotondo may perhaps be induced to extend his excursion to the little village of La Mentana, 2 m. on the l., which contains a baronial mansion of the Borghese family. It occupies the site of ancient Nomentum, but there are no remains now visible except some marbles and inscriptions. 4 m. from it is the village of *St. Angelo*, marking the site of Cornieulum; it is placed on the summit of a steep and precipitate hill, commanding a magnificent prospect extending from Soracte to the very verge of the Campagna. It was the birthplace of Servius Tullius, and one of the cities in the Montes Corniculani captured by Tarquinius Priscus. Considerable remains of its ancient walls, in Polygonal masonry, still exist.

The high road, after leaving Monte Rotondo on the l., proceeds by the Fonte di Papa, and below the hill of Sta. Colomba to Marcigliana, a farm belonging to Prince Borghese, situated on an eminence above the road. On the rt. hand, nearly opposite, are an ancient tumulus, a fountain, and a deep cutting, supposed by Sir W. Gell to be an ancient road. On the hill above it and at Marcigliana Vecchia are some ruins of Roman villas.

As the road approaches the Allia, the valley at Malpasso, supposed to be a necropolis of Fidenæ, comes in view. Beyond the Allia, and between the 6th and 5th milestones from Rome, the road passes through the ancient Sabine city of FIDENÆ, the ally of Veii, and so celebrated for its repeated wars with Rome, that Livy remarks, "it was almost more frequently captured than attacked." The most prominent objects which now mark its site are the *Castel Giubileo* on the rt., and the *Villa Spada* on the l. of the road. The Villa Spada stands on a projecting tongue of land, supposed to be the site of the villa of Phaon, where Nero destroyed himself, and where Metius, the treacherous leader of the Alban forces, took his station to witness the battle between Tullus Hostilius and the troops of Veii and Fidenæ. Castel Giubileo is supposed to occupy the site of the ancient arx or citadel of Fidenæ; below it towards the river some other excavations are seen.

"Making the circuit of Castel Giubileo, you are led round till you meet the road, where it issues from the hollow at the northern angle of the city. Besides the tombs which are found on both sides of the southern promontory of the city, there is a cave, running far into the rock, and branching off into several chambers and passages. Fidenæ, like Veii, is said to have been taken by a mine; and this cave might be supposed to indicate the spot, being subsequently enlarged into its present form, had not Livy stated that the *cuniculus* was on the opposite side of Fidenæ, where the cliffs were loftiest, and that it was carried into the Arx. The chief necropolis of Fidenæ was probably on the heights to the N.E., called Poggio de' Sette Bagni, where are a number of caves; and here, also, are traces of quarries, probably those of the soft rock for which Fidenæ was famed in ancient times. The walls of Fidenæ have utterly disappeared; not one stone remains on another, and the broken pottery and the tombs around are the sole evidences of its existence. Yet, as Nibby observes, ' few ancient cities, of which few or no vestiges remain, have had the good fortune to have their sites so well determined as Fidenæ.' Its distance of 40 stadia, or 5 m. from Rome, mentioned by Dionysius, and its position relative to Veii, to the Tiber, and to the confluence of the Anio with that stream, as set forth by Livy, leave not a doubt of its true site."—*Dennis.*

The plain traversed by the road was the scene of many a bloody fight between the Romans and Etruscans subsequent to the kingly period; and Hannibal is supposed to have pitched his camp there on his march from Capua.

The road crosses the Anio by the Ponte Salaro, a fine bridge of 3 arches, built of tufa in the Etruscan style, and faced with travertine by Narses in the 6th century. This venerable structure was partially destroyed by the French during the siege operations of 1849, which is the more to be regretted as it seems old enough to have been the identical bridge on which Manlius Torquatus conquered the Gaulish giant. After passing this bridge is a green hill on the rt., upon whose summit stood the Sabine city of ANTEMNÆ, one of the 3 cities whose daughters became the mothers of the Roman race:—

" Quinque adeo magnæ positis incudibus urbes
Tela novant, Ætina potens, Tiburque superbum,
Ardea, Crustumerique et turrigeræ Antemnæ."
Virg. Æn. vii.

" It seems that the high point nearest the road was the citadel of Antemnæ; and the descent of 2 roads now scarcely perceptible, one towards Fidenæ and the bridge, and the other towards Rome, marks the site of a gate. On the other side of the knoll of the citadel is a cave, with signs of artificial cutting in the rock, being a sepulchre under the walls. There was evidently a gate also in the hollow which runs from the platform of the city to the junction of the Aniene and the Tiber, where there is now a little islet. Probably there was another gate towards the meadows, on the side of the Acqua Acetosa, and another opposite; and from these 2 gates, which the nature of the soil points out, one road must have run up a valley tending in the direction of the original Palatium of Rome; and the other must have passed by a ferry towards Veii, up the valley near the present Tor di Quinto. It is not uninteresting to observe how a city, destroyed at a period previous to what is now called that of authentic history, should, without even one stone remaining, preserve indications of its former existence. From the height of Antemnæ is a fine view of the field of battle between the Romans and the Fidenates, whence Tullus Hostilius despatched M. Horatius to destroy the city of Alba Longa. The isthmus where the 2 roads from Palatium and Veii met unites with the city a higher eminence, which may have been another citadel. The beauty of the situation is such that it is impossible it should not have been selected as the site of a villa in the flourishing times of Rome."
—*Gell.*

From the Ponte Salaro the road, ascending through beds of volcanic ashes, proceeds almost in a straight line to Rome, which it enters by the Porta Salara, bordered on either side by elegant villas. Before reaching the gate it skirts on the l. the grounds of the Villa Albani.

14 m. ROME (Rte. 27).

ROUTE 25.

LEGHORN TO CIVITA VECCHIA, BY THE
SEA-COAST.

	Tuscan and Roman miles.
Leghorn to Cecina . . .	24
Cecina to San Vincenzio . .	17
San Vincenzio to Follonica .	18
Follonica to La Potassa . .	15
La Potassa to Grosseto . .	15
Grosseto to Orbetello . . .	30
Orbetello to Montalto . . .	24
Montalto to Corneto . . .	12
Corneto to Civita Vecchia .	12
	167

The new road along the coast of Tuscany, called the Strada del Littorale, has been constructed of late years by the grand ducal government as a part of their extensive operations in the Maremma. The route, however, ought not to be attempted between the beginning of June and the end of October, during which period the malaria compels even the residents to desert the coast; nor at any season by persons who are not inclined to put up with much discomfort: indeed it offers few attractions for any class of travellers, the interesting places upon it being more easily reached from other points than from Leghorn. The distances and stations, as given above, must at present be considered provisional. There are no post-horses on it, and the Inns in general are so bad as scarcely to deserve the name. There is a diligence that leaves Leghorn (with a good open cabriolet) every evening at 5 P.M. for Follonica, and 3 times a week at the same hour for Grosseto.

Before starting from Leghorn the traveller will do well to take provisions for the journey.

The road, soon after quitting Leghorn by the Porta di Maremma, crosses the Rio Maggiore, and then proceeds along the base of the group of hills, on the summit of which is situated Monte Nero. At first these hills are covered with villas; but those which follow gradually become bare of everything except heath, myrtle, arbutus, and broom, which, with the red soil peeping through here and there, have a very picturesque effect. Near the 12th milestone is a neat looking Locanda near the Promontory and Torre of *Castiglioncello.* 1 m. beyond it, the road enters the plain, and soon afterwards crosses the river Fine by a good bridge. At Collenzano, 1 m. before reaching the river Cecina, it is joined by the road from Pisa, and by that from Volterra (24 miles), the latter descending along the rt. bank of the river, the Cecina is crossed near some ruined iron-works (la Magona), about 2 m. to the westward of which is its mouth and the small village of San Giovanni, defended by a fort. At this point the milestones take up the distance from Pisa, so that the traveller must henceforth deduct 8 m. from the distances stated on the stones, which will give very nearly the distances from Leghorn.

24 At *Cecina* there are 2 inns, L'Europa and the Albergo di Colle à Mezzano, the latter tolerably clean and moderate for such accommodation as it affords. This is sometimes made the first sleeping-place out of Leghorn, though, with good horses, it is possible to push on another stage to

17 San Vincenzio, where beds can also be obtained. San Vincenzio is the most convenient point from which the traveller can visit the ruins of POPULONIA, the naval arsenal of Etruria, the great mart of her commerce, and the powerful city which Virgil represents as sending 600 warriors to assist Æneas. As it was ruined in the time of Strabo, it is not surprising that there are very few remains now visible. These are situated on a little isthmus on the coast, about 10 m. from San Vincenzio, from which there is a good road; and from Populonia it is possible to proceed in a carriage to Piombino, 6 m. distant, over the mountains, and from Piombino through the sandy tract of pine forest called the Tombolo to Follonica, 15 m. farther; in wet weather, however, the road through the Tombolo is not practicable for vehicles; indeed the least fatiguir

mode of reaching Follonica from Piombino will be by a boat, which in ordinary weather will perform the voyage in less than 3 hours. Populonia is distinguished for a considerable distance by its picturesque feudal castle, with machicolated battlements and turrets, belonging to the Desiderj family. Of the ancient city the walls alone remain, and are traceable for about 1½ m. on the summit of the hill. The largest masses are on the W., and are built in horizontal courses, though the blocks are so much more irregular than usual in Etruscan masonry as to give the walls in places a polygonal appearance. The blocks vary from 1 to 7 feet in length. Within the walls there are 6 vaults, supposed by some to be the remains of an amphitheatre, a mosaic representing fishes, and some reservoirs, all of Roman times. A few tombs are found in the slopes of the hill; and in a dense wood, half a mile S. of the walls, are some circular vaults in the sandstone cliffs called " Le Buche delle Fate." On the hill to the E. are several tumuli, some of which, called " Le Grotte," were opened in 1840, but they contained nothing of great value, and had evidently been rifled in ancient times. *Piombino*, though the capital of a principality, is a miserable town of 1700 souls, including the small garrison in its citadel. It is situated on a peninsula, which shelters a small harbour, Porto Vecchio, from which small vessels keep up a communication with Elba on stated days. The distance to Portoferrajo is 12 m. If the traveller, who does not turn off the road to Populonia and Piombino, should have slept at Cecina, he will probably make S. Vincenzio his half-way resting place on the second day, and sleep at Follonica. If, however, he does not wish to turn off to the latter place, he will find, before reaching the 49th milestone, the Locanda dell' Alummiere, a small and very miserable single house, 2 m from Campiglia, at Le Caldane, the " Aquæ Calidæ ad Vetulonios " of Pliny, which still retains its hot baths, as its name imports. *Campiglia*, with its picturesque ruined castle, though lying

off the road, is not unworthy of a visit if the traveller have time at his disposal. It is a town of 2000 souls, and has a very decent locanda, kept by Giovanni Dini. In the neighbourhood of Campiglia, on very doubtful authority, some of the older antiquaries placed the site of Vetulonia. There are no remains of antiquity at Campiglia, though some Etruscan tombs and Roman ruins have been found in its neighbourhood. The view from the hill above the town, called Campeglia Vecchia, is one of the finest in the whole of the Maremma, extending from the island of Gorgona on the N. to that of the Giglio on the S., and embracing to seaward the islands of Corsica, Capraja, Elba, Pianosa, and Monte Cristo. Near the 53rd milestone the road crosses the river Cornia by a good stone bridge, and for a considerable distance passes through the dense pine forest called Il Tombolo, abounding with thick cover of tall heath, cork trees, myrtle, arbutus, and broom, among which the wild boar and roebuck find a shelter. Near the 60th milestone, a road on the rt. branches off to

18 Follonica, about a mile distant on the sea-coast, an industrious little village and a small port, deserted always in the summer season, the seat of the Granducal iron-works, which produce 10 millions of Tuscan pounds of metal annually. The ore is brought from the mines of Rio in the island of Elba, and the combustible from the forests of the mountains of the Maremma. In consequence of the malaria the works are only in operation from December until May; the iron produced is of excellent quality, and forms a source of considerable revenue to the government, in whose hands the manufacture is a monopoly. It is the last station on this route upon the coast, which travellers often make the second sleeping place out of Leghorn; the inn is much more comfortable than the roadside Alummiere which we have just mentioned. Leaving Follonica by a road leading to Massa Maritima (14 m.), we quit the shores of the Mediterranean to re-enter the high road which crosses it at right angles, and commands a view of Massa

perched upon a height to the l. *Massa* is an episcopal town of 3000 souls ; but in spite of its imposing position amidst some charming scenery, it is a miserable place, with an apology for an inn, Locanda del Sole. The cathedral, dedicated to S. Cerbone, which dates from the 13th century, has 3 tiers of arcades in its façade, and is the only object of interest in the town. The view from the hill, however, is so magnificent that it almost repays a visit. The road beyond the branch to Massa traverses a long barren valley, with some clearances more or less advanced, and about the 69th milestone reaches

15 La Potassa, a wretched looking locanda, where some refreshments may be obtained. About 5 m. further, lying a little off the road on the left hand, and therefore easily passed without notice, is the Locanda called " Il Gran Lupo." *Colonna*, perched upon a wooded hill on the rt., is supposed to represent Colonia, the scene of the battle of Telamon, in which the Gauls were routed A. U. C. 529. It is said to still retain some fragment of polygonal walls, and some other remains of Roman times. At the 77th mile-stone the road enters on an extensive morass, called the Lago di Castiglione, the Lacus Prelius of Cicero, which the government are gradually filling up by means of river deposits or *colmates*, on the plan adopted in the Val di Chiana. The road soon strikes across the plain to the E., passing the river Bruna by a wooden bridge on brick piers. At the mouth of the Bruna is the little port of Castiglione della Pescaja, busy with its anchovy fishery, and its trade in timber and salt, the latter being imported from Elba. The fortress commands an extensive view of the coast. Near the 80th milestone, lying off the road on the rt., is a locanda called " La Società," where indifferent refreshment may be obtained. A drive of 9 m. over a dreary flat brings the traveller to

15 GROSSETO, the capital of the Maremma, a regularly fortified town, the walls of which form a pentagon, with brick bastions and 2 gates. It is

an episcopal town of 3000 souls, and possesses both a cathedral and a theatre. After entering the gate, a street on the l. hand leads to the inn " L'Aquila," kept by the Vedova Palandri, which is clean and comfortable. This is usually the third sleeping-place from Leghorn. There is a road from Grosseto to Siena 50 m. distant, by Batignano, and Paganico (on the Ombrone, the ancient Umbro). Route 26E.

Before leaving Grosseto the classical tourist may pay a visit to the ruins of the ancient city of *Rusellæ*, about 6 m. off. About 4 m. from Grosseto are the sulphur springs, called the Bagni di Roselle, where guides to the ruins may be obtained. The pathway leads along the side of the hill of Moscona, which is covered with the ruins of a circular fortress of the Middle Ages, with large subterranean vaults of apparently a much earlier period. 2 m. beyond it is the isolated hill on which we may still trace, for a circuit of 2 m., the stupendous walls of Rusellæ, celebrated for its antiquity even by the Roman writers, and so powerful as to have been one of the 12 cities of the Etruscan League. The site has been utterly deserted since the middle of the 12th century. During the 7 centuries which have since elapsed, the place has become a perfect wilderness, overgrown with dense thickets of underwood, through which, in parts, it is quite impossible to penetrate. Many parts of the walls are unapproachable, and a large portion of the area within them appears as if it would never again be trodden by the foot of man. The walls, wherever we can approach them, are of exceeding interest ; in some portions of their circuit they present the usual horizontal and rectangular character of Etruscan masonry ; but on the northern and eastern sides, they are formed of enormous masses, piled together in the primitive style of Pelasgic construction, and in some places resembling the rudest specimens of Cyclopean. Some of these blocks are from 6 to 8 feet high, and from 7 to 12 feet long. In some places there are traces of an inner wall more regularly built, with smaller blocks of rectangular masonry. Several gates are to be traced, and at the S.E. angle is a triple square of masonry, supposed by Micali to have been the Arx. A circular ruin, with vaulted apartments of Roman work, has been described as an amphitheatre. All trace of the Etruscan necropolis is lost amidst the dense woods which cover the site, and the only tomb now known in the neighbourhood is a square chamber covered with slabs of stone, and bearing undoubted marks of high antiquity.

The milestones end at Grosseto, and we do not meet with them again until we reach Corneto. The distance from Grosseto to Orbetello is said to be 30 m. There are 3 ferries to be passed: the first, and the worst, 2 m. distant, is over the Ombrone; the second, 14 m. further, is over the Osa; and the third, 4 m. further, is over the Albegna. The boats at these ferries are very bad, and none of them will take a carriage without removing the leaders. 3 pauls is the tariff in each of them for any kind of carriage.

Beyond the Ombrone, and after passing the quarries of Alberese, the road traverses a wooded valley bounded towards the sea by a range of hills, celebrated among the sportsmen of Central Italy as a favourite hunting-ground of the wild boar. A road-side *locanda* called *Collecchio* is much frequented by sportsmen during the hunting season. Between Collecchio and the sea is a ruined castle belonging to the Marsigli family of Siena, the name of which (Bella Marsilia) still celebrates the "Bella Marsigli," whose beauty induced some Turkish cruisers to carry her off to Constantinople, where she became a sultana.

At the opposite extremity of the marsh, distant 2 m. from the high road, is the miserable and sickly village of *Talamone*, the ancient TELAMON, where Marius landed on his return from Africa, and where the Romans defeated the Gauls, A.U.C. 529. There is little to detain the traveller in this place: no Etruscan masonry is to be seen; but the stones are covered with fragments of ruins, the remains apparently of

Roman villas; and at Telamonaccio, in the opposite angle of the bay, are some hot springs, which are supposed to be those mentioned by Pliny as existing in the neighbourhood of Vetulonia, the site of which has recently been discovered in this neighbourhood. The position of this long-lost city, on an insulated hill about 6 m. distant from the coast, renders it more than probable that Telamon was its port, as Graviscæ was that of Tarquinii, and Pyrgos of Cære. To reach the site of Vetulonia from the present road, we must either take the bridle-path which strikes off from the high road towards the l., before we reach the Osa, and leads to Magliano, or we must strike off by the new carriage-road, which connects Magliano with the salt-works at the mouth of the Albegna.

21 m. from Grosseto we cross the Osa, the ancient Ossa. The remains of the Roman bridge, by which the Via Aurelia was carried over the river, are still visible in some vast masses of masonry lying in the stream. 4 m. further, we cross the Albegna, the Albinia of the Itineraries.

At the mouth of the Albegna are the Saline or salt works, from which the grand ducal government in 1842 constructed a high road to *Magliano*, a village of 300 souls; the ruins of whose mediæval castle form a picturesque and striking object as we approach it. Magliano lies about 10 m. from the high road, but, as it is destitute of accommodation for the traveller, it must be visited *en route* either to Grosseto or Orbetello, unless indeed the roadside locanda of Collecchio be made the head-quarters for this excursion. During the operations for the new road, Signor Pasquinelli, the engineer, in exploring the district for materials for his foundations, discovered beneath the surface the walls of an ancient city, which supplied him with the stones necessary for his purpose. These he destroyed as soon as they were excavated, but as the quantity he required was considerable, he was compelled to lay bare the whole circuit of the walls.

By these operations, destructive as they were, Signor Pasquinelli brought to light a long-buried and forgotten city, which Mr. Dennis has identified with VETULONIA, one of the most ancient and powerful cities of the Etruscan League. The form of the city, as traced by Signor Pasquinelli, was that of an irregular square, rather more than 1¼ m. in length, and ¾ m. in breadth; the whole circuit of the walls being upwards of 4 m. The blocks of stone of which the walls were built were found in many places overturned and mingled with fused metal and burnt matter, as if the city had been destroyed by some violent catastrophe. The blocks, however, had been put together without cement in the horizontal manner; and though generally of comparatively small size, there were some among them 9 or 10 feet in length. In the course of these excavations several bronzes and earthen pots were dug up, which sufficiently proved the Etruscan character of the site; and, beyond the walls, some tumuli, encircled with masonry at their base, were discovered and destroyed during the progress of the road. On some of the neighbouring heights several painted tombs had been opened by various explorers long before the existence of the city was ascertained, and there is little doubt that much more would be brought to light by judicious excavations.

As we approach Orbetello, and indeed for some miles along the road between the Osa and Albegna, we command very striking views of the noble promontory of Monte Argentaro, the Mons Argentarius of the ancients, with its double peak, one of which is crowned by the Passionist convent of Il Ritiro. Within the northern bay of this headland is the fortified port of San Stefano, to which a road leads from the Bocca d' Albegna, along one of the necks of sand by which Monte Argentaro is united to the mainland. At the south-eastern base of this mountain is the fortified harbour of Port' Ercole, the Portus Herculis of the ancients. This and all the other small ports on this coast are actively engaged in the tunny fisheries, and many of the towers which are seen upon the coast are used to watch the shoals during the fishing season. Immediately at the back of Monte Argentaro, and separating it from the mainland, is the great salt-lake or lagoon, which fills the surrounding country with malaria in summer, and at other seasons supplies it with fish, which are caught at night by the harpoon and lights. The high-road runs along its eastern shore, and by a détour of 2 m. reaches,

80 m. ORBETELLO, a strongly fortified town, of 3000 souls, built on the long and sandy tongue of land which here projects into the lake, and the extreme point of which has been connected recently with Monte Argentaro by an artificial causeway. There are 2 *inns* here, the Locanda dell' Ussero, and the Chiave d'Oro, both very indifferent. One of them is usually made the fourth sleeping-place from Leghorn. The fortifications of Orbetello, which are on the land side, were built chiefly by the Spaniards, in the 16th and 17th centuries. The sea-wall, which protects it on the side of the lagoon, rests upon stupendous masses of ancient masonry, whose polygonal blocks, put together without cement, bespeak at once their very ancient character. On the sandy isthmus, between the glacis or the "Spalti" and the mainland, several ruins of Etruscan tombs have been discovered, from which sarcophagi, vases, and bronze articles have been obtained.

No traveller should leave Orbetello without devoting a few hours to visit *Ansedonia*, the site of the ancient city of COSA, the Cosæ of Virgil, who mentions it among the Etruscan cities which sent assistance to Æneas. It is only 5 m. from Orbetello, and the high-road to Montalto and Civita Vecchia passes close to it. It is situated on the summit of an isolated hill on the sea-shore, at the extremity of the neck of sand which separates the lake of Orbetello from the sea. The ascent of the summit is about a mile long, and still traverses the ancient pavement. The walls are more perfectly preserved than those of any other city of ancient Italy; they are about a mile in circuit, and exhibit 2 distinct kinds of masonry—the upper courses being horizontal, like those of the Etruscan cities generally; the lower being composed of stupendous blocks of polygonal stones, fitted together with the utmost nicety, and without cement, like those of the Pelasgic city of Alatri, described in the Handbook for Southern Italy. The walls vary in height from 12 to 30 feet, and in thickness from 5 to 6. At intervals they are strengthened by towers from 20 to 40 feet square; 14 of which are still traceable, no less than 11 occurring in 2 sides of the angle which faced the sea, and was therefore more open to attack. The external surface of the walls, like those of Alatri and Arpino, has been worked down to a smooth face, but the inner surface has been left in its rough state. There are 3 double gates, situated in the northern, southern and eastern walls; the latter is the most perfect, and exhibits in high perfection all the peculiarities of structure for which Cosa is remarkable. Like the great gate of Arpino, all the gates of Cosa must have been covered with flat slabs of stone, or have had lintels of wood. In the S.E. angle the ground rises into a small plateau, which must have formed the Arx of the city. On this height may be recognised 3 or 4 specimens of masonry, of as many different periods; the lowest being Pelasgic, like the city walls; the next Etruscan; the next Roman; and the most recent mediæval. The polygonal architecture of Cosa was long considered to be the only example of that style within the limits of ancient Etruria; and considerable controversy has been carried on by the Italian and German archæologists in regard to its antiquity. The Italian antiquaries, with few exceptions, regard Cosa as a more recent Etruscan city than Cortona, Volterra, Tarquinii, and others in which the horizontal style is found in its greatest purity; and have therefore concluded that its polygonal substructions do not denote that high antiquity of which they are the signs in cities of Pelasgic origin.

Orbetello is a convenient place from which to make an excursion to the ruins of SATURNIA and SOVANA. Saturnia is 30 m. distant; the road ascends the valley of the Albegna by its l. banks, and is practicable for carriages as far as Montemerano, whence a bridle path of 8 m. leads us to Saturnia. Another bridle-path of 10 or 12 m. across the mountains leads to Sovana and Pitigliano; or if the carriage road be preferred, an excellent road of 17 m. leads from Montemerano to Manciano and Pitigliano, where the traveller may obtain accommodation at the Casa Bertocci. On his return the traveller may visit the Ponte della Badia (Vulci), Toscanella, and Corneto. All these places, including Saturnia and Sovana, and the roads by which they may be approached, are noticed in detail in our Excursions to the Etruscan Cities, at the close of this volume.

Leaving Orbetello for Civita Vecchia, the road passes at the bottom of the Hill of Cossa, and along the Lago of Burano on the rt., at the distance of 15 m., the river Chiarone is reached, and the Tuscan dogana, a large house with plenty of rooms and beds, but no *cuisine*. 9 m. further, along an indifferent road, the river Fiora is passed, from which a steep ascent brings us to

24 m. *Montalto*, the ancient Forum Aurelii, now the Papal dogana, a miserable town with dark, crooked, narrow streets, and an indifferent *inn*, in the Piazza, kept by Cesarini. The charge for barriers here is very heavy; it is everywhere on entering the Papal States; and duty is levied on carriages and horses, unless the traveller find security in Rome for their re-exportation. The Roman milestones begin here, and continue to Civita Vecchia.

From Montalto the traveller can more easily visit than from any other point the ruins of the ancient Vulci, the Ponte dell' Abbadia, and the more recent Roman ruins about Musignano and Canino. From Montalto upwards the banks of the Fiora are very picturesque, especially as we approach the Ponte dell' Abbadia: the distance from Montalto to the latter is less than 8 m., and may easily be performed on horseback, but ought not to be attempted, from the insalubrity of the climate, *after the middle of May.*

The road, after leaving Montalto, is very hilly. 3 miles beyond it we cross the Arrone; and 7 m. farther, before we cross the river Marta, we pass on our r. hand, upon the coast, the site of *Gravisca*, the ancient port of Tarquinii, now marked only by some blocks of tufa and broken columns, and by a magnificent arch 14 feet in span, called the Pontone, which formed the mouth of a cloaca, and opens into an embankment of massive masonry which was doubtless the quay of the Etruscan port. Beyond the Marta, on the coast, is *Porto San Clementino*, a small harbour for the export of salt and grain, which is full of bustle and activity in the winter, but in summer is deserted on account of the malaria.

Soon after crossing the Marta, the road passes below Corneto, about half way to Civita Vecchia, but does not enter it. Corneto is described in our Excursions from Rome. At the junction of the branch-road leading to the town is a wretched locanda; but there is a very tolerable inn at Corneto itself. The road from this point is in good order, and about midway between Corneto and Civita Vecchia it crosses the Mignone, at whose mouth the Tower of Bertaldo or Sant' Agostino marks the site of Rapinium,—the scene of St. Augustine's reproof by the angel for entertaining doubts on the subject of the Trinity.

CIVITA VECCHIA (*Inns:* Isole Britanniche, or Orlandi's Hotel; a new and excellent hotel, but rather expensive. Hôtel de l'Europe, also belonging to Orlandi). At both hotels travellers may obtain every information respecting packets, and may engage horses and carriages for excursions to Corneto, &c. Civita Vecchia is one of the numerous places which steam navigation has raised from comparative insignificance. A large proportion, if not the majority, of travellers land here on their first entrance into Southern Italy; and the several lines of steamers which regularly touch here on their voyages between Marseilles, Naples, and the Levant, have given an importance and activity to the town which it never could otherwise have acquired.

As the principal port of the Papal States on the Mediterranean, and as the modern port of the capital itself, Civita Vecchia has some commercial importance: a large quantity of the exports of the States are brought here for shipment, and English vessels may frequently be recognized in the harbour. As a proof of the immense advantages which steam communication has conferred upon the town, it may be sufficient to mention that the vessels of each of the lines of steamers which run between Marseilles, Genoa, Leghorn, and Naples, touch here 3 times a month each way, so that there are seldom less than 30 arrivals and departures of steamers monthly from this port; the French government packets afford additional facilities by extending their voyages to Malta and the Levant. These steamers have brought Rome within a journey of 7 days from London, and have made Civita Vecchia the central point from which travellers may calculate on a rapid and certain conveyance to any part of the Mediterranean.

Travellers are not allowed to land until the captain has exhibited his papers and the passports have been duly examined. A few years ago this arrangement caused a delay from 8 A.M. until noon or later—a serious inconvenience to those who were anxious to reach Rome before dark; but the great increase of visitors has latterly produced a relaxation of the rule, and passengers may now land as soon after daylight as the captain has gone through the required formalities. As soon as the traveller lands he is beset with porters (*facchini*); he should therefore make his bargain before leaving the steamer. 2 pauls for landing, including a truck to convey the luggage to the custom-house, are sufficient. On leaving the town the luggage is examined by the police, and by the custom-house officers, who insist on plumbing it, for which a few baiocchi are paid, which may save another examination on entering Rome. English travellers have also to pay 5 pauls to the English vice-consul for his visa to the passport, which is required by the police before they will sign it

Finally, on leaving the town a fee of 2 or 3 pauls is demanded at the gate.

The *Port*, with its massive construction, is one of the most remarkable works of Trajan, and as the "Portus Trajani" it is well known by the description of the younger Pliny. Though the moles, quays, and fortress which we now see were erected after the destruction of the town by the Saracens in the 9th century, their foundations are easily recognised as Roman. Civita Vecchia was made a free port by Clement XII.; its fortress was begun in 1512 by Julius II., from the designs of Michael Angelo, and finished by Paul III. The walls of the town were built by Urban VII. in 1590. The brightness of the ramparts and the lazzaretto, and the massive architecture of the buildings around the harbour, give it a striking appearance as we approach it by sea; but the anticipations to which they give rise are not realised by the town itself.

Civita Vecchia is the capital of the smallest Delegation of the Papal States, which embraces a superficial extent of 443 square m., and a pop. of only 24,700 souls, being less than that of the isolated territory of Benevento. The pop. of the town itself is upwards of 10,000. It occupies the site of the Roman settlement of Centumcellæ. On the destruction of that town by the Saracens in 828, the inhab. removed to a position farther inland, but returned to the former site in 854, from which circumstance the name Civita *Vecchia*, or the old town, is said to be derived. It was made an episcopal see by Leo XII. in 1825. It is now united with the more ancient dioceses of Porto and Sta. Rufina. The *prisons* of Civita Vecchia are calculated to hold 1200 persons, and the number in confinement is seldom much below that amount. A large proportion of the criminals recently confined there had been guilty of homicide; a fifth were under sentence of imprisonment for life, and nearly one-half for the term of 20 years.

Numerous antiquities and coins have been found in the vicinity of the town. About 3 miles distant are the *Bagni di Ferrata*, mineral springs, mentioned by Pliny as the Aquæ Tauri. The aque-duct constructed on the foundations of that built by Trajan is a remarkable work, by which water is conveyed from the Mignone, a distance, it is said, of 23 m. At La Tolfa, 12 m. distant, are some lead mines and the Alumiere, or alum works, which formerly gave a considerable annual sum to the treasury.

Civita Vecchia is the most convenient point from which travellers who may desire to visit the ruins of the ancient cities of S.-western Etruria can take their departure. Many, however, who are anxious to reach Rome will hardly be induced to delay their journey for the purpose of making a complete tour through these interesting localities; and as there are many who do not enter Italy by Civita Vecchia, it has been considered desirable to give an account of the tour under 'Excursions from Rome,' where good introductions may be obtained. Corneto, however, is within an easy distance of Civita Vecchia, and travellers who are detained here for a day cannot employ it more profitably than by devoting it to an excursion to that town. A *calessa* for one person to go and return costs 2 scudi. There is a small gallery of Etruscan antiquities in the Town Hall of Civita Vecchia, consisting of sarcophagi, female heads in painted stone, monumental tablets, and some Roman milestones. There is another collection belonging to Signor Guglielmi, of articles found upon his own lands; and Signor Bucci has a collection of bronzes and vases for sale.

ROUTE 25A.

CIVITA VECCHIA TO ROME.

52 miles.

	Posta.
Civita Vecchia to Santa Severa	2
Santa Severa to Palo	1¼
Palo to Castel di Guido	1½
Castel di Guido to Rome	2
	7

A regular Post-office diligence leaves Civita Vecchia for Rome every evening at 7, reaching Rome the next morning at 4 a.m., and supplementary diligences on the arrival of every steamer, as soon as the passengers have cleared their luggage at the Custom-house and obtained their passports; fare, postilions included, 13 francs. Time employed on the journey, 8 hours. Persons who wish to proceed to Rome at their own convenience, may hire a post-diligence, leaving Civita Vecchia at any hour by paying 11 scudi and 9 pauls, the carriage taking as many as 4 passengers; this mode of proceeding will best suit families, who, upon their arrival at Rome, *instead of being set down at the coach-office, are taken direct to their hotel ;* it will also enable them to stop on the road at Palo, to make from thence an excursion to Cere and Cervetri, and to leave Civita Vecchia at their own hour. There are plenty of vetturini always ready to start from Civita Vecchia, who convey passengers to Rome for 16 pauls, but as they seldom change horses on the road, they seldom perform the journey in less than 12 hours. This road, the only one now travelled between Civita Vecchia to Rome, runs near to the coast as far as Palo; on leaving the town it follows the sea-shore to Cape Linaro, where it takes a sudden bend, passing by Torre Chiarruccia, the Roman station of Castrum Novum, on the Via Aurelia, from thence to Santa Marinella, the ancient Punicium, 2 m. beyond which are ruins of 2 ancient bridges, built of massive blocks of stone, by which the Via Aurelia crossed a small stream. About 6 m. farther we arrive at

2 Santa Severa, a post station, with a picturesque fortress of the middle ages, originally a fief of the Counts of Galera, from whom it passed to the Orsini, and now belongs to the Patrizi family ; it is supposed to occupy the site of Pyrgos, the port and arsenal of Cære, the "Pyrgi Veteres" of Virgil: it is mentioned by Strabo as remarkable for its fine walls and towers, and for its temple of Lucina, plundered by Dionysius of Syracuse. Several massive fragments of masonry, some polygonal, may be still seen, forming a part of the quadrangular enclosure by which the ancient town was surrounded. From Santa Severa the road crosses

several small streams, descending from the chain of La Tolfa, and the Vaccinia, from Cervetri and the hills of Bracciano, 4 m. before reaching

1½ Palo, a small village with a fortress and castle of the 15th cent. to defend its unsafe roadstead. Palo occupies the site of the Etruscan Alsium, near which Pompey and Antoninus Pius had villas; the only ruins now visible are some of the Roman period, probably of a villa, about 1 m. eastward of the castle. Palo is a good deal frequented by small coasting vessels, which bring from Elba the iron-ore used in the smelting furnaces of Bracciano, to which it is carried on carts by a road of about 15 m. The Inn opposite the post-house is very indifferent, but it can be made a resting-place for travellers who may wish to visit Cære. Spending the night here after the 1st of June ought to be avoided, as, like all the places on the coast, malaria sets in soon after that period of the year. The description of Cervetri and Cære will be found under the chapter of Excursions from Rome. On leaving Palo, the old post station of Monterone, 1 m. distant, is soon reached, and from Monterone a road of 4 m. along the Sanguinara torrent leads to Cære. Near Monterone are the Tumuli, called the Colli Tufarini, which being explored in 1838, were found to be Etruscan sepulchres, similar to those of Vulci ; they probably formed part of the necropolis of the neighbouring Alsium. From Monterone the road gradually ascends, leaving the sea-coast more to the r., and crossing several streams descending from the higher country on the S. side of the lake of Bracciano : of these streams the most considerable is the Arrone, the natural outlet of that lake, which is spanned by its Roman bridge of 2 arches, a good specimen of ancient masonry. From the Arrone the road ascends to Castel di Guido, on the ridge of hills that separate the waters of the Arrone, emptying themselves into the Mediterranean, and of the Galera, which falls into the Tiber.

1½ Castel di Guido, a possession of the Orsini family, on or near the site of the ancient Loricum, the scene of the early education and of the death of the Emperor Antoninus Pius.

From Castel di Guido the road becomes very hilly and uninteresting, similar in many respects to the rest of the northern Campagna: descending into the valley of the Galera, called here the Fossa d'Acqua Sona, that river is crossed at the rude osteria of Malagrotta, and 2 m. farther on, the Maglianella and the Magliano. Soon after passing the latter stream, and at the 3rd milestone from the gates of Rome, the modern road leaves on the rt. the Via Aurelia, which proceeds in a more direct line to the city, passing under the walls of the Villa Pamfili Doria to the Porta San Pancrazia, on the site of the ancient Porta Aurelia. 2 m. from Rome, the aqueduct conveying the Acqua Paola to Rome is crossed by the post-road; a deep valley succeeds, followed by a corresponding ascent, at the top of which we find ourselves in front of the bastions of the Vatican; it was at this place that the French sustained so serious a check in their first approach to Rome in 1849, when they were repulsed with serious loss by a few pieces of cannon judiciously placed and manned by a set of brave fellows posted at the western angle of the bastion in the garden of the Pope. From this point the road descends along the fortified wall of the city to the Porta de' Cavallegieri, where passports are demanded, and from whence, if the traveller be unprovided with a *Lascia Passare*, his carriage is escorted to the Dogana. A few hundred yards beyond this gate, the meanest in appearance and the least interesting in its historical recollections of all those by which Rome is entered, the traveller finds himself on a sudden turning in the midst of the Piazza of St. Peter's, with that magnificent pile and the palace of the Vatican before him. As he traverses this magnificent scene, he will soon forget the dreary road and the fatiguing journey of the last 8 hours: advancing from thence he enters the Borgo, passes before the palace which was once the residence of the representative of Roman Ca-

tholic England, the Castel of St. Angelo, and over the Elian Bridge, from which he for the first time descries the waters of the yellow Tiber: here, however, all his illusions of Roman grandeur will momentarily cease; a dirty, narrow street, so unlike those he has already passed through, and so unworthy even of modern Rome, conducts to the quarter usually frequented by our countrymen in the capital of the Christian world.

ROUTE 26.

FLORENCE TO ROME, BY SIENA AND VITERBO.

About 200 m.

The completion of the railroad from Florence to Siena has rendered this rte. more available to travellers: as regards actual distances it is the shortest to Rome, and may easily be performed in 3 days with post horses, and in 4 by vetturino, from Siena.

An excellent diligence runs 3 times a week between Florence and Rome, performing the journey in 36 hours, including a stoppage of 2 hours at Siena. Passengers leave Florence by the morning train at 7·30 A.M., and Siena at 1 P.M., arriving at Rome the following day at 7 P.M. The fares (13½ and 12½ scudi for coupé and intérior from Siena) are exorbitant (5d. per English mile), considering the distance, and the slow mode of travelling.

Persons disliking railway travelling, or who, having their own carriages, may prefer the high road, can reach Siena by post in 7, and with vetturino horses in 10 hours by Rte. 26A.

The Malle Poste from Florence to Rome takes 2 passengers, and is a more comfortable and expeditious conveyance; it leaves Florence in the evening, and arrives at Rome by daybreak on the next morning but one; it follows the post road between Florence and Siena.

The traveller, by leaving Florence early, will arrive at Siena before 11 A.M., which will afford him ample time to see the city, and to leave on the day following by diligence or vetturino for Rome.

Another facility which the railroad affords is to enable the tourist to visit the interesting sites of Certaldo, the country of Boccaccio, and the very curious town of St. Gemigniano, and to reach Siena on the same evening.

Railway trains for Siena leave Florence 3 times a day in summer, at 7 and 10.30 A.M. and 5.30 P.M., and 3 times a day in winter, at 7.40; 11.0, and 4.30 P.M., performing the journey in 3½ hours; fares, 1st class, 10½ pauls; 2nd class, 7¾; the carriages of the latter class are very good, clean, and comfortable.

The station of the Leopolda Railway at Florence is outside and close to the gate leading to the Cascine; the line is the same as that to Pisa and Leghorn (see Hand-book for Northern Italy, Rte. 42) as far as Empoli, from whence the branch to Siena ascends the Val d'Elsa; on leaving the Florence station, the line runs parallel to the Arno, along the north side of the Cascine, passing by the populous village of Brozzi to

San Donino Stat. The country between this and the next stat. is a perfect garden, in one of the most productive regions of the valley of the Arno; the river Bisenzio, which descends from the Apennines, and passes by Prato, is crossed by a handsome bridge, before arriving at

Signa Stat. The village of Signa on the right bank of the Arno, and of Lastra on the left, are connected by a bridge; these two towns are the centre of the straw plait manufactory. Soon after leaving Signa, the rly. crosses the Ombrone river from Pistoia, and enters the narrow ravine or gorge of La Gonfolina, by which the middle valley of the Arno or that of Florence communicates with the lower one, or that of Pisa. The railroad runs close to the river throughout this ravine, and in carrying it through, great engineering difficulties had to be surmounted. At the western extremity we arrive at the

Montelupo Stat. (see Handbook of N. Italy). On leaving this stat., the river Pesa is crossed, where it separates Montelupo from the old post stat. of Ambrogiana. Here the Val d'Arno

Inferiore may be said to commence; the rly. follows it in a straight line to *Empoli* stat. As passengers change carriages here, they will do well to see that their luggage is properly transferred to the Siena line. Passengers arriving from Florence have in general to wait some time before starting for Siena, until the up train arrives from Leghorn and Pisa. At Empoli the railway to Siena branches off to the l., takes a more southerly direction, and enters the valley of the Elsa at Ponte a Elsa, running parallel to the old post road.

Granajuolo Stat. From this portion of the road the town of San Miniato dei Tedeschi, with its high mediæval towers, forms a very picturesque object on the summit of hills on the rt.; the traveller who takes an interest in Tuscan agriculture will do well to visit from this stat. the Agricultural School, founded by the Marquis Ridolfi at Mileto, about 2 m. distant, on the opposite side of the Elsa. A district rich in corn, vines, and mulberry-trees is passed before arriving at

Castel Fiorentino Stat. The town is situated on the hill to the l. of the stat., and contains a population of 2300 souls. It is the principal place in the Val d'Elsa, and in former times was one of considerable importance, commanding the high road from the Val d'Arno to Siena. Continuing along the banks of the river, through an equally fertile country, we arrive at

Certaldo Stat. Here, as at the last, the station is in the plain, and the town on the declivity of the hill on the left, overlooking the river and its beautiful valley. The traveller will do well to employ the interval between two trains to visit this picturesque village, immortalized by its connexion with Boccaccio, who assumed the name of Certaldese to commemorate the country of his family. Certaldo will well repay a visit to those who take an interest in Italian history, and in the beautiful language of which Boccaccio was one of the founders. Here he spent the greater part of his life on his return from Paris, and was buried in the ch. of St. Michael and St. James, still called the Canonica.

" Boccaccio to his parent earth bequeath'd
  His dust—and lies it not her Great among,
  With many a sweet and solemn requiem
    breathed
  O'er him who form'd the Tuscan's siren
    tongue ?
  That music in itself, whose sounds are song,
  The poetry of speech ? No ;—even his tomb,
  Uptorn, must bear the hyæna bigot's wrong,
  No more amidst the meaner dead find room,
  Nor claim a passing sigh, because it told for
    whom !"   *Childe Harold.*

"Boccaccio's sepulchre," says M. Valery, " formerly stood in the centre of the ch.; against the wall close by was the epitaph written by himself, and an additional one by his illustrious friend Colluccio Salutati, chancellor of the Seigniory of Florence. The podestà of Certaldo, Lattanzio Tedaldi, erected a more magnificent monument to him, in 1503, on the interior front of the ch., which was honourably transferred to a spot facing the pulpit on the construction of an orchestra. Boccaccio was represented half length, holding on his breast, with both hands, a folio volume on which was inscribed *Decameron*, a singular book to be placed just facing a preacher, and a proof of liberality on the part of the clergy. The tomb has experienced the most melancholy changes. For more than 4 centuries it had been the honour of Certaldo, and had attracted many travellers to the Canonica, when in 1783 it was removed by a false interpretation of the law of Leopold against burying in churches; the hyæna bigots of Certaldo, against whom Childe Harold and his annotator declaim, had nothing to do with it. The stone that covered this tomb was broken and thrown aside as useless in the cloister adjoining. It is said that Boccaccio's skull and bones were then exhumed, and a copper or lead tube containing sundry parchments of the same century. These precious fragments, now lost, were long preserved by the rector of the ch., who ten years after accepted a benefice in the upper Val d' Arno. It is stated by tradition that they were still at that epoch an object of curiosity to strangers, who went to the rector's house to see them. It is difficult to explain the culpable negligence that allowed the remains of Boccaccio to be lost, when we consider

the unceasing popularity, at Certaldo, of this eloquent, admirable writer, this limner, so true, graceful, touching, profound, and mirthful, the perfect impersonation of Tuscan genius.'' Boccaccio's house, built of brick, with a small tower, was repaired in 1823 by the Marchioness Lenzoni Medici, one of the last descendants of the illustrious house whose name she bears, who " reconstructed the staircase, decorated Boccaccio's chamber with his portrait, a large fresco by Benvenuti, and a bookcase of his works. The small windows are of the time. The furniture is the oldest that could be found at Certaldo, with some imitated from paintings of that period. The lamp seems the most authentic article of the whole, as it was found in the house, and the hardness of the oil proved its antiquity. A well, a bath, and a terrace are shown, which, according to an old tradition, belonged to Boccaccio. The fragments of stone which covered his grave for more than 4 centuries was religiously collected by the Marchesa Lenzoni in 1826, and placed in this house with an inscription by her friend, Signor Giordani."

As there is little interest in the country between Certaldo and the next station, Poggibonsi, the railway continuing to run in a less fertile district along the foot of the hills formed of tertiary sandstones that bound the Val d' Elsa on the E., the tourist may make a very interesting excursion to the town of San Gimignano. The distance from Certaldo is about 8 m.; but as the road is hilly the pedestrian would require 3 and a light gig 2 hours to reach it : vehicles for the purpose may be easily procured at the railway station, and on hiring them an agreement should be made that, instead of returning to Certaldo, the traveller will be conveyed to Poggibonsi. Crossing the Elsa, the road ascends the valley of the Casciani torrent, from which it ascends to the hamlet of Pancole—the hills on this as on the opposite side of the Elsa, being composed of tertiary sands abounding in marine remains.

San Gimignano, a very ancient town of about 2000 Inhab. on the top of a hill 1220 feet above the sea. There is a tolerable inn in the town, the Albergo della Pace, where a traveller can put up: a few hours will enable him to see everything of interest and to return either to Certaldo or Poggibonsi. One of the most remarkable features in this strange and primitive, unaltered mediæval town is the number of lofty square towers in so small a space, from which it has received the distinctive appellation of St. G. delle Belle Torre. The Palazzo del Podestà or del Commune is an edifice of the 14th century; in the principal hall, that where the council held its meetings, there is a very interesting fresco, painted in 1317, by the Sienese painter Lippo di Memmo, and restored, according to the inscription beneath it, by Benozzo Gozzoli, in 1467: it represents a Podestà, Nello dei Tolomei, on his knees before the Virgin surrounded by 28 saints: close to the palace is the highest of the 14 towers of San Gimigniano: it is built on an arch, under which passes a street: it was raised in 1290, and from a fund to which each chief magistrate was obliged to contribute ' on going out of office for the privilege of having his armorial bearings affixed to it. Of 3 bells which it contains, the largest, weighing 12,000 Tuscan pounds, was cast in 1326.

The Palazzo del Oriolo, now the theatre, has also a tower close to it; it is opposite the collegiate church.

Of all the towers of S. Gimignano, the most elegant are the twin Torri degl. Ardinghelli, built by the noble family of that name in the 13th century.

Of the 36 churches that formerly existed in this small town, many are in ruins; those worthy of a visit are:

The *Collegiata*, or the Asunta, was made a collegiate church by Sixtus IV., although existing previously from the 12th century; its interior is remarkable for some frescoes by Bartolo Fredi (1316), representing subjects of the Old Testament; for 3 large frescoes of the Inferno, the Paradiso and 12 apostles, by Taddeo Bartolo (1393); and for that of Saint Sebastian, painted between the two western doors by Benozzo Gozzoli in 1465. In the chapel of S. Fina some frescoes by D.

Ghirlandajo and his pupil Mainardi. In the Sacristy there is a fine marble bust of Onofrio Vanni by Benedetto da Majano, for which the sculptor received 10 florins in gold. The ch. of St. Augustin, although begun in the 13th, was not completed until the end of the following century; the cloister was added 100 years later, when Benozzo Gozzoli (1465 — 66) painted the beautiful frescoes in the choir representing scenes of the life of St. Augustin.

There is an altar-piece of the Virgin surrounded by Cherubim, by Pinturricchio, in the church of the Ulivitani; and a Deposition by Cigoli in that of the Capucins outside the town.

San Gimignano has at all periods possessed an exuberance of monastic institutions: a century ago it contained 235 monks and priests out of a population of 1300 souls; and even now, out of 2000 inhab., there are 120 priests and friars.

There has been of late years established in the suppressed monastery of S. Domenico a Penitentiary, or House of Correction for convicted females, who are sent here from all parts of the Grand Duchy.

The road from S. Gimignano to Poggibonsi descends along the Foci torrent: the distance is less than from Certaldo—scarcely 6 miles.

Poggibonsi Stat.—A town of nearly 3000 souls, situated in the angle formed by the junction of the Elsa and Staggia torrents. There is a very fair inn here, the Aquila Nera, provided you fix your price. It derives its name from the high hill, Poggio Bonzi, at the foot of which it is situated, and which is surmounted by an old castle built in the middle of the 15th century, during the wars between the Sienese and the Florentines. 4 m. S. W. of Poggibonsi is the town of Colle, to which there is an excellent road, the post route between Florence and Siena. From Poggibonsi the rly. follows the valley of the Staggia nearly to the source of the river: the ascent is very rapid, being about 750 feet in a distance of 16 m. 5 m. after leaving Poggibonsi the line passes the village of Staggia on the rt., and at an equal distance farther on the old square castle of Monte Riggioni, which forms a very picturesque object in the landscape. All along this upper valley of the Staggia, the geologist will observe very considerable deposits of travertine, not only of fresh water origin, but interstratified in the marine beds of the tertiary marine formation. 2 m. before arriving at Siena the railroad enters a long tunnel, pierced in the hill of San Dalmazzo, which here forms the summit level, that separates the waters flowing into the Elsa and the Arno on the N., and into the Ombrone on the S. A mile beyond this tunnel we arrive at the

Siena Stat., close to the newly opened Porta di San Lorenzo, which leads into the principal street of the city. Luggage is sometimes examined at the gate, but passports are only required at the hotels where travellers pass the night. The offices of the diligences to Rome and to Chiusi are at short distances within the gate, and persons about to proceed even on the morrow by these conveyances will do well to deposit here their luggage on the way to their hotels.

SIENA (*Inns:* Arme di Inghilterra kept by Seggi, the nearest to the rly. station and diligence offices, very fair; Aquila Nera, equally good. There are very good apartments for families in both these hotels, and the charges are reasonable. I Tre Re, a small but clean-looking inn. There is an excellent café (del Greco), nearly opposite the Loggia of the Casino dei Nobili. This ancient city occupies the irregular summit of a hill of tertiary sandstone, rising on the borders of the dreary and barren tract which forms the southern province of Tuscany. The whole district bears a desolate appearance, and, consists of bare clay hills capped with marine sandstone. The street entered by the post road at the Porta Camollia, or the Florentine gate, divides the city into two nearly equal portions; the streets are generally narrow and irregular, frequently so steep as to be impassable

in carriages, and many of them are mere narrow lanes; the smaller streets are mostly paved with tiles, in the manner described by Pliny as the "spicata testacea." The wider ones are generally bordered with immense mansions called palaces, some of which have lofty towers and rings near the entrance, like the old mansions of Florence. In the days when Siena, as a republic, was the great rival of Florence, it contained nearly 200,000 inhab.; the present population is about 22,000, and in the extreme quarters of the city grass is growing on the pavement.

Siena preserves, almost without change, the name of Sena Julia, and is supposed to have been a colony established by Julius Cæsar. Though in the heart of Tuscany, it does not possess a vestige of Etruscan antiquity. The interest of the existing city is derived from its prominent position among the free cities of the middle ages. In the early part of the 12th century it had thrown off the yoke of the Countess Matilda, and declared itself an independent republic. The nobles fell early before the power of the people, and were compelled to retire from the city. The popular party, although divided by the rivalry of their leaders, warmly embraced the Ghibelline cause; and on the expulsion of Farinata degli Uberti from Florence, all the Florentine Ghibelines who were implicated in the conspiracy of that celebrated personage were received favourably at Siena. During the hostilities which followed, the whole power of the Guelph party in Tuscany was defeated by the combined forces of Siena and Pisa, under the command of Farinata and the generals of Manfred, at Monte Aperto, about 5 miles from Siena. This memorable battle, commemorated by Dante, in which the Guelphs left no less than 10,000 dead upon the field, was fought on the 4th Sept. 1260; it not only established the supremacy of the Ghibelines, but left in the hands of the Sienese the great standard of Florence, whose poles are still preserved as trophies in the cathedral.

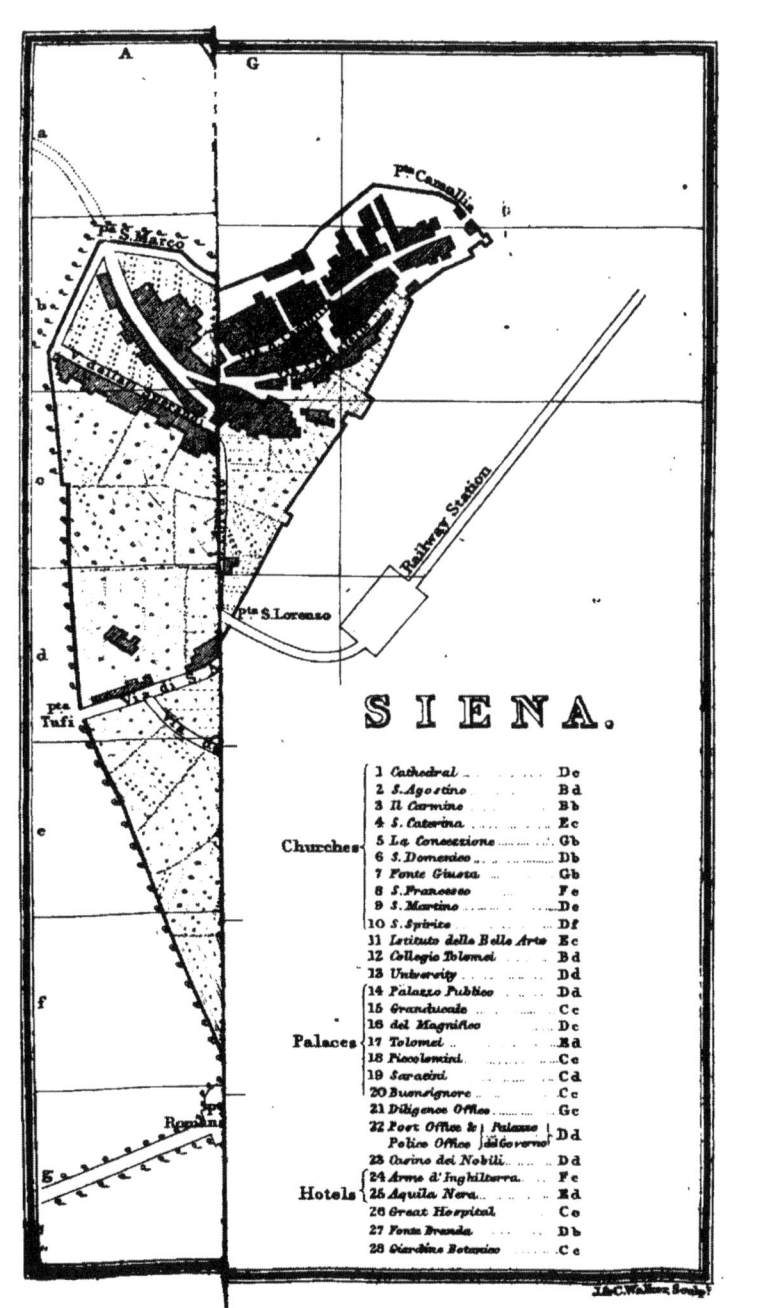

SIENA.

	1	Cathedral	D e
	2	S. Agostino	B d
	3	Il Carmine	B b
	4	S. Caterina	E c
	5	La Concezione	G b
Churches	6	S. Domenico	D b
	7	Fonte Giusta	G b
	8	S. Francesco	F e
	9	S. Martino	D e
	10	S. Spirito	D f
	11	Istituto della Belle Arte	E c
	12	Collegio Tolomei	B d
	13	University	D d
	14	Palazzo Pubico	D d
	15	Granducale	C c
	16	del Magnifico	D c
Palaces	17	Tolomei	B d
	18	Piccolomini	C c
	19	Saracini	C d
	20	Buonsignore	C c
	21	Diligence Office	G c
	22	Post Office & Palazzo Police Office del Governo	D d
	23	Casino dei Nobili	D d
	24	Arme d'Inghilterra	F e
Hotels	25	Aquila Nera	E d
	26	Great Hospital	C e
	27	Fonte Branda	D b
	28	Giardino Botanico	C e

J.&C.Walker Sculp.

This decisive action brought back to Siena a great number of her exiled nobles, either to become citizens and traders, or to live a distinct and isolated class in a separate quarter of the city, which still retains the name of " Casato." After numerous contests between the people and the rich merchants, who formed a kind of burgher aristocracy on the overthrow of the nobles, Charles IV. in vain endeavoured to acquire the *signoria ;* but the city, although able to resist his schemes, was too much weakened in her principles of liberty by the tyranny of Pandolfo Petrucci and other popular usurpers to withstand the encroachments of the Medici, who found means to destroy by treachery the last remnant of her freedom.

It was during this last struggle that the ferocious Marquis de Marignano, whom Cosmo de' Medici had commissioned to reduce the citizens by famine, inhumanly destroyed the population of the Sienese Maremma, and carried desolation into the whole of that once fertile district. Malaria inevitably followed this cruel policy, and " those," says Sismondi, " who at the peace returned to reap the inheritance of the victims of Marignano, soon fell themselves the victims of that disease." During the period of its freedom the territory of Siena was large and populous ; 200,000 men were found within its walls ; it had 39 gates, of which all but 8 are now closed ; the arts were encouraged, the city became the seat of a school of painting, and its commerce was so extensive as to excite the jealousy even of the Florentines.

Siena is now the chief city of one of the 5 Compartimenti of Tuscany, the seat of an archbishop, and of a military governor.

The *School of Siena* is so remarkable a feature in the history of the city, that it will be desirable to give a brief epitome of its character and its masters, in order that the works of art in its public gallery and churches may be the more thoroughly appreciated. The prevailing characteristics of this school are deep religious feeling, and a peculiar beauty and tenderness of expression inspired by devotional enthusiasm, differing altogether from that style which classical study had introduced into the northern schools of Italy. In antiquity the Sienese school is nearly equal to that of Florence, and there is no doubt that it exercised an important influence on the great masters of the 15th century. The patronage of the republic as early as the 13th encouraged if it did not create a society of artists, of which Guiduccio, Dietisalvi, Guido da Siena, and Duccio di Buoninsegna were the leading members. The most remarkable among the early masters is Simone Memmi, the contemporary of Giotto, and friend of Petrarch, who dedicated to him two of his sonnets as the painter of the portrait of Laura. He died in 1345 ; among his scholars were his relative Lippo Memmi, and Pietro and Ambrogio Lorenzetti. In the 15th century Andrea di Vanni, Berna da Siena, Taddeo Bartolo, and Jacopo Pacchiarotto were the principal representatives of the school. The school afterwards declined, until the time of Sodoma, a follower and perhaps a pupil of Leonardo da Vinci, whose merits were so great that he was employed on the decorations of the Vatican and the Farnesina Palace at Rome. Among his pupils were Michaelangelo da Siena (Anselmi) and Bartolommeo Neroni (Riccio), and the most eminent of all, Beccafumi, well known by the pavement of the cathedral. The last names of note in the Siena school are those of Baldassare Peruzzi, and Marco da Siena, generally considered as his pupil. The subsequent history of the Sienese school presents no artists of great eminence, although the names of Salimbeni and Francesco Vanni occur during the latter half of the 16th century.

The *Istituto delle Belle Arte* contains a most interesting collection of works by the older Sienese masters, arranged chronologically in 5 rooms, and a large miscellaneous collection in 3 others. The pictures of the old Sienese masters have been chiefly obtained from suppressed religious establishments, and from the municipality of Siena. The most remarkable of them are: 1st room, 6, *Guido da Siena* (1221), Madonna and Child ; 14, *Mar-*

I 3

garitone d' Arezzo, Portrait of St. Francis, signed (1270); 15, *Maestro Gilio* (1257), and *Dietisalvi* (1264), Portrait of a Monk of S. Galgano, and of Ildrobrandino Pagliaresi; 18, *Duccio*, Madonna and Child, with 4 saints; 22, a very interesting Tritico, representing the Virgin and Child, with S. Peter and S. Paul; 42 to 49, *Ambrogio Lorenzetti*, a very curious series of pictures by this old painter of the middle of the 14th century, from different suppressed convents and churches; 63, *Nicolo di Segna* (1345), a painted Crucifix; 82, *Lippo Memmi*, a very beautiful picture of the Virgin and Child surrounded by angels and saints; 95, *Mino del Pellicciajo* (1362), a large picture of the Virgin and Saints. 2nd room, 13, 14, *Spinello Aretino* (1400), Swoon of the Madonna, and Coronation of the Virgin, and 20 pictures of unknown authors. 3rd room, 15th century, 1—6, an interesting series of authentic pictures by *Taddeo Bartolo*; 19, 25, and 68, 70, *Sano di Pietro* (1460, 1480); 26, 30, *Matteo di Siena*, a very curious suite of this celebrated master; 32, *Francesco di Giorgio*, the Birth of our Saviour, from the suppressed Convent of Monte Uliveto; 44, *Guiduccio*, 2 interesting small pictures presenting views of Siena, and executed for the municipality in 1484, 1488. 4th room, 5 and 7, *Sano di Pietro*, sitting figure of S. Jerome, and Apparition of the Virgin to Calixtus III., with her address and the Pope's reply; 9, *Sodoma*, the magnificent fresco of Christ bound to the column, one of the finest productions of the Sienese school, formerly in the cloister of the Convent of San Francesco; 10, *Taddeo Bartolo*; 11, 13, 17, and 29 to 31, pictures by *Sano di Pietro*; 26, 27, *Luca Signorelli*, 2 frescoes removed from the Petrucci palace. The 8 pilasters, and the frames containing the above frescoes, are fine specimens of wood carving by *Antonio Barili*, by whom they were made (in 1511) for a room in the palace of Pandolfo Petrucci. 5th room, 20, *Sano di Pietro*, the Padre Eterno, painted in 1470 for the Directors of the Gabella; 35, *Taddeo Bartolo*, a Tritico, the Madonna, St. Francis, and 2 Angels. In

a room called *the Sala dell' Esposizione*, 2, 3, *Sodoma*, frescoes removed from the suppressed Convent of Santa Croce; 17, *Vasari*, the Resurrection; 16 and 22, *Beccafumi*, the Fall of the Angels, and a Tritico representing the Trinity and Saints; 45, *Sodoma*, Judith. In a large room called *Stanza dei Quadri di diverse Scuole* are more than 100 pictures recently presented to the Institute, of which the following are the most remarkable: 2, *Fra Bartolommeo*, the Magdalen; 24, *Palma Giovane*, the Bronze Serpent—this picture is signed and dated 1598; 34, *Breughel*, a Storm at Sea; 36, *Annibal Caracci*, a Madonna and Child; 56, *Titian*, Christ at Emmaus; 64, *Sodoma*, an Adoration of the Magi; 65, *Pinturicchio*, a Holy Family; 77, 78, 79, 80, *Beccafumi*, St. Catherine receiving the Stigmata, and 3 smaller pictures forming the gradino from the Ch. of the Ulivetani; 84, *Sodoma*, St. Catherine; 104, *Fra Bartolommeo*, Martyrdom of St. Catherine. In the large room of Casts of Ancient Statues are the 7 Original Cartoons by *Beccafumi*, copied in mosaic at the Duomo: they represent Moses on Mount Sinai, Moses breaking the Golden Calf; the Destruction of the Adorers of the latter, Moses striking the Rock, Elias and Acabus, a shield supported by 2 angels, Moses breaking the Tables of the Law. There are some good specimens of wood carving in the Istituto—a branch of art for which Siena has been more celebrated than any other town in Italy, a superiority which it still maintains. This branch of art, which attained a great degree of perfection under the two Barilis in the 15th and 16th centuries, is continued at the present time by Giusti, some of whose productions were much admired and rewarded at the great Exhibition in 1851, and whose studio, in the cloisters of the suppressed Convent of San Domenico, is well worth a visit.

The *Duomo* or Cathedral, which is situated on the highest point of the hill of Siena, was commenced after the election of Nicholas II., 1059, and consecrated in 1179 by Alexander III.: it is supposed to stand on the site of a temple of Minerva, and subsequently of an early Christian ch. dedicated to the Virgin of the Assumption. The present cathedral is only a portion (the transept) of a much vaster edifice, which was never completed; but the beautiful unfinished S. front and the gigantic nave and aisles may be still seen near the present ch., partly hidden by the stables and coach-houses attached to the modern palace of the Grand Duke, and the drawings made by the architect, Maestro Landi, still exist in the archives of the Duomo. Mr. Hope, speaking of the cathedral as it now stands, says, " The front was first completed about the middle of the 13th century by Giovanni da Siena; but not being approved of, was demolished, the nave lengthened, and the new front begun, in 1284, it is supposed, on the designs of Niccolò di Pisa, and finished by Lorenzo Maitani, a native of Siena, in 1290. It is inlaid with black, red, and white marble, relieved with other colours, painting, and gilding, and offers a bastard pointed style, or rather a jumble of different styles; the centre porch being round, and those of the sides pointed, and the higher parts not rising insensibly out of the lower, but seeming stuck on these *après coup;* the pediments only like triangular screens or plates, placed before and unconnected with the roof." The façade is covered with ornaments and sculptures, among which are several animals symbolical of the cities which were allied to Siena at different periods. Over the door are busts of the 3 saints, Catherine, Bernardin, and Ansan, who were natives of the city. The most remarkable sculptures of this front are the Prophets and the 2 Angels by Jacopo della Quercia. The columns of the great doorway are surmounted by lions, the emblems of Florence and Massa. *The Campanile* was built by the Bisdomini; but its marble coating and other ornaments are by Agostino and Aguolo da Siena. One of the bells bears the date of 1148. *The interior* of the cathedral exhibits but a small portion of the building as it was originally designed; it was intended to have formed the transept of a much more magnificent Basilica which was carried on by Maestro Landi until 1356, when the plague, which made such ravages at Siena, and other causes, led to its being abandoned. The pillars are clustered, and the capitals are ornamented with foliage and figures. The lower arches are semicircular, but those of the clerestory and its windows are pointed. The choir is lighted, and in both ends is a rich wheel-window. Over the lower arches of the nave the frieze is ornamented with a series of terra-cotta heads of all the popes down to Alexander III. in alto-relievo, among which that of Pope Zacharias was originally the bust of Pope Joan, and had the inscription, *Johannes VIII., Femina de Anglia.* It was metamorphosed in 1600 by the grand-duke, at the suggestion, it is said, of Clement VIII. and Cardinal Tarugi. Many of the antipopes are in the series, but, like all collections professing to be complete, several are either inventions or duplicates. The roof is painted blue, and studded with gold stars, as also the dome, but with the stars in panels. The two large columns of the door, sculptured in 1483, sustain an elegant tribune with four bas-reliefs, representing the Visitation, the Marriage of the Virgin, the raising of her Body, and her Assumption. The beautiful painted glass of the N. wheel-window was designed by Pierino del Vaga, and executed by Pastorino of Siena, in 1549. The wheel-window at the opposite extremity of the ch. is also very beautiful, and more in the style of the 15th century. The cupola is an irregular hexagon, with a zone of small pillars running round the tympanum. The pavement is unique and unrivalled as a work of art in its own peculiar class. It has not the tessellation of mosaic; it consists of a dark grey marble inlaid upon white, with lines of shading resembling niello. The oldest of these works are the Samson, Judas Maccabæus, Moses, the five kings of the Amorites taken in the cave of Makkedah (Joshua x., 16), and the Solomon and Joshua are by *Duccio:* Absalom hanging by his Hair is also attributed to this master. The grandest compositions are those by *Beccafumi*, particularly the Sacrifice of Isaac, the Adam and Eve after the Fall, and the Moses on Mount Sinai, said to have been his latest work. 7 of the original cartoons from which Beccafumi executed them have been recently discovered, and are now preserved in the Istituto delle Belle Arte. The symbols of Siena and her allied cities—the Hermes Trismegistus offering the Pimandra to a Gentile and a Christian, Socrates and Crates climbing the Mountain of Virtue, the Wheel of Fortune, with the Four Philosophers in the angles, are among the most curious of these works, but their authors' names have not been handed down. The mosaics of the Sibyls in the nave are from designs of Benvenuto, Matteo di Giovanni, Neroccio, and Guidoccio, painters of the 15th century. The Erythræan Sibyl, the Seven Ages of Man, the figures of Religion, Faith, Hope, and Charity, are by *Antonio Federighi*, who also designed the Battle of Jephthah, executed by *Bastiano di Francesco*. In front of the entrance are mosaics on the floor representing the emblems of the several towns which were allied to Siena at different periods. The pavement of the choir was covered with boards about 2 centuries ago, in consequence of the injury it received from the constant tread of visitors. On great festivals the planks are removed, but at other times the custode who shows the library will raise the planks, to enable the visitor to inspect these curious mosaics. In the choir the beautiful carvings of the stalls were begun in 1387 by *Francesco Tonghi*, by *Bartolino* of Siena and *Benedetto* of Montepulciano, from the designs of *Riccio* (Bartolommeo Neroni), and completed in 1506 by the two Barilis, when the choir was removed from beneath the cupola to its present situation. The *Tarsia* work is by the celebrated Fra Giovanni da Verona, and formerly existed in the ch. of Monte Uliveto. The high altar is by *Baldassare Peruzzi*. The magnificent tabernacle in bronze, the work of *Lorenzo di Pietro*, was completed in 1472, after a labour of 9 years. On the consoles are 8 angels in

bronze, by *Beccafumi*. The octagonal pulpit of white marble, supported by a circle of columns, 1 in the centre and 8 around it, 4 of which rest on lions playing with their cubs, is a remarkable work of *Niccolò di Pisa*, with the date 1226, aided by his son Giovanni, and Arnolfo; the Last Judgment, represented in two of its bas-reliefs, is perhaps one of the finest productions of this illustrious artist. On the pilasters of the cupola are fastened 2 poles of the *Carroccio*, captured by the Sienese at the great battle of Monte Aperto in 1260. On one of the neighbouring altars is still preserved the crucifix carried by the Sienese in this battle. In the chapels on each side before entering the choir are 2 portions of a painting by *Duccio di Buoninsegna*, which are extremely interesting in the history of art; on one of them is his name, and was so highly prized at the period of its execution, that it was honoured with a public procession like that of Cimabue at Florence. The panel was originally painted on both sides, the picture having stood over the main altar of the cathedral, then placed under the cupola; but these have been separated, and are both attached to the walls of the chapels. One, in the chapel of the Holy Sacrament on the rt. of the choir represents the Passion of Christ in small compartments; and the other, in the opposite chapel of Sant' Ansano, the Madonna and Child, with several Saints. Some notion may be formed of the estimation in which the fine arts were held at Siena at the period of Duccio (1311) from the circumstance lately come to light, that he received in payment for this picture the enormous sum of 3000 golden florins. The *Chapel of St. John the Baptist*, a circular building, was designed by *Baldassare Peruzzi*; there are some bas-reliefs of the history of Adam and Eve by *Jacopo della Quercia* on the altar, and a good statue of St. John by *Donatello*, besides several ornamental works by Sienese sculptors of less eminence. In this chapel is preserved the Baptist's right arm, presented by Pius II. in 1464. The *Capella del Voto*, or the *Chigi Chapel*, built by Alexander VII., is rich in lapis lazuli, marbles, and gilding. It contains a statue of St. Jerome and a Magdalen by *Bernini*, who is said to have transformed the latter from a statue of Andromeda; St. Catherine and St. Bernardino are by his pupils *Raggi* and *Ercole Ferrata*, who also executed the statue of the Pope from Bernini's designs. The Visitation is a copy in mosaic of a picture by Carlo Maratta, and the St. Bernardino is by *Cav. Calabrese.* Opposite the Chigi Chapel is the room once called the Sala Piccolominea, but now the *Library*, decorated with 10 frescoes, illustrating different events in the life of Pius II. (Æneas Sylvius Piccolomini); outside is an 11th, representing the coronation of his nephew Pius III. These works, which are particularly remarkable for the preservation of their colours, were painted as a commission from the latter pontiff when Cardinal Piccolomini, by *Pinturicchio*, assisted by the advice of Raphael, then in his 20th year, who furnished some of the designs, 2 of which are still preserved—1 at Florence, the other in the Casa Baldeschi at Perugia. It is even believed that the whole of that nearest to the windows on the rt. hand, representing the journey of Pius II., when a young man, in the suite of Cardinal Capranica, to the Council of Basil, is from the design of Raphael. The roof is covered with mythological pictures. In the library is also preserved the exquisite antique group of the Graces in Greek marble, found under the foundations in the 13th century. This group, one of the finest known specimens of Grecian sculpture, was copied by Canova, and was so much admired by Raphael that he made a sketch of it, which is still preserved in the Academy of Venice. It is also supposed to have suggested the picture of the Graces by Raphael, formerly in Sir Thomas Lawrence's collection. The choir books, 50 in number, which give the name of library to this apartment, contain some beautiful miniatures by *Fra Benedetto da Matera*, a Benedictine of Monte Casino, and *Fra Gabriele Mattei* of Siena; one of the missals is illuminated by *Liberale* of Verona. The collection was formerly much larger, but many of the duplicates were carried to Spain, being presented to Charles V. Some modern monuments have been injudiciously put up in this beautiful hall: one to a former governor, Giulio Bianchi, by *Tenerani*; the other to Mascagni, the anatomist, by *Ricci.* The monument of Bandino Bandini, in the ch., remarkable for a statue of Christ risen from the dead, a Seraph, and 2 Angels by *Michael Angelo* in his early youth. There is also a bronze bas-relief on the floor of the ch. by *Donatello*, covering the grave of Giovanni Pecci, bishop of Grosseto. Of the 2 vases for holy water, 1 is an ancient candelabrum, covered with mythological sculptures; the other is an able work of *Jacopo della Quercia.* The *Sacristy* contains several small pictures by *Duccio*, which formed the Predella, and *encadrement* of those in the chapels of Sant' Ansano and the Sacrament, and 1 by *Pietro Lorenzetti.*

Under the cathedral, or rather under the choir, is the ancient *Baptistery*, now the ch. of St. John the Baptist; a long flight of steps descends into it. Its front is a much purer Gothic than the cathedral, and is attributed to Agostino and Agnolo; the floor bears the date of 1486. "Its pilasters are panelled in lozenges, alternately with quatrefoils, heads of St. John the Baptist, and lions' heads exquisitely beautiful. Its interior is very shallow, and to the E. of it a lofty flight of steps leads through a beautiful marble gate, in the pointed style, to the piazza of the duomo, which in the original design was intended as a lateral door into the great nave of the cathedral."—*Hope.* Among the beautiful ornaments of the Font, in gilt bronze, are the Baptism of the Saviour, and the St. John before Herod, by *Lorenzo Ghiberti*; the Banquet of Herod, by *Pietro Pollajolo*, an able Florentine sculptor and goldsmith of the 15th century; the St. Joachim by *Donatello*; the Birth of St. John, and his Preaching in the Desert, by *Jacopo della Quercia.* The marble bas-reliefs in the tabernacle are by *Lorenzo di Pietro* (Vecchietta). The frescoes over the altar and on the roof are by Sienese painters of the 15th century; that over the altar, on the l., is supposed to have been painted by

Gentile di Fabriano, and the St. Peter by *Becoafumi*.

Several of the churches in Siena are remarkable for their paintings.

The Ch. of *S. Agostino*, restored and finished by Vanvitelli in 1755, has a beautiful Nativity by *Sodoma*; a fine Christ at the Cross, by *Perugino*; the Massacre of the Innocents, a celebrated picture, by *Matteo da Siena*; the St. Jerome by *Spagnoletto*; and the Baptism of Constantine by *Francesco Vanni*; and in the Piccolomini chapel a statue of Pius II., by *Dupré*, recently erected at the public expense. The adjoining Convent is now appropriated to the use of the Tolomei college, one of the most celebrated educational establishments in Italy, under the direction of the Fathers of the Scuole Pie.

The conventual ch. of the *Carmine* is remarkable for its steeple and cloisters, by Baldassare Peruzzi. The Madonna throned in the choir is by *Bernardino Fungai*, 1503. The St. Michael is by *Beccafumi*; the Martyrdom of St. Bartholomew by *Casolani*; the Nativity was begun by *Riccio*, and finished by *Arcangelo Salimbeni*. In the court of the convent is a deep well, called the Pozzo di Diana, which was believed to communicate with the fabulous mine of Diana, ridiculed by Dante (Purgat. xiii.)

La Concezzione, more generally known as the Chiesà dei Servi, a fine ch. from the designs of Baldassare Peruzzi, has a Coronation of the Virgin, by *Bernardino Fungai*; 2 Annunciations, by *Francesco Vanni*; a Massacre of the Innocents, by *Matteo da Siena*; the picture called the Vergine del Popolo by *Lippo di Memmo*; the Nativity of the Virgin, by *Manetti*; and a good Nativity, by *Casolani*.

San Domenico, begun in 1220 and not finished till 1465, is an interesting and imposing edifice, 75 feet wide; spanned by a pointed arch of singular boldness, which sustains the transepts, and is well worthy the study of architects. Among its pictures are, in a chapel on the l. of the choir, the celebrated Madonna by *Guido da Siena*, with the date 1221, 19 years before the birth of Cimabue, on the strength of which the Sienese claim the honour of being the earliest school of art; on the wall of the same chapel a Santa Barbara by *Matteo da Siena*, dated 1479; a Madonna and Saints, by *Giovanni di Paolo*, 1426; a Crucifixion, by *Ventura Salimbeni*; the Martyrdom of St. Peter, by *Arcangelo Salimbeni*; the Adoration of the Shepherds, by *Luca Signorelli*; the Nativity of the Virgin, by *Casolani*. On one side of the altar is the fine picture of St. Catherine fainting in the arms of two nuns at the appearance of the Saviour, by *Sodoma*; on the other side of the altar is St. Catherine in ecstasy, and the Almighty, with the Madonna and Child, attended by angels, appearing to her. The Demoniac is by *Francesco Vanni*. The marble tabernacle and the two Angels are attributed to *Michael Angelo*. Over the door leading to the chapel, in the extremity of the ch., is the Crucifixion, attributed to *Giotto*, and over the altar the portrait of St. Catherine, by her friend *F. Vanni*.

San Francesco, a fine and very spacious church built from the designs of Agnolo and Agostino da Siena in 1326; the general form of this church is the same as that of Santa Croce at Florence, with a fine transept, having 4 chapels on pointed arches on each side of the choir. It contains a masterpiece of *Sodoma*, the Deposition, which Annibale Caracci admired so much as to say he found few pictures equal to it. The Holy Fathers in Purgatory is by *Beccafumi*.

The *Ch. of Fonte Giusta*, built in commemoration of the victory of Siena over Florence in 1482, contains the celebrated picture by *Baldassare Peruzzi*, representing the Sibyl announcing to Augustus the birth of Christ, a noble painting, justly regarded as the masterpiece of that accomplished artist. The Sibyl is a sublime and expressive figure. So highly was this picture admired by Lanzi, that he says Peruzzi "gave it so divine an enthusiasm, that Raphael treating the same subject, as well as Guido and Guercino, whose sibyls are so often met with, probably never surpassed it." The marble altar, sculptured in 1517 by Marzini, is an elaborate work. Among the *ex-voto* offerings preserved in this church are a sword, a small wooden shield bound with iron, and a large bone of a whale, consecrated to the Madonna of Fonte Giusta by Columbus on his return to Europe.

San Giorgio contains the tomb of Francesco Vanni, the painter. The tower has 38 windows, said to allude to the 38 companies which fought at the great battle of Monte Aperto.

San Martino, a handsome ch. with a front built by Giovanni Fontana, of Como, an architect of the 17th century, is remarkable for the Circumcision, by *Guido*; the Martyrdom of St. Bartholomew, by *Guercino*, for which he was partly paid in *peluzzo*, or plush, for the manufacture of which Siena was then celebrated. The picture of the Victory of the Sienese at the Porta Camollia in 1526 is by *Lorenzo Cini*. There are several interesting statues in terracotta, by *Jacopo della Quercia*, which have been coloured in recent years.

San Quirico, in the highest part of the town, supposed to occupy the site of a Temple of Romulus, has two fine works by *Francesco Vanni*, the Flight out of Egypt, and the Ecce Homo. The Deposition, by *Casolani*, and the Angel with the Virgin at the Sepulchre, by *Salimbeni*, are also to be noticed.

San Spirito, with a noble doorway by Baldassare Peruzzi, has some fine paintings; the most remarkable are the Madonna throned with Saints, by *Sodoma*; four subjects from the life of S. Jacinto, by *Salimbeni*; a fresco of the Crucifixion, with the Madonna, St. John, and the Magdalen, by *Fra Bartolommeo*, in the cloister; the Coronation of the Virgin, by *Pacchiarotto*; S. Jacinto, by *Francesco Vanni*.

La Trinità is remarkable for its fine ceiling by *Ventura Salimbeni*; a Madonna by *Matteo di Giovanni*; and the Victory of Clovis over Alaric, by *Raffaele Vanni*.

Of the numerous *Oratories*, the most interesting are those occupying the house of St. Catherine of Siena, and the ancient Fullonica of her father, who was a dyer and fuller beneath. In the latter are St. Catherine receiving the Stigmata by *Sodoma*; her Pilgrimage to the tomb of St. Agnes of Montepul-

ciano, by *Pacchiarotto*; and her pursuit by the Florentines, by *Ventura Salimbeni*. In the house are representations of various marvellous events in the life of the Saint by *Vanni, Serri, Nasini*, &c., and the Miraculous Crucifix, by *Giunta da Pisa*, from which the church tradition states that she received the Stigmata.

The *Palazzo Pubblico*, with its lofty tower *Della Mangia*, stands in the Piazza del Campo, a large open space more nearly resembling the form of an escalop shell than anything else to which it has been compared. Its entire circuit is said to be 1000 feet: it is sloped like an ancient theatre for public games, and its artificial soil is supported by strong walls. It is difficult to imagine anything more perfectly in accordance with the idea of republican greatness than the aspect and arrangement of this forum; it was the scene of many popular tumults during the middle ages, and derives its name, "del campo," from the passage of Dante:

" Quando vivea più glorioso, disse,
    Liberamente nel Campo di Siena,
    Ogni vergogna deposta, si affisse."
                        Purg. xi.

It is now the site of the vegetable, fish, and game market, the scene of the annual horse-race, called the Palio, which takes place on the 15th August, and is contested by the several wards of the city with a spirit of rivalry which recalls the factions of ancient Rome. The *Loggia di San Paolo*, built in 1417 by the merchants of the city, and now the *Casino de' Nobili*, has its principal front in a neighbouring street; it was remarkable in the middle ages as the most impartial commercial tribunal in Italy; its laws were recognised by nearly all the other republics, and its decisions were considered equally binding. The marble seat was designed by *Peruzzi*. The statues of St. Peter and St. Paul are by *Antonio Federighi*; the S. Vittore and S. Ansano are by *Urbano da Cortona*; the latter is said to have been much admired by Michael Angelo.

The Palazzo Pubblico was begun in 1295 and finished in 1327, from the designs of Agostino and Agnolo da Siena; it is now converted into public offices, courts of law, and prisons. The chapel dedicated to the Virgin was built to commemorate the cessation of the plague of 1348, which carried off 80,000 persons. The halls of the ancient tribunal di Biccherna, instituted for the management of the taxes and civil affairs of the republic, contain numerous paintings of the native school : among these are the Madonna with Saints by *Sodoma ;* and the Coronation of the Virgin by *Pietro Lorenzetti,* in 1345. The ceiling is painted chiefly by *Petrazzi ;* the principal subjects are the Coronation of Pius II., the Donation of Radicofani by the same pope, and the privileges conferred by him on his adopted city. The Sala delle Balestre is covered with frescoes by *Ambrogio Lorenzetti* (1338), illustrating the results of good and bad government. The Sala del gran Consiglio contains the immense fresco of the Madonna and Child with saints under a baldacchino, the poles of which are held by the apostles and patrons of the city, by *Sermino di Simone,* in 1287, retouched by *Simone Memmi* (di Martino) in 1321. The fresco in chiaroscuro, representing Guido Ricci at the assault of Monte Massi, is attributed to *Simone Memmi,* and is curious for the great variety of military engines introduced. The S. Ansan, S. Victor, and S. Bernardin are by *Sodoma.* The adjoining chapel is covered with very graceful and expressive frescoes, illustrating the history of the Virgin, by *Taddeo Bartolo ;* the altarpiece of the Holy Family and S. Calisto is by *Sodoma.* The adjoining room has a curious gallery of portraits of illustrious persons, republicans and others, among whom Cicero, Cato, heathen gods and warriors, are found ranged with Judas Maccabæus and St. Ambrose ; they are also by *Taddeo Bartolo* (1414). In the Sala del Cousistorio, the roof painted by *Beccafumi,* and so much admired by Vasari and Lanzi, represents the burning of the enemies of Rome ; the walls are hung with portraits of 8 popes and 39 cardinals, natives of the city. The paintings of *Spinello Aretino* are also

remarkable : they represent the leading facts in the history of Frederick Barbarossa and Alexander III., from their first election to the triumph of the pope over the emperor, and their final reconciliation. Several of the pictures by the early Sienese masters have been recently removed from the Palace to the Istituto delle Belle Arte.

The archives, a portion of which were carried off by the French and restored at the peace, contain an invaluable collection of state papers during the republican times, some of which are illustrated with miniatures.

The council-chamber was converted into a theatre from the designs of *Bibiena :* operas are occasionally performed here. The tower, called *della Mangia,* begun in 1325, is said to have been greatly admired by Leonardo da Vinci, who came here to examine its construction in 1502.

The *Fountain,* in the Piazza del Campo, called the *Fonte Gaja,* gave the name "della Fonte" to *Jacopo della Quercia,* who executed the marble bas-reliefs, representing various subjects of Scripture history, now unfortunately much damaged. The subterranean aqueducts which supply it with water, are 15 m. in length. It is related that Charles V., when he examined them, declared that Siena was more admirable below than above ground.

Among the many remarkable events which have taken place in this piazza, the summary punishment of Charles IV. for his attempt to seize the signoria in 1369 is not the least singular. The people, on the first manifestation of his design, broke into the palace in which he was lodged, disarmed his followers, and left him alone in this square, "addressing himself in turn to the armed troops which closed the entrance of every street, and which, immoveable and silent, remained insensible to all his entreaties. It was not till he began to suffer from hunger that his equipages were restored to him, and he was permitted to leave the town."

The *Palaces* of Siena are more remarkable as examples of the domestic architecture of the middle ages than for the works of art which they contain. They present that peculiar style which marks all the works of Agostino and Agnolo, the two great architects of the republic. A few of these have small galleries of paintings by the native school, but they present the works of few masters who may not be better studied in the churches already described.

The *Palazzo del Magnifico*, with the fine bronze ornaments and rings on the outer wall, cast by Mazzini and Cozzarelli, was erected in 1504 by Pandolfo Petrucci, the celebrated tyrant of Siena, called Il Magnifico; the frescoes by Luca Signorelli, and the fine wood carvings by Barili, have been recently removed to the Istituto delle Belle Arte. The *Palazzo Saracini* has a collection of paintings by the Sienese masters, the most interesting of which is the Christ in the Garden by *Sodoma*. The *Palazzo Buonsignori* is a fine example of Gothic, with a terra-cotta front. The *Palazzo Piccolomini* has 2 halls painted by *Bernhard von Orley*, a favourite pupil of Raphael. The *Palazzo Piccolomineo*, now the Palazzo del Governo, one of the finest in the city, built by Pius II. from the designs of *Francesco di Giorgio*. Near it is the elegant Loggia by the same architect, also erected by Pius II. in 1460—"gentilibus suis,"—as the inscription over it states. The *Palazzo Pannilini*, from the designs of *Riccio*, contains some mythological subjects by Beccafumi and Baldassare Peruzzi. The *Palazzo Pollini*, attributed to Peruzzi, has some frescoes by *Sodoma*, the principal of which are the Susanna, the Scipio, and the Burning of Troy, with the Judgment of Paris, afterwards altered to represent the history of Lot. *Palazzo Tolomei*, a good specimen of the domestic architecture of the early part of the 13th century, having been built by Il Tozzo in 1205. The *House of Beccafumi*, a small brick building erected by himself, is interesting among the other records of the Sienese school: it is in the street still called "dei Maestri," from the number of artists who occupied it during the flourishing times of the republic.

Near the Piccolomini Palace is the *Fonte di Fullonica*, begun in 1249, and presented to the city by the native architect Francesco di Giorgio in 1489. The ancient Gothic *Fonte Branda*, at the foot of the Hill of San Domenico, constructed by Bellamino in 1193 at the command of the consuls of Siena, is immortalised by Dante:

" Ma se io vedessi qui l' anima trista
  Di Guido o di Alessandro, o di lor frate,
  Per fonte Branda non darei la vista."
                                Inf. xxx.

The *Fonte Nuova*, built in 1259, is also a remarkable work.

The *University*, of late years removed to the Jesuits' college of S. Vigilio, dates from 1203: it is now very flourishing, since the recent transfer to Siena of the faculties of law and philosophy from Pisa; the number of students exceeding 500. In the entrance cloister is the tomb of the celebrated jurist Nicolo Aringhieri (1374), remarkable for its bas-reliefs, and attributed by Cicognara to Goro di Gregorio da Siena. It stood originally in the ch. of S. Domenico.

The *Library* occupies the great hall of the Accademia degli Intronati, considered to be the oldest in Europe. This academy was one of the most famous among the 16 for which Siena was remarkable in the 16th and 17th centuries. Indeed, so great was the passion of the citizens for academies, that one for females, called Delle Assicurate, was founded here in 1654 by the Grand Duchess Vittoria. The library contains about 40,000 vols. and 5000 MSS. The most ancient of the latter are the Greek Gospels of the 8th or 9th century, with miniatures, originally in the Imperial Chapel at Constantinople, and purchased at Venice on the fall of the Greek empire for the great hospital of this city. An Italian prose translation of the "Æneid," of the 13th century, is curious as one of the earliest examples of Italian versions of the classics. The " Ordo Officiorum Senensis Ecclesiæ" is remarkable for its miniatures of 1213 by *Oderigi da Gubbio*, the friend of Dante, who has immortalised him in a fine passage of the "Paradiso."

The manuscript notes of Francesco di Giorgio on architecture and engineering, illustrated with drawings, are exceedingly curious; the engineer will find them full of valuable suggestions, many of which were adopted at a later period in military tactics by Pietro Navarra and others, who appropriated the merit of their discovery. Two objects of even higher interest are the portfolios of Baldassare Peruzzi and Giuliano Sangallo. Both of them contain sketches, ornaments, and architectural subjects; among those of the former is the original study for the Sibyl in the ch. of Fonte Giusta.

Among the autograph letters preserved here are those of St. Catherine of Siena, Metastasio, and Socinus: many of them have been published.

The *Collegio Tolomei*, founded in 1668, for the purpose of educating the sons of the Sienese nobility, has become of late years one of the first scholastic institutions in Italy. Originally confided to the Jesuits, since the suppression of that order it has passed under the management of the *Fathers* of the Scuole Pie, and has acquired a well-merited celebrity; it contains about 100 in-door pupils, each paying about 40*l*. a year, for which they receive an excellent classical education, the elements of the natural and physical sciences, &c.: the greatest care and attention is paid to the boys, and every kind of rational amusement afforded to them. Situated as Siena is, in the part of Italy where the language is most purely spoken, young men are sent to the Collegio Tolomei from every part of the peninsula. The original rule that none but patricians could be admitted is no longer rigorously adhered to, although the great proportion of the inmates still belong to noble families.

The *Hospital* (Spedale di Santa Maria della Scala), a spacious Gothic building, is one of the most ancient hospitals in Europe; it was founded by Fra Sorore, an Augustin monk, in 832. It contains upwards of 300 beds, and has in late years derived great honour from the anatomical labours of Mascagni, one of its most distinguished professors. The Church attached to it dates from the middle of the 13th century; it has 5 remarkable frescoes by *Domenico Bartolo*, re-

presenting, 1. Several saints and patriarchs; 2. The Life of the Beato Agostino Novello; 3. The Indulgence granted to the Hospital by Celestin III.; 4. The Marriage of the young Maidens of Siena; 5. Acts of Charity towards the Sick and Infirm. The large painting in the tribune of the Pool of Bethesda is by *Sebastiano Conca*; the bas-relief of the dead body of Christ is by *Giuseppe Muzzuola* of Volterra, a sculptor of the last century; the bronze statue of the Saviour at the high altar is by *Lorenzo di Pietro* (1446). In the ward of the Pellegrinajo are several paintings by Sienese masters of the 14th and 15th centuries.

The *Gates* of Siena are in many respects remarkable. The most interesting of these are the Porta Camollia, already described; the Porta San Viene; and the Porta Romana. The *P. San Viene*, more generally called *di Pispini*, takes its name from the exclamations of the people during the solemn entry of the body of St. Ansan, which was welcomed by a public procession of the citizens shouting "Il santo viene!" The gate was built by Moccio, and was ornamented in 1526 by a Nativity by *Sodoma*. The *Porta Romana*, built in 1327 by Agostino and Agnolo, is an interesting example of those great architects; like San Viene, it has also its painting—the Coronation of the Virgin, by *Sano di Pietro*, in 1459; and the Porta di San Lorenzo, recently opened, and close to the fly. stat.

The *Citadel* of Siena was built by Cosmo I. in the form of a square with 4 bastions; it is at the N. W. extremity of the town.

The *Lizza*, which adjoins the Citadel, celebrated by Alfieri for its "fresco ventolino," occupies the site of a fortress erected by Charles V. in 1551, and destroyed by the citizens soon afterwards; it is ornamented with statues, and is the favourite walk of the inhabitants.

The great festival of Siena is that in honour of St. Catherine. This popular saint was the daughter of a dyer; she was born in 1347, and took the vows when only eight years of age. Her revelations and miracles gained her so high a repute, that she succeeded in inducing Gregory XI. to remove the Holy See from Avignon after it had been fixed there for seventy years. She died in 1380, and was canonised in 1461. Another saint of Siena, San Bernardino, was born in 1380; he joined the Franciscans, by whom he was sent on a mission to the Holy Land. On his return, he founded 300 monasteries and died in 1444.

In the neighbourhood of Siena is the large Franciscan Convent of *L'Osservanza,* erected in 1423 by Francesco di Giorgio, by order of Pandolfo Petrucci, the celebrated tyrant of Siena, cited by his friend Machiavelli as one of the best types of a usurper. He died in 1512, and was buried here; his tomb and that of Celia Petrucci, in the crypt, are the works of scholars of Peruzzi. The ch. also contains some fine works by *Luca della Robbia,* in terra cotta, representing the Coronation of the Virgin, and several pictures of early Sienese masters.

About 3 m. from Siena is the *Castle of Belcaro,* celebrated in the history of the treacherous siege of Siena by Cosmo I. in 1554, when it was the head quarters of the Marquis di Marignano mentioned in a previous page. The ramparts still show several cannon balls imbedded in the walls. During the 13th century Belcaro was chosen by St. Catherine as the seat of a convent; in the 16th century it became more famous as the residence of Crescentius Turamini, the rich banker of Siena. Unlike his fellow-citizen Buonsignori, who emigrated to France to found the "Bank of the Great Table," or his vain contemporary Agostino Chigi, who ordered the silver plate used at the banquet he gave to Leo X. at the Farnesina Palace to be thrown into the Tiber as it was removed from table, Turamini devoted his wealth to the encouragement of native art, and employed *Baldassare Peruzzi* to decorate Belcaro with his pencil. The loggia was entirely covered with his frescoes; they were unfortunately defaced in the last century, but the whitewash has lately been removed, and several of the subjects are now cleverly restored. The chapel was entirely built by this great artist; its roof was ornamented by him with the most delicate frescoes, showing that in fancy and in grace he had derived no common inspiration from the works of Raphael, of whom he professed to be an imitator. The vestibule of the villa presents, however, on its ceiling a still more celebrated work, the great fresco of the Judgment of Paris, considered by Lanzi to be one of those in which Peruzzi most closely approached the genius of Raphael. It is now believed to have been painted from his design, since the engraving of Marc Antonio, professing to be from a drawing by Raphael, precisely corresponds with this fresco.

The manners and language of the Sienese remain to be noticed. The epithet which Dante fixed upon the citizens in more than one passage has probably tended to give a notoriety, if not a celebrity, to their national vanity, which promises to outlive the failing:

" Ed io dissi al poeta: or fu giammai
  Gente sì vana come la Sanese ?
  Certo non la Francesca sì di assai."
                                   Inf. xxix.

The pronunciation and accent of the Sienese are celebrated for their purity, and the Tuscan dialect is said to be spoken there without that guttural harshness or those strong aspirates which are so disagreeable at Florence. Perhaps, however, in spite of the claims of Siena, the more an English traveller becomes acquainted with Italy, the more will he be disposed to assent to the proverb,

" Lingua Toscana in bocca *Romana.*"

Siena is one of the places selected as a summer residence by English visitors who pass the season in Italy; it is free from mosquitos, and its climate is considered healthy. The inhabitants boast, as a proof of this fact, that they escaped both visitations of the cholera. "Siena," says Sir James Clark, "affords a healthy summer residence for persons who are not very liable to suffer from rapid changes of temperature, which often occur here during the summer, owing to the high and exposed situation of the place. Siena is considerably cooler in the summer and much colder in the winter,

Naples, Rome, Pisa, or Nice. The annual mean temperature is 55°·60, being 6° less than Naples, and only about 5° more than London; but this arises from the coldness of its winter, which is only 1°·38 warmer than that of London. Its summer temperature is about the same as that of Capo di Monte at Naples, but 3° warmer than that of the baths of Lucca. Its daily range of temperature is very great. It is dry and cool, from its great elevation (1330 feet above the sea), and altogether a safe summer residence. For persons disposed to, or labouring under pulmonary affections, however, Siena is an unfavourable climate at all seasons. For nervous, relaxed people it forms a better summer retreat than either Naples or the baths of Lucca."

There are several excellent roads from Siena : to Arezzo by Monte Savino (Rte. 26B), 42 m.; to Chiusi by Rapolano and Torrita (Rte. 26c), 40 m.; to Chiusi by Asciano and Montepulciano, 48 m.; to Grosseto and the Tuscan Maremma, 52 m. 26E.

Diligences run three times a-week between Siena and the following places: to Arezzo in 10 hrs., to Chiusi in 8 to 10 hrs., to Grosseto in 15 hrs., to Rome in 29 to 32 hrs., according to the season; as well as a daily Malle Poste to Rome in 26 hrs.

Leaving Siena, the following are the Post-stations on the road to Rome :

	Posts.
Siena to Monterone	1
Monterone to Torrenieri	1½
Torrenieri to Poderina	1
Poderina to Ricorsi	1
Ricorsi to Radicofani	1
Radicofani to Ponte Centino . .	1
P. Centino to Acquapendente . .	1
Acquapendente to S. Lorenzo . .	0¾
S. Lorenzo to Bolsena	1
Bolsena to Montefiascone. . . .	1
Montefiascone to Viterbo . . .	1
Viterbo to L'Imposta	1
L'Imposta to Ronciglione . . .	1
Ronciglione to Monterosi . . .	1
Monterosi to Baccano	1
Baccano to La Storta	1
Là Storta to Rome	1½
	—
Total from Siena (135 Eng. miles)	17½

The road from Siena to the Papal frontier passes over one of the most barren districts in the whole of Italy ; its bare clay hills are generally destitute of trees, and the entire country, as far as the eye can reach, is dreary and desolate beyond description. On leaving Siena the road descends into the valley of the Arbia, and follows its rt. bank for nearly 2 stages. Nothing can be more dismal than the look of the bleak region extending to the E., contrasting with the distant green and wooded hills of the Montagnuola of Siena in the opposite direction.

1 Monterone.

The Arbia and the Ombrone are crossed shortly before reaching

Buonconvento, surrounded by ancient walls, situated on the Arbia, near its junction with the Ombrone, in a fertile and richly cultivated valley, presenting a singular contrast with the barren clay hills by which it is surrounded. [There are two *Inns* here, the Cavallo Inglese and the Europa; neither very comfortable.] The ancient castle of Buonconvento, one of the best preserved in Tuscany, is infamous in Italian history as the scene of the death of the Emperor Henry VII. The emperor was on his march towards Rome, in order to give battle to the Guelph party under Robert of Naples, when he stopped here to celebrate the feast of St. Bartholomew, August 24, 1313. He received the communion from the hands of a Dominican monk of Montepulciano, and expired in a few hours. " It was said," says Sismondi, "that the monk had mixed the juice of napel in the consecrated cup ; it was said also that Henry was already attacked by a malady which he concealed—a carbuncle had manifested itself below the knee, and a cold bath, which he took to calm the burning irritation, perhaps occasioned his sudden and unexpected death." The contemporary writers nearly all agree in ascribing the event to poison, but recent critics appear inclined to regard it as a fiction of the Ghibelines, who found the people too willing to believe it. From Buonconvento, a road of 7 m. leads up the valley of the Ombrone to the Benedictine convent of *Monte Uliveto Maggiore;* worth visiting on account of its fine frescoes by *Luca Signorelli,* representing events in the life of St. Benedict, and for some of the earliest productions of *Sodoma.* The Pereta and the Serlate torrents are crossed between Buonconvento and Torrenieri. The road is a continued and wearisome ascent; on a hill, 5 m. on the rt., is the town of Montalcino, celebrated for its wines.

1½ Torrenieri (an additional horse from this place to Poderina, and *vice versâ*). Beyond this station the Asso and the Tuoma are crossed. Another steep ascent over barren hills brings us to *San Quirico,* where a road on the left hand strikes off to *Pienza* (6 m.), the birth-place of Pius II. (Æneas Sylvius), and of his nephew Pius III., who built the immense Piccolomini palace in the town. An interesting excursion may be made from San Quirico to Montepulciano and Chiusi (25 m.), both Etruscan cities of high antiquity, whence a good road leads through Città della Pieve to Orvieto (32½ m.), and thence to Montefiascone (18 m.).—(See Rte. 23.) San Quirico has two small *Inns,* the Aquila Nera, clean and good of its kind, and Il Sole, which the vetturini sometimes make their first night's sleeping-place from Siena. The Gothic church, the Piccolomini palace, and the old square tower, supposed to be of Roman origin, are the only objects of interest in the village.

1 La Poderina, on the river Orcia. 3 m. beyond it is the *osteria* of La Scala, now much improved, generally made the first day's resting-place of the vetturini on leaving Siena. Numerous torrents flow down from the flanks of Mont' Amiata into the Orcia between this and

1 Ricorsi. The small Inn here is almost the only house. It is very indifferent, but the people are obliging. (An additional horse to Radicofani.) Near to this place are the baths of San Filippo, the deposit from the calcareous waters of which is turned to a profitable account in the manufacture of casts. The water, when allowed to

fall upon the moulds of medals or gems, leaves a precipitate which hardens into the most beautiful impressions; and when sulphur moulds are used, very fine fac-similes are produced. A wild and dreary road winds up the barren volcanic mountain of Radicofani, through the deep ravine of the Formone. Nothing can exceed the desolation of the scene; huge masses of basalt encumber the mountain's sides, and vegetation seems to have entirely ceased.

1 *Radicofani* (*Inn*, La Posta: lately improved, but exorbitant, *if the prices are not agreed upon beforehand,* and the best sleeping-place for the first night from Siena for persons travelling post with horses; it was once a hunting palace of the grand dukes. The house has lately been fitted up and painted, but in former times its vast range of apartments, with their high black raftered roofs and the long passages, were considered by Mr. Beckford a fitting scene of a sabbath of witches). The mountain of Radicofani is 2470 ft. above the sea, and from its great height it commands all the surrounding country. The geology of the mountain is interesting; it is composed of Subapennine marl, covered with an enormous erupted mass of volcanic matter, which forms very regular basaltic columns. The village is higher up the mountain than the road; it is surrounded with strong walls, but contains nothing to attract attention, except the dress and wild appearance of its inhabitants. Still higher, occupying the summit of the cone, is the ruined castle of Ghino di Tacco, the robber-knight, whose seizure of the abbot of Cluny when on his way to take the mineral waters of Tuscany is celebrated by Boccaccio. The abbot's ailments appeared to Ghino capable of a simple remedy, for he put him on a regimen of bread and white wine, and it is said so effectually cured him, that he found it quite unnecessary to drink the waters. The Fort was a place of some importance in much later times. During the last century it was garrisoned, but the powder-magazine having blown up, the Tuscan government

has not thought it worth while to re-build it. At the Dogana, by the road-side, passports are examined and *viséed*, and luggage is examined on entering Tuscany. A good mountain road of 12 m. leads from Radicofani to Sarteano, and another from Novella to San Casciano de' Bagni, of some celebrity as a watering place. The high pointed peak seen to the E. of Radicofani is the Dolomitic Peak above Cetona.

A rapid descent leads down the valley of the Rigo, passing the *osteria* of Novella before crossing the Rigo, which here falls into the Paglia. Following the course of the torrent, we cross the Elvella, which divides Tuscany from the Papal States at the *osteria* of Torricella, and arrive at

1½ *Ponte Centino*, the Papal frontier station and custom-house, on the l. bank of the Elvella, near the point where that torrent and the Siele fall into the Paglia. Passports are signed here, but persons travelling by diligence are not annoyed by an examination of their luggage, an operation which in their case takes place at Rome, as it may for those travelling by post or Vetturino, on the administration of a small fee, or provided they have obtained a *Lascia passare.*

[An additional horse from Ponte Centino to Radicofani, and also to Acquapendente. For carriages with 4 or 6 horses, besides the 2 additional required by the tariff, the postmaster of Ponte Centino is allowed to attach a pair of oxen from the Osteria di Novella to Radicofani, at a charge of 60 bajocchi. In this case the course for the two additional horses, estimated at 1½ post, is fixed at 60 bajocchi per horse. Carriages of couriers and others with only 2 horses are not subject to the regulation as regards the oxen. An additional horse from Ponte Centino to Acquapendente.]

The road proceeds along the left side of the Paglia, which receives so many torrents in its course that the route between Radicofani and Acquapendente is often impassable after heavy rains. The scenery of the frontier continues, for some miles, of the most dreary character, but it improves as we approach Acquapendente. The Paglia is crossed by the Ponte Gregoriano, and a long and steep ascent leads to

1 *Acquapendente* (*Inn*, Tre Corone d'Oro, in a large old mansion, rather desolate and ill furnished at present, but not otherwise objectionable). Passports are again *viséd* here, for which a charge of 1 paul is made. The approach to this, the first town of the Papal States, offers the most cheering contrast to the wild ravines and dreary hills of the Tuscan frontier. The road winds up the hill amidst fine old oaks and terraces covered with vegetation. The town is picturesquely situated on the summit of a precipitous mass of rock, over which several pretty cascades, from which it derives its name, dash into the ravine below. This hill is composed chiefly of the Subapennine marls, capped with volcanic tufa and basalt. During the ascent on the right hand, some short basaltic columns are seen. Acquapendente is a dull and dirty episcopal town, possessing no interest whatever except that derived from its romantic position. It was, previously to the 17th century, a mere stronghold, with few inhabitants, but it became a place of some importance after Innocent X., in 1647, removed here the episcopal see from Castro, which was destroyed as a punishment upon the inhabitants for the murder of their bishop. The population in 1833 was 3300. The medical traveller will not pass through the town without recollecting the fame of Fabricius ab Acquapendente, born here in 1537. Fabricius was the successor of Fallopius at Padua, where he filled the professor's chair for nearly half a century. His name is celebrated in medical science as the discoverer of the valves of the veins. To the English traveller it is particularly interesting, since Harvey studied under him at Padua, and probably received from his discoveries his first impulse in investigating the circulation of the blood. Fabricius died in 1619, the year in which his illustrious pupil began to teach publicly in London the doctrine of the circulation.

The aspect of the country gradually improves after leaving this town; many of the tufa hills are filled with grottoes, which serve as habitations for the shepherds. A gradual ascent brings us to

¾ San Lorenzo Nuovo (*Inns*, Aquila Nera, and L'Ecu de France), a formal village built on the brow of the hill by Pius VI., as a refuge for the inhabitants of the old town, situated lower down and nearer the margin of the lake, which was desolated by malaria. From this point the traveller enjoys the first view of the lake of Bolsena, with its picturesque shores surrounded by lofty hills covered with trees to their very summit. On the descent the ruined town or station of San Lorenzo Vecchio, surmounted by an old tower covered with ivy, forms a striking feature in the landscape. It occupies an Etruscan site, and numerous sepulchres are still traceable in the cliffs beneath its walls.

1 *Bolsena* (*Inn*, Aquila d'Oro, described by some travellers as very dirty and uncivil, and by others as comfortable and clean), a small town of 1700 souls, situated on the margin of the lake, on the site of the Roman city which supplanted the Etruscan city of Volsinii, after the latter had been conquered and razed to the ground. Volsinii was one of the most ancient and most powerful cities of the Etruscan league, and was so opulent when it was last conquered by the Romans, that it is stated by Pliny to have contained no less than 2000 statues (B.C. 280). An account of its various contests with Rome will be found in Livy, who notices the worship of Norcia, and states that the years were marked by fixing nails in her temple. The common story of the citizens becoming after the loss of their independence so sunk in luxury as to fall under subjection to their own slaves is rejected by Niebuhr, who considers that the insurgents called "slaves" by the Roman writers were not domestic slaves, but serfs who had aided the Volsinienses in the defence of their common home,

and had obtained as their reward the rights of citizenship. At a later period Volsinii was remarkable as the birthplace of Sejanus, the favourite of Tiberius, but we have very few other notices of it in Roman history. The Etruscan city is supposed to have been situated on the table-land on the summit of the hill called "Il Piazzano," above the amphitheatre, but there is not a vestige of wall or temple to be traced. The remains of the Roman city are more numerous. At the entrance of the town is a confused heap of architectural fragments which deserve examination. Among them are broken columns, Corinthian capitals, several altars and inscribed stones. Nearer the gate are numerous granite columns, the remains of an ancient temple supposed to be that of the Etruscan goddess Norcia. Among the ruins is a Roman bas-relief of the sacrifice of the Arvales. Besides these antiquities, numerous sepulchres and tumuli exist in the neighbourhood of the town, together with some remains of a Roman amphitheatre, approached by a Roman road of basaltic pavement. Large quantities of Etruscan vases, statues, and other relics have been found here in recent years: the statue called the Arringatore, now in the gallery at Florence, is perhaps the most remarkable of these discoveries. The triple church of *Sta. Cristina* has a façade ornamented with some bas-reliefs collected from the ancient temple in 1512 by Cardinal de' Medici, and a marble sarcophagus, with a bas-relief of the triumph of Bacchus. It is more interesting, however, as the alleged scene of the miracle to which the genius of Raphael has added immortal celebrity. The miracle is said to have taken place in 1263, when a Bohemian priest, who doubted the doctrine of transubstantiation, was convinced by blood flowing from the Host he was consecrating. In commemoration of this event, Urban IV., then residing at Orvieto, instituted the festival of the Corpus Domini. A dark and dirty vault, forming a kind of chapel, is pointed out as the actual scene of the miracle. The spot where the blood is said to have fallen is covered with an iron grating.

The Upper Town of Bolsena is worth a visit, not so much for its beauty as for its singularity; from every point of high ground the scenery and fine views will amply repay the trouble of the ascent.

The Lake of Bolsena is a noble expanse of water, whose circumference is estimated by Calindri at 43,000 metres, 26¼ English ms. It has the form of an extinct crater, and, being bounded by volcanic rocks, has been frequently regarded as such; but that hypothesis can scarcely be admitted when the great extent of the lake is considered. The investigation of its geology would, however, be a dangerous task, for the treacherous beauty of the lake conceals *malaria* in its most fatal forms; and the shores, although there are no traces of a marsh, are deserted, excepting where a few sickly hamlets are scattered on their western slopes. The ground is cultivated in many parts down to the water's edge, but the labourers dare not sleep for a single night during the summer or autumn on the plains where they work by day; and a vast tract of beautiful and productive country is reduced to a perfect solitude by this invisible calamity. Nothing can be more striking than the appearance of the lake, without a single sail upon its waters, and with scarcely a human habitation within sight of Bolsena; and nothing perhaps can give the traveller who visits Italy for the first time a more impressive idea of the effects of malaria. The 2 small islands, the largest called *Bisentina*, and the smallest *Martana*, are picturesque objects from the hills. The latter is memorable as the scene of the imprisonment and murder of Amalasontha, queen of the Goths, the only daughter of Theodoric and grandaughter of Clovis; she was strangled in her bath, A.D. 535, by the order or with the connivance of her cousin Theodatus, whom she had raised to a share in the kingdom. Some steps in the rock are shown as the stair which led to her prison. The church on the island of Bi-

sentina was built by the Farnese family, and decorated by the Caracci; it contains the relics of Sta. Cristina, the virgin saint of Bolsena, whose footsteps on the rocks at the bottom of the lake are still shown as proofs of her miraculous preservation from the death by drowning, to which she had been consigned by her pagan persecutors. The Farnesi had 2 villas on these islands, where Leo X., after visiting Viterbo, resided for the purpose of fishing. The lake has always been famous for its fish; its eels are commemorated by Dante, who says that Pope Martin IV. killed himself by eating them to excess:

> "E quella faccia
> Di là da lui, più che le altre trapunta,
> Ebbe la santa chiesa in le sue braccia;
> Dal Torso fu, e purga per digiuna
> Le anguille di Bolsena e la vernaccia."
> *Purgat.*, xxiv.

In the S.W. bend of the lake, near the island of Martana, is the little river Marta, by which it is drained; it flows beneath Toscanella, and falls into the sea at Corneto. Pliny's description of the lake, which he calls the Tarquinian lake, and his account of its 2 floating islands, will interest the classical tourist (Epist. ii. 96); the islands, if they ever existed, have disappeared, for the description cannot apply to Bisentina and Martana.

The traveller who wishes to visit the fine cathedral of Orvieto, without encountering the details of Rte. 23, may, in a light gig, easily go to Bolsena and return on the same day. The road is good, but hilly; the distance 12 m., but charged 2 posts by the postmaster. The cross-road from Bolsena offers the easiest and most rapid mode of visiting Orvieto.

An additional horse is required from Bolsena to San Lorenzo; and also from Bolsena to Montefiascone, but not *vice versâ* in either case.

About a mile from Bolsena the traveller should leave the carriage, to examine the basaltic columns on the steep slopes of the hill overlooking the lake. They are thickly clustered, and present generally 5 or 6-sided prisms, from 2 to 4 ft. in height. The ascent of the hill now leads us through a wood abounding in oaks, and presenting some exquisite prospects over the lake. The wood has been cleared for some hundred yards on either side of the road, in order to prevent the concealment of banditti, who formerly gave the hill of Bolsena a disagreeable notoriety. After a long ascent we reach the town of Montefiascone, situated on an isolated hill crowned by an old castle of the middle ages, and commanding an extensive view of the lake and its surrounding scenery.

1 Montefiascone (*Inns:* La Posta, dear and unaccommodating, before coming up to the gate on the Bolsena side; Aquila Nera, clean and civil, at the foot of the hill beyond the gate), an episcopal town of 5500 souls, occupying the site of an ancient Etruscan city, of which some sepulchres still exist, though antiquaries are not agreed upon its name. The cathedral, dedicated to St. Margaret, in spite of its unfinished front, has an imposing air; its octagonal cupola is one of the earliest and most interesting works of San Michele. Near the gate is the ch. of *San Flaviano*, a Gothic building founded in 1030, and restored by Urban IV. in 1262, presenting a singular mixture of round and pointed arches. From the gallery in front this pope is said to have given his benediction to the people. In the subterranean chapel is the monument of Bishop Johann Fugger, of a wealthy and distinguished family of Augsburg, who so frequently replenished the coffers of the emperors and entertained them at their palace, now well known as the hotel of the Drei Mohren. The bishop is represented lying on his tomb, with a goblet on each side of his mitre and under his arms. The death of this prelate, which took place in the town, was caused by his drinking too freely of the wine to which he has given such extraordinary celebrity. The following is his epitaph, written by his valet: *Est, Est, Est. Propter nimium est, Joannes de Foucris, Dominus meus, mortuus est.* The explanation of this singular inscription, which has

Cent. It.

given rise to abundant controversy, appears to be simply this: the bishop was in the habit of sending on his valet beforehand in order to ascertain whether the wines were good, in which case he wrote on the walls the word *est* (*it is good*). At Montefiascone he is said to have been so pleased with its sweet wine, that he wrote the *est* three times, a mode of expressing the superiority of liquors which recalls the XXX of the London brewers. The fact is likely to be perpetuated much longer than the luxurious prelate would probably have desired, for the best wine still bears the name of the fatal treble *est*.

Near the inn of the Aquila Nera, at Montefiascone, a hilly road branches off to Orvieto (18 m.), and to Città della Pieve (44½ m.), whence the traveller may proceed either to Perugia (26 m.), or to Chiusi (6 m.), and Montepulciano (22 m.) All these roads are hilly. (See Route 23.)

From Montefiascone to Viterbo the road, after a steep descent, crosses a dreary and unenclosed country destitute of interest—the great Etruscan Plain, between the volcanic groups of Monte Cimino and of the Lake of Bolsena. About midway between the towns, and about a mile from the road on the l., are the ruins of *Ferento*, the Etruscan Ferentinum, mentioned by Horace, in whose time it was a Roman colony; it afterwards became the birth-place of the Emperor Otho and an episcopal see, but was destroyed by the citizens of Viterbo, in the 11th century, on account of the alleged heresy of its inhabitants, in representing our Saviour on the cross with the eyes open, instead of shut. The ruins are interesting. Those of the theatre are remarkable for their massive substructions of Etruscan masonry, their 7 gates, and their *scena*, which is supposed to be the most perfect in Italy. Beyond it is the village of *Vitorchiano*, which enjoys the singular privilege of supplying the senator and municipality of Rome with servants, a privilege derived from its fidelity to Rome in the middle ages, as recorded by an inscription in the palace of the Conservatori at the

K

Capitol. About 7 m. beyond Férento is *Bomarzo,* celebrated within the last 20 years for the Etruscan tombs which have been explored by Prince Borghese with so much success, and to which we are indebted for the interesting sarcophagus with knotted serpents on its temple roof, now in the British Museum; and for the bronze shield with a lance thrust in it, and its braces of leather still perfect, which now forms one of the most remarkable objects in the Museo Gregoriano, at the Vatican. Also about midway between Montefiascone and Viterbo, near the Osteria delle Fontanile, a few yards from the road on the rt. hand, is a considerable portion of the *Via Cassia,* which connected Florence and Rome, passing through Chiusi, Bolsena, Bagni di Serpa, Vetralla, and Sutri, and joining the Via Amerina at Baccano, from which place the united roads entered Rome under the name of the Via Cassia. Beyond this fragment of the ancient road, and at about the distance of 2 miles from Viterbo, a small column of vapour marks the position of the warm sulphurous lake called the *Bulicame,* celebrated by Dante:

" Quale del Bulicame esce ruscello,
  Che parton poi tra lor le peccatrici,
  Tal per l' arena giù sen giva quella."
      Inf. xiv.

1 VITERBO.—(*Inns,* Aquila Nera, at the post-house, and inside the Florence gate, good as to rooms and beds, and generally improved, but charges high to persons travelling by post; Angelo, in the Piazza, very second-rate.) From Viterbo to Montefiascone the post is reckoned at 1½, and an additional horse is required by the tariff, but not *vice versâ.*

Viterbo, situated at the northern foot of Monte Cimino, is the capital of one of the most extensive delegations of the Papal States, embracing a superficial extent of 1348 square m., and a population of 124,000 souls. It is the seat of a bishop, and the residence of the delegate. The population of the city is 14,500. It is surrounded by walls and towers built chiefly by the Lombard kings; its streets, though narrow and

dirty, are paved with flag-stones, like those of Florence. By the old Italian writers it is called the city of handsome fountains and beautiful women.

It is supposed to occupy the site of the ancient *Fanum Voltumnæ,* celebrated as the spot where the Etruscan cities held their general assemblies. The present town was raised to the rank of a city by Celestin III., in 1194; during the 13th century it was the residence of several popes, and the scene of numerous conclaves, at which the following pontiffs were elected: Urban IV., in 1261; Clement IV., in 1264; B. Gregory X., in 1271; John XXI., in 1276; Nicholas III., in 1277; and Martin IV., at the dictation of Charles of Anjou, in 1281. It was the chief city of those allodial possessions of the Countess Matilda, extending from Rome to Bolsena, and embracing the whole coast, from the mouth of the Tiber to the Tuscan frontier, which that princess bequeathed to the Holy See in the 12th century, and which constitute what is now known as the patrimony of St. Peter.

The *Cathedral,* dedicated to San Lorenzo, is a Gothic edifice, built on the site of an ancient temple of Hercules. It contains the tombs of popes John XXI., Alexander IV., and Clement IV. At the high altar is the picture of S. Lorenzo in Glory, by *Gio. Francesco Romanelli,* a native painter. The pictures illustrating various incidents in the history of S. Lorenzo are by his son *Urbano.* The subjects from the life of S. Lorenzo and St. Stephen are by *Marco Benefial.* In the Sacristy is a large picture of the Saviour and the four Evangelists, attributed to *Albert Durer* (?); the medallion on the roof is by *Carlo Maratta.* But these works of art will fail to interest the English traveller as much as the recollection of the atrocity which has associated this ancient edifice with the history of England. It was at the high altar of this cathedral that Prince Henry of England, son of the Earl of Cornwall, was murdered by Guy de Montfort, the 4th son of Simon de Montfort, Earl of Leicester, who was killed in 1265 at the battle of Evesham, fighting against

Henry III. On that occasion the body of the Earl was dragged in the dust by the royalists; his son, Guy de Montfort, who was also present in the battle, vowed vengeance against the king and his family for this outrage. No opportunity, however, occurred for a few years; but the grandson of the notorious persecutor of the Albigenses was not likely to forget his vow, and an accidental visit to this city at length threw one of the young princes of England in his way. After the battle of Tagliacozzo, Charles of Anjou was summoned from his conquests to accompany his brother St. Louis on a second crusade against Tunis. His stay, however, was short, and he soon returned to Naples. The College of Cardinals being then at Viterbo, Charles proceeded to that city in order to induce the cardinals to bring the long interregnum to a close, and elect a successor to the chair of St. Peter. During his residence at Viterbo, many of the crusaders who had returned from Tunis had assembled there, together with his great officers of state. Among the latter was Guy de Montfort, the lieutenant of Charles in Tuscany. On a certain day he met, in this cathedral, Henry, son of Richard Earl of Cornwall, king of the Romans, and brother of king Henry III. of England. The prince was passing through Viterbo on his return from Africa, whither he had accompanied his cousin Edward. The young prince was kneeling at the altar during the celebration of mass, when Guy de Montfort rushed upon him and ran him through with his sword. The prince instantly expired, and the murderer walked out of the ch. unmolested. He said to his attendants at the door, "I have been avenged." "How?" said one of them, "was not your father dragged in the dust?" At these words he returned to the altar, seized the body of the prince by the hair, and dragged it into the public square. He then fled and took refuge in the Maremma, but Charles was afraid to punish him for the crime. Prince Edward, the son and successor of Henry III., and Philippe le Hardi, of France, were both in Viterbo at the time, but

they quitted it immediately, indignant at the weakness of Charles in allowing the murderer to go unpunished. Giovanni Villani, the principal authority for these facts, states that "the heart of Henry was put into a golden cup, and placed on a pillar at London Bridge, over the river Thames, for a memorial to the English of the said outrage." (Lib. vii. c. 40.) Dante, the true historian of the middle ages, has also commemorated this circumstance, and has placed the murderer in hell, in that 7th circle guarded by the Minotaur and the Centaurs, which is surrounded by a river of boiling blood, in which those whose sins have been tyranny or cruelty towards mankind are punished:

" Poco più oltre il Centauro si affissi
   Sovra una gente, che infino alla gola
   Parea che di quel bulicame uscisse.
Mostrocci una ombra dalla un canto sola,
   Dicendo : colui fesse in grembo a dio
   Lo cor, che in su Tamigi ancor si cola."
                                   Inf. xii.

Besides this event, there is another historical incident which gives the cathedral of Viterbo additional interest in the estimation of English travellers: it was in the square before it that Adrian IV., the only Englishman who ever wore the tiara, compelled Frederick Barbarossa to humble himself in the presence of the papal and imperial courts by holding his stirrup while he dismounted from his mule. The haughty emperor only yielded at the persuasion of his courtiers, who suggested the precedent of Lothaire; but Frederick deeply felt the injury, and consoled himself, according to the contemporary historians, by declaring that he paid this homage not to the pope, but to the apostle of whom he was the recognised representative.

Close to the cathedral is the Episcopal Palace of the 13th century, now greatly ruined, but still retaining many points of interest connected with the history of the popes. The great hall is still shown in which the conclave was assembled at the command of Charles of Anjou, at the time of the murder of Prince Henry, when, after a deliberation of 33 months, they elected Tebaldo Visconti to the papal chair, under the name of Gregory X. In the same hall the cardinals afterwards elected Martin

K 2

IV., after an interregnum of 6 months, though not until Charles of Anjou had excited an insurrection against them among the inhabitants of Viterbo. At the suggestion of that monarch the citizens removed the roof in order to force them to an election ; they then arrested and imprisoned the cardinals Orsini and Latino, whom Charles, for his own personal interests, wished to be removed from the council. It is said that the municipal archives still preserve letters of these cardinals dated from " the roofless palace." Another chamber is shown, in which John XXI. was killed by the fall of the roof in 1277.

. The ch. (entirely modernised) of the *Convent of Sta. Rosa* contains the body of the saint, one of the heroines of the 13th century, whose history, like that of Joan of Arc, presents a strange combination of religious and political enthusiasm. She first roused the people against the emperor Frederick II.; after the success of the Ghibeline party she retired into exile, and on the death of the great emperor returned in triumph to Viterbo, where she died, and was soon afterwards canonized by the Guelph party. Her body, resembling that of a black mummy, is preserved in a gilt tomb, and is the object of great veneration on account of her numerous reputed miracles.

The Ch. of *S. Francesco,* behind the hotel, a good specimen of Italian Gothic, contains the celebrated Deposition from the Cross, by *Sebastiano del Piombo,* painted, as we learn from Vasari, from the designs of Michael Angelo : " L' invenzione però ed il cartone fu di Michelagnolo ; fu quell' opera tenuta da chiunque lo vide veramente bellissima, onde acquistò Sebastiano grandissimo credito, e confermò il dire di coloro che lo favorivano." Lanzi also cites this work as one of those in which Sebastian del Piombo was assisted by Michael Angelo, who patronised him after the death of Raphael, to the prejudice of Giulio Romano and the other eminent followers of the rival school. In the rt. hand transept is the tomb of Adrian the Fifth (Ottoboni Fieschi), who died at Viterbo in 1276 : the re-

cumbent statue of the Pontiff, and the monument in general, are in a good style and in excellent preservation. ·

The Ch. of the *Osservanti del Paradiso* has another work of *Sebastiano del Piombo,* the Flagellation, which, according to Lanzi, was considered the finest picture in Viterbo. On the outside is a fresco of the Madonna with saints, attributed to *Leonardo da Vinci.*

· The Ch. called *della Morte* has a picture of the Incredulity of St. Thomas, by *Salvator Rosa.*

S. Ignazio has a picture of the saint at the high altar, by *Cav. d'Arpino,* and in the sacristy a small painting of Christ in the Garden, by *Marcello Venusti,* another artist, whom Lanzi mentions with great praise for his skill in embodying the ideas of Michael Angelo, by whom this work is supposed to have been designed.

Sta. Maria della Verità has a remarkable fresco of the Sposalizio, by *Lorenzo di Giacomo da Viterbo,* who completed it in 1469, after a labour of 25 years. It is highly curious in the history of art, independently of the fact that all the heads in the picture are portraits of the principal citizens, and it is scarcely less interesting as a study of the costume of the 15th century.

S. Angelo in Spata presents in its façade a Roman sarcophagus, with a fine bas-relief of a lion fighting a boar, and an inscription recording that it contains the ashes of Galiana, the most beautiful woman in Italy. This celebrated personage was the Helen of the middle ages (1138), and her beauty gave rise to a war between Rome and Viterbo, during which the Romans were defeated. In the capitulation which followed, the Romans stipulated that they were to be allowed a last sight of Galiana, who was accordingly shown to them from one of the windows still existing in the exterior of an old tower of the ancient gate of St. Antony.

The *Palazzo Pubblico,* begun in 1264, deserves a visit. Its court contains 2 large Etruscan tombs, with figures in relief and inscriptions, and an elegant fountain. In the hall of the Academia degli Ardenti are the frescoes of *Bal-*

dassare Croce, a scholar of Annibale Caracci. In another apartment are the marble tablet, containing the pretended edict of King Desiderius, the last of the Lombard kings, and the Tabula Cibellaria, another of the forgeries by which Annius, the well-known literary impostor, attempted to claim for Viterbo an antiquity greater than that of Troy. The museum of the academy is interesting on account of its local antiquities: it contains some fine Etruscan tombs in terra-cotta, vases, and other Etruscan remains, some Roman inscriptions and sarcophagi. Among the paintings is a Visitation, by *Francesco Romanelli.*

The principal fountains of Viterbo, which divide with its pretty women the honour of the proverb already mentioned, are the *Fontana Grande*, begun in 1206; the fountain in the market-place; that in the Piazza della Rocca, constructed in 1566 by Cardinal Farnese, and attributed to Vignola; and that in the court of the Palazzo Pubblico.

Outside the Roman gate is the *Domenican Convent*, remarkable as the residence of Fra Giovanni Nanni, better known as Annius of Viterbo.

The *Palazzo San Martino*, belonging to the Doria family, deserves a visit for its noble staircase *a cordoni*, by which a carriage may ascend to the upper stories. It also contains the portrait of the dissolute Olimpia Maidalchini Pamfili, sister-in-law and mistress of Innocent X., with her bed and its leather furniture.

The immediate neighbourhood of Viterbo is memorable for a battle fought there in 1234, between the army of the emperor in conjunction with the forces of the pope, and the troops of Rome, then in opposition to their own pontiff, who by a more singular coincidence formed an alliance with his hereditary enemy for the purpose of repressing the insurrection of his subjects. The papal forces on this occasion were commanded by an English prelate, Peter de Rupibus, bishop of Winchester, by whom the Romans were defeated with immense loss.

On the road to Orte and Narni are two objects of some interest: the sanc-tuary and Domenican convent of the *Madonna della Quercia*, and the *Villa Lante* at *Bagnaja*. The Madonna della Quercia, built from the designs of Bramante, is remarkable for its splendid roof, an imitation of that of Sta. Maria Maggiore. Over its three doors are some beautiful bas-reliefs in terra-cotta, by *Luca della Robbia*. Behind the altar is the image of the Madonna on the oak from which it was found suspended, and which gives name to the church. The campanile contains a bell said to weigh 13,500 lbs. On the ground in front of this convent are held the 2 famous fairs of Viterbo. the 1st, established by Leo X. in 1513, begins on the day of Pentecost, and lasts 15 days; the 2nd, founded by the Emperor Frederick II. in 1240, begins on the 22nd Sept., and ends on the 6th Oct. The *Villa Lante* is remarkable for its imposing architecture, said to be the design of Vignola. It was begun by Cardinal Riario, and finished by Cardinal Gambara, in allusion to whose name and armorial bearings a cascade was formerly made to assume in its fall from the mountain the form of an immense lobster. It is now almost deserted. It is related that, when St. Carlo Borromeo visited the villa, he suggested how much good the money lavished upon it would have done if distributed among the poor; to which Cardinal Gambara replied that he had made them earn it by their labours. On the summit of the mountain, 4 m. distant, above the Villa, is the *Menicatore*, or Logan stone of Italy, a large mass of rock, 22 feet long, and 9 feet high, said to weigh 220 tons, which still "logs" as easily as the celebrated "Logan rock" of Cornwall.

Orte, a few m. beyond this, picturesquely placed on an isolated ridge on the rt. bank of the Tiber, with a little inn called the Campana, occupies the site of ancient Horta, one of the military colonies of Augustus. It has the ruins of a fine bridge, called the bridge of Augustus, and some extensive remains of baths. To the south, the picturesque town of *Bassanello*, with its mediæval walls, marks the site of Castellum Amerinum, near which was the estate of Calpurnius, father-in-law of Pliny the younger. In the Val d'Orte the small lake called the Valdemone or Lago di Bassano, choked up with rushes, is the ancient Lake Vadimon, whose floating islands are beautifully described in the 8th epistle of Pliny, whose residence at the villa of his father-in-law gave him leisure and opportunity to observe them. The banks of the lake are celebrated for the total defeat of the Etruscans by the Romans, B. C. 309, which completely destroyed their political existence as an independent nation. A subsequent battle was fought here by the Etruscans in alliance with the Gauls and Boii, but they were again defeated by the Romans under Dolabella. A few m. S. of Bassanello, *Gallese*, a town of some consequence in the middle ages, is supposed to mark the site of the ancient Faliscan city of Fescennium, noted for the nuptial songs to which it gave the name of Carmina Fescennina. Near it and about 7 m. S. of Bassanello is the miserable village of *Corchiano*, occupying the site of an Etruscan town, the name of which is lost. Half a m. from it, on the road to Civita Castellana, is the Etruscan name "Larth Vel Arnies," in letters 15 inches in length, cut in the tufa rock through which the ancient Via Amerina is carried. 2 m. from Corchiano, on the road to Bassanello, is a curious Etruscan tomb, called *Puntone del Ponte.*

EXCURSION TO CASTEL D'ASSO, NORCHIA, AND BIEDA.

By far the most interesting excursion which can be made from this road is that to Castel d'Asso, Norchia, and Bieda. *Castel d'Asso*, or, as it is called by the peasantry, Castellaccio, was the necropolis of the Etruscan city of Castellum Axia, distant about 5 m. from Viterbo. When it is stated that the cliffs of this and the 4 adjoining valleys are excavated into a continued series of cavern-sepulchres of enormous size, resembling nothing else in Europe, and only to be compared with the tombs of the kings of Thebes, the traveller may perhaps be induced to prolong his journey for the purpose of visiting so remarkable a spot. It will be much more desirable to hire horses or donkeys for the excursion, than to attempt it in a carriage; and those who do not wish to return to Viterbo may proceed by Vetralla, the Vicus Matrini, the wayside inn called Le Capanacce, and thence through Capranica and Sutri (both of which are noticed at the end of this Rte.), to Ronciglione, the next post station on the high road to Rome. It will also be necessary to carry provisions from Viterbo, and on no account to omit to take torches, without which it is impossible to examine the tombs. The best guides to be obtained at Viterbo are Ruggieri, a coffee-house keeper, and Giuseppe Perugini, a barber. As there is much to explore, travellers should start from Viterbo at a very early hour, in order to have the day before them; they may then visit the 4 valleys, and reach Viterbo or Ronciglione in good time before dark. The principal of these valleys are those of Bieda (the Blera of Cicero) and San Giovanni di Bieda, to which a pathway leads off the high road of Vetralla. The 1st object which attracts attention after leaving the road is a remarkable ruined fortress of the 15th century, called Castel d'Asso, marking by its name, as well as by the Etruscan foundations around it, the site of Castellum Axia, mentioned by Cicero as one of the strongholds of Etruria. Nothing can be imagined more grand or imposing than the appearance of this ruined fortress from all parts of the valley, and the artist might find abundant occupation in the fine combinations it makes with the surrounding scenery. Immediately in front of the castle, and far down in the glen, commences the long line of cavern-sepulchres, completely occupying the face of the cliff opposite the castle, and running up both sides of the valleys which fall into it. These extraordinary tombs were discovered by Signor Anselmi of Viterbo, and first made known by Professor Orioli. Elaborate drawings of them have been since given in Canina's " Etruria Maritima." Their general appearance resembles the Egyptian style, particularly in the doors, which are narrower at top than at bottom; over many of them are deep inscriptions in the oldest Etruscan-character, the letters of which in several instances are a foot high. They are also interesting in the history of Etruscan architecture, as presenting some fine examples of mouldings; but they want the projecting cornice which would be necessary to give them a complete resemblance to Egyptian structures. These lofty doorways, however, like those observed in the sepulchres of Lycia, Phrygia, and Egypt, are merely sculptured in the cliff; a smaller door at their base, easily concealed by earth, leads into the ante-chambers, which have similar false doors, at the base of which are the real entrances into the sepulchral chambers. Most of these are single chambers, but some are double, the inner apartment being much smaller and lower than the outer. They present a great diversity of size, and the roofs are frequently vaulted. In some of the tombs the receptacles for the dead are sunk side by side in the rocky floor of the chamber, in others they radiate from the centre, and in others there are ledges of rock along the sides of the apartment, in which sarcophagi were placed. Nearly every tomb appears to have been a family sepulchre. In the neighbourhood of Bieda bronze and marble figures, vases, and scarabæi are said to have been discovered in great abundance; but all the tombs have evidently been plundered, probably by the Romans. In regard to the inscriptions occasionally visible on these tombs, the visitor will be struck by the frequent repetition of the word *Ecasu,* or *Ecasuthinesl,* so commonly met with in Etruscan tombs in other parts of the country. It has been supposed to signify "*adieu;*" and "it would seem," says Sir William Gell, "that some general meaning must be expressed by words so frequently repeated, but nothing satisfactory has yet appeared as an interpretation. The interpretation of the inscription at Castel d'Asso, and other Etrurian cities, has hitherto wholly defied the efforts of the learned. It is in vain that Lanzi and Passeri have with great toil and learn-

ing succeeded to a certain degree in the interpretation of the Umbrian or Eugubian tables: notwithstanding the numerous remains of Etruscan, '*Ril avil*' (vixit annos, or annos vixit) and some proper names are all that have ever been satisfactorily made out in this language. It may be observed that brass arms have been found in these sepulchres, which seem to refer them to a very ancient period. It is remarkable that scarabæi also, in cornelian and other stones, are frequently met with here, as in Egypt, but always with Greek or Etruscan subjects engraved upon them."

After exploring the valley of Castel d'Asso, travellers should proceed to *Vetralla,* a town of 6000 souls, situated on the edge of the great plain of Etruria, and near the site of Forum Cassii, from which they may easily explore the marvellous necropolis of Norchia and the site of Bieda, each about 6 m. distant. There is a small inn, or *osteria,* at Vetralla, but the accommodation it affords is only indifferent, though the people are obliging, and Giacomo Zeppa, who lives hard by, may be employed as a guide. The road to *Norchia* lies over bare moors, and is practicable only on foot or horseback. The valley which contains the tombs is a perfect amphitheatre in form, and as the eye ranges along the face of the cliff on one side of it, nearly 300 ft. above the stream which flows at the bottom, it traces a long and almost unbroken line of tombs, adorned with pediments and cornices like those at Castel d'Asso, but more imposing in effect. Almost at the extremity of the line are the 2 sculptured tombs with pediments and Doric friezes, which have made the name of Norchia celebrated among the archæologists of Europe. Of these tombs one only of the pediments is complete; the half of the other was found buried in the earth near it, and was lately for sale at Viterbo. The tympana of the pediments are filled with figures in high relief, and the wall under the pediment is covered with other figures in bas-relief, nearly as large as life. The upper figures represent the various incidents of a combat;

the lower ones represent, probably, a funeral or religious procession; above the figures may be recognized, as suspended from the wall, a circular shield, a winged genius, a helmet, and 2 swords, and the 3 figures which close the procession bear the twisted rods, which are seen in no other place except the Typhon tomb at Tarquinii. Professor Orioli, who first described these tombs, considers that their Greek character and their execution mark their age as that of the 5th or 6th century of Rome. Their interior presents no magnificence whatever, and differs in no degree from that of the ordinary tombs in the vicinity. Although there are many more tombs in this necropolis than there are at Castel d' Asso, it is remarkable that no vestige of an Etruscan inscription has ever been found here. The picturesque Lombard church of Norchia, now in ruins, marks the site of the ancient Etruscan city, but its ancient name is lost, and nothing more is known respecting it than that it was called Orcle in the 9th century.

The second remarkable site to be visited from Vetralla is *Bieda*, distant within 6 m., a wretched modern village, occupying the site of the Etruscan city of Blera, on the Via Clodia, which passed through it, and of which the ancient Etruscan bridge still exists, under the name of the Ponte della Rocca. There is no inn at Bieda, and the only respectable house in the village is that of the proprietor, the Piedmontese Count di San Giorgio, who recently bought this property, and with it the feudal title of Duke of Bieda and sundry feudal privileges connected with it. The ch., however, contains a picture of the Flagellation, by *Annibale Caracci*, and has a Roman sarcophagus in front of it, which was found in the neighbourhood. Both the modern and the ancient town were placed at the extremity of a long narrow tongue of land, projecting into deep ravines, and communicating with them by narrow and almost precipitous clefts in the tufa rock. The sides of these ravines, in every direction, excepting where the cliffs face the north and east, are literally honeycombed with sepulchral chambers, rising above each other in terraces, and generally shaped into the forms of houses, with sloping roofs and moulded doorways, like those of Norchia. In fact, Bieda surpasses all other Etruscan sites in the architectural variety and interest of its tombs. In the ravine on the east of the town is a conical mass of rock, forming internally a tomb of 2 chambers, and hewn externally into a series of circular steps, contracting towards the summit, which probably supported a figure like those of Vulci and Tarquinii. In the ravine on the W. of the town is an ancient bridge of three arches, the central of which is semicircular and split throughout its entire length. The architecture of this bridge is superior in its construction to that of the bridge already mentioned, and for that reason, though perfectly Etruscan in its character, it is considered to belong to a period subsequent to the Roman conquest of Etruria. The scenery of the ravines around Bieda is of the wildest and most impressive character, and artists who have exhausted even the grand scenery of Civita Castellana will find in these solitary glens combinations of ancient art and romantic nature, at once novel and inexhaustible.

If an examination of these extraordinary valleys should lead the traveller to desire a more minute acquaintance with this district of Etruria, he will be able to make an excursion from Vetralla to Corneto (Tarquinii), 18 m. distant by the high road, which leads through it from Viterbo to Civita Vecchia; but as this would lead him altogether away from the Roman road, and would require preparations in the way of introductions, we shall make it the subject of a separate journey, and shall therefore describe it under "Excursions from Rome."

The traveller who is desirous of proceeding to Rome without returning to Viterbo, can do so by following the Via Cassia from Vetralla to Monterosi, visiting Sutri on his way. A diligence runs three times a week between Viterbo and Rome, passing by Vetralla, performing the distance professedly in 10 hours. On leaving Vetralla, a gradual ascent leads us thence over the shoulder of the Monte Cimino, beyond which is the roadside osteria called Le Capanacce, in whose walls are embedded many relics of the Vicus Matrini, a Roman station, situated nearly 2 miles beyond it, and still retaining its ancient name. 3 or 4 m. further we arrive at *Capranica*, a small modern town, which occupies the site of an Etruscan one whose name is lost, and is celebrated throughout the Papal States for its mineral waters, called by the peasantry the Fonte Carbonari, which are in high repute in diseases of the bladder and kidneys. There is no inn at present at Capranica, but travellers may obtain acccommodation at the house of a very civil and obliging butcher called Ferri. There are some interesting Gothic tombs in the Ch. outside the gate, and a fine portal, ornamented with early Christian sculptures, in the street opposite, and which once formed a part of a church that has been destroyed. About 3 m. beyond Capranica is *Sutri*, a description of which will be found at the end of the present Route.

Returning to Viterbo—

[An additional horse is required from Viterbo to l'Imposta.]

The road on leaving Viterbo begins immediately to ascend the steep volcanic hill of Monte Cimino, the classical Ciminus, whose dense forests served as a barrier to Etruria against Rome for so many ages prior to the memorable march of Fabius. It is clothed with Spanish broom, heath, and brushwood, among which there are still some noble oaks and chesnut-trees, interspersed occasionally with stone-pines.

1 L'Imposta, a solitary post-house, from which the road still continues to ascend before it reaches the summit. It is impossible to imagine a grander panorama than bursts upon the traveller from this point, 2900 feet above the sea: in very clear weather he may descry Rome for the first time. It embraces on one side the whole chain of the Apennines from Otricoli to Palestrina, the Alban hills, and even the distant Vol-

scian range, with the valleys of the Sacco and the Liris separating them from the central Apennines, whilst the Tiber may be seen in the foreground winding its course through the desolate Campagne at their base. Soracte is almost at the traveller's feet on one side, whilst behind in the distance majestically rise the sharp peaks of Montamiata and Cetona. Below is the beautiful little lake called the Lago di Vico, or Lacus Cimini:

> " Et Cimini cum monte lacum, lucosque
> Capenos." *Virg. Æn.*, vii.

The road soon skirts the eastern margin of this beautiful basin, about 3 m. in circumference, whose steep sides are covered with luxuriant forests. The Lake of Vico occupies the site of a great volcanic crater contemporaneous with the elevation of the eruptive mass of the Cimino. Its volcanic origin is evident from the physical structure of the surrounding hills, confirmed by an ancient tradition that it was caused by a sudden sinking, during which a city called Succinium was swallowed up. Several ancient writers mention that when the water was clear, the ruins of this city might be seen at the bottom of the lake.

Before reaching Ronciglione a narrow road on the l. hand leads through a forest abounding in some charming scenery to the castle of *Caprarola*, the masterpiece of Vignola. It was built by that eminent architect for Cardinal Alessandro Farnese, nephew of Paul III., on the slopes of Monte Cimino. As a specimen of the fortified domestic architecture of the 16th century, it is perhaps unrivalled in Italy. It is of a pentagonal form, and is surrounded with bastions and a fosse. The substructions of the palace are of the most solid and imposing kind. The apartments are decorated with frescoes and arabesques, by Federigo, Ottaviano, and Taddeo Zuccari, by Tempesta, and by Vignola himself, whose perspectives are by no means the least remarkable of the many interesting works of art for which this castle is remarkable. Each room is devoted to some incident in the history of the Farnese family, or to some allegorical subjects. The Sala degli Annali has the fine fresco of Taddeo Zuccari, representing the entry of Charles V. into Paris between Francis I. and Cardinal Farnese, who is riding on a mule. Taddeo has introduced himself and his two brothers as the supporters of the canopy. The Stanza del Sonno is remarkable for its fine poetical subjects, now nearly destroyed, which were suggested by Annibale Caro. All the subjects illustrated by the Zuccari are engraved in Prenner's " Illustri Fatti Farnesiani," Rome, 1748. The arabesques of Tempesta are also interesting ; on the top of the stairs he has represented himself on horseback in the female dress which he assumed for the purpose of escaping from his work, but he was pursued and overtaken by the people of the castle, who compelled him to return and complete his engagements. In the gardens is the elegant *Palazzuolo*, designed by Vignola as the casino of the castle, worthy of a visit for the beautiful prospect over the surrounding country from its upper terrace. It is stated that Cardinal Borromeo, afterwards St. Charles, during his visit to Caprarola, made an observation similar to that already recorded in the account of the Villa Lanti at Viterbo: "Che sarà il paradiso !" he remarked; "Oh! meglio sarebbe stato aver dato a' poveri tanto denaro spesovi." The answer of Cardinal Farnese may be regarded as a suitable reply to all similar observations of mistaken philanthropists: "Di averlo egli dato a' poveri a poco a poco, ma fattoglielo guadagnare *con i loro sudori.*"

1 Ronciglione (*Inns* much improved within the last 3 or 4 years. La Posta, formerly bad and dirty, is now said to be respectably conducted; the Aquila Nera is clean and comfortable, with a civil landlord). [An additional horse from Ronciglione to l'Imposta.] This is the last place entirely free from malaria between Viterbo and Rome. It is a dirty and ruinous town, of 6000 souls, romantically situated on a precipitous point of rock above a deep and wooded ravine, in the sides of which are several sepulchral cham-

bers marking the site of an Etruscan town, the name of which has been lost. Its ruined Gothic castle is a striking object on approaching the town. Ronciglione was burnt by the French during the first invasion; it has some iron works. The iron is brought from Bracciano, where it is obtained by smelting the iron ores from Elba. Notwithstanding the impulse given to the town by these establishments, many of its fine old palaces are comparatively deserted, and fast falling to decay. The Roman gate bears the name of Odoardo Farnese. On leaving the town we enter upon the celebrated region so well known as the Campagna of Rome, a tract of country stretching from the hills of Etruria to the Circæan promontory near Terracina, bounded on the east by the mountains, and by the Mediterranean on the west.

From Ronciglione, a road leads to the Etruscan town of Sutri (3 m.), whence a good road fit for carriages communicates with the high post-road near Monterosi (7 or 8 m.); so that travellers encumbered with heavy carriages might make a détour from Ronciglione, either in the light *caritelle* of the country or on horseback, and rejoin their carriages at Monterosi. A good diligence from Viterbo to Rome passes by Sutri 3 times a-week. Sutri may also be very conveniently visited from Viterbo and Vetralla, and included in the tour from the former town, embracing the Etruscan sites on the declivities of the Monte Cimino, Castel d'Azzo, Vetralla, Norchia, Bieda, and Capranica (see ante, p. 198).

EXCURSION TO SUTRI.

There is no inn at Sutri, but clean beds and tolerable accommodation may be obtained at the house of a butcher, called Francocci.

SUTRI occupies the precise site of the ancient Etruscan city of Sutrium, whose alliance with Rome exposed it to frequent attacks and sieges from the other tribes of Etruria. In these operations the military prowess of Camillus, of Fabius, and of other warriors illustrious in Roman history, was instrumental in saving Sutrium from its enemies. The proverb "ire Sutrium" commemorates an incident which took place during the most remarkable of these attacks in 365, when, at the urgent entreaty of the citizens, Camillus and the Roman army recovered the city from the confederated Etruscans on the very day on which they entered it as conquerors. From the rapidity of this double exploit, "ire Sutrium" became a proverb. The city is situated on a long insulated rock of volcanic tufa, forming, in combination with the ravines by which it is surrounded, an exceedingly striking picture. A bridge formerly connected it with the high table-land adjoining, but it was broken down by the French in 1798. In the deep valley passed on approaching the gate from this side are numerous sepulchral chambers, but they are not so remarkable as those we shall observe in the lower valley on leaving the town for Monterosi. On the south side of the town are some fine fragments of the ancient walls. Of the five gates now observable, three are ancient, viz. the two in the southern wall, and one in the northern, now blocked up, but still called the Porta Furia, from the tradition that it was that by which the city was entered by Camillus. The latter has a slightly pointed arch, and is considered by many as more recent than the others. The two remaining gates, one at each extremity of the town, are modern, although one of them bears an inscription attributing the foundation of Sutrium to the Pelasgi (!) and the other setting forth the antiquity of the city. At the foot of an insulated eminence, crowned by the villa of the Marchese Savorelli, embosomed in a thick and picturesque grove of ilex and cypress, is the ancient amphitheatre of Statilius Taurus, excavated in the tufa, and so perfect as to be regarded unique. The steps are worn in a few places, but all its corridors and vomitories and six rows of its stages are preserved. In a few places some brickwork may be recognised, but only

where there existed obvious deficiencies in the rock; with this exception the amphitheatre has no masonry, but is hewn out of the solid rock. The length of the arena is about 160 feet, and its greatest breadth about 132 feet. Some doubt exists whether this interesting structure is of Etruscan or Roman workmanship ; if it be Etruscan, it may be regarded as the type of all the amphitheatres built by Imperial Rome. Micali considers it Etruscan, Nibby refers it to the time of Augustus, and Canina regards it as Roman, on the ground, principally, that the character of the architectural details is Roman. The most reasonable conjecture probably is that which makes it an Etruscan work of a period subsequent to Etruscan independence, and yet before Etruria had lost all her national characteristics under the Roman yoke. In the face of the cliff, above the amphitheatre, are numerous sepulchral caverns, one of which has been converted into a ch. These and the subterranean passages which are known to exist beneath the cliffs of Sutri, and which tradition has invested with mysterious histories, are believed to have been used, both as places of divine worship and of burial, by the early Christians, during the persecutions of the Emperors. Nearer the town, in the midst of a thick wood, is a sepulchral chamber with a pillar in the centre, called the "Grotta d' Orlando," in which tradition relates that Charlemagne's celebrated Paladin was born; the inhabitants also claim Pontius Pilate as a native of Sutri, which is disputed by Marta on the lake of Bolsena. The modern town has a population of 2000 souls, but, although several popes in the 11th and 12th centuries held councils there, it contains nothing of remarkable interest; the views from some of its old houses overlooking the valley are very beautiful. On descending from the Porta Romana, a perpendicular face of rock, on the rt. hand, is seen filled with sepulchral chambers, many of which have traces of columns, pediments, and architectural façades. Several of these have apparently been fronted with stone of a different quality, but these ornaments have been removed, and nothing remains but the cavities which received them. These chambers are well worthy of examination; and indeed Sutri has been so little explored that it offers a more ample field perhaps than any other Etruscan settlement so easily accessible from the high road. Capranica and the road from Sutri to Vetralla are described in a previous page. Leaving Sutri for Rome, we again join the Roman road near the junction of the two roads from Siena and Perugia, and soon reach Monterosi.

———

The direct road from Ronciglione to Monterosi presents nothing worthy of particular notice.

1 Monterosi,	
1 Baccano,	Described in
1 La Storta,	Route 27.
1¼ Rome,	

ROUTE 26A.

FLORENCE TO SIENA, BY THE POST ROAD,
41 English m.

	Posts.
Florence to San Casciano	1
S. Casciano to Poggibonsi	2
Poggibonsi to Siena	2
	—
	5

The 1st stage out of Florence being very hilly, an additional horse is required by the tariff. The road leaves Florence by the Porta Romana, from which a steep ascent leads to the village of S. Gaggio, having the Granducal villa of Poggio Imperiale on the l., and the hill of Bellosguardo covered with villas on the opposite side. 3 m. from the city gate is the large village of Galuzzo, beyond which the road passes on the rt. the *Certosa*, situated on a commanding eminence, in the angle formed by the junction of the rivers Greve and Emo. This celebrated Carthusian convent was founded, by Niccolò Acciajoli, grand seneschal of Naples, in 1341. The subterranean chapel contains the tombs of Acciajoli, by Orcagna, and of some other members of his family; that of Cardinal Angelo Acciajoli is by Donatello and Giuliano Sangallo. In this convent, Pius VI. found a retreat during those political troubles which marked the latter years of his eventful pontificate: he was arrested within its walls, and carried a prisoner to France. 2 m. farther, at Monte Buoni, a road strikes off on the l. to L' Impruneta, where the ch., Sta. Maria, is celebrated for a miraculous image of the Virgin, which attracts, on certain festivals, an immense concourse of devotees from all parts of Tuscany. The country around the village of L' Impruneta is of great interest to the geologist, being composed of eruptions of serpentine through the secondary limestones; the well-known green marble called verde dell' Impruneta is found here. Great numbers of oil jars, and of the beautiful earthen flower and shrub vases in such general use in the Tuscan gardens, are manufactured in this neighbourhood.

The road from Monte Buoni is a continued ascent to

1 San Casciano (*Inn*, La Campana), on the summit level between the valley of the Arno and of the Pesa. In the neighbourhood of San Casciano is the villa of Machiavelli, now the property of the Maffei family. In this house it is said that he wrote " The Prince " and several other works. On leaving the town we descend to the rt. bank of the Pesa. At the bridge called Ponte Rotto a hilly road branches off on the rt. to Certaldo, ascending the Pesa for 3 m.: the river is crossed at Ponte Nuovo, where another hilly road branches off on the l. to Sambuca and Castellina, in the wine-growing province of Chianti, and to Siena. A steep ascent of 4 m. brings us to Barberino, a large village, in a beautiful situation, on the top of the ridge between the Pesa and Elsa valleys. There is a good inn at Barberino where vetturini stop on their way to Siena; from Barberino the road is a descent along the Drove torrent to

2 *Poggibonsi* (*Inns*: Aquila Nera, cheap, if you name your own prices; La Corona; both very tolerable).

———

Leaving Poggibonsi for Siena, we ascend the valley of the Staggia, leaving on the l. hand the hilly district of the *Chianti*, which gives name to a wine well known to travellers on this route, and thus celebrated by Redi:

" Del buon Chianti il vin decrepito,
    Maestoso,
    Imperioso.
Mi passeggia dentro il core ;
Esso scaccia senza strepito
Ogni affanno e ogni dolore."

And on the rt. the upper valley of the Elsa and the large town of Colle, to which a good road strikes off on the l., and continues to Volterra. After leaving Poggibonsi, 4 m. farther, the picturesque Castle of Monte Riggione is passed, from which commences the ascent of the hills that separate the waters flowing into the Arno and Ombrone—the highest point of the road being near San Dalmazio, over the great tunnel of the Siena Railway. Shortly afterwards we pass a column, erected on the spot where Frederick II. met his consort Eleonora of Portugal, conducted by Æneas Sylvius and by 400 ladies of the city.

Siena is entered by the Porta Camollia, over which is the inscription said to have been put up in 1604 for the Grand Duke Ferdinand :

" Cor magis tibi Sena pandit."

ROUTE 26B.

SIENA TO AREZZO, BY MONTE SAN SAVINO.

About 42 m.

This is a very good, but hilly road, and may be performed in a day in a light carriage ; a diligence runs along it 3 times a week, performing the journey in 10 hours.

On leaving Siena by the Porta Pispini, the road descends for 4 m. to Ruffolo, where it crosses the Bozzone torrent, and, 1 m. farther, the river Arbia on a handsome bridge at Taverne d' Arbia. Beyond this we enter the bleak and arid region of the Crete Sanese, or blue tertiary marls, hereabouts extremely abundant in fossil

shells, and which continues for 8 m. farther ; ½ m. after crossing the Arbia a road to Asciano and to Montepulciano branches off on the rt. About 15 m. from Siena we reach the hamlet of S. Quirico on the upper Ombrone, where the roads to Arezzo and to Chiusi (Rte. 26c) separate, and from which we commence to ascend for 6 m. the range of hills that separate the valley of the Ombrone from that of the Chiana ; the highest point of the road is near Palazzuolo, 2000 ft. above the level of the sea. Descending from thence, by a very tortuous route, we pass the large village of Monte San Savino, situated on a hill above the river Esse, one of the large affluents of the Chiana ; between the Esse and the Chiana the road crosses obliquely 2 low ranges of tertiary hills parallel to the latter river, and 7 m. before arriving at Arezzo enters the Val di Chiana at the Pieve al Intoppo, 1 m. before reaching the Chiana. From this point the drive to the gates of the city over the low hills of L'Olmo, and across the Piano di Arezzo, is through an extremely rich and fertile country.

Arezzo. (See Rte. 27.)

ROUTE 26c.

CHIUSI TO SIENA, BY THE VAL DI CHIANA.

About 42 m.

There are 2 roads by which the traveller can proceed from Chiusi to Siena: the one by Rapolano, the other by Chianciano, Montepulciano, Torrita, and Asciano ; the latter is by several m. the longest, and with vetturino horses—for there are no post-stations on the road—will require 2 days, but it is by far the most interesting to those not pressed for time, as it will enable the tourist to visit the Baths at Chianciano, and the interesting town of Montepulciano ; the latter, where there is a tolerable locanda, may be reached in a morning's drive from Chiusi, and made the first day's resting-place.

The more direct road by Rapolano is

now travelled by a diligence, which, leaving Chiusi at a very early hour, arrives at Siena about 1 o'clock, in time for the railway train that reaches Florence at 6.45, and Leghorn at 8.30, on the same evening.

The road, on leaving Chiusi, runs round the base of the hill on which the town is built; that to Chianciano branching off to the l. soon afterwards. 3 m. farther, after passing the Granducal *fattoria* (farm) of Dolciano on the rt., it enters a marshy plain which separates the Lakes of Chiusi and Montepulciano, where malaria now exists to a greater degree than in any part of the Val di Chiana; following the l. bank of the latter lake to Acquaviva, near which there is another large Granducal farm, the road enters a series of low hills, passing by Nottula at the foot of the mountain on which Montepulciano stands; from here to Torrita the country is very beautiful.

Torrita. The town offers nothing of interest; there is a poor locanda outside the gate, where vetturini stop.

We do not enter the village, which is upon an elevation on the l.; before reaching Torrita the road from Montepulciano to Arezzo by Fojano branches off on the rt.

On leaving Torrita, the picturesquely situated town of Asinalunga (one of the several that, placed on the range of hills bordering the Val di Chiana, were out of the reach of its once pestilential malaria) is passed on the l.; near this a good road to Siena by Asciano branches off on the l. Here we enter the valley of the Föenna, one of the largest tributaries of the Chiana. At the Osteria of Palazzolo, the only place where the diligence changes horses, the traveller may obtain some refreshment in the shape of breakfast. The town perched on the hill above it is Rigomagno. A very gradual ascent of 4 m. through a well wooded valley leads to the highest point of the road, where the chain of hills forming the water-shed between the Chiana and the Ombrone is crossed by a low col (1260 feet above the level of the sea); across this pass it is proposed to carry the railway from Siena to Arezzo and the valley of

the Tiber. Near the summit is the small village of Serre, an important place in the mediæval warfare of the Tuscan republics. From Serre a very steep descent, by far the worst part of the road between Chiusi and Siena, brings us to

Rapolano, a picturesquely situated little town on a height, surrounded by walls, with a population of 2000 souls; it has some reputation as a watering-place, and is much frequented during the months of July and Aug. The waters, which contain a large proportion of carbonic and of sulphuretted hydrogen gases, are very efficacious in cutaneous complaints, and in rheumatic affections. The springs issue from the secondary limestone rock which constitutes the ridge of hills over which we have passed, although where they come to the surface they are surrounded by an extensive modern travertine deposit. The traveller who may wish to explore the surrounding country will find a very fair inn here, and, in the summer months, abundance of gaiety and society.

From Rapolano we enter the dreary region of the Crete Sanese, ascending the upper valley of the Ombrone to San Quirico. The contrast between this sterile region and the fertile Val di Chiana, which we have just traversed, is very striking. No country can be less interesting than the 10 m. from San Quirico to Taverne d' Arbia, 5 m. before reaching Siena, except to the palæontologist, who may make here an abundant and varied collection of the fossil marine shells of the subapennine formation.

Siena. (See Rte. 26.)

ROUTE 26D.

SIENA TO GROSSETO.

About 50 m.

This is a long day's journey, and has little to interest the traveller except Grosseto itself. It forms, connected with the rly., the most direct route between Florence and the southern Tuscan Maremma. A public conveyance starts from Siena during the winter months 3 times a-week, performing the journey in 15 hours.

4 m. from Siena a road branches off to the rt. at San Galgano, leading to Chiusdino, a forest district in the chain of secondary mountains W. of Siena, called the Montagnuola—the road to Grosseto continuing along the rt. side of the Merse to the Osteria of the Ponte a Macereto, from which continuing along the l. bank to Petriolo on the Farma, a steep ascent of 5 m. brings us to Casale, and a descent of 10 m. more to the village of Paganico, near the rt. bank of the Ombrone. Between this and Grosseto the road is hilly, but in excellent repair. At Batignano commences the descent into the plain of the Maremma along the Salica torrent, passing about 2 m. (on the l.) from the ruins of Roselle, and farther on the baths at the foot of the hill of Moscona; hence to Grosseto over a level tract of 5 m.

For Grosseto, see Rte. 25.

ROUTE 26 E.

FLORENCE TO VOLTERRA, THE BORACIC ACID LAGONI, AND MASSA MARITIMA.

The easiest and most economical mode of reaching Volterra from Florence or Leghorn is by Pontedera, on the Leopolda Railway. A diligence leaves the Pontedera Station every Tuesday, Thursday, and Saturday, on the arrival of the 2nd train from Florence, or about 12 o'clock, and reaches Volterra at 6 in the evening. Travellers arriving at Pontedera will always find vehicles for hire. A calessa for 1 person costs 15 pauls, and will perform the journey in 5 hours. Parties proceeding to Volterra will find very good calèches, which require but 5 hours on the road. A vetturino named Gambacorta has an excellent carriage and good horses, and can be strongly recommended for his attention and honesty. By writing to him before-

hand, at Pontedera, parties will save themselves trouble and extortion.

The road from Florence to Pontedera is described in the 'Handbook of N. Italy,' Rte. 42, and at p. 173, as far as Empoli, beyond which the stations are—

> San Pierino,
> La Rotta,
> San Romano, and
> Pontedera.

From the Railway station the road turns to the l., leaves the valley of the Arno to enter into that of the Era, and follows the W. side of the latter during the greater part of its length. The country is highly cultivated, producing corn, maize, grapes, and mulberry trees, whilst the hills on either side are covered with rich arborescent vegetation, and crowned with picturesque villages—the Val d' Era, in its lower part particularly, being considered one of the most fertile districts of Tuscany. 4 m. from Pontedera the road passes through the village of Ponsacco, and near the 8th mile that of Cassinoli, where there is a large villa belonging to the Bacciocchi family. A little farther on beyond the Era is seen the picturesque village of Piccioli, on a beautiful wooded declivity. Higher up, the river Sterza is crossed by a handsome bridge, about a m. above its junction with the Era. From this point the valley narrows, the soil becomes less productive—to the rich alluvial soil of lower down succeed the tertiary marine marls and sands. As we ascend the valley fine peeps of Volterra and of the mountains of Monte Catini come into view, the country becoming more bleak and barren. The village of Lajatico, a fief of the Corsini family, is left on the right, and after a gradual rise along the Ragone torrent the road reaches its highest point, the summit level between the valleys of the Era and Cecina, near the Osteria di Bachetona, 500 feet above the Arno at Pontedera. 3 roads branch off from this point, on the rt. to Monte Catini, on the l. to Volterra, whilst the continuation before us leads to the ford over the Cecina,

Pomarance, and to the Lagoni, and from thence to Massa.

The view from the Pass of La Bachetona is very fine, to the N. embracing the whole extent of the valley of the Era. closed by the rounded group of the Pisan hills, beyond which rise the Apennines of Modena and Lucca, amongst which the Peaks of La Pania form very remarkable objects in the panorama; in front and to the S. the clayey, arid region over which Volterra towers, with the river Cecina at its base, and beyond the wooded range of the Maremma, behind Pomarance, crowned by the mediæval castles of Rocca Silana, Monte Castelli, and Libiano, whilst on the rt. and nearer to where we are standing is the eruptive group of hills of Monte Catini, the village grouped round its high square tower, and the prolongation of the range by the mountains of Castellina and Monte Vaso to the shores of the Mediterranean.

From La Bachetona a good road of 5 miles leads to Volterra, ascending gradually along the summit of the ridge that separates the waters of the Cecina from those of the Era. Before reaching the city the ascent becomes more rapid, the road passing along the newly constructed promenade at the base of the Castle Hill, from which the prospect over the Val Cecina and Mediterranean is extremely fine.

Volterra (*Inns*, the Unione, kept by Ottaviano Callai, clean, comfortable, and moderate charges; La Corona, indifferent, chiefly frequented by people of the country. Giuseppe Callai, nephew of the master of the Unione, is a good cicerone). This is one of the most interesting towns in Italy, and travellers who are desirous of investigating the remains of one of the grandest Etruscan cities should not fail to visit it. Volterra retains more of its ancient character than any other Etruscan settlement. The remark of Maffei, that those who have not been at Volterra know nothing of Etruscan antiquity, although true, must be regarded as the testimony of a too partial witness. The town is situated on a lofty and commanding eminence, capped by

a tertiary sandstone full of marine shells, which rests upon a mass of blue clay, whose soft soil is so frequently washed away by the rains and torrents, that the neighbouring country presents a singular appearance of wild and sterile desolation. The hill of Volterra is bounded by the Era on the N., and by the Cecina on the S.; it is 1900 feet above the level of the sea. From all sides the ascent to the town is long and rapid. In spite of the dreary aspect of the country, the view from the summit of the hill, and especially from the citadel, is particularly striking; in clear weather it extends to the hills above Pisa and the distant Apennines, and commands a long line of sea, including Corsica and the northern extremity of the island of Caparaja. The pop. of the town is 4500.

Volterra nearly retains its ancient name of Velathri or Volaterræ. Although less is known of its early history than of that of Cortona, there is no doubt that it was a city of the league, and one of the most ancient settlements of Etruria. Its interest is so entirely Etruscan, that it would almost appear out of place to enter into details of its history during the middle ages, when its strong position between the republics of Pisa, Florence, and Siena naturally made it a place of great importance in the contests of the free cities. Like many other small towns of central Italy, it was for some time able to assert its independence, and was governed by its own consuls; but it gradually fell under the power of Florence, and from that time its history is to be traced in that of the Florentine republic.

The ancient walls are among the best characterised specimens of Etruscan architecture; they are constructed in horizontal courses without cement, and are composed of massive blocks of tertiary sandstone, here called *Panchina*. The greater part of the walls were ruined during the sieges of the middle ages, particularly in the capture of the city by Federigo di Montefeltro in 1472. They are supposed, from the remains still visible, to have been 6 m. in circuit, or about double the extent of those of Cortona and Fiesole. The most perfect fragments are seen outside the modern gates, below the ch. of Sta. Chiara, at a quarter of an hour's walk from the inn. Of 5 detached fragments one is 40 feet in height, and about 14 feet in thickness; the largest blocks being 10 feet long by 3 feet high. 2 of them have 2 square open sewers, with projecting sills, about 10 feet from the ground. The soil near them is gradually wasting away by the encroachments of the ravines, which threaten to undermine the foundations at no very distant period. One of the ancient gateways is still standing, in a fine state of preservation. It is called the *Porta all' Arco*, and is a circular double arch, nearly 30 feet deep and 21 feet high, formed of 19 immense masses, put together without cement. The keystone and the two pilasters have colossal heads sculptured on them, which were formerly supposed to be lions; but a bas-relief on one of the cinerary urns in the Museum, which appears to represent this gate, shows that they were probably human heads, representing the tutelary deities of the city. Within the gate the channel for the portcullis is still visible. Another gate, called the *Porta di Diana*, has been much altered; near it the ancient walls may also be traced for a considerable distance. Beyond this, about half-way down the hill, is the Necropolis, in the tombs of which were found the valuable objects now in the Museum. One tomb has been preserved in its original state, for the sake of travellers. It is a circular chamber, 18 feet in diameter, and about 6 feet in height; it is supported by a column forming part of the surrounding rock in the centre, and is surrounded by a triple tier of benches, on which are placed 40 or 50 small sarcophagi.

Of the other antiquities, of which some vestiges are still traceable, the most remarkable are the piscina and the baths. The *Piscina*, outside the gate of the fortress, can only be seen by permission of the bishop, and must be entered by a long ladder. It is a fine specimen of Etruscan architecture: the arches are sustained by 6 columns, and constructed with blocks of great solidity; in the vault are some apertures, evidently for the water-pipes. The *Thermæ* near the fountain of San Felice are clearly Roman, and consist of two baths and some smaller chambers, in which we may trace fragments of mosaic pavement and marble bas-reliefs. One bath is circular, the other square; from the substructions they appear to have been vapour-baths. In the Borgo di Montebradoni are remains of an Etruscan hypogeum, with some cinerary urns, &c. Near the Florence gate are traces of a Roman amphitheatre: but all these remains yield in interest to the museum in the Palazzo Pubblico, where most of the objects discovered in the tombs and ruins have been carefully preserved.

The *Palazzo Pubblico* was begun in 1208, and finished in 1257, as recorded in an inscription in the quaint Latin rhyme of the period. The tower was much shattered by the earthquake of 1826, and has been since rebuilt. The Gothic façade is covered with armorial shields; but the windows, as in most of the buildings which surround it, have been modernized. The two lions sustaining the arms of Florence were added when the Florentine republic acquired the sovereignty of Volterra, and appointed one of its own citizens to be captain of the people. The Palazzo contains the museum and public library. The *Museum* is one of the most interesting local collections in Italy; it was opened in 1731, and is chiefly indebted for its treasures to the munificence of Monsignore Mario Guarnacci, who bequeathed his Etruscan collections to the town in 1761; it is filled with tombs, statues, vases, coins, bronzes, pateræ, gold ornaments, mosaics, &c., collected in the Necropolis. The whole are arranged in 9 rooms. There are upwards of 400 cinerary urns, mostly of alabaster; some however are of tufa, and a few, the most ancient probably, in terracotta; they are square, and from 2 to 3 feet in length. On the lids are the recumbent figures of the deceased. Several of the urns have inscriptions

—among which the Cæcina (Ceicna), Flavia (Vlave), Gracchia (Cracne), and other well-known Etruscan families, may be recognised. The bas-reliefs of these urns, independently of their interest as works of art, are as instructive in affording an insight into the costumes and manners of the Etruscans. In truth, there is no place in Italy where the habits and civilization of Etruria can be better studied than in this museum. The bas-reliefs on some of the urns are coloured red, and one still retains traces of gilding. These sculptures represent various incidents of domestic life, and a most remarkable series of subjects illustrating every period of the Greek mythology. Among the scenes of domestic life are many of a very affecting character; death-bed scenes are favourite subjects, and the parting of husband and wife is frequently represented in various but touching forms. In some cases, the soul, symbolised by a figure on horseback, is represented setting out on its long journey, while a child, the sister probably of the deceased, is striving to detain it, and the messenger of death is hurrying it on, carrying over his shoulder a long sack like a purse, one end containing the good, the other the bad deeds of the deceased. In other bas reliefs, the soul on horseback is proceeding on its journey to the next world attended by Charon and a good genius. On another urn we see the funeral car drawn by horses with their heads hanging down as if in grief, conveying the body and the mourners to the tomb. On some, we see human sacrifices, and on others, sacrifices of asses, bulls, and wolves. On many of the urns are sculptured flowers; which are represented half-blown when the deceased was young, and full-blown when he was an adult. Funeral processions, triumphal processions, and the solemn processions of the judges, occur almost side by side with banquetings, and other familiar scenes of an Etruscan home; and even the representation of a female school is not wanting. Boar hunts, bull-fights, gladiatorial combats, and horse-races in the circus,

supply an instructive series of illustrations of Etruscan sports; while the events of ancient mythology, which are here represented, include almost every popular topic of ancient history or fable. Without entering into minute details, we may mention the following as the principal subjects of these sculptures: —Ulysses and the Syrens, Ulysses and Circe, the Rape of Helen, the Murder of Polites by Pyrrhus, the Death of Pyrrhus at Delphi, the Death of Clytemnestra, Orestes and Pylades, Orestes and the Furies, the Seven Chiefs before Thebes (three examples, one of which has a representation of the gate of Volterra), Polynices and Eteocles, Amphiaraus and Eriphyle, Œdipus and the Sphinx, Œdipus slaying his father Laius, Cadmus and the Dragon, Cadmus fighting the armed men who have sprung from the teeth of the Dragon, Perseus and Andromeda, the Centaurs and Lapithæ, Actæon and the Dogs, Cupid and Psyche, and the Rape of Proserpine. The 2 large urns or sarcophagi, which are rather more than 5 feet long, were found in 1760, in the tomb of the Flavian family. The one which bears a male figure on the lid has on its front a funeral procession; the other, which bears a female figure, has two very touching groups representing a mother with her children taking leave of her husband, and the same mother fondling her child after her bereavement. The walls of the 8th chamber are covered with Etruscan inscriptions, and with fragments from the Roman baths. In the 9th is a portion of a mosaic found in the baths in 1761; and the headless statue of a female with a child in her arms, discovered by Maffei in the amphitheatre, and supposed by Gori to be the Dea Norcia of the Etruscans. It bears an inscription on the right arm, which has been illustrated by Lanzi. A bas-relief representing a bearded soldier the size of life, with an Etruscan inscription, is considered by Micali, Gori, and other archæologists, as the oldest relic in the museum; it formed probably the side of the door to a sepulchre. In presses ranged round this room are contained numerous smaller Etruscan antiquities

—bronzes, smaller vases, inscriptions, &c.; some of the bronzes are very beautiful—such as handles of vases, ornaments of horse-trappings, &c.; there is also a good collection of coins, those of Volterra of a very rude style, presenting the principal interest. A small series of cameos and intaglios, and a fine specimen in silver gilt of that peculiar ornament, the *bulla*, so frequently represented in Etruscan costumes, recently found in one of the Volterra tombs. In the great Hall of the Magistratura, in the Palazzo Pubblico, and above the Museum, is the Public Library, containing 13,000 volumes: it was also founded and endowed by the same public spirited prelate, Guarnacci. Besides the printed books it contains a series of the Acts of the Law Courts of the City extending as far back as the end of the 13th century. There are also some good ivory sculptures, in the form of boxes for wedding presents, and 2 very fine crozier heads also in ivory, which belonged to the Abbot of the Carthusian Monastery of the Badia, and to a Bishop of Volterra in the 12th century. At one extremity of the Sala de la Magistratura, the wall is covered by a large fresco, attributed to one of the Orcagnas; it represents the Annunciation and Saints; unfortunately it has suffered a good deal by modern retouches.

The *Cathedral*, consecrated by Calixtus II. in 1120, was enlarged in 1254 by *Niccolò di Pisa*, and restored and embellished in the 16th century by Leonardo Ricciarelli, a nephew of Daniele da Volterra. The façade is entirely of the 13th century, but the door of black and white marble appears to be more recent. The interior is imposing. It is in the form of a Latin cross, and retains all the characteristics of the original design of *Niccolò di Pisa.* The Corinthian capitals in stucco were added to the columns in 1574 by *Leonardo Ricciarelli,* who adorned the roof of the side aisles with the armorial bearings of the families which had contributed to the embellishment of the fabric. Inside the principal door are bas-reliefs representing the translation of the body of St. Octavian to this cathedral; it was originally interred in the ch. dedicated to the saint on a hill 4 m. N. of Volterra, and was brought hither in the year 820 by Bishop Andrea. The bas-reliefs were formerly placed on the exterior wall of the cathedral, and were removed to their present position in 1767. Near this is an altar of mosaic, a great part of which was the work of *Mino da Fiesole,* who was also the sculptor of the two kneeling angels on the beautiful spiral columns on each side of the choir. On the l. of the great door is the marble tomb of the learned Marie Maffei, bishop of Cavaillon, secretary of the Sacred College, and Nuncio of Julius II. at Paris, and on the rt. that of Archbishop Incontri, a good modern work by Costoli. The vault of the choir was once covered with frescoes by Niccolò Circignani; nothing now remains of these works but the painting representing the Almighty. The marble pulpit is covered with bas-reliefs, which are probably not later than the 13th century. It is supported by 4 columns of Elba granite, resting on the backs of monsters. The bas-relief in the front represents the Last Supper; in the interior are 3 others, Abraham sacrificing Isaac, the Salutation, and the Annunciation, with the names of each person engraved above them. In the chapel of the Inghirami family, in the N. transept, are some frescoes by *Giovanni da S. Giovanni,* representing events in the life of St. Paul, and a painting by *Domenichino,* of his conversion, much injured by retouching; it is said that Domenichino received for this work 800 scudi. The other pictures of the chapel are the Martyrdom of St. Paul by *Francesco Curradi,* formerly attributed to Guercino; and the Saint receiving letters relating to the Christians of Damascus, by *Matteo Rosselli.* This chapel was built in 1615 by Gen. Jacopo Inghirami, a celebrated captain of the 16th century, called the "flagello de' Barbereschi e de' Turchi." In the chapel of the SS. Sacramento, built by Bishop Serguidi, is the Resurrection of Lazarus by *Santi di Tito,* with the inscription Santi Titi, F. 1592. The altar was designed by Vasari. The side walls are painted by *Giovanni Balducci* ·

and the stuccoes of the vault are by *Leonardo Ricciarelli,* whose portrait has been introduced by Balducci. In the Gherardi chapel is an Annunciation, with an inscription on the back, B.M.F. ("Bartolommeo me fece"); it was formerly attributed to Ghirlandaio. The fine Presentation in the Temple is by *Giobattista Naldini.* Over the door of the cloister is a bust of S. Lino by *Luca della Robbia.* In the chapel of the Rosary is the St. Sebastian, by *Francesco Cungi* of Borgo S. Sepolcro. In the chapel dedicated to St. Octavian is the beautiful marble tomb of the saint, executed by *Raffaello Cioli deo Settignano,* in 1525, at the expense of the people of Volterra, who were desirous of commemorating their delivery from the plague of 1522 through the supposed intercession of the saint. The 2 angels at the sides are by *Andrea Ferruzzi.* The fine picture of the Virgin, with St. Francis, St. John, and other saints at the high altar, is considered the master-piece of *Il Volterrano :* the beauty of the head of St. John is particularly remarkable. The oratory of San Carlo; an Annunciation by *Luca Signorelli,* painted in 1491; the Virgin with saints and angels, a beautiful work, by *Leonardo da Pistoja;* the Magdalen *della Radice,* by *Camillo Incontri,* a scholar of Guido, who retouched the head and some other portions; and the Nativity by *Benvenuto da Siena,* dated 1470; a Crucifixion, by *Rosso Fiorentino;* a Virgin and Child, by *Filippo Lippi;* S. Joseph, by *Il Volterrano,* one of his earliest works; a small Crucifixion, by *Sodoma.* The chapel of the Virgin contains the frescoes of *Benozzo Gozzoli,* representing the Nativity and the Adoration of the Magi; the representation of the SS. Nome di Gesu, executed on wood by *S. Bernardino da Siena,* was presented by him to the town in 1424, when he introduced his new religious order. There is an epitaph in this cathedral to the memory of Bishop Cæcina of Volterra, who died in 1765, and who is supposed to have been the last of the illustrious race of Cæcina, whose name for so many ages had been associated with Volterra. The Sacristy, celebrated for its relics, has a silver reliquiary, re-markable for its elaborate workmanship, containing 4 pieces of the true cross.

The neighbouring ch. of *S. Giovanni,* supposed to occupy the site of a Temple of the Sun, is an octagonal Gothic building, referred to the 7th century. The doorway of black and white marble is very curious, and the capitals of the Gothic columns are full of animals and birds. Over the architrave are 13 heads in bas-relief representing the Virgin and the Twelve Apostles. The rich arch of the high altar is covered with festoons of flowers and fruits, beautifully sculptured by *Balsimelli da Settignano* in the 16th century. The fine picture of the Ascension is by *Niccolò Circignani;* it bears his name and the date 1591. The ancient Baptismal font, now used as an altar-table, with its beautiful bas-reliefs, was sculptured by *Andrea Sansovino* in 1502, and the *Ciborio,* formerly on the high altar of the Cathedral, bears the name of *Mino da Fiesole,* with the date 1471.

The ch. and monastery of *San Lino* were founded in 1480 by Raffaello Maffei, and finished in 1517, at the cost of 80,000 scudi. It contains the tomb of the founder, erected by his brother Mario, whose mausoleum has been mentioned in the description of the cathedral. The tomb is of white marble; the statue of Maffei is by *Mino da Fiesole;* the ornaments are by *Fra Angelo Montorsoli;* and the statues of the Archangel Raphael and of the Beato Gherardo Maffei, the Franciscan, are by *Stagio.* Raffaello Maffei, who was born at Volterra in 1451, obtained considerable reputation as a theologian and philosopher; he was the founder of the Accademia Letteraria de' Sepolti, the author of the "Commentarii Urbani," dedicated to Julius II., and the translator of the Odyssey. He was appointed by Sixtus IV. secretary to the Cardinal of Aragon on his mission into Hungary, and was employed by the same pope in other important negotiations. His brother Antonio Volterrano is well known as one of the leading personages in the conspiracy of the Pazzi. The picture of the Virgin and S. Lino is by *Francesco Curradi,* and is inscribed "Ser

Curradi, 1597." The 5 lunettes and 1 of the altarpieces are by *Cosimo Daddi.*

The ch. of *S. Francesco,* founded in the 13th century by the Comune and citizens, was rebuilt in 1623, and has undergone many subsequent alterations. It contains several tombs of the Guidi family, among which is that of Jacopo Guidi, bishop of Penna and Atri, the pupil of Guicciardini, with whom he was sent on a mission from Cosmo I. to the courts of Madrid and Paris. He wrote a life of the grand duke, and died in 1588. At the altar of the Maffei family is a picture of the Virgin and Child with saints, by *Luca Signorelli.* The Gabbretani altar has a clever Nativity by *Giovanni Balducci,* in 1591. The Conception is by *Giobattista Naldini,* 1585. The altarpiece of the Guarnacci chapel is by *Cosimo Daddi.* The celebrated Mario Guarnacci, founder of the museum, and one of the very earliest Etruscan scholars, is buried here. His tomb was erected in his lifetime.

Adjoining this Ch. is the Gothic chapel belonging to the *Confraternità della Croce di Giorno,* built in 1315. The interior is covered with frescoes which have suffered much from the effects of damp and time, and some of them are partially defaced. On the blue vault are the 4 Evangelists, by *Jacopo Orcagna,* in 1410. The paintings on the walls by Cenno di Francesco di Ser Cenni, according to the inscription, represent, in different compartments, the Massacre of the Innocents, the Recovery of the True Cross, &c. These frescoes are interesting for the costumes of the period which they represent, especially of the females, so little different from those now in use. This Cenno di Ser Cenni is supposed to be *Cennino Cennini da Colle,* the pupil of Agnolo Gaddi. The Crucifixion at the high altar is by *Sodoma.*

The *Ch. of S. Agostino,* built in the 16th century, and restored in 1728, contains a Crucifixion by *Francesco Curradi,* dated 1611, and 2 paintings by *Il Volterrano* (Franceschini): 1 with an inscription, and the date 1669; the other representing the . Purification,

painted in 1630, when he fled to Volterra to escape the danger of the plague, which was then raging in Florence. This Ch. is celebrated for its relics; the miraculous picture of the Crucifixion, at the Falconcini altar, is still regarded with great veneration.

The *Ch. of S. Michele,* founded in 1285, and restored by the Fathers of the Scuole Pie in 1828, contains a fine picture of the Madonna and Child with St. Joseph, by *Carlo Maratta.* At the altar of S. Giuseppe Calasanzio, founder of this order, is a painting of the saint by *Giuseppe Zocchi.* The Scuole Pie were established in the adjoining convent in 1711. The present Pope Pius IX. received his education here.

The *Ch. of San Giusto,* in the suburb of the same name, is a good specimen of the architecture of the 16th century.

The *Citadel* is divided into 2 portions: the Cassero, or the Rocca Vecchia, and the Rocca Nuova. The Cassero was built in 1343 by Walther de Brienne, duke of Athens, then lord of Volterra. Its foundations partly rest on the ancient Etruscan walls. The Rocca Nuova was built by the Florentines, after they had reduced the city to obedience. At the same time they constructed, on the site of the old episcopal palace, the famous prison called *Il Mastio.* This is one of the most formidable prisons of Tuscany, and was formerly used for state offenders. It has acquired some celebrity as the scene of the long confinement of the great mathematician Lorenzo Lorenzini, the scholar of Viviani. He was imprisoned here in 1682 by Cosmo III., on the unfounded suspicion of being one of the chief instruments in the correspondence between the Grand-Duchess Margaret of Orleans and Prince Ferdinand, to whose court he was attached. He remained a prisoner until the prince's death in 1693. During the 11 years of his captivity he composed the work on Conic Sections which exists in manuscript, in the Magliabecchiana library at Florence. The Citadel has of late years been converted into a prison for men condemned to lengthened periods of imprisonment. The cellular and silent system is now adopted in it.

At present it contains upwards of 300 prisoners, some for most atrocious crimes, others for political offences, the Torre del Mastio being exclusively set apart for the latter class of offences. Permission may easily be obtained on application to the *Pretore* or Governor of Volterra to visit the prisons in all their details.

Behind the hospital of S. Maria Maddalena is a building erroneously called the Torre degli Auguri. An inscription still visible over the door in Gothic characters shows that it was built in 1299 by the Hospitalers of S. Giacomo in Altopascio.

The *Casa Guarnacci* with its 3 towers has an inscription over the door in Gothic characters, which shows that the first tower was erected at the beginning of the 13th century, and records the name of its architect, Giroldo da Lugano.

The *Casa Ducci* is remarkable for the inscription on the façade commemorating a young child of the family of Persius, who is claimed as a native of Volterra. The inscription is as follows:—A. PERSIVS A. F. SEVERVS V. ANN. VIII. M. III. D. XIX.

The *Casa Ricciarelli*, still occupied by the descendants of *Daniele da Volterra*. It contains a fine oil painting of Elijah by that great artist, who was born here in 1509, and died in Paris in 1566. The *Casa Masselli* in the Via del Crocifisso contains another example of this master in the ceiling of a small room which he painted in fresco.

The *Fountain of San Felice*, near the gate of the same name, has obtained some repute for its mineral waters, which possess the aperient properties of the sea-water. They are much used in dyspeptic complaints.

The *Alabaster Manufactories* of Volterra are well worth visiting; they have much increased in importance of late years, and not less than one-half of the male pop. of Volterra are employed in one way or other in the trade; the great markets being the United States, India, China, and in Europe, Russia. Nearly all the vases and ornamental works seen in the shops of Florence and Leghorn come from Volterra, hence they can be obtained cheaper here, and as there are several shops in the place, travellers will be able to make their selection on the spot, and at prices inferior to those asked at Florence and Leghorn. The commoner varieties of alabaster used for vases, &c., are found in the vicinity of the town, but the finer qualities of white statuary alabaster have been brought until lately from the quarries of La Castellina, S. of Leghorn. The landlord of the Unione will have any objects carefully packed, and forwarded to England or the United States.

The *Environs* of Volterra abound in objects which would afford interesting occupation to the traveller for many days. The *Villa Inghirami*, in the valley to the E. of the town, is remarkable for the extraordinary labyrinth in the rock, called the *Buche de' Saracini*, on the principle which assigns to the Saracens every wonder on the coast of Italy. One of the most remarkable objects in the neighbourhood of Volterra is the deep chasm called the *Balze*, produced by the action of water during many centuries on the clayey and marly soil of the surrounding hills. There is no place in Tuscany where the operation of this cause has been attended with more disastrous consequences. The upper part of the ravine or chasm is composed, like the tableland on which Volterra stands, of a tertiary sandstone resting on a thick bed of blue clay; as the subjacent marls are washed away by the rains, large portions of the more solid superincumbent rock are continually falling from the top without having any apparent effect in filling up the abyss. It is known from authentic documents that the site now occupied by the ravine was a highly cultivated spot, well wooded, and covered with habitations in the 7th century; about the end of the 16th century the sides were observed to be gradually undermined by the water which had penetrated through the porous strata; in 1627 the ch. of San Giusto was engulfed; and in 1651 its rapid increase compelled the removal of another ch., which had previously appeared to be beyond the reach of danger. Cosmo II. made an attempt to check the progress of this mischief, and several plans were subsequently tried to collect the waters into another channel; but all have been unsuccessful, and the inhabitants observe with great regret that the danger is gradually approaching the celebrated Camaldolese monastery of S. Salvatore.

The Camaldolese monastery called the *Badia di San Salvatore,* situated on the N.W. extremity of the hill of Volterra, and about 1 m. from the town, was founded in the 11th century for the Camaldolese monks. It has a noble cloister, and contains many fine works of art well worthy of a visit. At the altar of S. Romualdo is the fine picture by *Domenico Ghirlandaio* representing S. Romualdo, S. Benedict, S. Attina, and S. Greciniana. It is in admirable preservation, and is well known to artists by the engraving of Diana Mantovana, wife of the architect Capriani. At the altar of the SS. Sacramento is the Nativity of the Virgin, by *Donato Mascagni* (1599). At the altar della Pietà is the Deposition from the Cross, by *Gio. Paolo Rossetti,* and at another altar is the Nativity of the Saviour by the same master. The S. Benedict and S. Romualdo at the sides of the organ are by *Il Volterrano.* In the apartment of the Abbot is the fine picture of Job by *Donato Mascagni,* by whom are the frescoes relative to the life of S. Giusto, and the oil painting of the Marriage of Cana, in the Refectory. In one of the adjoining rooms there is a series of pictures representing various events in the history of Volterra, attributed to *Ghirlandaio.*

A very interesting excursion may be made from Volterra to the Copper Mines of La Cava, near Monte Catini, 7 m. distant. A light gig may be hired to go and return for 12 pauls. Leaving the city, we follow the same road as far as the Inn of La Bachetona, from which another excellent one, made by the proprietors of the mines, brings us, in ¼ an hour, to the village of Monte Catini, where there is a very fair country Inn and Café, in which the geological traveller who may wish to prolong his stay in this interesting district, will find fair accommodation.

The village of Monte Catini is situated on the summit of a hill on the l. of the road; it presents nothing remarkable except the high square tower, all that remains of the ancient Castle, and which forms so striking an object in the landscape for many miles around. About a m. beyond the town is the Mining establishment of Caporciano or La Cava. The mines of Monte Catini have of late years acquired much celebrity from the richness and abundance of their copper ores, and are now very productive. They appear to have been worked as far back as the 17th century: in 1827 they were re-opened by a company, who, after 10 years' labour, abandoned them, when they became the property of some English gentlemen, Messrs. Sloane and Hall, since which they have attained an unexampled prosperity, at least in the history of Italian mining.

The country in which they are situated is of a very peculiar geological character. As the traveller reaches Monte Catini, he will observe that it forms part of a group of pointed hills, very different in form and general appearance from all others in the surrounding country. They are also very different mineralogically, being formed of a singular rock of igneous or eruptive origin, which, from its colour, has been called *Gabbro Rosso* by the Tuscan geologists, and which has much analogy with certain porphyries, and especially with those so rich in mineral wealth in the New World; this *Gabbro Rosso,* which has risen through the surrounding limestone at a comparatively recent period, constitutes the peaks of Monte S. Antonio, Poggio alle Croce, and Monte Massi. The mine of La Cava is excavated entirely in the latter hill—the house or villa of La Cava and the principal works being at its base. The metalliferous deposit is of as peculiar nature as the rock in which it is situated, commencing at the surface in the form of a narrow vein, which gradually widens on descending, and which swells out in some places to the breadth of several feet. The ore being in the form of large globular masses, imbedded in a steatite rock, which fills up the vein. The geologist will obtain, on application to the very intelligent engineer, Mr. Schneider, who directs the works, every facility for examining them. The mine is now worked on 5 different levels, the lowest 510 feet below the surface. Hitherto the only power used for removing the water and the ores has been by horses; but in consequence of the extension of the works and the accumulation of the water, a magnificent adit-level, of nearly an English m. in length, is nearly completed. The ores consist of various sulphurets of copper, varying in richness from 20 to 80 per cent., but averaging nearly 30; the quantity extracted is upwards of 1000 tons annually, and which will be considerably increased when the new adit has reached the vein. From the want of fuel and of the necessary water-power for dressing the ores near the mine, they are carried to the smelting establishment of La Briglia, in the valley of the Bisenzio, near Prato. The quantity of copper produced from the ores of La Cava at present approaches 300 tons annually, the whole of which is either consumed in Tuscany or in the neighbouring Italian States.

The visitor to the works of La Cava will be not less gratified with the admirable manner in which the underground works are conducted than with the general system of management at the surface. Schools of both sexes for the miners' children have been established, a handsome church has been erected and liberally endowed, savings banks formed, and, at stated periods, marriage portions awarded to the young females of the workmen's families; music and drawing-schools established for the occupation of the workmen during their leisure hours; and all this by the owners of the mine, from their profits in the undertaking. No care or expense is spared by these benevolent gentlemen in contributing to the moral and physical wants of their dependants; and every one who may visit La Cava will come away gratified to have wit-

nessed such a degree of comfort and contentment amongst the working population, as is rarely met with in mining disticts.

Before leaving La Cava, the traveller ought to ascend to the summit of the Monte Massi—a walk of ½ an hour; there is, perhaps, no point in Central Italy from which a more magnificent panorama will open before him, embracing from the Mountains of Massa and Carrara, at the N.-western extremity of Tuscany, to Mont' Amiata, at its southern limit; from no place will he be able to form a more correct notion of the physical features of Central Italy generally, and of the immediate provinces of Volterra and the Maremma. Monte Massi is 1910 feet above the sea, and 1800 above the subjacent valley of the Cecina.

The geological tourist will find Monte Catini the most convenient point from which he can visit the mines of Miemo, Castellina, and Monte Vaso. There will be much to interest him in the vicinity connected with the metamorphic action of the igneous Gabbro Rosso on the stratified rocks through which it has made its way to the surface. There is perhaps no point in Europe more interesting in this respect; the sections laid open in making the new road between the village of Monte Catini and La Cava are most instructive.

On leaving Monte Catini the traveller need not return to Volterra, but proceed from the Osteria of La Bachetona by the direct road to Pomarance, 11 m. distant.

A rapid descent of 5 m., in the midst of bare marl hills, leads from La Bachetona to the Moje, or salt works of S. Leopoldo, (to which there is also a direct road of the same length from Volterra. These works, which furnish the principal supply of salt for Tuscany, produce annually upwards of 22 millions of pounds, entirely derived from the evaporation of the neighbouring brine springs. The springs, now 8 in number, are situated at a short distance from the evaporating-pans, to which the salt water is conveyed by means of wooden pipes; the wells varying in depth from 80 to 100 feet, are sunk in the tertiary shelly marls which form the soil on either side of the Cecina, and, from recent borings, there can be no doubt as to their origin, 4 very thick beds of rock-salt having been met with between the surface and the depth of 300 feet. There are many other brine-springs on either side of the Cecina, but are not used, the production of salt being a government monopoly, and those of Le Moje sufficing for the consumption of the Duchy. The fuel employed for the 4 evaporating-pans is exclusively wood, which the forests of the neighbouring hills furnish in abundance, and which the owners, under certain conditions, are obliged to dispose of to the government. The salt produced is beautifully white and pure: from its sale the Granducal Treasury derives a revenue of 4,100,000 lire, = 137,000*l.* Attached to the works is a Palace, inhabited by the director, and where the Grand Duke sometimes resides; but the malaria is so dangerous here during the summer and autumnal months as to oblige the principal employés to take refuge at Volterra.

Leaving the Moje, a low range of hills is crossed before reaching the Cecina, which must now be forded, the suspension-bridge that formerly existed having been carried away, and not replaced, to the very great inconvenience of the countries beyond the river. In ordinary times there is little danger in crossing the Cecina, but in the rainy season the passage is often rendered impossible for days together. During the floods no one ought to attempt the ford without an experienced guide. From the opposite bank a good road of 5 m. leads to Pomarance, constantly ascending over the tertiary shelly marls, here very abundant in beds of white gypsum or alabaster. Pomarance is situated at the summit of the ascent, although it cannot be seen until we arrive close to the gate.

There is little to interest the stranger in this small town; in the principal ch. there is a picture by *Pomerancio* (Cristoforo Roncalli), who was born here. Pomarance is also the country of the celebrated anatomist Mascagni,

Cent. It.

as we are told by an inscription over the door of the house where he was born. Count Lardarel has a very large palace in the town, where all strangers, known to him, will be most hospitably received. There is a small road-side inn, where persons intending to visit the Boracic Acid Works will find decent accommodation.

Lardarello, formerly called the Lagoni di Monte Cerboli, is the principal of Count Lardarel's establishments, and where the different manufacturing operations, as well as the singular circumstances that accompany the production of the boracic acid, can be most conveniently examined and studied. It is about 6 m. from Pomarance, by a good carriage-road, the high road to Massa, and the innkeeper of the Locanda will supply the necessary vehicle to reach it: every facility will be afforded to strangers by the director of the works, to whom they should apply on arrival at Lardarello. If scientifically disposed, the traveller will find a very obliging and well-informed guide in the resident apothecary of Count Lardarel's establishment.

Although some changes have occurred since it was written, we cannot do better than insert the following account of the works, as furnished to the editor by Mr. Babbage:—

"The district in which the Lagoni occur is one of the most singular countries in the world. Near the village of Monte Cerboli, in the midst of a deep, rugged and broken ravine, is one of the 8 establishments for extracting boracic acid from the earth. From the whole surface of a large space, probably a square mile of the broken ground, there issues a large volume of steam, which rises high in the atmosphere before it is absorbed, and may be seen at the distance of many miles. In the midst of this fog of steam, on a small plain forming a kind of island, stands a village containing the cottages of the workmen, the evaporating chambers, the store-houses, and a church recently built. The process of preparing the boracic acid is the following: on excavating a few inches into any part of the broken

L

ground, steam issues with great force, driving with it mud and even stones with a violent noise. One or two feet is quite deep enough for the object required. A small dwarf wall is rudely made round this opening, and thus a large cup-shaped pool is formed of from 10 to 40 feet in diameter. Into this cavity a small stream of water is conveyed until it is nearly full. The cold water going down into the cavity becomes greatly heated, and is driven violently upward by the steam thus formed. The whole of the water becomes heated by this constant regurgitation from the heated cavity, and at the end of about 24 hours it has absorbed nearly 1 per cent. of boracic acid. After a period of repose in another excavation, in which the mud is deposited, this solution is conveyed into large evaporating pans. A powerful jet of steam from one of the large holes made in the broken ground is conveyed in a kind of drain to the evaporating-house, and passes in flues under every part of the evaporating-vessels. The water is thus carried off into the atmosphere, and the boracic acid remains. These works are now in the most flourishing condition owing to the sagacity of the Chevalier Lardarel, now Count of Monte Cerboli. About 10 years since, the cost of the fuel by which the water was evaporated was so great that little boracic acid was procured, and it scarcely repaid the labour and cost of production. The Count conceived the happy idea of employing the heat which nature so plentifully offered, and thus dispensed with the whole expense of fuel. The result of this plan of converting volcanic heat to commercial purposes has been the establishment of villages and a thriving population in a locality which was previously almost a desert. About 10 years ago the whole of the borax consumed in England was imported from the East Indies; at present more than half the demand is supplied from the boracic acid works of Tuscany."

To this very clear description we may add, that the quantity of boracic acid now produced falls little short of 4 millions of Tuscan pounds, or 1340 tons

annually; that the greater part of this is exported to England, where, being converted into borax, it is extensively employed in the manufacture of all kinds of pottery-ware, and even glass: that so great is the demand at present, that double the quantity produced would find a ready market; and that there is every reason to believe, ere many years have elapsed, the produce will be decupled under the improvements introduced by the enterprising owner of the Lagoni, aided by the discoveries in manufacturing chemistry.

The number of workmen employed at Lardarello exceeds 300, who are lodged on the spot, in most comfortable dwellings, at the expense of the proprietor, who has recently erected a very handsome villa for himself and his employés, a church and schools for the children of the workpeople. Everything is done here, as we have seen at La Cava, to contribute to the comfort and well being of his people by the proprietor; and however unhealthy their occupation may appear, or insalubrious the mephitic vapour in which they breathe, it is gratifying to know that there is less mortality than in most mining districts, and as the traveller may assure himself, that in no part of Italy is there to be met with a more healthy and robust class of men than the labourers at the Boracic Works of Lardarello.

It may not be irrelevant here to say a few words on the scientific history of these extraordinary emanations. As the traveller enters the valley of the Possera, in which the Lagoni of Lardarello are situated, he will find it nearly closed up at its northern extremity by a range of serpentine hills, on the highest of which are perched the ruins of a monastery, dedicated to St. Michael, whilst at its base, on a conical mount, is the picturesque village of Monte Cerboli, ½ m. beyond which is the modern town of Lardarello, entirely occupied by the Boracic Works and the dwellings of the workmen. This valley continues for about 3 m., closed at the opposite extremity by the mountain of Castel Novo, at the foot of which the high road to Massa crosses. The sides of this valley are formed of inclined strata of Alberese limestone, belonging to the same geological period as the chalk of our islands, and it is from the fissures in this rock that the boracic vapours issue. The space from which they rise does not exceed 2 square m.; it is impossible to say from what depth they proceed; on arriving at the surface their temperature is at least that of boiling water. They contain, in addition to boracic acid, sulphuretted hydrogen in considerable quantity, but no careful examination has hitherto been made of their chemical composition,

Although Lardarello is the most productive of all the Boracic Acid Works, it is only one of the nine establishments founded by Count Lardarel—the others being Castelnovo, Sasso, Monte Rotondo, Lago Lustignano, San Eduardo, San Federigo, and Serrazzano. If the traveller will cast his eye over the map of the district occupied by these several localities, he will see that it embraces a very limited area, scarcely 30 English square m., between the sources of the Cornia and Cecina, and that each of these gaseous emanations is situated in valleys descending like so many fissures or cracks from a central point, under which probably, but from what depth it is impossible to say, all these extraordinary eruptions emanate.

A tour to the different establishments of Count Lardárel will well repay the time spent by the scientific traveller: he will be received with the greatest attention at each, where the hospitable proprietor has a comfortable house, and we can assure him that he will find nowhere the door closed against him. Good carriage roads communicate between the different works. They may be visited at all seasons of the year, although the most favourable will be in the early spring, or after the rainy season in the autumn. The best mode of proceeding will be, after having visited Lardarello, to cross to Castelnovo, thence to Sasso, Monte Rotondo, Lago Lustignano, and Serrazzano, from which, by a fair country road of 9 m., the tourist can return to Pomarance.

Should the traveller not wish to prolong his journey to Massa, 16 m. from Castelnovo, he may make an interesting excursion to the ruined Castle of Rocca Silana, a curious monument of the middle ages; about 8 m. distant. For the first 4 m. the road is the same as that to Monte Cerboli, from which turning off to the l., it crosses the Possera by a curiously constructed bridge, one of the piers being upon an immense boulder, from which it ascends to the village of San Dalmazzo : here the carriage must be abandoned; the path ascends rapidly, although still suited for horses, for 3 m. through a very picturesque country, until the pinnacle on which Rocca Silana stands is reached.

The Castle of Rocca Silana is situated on the summit of a peak of serpentine, and in so elevated a position (1760 feet above the sea) as to be visible for many miles around, and to form one of the most prominent objects in the landscape of this part of the province of Volterra; it consists of a square castle in the centre, having remains of a keep, and 4 octagonal turrets at the angles; but the walls, instead of forming a plane surface from angle to angle, are convex outwards; the masonry is very beautiful, formed of square blocks of limestone below and of brick above, surmounted by a cornice. The interior, now a waste, is occupied by a continuous arched vaulting that runs round three of its sides, the fourth being occupied by the foundations of the tower, and the small door the only entrance.

A fortified line of wall, with square towers at intervals, surrounds the castle on 2 sides—the others being amply defended by the vertical precipice on which it stands. The gateway to this outer line of defence is a very good specimen of military mediæval architecture; the entrance is by a zigzag covered way, once furnished with 3 gates, the innermost being almost entire.

Little is known of the history of Rocca Silana, except that it was during the 13th and 14th centuries a constant subject of contention between Volterra and its more powerful neighbours of Siena and Florence. It is almost needless to say that there is not the most remote authority for supposing it to have been a Roman work, or to have any connexion with Sylla, as its name might imply, and as there exists a belief in the country around. The view from the Castle is magnificent, extending to the Apennines on one side and to Mont Amiata on the other, embracing a great part of the provinces of Volterra and Siena.

The tourist may prolong his excursion to the copper mines in the valley of the Pavone beneath, by a very accessible path for a pedestrian, and thence ascend to the village of Monte Castelli, situated at almost an equal elevation, and on the opposite side of the valley from Rocca Silana. These mines are situated on what has much the appearance of a vein in the serpentine, and belong to the owners of those of La Cava. They are well worked, but hitherto to little advantage. Their situation is a most picturesque one, at the bottom of a deep rent, through which the river has cut its way to the Cecina; the sides of the ravine, formed of black, arid serpentine, give to the scene around a picture of devastation and horror, with the ruined Castle of Rocca Silana frowning from its eagle's nest over the abyss beneath. Monte Castelli is a small village, chiefly inhabited by the miners. It has, as its name indicates, the ruins of a mediæval castle. From it there is a very fair road to San Dalmazzo, or instead of returning through it from the mines, the tourist can proceed on foot by a rugged path to S. Dalmazzo, passing the ruined ch. of La Pieve, a good specimen of the Lombardo Gothic style of the 13th century.

A very good, although hilly, carriage road of 26 m. leads from Pomarance to Massa, over the first 6 of which we have already travelled in going to Lardarello. From the latter place the route continues along the Valley of the Possera 1 m. above the boracic acid works to Bagno a Morbo, where there is a bathing establishment, much frequented in the middle ages, mentioned by Dante, and celebrated for having effected the cure of Lorenzo de Medicis. There is a large lodging-house, close to the hot springs, where a good *pension* has been established for the bathers. The baths are efficacious in rheumatic and paralytic affections. There is a second bathing establishment, also much frequented in July and August, ½ m. higher up the valley. A gradual ascent of 2 m. farther brings us to the pass between the valleys of the Possera and Pavone, near to which we come on the line of Lagonis of Castelnovo, which extend to a much greater elevation than in the Valley of Monte Cerboli. The village of Castelnovo, with a population of 1500 souls, is built on the declivities of a hill about 1 m. from the rt. bank of the Pavone: it has a small dirty locanda. To persons wishing to visit Monte Rotondo, Sasso, and the mountain of Gerfalco, it may serve as a halting-place.

From Castelnovo to Massa the distance is called 16 m., but from the hilly nature of the road it can scarcely be travelled in less than 14 hours; it ascends the ridge of hills separating the upper sources of the Cornia and Pavone, leaving, about 2 m. on the rt., Bruciano, Sasso, and Monte Rotondo. Arrived at the summit of the pass, there is a fine view of the valley of the Cornia, extending to the Mediterranean, the island of Elba, &c. From this point we descend constantly to Massa. (See Rte. 25.) Instead of proceeding by the carriage-road, the pedestrian will do well to proceed from Castelnovo to Sasso, thence to Monte Rotondo, and by a cross bridle-road to the coal-mines (Lignite) of Monte Bamboli, 6 m. W.N.W. of Massa.

The high conical peak, called the Cornata of Gerfalco, forms a very remarkable object on our l. in the journey from Castelnovo to Massa. Although having a form so common in volcanic countries, it is formed entirely of secondary strata, and will be well worth a visit from the geological traveller. It consists of beds of limestone and of red calcareous shales, abundant in fossils analogous to those of the lias and inferior oolitic formations of Northern Europe.

ROUTE 27.

FLORENCE TO ROME, BY THE VAL D'ARNO DI SOPRA, AREZZO, CORTONA, PERUGIA, ASSISI, FOLIGNO, SPOLETO, AND CIVITA CASTELLANA.

204 m.

	Posts.
Florence to Incisa, by San Donato	2
Incisa to Levane	2
Levane to Arezzo	2
Arezzo to Camuscia	2
Camuscia to Case del Piano	1½
C. del Piano to Magione	1
Magione to Perugia	1½
Perugia to S. Maria degli Angeli	1
S. Maria to Foligno	1
Foligno to Le Vene	1
Le Vene to Spoleto	1
Spoleto to La Strettura	1
La Strettura to Terni	1
Terni to Narni	1
Narni to Otricoli	1
Otricoli to Borghetto	¾
Borghetto to Civita Castellana	¾
C. Castellana to Nepi	1
Nepi to Monterosi	¾
Monterosi to Baccano	1
Baccano to La Storta	1
La Storta to Rome	1½
Posts	26½

A week before leaving Florence persons travelling with their own carriage should write to their banker at Rome or to the British consul, to obtain a *lascia passare* for the Porta del Popolo. This beautiful road is longer than that by Siena, but surpasses it both in picturesque and in historical interest, and the inns on it are in general better. The post-route from Florence to Arezzo formerly followed the more level but circuitous defile of the Arno by Pontasieve, but since the commencement of 1853 the Post station at the latter place has been removed, and the more direct road by S. Donato adopted by the government. [An additional horse from Florence to Incisa, and *vice versâ.*]

Leaving Florence by the Porta di San Nicolo, the road follows the valley of the Arno for 3 m. to Bagno a Ripoli, from which it ascends to San Donato in Collina, crossing the range of hills which separate the Val d'Arno of Florence from the Val d'Arno di Sopra. From the summit of the pass of S. Donato, 1320 feet above the sea, the view looking back over the valley of Florence is extremely fine, and in clear weather extends to the snowy mountains of the Lucchese and Modenese Apennines. On the other side is a noble view of the upper Val d'Arno and of the mountains of La Falterona and Casentino. The road winds round the hill on which stands the villa di Torre à Cona, belonging to the Rinuccini family. The grounds of the villa command fine prospects.

1½ Incisa (*Inn*, La Posta, tolerable and civil, but too near the stables), a small town where the family of Petrarch had its origin. The bed of the Arno here cuts through the calcareous beds of the eocene formation. We now proceed along the l. bank of the Arno, passing through Figline, where there is a tolerable inn, (the Europa,) by a rich and level country as far as Levane.

Large quantities of fossil bones have at various times been discovered in the valleys N. of Figline, near Levane and Montevarchi, and in the plain of Arezzo. The Italian antiquaries, ignorant of natural history, and eager to connect everything on this road with Hannibal, at once proclaimed them to be the remains of the Carthaginian elephants. The fossil bones include those of the mastodon, hippopotamus, elephant, rhinoceros, hyæna, tiger, bear, and of several extinct species of deer. The upper Val d'Arno is remarkable for its interesting strata, abounding in fresh-water testacea, which may be studied to advantage at Monte Carlo, about 1 m. S.E. of San Giovanni. These curious formations, evidently the deposits of a fresh-water lake, will afford much interest to the geologist who has time to linger on this road.

S. Giovanni (*Inn*, Leone d'Oro). This little town is memorable as the birthplace of Masaccio; it recalls also the name of another native painter, Giovanni Mannozzi, better known as *Giovanni da S. Giovanni*, extolled by Lanzi as one of the best fresco-painters of his day. In the *Cathedral* are still to be seen some interesting examples of his bold and original style: at the high altar is the beheading of St. John, on the l. steps ascending to it is his fresco of the Annunciation; on the rt. the Sposalizio, and in the rt. aisle the St. Joseph. In the adjoining ch. of S. Lorenzo are a painting of the Virgin and Child, with saints, by the school of Siena, and some other *quattro-centisti* pictures; the Annunciation at the 3rd altar of the rt. aisle is by *Masaccio*. On the left of the door is shown the miserable spectacle of a withered body of a man, built up in the church-wall, and discovered a few years ago during some repairs. It still remains in its original position, but nothing is known of its history.

Half way between San Giovanni and Montevarchi, the large village of Terra-nova is seen on the opposite bank of the Arno.

Montevarchi is the chief market town of the Val d' Arno di Sopra; it is often made a sleeping-place by the vetturini; the inn, La Locanda Maggiore, outside the Florence gate, is only tolerable. It is the seat of the Accademia Val d'Arnese, the museum of which, rich in fossil remains of this district, is well worth a visit from the scientific traveller.

3 m. beyond Montevarchi, and before reaching Levane, we cross the Ambra, a considerable stream which descends from the hills of Chianti, and along which there is a good road to Siena and Chiusi, and the S. part of the Val di Chiana by Rapolano.

2 Levane (*Inn*, La Posta, very tolerable).

The road for the next 10 m. is very hilly, crossing several of the deep gullies (Borri) excavated in the clayey soil and slate rocks which form this part of the country. 4 m. from Levane, and 33 from Florence, is Poggio Bagnuoli, with a beautifully-situated and comfortable Inn, which vetturino travellers may make their first day's halting-place from Florence. 6 m. farther the road descends to the Prat'antico, where it crosses the Chiana.

About 1 m. on the rt. from Prat'antico is situated the Chiusa di Monaci, which will be well worthy of a visit from every traveller interested in hydraulic engineering: it consists of a series of locks and sluices, by which the drainage of the beautiful and fertile Val di Chiana, the ancient Palus Clusina, is regulated.

[An extra horse from Levane to Arezzo in the months of November, December, January, and February.]

After crossing the Chiana, the road enters the plain of Arezzo; and after passing through the village of S. Leo, and crossing the Castro stream, 2 m. we reach the Porta Fiorentina of

AREZZO. (*Inns:* Arme d'Inghilterra, La Posta, both very good; L'Europa.) This ancient city, the representative of one of the most powerful cities of the Etruscan league, is beautifully situated on the declivity of a range of hills overlooking its fertile plain. It abounds not only in ecclesiastical antiquities of the middle ages, but in historical associations with many illustrious names in Italian literature and art. It was the birthplace of Mecænas, Petrarch, Vasari, and a long list of eminent men in every branch of human knowledge — so long, indeed, that the historian Villani attributes their number to the influence of the air; and Michael Angelo, who was born at Caprese in the neighbourhood, good humouredly complimented Vasari, by attributing his talent to its climate: "Se io ho nulla di buono nell' ingegno, egli e venuto dal nascere nella sottilità dell' aria del vostro paese di Arezzo."

The pop. of Arezzo is rather more than 11,000 souls. It is a neat and well-paved city, with good streets.

Independently of its interest as one of the first cities of ancient Etruria, *Arretium* was celebrated in Roman times for its small vases of red clay of a bright coral colour, which Pliny says were equal to those of Samos and Saguntum. The Etruscan city twice contended against the Romans, but without success, and in later times became the head-quarters of Flaminius prior to the disastrous battle of Thrasimene. In the middle ages, during the feuds of the Guelphs and Ghibelines, Arezzo contended vigorously against Florence, but at length fell under her power. During the revolutionary excitement of 1799 the inhabitants rose against the French authorities, and committed great atrocities. They afterwards had the rashness to oppose the army of Gen. Mounier at Prat'antico; which the French general resented by sacking a large portion of the town and destroying its defences.

In the *Piazza Maggiore* are the magnificent *Loggie* constructed by *Vasari*, and considered his masterpiece in architecture.

The *Ch. of Sta. Maria della Pieve*, the most ancient in the city, dates from the beginning of the 9th century, and is supposed to occupy the site of a temple of Bacchus. It was repaired in 1216, by *Marchione*, a native architect, with the addition of the front and campanile. The front has 3 open colonnades, like the Duomo of Pisa, containing no less than 58 columns, some of which are round, some multangular, and some twisted; indeed the whole church bears evidence of being composed of fragments from other buildings. The middle column of the 3rd story is a Caryatid. The doorway is round-headed, resting on 6 columns with Corinthian capitals, and various bas-reliefs and statues. The campanile has 5 stories of columns with fantastic capitals. The whole building presents a singular mixture of facility of style with irregularity of detail. In the interior the arches are either semicircular or obtusely pointed; above the high altar is the fine picture of St. George, by *Vasari*, and in the rt. transept is a good Giottist Ancona or Gothic altar painted in compartments.

The *Cathedral*, in the Upper Town, is an imposing specimen of Italian Gothic. The piazza in which it stands recalls in many characteristic features the English cathedral close. It was commenced in 1177, from a design of Lapo, and under the direction of Margaritone di Arezzo: the altar and the Ubertini chapel were added about 1290. The interior of this majestic edifice is characterised by a gloomy magnificence which gives it a sombre effect. The compartments of its ceiling are covered with biblical subjects in fresco; and its brilliant painted windows were executed early in the 16th century by Guillaume de Marseilles, called Marcilla, a French Dominican monk, who was afterwards prior of his order at Arezzo. It is difficult to imagine anything finer than these paintings. The tall lancet windows of the Tribune have been compared and even preferred to the "Five Sisters" of York Minster; and another in the S. wall near the W. end, representing the Calling of Matthew, was so highly prized by Vasari, that he says "it cannot be considered glass, but rather something rained down from heaven for the consolation of men." At the high altar, the marble urn by *Giovanni di Pisa*, in 1286, covered with bas-reliefs representing events in the life of S. Donato, patron of the city, and with numerous small statues, is one of the best works of that great sculptor; in the middle compartment are the Madonna and Child; on one side is St. Donato, and on the other St. Gregory, whose bust is a portrait of Pope Honorius IV. The series representing the actions of S. Donato, and the bas-relief of the Death of the Virgin, are very fine. Vasari, in his description of this monument, says that it cost 30,000 golden florins, and was esteemed so precious, that Frederick Barbarossa passing through Arezzo after his coronation at Rome, extolled its beauty; "ed, in vero," he adds, "a gran ragione." The Crucifixion is by *Spinello Aretino*. The Magdalen by *Pietro della Francesca*, the celebrated painter of Borgo San Sepolcro, and whose other works executed in Arezzo are extremely interesting, they are said to have given Raphael the idea of some of his frescoes in the Vatican. The Cathedral also contains some works by Luca della Robbia.

The fine tomb of Guido Tarlati, of Pietramala, the warrior bishop and chief of the Ghibelines, excommunicated by the pope, whose life was one of the most dramatic in the history of the times, is another interesting specimen of the monumental sculpture of the 14th century. It was executed between 1320 and 1330, by *Agostino* and *Agnolo da Siena*, from the design, as Vasari supposed, of Giotto ; it appears doubtful, however, whether the great painter gave the design, though he certainly recommended Agnolo and Agostino as the fittest sculptors for the work. The history of the ambitious prelate is represented in 16 compartments, in which the figures, although short, are worked out with singular delicacy and precision, surprising works for the time, and worthy of the highest place among the early specimens of art after its revival. The subjects are as follows :— 1. Guido taking possession of his bishopric. 2. His election as their general-in-chief by the people of Arezzo in 1321. 3. Plunder of the city, which is represented under the form of an old man. 4. Guido installed Lord of Arezzo. 5. His restoration of the walls. 6. His capture of the fortress of Lucignano. 7. Capture of Chiusi ; 8. of Fronzola ; 9. of Pocognano ; 10. of Rondine ; 11. of Bucine ; 12. of Caprese ; 13. of Laterina ; 14. of Monte Sansavino. 15. The coronation of the Emperor Louis of Bavaria, in S. Ambrogio, at Milan. 16. The death of the Bishop. Besides these subjects, the figures of priests and bishops on the columns separating the compartments are beautiful as works of art.

The tomb of Pope Gregory X., executed shortly after his death, by *Margaritone*, is also worthy of attentive study. This enlightened pope was seized with illness at Arezzo, and died there suddenly in 1276. He was on his return to Rome to make the final preparations for a new crusade to the Holy Land, in which he had enlisted Rudolph of Hapsburg, Philippe le Hardi, Edward of England, the King of Arragon, and indeed all the principal potentates of Europe. Near it is a modern work, the martyrdom of S. Donato, which first established the reputation of *Benvenuti*, a native of Arezzo, and the most eminent of the modern Tuscan painters. His great picture, Judith showing the

head of Holofernes, one of the finest productions of modern art, although the figure of Judith is perhaps too theatrical, is in the large chapel of the Virgin, consecrated about 1802. In the same chapel is the fine painting of Abigail going to meet David, by *Sabatelli*, a contemporary artist, and several very good specimens of *Andrea della Robbia*. Over one of the side doors of this cathedral are suspended some fossil tusks, which the citizens still regard as relics of the elephants of Hannibal. Among other tombs of eminent natives is that of Redi, the natural philosopher, poet, and physician, celebrated for the purity of his language and style. He died in 1698. The archives of the cathedral contain about 2000 documents, among which is an almost complete series of Imperial diplomas, grants from Charlemagne to Frederick II., in favour of the ch. of Arezzo. The marble statue of Ferdinand de' Medici is by *John of Bologna*.

The ch. of the *Badia di Sta. Fiora* is remarkable for the architectural painting on its flat ceiling by the famous master of perspective *Padre Pozzi*. In the refectory is the immense painting of the Banquet of Ahasuerus by *Vasari*, who has introduced his own portrait under the disguise of an old man with a long beard.

The ch. of *S. Francesco* contains the remarkable frescoes by *Pietro della Francesca*, so much praised by Vasari ; they represent the History of the Cross, and the Vision and Victory of Constantine, which gave Raphael the idea of his great battle in the *Stanze* of the Vatican. They were much damaged during the last century by an earthquake. The sketch for the Vision was in Sir Thomas Lawrence's collection. There is a good specimen of Spinello Aretino over one of the altars in this Church.

A fresco of the Almighty supporting Christ on the Cross, by Spinello Aretino, remains in good preservation on the wall of the *Convent della Croce ;* on the great altar of which is an admirable picture of the Madonna and many Saints, by *Luca Signorelli*. In the ch. of *S. Agostino*, there is a good Presentation in the Temple, of the school of Perugino. Among the many fine productions of La Robbia ware in Arezzo may be mentioned the first altar on the l. in *S. Maria in Gradi.*

The *Palazzo Pubblico*, built in 1332, was originally Gothic, but has been modernized without the least regard to its ancient style of architecture. It contains a small collection of paintings by native artists; on the front is a curious series of armorial bearings of the successive Podestàs, amounting to many hundreds, and including some historical names.

The *Fraternità*, built in the 14th century, has a majestic Gothic front and porch of exceeding richness, flanked by 2 lancet windows; it was founded originally for the relief of the poor, and as a provision for widows and orphans; with these objects are now combined a museum of antiquities and natural history, and a library containing upwards of 10,000 volumes.

The *Museo Pubblico* contains a good collection of vases, bronzes, and cinerary urns. The vases are chiefly of the red ware of the city, and have been described in Dr. Fabroni's work on the Arezzo vases; there are also examples of the pottery of other Etruscan towns.

The *Museo Bacci* is much dilapidated, but it still contains some interesting bronzes and pottery. The large Etruscan vase with red figures, found near Arezzo in the middle of the last century, representing the Combat of the Amazons, Hercules slaying a warrior, and a dance of Bacchanals, is the best specimen of the kind in the collection. There are also some interesting vases of the red stamped clay described by Pliny, and for the manufacture of which Arezzo in his day was celebrated.

The walls of Arezzo were erroneously supposed to be Etruscan; they are not older than the middle ages; and the best founded opinion is, that the present town occupies not the site of the Etruscan city, but that of the Roman colony founded after the site on the hill above had been abandoned. On the hill called Poggio di San Cornelio, 3 m. S.E. of the town, several fragments of Etruscan masonry were discovered about 18 years ago, which are supposed to be the remains of city walls. Micali has published a plan of them. Modern antiquaries regard them as marking the site of the Etruscan Arretium.

Little now remains of the Roman ruins of Arezzo; the massive walls in the gardens of the Passionist monastery, which are shown as the most important, are supposed to be those of an amphitheatre. This spot is interesting for the fine view which it commands over the town.

Like Venice and Bologna, Arezzo has its illustrious houses, associated with the memories of great names. They are generally marked by marble tablets, inscribed with the names of those who were born within their walls; and they occur so numerously, that scarcely a street is without its record. This custom has been unjustly ridiculed by some recent travellers; few persons derive so much instruction by these memorials as travellers, and their more frequent adoption in England would associate many an interesting house with the greatest names in our history.

The most remarkable house in Arezzo is that in the Sobborgo del' Orto, close to the cathedral, in which *Petrarch* was born on Monday, July 20, 1504. A long inscription, put up in 1810, records the fact; the room shown as the scene of his birth has retained no trace of antiquity. Close to it is the well near which Boccaccio has placed the comic scene of Tofano and Monna Ghita, his wife.

In the Strada San Vito is the house of *Vasari*, still preserved nearly in its original state, and containing several excellent works by that celebrated artist biographer.

Among the eminent natives of Arezzo, beside those already mentioned, may be noticed Lionardo Aretino, the Florentine historian; Pietro Aretino, the satirist; Fra Guittone, the inventor of musical notation; Guittone, the poet, mentioned by Dante in the Purgatorio; and Margaritone, the painter, sculptor, and architect of the 13th century.

In modern times Arezzo has produced

2 of the most eminent men of Italy— Count Fossombroni, for many years prime minister of Tuscany, during whose administration the country enjoyed a degree of prosperity and tranquillity unknown elsewhere in Italy; and Benvenuti, the painter, celebrated, amongst his other works, for his frescoes in the Medicean chapel at San Lorenzo.

The red sparkling wine of Arezzo formerly enjoyed great celebrity; Redi thus noticed its fine qualities:—

> " O di quel che vermigliuzzo,
>   Brillantuzzo,
>   Fa superbo l' Aretino."

There is a handsome Public Promenade, with a statue of the late Grand Duke, Ferdinand III.

A good but hilly road (Rtes. 18 and 19) leads from Arezzo to Urbino, by Borgo San Sepolcro and Citta da Castello; to Siena by Monte Sansovino and Palazzuolo (Route 26 B), and to Chiusi by Fojano and Torrita.

Diligences leave Arezzo daily for Florence at day-break, arriving at 4 P.M.; for Siena 3 times a-week; and for Perugia 3 times a week, in correspondence with those for Rome by Todi, Narni, and the Tiber.

EXCURSION THROUGH THE VAL DI CHIANA TO CHIUSI.

A very interesting excursion may be made from Arezzo to Chiusi, through the Val di Chiana, one of the richest agricultural districts not only of Italy, but perhaps of Europe. As there are no post-horses the journey must be made by vetturino, or the traveller will easily find a gig-conveyance at Arezzo for the whole or a part of the road.

Leaving Arezzo, the road is the same as that to Siena as far as the Chiana, passing for 2 miles across the Piano di Arezzo, thence over the hills of L' Olmo to Pieve al Intoppo. 1 m. after crossing the river the road turns to the S., and after running through the plain for 12 m. parallel to the Chiana, passing through the village of Montagnana, reaches Fojano by a very steep ascent, where, to a carriage, oxen are often required.

Fojano, the ancient station of ad Græcos on the Via Cassia, is beautifully situated on the hill commanding a fine view of the valley beneath and of the distant mountains of Cortona, of the lake of Thrasimene, &c. The cathedral is very neat, and has a good altar-piece in Luca della Robbia Pottery. The position of Fojano, at a considerable elevation, 1080 feet, places it out of the reach of the malaria which, at certain seasons, renders the subjacent plain unhealthy. The Inns at Fojano are very indifferent: the best is on the l. hand on entering the town.

The most direct road to Chiusi, on leaving Fojano, is by Bettole and Torrita. Descending rapidly, it crosses the Esse torrent about 3 m. distant, to ascend to Bettole, a modern village on the height, also out of the reach of malaria. Here the tourist may visit one of the great farms or *fattorie* belonging to the Order of San Stefano, to which the greater part of the reclaimed land in the valley of the Chiana belongs. To each fattoria are attached several smaller farms (Podere). Descending from Bettole, we cross the Foënna torrent, one of the largest tributaries of the Chiana, 3 m. beyond which is Torrita. From Torrita to Chiusi a hilly road, passing at the base of the high hill on which Montepulciano stands, brings to the margin of the lakes of Montepulciano and Chiusi; it is the same as that from Siena to Chiusi, described Rte. 26 c.

The Tuscan portion of the valley of the Chiana (Clanis), extending from the lake of Chiusi to the Chiusa de' Monaci, near which it empties itself into the Arno, remained a pestilential marsh until towards the middle of the last century, when a mode of drainage was adopted peculiar to Italian hydraulic engineering,—that of *Colmates*, which is effected by carrying the torrents charged with alluvial matter into the marshy portions, allowing them to deposit the mud thus brought down, by which the subjacent soil is raised, and such a fall for all stagnant waters procured as to permit of the ordinary methods of drainage. By this means the valley of the Chiana, by which Dante illustrates the pestilent fevers of the tenth *bolgia* of the Inferno—

" Qual dolor fora, se degli Spedali
  Di Val di Chiana, tra' Luglio e' l Settembre *?*'

is now reduced to one of the most fertile districts of Tuscany, rich in corn, vines, and mulberry plantations, peopled by a healthy peasantry, and studded with numerous villages. These operations, begun under the direction of the celebrated mathematicians of the school of Galileo—Torricelli and Viviani—have been completed under that of the late patriotic prime minister of Tuscany, Count Fossombroni, one of the last of that celebrated school of mathematicians and engineers which has nearly ceased to exist with himself.

The agriculturist will do well to visit some of the different farm-houses erected by the Grand Duke (*fattorie*) on a very extensive scale, especially those of Crete, Fojano, Bettole, Dolciano, &c.; in which the mode of preserving grain in underground chambers or *Silos* is worth his notice.

To the scientific traveller the valley of the Chiana presents a phenomenon in physical geography almost unique —the change in the course, and in an opposite direction, which the waters of the Clanis have taken within historic periods. In the first centuries of our era the whole of the waters of the Clanis, with probably a portion of those of the Upper Arno, ran into the Tiber, and a considerable part of the former did so even in the middle ages; but in consequence of the elevation of the valley by natural means and by the hydraulic operations above alluded to, the whole of the waters of the Chiana, as far as Chiusi, now empty themselves into the Arno. We learn from Tacitus that this change in the course of the Clanis was contemplated by Tiberius, but the project was abandoned in consequence of the opposition of the Florentines, who represented that their lands would be flooded and destroyed if the course of the river were so diverted.

For a more detailed description of the means adopted to drain the valley, the reader is referred to Count Fossombroni's celebrated work, " Memorie Fisico-Storiche sopra lo Val di Chiana," recently reprinted in an 8vo. volume at Montepulciano.

As connected with the hydraulic works of the Val di Chiana, we would advise the traveller to visit the locks, or Chiusa de' Monaci, 3 m. from Arezzo, near to where the Chiana empties itself into the Arno; and the locks of Valiano, near Chiusi, by which the emptying of the lakes of Chiusi is regulated.

The Via Cassia ran along the W. side of the Val di Chiana; Fojano was one of its principal stations.

Leaving Arezzo for Rome [an extra horse is required from Arezzo to Camuscía, and vice versâ, during the months of November, December, January, and February only], the road proceeds along the Val di Chiana, skirting the base of the hills which bound it on the E.

A short distance from the walls of Arezzo is *L' Olmo,* a village so called from a gigantic elm, to which tradition had given an age as ancient as the time of Hannibal. It was so large that 10 men could hardly embrace it, and when destroyed by the French its boughs are said to have filled a hundred carts.

Between this and Camuscía the road passes through *Castiglione Fiorentino,* which the vetturini generally make one of the resting-places between Rome and Florence. The Leone Bianco is a very fair village inn, with a civil landlord. Castiglione is not without its pictures. The ch. of *Sta. Maria della Pieve,* in the upper town, built in the 14th century, contains a Madonna and S. Giuliano, and a St. Michael, by *Bartolommeo della Gatta,* whose works are so highly praised by Vasari, In *S. Francesco* is a painting by *Vasari,* representing the Virgin, St. Anne, St. Francis, and St. Silvester. The scenery from the terrace, below the old town, is magnificent. It commands the broad valley of the Chiana in all its length, scattered with villages, while in the foreground it presents one of the richest districts of Italy, abounding in vineyards and in every kind of agricultural produce. Beyond Castiglione the road passes below the village of Montecchio, a stronghold of former days to defend the road; and afterwards winding round the hill of Cortona, we reach at the foot of one of its spurs

2 Camuscía; a post-station and inn at the junction of the high post-road, with some country roads leading to towns in different parts of the valley; one of these leads to Fojano (9 m.), Lucignano, Asinalunga, &c.; another to Chiusi (22 m.) and Montepulciano; while a third conducts us (1 m.) up the mountain to *Cortona*.

EXCURSION TO CORTONA.

There is a very fair inn at Cortona, the Locanda Dragoni; but perhaps Camuscía had better be made the tourist's head-quarters, and Cortona visited from it. Close to Camuscía, on the road to Montepulciano, is the remarkable tomb discovered in 1842 by Signor Sergardi of Siena, from whom it derives the name of the "Grotto Sergardi." Many travellers may prefer visiting this curious monument before ascending to Cortona. It is a huge tumulus, called "Il Melone," within which were found 2 parallel tombs of double chambers, roofed on the principle of approaching stones, and built, not with the usual massive blocks of Etruscan masonry, but with small roughly-dressed stones, from the schistose formation of the spot, put together without cement, so as to resemble brick-work. The tombs had been rifled in past ages; but a smaller chamber was discovered above them, which contained several iron and bronze articles, and some vases containing human ashes. The chambers are almost inaccessible from the damp; but all the objects discovered in the tumulus may be seen in the neighbouring villa of Signor Sergardi.

CORTONA, one of the most ancient and interesting of the 12 cities of the Etruscan league, dating its origin from the Pelasgi, if not from a still earlier race, occupies a commanding position on the very summit of a mountain. As the Corythus of Virgil, it will at once be recognised by the classical tourist as the scene of the murder of Iasius by Dar-

danus, and of the subsequent flight of the latter into Asia Minor:

" Hinc illum Corythi Tyrrhenâ à sede profectum
  Aurea nunc solio stellantis regia coeli
  Adcipit, et numerum divorum altaribus addit."
                                Æn., vii. 205.

This mythological antiquity carries us back to an age anterior to Troy; and yet, while the site and even existence of the latter city is called in question, Cortona retains her ancient walls in many places unchanged. Its antiquity, indeed, independently of that given to it by poetical fiction, is proved by historical evidence to be equalled by few other towns in Italy. It was founded, according to Dionysius of Halicarnassus, by the Umbri, from whom it was captured by the Pelasgi, who advanced into Central Italy from their first settlement at the mouth of the Po, and there seized and fortified Cortona and other colonies.

The present town lies within its ancient circuit; the modern gates seem to occupy the same positions as the ancient; and the gigantic wall, formed of enormous rectangular blocks of sandstone, laid together in horizontal courses, without cement, is preserved for about 2 m., nearly two-thirds of its original extent. Here and there its course is interrupted by Roman works or modern repairs, but its magnificent masonry is generally well preserved beneath the modern fortifications, and still appears fitted to remain during another 3000 years. Near the fortress, beyond the modern wall, is a stupendous fragment 120 feet in length, composed of blocks varying from 7 to 14 feet in length, and from 3 to 5 feet in height; 7 courses remain in one part, where the wall is 25 feet high. In addition to the walls there are several other objects of Etruscan antiquity to engage attention. Within the town is the vault under the Palazzo Cecchetti, lined with regular uncemented masonry, about 13 feet square and 9 high, and apparently sepulchral. On the ascent to Sta. Margherita are some remains of Roman baths, miscalled the Temple of Bacchus. Outside the town, about ½ m. from the Porta S. Agostino, is an Etruscan tomb about 7 feet square, called the "Grotto of Pythagoras," a singular title, considering that the father of Pythagoras was reputed to be one of the Tyrrhenian or Pelasgic settlers, who retired to the islands of Asia Minor after their expulsion from Attica. It was entered by folding doors of stone, the sockets for which are still visible, though the doors have disappeared. The construction of its roof, and the massive blocks of sandstone which compose its sides, are equally remarkable. The walls are of enormous rectangular blocks, finished and put together with wonderful precision, and the roof is formed of 5 stupendous wedge-like stones, of very great length, resting on semicircular walls, and suggesting the impression that the architect must have understood the principle of the arch.

In the *Museum* of the Academy there is a small collection of antiquities, among which coins and bronzes predominate. The small bronze figure of Jupiter Tonans is the best figure in the collection; but the gem of the whole museum is the celebrated *Bronze Lamp*, whose beauty may be imagined from the description of Micali, who says that no other Etruscan work in bronze, except the larger statues, can rival it in mastery of art. It was discovered in a ditch at La Fratta in 1840, and was purchased by Signor Tommasi, of this city, for 700 dollars. It is a circular bowl, nearly 2 feet in diameter, having 16 lamps around the rim, alternating with heads of Bacchus, and a Gorgon's face of inexpressible fierceness at the bottom; the weight of it is said to be 170 Tuscan pounds. There are few vases of any interest in the Museum. There are 2 other Museums, the Museo Corazzi, whose chief treasures have found their way to Leyden, and the Museo Venuti.

The *Accademia Etrusca* was founded, in 1726, by the eminent antiquary Ridolfino Venuti; it is at present in the Palazzo Pretorio, where are also the library and museum. The Academy has published 10 volumes of memoirs; its president is honoured with the title of "Lucumo," the ancient name of the kings of Etruria. The Library, called the Biblioteca Ponbucci, has a beautifully written MS. of Dante, and a MS. called the "Notti Coritane," in 12 folio volumes, a collection of conversations on archæological subjects.

The *Cathedral*, said to be as old as the 10th century, was restored by Galilei, the Florentine architect of the last century. It has several fine paintings, among which are the Deposition from the Cross, by *Luca Signorelli*, who was a native of Cortona, and his pupils; his manner may here be traced from its early style in the Deposition from the Cross, to his most advanced, in his Last Supper, in the church of Gesù. The Annunciation is by *Pietro da Cortona*, another native painter. The most remarkable monument preserved here is the great Sarcophagus, which the local antiquaries, eager to identify everything with Hannibal's invasion, have honoured by calling it the tomb of the consul Flaminius. Its fine bas-relief, representing the combat of the Centaurs and Lapithæ, is clearly referable to a later period of Roman art, so that there can be no authority for the tradition which regards the sarcophagus as the sepulchre of the unfortunate consul. Another tomb is that of Giambattista Tommasi, Grand-Master of Malta in 1803.

The *Ch. of Gesù* also contains some remarkable pictures. The Last Supper, by Luca Signorelli, a most singularly expressive picture. It represents the Saviour standing in the midst of his disciples, distributing the bread to them as they kneel on either side. A Conception and a Nativity are by *Luca Signorelli*. A very expressive Annunciation is by the *Beato Angelico da Fiesole*, as are also two gradini admirably preserved, on which are depicted the lives of the Madonna and of S. Domenico. The unfinished Madonna throned, with St. Ubaldo and St. Roch, is by *Jacone*, the Florentine painter.

The *Ch. and Convent of Santa Margherita* occupy the summit of the mountain on which Cortona is placed; they are surrounded by plantations of cypresses, and the view they command is one of the finest panoramas which can be imagined. Its majestic Gothic architecture is by *Niccolò* and *Giovanni di Pisa*, whose names are seen inscribed on the tower. The Tomb of Sta. Margherita is a remarkable work of the 13th century; its silver front was presented, together with the crown of gold, by *Pietro da Cortona*, when he was raised to the dignity of a noble by his native city; the front is said to have been designed by him. Among the paintings are the Dead Christ, by *Luca Signorelli*; the St. Catherine, by *Baroccio*; the Conception, with St. Margaret, St. Francis, St. Domenic, and St. Louis, by the elder *Vanni*; the Virgin, with St. John the Baptist, St. Elizabeth of Hungary, and St. Biagio, by *Jacopo da Empoli*; and an old but expressive fresco representing St. Margaret finding the dead body of her lover.

The Gothic *Ch. of S. Francesco*, dating from the 13th century, has one of the finest works of *Cigoli*, the Miracle of St. Antony's Mule which converted a heretic, and an Annunciation by *P. da Cortona*.

The *Ch. of S. Domenico*, dating from the first half of the 13th century, contains another of those charming works by which *Fra Angelico* raised the purity and devotional character of early Italian art. It represents the Virgin surrounded by saints; a somewhat similar picture in the sacristy appears to be by one of his pupils. In the choir is one of the finest specimens known of the *Ancona*, or Gothic altar painted in compartments, by Lorenzo di Nicolo, with the date 1440, and an inscription stating that it was presented by Cosmo and Lorenzo de' Medici to the monks of this convent, on condition that they would pray for their souls. The Assumption with St. Jacinto is by *Palma Giovane*.

The *Ch. of S. Agostino* contains one of the best works of *Pietro da Cortona*, the Virgin, with St. John the Baptist, St. James, St. Stephen, and St. Francis; and a painting by *Jacopo da Empoli*, representing the Virgin, St. John the Baptist, and S. Antonio Abate.

A road of 3 m. from Cortona, through Contesse, leads into the high road a few m. north of Ossaja, without the necessity of returning to Camuscia.

Leaving Camuscia, the road soon reaches the Tuscan frontier village of *Ossaja*, the station of the custom-house, where in returning from Rome baggage and passports are examined. Between this and the Papal custom-house we traverse the ridge or chain of La Spelunca. From the summit of the ascent the traveller has a good view of the Lake of Thrasimene, and the Val di Chiana, and of the hills bounding them. From here the road descends to the borders of the lake.

The Papal custom-house is at Monte Gualandro, 5 m. from Ossaja, where a *lascia passare* is useful, as it prevents a search, but a fee generally saves all trouble. A short distance beyond the papal Dogana, after passing the *Ponte di Sanguinetto*, the road descends to the post-station of Case del Piano.

1½ Case del Piano. (*Inn*, La Posta.) A 3rd horse is required by the tariff from this place to Camuscia, and 2 additional for carriages with 4 or 6 horses.

On leaving Camuscia, the LAKE OF THRASIMENE will naturally recall to the classical traveller the memorable battle fought upon its banks, upon the very spot, indeed, which he must pass between that station and Passignano. The details of that disastrous action, "one of the few defeats," says Livy, "of the Roman people," are fully given by that historian and by Polybius; but the local features of the country, as they may still be traced, are nowhere more accurately described than in the following note of Sir John Hobhouse to the 4th canto of 'Childe Harold:'—

"The site of the battle of Thrasimene is not to be mistaken. The traveller from the village under Cortona to Case del Piano, the next stage on the way to Rome, has for the first 2 or 3 m. around him, but more particularly to the rt., that flat land which Hannibal laid waste in order to induce the Consul Flaminius to move from Arezzo. On his left, and in front of him, is a ridge of hills bending down towards the lake of Thrasimene, called by Livy

' montes Cortonenses,' and now named the Gualandro. These hills he approaches at Ossaja, a village which the itineraries pretend to have been so denominated from the bones found there : but there have been no bones found there, and the battle was fought on the other side of the hill. From Ossaja the road begins to rise a little, but does not pass into the roots of the mountains until the 69th milestone from Florence. The ascent thence is not steep, but continues for 20 minutes. The lake is soon seen below on the rt., with Borghetto, a round tower, close upon the water; and the undulating hills partially covered with wood, amongst which the road winds, sink by degrees into the marshes near to this tower. Lower than the road, down to the rt., amidst these woody hillocks, Hannibal placed his horse, in the jaws of, or rather above, the pass, which was between the lake and the present road, and most probably close to Borghetto, just under the lowest of the ' tumuli.' On a summit to the l., above the road, is an old circular ruin, which the peasants call ' the tower of Hannibal the Carthaginian.' Arrived at the highest point of the road, the traveller has a partial view of the fatal plain, which opens fully upon him as he descends the Gualandro. He soon finds himself in a vale enclosed to the l., and in front, and behind him, by the Gualandro hills, bending round in a segment larger than a semicircle, and running down at each end to the lake, which obliques to the rt. and forms the chord of this mountain arc. The position cannot be guessed at from the plains of Cortona, nor appears to be so completely enclosed unless to one who is fairly within the hills. It then, indeed, appears ' a place made as it were on purpose for a snare,' *locus insidiis natus*. Borghetto is then found to stand in a narrow marshy path close to the hill and to the lake, whilst there is no other outlet at the opposite turn of the mountains than through the little town of Passignano, which is pushed into the water by the foot of a high rocky acclivity. There is a woody eminence branching down from the mountains into the upper end of the plain nearer to the side of Passignano, and on this stands a white village called Torre. Polybius seems to allude to this eminence as the one on which Hannibal encamped, and drew out his heavy-armed Africans and Spaniards in a conspicuous position. From this spot he despatched his Balearic and light-armed troops round through the Gualandro heights to the rt., so as to arrive unseen and form an ambush among the broken acclivities which the road now passes, and to be ready to act upon the l. flank and above the enemy, whilst the horse shut up the pass behind. Flaminius came to the lake near Borghetto at sunset; and, without sending any spies before him, marched through the pass the next morning before the day had quite broken, so that he perceived nothing of the horse and light troops above and about him, and saw only the heavy-armed Carthaginians in front on the hill of Torre. The consul began to draw out his army in the flat, and in the mean time the horse in ambush occupied the pass behind him at Borghetto. Thus the Romans were completely enclosed, having the lake on the rt., the main army on the hill of Torre in front, the Gualandro hills filled with the light-armed on their l. flank, and being prevented from receding by the cavalry, who, the farther they advanced, stopped up all the outlets in the rear. A fog rising from the lake now spread itself over the army of the consul, but the high lands were in the sunshine, and all the different corps in ambush looked towards the hill of Torre for the order of attack. Hannibal gave the signal, and moved down from his post on the height. At the same moment all his troops on the eminences behind and in the flank of Flaminius rushed forwards as it were with one accord into the plain.

"There are 2 little rivulets which run from the Gualandro into the lake. The traveller crosses the first of these at about a mile after he comes into the plain, and this divides the Tuscan from the Papal territories. The second, about a quarter of a mile further on, is called 'the bloody rivulet;' and the peasants point out an open spot to the l. between the 'Sanguinetto' and the hills, which, they say, was the principal scene of slaughter. The other part of the plain is covered with the thick-set olive-trees in corn-grounds, and is nowhere quite level except near the edge of the lake. It is, indeed, most probable that the battle was fought near this end of the valley, for the 6000 Romans, who, at the beginning of the action, broke through the enemy, escaped to the summit of an eminence which must have been in this quarter, otherwise they would have had to traverse the whole plain, and to pierce through the main army of Hannibal.

"The Romans fought desperately for 3 hours (unheeding an earthquake which occurred at the time and overthrew many cities, and even mountains, in various parts of Italy); but the death of Flaminius was the signal for a general dispersion. The Carthaginian horse then burst in upon the fugitives; and the lake, the marsh about Borghetto, but chiefly the plain of the Sanguinetto and the passes of the Gualandro, were strewed with dead. Near some old walls on a bleak ridge to the l., above the rivulet, many human bones have been repeatedly found, and this has confirmed the pretensions and the name of the 'stream of blood.'" In the adjoining range of hills above Passignano and Ossaja, are 2 other localities called Pietra Mala and the Vallata Romana, the names of which are also supposed to refer to that fatal conflict.

The Lake of Thrasimene, which has scarcely changed its ancient name in the modern one of *Lago Trasimeno*, is a beautiful sheet of water about 30 English m. in circumference, and in some parts as much as 8 English m. across. It is surrounded by gentle eminences covered with oak and pine, and cultivated with olive-plantations, down to its very margin. The hills around it gradually increase in elevation as they recede from the lake, and rise into mountains in the distance. It has 3 islands, the Isola Maggiore and Minore, opposite Passignano, and the Isola Polvese in its southern angle. On the *Isola Maggiore* is a convent, from which the view over the lake and its shores is one of those glorious prospects so abundantly scattered across the path of the traveller in Italy. The lake abounds in fish, particularly in eels, carp, tench, and pike; a small fish called the *lasca*, a fresh-water herring (*Clupea*), and the *regina*, of the carp genus. The bed of the lake has been gradually filling up by the alluvial matter carried into it, and several suggestions for draining it have been made, which might be effected without much difficulty. The fishery at present lets for 4000 scudi, whilst, by drying, it would produce annually, according to the calculation of Signor Balducci, 122,892 scudi, and would employ at least 1300 persons as agricultural labourers. The level of the lake (967 feet above the sea) has evidently risen within historical periods. Some buildings, now 13 feet below its present level, were discovered recently at Passignano, which appeared to have belonged to a pig-house, as they contained straw, grass, seeds, maize, &c. Sig. Balducci attributes this to the elevation of the bed of the lake, which, by his own observations, was raised 9 inches by the alluvial matter carried into it by the torrents from 1819 to 1841, although the period was not very rainy; whilst other observations, founded on authentic documents, show this level to have increased 48 feet in a century. The older maps of the district also prove that the lake occupied a lesser area than it does at present, a change which the comparison of plans of it made at different periods shows to have been gradual. The greatest depth is now 21 feet between Castiglione del Lago and the Isola Maggiore, whereas 32 years ago a sounding is recorded near the same point which gave a depth of 33 to 39 feet. The Emissario, said to have been constructed by the Baglioni family, when lords of Perugia in the 15th century, to drain the superfluous water of the lake, has been injudiciously raised in recent times. Signor Balducci believes that it existed before the time of the Baglioni, for, if it had not, the shores of the lake mnst have been under water; whereas there is every reason to believe that at a remote period the plain extending round the lake was much more extensive than at present. This fact would explain the ancient accounts of the battle, and the stand made by Flaminius near the modern village of Passignano after his first defeat near Borghetto.

The Lake of Thrasimene and its historical associations give an interest to this road which is not felt in any other approach to Rome from the north.

" I roam
By Thrasimene's lake, in the defiles
Fatal to Roman rashness, more at home;
For there the Carthaginian's warlike wiles
Come back before me, as his skill beguiles
The host between the mountains and the shore,
Where Courage falls in her despairing files,
And torrents, swoll'n to rivers with their gore,
Reek through the sultry plain, with legions scatter'd o'er,

Like to a forest fell'd by mountain winds;
And such the storm of battle on this day,
And such the frenzy, whose convulsion blinds
To all save carnage, that, beneath the fray,
An earthquake reel'd unheededly away!
None felt stern Nature rocking at his feet,
And yawning forth a grave for those who lay
Upon their bucklers for a winding-sheet;
Such is the absorbing hate when warring nations meet!

Far other scene is Thrasimene now;
Her lake a sheet of silver, and her plain
Rent by no ravage save the gentle plough;
Her aged trees rise thick as once the slain
Lay where their roots are; but a brook hath ta'en—
A little rill of scanty stream and bed—
A name of blood from that day's sanguine rain;
And Sanguinetto tells ye where the dead
Made the earth wet, and turn'd the unwilling waters red." *Byron.*

An additional horse is required from Case del Piano to Magione.

Leaving Case del Piano, the road skirts the shore of the lake amidst beautiful scenery. *Passignano*, a dirty village through which it passes, built on the extremity of a rocky promontory of *pietra serena* jutting into the lake, is chosen by the vetturini as the 2nd day's resting-place from Florence: the *inn*, Il Genio, is large and clean, with a civil landlord. Following the shores of the lake for about 4 m., to the village of Torricella, situated on the water's edge, the road here commences to ascend the steep range of

hills: looking back over the lake from these elevations, is amongst the most charming prospects on the journey.

1 Magione, a post-house near the summit of a commanding eminence, about 390 feet above the Lake, surmounted by an isolated square tower of tall and imposing aspect, and still presenting its vaults, halls, and machicolations, which carry the mind back to the contests of Forte Braccio and Sforza, when the solitary tower must have been a place of some strength. An additional horse is required by the tariff between this station and Perugia, both going and returning.

From Magione the road descends rapidly into the valley of the Farmanuova, a small stream which it crosses; 2 m. beyond which it passes the Cina, a larger torrent, and then gradually rises as it approaches the long and lofty mountain-ridge of tertiary calcareous marl and grey limestone shale which divides the valleys of the Gerna and the Tiber, and on the top of which Perugia is built. The fine old Gothic monastery, formerly belonging to the Templars, and now a palace of Prince Doria, forms, with its ancient towers and lofty campanile, a conspicuous object from the road. The ascent from the foot of the hill of Perugia to the city gates is so steep, that additional horses or oxen are required to assist the post-horses in accomplishing it.

1½ PERUGIA. (*Inns:* L'Europa, in the Corso, kept by Angelo Banchi, an ancient palace: the father of the present owner, who established the hotel, lived for many years in English families. This hotel is very well spoken of; the landlord is civil and obliging. The Gran Bretagna, or Posta, on the opposite side of the street, kept by Casati, very fair, but the charges have been complained of.)

Perugia, the ancient Perusia, was one of the most important cities of the Etruscan league, and is scarcely inferior in antiquity to Cortona. Of its history in Etruscan times little more is known than that its citizens were 3 times defeated by Fabius, and that it fell under the power of Rome when all the other cities of Etruria lost their independence. In the reign of Augustus it was occupied by Lucius Antony, the brother of the triumvir, and besieged by Augustus, who starved it into a surrender. One of the citizens, however, set fire to his house to prevent it falling into the hands of the conqueror, and the flames unfortunately spreading reduced the whole city to ashes. Augustus rebuilt it as a Roman colony, and commemorated the event by the inscriptions which are still visible on 2 of its gates. Its history in the middle ages is not less interesting than that of Bologna or Siena, although the struggles of this free city against the growing power of the popes, and the contests which followed between the popular party and the nobles, differ little from those which were the immediate precursors of the fall of nearly all the Italian republics. But the events which peculiarly mark the history of this city bring before us one of the most extraordinary men whose characters were formed by the circumstances of this eventful period. This celebrated personage, Braccio da Montone, surnamed Fortebraccio, the rival of Sforza, and like him the founder of a new school of military tactics, was born at Perugia. As the commander of the Florentine army he attacked his native city, after its surrender to Ladislaus king of Naples, who was supported by his great rival Sforza. Braccio commenced this memorable siege of Perugia in 1416; the inhabitants gallantly resisted, and at length called to their aid Carlo Malatesta, lord of Rimini, who was defeated in the neighbourhood of the city by Tartaglia da Lavello, one of Braccio's lieutenants. The citizens then surrendered and received Braccio as their lord, July 19th, 1416. His rule was marked by a wise and conciliatory policy, and this eminent warrior proved himself one of the best rulers of his time. He recalled the nobility, reconciled the factions of the city, and administered justice with an impartial hand. The political existence of Perugia ended at his death, and the city returned under the dominion of the Church. Its affairs were administered by the Baglioni family, under the authority of the popes; but the ambition of this noble house brought them into collision both with the people and the Holy See. After several contests for supremacy, Paul III. succeeded in reducing the city to subjection, and, after destroying all remains of its ancient institutions, directed the construction of the present citadel as an effectual means of repressing any future outbreak. From that time Perugia has, with few exceptions, remained in passive obedience to the Church. During the disasters attendant on the French invasion it shared the fate of the other Italian cities, and became one of the component parts of the Roman republic.

In connection with these historical events, the plagues of Perugia may be noticed. During the 14th and 2 following centuries the city was frequently visited by this pestilence; in that of 1348, 100,000 persons are said to have perished, and in that of 1524 Pietro Perugino was among its victims.

Antiquities.—Considerable portions of the walls, and the foundations of many of the ancient gates, are still preserved; and though less massive than those of Cortona, they are fine specimens of Etruscan architecture.

The walls are composed of regular blocks of travertine; near the Porta S. Ercolano is a portion at least 40 ft. high. Of the gates, the S. Ercolano, the Arco di Augusto, the Arco di Bornia, and Porta Colonna, are Etruscan as high as the imposts; the Arco di S. Luca, the Porta di S. Pietro, and the Arco de' Buoni Tempi, have all Roman foundations; the Arco della Conca is mediæval. The celebrated gateway called the *Arch of Augustus*, from the inscription " Augusta Perusia " over it, is the finest and most imposing of the ancient gates. It is double, with an oblique arch about 30 ft. in height from the pavement to the keystone. It is built of massive blocks of travertine 3 or 4 ft. long, and laid in courses 18 in. high. In one of the spandrils are some remains of what seems to have been a colossal head. Above the arch is an Ionic frieze, ornamented with alternating shields and columns; from this frieze springs another arch, now blocked up, the whole of which was evidently added by the

Romans. The gate is flanked by 2 sq. towers, whose masonry, as high as the imposts of the arch, is probably Etruscan. Within the gate is a wall of rusticated masonry upwards of 50 ft. high, of the same workmanship as the gate itself, but now unconnected with it. The inscription, *Augusta Perusia,* as we have already stated, was added by Augustus. In confirmation of the high antiquity of this gateway, deduced from its characteristic masonry, the evident injury the arch has sustained by fire authorizes the conclusion that it existed prior to the general conflagration of the city which followed the surrender to Augustus. The *Porta Marzia,* another interesting gateway of Etruscan workmanship, was removed from its original position, together with a great portion of the ancient wall, when the citadel was built by Paul III. But fortunately Sangallo did not allow it to be destroyed, and the stones composing it were carefully preserved by building them up afterwards into the castle wall. The frieze is ornamented with 6 pilasters, alternating with 3 male figures and 2 heads of horses. In the upper part is the inscription *Colonia Vibia,* and in the lower part *Augusta Perusia,* both of which must have been added after the city became a Roman colony.

The *Necropolis* of Perugia was discovered in 1840, in the line of the new road to Rome, about ½ m. before it reaches the Ponte di San Giovanni. In that year a peasant discovered the sepulchre which has since become so celebrated as the "Tomb of the Volumnii;" and from that period to the present numerous other tombs have been brought to light, chiefly by the researches of Cav. Vermiglioli, the learned professor of archæology in the University, who has taken measures to preserve most of them as they were found. The tomb which was first discovered is called the "Grotta de' Volunni," and is still unsurpassed by any which have been since opened. It is one of the largest and most beautiful in Etruria, and is inferior in interest to none, although it is supposed to be of as late a date as the 6th century of Rome. The tomb is approached by a long flight of steps descending to the entrance in the hill side; the entrance was closed by a large slab of travertine, and on one of the doorposts is still seen, as fresh as on the day when it was first carved, an Etruscan inscription with the letters coloured in red, recording the names of Arnth and Larth Velimnas. The tomb consists of 10 chambers; the largest, with a beam and rafter roof, is 24 ft. by 12, and 16 ft. high: the 9 others which open into it are of much smaller size. In one of these are 7 *cinerary urns* of very fine workmanship, 1 of them being of marble and 6 of travertine. Of the latter, 5 have on their lids recumbent male figures in the attitude of revellers at a feast; the 6th has a female figure sitting on a pedestal; and the marble urn, which is in the form of a Roman temple, is remarkable as having a bilingual inscription in Latin and Etruscan; the Latin is "P. Volumnius A. F. Violens Cafatia Natus," and the Etruscan is evidently of corresponding import. All the other urns have inscriptions recording the name of "Velimnas" in pure Etruscan characters, and 4 of them have heads of Medusa on their fronts. The ceiling of this chamber is coffered in squares, and has in the centre a Gorgon's head of enormous size and of startling power of expression. Over the door is a large shield between 2 curved swords, bearing a head in relief, supposed to be that of either Medusa or Apollo. In the angles of the pediment are 2 busts of singular character, but the face of one has disappeared, and, though it is easy to see that the other wears a peasant's dress and bears the crooked staff, it is difficult to explain their real meaning. On the other walls of the chamber are figures of dragons or serpents, made of earthenware with metal tongues which seem ready to hiss at each intruder, and the remains of a colossal winged demon in relief. The tomb has been preserved in the state in which it was found, but most of the vases, lamps, bronze armour, weapons, paterae, ornaments, and bones, have been removed to the neighbouring villa of Count Baglioni, the proprietor of the ground, who very liberally allows them to be inspected by travellers. Many less distinguished tombs have since been opened, and are preserved with their painted urns just as they were found; among them we may mention those of the Etruscan families of Pumpuni (Pomponius), Ceisi (Cæsius), Veti (Vettius), Casni (Cesina), Pharu (Farrus), Petroni (Petronius), Acsi (Accius), Anani (Annianus), Vipi (Vibius). Among the many curious objects found within these tombs and now preserved in the Villa Baglioni are a bronze curule chair, coins, mirrors, curling-irons, lamps, helmets, greaves, and even eggs. The griffin of Perugia is one of the most frequent emblems on the urns.

About 2 m. from the city, at the hamlet of La Commenda, on the road to Florence, is the once celebrated Etruscan tomb called the "Tempio di San Manno," from the 2 altar-like masses of stone which it contains, with channels on their upper surface, as if to carry off the blood. This tomb has been known for ages, and, though now used as a cellar, it is still remarkable for its beautiful masonry, for its perfectly arched roof, and its wonderful state of preservation. It is, however, a mere vault, 27 ft. long by about 13 ft. wide, and 15 ft. high. Its finely arched roof is composed of blocks of travertine 16 ft. long. and 10 ft. high. On the l. side is the inscription in 3 lines called by Maffei "the queen of inscriptions," and still valued as one of the longest and most perfect known.

Perugia is now the capital of a delegation and is governed by a Prelate. The delegation includes a superficial extent of 1807 sq. m., and a population of 217,000. The population of the city and its suburbs amounts to 18,500. The bishopric of Perugia was founded A.D. 57; St. Herculanus one of the followers of St. Peter, was its first bishop.

School of Umbria.—As Perugia may be considered the centre of this school of painting, it will be useful to give a brief summary of such of its leading features as will enable the traveller more accurately to comprehend the examples he will meet with in its churches and galleries, and thus trace its influence on the masters of the Roman school. The school of Umbria is essentially characterised by the spiritual tendency of the art. The deep religious feeling and enthusiasm inspired by the great sanctuary of Assisi seem to have exercised an undivided sway over all the painters within the sphere of their influences; and the school of Umbria, like that of Siena, may be regarded as the transition from the classical style prevalent at Florence to that devotional style which attained its maturity under Raphael. The oldest painters of the Umbrian school are *Martinello, Matteo di Gualdo,* and *Pietro Antonio da Foligno* (1422), whose works we shall hereafter meet with at Assisi. In the latter half of the same century occurs Niccolò da Foligno, better known as *Niccolò Alunno,* a superior and expressive painter, whose works still exist at Assisi and in his native city. *Fiorenzo di Lorenzo,* his contemporary, and *Benedetto Bonfigli,* who seems to have followed the style of Gentile da Fabriano, were the immediate predecessors of Pietro Vannucci of Città della Pieve, called *Pietro Perugino* from the city of his adoption, who is the great master of this school. Perugino seems at first to have combined the styles of these earlier painters with many peculiarities of the Florentine school; and at length, striking out into an original path, introduced that style, peculiarly his own, which exercised so great an influence on the earlier works of his pupil Raphael. With Perugino may be associated *Bernardino Pinturicchio* and *Andrea del Ingegno,* his able contemporaries, and, according to Vasari, his scholars; but the Spanish *Lo Spagna* is considered, next to Raphael, the most eminent of all his pupils. Among the successors and imitators of Perugino are *Giannicola, Tiberio d'Assisi, Girolamo Genga,* and *Adone Doni.* To the Umbrian school some writers have also referred *Giovanni Santi* of Urbino, the father of Raphael, and *Francesco Francia* of Bologna. On the influence of the school of Umbria on the genius of Raphael, whose early powers were first developed here under the instructions of Perugino, it is not necessary to enter here. The question is treated fully in Kugler's ' Handbook of Painting,' to which the reader is referred for a more complete history of the several masters above mentioned.

The *Cathedral*, or Duomo, dedicated to San Lorenzo, dates from the end of the 15th century, and occupies the site of a more ancient ch. Its fine bold Gothic, although as much as possible transformed into the Roman style, still presents many features for study; most of its pointed windows have been closed up, but its wheel window still remains. The porch on the side of the Corso is by *Scalza*, the celebrated sculptor of Orvieto. The interior is imposing, but its effect is somewhat impaired by its parti-coloured appearance. The chapel of the l. nave contains the masterpiece of *Baroccio*, the Deposition from the Cross, painted while he was suffering from the effects of the poison given him while occupied at the Vatican, by some envious rivals who had invited him to a repast, in order that they might more easily accomplish their purpose. It was carried off by the French, and for some time after its restoration remained in the Vatican. The richly painted window of this chapel (1565) is by *Constantino da Rosaro* and *Fra di Barone Brunacci*, a monk of Monte Casino; the wood carvings of the stalls, after the designs of Raphael, are very beautiful. The Chapel of the SS. Sacramento is remarkable as the design of *Galeasso Alessi*, the great architect of Perugia; the stucco ornaments are by *Scalza*. In the rt. hand nave is a marble sarcophagus, containing the remains of 3 popes—Innocent III., Urban IV., and Martin IV. In the winter choir is an altarpiece by *Luca Signorelli*. The celebrated Sposalizio of Perugino, formerly in the Capella del Santo Anello, was removed with many other spoils after the disastrous treaty of Tolentino, and is now in the Museum of Caen in Normandy. Over the altar is a painting of the same subject by Cav. Wicar. This chapel is called "del Santo Anello," from an ancient ring of onyx or agate preserved in it, and highly venerated as the wedding-ring of the Virgin. The stalls are inlaid with very elegant arabesque designs. In the sacristy are 2 small pictures of St. Peter and St. Paul by *Giannicola*. The library contains several biblical rarities of great value; among which are a Codex of 42 leaves on papyrus, containing the ancient Italian version of the 12 chapters of the Gospel of St. Luke, in gilt letters, supposed to be of the 6th century, and a Breviary of the 9th.

There are upwards of 100 churches in Perugia, and about 50 monastic establishments. Of these the following are the most remarkable:—

The *Convent of St. Agnese* has 2 small chapels painted by *Pietro Perugino*. The first represents the Virgin, with St. Antony the Abbot, and St. Antony of Padua; the second the Almighty in his glory. It is necessary to obtain permission to see these works.

The Ch. of *S. Agostino* contains 2 works of *Perugino* on the rt. and l. of the entrance, one representing the Nativity, the other the Baptism of the Saviour. They originally formed a single picture, which was divided in 1603. In the rt. transept are 2 pictures by *Perugino*, the one representing the Almighty in the midst of the Seraphim, the other St. John and St. Jerome. The Adoration of the Magi is by *Domenico di Paris Alfani*. In the l. transept, over the door of the sacristy, is the Madonna, with St. Nicholas and St. Bernardin in glory, and St. Sebastian and St. Jerome below, by *Perugino*. The *intarsie* and bas-reliefs of the seats of the choir are by Agnolo Fiorentino, from the designs of Perugino. In the sacristy are 8 small framed pictures, of half-length figures of various Saints, by *Perugino*; a sketch by *Lod. Caracci*; another by *Guercino*; a fine head of the Saviour by the school of Michael Angelo; and 4 oblong pictures, much injured, representing Marriage of Cana, the Adoration of the Magi, the Circumcision, and the Preaching of St. John the Baptist, attributed to *Perugino*, but more probably executed by some of his able scholars; the Descent of the Holy Ghost is by *Taddeo Bartolo*, a remarkable painting, executed in 1403.

The *Confraternità di S. Agostino* adjoining has a superbly gilt roof, with paintings by *Orazio di Paris Alfani, Scaramuccia Gagliardi*, &c. In the sacristy is a painting of the school of Perugino, dated 1510, and representing the Madonna and Child with St. Sebastian and St. Augustin.

The Ch. of *S. Angelo*, a circular building, resembling S. Stefano Rotondo at Rome, has been considered a Roman building, or a temple dedicated to Neptune; it is more probable, however, that it was built in the 5th or 6th century, of ancient materials. The interior has 16 columns, evidently taken from other edifices, all differing in size, material, and in the form of the capitals. A Gothic doorway was added in the 14th century.

The Ch. of the Convent of *S. Antonio da Padoa*, formerly remarkable for its altar-piece by Raphael and its Nativity by Perugino, has been despoiled of its treasures. The altarpiece of Raphael was sold by piecemeal by the nuns, and the fragments have since been dispersed among various collections; the 2 principal portions are in the Museo Borbonico at Naples, and the 5 small subjects of the gradino are in England; 2 are at Dulwich, 1 in the collection of Mr. Samuel Rogers, 1 in that of Mr. Miles of Leigh Court, and the 5th in that of Mr. Whyte of Barron Hill.

The *Confraternità of S. Bernardino*, called also " La Giustizia," near the ch. of S. Francesco de' Conventuali, has a marble façade by *Agostino della Robbia*, interesting as a work of art, and curious as exhibiting the passage from the Gothic to the classic style. It is covered with arabesques and bas-reliefs, representing various miracles of the saint: in the niches are statues of S. Costanzo, S. Ercolano, the Angel Gabriel, and the Virgin at the Annunciation. The work bears this inscription, *Opus Augustini Fiorentini*, 1461.

In the ch. is a Cross with the Crucifixion on a gold ground by *Margaritone*, 1272. The altarpiece, representing St. Bernardin and the Saviour, is by *Benedetto Bonfigli*. In an inner chapel is a Madonna and Child, with St. Francis and St. Bernardin, by *Perugino*.

The ch. of *S. Domenico*, built in 1632 from the designs of Carlo Maderno, occupies the site of the famous ch. built by Giovanni di Pisa in 1304, which had fallen into decay. The W. end, however, with its superb Gothic window, has been preserved, and on its inner walls are still visible some terra-cotta ornaments and statues executed by *Agostino della Robbia* in 1459. The lancet window has 2 transoms, and is filled with the most beautiful painted glass, executed by Fra Bartolommeo of Perugia in 1411. Its great treasure, however, is the *Monument of Benedict XI.* by *Giovanni di Pisa*, in the l. transept, justly considered by Cicognara as one of the finest works of the revival. It was erected by the Cardinal di Prato to the memory of the murdered pontiff, who is represented in a reclining posture, full of grace and dignity, under a Gothic canopy, with 2 angels drawing aside the drapery. The canopy is supported by 2 spiral columns encrusted with mosaic; under its upper part are the Madonna and Saints. This able pope, who had been General of the Dominican order, and whose virtues and talents had raised him from an humble station to the highest honours of the Church, vainly endeavoured to reconcile the Bianchi and Neri of Florence, and to procure the recall of the latter from exile; he had to contend, on the one hand, with the most unscrupulous monarch of Christendom, Philippe le Bel, and on the other with the cardinals, who were jealous of his independent authority. Benedict, during his residence at Perugia, had issued 2 bulls against Guillaume de Nogaret and the other parties implicated in the seizure of Boniface VIII. at Anagni. Philippe le Bel considered himself compromised by these excommunications, and, fearful that the pope might adopt more direct measures, he employed Cardinal Orsini and Cardinal Le Moine to compass his immediate death. This was done by sending a person disguised as a servant of the nuns of Santa Petronilla to present to the pope, in the name of the abbess, a basket of poisoned figs. Giovanni Villani accuses the cardinals of the act, while Ferreto of Vicenza states that they employed the pope's esquires as their agents. The unhappy pontiff struggled 8 days against the poison, and at length died, July 6, 1304. The most remarkable painting in the ch. is the Adoration of the Magi in the l. aisle, by *Benedetto Bonfigli* or *Gentile da Fabriano*, with the date of 1460. The sacristy contains 2 tall pictures by *Giannicola*, one representing St. Elizabeth and St. John the Baptist, the other the Madonna and St. John the Evangelist; and a small picture by *Fra Angelico da Fiesole*, which seems part of the gradino representing the life of S. Nicolo di Bari in the Vatican Gallery. There are also some small figures by him. The massive campanile, reputed one of the largest in Italy, was even taller than it is at present, but was reduced by order of Paul III. when the citadel was erected.

The ch. of *S. Ercolano*, a Gothic structure, was founded in 1297, and rebuilt in 1325, from the design of Fra Bevignate, a monk. The frescoes of its walls and roof are by *Gian Andrea Carlone*, and bear the date of 1680.

The ch. of the Convent of *S. Francesco dei Conventuali*, originally a Gothic building, has still remaining several interesting paintings. On the rt. is the fine picture of St. John the Baptist, with St. Jerome, St. Sebastian, St. Francis, and St. Bernardin, by *Perugino*, or in the opinion of some by *Beato Angelico*. In the l. transept is the Martyrdom of St. Sebastian, by *Perugino*, painted in his 72nd year (1518). Among its other pictures are the Archangel Michael; the Dispute with the Doctors, which death prevented him from completing; the finely-finished Nativity, painted in 1546; all three by *Orazio Alfani;* and the Padre Eterno, above the latter picture,

has been attributed, but on insufficient grounds, to Raphael. Near it is the copy, by *Cav. d' Arpino*, of the Entombment by that great painter, now in the Borghese Gallery, which Paul V. substituted for the original picture. The chiari-scuri, representing Faith, Hope, and Charity, are copies of those which one of the monks is said to have cut off when the picture was removing; the originals are in the Pinacotheca of the Vatican. Over the altar near the sacristy is a Madonna and Child, with this inscription in Gothic characters : " ERUO, M. CCC. LXXXIIII, mense Juni," painted as an *ex voto* in time of pestilence, probably by some artist of the Sienese school. In the sacristy are 8 pictures of great value as studies of costume, representing the miracles and events of the life of S. Bernardin, by *Vittore Pisanello* (1473); and St. Peter and St. Paul, by *Fiorenzo di Lorenzo*. In a side chapel, enclosed in a miserable box, are preserved the skull and bones of the illustrious *Braccio Fortebraccio*. He fell at the siege of Aquila, June 5, 1424, a few months only after his heroic rival Sforza, then commanding the forces of Joanna of Naples, perished, by drowning, in the Pescara. The body of Braccio was sent to Rome, where the pope had it interred in unconsecrated ground, as being that of an excommunicated person. Perhaps this may account for the profanation still shown to the remains of that great and honourable warrior. The wanton manner in which they are now exposed to the curiosity of travellers is a national disgrace ; and it is a reproach to the Perugians that the bones of their illustrious captain have not yet received at their hands the honours of a tomb. The inscription on the box records that the bones were placed there in the pontificate of Eugenius IV., and designates Braccio as "Italiæ militiæ parens."

The Ch. of *S. Fiorenzo* likewise contains the ashes of *Galeasso Alessi*, the celebrated architect of Perugia, who was buried here in 1572. There is no monument, nor even an inscription, to this great artist, whose genius did so much to embellish the cities of Italy. Surely there is public spirit enough in Perugia to make an honourable though tardy reparation to these two most illustrious of its citizens.

The ch. of *Sta. Giuliana*, a Gothic edifice, built in 1292, is remarkable for its fine wheel window, and for a semicircular painting of the Almighty by *Perugino*.

The ch. of *Sta. Maria Nuova* contains some remarkable pictures. The Adoration of the Magi is an interesting work in the first manner of *Perugino*, who has introduced his own portrait when about 30 years of age. The altarpiece of the l. transept is an exquisite picture of the Annunciation, with God the Father in a glory; it is dated 1466, and is attributed by some to *Niccolò Alunno*, and by others to *Bonfigli*. Opposite is the Transfiguration by *Perugino*. 3 small pictures of the Annunciation, the Nativity, and the Baptism of the Saviour, in the sacristy, are also by *Perugino*, and the St. Sebastian and St. Roch is by *Sebastiano del Piombo*.

The ch. of the *Madonna della Luce* shows the passage of the Gothic into the classic style, from the designs of Giulio Danti. It has still a fine wheel window, composed of 7 smaller circles, and a double Gothic doorway. The celebrated picture of the Coronation of the Virgin, by Raphael, begun shortly previous to his death, and finished by Giulio Romano and Fransesco Penni, was taken away by the French, and is now in the Vatican. A modern copy has been sent to supply its place.

The Confraternità of *S. Pietro Martire*, near the ch. of *S. Domenico*, has an exquisite Madonna and Child between 2 angels, and worshipped by members of the Confraternità, by *Perugino*, a work of so much beauty that it has been attributed to Raphael. Numerous early works occur in nearly all the churches, many of which are elaborately finished, and with all that attention to detail which marks the works of Albert Durer and the early German masters.

The ch. of the Benedictine monastery of S. Pietro de' Casinensi presents a specimen of the ancient basilica, supported by 18 columns of granite and marble taken from some Roman edifice. It is quite a gallery of pictures. In the nave are 10 paintings by *Aliense*, representing the Life of the Saviour, 1 of which, among the 5 on the rt. side, was painted at Venice under the direction of Tintoretto; St. Peter Abbot sustaining the falling column, Totila kneeling to St. Benedict, and the Saviour commending his flock to St. Peter, by *Giacinto Gimignani*; the Resurrection, by *Orazio di Paris Alfani*; the Vision of St. Gregory at the castle of St. Angelo, by *Ventura Salimbeni*; copies from Guercino of the Christ bound, and the Flagellation, by *Aliense*; the Adoration of the Magi, by *Adone Doni*, very graceful; good copies of Raphael's Annunciation and Deposition, by *Sassoferrato*; and the Dead Christ, by *Perugino*. In the chapel of the Sacrament are, the St. Benedict sending St. Mauro and St. Placido into France, with a view of Monte Casino introduced, by *Gio. Fiammingo*; the St. Peter and St. Paul, by *Wicar*; the Madonna in fresco, by *Lo Spagna*; and 3 fine frescoes by *Vasari*, representing the Marriage of Cana, the Prophet Elijah, and St. Benedict. In the l. aisle are, a bas-relief of the Saviour, St. John, and St. Jerome, by *Mino da Fiesole*, dated 1473; a Deposition, by *Benedetto Bonfigli*, in 1468; the St. Peter and St. Paul, by *Gennari*, the master of Guercino. The other pictures are, the Judith of *Sassoferrato*; the Assumption, by *Paris Alfani*; and the Madonna and Child, by the school of *Perugino*. The Ascension, painted by Perugino for the high altar of this church, was carried off by the French, and is now in the public gallery at Lyons; and its *Predella*, representing the Adoration of the Magi, the Baptism and Resurrection of our Saviour, in the Museum at Rouen. Over the door of the sacristy are some excellent copies by *Sassoferrato* from Perugino and Raphael, representing Sta. Catherina, Sta. Apollonica, Sta. Flavia, and near them S. Placido and S. Mauro. In the sacristy are 5 beautiful little pictures by *Perugino*, framed, representing Sta. Scolastica, S. Ercolano, S. Pietro Abbate, S. Costanzo, and S. Mauro. St. John embracing the Infant Saviour is the earliest known work of *Raphael*, copied from one of Perugino's subjects. The Sta. Francesca is by *Caravaggio*; the Holy Family, by *Parmegiano* (?); the Head of the Saviour, by *Dosso Dossi*; the Crowning with Thorns, by *Bassano*; the Ecce Homo, said to be by *Titian*; the fine pictures of Christ Bound and the Flagellation, by *Guercino*; and 6 frescoes, by *Girolamo Danti*. The choir is enriched with stalls of walnut-wood, worked in bas-relief by Stefano da Bergamo from the designs of Raphael: they are all different, and the inimitable grace and exquisite fancy of the great master appear to have been here, as in the loggie of the Vatican, quite inexhaustible. Besides these, the doors and other portions of wood-work contain remarkable specimens of *tarsia* by Fra Damiano da Bergamo. The books of the choir are an invaluable series of illuminated works; they are rich in miniatures and initial letters of the 16th century, painted with exceeding beauty by monks of the Benedictine order. Behind the tribune a door opens out upon a balcony, which commands an extensive panoramic view, embracing the valley of the Tiber as far as Assisi.

The ch. of the Camaldolese convent of *S. Severo* contains the first fresco painted by *Raphael*. It is much damaged, but is highly interesting as a subject of study. It represents in a lunette the Almighty between 3 angels and the Holy Spirit, and below, the Saviour, a beautiful figure, with S. Mauro, S. Placido, S. Benedetto, S. Romualdo, S. Lorenzo, and S. Girolamo. The following inscription is underneath: *Raphael de Vrbino Octaviano Stephano Volaterrano Priore Sanctam Trinitatem Angelos astantes sanctosqve pinxit*, A.D. MDXV. Below it on the sides of the niche are St. Jerome, St. John the Evangelist, St. Gregory the Great, St. Boniface, Sta. Scolastica, and Sta. Martha, by *Perugino*. Underneath is the inscription, *Petrvs de Castro Plebis, Pervsinvs tempore Domini Silvestri Stephani Volaterrani a Destris, et Sinistris Cent. It.*

Div. Cristiferae sanctos sanctasqve pinxit, A.D. MDXXI. The picture by Raphael resembles in its composition the upper part of the Dispute of the Sacrament in the Stanze of the Vatican.

The Ch. of *S. Tommaso* contains an altarpiece representing the Incredulity of St. Thomas, the reputed masterpiece of *Giannicola*.

The *Piazza del Soprammuro* is so called from the monstrous subterranean masonry which supports it, filling up the space between the 2 hills on which stand the fortress and the cathedral. Some of these walls and vaults still preserve, in the name of *Muri di Braccio*, a record of the great captain of Perugia, by whom they were chiefly executed.

The *Fountain*, begun in 1274 and finished in 1280, is the work of *Nicola* and *Giovanni da Pisa*. It consists of 3 vases, or basins, arranged one over the other: the 2 lower ones are marble, the upper one is of bronze. 1. The 1st marble basin is a polygon of 24 sides, each of which is divided into 2 compartments, ornamented with bas-reliefs by these great sculptors. Among the subjects represented are the actions and occupations of human life during the 12 months of the year: the Lion, as the emblem of the Guelph party; the Griffin of Perugia; symbolical representations of the arts and sciences; Adam and Eve; Samson; David and Goliath; Romulus and Remus; the fables of the Stork and the Wolf, the Wolf and the Lamb, in allusion no doubt to the ancient emblems of the Tuscan republics. 2. The second basin, supported by columns, is also a polygon of 24 sides, in each of which is a small statue. The subjects begin with St. Peter, the Christian Church, and Rome, and are chiefly symbolical. The sculptures of this second basin are now supposed to be entirely by Nicola, whilst those of the lower basin are by Giovanni. 3. The 3rd basin is a shell of bronze, supported by a column of the same metal, and was executed in 1277 by Maestro Rosso. Out of its centre rise 3 nymphs and 3 griffins.

The *Piazza del Papa* is so called from the fine bronze statue of Julius III., re-

M

markable for its elaborate pontifical ornaments, executed by Vincenzio Danti in 1555. The citizens erected this statue to Julius III. in gratitude for his restoration of many of their privileges, which were taken from them by Paul III. after their rebellion against the salt-tax. The statue during the Italian revolutions had some singular vicissitudes: it was removed for safety from one place to another, and successively occupied the cellar of the Monaldi palace, the palace of the Inquisition, and the Fortress.

The majestic *Palazzo Comunale*, the residence of the delegate and of the magistracy, is supposed to have been designed by Bevignate in 1333, although some authorities date its foundation from 1281. Its front presents a melancholy aspect: many of its rich Gothic windows have been closed up, and new ones, in a more modern style, opened. The first story is the only one which has been tolerably preserved. The upper story has only 4 of the original windows, and their great beauty makes the traveller regret more deeply the loss of the others. Its lofty doorway, with its round-headed arch, is a fine specimen of Italian Gothic; it is covered with elaborate sculptures of animals and foliage, and its graceful spiral columns give it a great similarity to many of our own cathedral doors. Among its decorations are the arms of the cities in alliance with Perugia, viz. Rome, Bologna, Florence, Pisa, Naples, and Venice; the arms of the pope, and of the king of France; 3 statues of saints; 6 allegorical figures; the lions of the Guelphs; and 2 griffins tearing a wolf, the griffin being the emblem of Perugia, and the wolf that of Siena. The interior is not particularly remarkable: the grand hall was the place where the Perugians, as a free municipality, held their councils. One of the antechambers, formerly the chapel of the priors, has a fresco of *Benedetto Bonfigli*, in 1460, partly damaged. The hall, now used by the Magistratura, has a fresco representing Julius III., restoring to the city the magistrates who had been removed by Paul III., and an Ecce Homo, by *Perugino*. In the mu-

nicipal archives is an interesting literary curiosity, a complete code of laws for the administration of justice, digested in 1342, and written in Italian, which is of great value as an illustration of the language and habits of the people at that early period.

The *Sala del Cambio* (the Exchange), now no longer used for its original purpose, is covered with frescoes by *Perugino*, the best perhaps which he ever painted. On entering the hall, the paintings on the rt. wall are the Erythræan, Persian, Cumæan, Libyan, Tiburtine, and Delphic sibyls; the Prophets Isaiah, Moses, Daniel, David, Jeremiah, and Solomon; and above, the Almighty in glory. On the l. wall are several philosophers and warriors of antiquity, with allegorical figures of different virtues above them. They occur in the following order: Lucullus, Leonidas, Cocles, with the figure of Temperance; Camillus, Pittacus, Trajan, with the figure of Justice; Fabius Maximus, Socrates, and Numa Pompilius, with the figure of Prudence. On the wall opposite the entrance are the Nativity and Transfiguration. On a pilaster on the l. is a portrait of *Perugino* himself. Near the door is the figure of Cato. On the roof, amidst a profusion of beautiful arabesques, are the deities representing the 7 planets, with Apollo in the centre. In the execution of these graceful frescoes Perugino was assisted by *Raphael*; the Erythræan and Libyan sibyls, and the head of the Saviour in the Transfiguration, are said to be his works. In an adjoining chapel is an altarpiece, also by Perugino, representing the Baptism of our Saviour, with angels kneeling around, and other naked figures waiting to be baptized; both in the *Sala* and in the chapel, except on bright, sunny days, these beautiful frescoes are not seen to advantage. The frescoes of the Cambio were painted in 1500, as stated in the inscription beneath; and Perugino received for the work, from the College of Merchants, 350 golden ducats.

The *Palazzo Governativo*, in the Piazza del Duomo, is, like the P. Comunale, a Gothic building bearing the insignia of the lion and the griffin. It has little to require observation beyond its Gothic ornaments.

The *University* of Perugia, founded in 1320, occupies the old convent of the Olivetans. It was liberally endowed by various popes and emperors, and ranks next after those of Rome and Bologna in the Papal States for the number of its students. It has a botanic garden, a cabinet of mineralogy, and a museum of antiquities. The *Museum* is valuable to the student of Etruscan art. It has been enriched by gifts from various citizens, consisting of remains found in the neighbourhood of Perugia. It contains numerous cippi, with figures in bas-relief, several phallic pillars or columellæ, 2 or 3 feet high, with sepulchral inscriptions; numerous cinerary urns, bearing Latin as well as Etruscan inscriptions; a sarcophagus discovered in 1844, with reliefs on 3 sides, the principal one representing a procession of captives. The collection of inscriptions contains upwards of 100 specimens: the most valuable consists of 45 lines, and is the longest which has yet been found in the Etruscan character. It was discovered near the city in 1822, and occupies 2 sides of a block of travertine, 3½ feet high and 9 inches square: the letters are beautifully cut, and were coloured red. Archæologists are undecided as to the meaning of this inscription. Some of the coins and bronzes are also very interesting; the latter include a great variety of helmets, spears, strigils, mirrors, hinges, and other familiar articles. But the most remarkable objects are the silver and bronze plates, with bas-reliefs of arabesques, deities, mythological personages, and animals formerly supposed to belong to a biga, but now considered to have been the decorations of funeral furniture. They were found, together with numerous figures and sepulchral treasures in 1810, by a peasant of Castel San Mariano, 4 m. from Perugia, where it is supposed they had been buried for concealment. The silver plates were of course an object of speculation to the discoverers; some of them were melted down, and, of those which were fortunately preserved, a portion, including

the bas-relief of the charioteer in silver gilt, now in the British Museum, fell into the hands of Mr. Dodwell and Mr. M'llingen. The latter gentleman's share was purchased by Mr. Payne Knight, and presented by him to the British Museum. A beautiful Etruscan vase, 5 feet high, represents Penelope and Telemachus; another represents a bridal scene.

The *Pinacoteca,* or Gallery of the Academy of Fine Arts, although a small collection, contains some interesting works in the history of art. Among them is one of the finest productions of *Pinturicchio,* dated 1495, and composed of 6 pictures joined together, in which are represented with singular feeling and expression the Virgin, St. Augustin, St. Jerome, the Annunciation, a Pietà, and the Archangel Gabriel; it was formerly in the ch. of Sta. Anna. Other remarkable works by *Pinturicchio* are the 4 Evangelists, the St. Augustin, and a portion of a larger picture, representing various saints, painted, it is said, from the designs of Raphael. Another remarkable work is the exquisite Madonna and Child, with 2 angels, and St. Bernardin, by *Taddeo Bartolo.* The Virgin and 4 saints, with the Saviour, the Virgin, St. John, and 4 other saints on the plinth, is by *Benozzo Gozzoli.* The Virgin, with St. Francis and St. Bernardino, is by *Niccolò Alunno.* The Martyrdom of St. Catherine is by *Paris Alfani.* A painting with 2 series of figures,—1 representing St. Peter, St. Paul, and several other saints; the other representing the Saviour, the Virgin, and St. John the Baptist,—is a beautiful work of *Giannicola.* In a chapel above is a fine fresco by *Perugino,* representing the Madonna and Child, with St. Martin and St. Benedict; on the ceiling is a representation of the Almighty, with an angel on either side; the 2 latter are attributed to *Raphael.*

Private Galleries.—Many of the private galleries of Perugia have small but interesting collections; they contain numerous works by *Perugino,* several reputed works of *Raphael;* but a large number of the former were no doubt executed by Perugino's scholars, and few of the latter are complete'

M 2

authenticated. The following are the principal palaces:—

The *Palazzo Baglioni*, interesting chiefly from the recollections associated with the name during the mediæval history of Perugia, contains a picture of the Virgin and Child, by *Perugino;* and 3 paintings by the modern artists Camuccini and Landi, illustrative of the history of the family.

The *P. Baldeschi* in the Corso has the original drawing by *Raphael*, representing Æneas Sylvius, when a bishop, assisting at the betrothal of the Emperor Frederick III. with Eleonora infanta of Portugal. This beautiful design, of whose authenticity there is no doubt, was executed for the library of the cathedral of Siena.

The *P. Bracceschi* has a collection of Etruscan sepulchral urns, illustrated by Prof. Vermiglioli; and some pictures, among which are the Sta. Barbara by *Domenichino;* a St. Francis on copper by *Cigoli;* the Angelo Custode by *Cav. d'Arpino*, &c.

The *P. Camilletti* has an allegorical picture illustrating the " Vanitas Vanitarum," as inscribed upon it, by *Baroccio;* a head of a young man by *Pietro da Cortona;* a St. John Baptist attributed to *Caravaggio.*

Opposite to this is the house of *Perugino*, which will be regarded with exceeding interest. On one of the inner walls is a fresco of St. Christopher by the great artist, painted, it is said, as a compliment to his father, who bore the name.

The *P. Cenci* contains several pictures : the Seasons, by *Pietro da Cortona;* a Bacchus; a Madonna and Child, by the same; a Holy Family, by *Perino del Vaga;* Leda and the Swan, by the same; an Infant Saviour with angels, by *Domenichino;* St. Helena, by *Innocenzio da Imola;* St. Francis, by *Guido.*

The *P. Cesarei* has 2 designs attributed to *Raphael*, one representing Christ before Herod, the other Paul preaching at Athens; a pen-and-ink sketch by *Michael Angelo* for the full-length figure of the Saviour in the Minerva at Rome; and a design by *Baroccio*, representing the institution of the Eucharist.

The *P. Connestabili*, the palace of Count Staffa, has given name to one of the earliest and most beautiful works of *Raphael*, the Madonna and Child, well known as the "Staffa Madonna." It is a small round picture of exceeding beauty, in which the Virgin is represented reading; the Child is likewise looking into the book. This is one of the best authenticated and most charming pictures by the great artist; the family long possessed the original agreement for it between Raphael and Count Staffa; but it has unfortunately been lost. Among its other paintings are a portrait and a Virgin and Child, by *Pinturicchio;* 4 octagonal pictures representing different characters of heads, 2 of which are copies from Raphael, by *Sassoferrato;* a small picture of the Adoration of the Magi, attributed to *Raphael* in his early youth. There is also a collection of designs by *Perugino*, and a cabinet of coins.

The *P. degli Oddi* (di Porta Sole) is the second gallery in point of extent in Perugia. Among its pictures are the following :—by *Raphael*, 2 small pictures of the Presentation in the Temple, and the Adoration of the Magi; *Guido*, La Carità Romana, 2 pictures of children, and some studies; *Guercino*, Portia Judith, the Magdalen, and David; *Pietro da Cortona*, Head of a Magdalen; *Pinturicchio*, a design for a Holy Family, &c.; *Baroccio*, a St. Francis; *Domenichino*, a Virgin and Child; 2 pictures by *Andrea del Sarto;* a design by *Michael Angelo* for a Crucifixion; and some designs and studies by *Perugino.*

The *P. Donini* has a small gallery containing 2 original drawings by *Perugino*, representing the Annunciation, and 2 angels; 2 drawings of the Adoration of the Magi, and St. Michael, believed to be by *Raphael*. Among its pictures are the Madonna and Child, with St. Francis and St. Luke, by *Perugino;* 2 elaborate paintings on copper, representing the Adoration of the Magi, and the Murder of the Innocents, by *Titian;* a female head by *Baroccio;* and other works.

The *P. Monaldi* contains a large picture of Neptune in his sea chariot, receiving tribute from the Earth, painted by *Guido* for Cardinal Monaldi, when legate of Bologna. It contains also the sketch for this picture ; several designs by *Guercino*, and 2 pictures by him, — one representing the Saviour led to Judgment, the other the Flagellation.

The *P. Penna* is the most extensive gallery of Perugia, well arranged, each subject bearing the name of the painter. The following are the most remarkable : *Perugino*, a Madonna and Child throned and crowned by 5 angels, between St. Jerome and St. Francis ; *School of Fra Bartolommeo*, a Pietà, with 2 Apostles ; *Salvator Rosa*, 4 landscapes, and a sketch representing himself in the act of writing to his friend Cav. della Penna ; an original letter of Salvator's is preserved behind the sketch ; *School of Raphael*, a portrait, supposed to be that of Atalanta Baglioni, and an excellent copy of the Staffa Madonna ; *Luca Signorelli*, the Virgin and several Saints.

The *P. Sorbello* has a Madonna and Child, by *Perugino ;* a portrait by *Guido*, said to be that of Michael Angelo : a St. Anthony Abbot, by *Guido ;* a Madonna and Child, copied from Raphael, by *Andrea del Sarto ;* a small copy on copper of the Madonna della Seggiola, by *Domenichino*, &c.

The *Library* (Libreria Pubblica) contains nearly 30,000 volumes, among which are some MSS., a collection of Perugian editions of the 15th century, and a series of Aldines. Among the MSS. are the Stephanus Byzantinus of the 5th century, and the works of St. Augustin with miniatures of the 13th. Among the printed books is the first printed at Perugia, the Counsels of Benedetto Capra, a native jurist, in 1476.

The *Lunatic Asylum* of Perugia has acquired great celebrity throughout Italy. The system of non-restraint, now so universally commended in England, is adopted in it, and has been productive of the happiest results.

The fortress, called the *Citadella Paolina*, was begun in 1540, by Paul III., who destroyed one of the finest quarters of the town, and the palaces of the principal citizens, for the purpose. It was designed by *Sangallo*, and finished in 1544, by *Galeasso Alessi*. Its apartments and chapels were decorated with frescoes by Raffaello del Colle and other artists, but they were destroyed during the political troubles which followed the French invasion. After that time its ditches were filled up and converted into a public promenade, and the citadel itself was converted into a powder magazine. As, however, it still commanded the town without protecting the inhabitants from invasion, it was almost entirely dismantled by the citizens during the political troubles of 1849. The entrance gateway is by Galeasso Alessi ; the 2 statues of St. Peter and St. Paul in the first court are by *Scalza*, who was employed with *Mosca* in the ornamental sculpture of the building. The circumstances which preceded the construction of this fortress arose out of the salt-tax imposed by Paul III. The pope, careless of concealing his motive, recorded his opinion of the inhabitants in the following haughty inscription, long visible in the court : " Ad coercendam Perusinorum audaciam Paulus III., ædificavit." The first cannon is said to have been introduced in a corn-sack, and local tradition still preserves the record of the jealous feeling with which the Perugians regarded this encroachment on their liberty, in the popular distich—

" Giacchè così vuole il diavolo
Evviva Papa Paolo ! "

On the frieze of the first court of the citadel is an inscription recording the circumstances of its erection, but in terms more moderate than those of the pope : " Paulus III. Pont. Max. tyrannide ejecta, novo civitatis statu constituto, bonorum quieti, et improborum fræno, arcem a solo excitatam, mira celeritate munivit, Pont. sui an. sal. xliii." The incomparably beautiful view over the valley of the Tiber and the distant Umbrian Apennines from the castle terrace will fully repay the fatigue of the ascent.

There is a good *Casino letterario* at

Perugia, where newspapers and reviews are taken in, and to which strangers are admitted on proper introduction.

Outside the walls of the city are the ch. and convent of *S. Francesco del Monte*, founded by Fra Elias, the companion of S. Francesco d' Assisi. It contains a beautiful and touching fresco of the Nativity, by *Perugino* ; another expressive work by the same, representing, in 2 parts, 1st the Madonna, with St. John and the Magdalen, and, in the 2nd, the Madonna and Child, with the Apostles. It contains also several works by the school of Perugino. The ancient classical library for which this convent was formerly celebrated has been long dispersed.

The *Fairs* of Perugia, well known throughout Italy, occur twice in the year, and are attended by a great concourse of persons from different parts of the States. The first lasts from the 1st to the 14th of August for beasts, and to the 22nd of August for merchandise. It is called *La Fiera di Monte Luce*, and is held in the hamlet adjoining the monastery of *Clarisse*, a little way beyond the city walls. The second, called *La Fiera de' Morti*, for beasts and merchandise, lasts from the 1st to the 4th of November. It takes its name from the day fixed by Silvester II. for the commemoration of the dead, being the 2nd of the month.

The roads from Perugia to Città di Castello and Gubbio are described under Rte. 21 ; to Todi and Narni, and thence to Rome, by Pontefelice and the Tiber, under Rte. 22 ; by the latter, Terni may be reached without making the circuit by Foligno and Spoleto ; to Città della Pieve, and thence to Chiusi and Siena, under Rte. 22 A ; and to Orvieto, Rte. 23.

Diligences leave Perugia for Arezzo 3 times a week, on Mondays, Wednesdays, and Fridays, in the evening, corresponding with those from the latter place to Florence ; by these conveyances the distance is performed in 18 hours ; for Chiusi also 3 times a week, corresponding with that to Siena, and from the latter to Florence by railway, employing 36 hours, including 2 hours' stoppage at Città della Pieve, and passing the night at Chiusi ; for Todi, Narni, and Pontefelice, 3 times a week ; for Foligno daily ; and for Città di Castello and Gubbio 3 times a week.

Leaving Perugia for Foligno by the road completed in 1843, which passes by the Benedictine monastery of S. Pietro, we soon descend into the valley of the Tiber. This new road is much better engineered, but is 1½ m. longer than the old one, which led down into the plain by a steep descent of 3 m. The scenery which it commands, bounded by the picturesque outline of the mountains behind Assisi, is extremely beautiful, and the plains below are characterised by a high state of fertility and cultivation. On the line of the new road about a m. before reaching the Ponte di S. Giovanni, a peasant discovered, in 1840, an Etruscan tomb in what has since proved to be the ancient Necropolis of Perugia. This tomb and the others which have since been brought to light have already been described in our account of the antiquities of Perugia ; but we may again remark that travellers interested in Etruscan antiquities should not fail to visit them, as well as the collections in the villa of Count Baglioni at the foot of the hill. (See p. 235.) At the Tiber we reach the boundary of ancient Etruria, and, crossing it by a bridge of 5 arches, called Ponte di S. Giovanni, enter ancient *Umbria*. This will very probably be the first spot where the classical traveller will see the "yellow Tiber."

" Hunc inter fluvio Tiberinus amæno,
Vorticibus rapidis, et multa flavus arena,
In mare prorumpit."   *Æn.*, vii. 31.

This celebrated river rises under Monte Coronaro, just within the Tuscan frontier, below the village of Le Balze, one of the Papal frontier stations of the Forlì district, near where the Savio and the Marecchia likewise have their origin. According to Calindri, its course from its source to the sea is 249 m. in length, and it is said to receive during its passage no less than 40 tributary streams.

At Ponte San Giovanni the river is not very broad, but it has been dammed up for the purpose of turning several mills, which add in some measure to the picturesque character of its scenery. At San Giovanni the beds of Macigno (pietra serena) are seen dipping towards the S.W. in the bed of the Tiber. Further on the road crosses the Jescio and the Chiascio torrents at their junction. A cross road of about 3 m. from this point will enable the pedestrian to reach Assisi in an hour. The village of Bastia, ½ m. beyond this spot, has in the choir of its ch. an altarpiece composed of several small pictures by *Niccolò Alunno*, with the date 1499. Passing thence over a fertile and level plain, we reach, at the distance of about 10 m. from Perugia, the post-station of

1 Sta. Maria degli Angeli. A third horse is required by the tariff for carriages with 3 horses, and 2 for carriages with 4 or 6 horses, from here to Perugia, but not *vice versâ*.

This station takes its name from the magnificent ch. of Sta. Maria degli Angeli, built from the designs of Vignola, by Galeasso Alessi and Giulio Danti, to protect the small Gothic chapel in which St. Francis laid the foundation of his order and drew up its rules. During the earthquake of 1832 the ch. was almost wholly ruined, the tower was thrown down, the roof rent, and many of its columns gave way. The cupola, which had long been celebrated for the boldness of its design, was not materially damaged, and under it still remains undisturbed the original cell and the little chapel of St. Francis. The nave and choir, which were destroyed, have been rebuilt. The ch. is remarkable for its great modern fresco (1829), representing the Vision of St. Francis, regarded as the masterpiece of *Overbeck.* The Stanza di S. Francesco is also celebrated for its frescoes of the Companions of the Saint, a series of beautiful figures by *Lo Spagna*, now very much injured. There is a good bust of Cardinal Rivarola by Tenerani, in the sagrestia.

EXCURSION TO ASSISI.

At this place a road branches off to *Assisi*, distant about 1½ m. No traveller who takes an interest in the history of art, who is desirous of tracing the influence which the devotional fervour of St. Francis exercised on the painters of the 14th and 15th centuries, will fail to visit Assisi. To many the distance is not beyond the compass of a walk; but if the *impedimenta* of the travelling carriage be an insurmountable difficulty, arrangements may be made at Perugia for the excursion; the carriage may be sent on to Spello or to Foligno, and a light carriage of the country hired to ascend the mountain; it might then proceed to either of those places by the excellent road which leads direct from Assisi to Spello without the necessity of returning to the Madonna degli Angeli. There are no inns at Assisi worthy of the name. At the foot of the hill is the *Locanda della Palomba;* in the upper town the best appears to be that of *Cofanelli*, near the Piazza of Sta. Chiara. Those who wi to explore at leisure the curiosities of the place may have a bed and 2 meals here for 4 pauls a day. At the house of Lorenzo Carpinelli, architect, Via di S. Giacomo, the same entertainment costs 3½ pauls, of which moderate terms many artists avail themselves.

Assisi is the sanctuary of early Italian art, and the scene of those triumphs of Giotto to which Dante has given immortality:

"Credette Cimabue nella pintura
　　Tener lo campo, ed hora ha Giotto il grido,
　　Sì che la fama di colui è oscura."
　　　　　　　　　　　　Purg., xi. 94.

Surrounded by its battlements and towers, and commanded by its lofty and ruined citadel, with its long line of aqueducts stretching across the mountain, Assisi is one of the most picturesque spots in Italy. Its interest will be increased in the estimation of the Italian scholar by the beautiful description of Dante:

"Intra Tupino e l' acqua, che discende
　　Dal colle eletto dal beato Ubaldo,
　　Fertile costa di alto monte pende,
Onde Perugia sente freddo e caldo
　　Da Porta Sole, e dirieto le piange
　　Per greve giogo Nocera con Gualdo.
Di quella costa là, dov'ella frangè
　　Più sua rattezza, nacque al mondo un sole,
　　Come fa questo tal volta di Gange.
Però chi di esso loco fa parole,
　　Nom dica Assesi, che direbbe corto,
　　Ma Oriente, se proprio dir vuole."
　　　　　　　　　　　　Par., xi. 4?

The *Sagro Convento* belongs to the order of the SS. Apostoli (Black Friars), one of the reformed orders which have sprung from the original foundation of St. Francis. The brethren of this order are all *possidenti*, and their easy circumstances, added to the general cleanliness of their establishment, offer a striking contrast to the poverty inculcated by their great founder. It is an immense building, and within its walls were collected in former times a larger number of monks, than even in the great monastery of Monte Casino. It was begun in 1228, by the German architect Jacopo Tedesco, better known as *Jacopo di Lapo*, the father of Arnolfo, and was finished in 2 years. It has 2 conventual churches, piled one over the other; or, if we include the subterranean ch. excavated to receive the body of St. Francis, their number may be said to be 3. The German architect was sent by the emperor Frederick II. to Fra Elia, the general of the order; and hence these buildings have a peculiar value in the history of architecture, as one of the earliest examples where the introduction of the foreign Gothic can be established.

The first object which engages attention is the entrance, consisting of a fine pointed arch divided into 2 doorways; above it is a wheel window richly worked in red and white marble, of which the ch. is chiefly built, in the tessellated style.

The *Upper Church* is a fine and unmutilated specimen of Gothic, with a pentagonal choir, and lancet windows filled with painted glass of the richest colours, executed, by order of Sixtus IV. in 1476, by Fra Francesco di Terranova, and by Lodovico da Udine in 1485. The roof is painted by *Cimabue*. It consists of 5 compartments, 3 of which are ornamented with figures, and 2 with gold stars on a blue ground. The best preserved painting on the roof is that representing the 4 Doctors of the Church; the 4 Evangelists over the choir have almost disappeared, but the medallions, with figures of Christ, the Madonna, John the Baptist, and St. Francis, with the foliage, vases, and other ornaments which surround them,

are still traceable. On the upper portion of the walls of this nave is a series of paintings by *Cimabue*, representing various events of the Old and New Testament, from the Creation to the Descent from the Cross. The lower portion of the walls represents in 28 compartments the different events of the life of St. Francis; they bear sufficient evidence of being the work of the school of Cimabue, and some of them have been attributed to *Giotto*. Behind the altar, the frescoes forming the decorations round the window are attributed to *Giunta da Pisa*. In the angles of the nave are Gothic galleries, which appear to have originally been carried round it. In the choir are 102 seats, the whole of which were inlaid by Fra Domenico di San Severino, a monk of the convent, at the expense of Francesco Sansoni, the general of the order, at the end of the 15th century. The campanile of this ch. is a massive pile, with stairs *a cordoni:* there is a very extensive view from the summit of it.

Under the portico leading to the *Lower* or *Middle Church*, is a painting of the Virgin, St. Francis, and other saints, attributed to *Lo Spagna*. On descending into this ch., it has a gloomy and low appearance, but it contains treasures enough to justify the title of museum. The 4 triangular compartments of the vault are occupied with large paintings by *Giotto*, in which the great painter has represented the 3 principal virtues practised by St. Francis, namely, Poverty, Chastity, and Obedience, and his glorification. They are by far the finest frescoes of Giotto at Assisi, and are interesting as showing the influence exercised upon him by the allegorical descriptions of his friend Dante. The 1st virtue, Poverty, shows this in a striking manner; Poverty appears as a woman standing among thorns, whom Christ gives in marriage to St. Francis. In the 2nd, Chastity is represented as a young female sitting in a strong fortress, to which St. Francis is leading several monks, &c. In the 3rd, Obedience is represented with a yoke, but wrapped up in allegorical emblems which it is difficult to comprehend. In the 4th,

St. Francis is seated on a throne holding the cross and the rules of the order, while hosts of angels sing his praises. In the cross-aisle is the celebrated Crucifixion, by *Pietro Cavallini*, the pupil of Giotto, admired by Michael Angelo for its grandeur. It was painted for Walter de Brienne, Duke of Athens, during his temporary elevation as captain of the Florentine republic, in 1342. It is the finest work extant by this master; the afflicted angels in the upper part of the composition, and the groups of horsemen, soldiers, &c., in the lower portion, are full of expression and feeling. The portrait of Cavallini, with a cap on his head and his hands clasped in adoration, is below it. In the southern transept are several paintings attributed to *Puccio Capanna*, another scholar of Giotto; they represent the Last Supper, the Capture of Christ, the Flagellation, and Christ bearing the Cross; on the wall, by the same painter, are the Deposition from the Cross, the Entombment, the Resurrection, and the St. Francis receiving the Stigmata. In the other transept are the Massacre of the Innocents by *Taddeo Gaddi*; and various events in the Life of the Virgin, the Annunciation, the Visitation, the Nativity, the Adoration of the Magi, the Presentation in the Temple, and the Flight out of Egypt, all of which are attributed to *Giovanni da Melano*, the pupil of Taddeo Gaddi, who flourished about 1365. The chapel of St. Louis King of France, sometimes called also the chapel of S. Stefano, has a vault painted by *Adone Doni*, and by Andrea di Luigi, or *L'Ingegno*, the able pupil of Perugino. The 4 Prophets and the 4 Sibyls are by *L'Ingegno*, and are perhaps to be considered his finest works; in the "Disputa" *Adone Doni* has introduced his own portrait as an old man. The graceful and expressive altarpiece representing the Madonna and Child throned, with 3 saints on each side, is by *Lo Spagna*. The chapel of S. Antonio di Padova, formerly belonging to the dukes of Urbino was originally covered with the works of *Giottino*, but,

the roof having fallen in, they were destroyed, and replaced by the present frescoes by Cesare Sermei, an artist of Orvieto, at the close of the 16th century. The ch. still preserves, however, an example of *Giottino,*—the Coronation of the Virgin. The chapel of Sta. Bonaventura, or of Sta. Maria Maddalena, is rich is frescoes representing the Life of the Magdalen by *Buffalmacco*. The chapel of S. Martino has a vault covered with frescoes, attributed by some to *Giotto* (?), by others, with more probability, to *Simone Memmi*. The chapel of the SS. *Crucifisso* was built in 1354, by the celebrated Cardinal Albornoz, who is said to be buried near it, the body having been brought hither from Viterbo, where he died in 1367. Its paintings are supposed to be by *Pace da Faenza*, a scholar of Giotto. Vasari says that this chapel was painted by Buffalmacco, and that he was liberally rewarded by the cardinal; the value of this statement will be shown by the simple fact that Buffalmacco, whose death Vasari himself places in 1340, died 14 years before the chapel was founded. The chapel of S. Antonio Abate, originally painted by Pace da Faenza, has suffered greatly from the damp; its frescoes have been whitewashed over. It contains 2 sepulchral monuments of the family of Blasco, dukes of Spoleto, with an epitaph in Latin hexameters. Near the entrance to the ch., on the rt. hand, is a monument bearing the arms of the Cerchi family of Florence, and upon it is a porphyry vase, said to have been a present from Ecuba di Lusignano, the queen of Cyprus, who has been supposed to be buried near it in a magnificent mausoleum by Fuccio Fiorentino, in 1240. There appears, however, to be great obscurity about this tomb; the crowned head is a sufficient indication of royalty, but the attitude of the sitting statue is little in accordance with feminine grace or the dignity of a queen. It has been suggested that it is more probably that of Giovanni di Brenne, king of Jerusalem in the time of St. Francis, who entered the order and died in 1237; and that his daughter Maria de Lusignan, princess of Antioch, sister of Yolanda wife of the emperor Frederick II., erected this monument to his memory. The walls near it are covered with the remains of frescoes. said to be painted by Greek artists. In the sacristy is a curious portrait of St. Francis, attributed to *Giunta da Pisa*. Considerable speculation has been excited in regard to the precise spot in this ch. where the illustrious Ghibeline general of the 13th century, Guido di Montefeltro, was buried. Some doubt, indeed, exists whether the body was not removed from Assisi by his son Federigo. After a brilliant career of military glory, this celebrated captain, charmed by the enthusiasm of St. Francis, retired to Assisi and assumed the habit of the new order. From this seclusion he was summoned to Anagni by Boniface VIII., who was so anxious to have the advantage of his counsels during his contests with the house of Colonna, that he promised him plenary indulgence if he would assist in reducing Palestrina, the feudal stronghold of that noble family. Guido stipulated for a more express absolution for any crime he might commit in giving this advice, and then suggested the perfidious policy of promising much and performing little:

" Lunga promessa con lo attender corto."
                              Inf. xxvii.

After this Guido retired again to this convent, and died here in 1298. Dante has punished him for this treason by putting him in the Inferno, because his absolution preceded his penitence, and was therefore null. Below this ch. is a chamber excavated in the rock, which has been sometimes called the *Third Church*. It contains the body of St. Francis, which was discovered here in December, 1818, and again deposited in its urn of travertine, after it had been formally acknowledged by a deputation of cardinals and prelates. It is supported by the solid rock, which was left standing for the purpose, while the ch. was excavated around it. The whole is enclosed by an iron palisade; but

the general air of the mausoleum is too modern, and perhaps too obtrusive, for so remarkable a tomb.

The convent and its cloisters are scarcely less remarkable than the ch. A series of heads of eminent Franciscans by *Adone Doni* presents some interesting studies; and in the refectory is a fine painting of the Last Supper, by *Solimene*.

The ch. of *Sta. Chiara*, built by Fra Filippo da Campello, the pupil of Jacopo da Lapo, in 1253, a few years only after the death of the saint, still retains its fine wheel window; but the greater part of the ancient ch. which was in the Gothic of the 13th century, and painted internally by Giotto, has been replaced by modern innovations. It is interesting, however, as containing the body of Sta. Chiara, the first abbess of the order which bears her name, the celebrated maiden whom the enthusiasm of St. Francis induced to renounce her family and her riches, and whose hair he cut off with his own hand. She is buried under the high altar. The side wings still retain some frescoes illustrating the life of the Saint, attributed to *Giotto*, but probably executed by his able imitator Giottino.

The *Cathedral*, dedicated to St. Rufinus, its first bishop, under Fabian I., dates from the early part of the 12th century, and its crypt from 1028; it was modernised by Galeasso Alessi in the 16th century, but retains its Gothic front. An ancient marble sarcophagus serves as the high altar.

The ch. called the *Chiesa Nuova* is remarkable as occupying the site of the house in which St. Francis was born. The apartment is still shown in which his father confined him under the belief that his devotion and his charities were acts of madness.

In the Piazza is the magnificent portico of the ancient *Temple of Minerva;* it consists of 6 fluted columns of travertine and a pediment, beneath which some fragments of antiquity and Roman inscriptions have been collected for preservation. The ruin has been attached to a ch. to which it has given the name of Sta. Maria della Minerva.

The chapel of the confraternità of *Sta. Caterina* is remarkable for the remains of paintings on its exterior by *Martinello* (1422), and in the interior for the works of *Matteo da Gualdo* (1468) and *Pietro Antonio da Fuligno.*

The Ch. of *S. Pietro* deserves mention among the architectural remains of Assisi, for the 3 wheel windows which still remain of its original and imposing Gothic.

At the Convent of *S. Damiano* are preserved some relics of Sta. Chiara; within its walls the Church tradition states that she performed many of her miracles. In the dormitory is a door now walled up, where she is said to have repulsed the Saracens, who were on the point of scaling the convent.

Assisi, independently of the interest it derives from St. Francis, is remarkable as the birthplace of Metastasio. It has been the seat of a bishopric since A.D. 240. The present population by the last census was 6500, of which a very large proportion belong to Church and monastic establishments.

The great fair of Assisi begins on the 21st July and ends on the 1st August, during which time the indulgences granted draw people from all parts of Catholic Europe. Another fair takes place on the 4th October, at the festival of St. Francis.

Assisi has some celebrity for its manufactory of needles and files. The annual quantity of needles it produces is about 4000 lbs.

The high mountain behind Assisi is the Monte Subasio, 3620 feet above the level of the sea; in one of the ravines descending from it is the Sanctuary delle Carceri, where St. Francis retired to for his devotions.

A new and excellent branch road leads from Assisi into the post route, half way between St. Maria degli Angeli and Spello. The distance to Foligno is about 8 m. Travellers from Rome to Florence should make at Foligno the arrangements recommended in a previous page for visiting Assisi. They may thus diverge from the high road 4 m. beyond Spello, and rejoin their travelling carriage at Gli Angeli.

Leaving Sta. Maria degli Angeli, the road traverses the plain to Foligno, passing on the l. hand the ancient town of *Spello* (the Colonia Julia Hispellum of the Romans), built on a projecting spur of the red Apennine limestone. The road passes at the foot of the town. By the side of an ancient gate, before arriving at the modern entrance to the town, is an inscription recording the fabulous exploits of Orlando. The Roman gate, surmounted by 3 figures, a female in the centre, and a Senatorial on either side, is well preserved, and is still called the Porta Veneris. The streets of Spello are very narrow and irregular, and are mostly paved with brick. The Gothic *Cathedral* of S. M. Maggiore contains 2 companion frescoes by *Perugino*, a Pietà, with his name and the date 1521, and the Madonna and Child with 2 saints, but both show symptoms of the decline which marked his latter years. In the chapel of the Holy Sacrament, on the l., are the 3 large frescoes by *Pinturicchio*, painted in 1501, representing the Annunciation, a very beautiful painting, with the painter's portrait looking from a window, and his name; the Nativity, with various incidents, such as the approach of the Magi, and a fine landscape; Christ disputing with the Doctors, a series of fine groups with highly finished heads. On the rt. of the entrance to the ch. is a Roman tomb with bas-reliefs representing an equestrian figure and an inscription; it is now used as a vase for holy water. The ch. of *S. Francesco*, consecrated by Gregory IX. in 1228, contains a large altarpiece by *Pinturicchio*, representing the Madonna and Child throned, with several saints in adoration, and St. John at the foot of the throne writing the "Ecce Agnus" on the ribbon of his cross: a charming composition; the St. John has been attributed to Raphael. A highly interesting letter from Gentile Baglioni, lord of Perugia, to the painter, has been whimsically introduced by him under the throne. Among the antiquities of Spello, a house still bears the name of the "Casa di Propersio," and gives name to the street: even the tomb (?) of the poet is shown under its lower apartments, so determined are the inhabitants to claim him as their own, although he tells us himself that he was born at the neighbouring town of Mevania. In the plain below the town, near the roadside, are some traces of an amphitheatre, and there are some remains of an arch in the Via dell' Arco, with the inscription R. DIVI; it is said by Calindri to have been dedicated to the emperor Marcus Opilius Macrinus; and remains of another arch leading to the monastery at the top of the town. Some Roman inscriptions are built into the wall of the ch. of S. Lorenzo. At the highest point of the town is a convenient balcony, or terrace, which the traveller should visit, as it commands the whole plain of the Clitumnus, the town of Foligno, the upper valley of the Tiber, the city of Perugia, the ecclesiastical buildings of Assisi, and the tertiary chain separated from that on which Perugia stands by the valley in which the Tiber winds its way into the plain.

Before entering Foligno, the river Topino is crossed.

1 FOLIGNO (*Inns*: Tre Mori, Grande Albergo, La Posta, all indifferent), the ancient Fulginium, a place of some importance as the head of a confederacy of Umbrian cities. During the middle ages it long maintained its independence, but was at last reduced by its more powerful neighbours; in 1439 it was incorporated with the States of the Church. It is an active and industrious episcopal town of 8200 Inhab., and has a high reputation throughout the States for its cattle, its manufactures of woollens, parchment, and wax candles. Foligno and the neighbouring towns were subject to frequent earthquakes for many years prior to 1831, and it was a rare occurrence for 3 months to pass without one. In 1831, however, they lost their desultory and occasional character, and a violent series of shocks occurred which spread devastation and misery throughout the province. The first, fortunately, took place in the daytime, and did little injury, but the 2nd ruined several edifices, by the fall of which upwards of 70 persons lost their lives in Foligno and Spello. From 1831 the town remained free from their visit-

ations until October, 1839, when some undulatory shocks were felt, but fortunately without such serious consequences as attended those of 1831. It is remarkable that the towns which suffered most from the earthquakes of these years are on alluvial deposits, while those on the solid calcareous rock, as Spoleto, Assisi, and Perugia, suffered comparatively little. The *Cathedral*, dedicated to St. Felician, has preserved its Gothic front and pointed doorway of the 15th century, with the 2 lions of red marble; the interior has been modernised, and has a Baldacchino of gilt wood and bronze, in imitation of that in St. Peter's at Rome. The ch. of *S. Domenico* has a Gothic façade. The ch. of the Convent of Sant' Anna or le Contesse, with a cupola by Bramante, was remarkable in former days for the celebrated picture by Raphael, called, from the town, the "Madonna di Foligno," and now one of the treasures of the Vatican. The ch. contains a Madonna, said to be by *Perugino*(?), and a picture attributed to *Lodovico Caracci*, representing our Saviour discovering himself to his disciples by the breaking of bread. The ch. of *S. Niccolò* preserves a beautiful altarpiece by *Niccolò Alunno*, a native of this town, which was taken to Paris; and there are other remains of the same master to be traced in some of the other churches. The Palazzo Comunale is a fine building recently constructed in the Ionic style. The Corso, called the Canopia, affords an agreeable walk for the citizens along the ancient walls.

4 m. W. of Foligno, between the Topino and the Timia, is *Bevagna*, which still retains almost its ancient name Mevania, celebrated by the Latin poets for the richness of its pastures, and still famous for its fine breed of white cattle. "Strabo mentions Mevania as one of the most considerable towns of Umbria. Here Vitellius took post as if determined to make a last stand for the empire against Vespasian, but soon after withdrew his forces. This city is further memorable as the birthplace of Propertius, a fact of which he himself informs us."—*Dr. Cramer.*

On the hill, 6 m. S. of Bevagna, is the picturesque little town of *Montefalco* remarkable for 2 pictures by *Benozzo Gozzoli*, in the churches of S. Fortunato and S. Francesco.

The road from Perugia falls into the Flaminian Way at Foligno (Rte. 16). Another excellent road leads to Ancona, by Tolentino, Macerata, and Loreto, with branches to Camerino and Fabriano (Rte. 15). A third leads by the Furlo Pass to Fano (Rte. 16), and a fourth to Todi and Narni by Bevagna, following the ancient line of the Via Flaminia.

On leaving Foligno for Rome, passing S. Eraclio, the road runs through the beautiful vale of the Clitumnus, "the fame of which is united by the poetry of Virgil with the triumphs of Rome and the Capitol itself:"

> " Hinc albi, Clitumne, greges, et maxima
>   taurus
> Victima, sæpe tuo perfusi flumine sacro,
> Romanos ad templa deûm duxere triumphos."
> > *Georg.,* ii. 146.

About midway between Foligno and Le Vene, picturesquely placed on a mountain on the l., is the little town of *Trevi,* the Trebia of Pliny. In its ch. of La Madonna delle Lagrime is a fine large and well-preserved fresco by Perugino; it represents the Adoration of the Magi, contains several full-length figures, and bears the painter's name.

Shortly before arriving at Le Vene, on the rt., is the small ancient temple supposed to be the one described by Pliny as dedicated to the river-god Clitumnus. The road passes at the back of the temple, which travellers will do well to bear in mind, as they may otherwise miss noticing it. The river which rises near it is still called the *Clitunno.* There are, however, some points connected with the authenticity of the temple which require to be noticed. The temple itself is described by Pliny as being an ancient edifice in his day; and antiquaries and architects agree in regarding the present building as much more recent, bearing evidence of the corruption of art, and probably not more ancient than the time of Constantine. The representation of Christian emblems, such as bunches of grapes

and the cross on the façade, do not appear more recent than the rest of the building. Sir John Hobhouse has endeavoured to meet some of the objections by showing that, when the temple was converted into a chapel, the interior was modernised. " The temple," says a good authority on such points, " can hardly be that structure which the younger Pliny describes as ancient even in his time ; for, instead of columns bescratched with the nonsense of an album, here are columns coupled in the middle of the front with those on the antes, a thing not found in any classical antiquity ; here are spiral columns, which, so far from being characters of early art, are corruptions of its decline."—*Forsyth.*

In spite of these difficulties, the existing building may be considered to mark the site of the temple of the time of Pliny ; and English travellers will doubtless give due weight to the tradition which has been accepted and celebrated by Dryden, Addison, and Byron. The temple is now used as a chapel dedicated to S. Salvatore.

> " But thou, Clitumnus ! in thy sweetest wave
> Of the most living crystal that was e'er
> The haunt of river nymph, to gaze and lave
> Her limbs where nothing hid them, thou dost
>   rear
> Thy grassy banks whereon the milk-white
>   steer
> Grazes ; the purest god of gentle waters !
> And most serene of aspect, and most clear ;
> Surely that stream was unprofaned by
>   slaughters—
> A mirror and a bath for Beauty's youngest
>   daughters !
>
> And on thy happy shore a Temple still,
> Of small and delicate proportion, keeps
> Upon a mild declivity of hill
> Its memory of thee ; beneath it sweeps
> Thy current's calmness ; oft from out it leaps
> The finny darter with the glittering scales,
> Who dwells and revels in thy glassy deeps ;
> While, chance, some scatter'd water-lily sails'
> Down where the shallower wave still tells its
>   bubbling tales."   *Childe Harold.*

1 Le Vene (a name derived from the neighbouring fountains), a post-house. Close to this spot is the source of the Clitumnus ; it issues in one body from the Apennine limestone in a considerable stream of pure crystal water. About half way to Spoleto, in the ham-

let of *S. Giacomo*, is a ch. containing in the apsis some beautiful frescoes by *Lo Spagna*. Below is the portrait of the Saint and 2 of his miracles; above, the favourite Coronation of the Madonna, dated 1526. The chapel on the rt. has been repainted, but all the rest is admirably preserved.

The approach to Spoleto is extremely beautiful. It "offers a rich promise of enjoyment to the picturesque traveller, in its towers, castles, and forest background; and few places afford so many grand and beautiful objects for the sketch-book; its old fortress, and its vast aqueduct, one of the loftiest known, spanning a ravine in which it is a singularly fine object when seen from the various heights, make up, with the beautiful country around them, some of the' very finest landscapes in nature."—*Brockedon*.

1 SPOLETO (*Inns:* the Albergo Nuovo, a new house kept by Mancini; la Posta, indifferent, and said to be exorbitant in its charges). This ancient city is the capital of a Delegation, embracing a superficial extent of 1375 sq. m., and a population of 126,700 souls. The city itself contains 6800. It is the seat of an archbishopric for the united dioceses of Spoleto, Bevagna, and Trevi; its bishopric is as ancient as the time of St. Peter, the 1st bishop being St. Brizius, A.D. 50. Spoleto has the manufactory of woollens in the Papal States next in importance to that of Rome.

Spoleto was the *Spoletium* of the Romans, "colonised A.U.C. 512. 25 years afterwards it withstood, according to Livy, the attack of Hannibal, who was on his march through Umbria, after the battle of Thrasimene. This resistance had the effect of checking the advance of the Carthaginian general towards Rome, and compelled him to draw off his forces into Picenum. It should be mentioned, however, that Polybius makes no mention of this attack upon Spoleto, but expressly states that it was not Hannibal's intention to approach Rome at that time, but to lead his army to the sea-coast. Spoletium appears to have ranked high among the municipal cities of Italy, but it

suffered severely from proscription in the civil wars of Marius and Sylla."—*Dr. Cramer*.

During the middle ages Spoleto and Benevento were the first 2 Lombard States which established a duchy with a kind of independent sovereignty. While that of Benevento, which set the first example, had spread over half of the present kingdom of Naples, Spoleto included within her territory nearly the whole of Umbria. After the overthrow of the Lombard kingdom by Charlemagne, the dukes of Spoleto, like the other petty princes of Italy, became vassals of the empire; but it was not long before they reasserted their independence, and exercised their ancient Lombard rights. About the time of Gregory VII. the countess Matilda of Tuscany had bequeathed to the Holy See her extensive fiefs of the March of Ancona and the duchy of Spoleto; notwithstanding which, Spoleto continued to preserve its municipal government, and indeed maintained it so effectually that the popes found it necessary to issue specific decrees for depriving it of its rights. Among the casualties to which its strong position and independent government exposed it in the middle ages, one of the most remarkable was its siege by Frederick Barbarossa; the citizens sallied from their walls and gave him battle, but they fled before the charge of the German cavalry: the town was given up to pillage for 2 days, and a large portion of it perished by fire. During the events which followed the French revolution, and the subsequent invasion of Italy, Spoleto, Perugia, and the other neighbouring towns, were incorporated with the Roman republic.

The *Cathedral*, dedicated to Sta. Maria Assunta, occupies a commanding situation: it dates from the period of its Lombard dukes, and still retains many vestiges of its original pointed architecture. The 5 Gothic arches of the façade are supported by Grecian columns, introduced, it is said, from the design of Bramante when the edifice was modernised. The frieze is ornamented with griffins and arabesques, and at each extremity is a stone pulpit facing the piazza. Over the portico is a large mosaic, representing the Saviour throned between the Virgin and St. John, and bearing the name of the painter, *Salsernus,* with the date 1207, a work of great interest in the history of the revival. The central Gothic window is filled with painted glass, and bears the symbols of the 4 evangelists. The interior of the cathedral is also interesting, though modernised in 1644 by a cardinal archbishop of the Barberini family. In the choir are the interesting frescoes of *Filippo Lippi,* representing the Annunciation, the Nativity, the Death of the Virgin, and her Coronation, but they have suffered from time and restorations. The chapel on the l. of the choir contains the tomb of this painter, who died here in 1469, from the effects of poison administered by the family of a noble lady, Lucrezia Bieti, whose affections he had won, and whom he had carried off from the convent of Sta. Margherita at Prato. His monument was erected by Lorenzo de' Medici, after an ineffectual attempt to induce the magistrates to allow him to remove the ashes of Lippi to Florence: the epitaph was written by Politian. Opposite is a fine monument to one of the Orsini family. The only other painting to be noticed in this cathedral is a Madonna by *Annibale Carracci,* much injured by recent attempts to restore it. In one of the lateral chapels are some carved arabesques in wood. The chapel, which now serves as a baptistery, is beautifully painted in fresco, with subjects from the history of Adam and Eve, by *Giacomo Siciliano,* in the manner of Lo Spagna. The font is sculptured with bas-reliefs of the Life of Christ: the octagonal baptistery, which is detached from the cathedral, is no longer used for its original purpose.

The Gothic ch. of *S. Domenico* is remarkable for a fine copy of the Transfiguration of Raphael, which the inhabitants attribute to *Giulio Romano.* The Gothic ch. of S. Giovanni has a rich doorway of the 16th century. The collegiate ch. of *S. Pietro,* outside the Roman gate, is worthy of a visit, as an example of Lombard architecture; the

front is noticed by Mr. Hope for its great profusion of sculpture.

The *Palazzo Pubblico* contains an interesting fresco by *Lo Spagna,* formerly on one of the inner walls of the citadel, and removed here for better preservation.

The *Piazza della Porta Nuova* has a small Madonna, with a blue veil, in fresco, remarkable for its excellent preservation; it was painted in 1502 by *Crivelli,* a native artist.

The *Citadel* should be visited by every traveller who wishes to enjoy one of the most extensive views in Italy. Permission is readily granted, on application to the commanding officer. It is a massive building surrounded with a strong rampart, and occupies a picturesque and commanding position, which completely overlooks the town: it was built by Theodoric, destroyed during the Gothic war, and repaired by Narses. It was subsequently rebuilt by Cardinal Albornoz, and enlarged by Nicholas V. It is now used as a prison. According to the returns published by the government it will hold 500 prisoners, who are generally persons convicted of homicides and felonies, political prisoners being rarely sent here. The view from the castle walls is extremely grand, commanding the whole valley of the Clitumnus, the Apennines from the Pass of Monte Somma to the high peak above S. Angelo in Vado and Città di Castello, the cities of Perugia and Foligno, the churches and convents of Assisi, Spello, Castelfranco, and scores of villages scattered upon the plain. Among the foundations of the castle, near the city gate, some remains of the polygonal walls are still visible.

The *Aqueduct,* called delle Torre, crossing the deep valley which separates the almost insulated hill on which the city is built from the opposite mountain, serves both as an aqueduct and a bridge. Calindri gives the height as 81 metres (about 266 ft.), and the length as 205·98 (rather more than 676 ft.). Scarcely any two travellers agree in their accounts of these measurements, and therefore the estimate of Calindri, the celebrated engineer of Perugia, and author of the 'Saggio Statistico Storico.'

of the Papal States, may be considered useful. The aqueduct is supported by a range of 10 pointed brick arches on stone piers, and is said by the same authority to have been built by Theodelapius III., duke of Spoleto, in 604. It bears, however, sufficient evidence of repairs and additions long subsequently to the Lombard times, and its substructions, and the body of the 9 piers, are perhaps all that can safely be regarded as belonging to the Lombard foundation. We have already stated that the structure serves both for an aqueduct and bridge. The water which supplies the town and castle is carried over it by a covered canal from Monte Luco; and at a lower level, but still at a frightful elevation above the valley, is the road over which vehicles pass: it is supplied with an opening and benches in the centre, to allow the passenger a view of the fine scenery around.

The Roman antiquities of Spoleto consist of the arch through which the street is carried, called the *Porta Fuga* and *Porta d'Annibale*, from the local tradition that Hannibal was repulsed in his attempt to force it. It is a plain arch, with a device of the middle ages, representing a lion devouring a lamb. Some of the churches present remains of Roman temples; that of the *Crocifisso* is supposed to preserve part of the walls of the Temple of Concord; in that of *S. Andrea* the fluted marble columns, in the Corinthian style, are said to have belonged to a temple of Jupiter; and in that of *S. Giuliano* are some fragments of the Temple of Mars. Besides these there are some remains of an ancient theatre; and the ruin still called the Palace of Theodoric. Outside the city gate a Roman bridge, which had remained buried and unknown for centuries, in consequence of the torrent over which it was erected having changed its bed, was discovered a few years since; but unfortunately the authorities have recently allowed it to be again buried, in constructing the new gate leading to Foligno.

1 m. E. of the town, beyond the aqueduct, picturesquely situated and beauti-fully wooded, is *Monte Luco*, with its monastery of S. Giuliano, the ch. of the Madonna delle Grazie, and its numerous hermitages. Monte Luco was made a place of religious pilgrimage by St. Isaac of Syria, A.D. 528, and it has since had great celebrity among the monastic establishments of Italy. The road leading to it commands some of the most magnificent scenery of the valley. The monastery dates from the 10th century; but the great attraction of the spot is its beautiful position, and its grove of oaks, which have been singularly protected and preserved by the ancient municipal laws of Spoleto. One of these fine trees is said to be not less than 105 ft. high, and 41 in circumference.

An additional horse is required by the tariff between Spoleto and La Strettura, both ways.

On leaving Spoleto the road winds over the steep ascent of the Monte Somma, which rises at the Pass to 3738 feet above the sea. The ascent commands, in fine weather, magnificent views over the valley of the Clitumnus, as far as Foligno and Spello, backed by the ridge of the Apennines. The upper parts of the mountain are covered with oaks, among which are thinly scattered trees of the Abruzzi pine. Lower down, the sides are clothed with small forests of ilex, mixed with arborescent heaths, and lower still with olive-trees. The descent from the summit of the pass to Terni is longer and much wilder in its character. In former days the glen was famous for its banditti; it is now infested with beggars. The long descent at length brings us into the plain of Terni, celebrated in ancient times as the most productive in Italy, and still so fertile that the meadows produce several successive crops in the year, precisely as they did in the days of Pliny.

1 La Strettura, beyond the pass; a post-station with a miserable *osteria*; a m. before reaching it, and higher up, is a large house, called the Casa del Papa, formerly the villa of Leo XII., who built it as his country residence. It has latterly been used as an inn, and is about to be supplied with addi-

tional accommodations for travellers. The road from La Strettura to Terni first descends a narrow valley, and then crosses the plain of the Nera for about 3 m., to

1 TERNI (*Inns:* Europa; Isole Britanniche; La Fortuna, good; la Posta). This interesting little town, occupying the site of ancient *Interamna*, is one of the most thriving second-rate cities of the Papal States. It has a Pop. of 9700 souls, and has manufactures of woollen cloths and iron, and upwards of 1000 boilers for winding silk from the cocoons. It claims the honour of being the birthplace of Tacitus the historian, and of the emperors Tacitus and Florian. It has been the seat of a bishopric since the year 138.

The *Cathedral*, dedicated to Sta. Maria Assunta, is said to have been built from the designs of Bernini. Its altar is rich in marbles, and there is a small collection of ancient inscriptions preserved there; but there is little in this or the other churches of Terni to require notice.

The *Antiquities* consist of some remains of an amphitheatre in the gardens of the episcopal palace; of a temple in the circular ch. of San Salvador, called by the local antiquaries the Temple of the Sun; vestiges of another building, called the Temple of Hercules, in the cells of the college of San Siro; and some remains of baths in the villa of the Spada family. Some inscriptions are also preserved in the Palazzo Pubblico, and in other parts of the town.

The great interest of Terni is derived from the *Caduta delle Marmore*, one of the wonders of Italy, and celebrated throughout Europe as the 'FALLS OF TERNI.' They are distant about 5 m. from the town, and the excursion will occupy 3 or 4 hours or more, as the taste and feelings of the traveller may influence him to prolong his visit. To those who are desirous of enjoying the scene as it ought to be enjoyed, a day will hardly seem too much to devote to the excursion. The charges for conveyance were formerly exorbitant, the service being a monopoly in the hands of the postmaster, conceded to him by government: a light carriage for 2 persons hired at the inn cost 5 pauls, each person paying 8 pauls more; so that for a party of 4 the charge was 3 scudi and 7 pauls. Recent travellers have obtained a carriage for 2½ scudi, everything included. The post tariff is 8 pauls for each person if more than 1, and 3 pauls for each carriage; but, if there be only 1 person, he pays 18 pauls and 3 for the carriage, in addition to the buonamano to the postilion of about 5 pauls. The postmaster, however, is not unfrequently ready to reduce these exorbitant charges, especially as donkeys are now to be hired very reasonably. The cicerone expects from 5 to 7 pauls, and the driver 5 pauls. *All this should be arranged with the landlord before starting*, to prevent subsequent imposition. By many a cicerone from the inn is considered an unnecessary expense; for the traveller is beset by scores at the Falls, whom a paul will content. The cicerone, however, may be useful in keeping off the beggars who assail the traveller in all parts of the valley; and for an extra fee of 2 pauls he will pay all the *custodi*, doorkeepers, &c., and relieve the traveller of all trouble. Pedestrians may reach the Falls in 1½ hour, and ladies who can walk 2 m. to the bottom of the ascent will find donkeys, for 3 pauls, to carry them to the Cascades.

After leaving the town the road for nearly 3 m. ascends the valley of the Nar, following the high road between Terni and Rieti as far as Papigno, a small mountain village, where a road leading to the bottom of the Falls branches off. The road then ascends the hill, and about ½ a mile from the summit reaches the spot where the Velino dashes over the precipice. There are therefore two points of view—that from above and that from below—seen from the opposite side of the valley. The latter, or the lower view, is by far the best; but travellers should see both, and accordingly should follow the directions of the guides, and go to the upper one first. The bed of the river above the Falls is about 50 feet wide, and the rapidity of the stream is said to be 7 m. an hour. After seeing the

Falls from the summit, the next point of view is that afforded by a small building on a projecting mass of rock, some hundreds of feet above the bottom, and which was erected, it is said, by Pius VI. for the accommodation of Napoleon. The lower part of the Falls is not visible from this point, but the scene notwithstanding is full of grandeur. A path leads from this building down the valley to a point where the Nar is crossed by a bridge, whence a road on the opposite bank leads the traveller through groves of ilex to the point where he finds himself immediately opposite the cataract. Nothing can surpass the view afforded by this side of the valley, particularly from the little summer-house in the side of the hill, which commands a view of the whole cataract, from top to bottom, in all its magnificence. Those travellers who have only time for one view should bear in mind that this is much to be preferred. There is another point of view from the summit of this hill which shows the Falls in relation to the surrounding country: it embraces the whole plain of the Velino as far as the mountains behind the Piè di Luco, described in Rte. 46 of Handbook of S. Italy.

The falls of Terni have been so frequently described, that we shall leave travellers to their own impressions, merely adding such historical and other facts as may be useful, and quoting the following beautiful passage from Lord Byron, in whose judgment, " either from above or below, they are worth all the cascades and torrents of Switzerland put together; the Staubach, Reichenbach, Pisse Vache, Fall of Arpenaz, &c., are rills in comparative appearance:"

" The roar of waters!—from the headlong height
Velino cleaves the wave-worn precipice;
The fall of waters! rapid as the light
The flashing mass foams shaking the abyss;
The hell of waters! where they howl and hiss,
And boil in endless torture; while the sweat
Of their great agony, wrung out from this
Their Phlegethon, curls round the rocks of jet
That gird the gulf around, in pitiless horror set,

And mounts in sprays the skies, and thence again
Returns in an unceasing shower, which round,
With its unemptied cloud of gentle rain,
Is an eternal April to the ground,

Making it all one emerald:—how profound
The gulf! and how the giant element
From rock to rock leaps with delirious bound,
Crushing the cliffs, which, downward worn and rent
With his fierce footsteps, yield in chasms a fearful vent

To the broad column which rolls on, and shows
More like the fountain of an infant sea
Torn from the womb of mountains by the throes
Of a new world, than only thus to be
Parent of rivers, which flow gushingly,
With many windings, through the vale:—Look back!
Lo! where it comes like an eternity,
As if to sweep down all things in its track,
Charming the eye with dread,—a matchless cataract,

Horribly beautiful! but on the verge,
From side to side, beneath the glittering morn,
An Iris sits, amidst the infernal surge,
Like Hope upon a death-bed, and, unworn
Its steady dyes, while all around is torn
By the distracted waters, bears serene
Its brilliant hues with all their beams unshorn:
Resembling, 'mid the torture of the scene,
Love watching Madness with unalterable mien."
Childe Harold.

Lord Byron, in a note to these stanzas, remarks the singular circumstance " that 2 of the finest cascades in Europe should be artificial—this of the Velino, and the one at Tivoli."

The formation of this cascade was the work of the Romans. The valley of the Velinus was subject to frequent inundations from the river, which was so charged with calcareous matter that it filled its bed with deposits, and thus subjected the rich plains of Rieti to constant overflows from the lakes which it forms at that part of its course. " The drainage of the stagnant waters produced by the occasional overflow of these lakes and of the river was first attempted by Curius Dentatus, the conqueror of the Sabines (B.C. 271). He caused a channel to be made for the Velinus, through which the waters of that river were carried into the Nera over a precipice of several hundred feet. It appears from Cicero and from Tacitus that the draining of the Velinus and Nera not unfrequently gave rise to disputes between the inhabitants of Reate and Interamna."—*Dr. Cramer.*

In these disputes, which happened in the year of Rome 700, Cicero was consulted by the inhabitants of Rieti, who erected a statue to him for his services. For about 1500 years from its first construction the channel continued to relieve the valley of its superabundant water; but in 1400 it was so much obstructed that the people of Rieti opened a new channel, which affected the lower valley and inundated Terni. Braccio di Montone, the lord of Perugia, interposed, and had a new channel made, but it was of little service, and speedily filled up. From that time to the end of the 16th century the inundations either above or below the Falls gave rise to constant contentions between the 2 cities; and the celebrated architects Sangallo and Fontana were employed upon the works, but with little success. Fontana adopted the old Roman channel until he reached the obtuse angle which it made towards the precipice; he then continued the channel in a straight line, so that the waters entered the Nar at right angles. This arrangement, added to the contracted state of the Nar at that point, blocked up that river with the masses of rock brought down by the Velino, and fresh inundations occurred in the valley of Terni. This was not corrected until 1785, when it was found necessary to adopt some further measures to protect the landholders of Terni, and a new channel was accordingly cut, by which the Velino is brought into the Nar at an oblique angle, which has obviated the mischief in the lower valley, and secured the effectual drainage of the plains of Rieti.

Considerable difference exists as to the actual height of the Falls. Calindri, the engineer, in his great work on the Papal States, gives it as 375 metres, or 1230 English feet; Ricardi, the architect, of Terni, who is more likely, as a resident engineer, to have taken greater pains in his measurements, estimates the upper Fall at 50 feet; the second, or the perpendicular Fall, from 500 to 600 feet; and the long sheet of foam, which forms the third Fall, extending from the base of the second to the Nar, at 240 feet: making a total height of between 800 and 900 feet, which may be taken as the nearest approximation to truth.

The road by which travellers who have descended to the lower Fall return to Terni is carried along the beautiful valley of the united rivers through groves of ilex. It passes through the grounds of the Villa Graziani, one of the residences of Queen Caroline when Princess of Wales. The scenery of this valley is exceedingly beautiful, and artists might fill their sketch-books with the varied and charming landscapes it presents. The mountain-sides are covered with timber, among which the ilex, the judas-tree, the chestnut, and the olive are conspicuous, while the lower slopes are rich in mulberry and orange plantations, and in vineyards. Travellers rejoin their carriages at Papigno, to which place they must be sent back after conveying the party to the upper Fall.

From Terni a very interesting road proceeds through Rieti and Aquila direct to Naples. (Handbook for Southern Italy, Rte. 46.)

From Terni to Rome is 62 m., which may be done in 1 day by post. An excellent road along the rich valley of Terni brings us to the foot of the hill on which Narni is built.

1 *Narni* (*Inn:* La Campana, very good, kept by Martellotti, a respectable landlord). Narni is an ancient Umbrian city, beautifully situated on a lofty hill commanding the valley of the Nar, and an immense extent of fertile and varied country as far as the Apennines. Its old convent towers and castle give it an air of picturesque beauty from many parts of the neighbouring country, but internally it is badly built, and its streets are narrow and dirty. It is the Narnia or Nequinum of the Romans, the birthplace of the emperor Nerva, of Pope John XVIII., and of Gattamelata. It is the seat of a bishopric, and has a pop. of 3500 souls. The castle is now used as a prison for criminals.

The great object of interest in Narni is the ruined Bridge, which has for ages been regarded as one of the noblest relics of imperial times. The master of the Campana has a light carriage which may be hired to take travellers by the road (about 3 m.), for 8 ⌐ ˙

but those who are able to do so should walk down the picturesque cliffs to the river. A rugged path of less than 1 m. leads from the town to the point where the Nar enters the deep and wooded glen, through which it flows from the plains of Terni to its junction with the Tiber. At this spot the *Bridge of Augustus,* which formerly joined the lofty hills above the river for the passage of the Flaminian Way, still spans the stream with its massive ruins. Nothing can be imagined grander in its general effect, or more striking in its details, than this magnificent ruin, and the picturesque scenery by which it is surrounded. The bridge was originally of 3 arches, built of massive blocks of marble, apparently without cement or cramps of any description. The foundations of the middle pier seem to have given way, and to have thus produced the fall of the 2 arches on the rt. bank of the river. The arch on the l. bank is still entire: its height is upwards of 60 feet, and the breadth of the piers is little less than 30 feet. These arches are described by the Roman writers as the highest known. Martial alludes to the bridge in the following passage:—

" Se jam parce mihi, nec abutere Narnia Quincto ;
 Perpetuo liceat sic tibi ponte frui."
                    Ep. 92.

The poets gave the Nar at this place the epithet *sulfurea:* its waters are still turbid, and contain a small quantity of sulphuretted hydrogen gas, which may be traced in most of the waters descending from the calcareous mountains of the Apennines. The best point for commanding a fine view of the ruins is the modern bridge, which crosses the river a short distance above them. It presents many picturesque combinations for the sketch-book, particularly where the convent of San Casciano, which forms so beautiful an object in the distance, is seen through the arch on the l. bank. The mass of ruin between the 2 northern piers, which at first sight would be taken for a pier, and is so represented in several drawings, is more probably a fragment of a ruined fortress erected on the

bridge in the middle ages. An examination of the structure will show that it had no connexion with the Roman work.

The *Cathedral* of Narni, dedicated to S. Giovenale, the first bishop of the see, A.D. 369, under St. Damascus I., is remarkable as a specimen of the pointed architecture of the 13th century. It contains a good picture of the saint. The convent of the *Zoccolanti* contains one of the finest works of *Lo Spagna,* the pupil of Perugino. It represents the Coronation of the Madonna, amid a heavenly choir, while an assemblage of apostles and saints adore the Madonna from below, and is so remarkable both for colouring and composition, that it was long regarded and described as a work of Raphael. It may be best seen in the evening. A lunette of the Madonna and Saints, in fresco, over the ch.-door, is a good work of the Umbrian school of the 15th century.

Travellers by post from Rome to Florence frequently make Narni their sleeping-place for the first night. They may then reach Terni early enough on the second day to see the falls with comfort, and sleep at Terni. On the third day they may reach Perugia.

There is a good but hilly road from Narni to Perugia through Todi and the Sette Valle (51 m.) (Rte. 22). An additional horse is required between Narni and Otricoli, both ways.

The road from Narni to Civita Castellana is extremely interesting: it follows the course of the ancient Via Flaminia for the two first stages to Borghetto; emerging from that great ravine of the Apennines which it entered at La Strettura, and approaching the plains of the Tiber. The highly cultivated country on the l., varied with gentle undulations and covered with oaks, forms in itself a scene of perfect beauty ; and near Otricoli, Soracte gives a new feature to the landscape, and continues for several stages to be a prominent object from the road. From its great height it appears much nearer than it really is, and seems to follow the traveller, so extensive is the circuit which the road makes round it. Before reaching Otricoli a number of ancient tombs are seen on the rt. of the road, marking the line of the Via Flaminia.

1 Otricoli, a small village of 800 souls, retaining the name and site of the ancient city of Ocriculum, the first city of Umbria which voluntarily submitted to Rome. The inn here is wretched. At Otricoli we meet with the argillaceous marls of the tertiary beds full of shells, with calcareous gravel beds resting on them, and forming the upper part of this formation. Some traces of volcanic tufa are met with on descending from Otricoli to the Tiber.

From Otricoli the road descends rapidly. Shortly before reaching the village of Borghetto it crosses the Tiber by a fine bridge, called the Ponte Felice, built by Augustus and repaired by Sixtus V.; it united Umbria with Etruria, which we again enter at this spot. The plain on the l. hand is memorable for the gallant manner in which Macdonald, during the retreat of the French, in December 1798, cut his way through the Neapolitan army under Mack. Macdonald's force, which had not then been joined by Championnet, did not number 8000 men, while that of his incapable opponent is admitted by Neapolitan authorities to have been three times as large. The skirmishing lasted 7 days, when Macdonald, weary of acting on the defensive, attacked and completely routed the Italians, and crossed the Tiber.

A steamer leaves Ponte Felice twice a week, on Tuesday and Friday, at sunrise, for Rome, performing the voyage in 8 to 10 hours, and stopping to land and take in passengers at Ponsano, Torrita, and Fiano : fares extremely moderate, 7 pauls. When there is little water in the river the boat starts from the Porto della Rosa, 12 m. lower down. The accommodation on board is bad as to *restaurant*, &c., and the vessel dirty, being generally crowded with labourers from the Sabine mountains and cattle. Still the conveyance is rapid and economical, and will afford an opportunity of visiting the banks of the Tiber in its most interesting and historical portion, and which cannot easily be done by other means.

¼ Borghetto, a post-station with a few scattered houses. There is now a tolerable Inn here. Its picturesque old dismantled fortress of the middle ages was more than once occupied during the contests just described. It stands on the gravel-beds which we have seen at Otricoli, forming the upper part of the tertiary formations, covered apparently with a very thin mass of volcanic tufa. On ascending from the Tiber the traveller meets the volcanic formations of the Campagna. Above Borghetto the geologist will be much interested in a fine mass of lava, filled with crystals, which continues nearly to Civita Castellana. This leucitic lava rests on tufa, beneath which are the tertiary gravel-beds justs described.

An additional horse is required from Borghetto to Otricoli, but not *vice versâ*. An additional horse to Civita Castellana, but not *vice versâ*. There is a road from Borghetto to Orta of about 10 m., through Bagnuolo; and from Orta to Amelia, a picturesque village in the mountains between the Nera and Tiber, there is a bridle-road of 10 m. more.

The country as Civita Castellana is approached is very beautiful ; no writer who has described the approach from Borghetto has failed to admire its singularly picturesque position.

⅞ Civita Castellana. (*Inn :* La Posta, recently so much improved as to be one of the best inns between Florence and Rome. The Croce Bianca, in the Gran Piazza, and Il Moro, are tolerable vetturino inns. The Croce Bianca is kept by the same landlord as the Posta.) The best guide to the Etruscan remains, both of Civita Castellana and of Falleri, is Domenico Mancini, whose services may be obtained for a few pauls a day, and who will provide horses. The road, immediately before it enters the gate of the city, is carried over the ravine at a height of 120 feet above the bottom by the magnificent bridge built by Cardinal Imperiali in 1712. Civita Castellana, romantically situated on a plateau of red volcanic tufa, is a fortified episcopal town of 3300 Inhab. ; the high road runs through its principal street, but, with the exception of its Etruscan antiquities, there is little in the town to detain the traveller. The Cathedral, a pointed Gothic building, bears the date MCCX. The side pillars of its Lombard doorway rest on lions, and are covered with ancient mosaics. On the front of the portico, over it, are the remains of a mosaic frieze, with an inscription now illegible. On the walls of the ch. are some curious sepulchral tablets with effigies, dating from the 15th century. The interior has been modernised. The bodies of S. Gracilian and Sta. Felicissima, who suffered martyrdom in this town in the 3rd century, are preserved in it. The Citadel, now used as a state prison, occupies the isthmus by which the town is connected with the higher ground; it was begun by Pope Alexander VI., from the designs of Sangallo, in 1500, and completed by Julius II. and Leo. X. It is an octagonal tower, with triangular outworks; but is wholly inadequate to defend this important position. The ravines, which almost insulate the town, and the fine scenes commanded by the higher ground, extending over the Campagna and embracing the plain of the Tiber and Soracte, will afford occupation for some days to the archæologist and the artist. In the bottom of these ravines flow the streams called the Rio Maggiore and Treja, which unite below the town, and fall into the Tiber under the latter name 7 m. lower down at Torre Giuliana.

Civita Castellana occupies the site of the most ancient of the two cities of Falerium or Falerii, the capital of the ancient Falisci, and one of the 12 cities of the Etruscan league.

" Faliscis
Mœnia contigimus victa, Camille, tibi."
Ovid.

Considerable difficulty formerly existed in regard to the actual position of this city, in consequence of some apparent contradictions in the accounts of the Roman writers, and also from the circumstance that many of the early topographers were unacquainted with the exact localities. Sir William Gell and Müller, following the opinion of Nardini and the older Italian antiquaries, supposed that C. Castellana marked the site

of Fescennium, which is more correctly placed at Gallese, 8 m. distant. It is now known, however, that the Latin accounts of 2 cities bearing the same name are perfectly correct; the first, or *Falerium Vetus,* founded by the Pelasgi shortly after the Trojan war, occupied the site of Civita Castellana; and the second, or *Falerii Novi,* was built in the plain about 4 m. distant, after the destruction of the old city by the Romans, about the year of Rome 512. To Civita Castellana, therefore, as the representative of Falerium Vetus, the allusions of Plutarch, of Livy, and of Ovid apply; and among the historical associations which these names will call before the mind of the classical tourist, the celebrated story of Camillus and the schoolmaster will not be forgotten. The second city, though built by the Romans, was constructed after the Etruscan model, and continued to be inhabited by Etruscans, although it was nominally a Roman colony.

The remains of the first and oldest of these Etruscan cities will be found in the deep ravines which surround the plateau on which Civita Castellana is built. Near the viaduct at the entrance of the town, forming an angle on the edge of the cliff, some portions of the ancient wall are met with, constructed of masses of stone 4 feet long and 2 feet deep, and in one part 18 courses high. At the N.E. angle of the town, near the convent of Sta. Agata, we meet with an Etruscan road bordered with tombs and sepulchral chambers, and still presenting the watercourse cut in the tufa, and the mouths of several sewers. The road winds down into the valley, passing 2 ruined gateways of the middle ages, and commanding in the descent occasional glimpses of the Etruscan walls, placed upon the very brink of the cliff, and surmounted by less massive masonry of the middle ages. Turning into the ravine watered by the Vicano torrent, we still trace along the brink of the cliff numerous fragments of the Etruscan walls, in many places serving as foundations for mediæval or more modern ones. Crossing the stream and returning towards the town in the direction of the citadel, we notice numerous tombs hollowed in the rock, many of them being large conical pits, 9 feet high, and bearing such a resemblance to corn-pits that many writers have described them as such. At the picturesque bridge called Ponte del Terreno the cliffs on all sides are perforated with innumerable tombs and sepulchral niches of every variety of form except the circular, most of which are supplied with spiramina or trap-doors, by which they could be ventilated or entered after the ordinary entrance had been closed. One tomb bears on its exterior the inscription "Tucthnu," in Etruscan letters, and the interior of another has an inscription in letters a foot in height, which has been quoted by Lanzi and other Italian writers on Etruscan art. The Ponte del Terreno itself is worthy a minute examination; the basement of the northern pier, to the height of 10 courses, is of massive Etruscan masonry; the arch which rests upon this, and spans the ravine watered by the Rio Maggiore, is of mediæval architecture; above this arch is a second, which also spans the ravine and carries the road; and above that again is the modern aqueduct, which supplies the town with water. The ancient road to the second city of Falerii passes by this bridge.

The second city of Falerii, built by the Romans, although occupied by Etruscans from the ancient city, is situated at the distance of 4 m. from Civita Castellana, at a spot called *Sta. Maria di Falleri*. Its walls are nearly perfect, and it is perhaps not too much to say that they present the most extraordinary specimen of ancient military architecture now extant. Travellers may go there in a light carriage, or still better on horseback: there is no difficulty in obtaining a proper conveyance from the inn. Those who are not pressed for time will probably prefer making it a pedestrian excursion. It derives its name of Sta. Maria from an old convent within its walls, built of the ruins of the ancient city. On leaving Civita Castellana, the road for about

½ m. follows that to Borghetto; it then turns off to the l. through a prettily wooded country. As it approaches the ruins it falls in with portions of the ancient road. Before we come in sight of the ruins we pass near a tomb, with a portico of 3 large arches, a bold cornice of masonry, and architectural mouldings and decorations of Roman character; near it is a group of tombs with porticos, one of which has a Latin inscription, proving that, if these tombs were originally Etruscan, they were afterwards converted by the Romans to their own use. The plan of the city is nearly a triangle, of which the W. and S.E. angles are abruptly cut off. The walls are built of tufa, and are nearly complete; they are defended by quadrilateral towers placed at unequal distances, and remarkably solid in their construction. Approaching the city from C. Castellana, we come first upon the eastern side, where a Roman tomb on a square foundation is a conspicuous object. One of the principal gateways of the city is close to this spot, and further on, in the truncated N.E. angle, is another gateway arched with a tower on its l. This eastern line of wall has 19 towers more or less perfect. The northern line also has 19 towers nearly perfect; in the middle of the line is a little gate, arched with small stones, and still very complete. At this spot are traces of the ancient pavement, and several Roman tombs, one of which is pyramidal. At the N.W. apex of the triangle is a fine massive gateway 18 feet high, with an arch formed of 19 blocks, flanked by towers, and called the Porta di Giove, from a head of Jupiter on the keystone. This is the most perfect of all the gates. The walls here are composed of 15 courses, and are about 32 feet high. The S. side was defended by the deep glen through which the little torrent Miccino runs in its course towards the Rio Maggiore. Its walls and towers have suffered more than the other sides of the city, but the 3 gates are still traceable. One of these near the S.E. angle is called the Porta del Bove from the Bull's head on the keystone; the height of the walls

54 feet, and some of the stones are 6 feet long and 2 feet high. The Necropolis was evidently in the dell below. The cliffs are perforated with sepulchral niches, and on the opposite side of the stream are remains of numerous Roman tombs, one of which has been found to bear an early Christian inscription. Within the walls the principal remains are those of the theatre near the Porta del Bove, Etruscan in its foundations, but evidently Roman in the superstructure and decorations. A fine statue of the Argive Juno, and several Roman statues and fragments of sculpture have been found among its ruins; but there is no doubt that there is still much to be brought to light by judicious excavations. There are also the remains of the Piscina, and of what is supposed to be the Forum. Just inside the Porta di Giove is the *Abadià di Sta. Maria*, an interesting example of Lombard architecture of the 12th century; its 3 naves are divided by columns evidently taken from ancient edifices. Over the door is an ancient capital, and these inscriptions: "Laurentius cum Jacopo filio suo fecit hoc opus:" "Hoc opus Q. Intavall. fieri fecit." The roof of this ch. fell in 1829, and it is now in ruins.

The ruins of Falerii have been admirably illustrated by Canina in his beautiful work entitled, 'L'Antica Etruria Maritima, nella Dizione Ponteficia,' 3 vols. folio, which the traveller should consult before visiting this as well as the other Etruscan towns described and delineated in that splendid publication, which contains not only the topographical details of each locality, and the present state of their ruins, but their restoration by the pencil of one who unites the knowledge of the archæologist and architect with the talent of the artist.

EXCURSION TO SORACTE.

Another excursion from Civita Castellana is to the *Mons Soracte*, or Sant' Oreste, as it is now called. It is about 10 m. distant, and is interesting classical recollections and for tiful scenery which it com-

" Vides ut alta stet nive candidum
　　Soracte."　　　　Hor., Od. i. 9.

" The lone Soracte's heights display'd,
Not *now* in snow, which asks the lyric Roman's aid
For our remembrance, and from out the plain
Heaves like a long-swept wave about to break,
And on the curl hangs pausing."
　　　　　　　　Childe Harold, iv.

The road is perfectly practicable for carriages to the foot of the mountain, but the ascent to the village of St. Oreste is extremely steep in parts. St. Oreste, supposed to occupy the site of the Etruscan town of Feronia, has about 1200 Inhab., but no inn; travellers, however, are received in a house outside the gates by a wealthy family who seem to take pleasure in showing attention to strangers. The summit of the mountain, far above the town, is 2270 feet above the level of the sea; it is occupied by the convent of S. Silvestro, founded in the 8th century by Carloman, uncle of Charlemagne, on the site of a ch. built by St. Silvester, previous to his accession to the popedom, on the conversion of Constantine the Great The original site was probably occupied by the temple of Apollo alluded to by Virgil. The garden of St. Silvester is still shown by the monks, and the place is much frequented by pilgrims. The view from the summit is singularly imposing; on the S. it embraces the Campagna as far as Albano; on the W. the lake of Bracciano; while towards the N. and E. its prospect is bounded by the Monte Cimino, the Peak of Soriano, and the Sabine Apennines. On the eastern declivity of Soracte, near the ch. of Sta. Romana, are an ancient grotto and a number of deep fissures, described by Pliny, from which violent gusts of wind still issue. Not far from it is the Acqua forte, an abundant natural stream, issuing from the rock, alluded to by the Roman writers. A great part of the mountain is beautifully wooded, and numerous fine landscapes will afford agreeable occupation to the artist. In a geological point of view Soracte is likewise interesting: it consists of a mass of secondary limestone, projecting like an island from the midst of the volcanic tufa which forms the subjacent Campagna.

From Civita Castellana to Rome the old and more direct road joined the Flaminian Way, skirting the base of Soracte, and proceeding through Capannacce, Rignano, Borghettacia, and Prima Porta; but it has fallen into disuse since Pius VI. constructed the new post-road through Nepi, in order to unite this with the road from Florence, Siena, and Viterbo to Rome. Rignano, which gives a Ducal title to the elder branch of the House of Massimi, is said to be the birthplace of Cesar Borgia, and is about 7 m. distant from the hill of San Martino, the site of the Etruscan city of Capena, retaining nothing but the beauty of its situation.

On leaving Civita Castellana the road descends into the plain formerly celebrated for the ancient Ciminian forest, and proceeds through groves of oaks to Nepi, passing, before entering the walls, its fine aqueduct of 2 tiers of arches, built by Paul III.

1 *Nepi* (*Inns*, La Fontana or Posta, very poor; La Pace, tolerable, but dear), the ancient Nepete or Nepe, its name having undergone scarcely any change. Nepi is an episcopal town of 1700 Inhab. It is remarkable chiefly from its picturesque position on the edge of a deep ravine of volcanic tufa; it is surrounded by fortifications of the middle ages, and on the side of Rome particularly the towers and machicolated battlements produce a very fine effect. Some of these fortifications rest on the ruins of the Etruscan walls, of which a fine specimen in 19 courses and 36 feet in height may be seen near the southern gate. Another fragment of 10 courses is found within the inner gate, and on the very brink of the ravine which bounds the town on the S. is a very interesting specimen in perfect preservation, but only 4 courses high. Some of these fragments must have been the very walls scaled by Camillus when he stormed Nepete B.C. 386. The oldest fortifications bear the arms of Calixtus III., who died in 1458, and the more recent were built by Sangallo, for Paul III., in the 16th century. The *Cent. It.*

French set fire to the town in 1799, and nearly destroyed it; there is little now to detain the traveller excepting its ancient ch., and the town-hall with its ancient front ornamented with statues and inscriptions. Beneath the town-hall are several Roman altars and statues found in the neighbourhood, and an antique fountain ornamented with lions' heads. On the opposite side of the piazza is a bas-relief of a winged lion much mutilated. This little town appears to have been the seat of a duchy for a short time during the middle ages; and in the 13th century it was besieged and finally taken by the emperor Frederick II. Its bishopric is one of the oldest in Italy, having been founded in the time of St. Peter: its first bishop was St. Romanus, A.D. 46. Nepi is 5 m. from the ruins of Falleri described in a preceding page, following a pathway through the woods, marking the line of the Via Amerina; it is 7 m. from Sutri by a short cut, and 9 m. by the high road.

The road now loses its picturesque character, and enters on a bare volcanic country, which lasts during the remainder of the journey. The road from Siena to Rome falls into this route shortly before reaching Monterosi, where we enter on the Via Cassia.

1 Monterosi (*Inns*, La Posta and L'Angelo, both far from good, but preferred by some to Baccano, the next station, on account of being on higher ground and more free from malaria). The conical hill above Monterosi is Monte di Lucchetti, or Rocca Romana, a portion of the volcanic group that surrounds the Lake of Bracciano, crested with some mediæval ruins. There is a good carriage-road from Monterosi to *Sutri*, about 7 m. distant, and another from Sutri to Ronciglione, which will afford the traveller a better resting-place. Sutri is described in Route 26. At Monterosi we enter the Comarca of Rome.

Between this and Baccano, and about midway between the two, is a large and good inn, called *Le Sette Vene*, certainly the best between Civita Castellana and Rome, being 16 m. from · · and 22 m. from the latte prietor has recently taken the 2 post relays of Monterosi and Nepi, so that travellers can be forwarded on their route at any time on the scale of the government tariff. The vetturini very properly prefer Sette Vene as a resting-place to either Monterosi or Baccano. Close to the inn may be seen an ancient Roman bridge of one arch over the Triglia, by which the Via Amerina was carried direct from Todi through Sta. Maria di Falleri and Nepi into the Via Cassia; and on the l. of the road the extremity of a current of lava descending from the hills above. A few miles beyond Sette Vene the road crosses the lip of the crater in which Baccano is situated. From this high ground the outline of the crater is well defined. On the hill above the post-house, called Monte Razzano, which commands a most interesting view, are some ruins, supposed to be those of a temple of Bacchus, and denoting the site of the Statio ad Baccanas, on the Via Cassia.

1 Baccano (*Inn*, the Post, civil and reasonable, and by no means the worst inn on this road, although the situation is objectionable in the summer and autumn on account of malaria). It is situated in a plain which forms the bottom of an extinct crater, 3 m. at least in diameter, the sides of which are formed of beds of ashes and pumice. In the centre of this crater is a sulphurous pool whose waters are supposed to render the atmosphere unwholesome. Beyond the south-western ridge of the crater are 2 small lakes, one of which is the Lacus Alsietinus, now called the Lago di Martignano, lying between the crater of Baccano and the lake of Bracciano. Traces of the ancient *Emissarii* made formerly to drain the lake may be seen from the road after leaving the inn at Baccano; and on the upper part of the hill are several openings of great depth, called *pozzi* by the peasantry, which were probably the air-shafts to these subterranean canals.

The road commences, soon after leaving Baccano, to rise over the S. edge of its crater. Arrived at the . . . . . st point of the Pass, let the tra- . . . . . lalt, and, leaving his carriage,

ascend one of the low hills close to the road, and, provided he be favoured with fine weather, such a panorama will burst before him as he has seldom witnessed; there are few situations from which he will be able to form a more correct idea of the topography of the environs of the Eternal City. Looking southwards, or in the direction of Rome, he will have on his l. the range of the Umbrian and Sabine Apennines, and which, in spring and winter being covered with snow, adds much to their grandeur, with the Tiber winding in the plain at their foot. Lower down, the pointed peak of Monte Genaro, the Mons Lucretilis, and at its base the lower pyramidal hills of Monticelli and Sant-angelo, the latter crowned by a mediæval castle occupying the site of the ancient Corniculum; a little farther S. the gorge by which the Anio breaks into the plain from its mountain valley, with a part of Tivoli, may be easily distinguished; and still farther, the range of the Sabine mountains, as far as the precipitous bluff on which Palestrina, the ancient Præneste, stands. A wide plain, continuous apparently with the Campagna, there intervenes between the Apennines and the detached group of the Alban hills, and the Volscian range: this is the great Latin valley, extending from the Campagna of Rome to the Campania Felice of Naples, watered by the Sacco and the Liris. The high peak seen in the Volscian Mountains is the Monte Lupone, which towers over the Pelasgic cities of Segni, Cori, and Norba. Nearer the spectator are the Alban hills, with the village of Colonna, the ancient Labicum, at one extremity, and the solitary tower of the Savelli, that marks the site of Corioli, on the other; whilst towering above all is the Mons Lazialis, the modern Monte Cave, overlooking the towns of Frascati Marino, Castel Gandolfo, and Albano, situated on its declivities: of Rome itself no part is seen except the cupola of St. Peter's, which may be easily descried over the low hills of Monte Mario; and nearer to the spectator still the mediæval tower above the Post station of La Storta, and the wooded knolls which surround the ruins of Etruscan Veii. A dreary, and, as it appears at this distance, a monotonous flat extends from the foot of the Alban hills to the shores of the Mediterranean, whilst on our rt. rise the hills surrounding the Lake of Bracciano, with their pointed peak of Monte Virginio, and, farther off, those of La Tolfa, ending in Cape Linaro, the headland projecting into the sea on our extreme rt., and behind which lies the modern town of Civita Vecchia.

It is from hereabouts that the traveller from Florence by this route will enjoy the first view of St. Peter's.

" Oh Rome! my country! city of the soul!
The orphans of the heart must turn to thee,
Lone mother of dead empires! and control
In their shut breasts their petty misery.
What are our woes and sufferance? Come and
    see
The cypress, hear the owl, and plod your way
O'er steps of broken thrones and temples! ye,
Whose agonies are evils of a day—
A world is at our feet as fragile as our clay.

The Niobe of nations! there she stands,
Childless and crownless, in her voiceless woe;
An empty urn within her wither'd hands,
Whose holy dust was scatter'd long ago;
The Scipios' tomb contains no ashes now;
The very sepulchres lie tenantless
Of their heroic dwellers: dost thou flow,
Old Tiber! through a marble wilderness?
Rise, with thy yellow waves, and mantle her
    distress."   *Childe Harold,* iv.

A very gradual descent leads from this point for the next 4 m. to the Osteria del Fosso, a lonely wayside Inn, so called from being situated in a ravine, through which descends a branch of the Cremera, that drains this part of the valley. Between this spot and La Storta our route skirts the ridge beyond which (on the l.) *Veii*, the great rival of Rome, was situated. The intervening hills allow scarcely a glimpse of its interesting ruins, a description of which will be found under "the Excursions from Rome."

1¼ La Storta, the last post to Rome. As we draw nearer the Eternal City the road winds over the gentle elevations which mark the desolate Campagna, but there are no villages or country-seats to denote the approach to a great capital; some old brick towers of the middle ages, a few farm-houses, and here and there the ruins of an ancient sepulchre, are the only objects which break the

monotony of the scene. If the present aspect of the Campagna should excite a contrast with the eventful drama once enacted on its surface, there is perhaps no description which will more completely embody the feelings of the classical tourist than that of Milton in the fourth book of the Paradise Regained, which Mr. Beckford seems to have paraphrased in the well-known description of his entrance into Rome. About the 7th milestone a turn in the road brings the towers and cupolas of Rome more prominently into view; but with the exception of St. Peter's and the Castle of St. Angelo, there are no objects of striking interest in the prospect. The Coliseum, the Aqueducts, the Forum, the Capitol, and the numerous antiquities whose names suggest themselves almost involuntarily at the first sight of Rome, all lie on the other side; the stranger may be disappointed to find that there is no point on this route which commands a view over the whole city.

As we advance the appearance of the country becomes more pleasing, and the vegetation less scanty. Monte Mario, with its wooded platform capped with cypresses, bounds the prospect on the rt.; the hills of Frascati and Albano stretch far away in the distance in front; while on the l. the plain of the Tiber is spread out before us. Near the 5th milestone from Rome a sarcophagus on a ruined base rises above the road on the rt., erroneously called the *Tomb of Nero*, although an inscription yet legible shows that it was that of Publius Vibius Marianus and of Reginia Maxima, his wife; a circumstance which may serve to prepare the traveller for the antiquarian misnomers in Rome itself.

2 m. beyond this the pretty valley of the Acqua Traversa is crossed: another ascent brings us to an elevation crowned with villas and farm-houses, from which the road descends to the Tiber, which it crosses by the modern *Ponte Molle*, built on the foundations of the Milvian bridge, constructed by Æmilius Scaurus. The ancient bridge is memorable in the history for Cicero's arrest of the

N

of the Allobroges, the accomplices of Catiline, and for the battle fought near it between Constantine and Maxentius, a religious victory which the genius of Raphael has invested with additional interest by the well-known fresco in the Vatican. It was also the scene of Constantine's Vision. From its parapet the body of Maxentius was precipitated into the Tiber; and on the same occasion the 7-branched candlestick of massive gold, brought by Titus from the Temple of Jerusalem, fell from the bridge into the river, in whose sands it is still imbedded with other valuable relics of ancient art. The present bridge was almost entirely rebuilt by Pius VII. in 1815. The old tower was then cut into the form of a triumphal arch; statues of St. John baptizing the Saviour, by Mochi, were erected at its northern, and of the Virgin and of St. John of Nepomucene at its southern extremity. On the night of the 13th of May, 1849, during the siege of Rome by General Oudinot, a body of French troops attempted to carry the bridge by a *coup-de-main*, upon which the Romans fired the mines which had been previously laid, and blew up one arch of the venerable structure. The bridge was restored in the following December. The river at this point is about 400 feet in breadth, but its banks are bare and destitute of timber, and its colour fully justifies the epithet *flavus* given to it by the Latin poets. The Cassian and Flaminian ways join on the N. bank of the Tiber, which here separated Etruria from Latium. Beyond the bridge, on a low hill, is the interesting little chapel erected by Pius II. on the spot where he met the procession which accompanied the head of St. Andrew on its arrival from the Peloponnesus in 1462. The altar is still standing on which this pope celebrated high mass on that occasion before he carried the head with his own hands to St. Peter's, where it was preserved among the most precious relics of the Holy See until 1850, when it was stolen; it has since however been recovered. A straight road now leads between the high walls of villas and gardens, which exclude all view of the city, to the Porta del Popolo, passing on the l. hand the elegant ch. of St. Andrew, built by Julius III. from the designs of Vignola, as a memorial of his deliverance on St. Andrew's day, 1527, from the German soldiery during the sack of Rome. Farther on, we pass the Casino del Papa Giulio, also designed by Vignola for the same pope, and finished by St. Carlo Borromeo; and the noble Palazzo Giulio, another fine building designed by Vignola, and decorated with frescoes by Taddeo Zuccari. It long served as the temporary residence of sovereigns and ambassadors previous to their public entry into Rome. Farther on we leave on the l. hand the road leading along the walls to the Villa Borghese, and on the rt., and close to the gate, the building appropriated as the Protestant church.

1¼ ROME. [From Rome to La Storta this post is charged as 2. Passports are demanded at the gate, and, unless a *lascia passare* be previously lodged with the officer by the banker or correspondent of the traveller, the carriage must proceed to the Dogana—a vexatious arrangement, from which a fee of 5 or 10 pauls sometimes fails to procure an exemption. This *lascia passare* is not granted to persons travelling by public carriages. Persons arriving by diligence have their luggage examined at the coach-office, and suffer no delay at the gate. A small fee will expedite matters with the passport-officer. In the event of the luggage being taken to the custom-house, a timely fee to the searcher will not only facilitate matters, but will generally render the examination a mere matter of form. *The traveller should be on his guard against individuals who station themselves at the gates of Rome, the Diligence offices, and Custom-house*, as agents for Inns. These persons endeavour to ascertain the name of the hotel at which the traveller intends to stop, and then represent that there is "no room," with the view of drawing him to another house. The same trick is also resorted to occasionally by vetturini and postboys.]

Rome is entered by the *Porta del Popolo*, the modern substitute for the Porta

Flaminia, which stood a little farther on the l. It was built by Vignola, from the designs of Michael Angelo, in 1561, during the pontificate of Pius IV. It has 4 columns of the Doric order, with statues of St. Peter and St. Paul, by Mochi, in the intercolumniations. The inner front was ornamented by Alexander VII., from the designs of Bernini, in honour of the visit of Christina queen of Sweden, in 1657. Although this entrance fails to excite that classical enthusiasm which no traveller can repress when Rome is entered by the road from Naples, it is still imposing. The gate opens upon the spacious Piazza del Popolo, an irregular area at the foot of Monte Pincio, which bounds it on the l. In its centre rises the fine obelisk of Rhamses I., one of the two erected by that great king before the Temple of the Sun at Heliopolis. In front, the twin churches of Sta. Maria in Monte Santo, and Sta. Maria de' Miracoli, built by Cardinal Gastaldi, divide the 3 streets which diverge from this northern entrance. The central one, called the *Corso*, follows in a straight line the course of the ancient Via Flaminia to the Capitol, the tower of which closes the *vista* in that direction. The street on the rt., called the *Ripetta*, runs parallel to the l. bank of the Tiber and into the heart of the ancient city; and that on the l., the *Via Babuino*, leads along the foot of the Pincian hill to the Piazza di Spagna—the quarter of Rome most inhabited by our countrymen and foreigners generally.

INDEX.

ABATE.

A.

ABATE, Niccolò dell', works by, 58.
Abadia di Sta. Maria, 264.
Academy at Bologna, 29.
—— at Ferrara, 19.
—— at Perugia, 243.
—— at Ravenna, 90.
Accademia degli Ardenti, 196.
—— Val d' Arnese, 222.
—— delle Assicurate, 185.
—— Etrusca, 229.
—— degli Intronati, Siena, 185.
Acciajoli, Niccolò, 204.
Acqua Buja, the, 66.
Acqua forte, the, 264.
Acqualagna, 127.
Acqua Paola, 172.
Acquapendente, the birthplace of Fabricius, 190.
Acqua Traversa, valley, 267.
Acquaviva, 206.
Adige, the, 10.
Adrian V., tomb of, 196.
Agostino, Sant', Tower of, 169.
Agricola, works by, 89.
Agriculture of the Papal States, xv.
Alabaster manufactories at Volterra, 214.
Albani, origin of the family, 132.
Albani, Francesco, works by, 31, 43, 46, 48, 53, 56, 58, 90, 109, 153, 154.
Albegna, the, 166, 168.
Alberese, quarries of, 166.
Alberti, Cherubino, works by, 143.
—— Durante, works by, 143.
—— Giovanni, works by, 143.
—— Leon Battista, works by, 103.
Albornoz, Card., 249.
Aldrovandi, Cardinal Pompeo, 55.
Alessi, Galeazzo, works by, 54, 237, 245, 247, 250.
—— tomb of, 239.
Alexander IV., tomb of, 194.
Alfani, Domenico di Paris, works by, 237.
—— Orazio di Paris, works by, 238, 239, 240, 243.

ANTIQUITIES.

Alfieri, Enrico, monument of, 85.
—— the poet, at the tomb of Dante, 88.
Alfonso, duke of Ferrara, at the battle of Ravenna, 95.
Algardi, Alessandro, works by, 51, 57.
Alidosi, cardinal, death of, 132.
Aliense, works by, 240.
Allia, the, 161.
Alsium, 171.
Altar, silver, at Città di Castello, 137.
Alunno, Niccolò, works by, 240, 243, 247, 252.
Amalasontha, 192.
Ambra, river, 222.
Ambrogiana, 173.
Amelia, 261.
Amphitheatre, remains of, at Ancona, 115.
—— near Sambuchetto, 123.
Ancona:—Inns, 112. Historical notice, 112. Port, 113. Triumphal arch of Trajan, 113; and of Clement XII., 114. Mole, 114. Forts, 114. Lazzaretto, 114. Cathedral, 114. Churches, 115. Exchange, 115. Palaces, 115. Prisons, 115. Women, 116. Steamers and diligences, 116.
Ancona to Bologna, 96.
—— to Foligno, 116.
Ancona (Gothic altar painted in compartments), 230.
Ancona, Andrea di, works by, 115.
Andrea, Novella d', 33.
Andreoli, Giorgio, painting by, 133.
Angelico, Fra, works by, 152, 230.
Anghiari, 144.
Anio, the, 162.
Anjou, Charles of, 195.
Annius, 197.
Ansau, St., 186.
Ansedonia, 167.
Anselmi, Sig., of Viterbo, 198.
Antemnæ, site of, 162.
Antiquities at Bagnacavallo, 77.
—— at Bologna, 34.

AREZZO.

Antiquities near Cesena, 101.
—— at Cetona, 159.
—— at Chiusi, 156.
—— at Città di Castello, 141.
—— at Ferrara, 19.
—— at Longiano, 101.
—— at Montepulciano, 159.
—— at Sarteano, 159.
Antoninus Pius, 172.
Apennines, the, 65, 70, 72, 125, 126, 129, 260.
Apostoli, SS., order of the, 248.
Aquæ Tauri, 170.
Aqueduct at Civita Vecchia, 170.
—— at Loreto, 122.
—— at Nepi, 265.
—— at Spoleto, 255.
Arbia, valley of the, 188, 205.
Arca, Niccolò dell', works by, 46, 54.
Arch of Augustus, 102, 108.
—— of Clement XII., 114.
—— at Macerata, 124.
—— of Trajan, 113.
Architecture, Christian, xxiii.
—— Cyclopean, xx.
—— Etruscan, 209, 234.
—— Gothic, 248.
—— Pelasgic, xviii.
—— specimen of the fortified domestic, 201.
Archives at Ravenna, 89.
Arco di Meloncello, 62.
Aretino, Lionardo, birthplace of, 225.
—— Pietro, birthplace of, 225.
—— Spinello, works by, 178, 184, 223, 224.
Aretusi, works by, 37, 44, 53.
Arezzo:—Inns, 222. Diligences, 226. Loggie by Vasari, 223. Cathedral, 223. Churches, 223, 224. Convent della Croce, 224. Palazzo Pubblico, 225. Fraternità, 225. Museo Pubblico, 225. M. Bacci, 225. House in which Petrarch was born, 225. House of Vasari, 225. Promenade, 226.
Excursions from: Through the Val di Chiana to Chiusi, 226.
Arezzo to San Giustino, 142.
—— to Siena, 205.

AREZZO.

Arezzo, Margaritone d', 178, 223, 224, 238.
—— Plain of, 144, 205, 222.
Argenta, 75.
Aringhieri, Nicolo, tomb of, 185.
Ariosto, bust of, 17.
—— MSS. of, 19.
—— tomb of, 20.
—— residence of, 20.
—— at the battle of Ravenna, 95.
Aristophanes, MS. of, 89.'
Army, Papal, xii.
Arno, valley of the, 173, 207.
Arnolfo, works by, 153.
Arpino, Cav. d', 109, 196, 239, 244.
Arretium, 222, 225.
Arringatore, 191.
Arrone, 169, 171.
Art, school of, at Ferrara, 11.
—— at Bologna, 27.
—— at Perugia, 236.
—— at Siena, 177.
Arvales, Roman bas-relief of the sacrifice, 191.
Aadrubal, death of, 127.
Asinalunga, 206.
Asinelli tower, 58.
Aspertini, Amico, works by, 45, 50, 63.
—— Guido, painting by, 29.
Assisi :—Inns, 247. Sagro Convento, 248. Cathedral, 250. Churches, 248-251. Portico of the ancient Temple of Minerva, 250. Tomb of St. Francis, 250. Fairs, 251. Manufactures, 251.
Asso, 189.
Astrone, the, 159.
Augustus, arch of, 102, 108.
—— bridge of, 102, 260.
Auximum, ruins of, 117.
Avanzi, Jacopo, works by, 46, 55, 61.
Azzolini, Francesco, 35.

B.

BABBAGE, Mr., his account of the Boracic Acid Works of Lardarello, 217.
Raccano, 266.
—— crater of, 266.
Bachetona, 207, 208.
Baciocchi, Princess Eliza, tomb of, 19.
Baglioni, Count, 235.
—— family, 232, 234.
Bagnacavallo, town, 77.
Bagnacavallo, works by, 29, 37, 43, 49, 53, 60.
Bagnaja, 197.
Bagnarea, 149.
Bagni, 154.
Bagni di Ferrata, 170.

BELLA.

Bagni, San Casciano de', 190.
—— a Morbo, 220.
—— di Roselle, 165.
Balducci, Giovanni, works by, 211.
—— Sig., remarks of, on the Thrasimene Lake, 232.
Balze, chasm, 214.
—— le, village, 246.
Baptisteries at Bologna, 36, 38.
—— at Loreto, 120.
—— at Ravenna, 81, 85.
—— at Siena, 181.
Barbarossa, Frederick, 184, 195.
Barberino, 204.
Barbiani, Andrea, works by, 83.
—— Giambattista, works by, 83, 86.
Barbioni, Niccolò, works by, 137, 139.
Barilli, Antonio, works by, 178, 180, 185.
Baroccio, Ambrogio, works by, 133.
—— painter, works by, 43, 46, 58, 90, 128, 133, 135, 154, 230, 237, 244.
Bartolo, Domenico, works by, 186.
—— Taddeo, works by, 175, 177, 178, 184, 238, 243.
Bartolommeo, Fra, works by, 178, 183, 238, 245.
Basilicas at Ravenna, 81, 83.
—— S. Apollinare in Classe, 92.
—— at Perugia, 240.
Bassanello, 197.
Bassano, works by, 241.
Bassi, Laura, 33.
Bastaruolo, 18.
Bastia, village, 247.
Bastianino, 15, 17, 18, 19.
Baths of Le Caldane, 164.
—— of Chianciano, 205.
—— San Filippo, 189.
—— of Marius, 62.
—— of Moscona, 207.
Batignano, 165, 207.
Battle of Anghiari, 144.
—— Casalecchio, 68.
—— Castel Bolognese, 97.
—— Fossalta, 27.
—— Monte Aperto, 176, 180, 183.
—— Ponte Felice, 261.
—— Ravenna, 80, 95.
—— Sentinum, 129.
—— Tadinum, 129.
—— Thrasimene, 230.
—— Tolentino, 124.
Beccafumi, works by, 177, 178, 180, 182, 184, 185 ; his house, 185.
Beckford, Mr., his designation of Bologna, 64.
Belcaro, castle of, 187.
Belforte, 125.
Belisarius at the siege of Osimo, 116.
Bella Marsilia, castle of, 166.

BOLOGNA.

Bellamino, works by, 185.
Bellini, works by, 103, 107, 115.
Bellosguardo, 204.
Benedetto, San, monastery of, at Ferrara, 16.
Benedict XI., monument of, 238.
Benedictine convent of Monte Uliveto Maggiore, 189.
Benefial, Marco, works by, 115, 137, 194.
Bentivoglio, family of, 27. Supposed origin of, 55.
—— Antonio, monument of, 46.
—— Francesca, 98.
—— Giovanni, murder of, 68.
Benvenuti, works by, 174, 224.
—— birthplace of, 226.
Benvenuto, works by, 180.
Bergamo, Stefano da, works by, 241.
—— Fra Damiano da, works by, 241.
Berghem, works by, 90.
Bernini, works by, 89, 181, 269.
Beroaldi, Filippo, monument of, 50.
Bertaldo, tower of, 169.
Bertinoro, 100.
Bettole, 226.
Bevagna, 252.
Bevignate, Fra, works by, 239, 242.
Bianca, Santa, 10.
Bibiena, Antonio, works by, 54, 56, 60, 63, 184.
—— Gio., works by, 44.
Biccherna, tribunal di, 184.
Bieda, 198, 200.
—— San Giovanni di, 198.
Biforca, la, 71.
Bigari, Angelo, works by, 37, 54.
Bindelli, 15.
Bisdomini, works by, 179.
Bisentina, 192.
Bisenzio, river, 171.
Bishops of Rome, list of, xxxiii.
Black Friars, order of the, 248.
Blasco, family of, 249.
Biera, 198, 200.
Boccaccio's tomb, 173, 174.
Bocca d' Albegna, 167.
—— Trabaria, la, 135.
Bologna :—Inns, 25. Situation, importance, and prosperity, 26. Historical notice, 26. School of art, 27. Accademia delle Belle Arte, 29. University, 32. Palazzo Cellesi, 33. Museums, 34. Observatory, 34. University library, 34. Gardens, 35. Hospitals, 35.
Churches : — S. Bartolommeo di Porta Ravegnana, 43 ; S. Bartolommeo di Reno, 44 ; S. Benedetto, 44 ; della Carità, 44 ; Cathedral, 37 ; Sta. Cecilia, 44 ; Celestir

BOLOGNA.

Corpus Domini, 45; S. Cristina, 45; S. Domenico, 41; S. Giacomo Maggiore, 45; S. Giorgio, 46; S. Giovanni in Monte, 47; S. Gregorio, 47; S. Leonardo, 47; Sta. Lucia, 47; Madonna del Baraccano, 48; Madonna di S. Colombano, 48; Madonna di Galliera, 48; Madonna del Soccorso, 48; Sta. Maria Maddalena, 49; La Maddalena, 49; Sta. Maria Maggiore, 49; Sta. Maria della Vita, 49; S. Martino Maggiore, 49; S. Mattéa, 50; I Mendicanti, 50; S. Michele de' Leprosetti, 50; S. Niccolò di S. Felice, 50; S. Paolo, 51; S. Petronio, 38; S. Procolo, 51; S. Rocco, 51; Santissimo Salvatore, 52; Servi, 52; S. Stefano, 36; 88. Trinità, 53; S. Vitale ed Agricola, 53. Piazza of S. Domenico, 41. Convent of S. Domenico, 43. Biblioteca Communale, 43. Piazzo Maggiore, 53. Fontana Pubblica, 53. Palazzo Maggiore del Pubblico, 54. Palazzo del Podestà, 54. Torrazzo dell' Aringo, 55. Portico de' Banchi, 55. Il Registro, 55. Private palaces, 55-58. Private houses, 55-58. Foro de' Mercanti, 58. Torre Asinelli, 58. Torre Garisenda, 59. Scuole Pie, 59. Colleges, 59, 60. Custom-house, Mint, 60. Theatres, Casino, 60. Accademia de' Filarmonici, 60. Liceo Filarmonico, 60. Montagnuola, 61. Dogs, 64. Climate, 64. Dialect, 64. Character of the people, 64. Conveyances, 65.
Environs.—Churches: Misericordia, 61; Annunziata, 61; Madonna di Mezzarata, 61; S. Paolo in Monte, 62; S. Michele in Bosco, 62; Madonna di S. Luca, 63; Capuccini, 64; Scalzi, 64. Bagni di Mario, 62. Olivetan Monastery and library, 62. Portico of the Canon Zeneroli, 62. Arco di Meloncello, 62. Certosa, 63. Cemetery, 63. Portico degli Scalzi, 64.
Bologna to Ancona, 96.
—— to Ferrara, 23.
—— to Florence by Pietramala, &c., 65.
—— —— by La Porretta, &c., 68.
—— to Modena, 25.
—— to Ravenna by Imola and Lugo, 76.
—— —— by Medicina and Lugo, 95.

BRIDGE.

Bologna, Giovanni di, works by, 53, 58, 151, 224.
—— Simone da, works by, 29, 36, 37, 42, 46, 49, 61.
—— Vitale da, works by, 29, 61.
Bolognese, Franco, his school and followers, 28.
Bolognini, Gio. Battista, works by, 47, 54.
Bolsena, lake of, 191.
Bolsena, Roman remains at, 191; fine views from the upper town, 192; the lake, 192; basaltic columns, 192.
Bondeno, 10.
Bonfigli, Benedetto, works by, 238, 239, 240, 242.
Bonone, Carlo, 16, 17, 18, 52, 81, 109.
Bomazzo, Etruscan tombs at, 194.
Bomporto, 10.
Books on Central Italy, xxviii.
Boracic Acid Works of Lardarello, 217.
Borghese, Cavaliere, 106.
—— Prince, 194.
Borghetto, 231, 261.
Borgia, Cesar, massacre of his allies by, at Sinigallia, 110. His birthplace, 265.
Borgo, 105, 172.
Borgo San Lorenzo, 71.
Borgo San Sepolcro :—Native artists, 142. Cathedral, 142. Churches, 143. Monte di Pietà, 143.
—— to San Giustino, 142.
Borgo Pace, 135.
Borgo Vecchio, 159.
Borgonzoni, Lorenzo, works by, 52.
Borri, 222.
Borromeo, S. Carlo, 197, 202, 268.
Bozzone torrent, 205.
Bracciano, 171.
Braccio da Montone, 234, 239.
—— Muri di, 241.
Braccio-forte, the, 85.
Bramante, works by, 54, 118, 148, 197.
Breughel, works by, 178.
Bridge of Augustus at Narni, 260.
—— —— at Orte, 197.
—— —— at Rimini, 102.
—— at Bieda, 200.
—— near Cagli, 128.
—— at Civita Castellana, 261, 263.
—— Elian, 172.
—— at Fossombrone, 127.
—— Milvian, 267.
—— Roman, 154, 166, 256, 266.
—— over the Santerno, 97.
—— of Savignano, 101.
—— over the Savio, 100.
—— near Schieggia, 128.

CAMPAGNA.

Bridge over the Tiber, 261.
—— over the Uso, 101.
Brienne, Walter de, 213, 249.
Briglia, la, 216.
Brisighella, 71.
Brizzi, Francesco, works by, 39, 42, 46, 52, 56, 57.
—— Filippo, works by, 40.
Bronzes, Etruscan, 211, 243.
Bronze baptistery at Loreto, 120.
—— fountain, 122.
—— lamp at Cortona, 229.
—— statue of Julius III., 241.
—— tables at Gubbio, 146.
Brun, Charles le, works by, 120.
Bruna, the, 165.
Brunacci, Fra di Barone, works by, 237.
Bucci, Sig., 170.
Buche delle Fate, 164.
—— de' Saracini, 214.
Budrio, G. L. da, works by, 61.
Buffalmacco, works by, 249.
Bulicame, lake, 194.
Bulla, 211.
Buonconvento, 188.
Buoninsegna, Duccio di, works by, 177, 180.
Buonsignori, 187.
Burano, the, 127.
Busco, 145.
Buzzio, Ippolito, works by, 151.
Byron, Lord, at the tomb of Dante, 88. His residence at Ravenna, 88. On the Falls of Terni, 258. On the Thrasimene Lake, 233.

C.

ÇA, La, 66.
Caccini, Giovanni, works by, 151.
Caduta delle Marmore, 257.
Cæcina, Bp., 212.
Carre, 171.
Cafaggiolo, 67.
Cagli, 128.
Calabrese, Cav., works by, 181.
Calcagni, works by, 118, 120.
Calcagnini, Celio, 17.
Calcinelli, 126.
Caldane, le, 164.
Caldarola, 125.
Calindri, 192.
Callis, site of, 128.
Calpurnius, 198.
Calvart, works by, 39, 42, 45, 46, 47, 48, 52, 53.
Calvin at Ferrara, 13, 19.
Camaldolese monastery at Volterra, 215.
Camerino, town and delegation of, 125.
Cametti, Bernardino, works by, 151.
Camillus, 203.
Campagna of Rome, 202.

CAMPAGNA.

Campagna, Girolamo, works by, 39.
Campello, Fra Filippo da, works by, 250.
Campiglia, 164.
—— Vecchia, 164.
Campigno torrent, 71.
Campolorzo, 125.
Campo Riggiano, Abbadia of, 145.
Camuccini, works by, 81, 244.
Camullo, Francesco, works by, 51.
Camuscía, 228.
Canal di Loreo, 74.
—— di Valle, 74.
—— Zanelli, 98.
Canale di Cento, 23.
—— Naviglio, 91.
Candigliano, the, 127.
Cangiasi, Luca, works by, 43.
Canina's 'Etruria Maritima,' 198.
—— works on Antiquities of Rome, xxix.
Canova, works by, 181.
Cantarini, Simone, works by, 46, 52, 103, 107, 109, 141.
Cantiano, 128.
Canuti, works by, 57, 62, 63, 64.
Capanacce, le, 198, 201.
Capanna, Puccio, works by, 249.
Capena, site of, 265.
Capo d' Argine, 23.
Caporciano, 215.
Capranica, 198, 201.
—— Card., 181.
Caprarola, castle of, 201.
Caprese, 144.
Caracci, the, their school and followers, 28.
—— Agostino, works by, 19, 30, 44, 56, 57, 58.
—— Annibale, works by, 30, 45, 47, 49, 51, 56, 57, 60, 64, 121, 141, 153, 154, 178, 200, 255.
—— Antonio, works by, 48.
—— Francesco, works by, 52.
—— Lodovico, works by, 29, 30, 37, 42, 43, 44, 45, 46, 47, 48, 50, 51, 56, 57, 58, 63, 109, 237.
—— Paolo, works by, 48, 52, 61.
Caravaggio, works by, 58, 241, 244.
Carbonara, 129.
Carceri, Sanctuary delle, 251.
Carione, Gian Andrea, works by, 138, 239.
Caro, Annibale, works by, 202.
Carpaccio, Vittore, works by, 16, 107.
Carpi, works by, 16, 49, 52.
Carriages, regulations as to, 7.
Carsoli, 148.
Cartoons at Orvieto, 153.
Carving, wood, 178, 180.
Curza torrent, 67.
Carsaglia, pass of, 71.

CATHEDRAL.

Casale, 207.
Casalecchio, 68.
Casario, Lazzaro, works by, 60.
Casato, 177.
Case Bruciate, 112.
—— del Piano, 230.
—— Nuove, 126.
Casting of the Santa Casa at Loreto, sculptures of, 119.
Casolani, works by, 182, 183.
Cassinoli, 207.
Castel di St. Angelo, 172.
—— d' Asso, 198.
—— Belcaro, 187.
—— Bolognese, 97.
—— Buonconvento, 188.
—— Caprarola, 201.
—— Fiorentino, 173.
—— Franco, 25.
—— Guibileo, 161.
—— di Guido, 171.
—— di S. Leo, 104.
—— Malatesta, 104.
—— Monte Riggioni, 176.
—— Novo, 218.
—— S. Pietro, 96.
—— Todino, 148.
—— del Vescovo, 68.
Castellaccio, 198.
Castellina, 204.
Castello, Francesca da, works by, 138.
Castellucci, Salvi, works by, 138.
Castellum Amerinum, 197.
Castellum Axia, 198.
Castelnovo, 220.
Castiglioncello, 163.
Castiglione Fiorentino, 227.
—— della Pescaja, 165.
Castro, 190.
Castro Caro, 73.
Castro river, 222.
Castrum Novum, 171.
Casuccini, Signor, his museum of Etruscan antiquities at Chiusi, 156.
—— Deposito del Colle, 158.
Catarina, Santa, 23.
Catelani, Fra Bernardo, pietà by, 128.
Cathedral of Ancona, 114.
—— Arezzo, 223.
—— Bologna, 37.
—— Borgo San Sepolcro, 142.
—— Camerino, 125.
—— Chiusi, 158.
—— Città di Castello, 136.
—— Città della Pieve, 155.
—— Civita Castellana, 262.
—— Cortona, 229.
—— Faenza, 98.
—— Fano, 109.
—— Ferrara, 14.
—— Foligno, 252.
—— Forlì, 99.
—— Fossombrone, 127.
—— S. Giovanni, 222.
—— Grosseto, 165.
—— Gubbio, 145.

CESENATICO.

Cathedral of Imola, 96.
—— Macerata, 123.
—— Massa, 165.
—— Montefiascone, 193.
—— Narni, 260.
—— Orvieto, 150.
—— Osimo, 117.
—— Perugia, 237.
—— Pesara, 107.
—— Ravenna, 80.
—— Recanati, 122.
—— Rimini, 103.
—— Schieggia, 128.
—— Siena, 178.
—— Spello, 251.
—— Spoleto, 254.
—— Terni, 257.
—— Todi, 148.
—— Tolentino, 124.
—— Urbino, 133.
—— Viterbo, 194.
—— Volterra, 211.
Cattolica, la, 106.
Cava, la, copper-mines of, 215.
Cavallini, Pietro, works by, 249.
Cavallucci, Antonio, works by, 142.
Cavanella di Pò, 74.
Cavedone, Giacomo, works by, 30, 44, 45, 46, 49, 50, 51, 52.
—— death of, 49.
Cavo Tassone, 23.
Caverns at Borgo, 106.
—— at Case Nuove, 126.
—— at Cesi, 148.
—— of Poggio de Sette Bagni, 162.
—— at Sigillo, 129.
Ceccarini, works by, 109.
Cecina, town and river, 163.
—— valley, 207.
—— ford, 217.
Cellini, Benvenuto, works by, 58.
Cemetery of Bologna, 63.
Cenni, Cenno di Francesco di Ser, works by, 213.
Cento, 24. Casa di Guercino, 24. Chiesa del Rosario, 24. Fair, 25.
—— Pieve di, 25.
Centumcellæ, 170.
Cerchi family, 249.
Cere, 171.
Cerfone, valley of the, 143.
Cerochi, 171.
Certaldo, 173. Boccaccio's tomb 174; his house, 174.
Certosa of Bologna, 63.
—— of Galuzzo, 204.
Cervellato, 64.
Cervetri, 171.
Cervia, 95.
Cesano, valley of the, 127.
Cesarea, relic of the city, 92.
Cesena, 100. Palazzo Pubblico, 100. Library, 101. Church near, 101. Sulphur-mines near, 101.
Cesenatico, 96.

CESI.

Cesi, 148.
Cesi, Bartolommeo, works by, 42, 46, 47, 50, 51, 56, 63.
—— Cetona, 159.
Charles IV., his attempt to seize the signoria, 177, 184.
Charles V. at Siena, 184.
Characteristics of the Papal States, xvi.
Chateaubriand at the tomb of Dante, 88.
Chenda, works by, 16.
Chialli, works by, 138, 139, 142.
Chiana, valley and river, 148, 154, 205, 226.
—— plain of the, 155.
Chianciano, 159.
Chianti, 204, 205.
Chiara, Sta., tomb of, 250.
Chiarone, the, 168.
Chiarruccia, Torre, 171.
Chiascio torrent, 247.
Chiassa torrent, 144.
Chienti, the, 124, 125.
Chigi, Agostino, 187.
Chiodarolo, works by, 45.
Chioggia, 74.
Chiusa di Monaci, 222, 227.
Chiusdino, 207.
Chiusi:—Guide, 155. Historical notice, 155. Walls, 156. Subterranean passages, 156. Museum of Signor Casuccini, 156. Collection of Signor Paolozzi, 156. Vases, 157. Tombs, 157. Cathedral, 158.
Chiusi to Montefiascone, 149.
—— to Siena by the Val di Chiana, 205.
Christian architecture, xxiii.
—— sculpture, xxv.
Christina of Sweden, 24.
Chronological tables, xxx.
Church of La Pieve, 220.
Churches at Ancona, 115.
—— S. Angelo in Vado, 135.
—— Arezzo, 223, 224.
—— Assisi, 248.
—— Bieda, 200.
—— Bologna, 36.
—— Bolsena, 191.
—— Borgo San Sepolcro, 143.
—— Cagli, 128.
—— Castiglione Fiorentino, 227.
—— Certaldo, 173.
—— Citerna, 143.
—— Città di Castello, 137.
—— Città della Pieve, 155.
—— Correse, 160.
—— Fano, 109.
—— Ferrara, 14.
—— Foligno, 252.
—— Forlì, 99.
—— Fratta, 144.
—— S. Giacomo, 254.
—— S. Gimignano, 175.
—— Gubbio, 145.
—— L'Impruneta, 204.
—— Loreto, 118.

CITTA.

Churches at Macerata, 123.
—— Sta. Maria degli Angeli, 247.
—— Montefalco, 253.
—— Montefiascone, 193.
—— Montepulciano, 159.
—— Nepi, 265.
—— Orvieto, 153.
—— Osimo, 117.
—— Perugia, 237.
—— S. Quirico, 189.
—— Ravenna, 80.
—— Recanati, 122.
—— Rimini, 103.
—— Spello, 251.
—— Spoleto, 255, 256.
—— Todi, 148.
—— Trevi, 253.
—— Urbania, 135.
—— Urbino, 133.
—— Viterbo, 196.
—— Volterra, 212.
Cignani, Carlo, works by, 47, 52, 54, 86, 99, 154.
Cignani, Felice, works by, 44, 46.
Cignaroli, 18.
Cigoli, works by, 175, 230, 244.
Cimabue, works by, 248.
Ciminus, Mons, 201.
Cina, torrent, 233.
Cini, Lorenzo, works by, 183.
Cinquemiglia, plain of, 125.
Cioli, Raffaello, works by, 212.
—— Simone, works by, 119, 120.
Circignani, Antonio, works by, 137.
—— Niccolò, works by, 137, 138, 141, 143, 144, 153, 211, 212.
Circus at Forlì, 99.
Citadel of Ferrara, 22.
—— of Forlì, 99.
Citerna, 143.
Città di Castello:—Inns, 135. Historical notice, 136. Churches:— S. Agostino, 138; S. Bartolommeo, 138; Sta. Caterina, 138; Cathedral, 136; Sta. Cecilia, 138; S. Domenico, 138; S. Francesco, 137; Sta. Maria Maggiore, 139; S. Michele Archangelo, 139; the Servites, 139; SS. Trinità, 139; other churches, 139. Palaces:— Palazzo Comunale, 139; P. Vescovile, 139; P. Apostolico, 139; Vitelli Palaces, 139-141; P. Bufalini, 141; P. Mancini, 141. Hospital, 139. Torre del Vescovo, 139. Monte di Belvedere, 141. Fair, 141.
Città di Castello to Gubbio, 144.
—— to Perugia, 147.
—— to Urbino, 134.
Città della Pieve, 154. Churches and works of Perugino, 155.

CONTESSE.

Città della Pieve to Chiusi, 155.
—— to Montefiascone, 149.
—— to Perugia, 148.
Civita Castellana:—Inns, 261. Guide, 261. Bridge, 261. Cathedral, citadel, ravines, 262. Remains, 262.
Civita Vecchia:— Inns, 169. Packets, 169. Facchini, 169. Diligence, 170. Vetturini, 171. Port, 170. Prisons, 170. Antiquities and coins, 170. Mineral springs, 170. Lead-mines and alum-works, 170. Etruscan antiquities, 170.
Civita Vecchia to Leghorn, 163.
—— to Rome, 170.
Civitanuova, 125.
Civitella Ranieri, 145.
Clanis, 226.
Clarisse, monastery of, 246.
Classis, ancient town of, 94.
Clement IV., tomb of, 194.
Climate of Bologna, 64.
—— of Siena, 187.
Clitumnus, vale of the, 126, 253.
—— source of the, 253.
—— temple of, 253.
Clitunno, the, 253.
Coal-mines (lignite) of Monte Bamboli, 220.
Coinage, Roman, 3.
—— table of, 4.
Coins, Etruscan, 211, 243.
Colbordolo, 134.
Coldazzo, 134.
Colfiorito, 126.
Colle, 125, 175, 205.
Colle, Cennino Cennini da, works by, 213.
Collecchio, 166.
Colleges at Bologna, 59.
—— at Faenza, 97.
—— at Fano, 109.
—— at Urbino, 134.
Collenzano, 163.
Colli Tufarini, 171.
Collina pass, 70.
Colmates, 226.
Colonna, 165.
Colonna de' Francesi, near Ravenna, 94.
Colonna, Michael Angelo, works by, 42, 44, 48, 52, 54, 57, 60.
Columbus, ex-voto offerings by, at Siena, 183.
Commacchio, 74.
Comarca of Rome, 265.
Commenda, la, 236.
Commerce of the Papal States, xiii.
Conca, the, 106.
Conca, Sebastiano, works by, 186.
—— Tommaso, works by, 137.
Conduits, Roman, 128.
Conegliano, Cima da, works by, 32.
Contesse, 230.

CONVENT.

Convent of Sta. Chiara, 86.
—— Capuchin, at Faenza, 98.
—— of the Padri Riformati at Sinigallia, 111.
—— Capuchin, at Urbino, 134.
—— of S. Albertino, on Monte Catria, 135.
—— of Il Ritoro, 167.
—— of S. Silvester, on Mons Soracte, 264.
Copper-mines of La Cava, 215; in the valley of the Pavone, 220.
Coppi, Jacobi, works by, 52.
Corchiano, 198.
Corneto, 168, 169, 170.
Cornia, the, 164.
—— valley, 220.
Corpus Domini, festival of the, 191.
Correggio, works by, 90, 122.
Correse, 160.
Cortona :—Inns, 228. Gates and wall, 228. Museums, 229. Bronze lamp, 229. Accademia Etrusca, 229. Library, 229. Cathedral, 229. Churches, 229.
Cortona, Pietro da, works by, 229, 230, 244.
—— Urbano da, works by, 183.
Corythus, 228.
Cosa, site of, 167.
Cosmé, works by, 15, 19.
Cosmo I., 186, 187.
Cospaja, 135, 142.
Cossa, Francesco, works by, 48.
Cossa, hill of, 168.
Costa, Lorenza, works by, 29, 39, 40, 44, 45, 46, 47, 50, 61.
Costacciaro, 129.
Costoli, works by, 211.
Cotignola, 77.
Cotignola, Francesco da, works by, 85, 86, 90.
—— Girolamo Marchesi da, works by, 29.
Council of Ferrara, 18.
—— of Rimini, 102.
Covigliajo, 66.
Cozzarelli, works by, 185.
Cremera, the, 267.
Cremonesi, Giuseppe, works by, 16.
Crespi, Giuseppe, works by, 49.
Crespino, 71.
Crete Sanese, 205, 206.
Creti, Donati, works by, 37, 57.
Cristina, Sta., relics of, 192.
Crivelli, works by, 255.
Croce, la, 154.
Croce, Baldassare, works by, 196.
Crucifixes, miraculous, 49, 84.
Cungi, Francesco, works by, 212.
—— Gio. Battista, works by, 143.
Cunio castle, ruins of, 77.

ECASU.

Cures, site of, 160.
Curradi, Francesco, works by, 211, 212, 213.
Custom-houses, 3.
Cyclopean architecture, xx.

D.

DADDI, Cosimo, works by, 213.
Dalmasio, Lippo, works by, 36, 42, 43, 47, 48, 51, 53, 61, 64.
Dante, tomb of, 87, 36. MS. of, 89. His description of Assisi, 247.
Danti's meridian, 40.
Danti, Girolamo, works by, 241.
—— Giulio, works by, 240, 247.
—— Vincenzio, works by, 242.
Del, Deposito de', 158.
Demaria, Prof., bust by, 60.
Dentone, works by, 50, 53.
Desani, Pietro, works by, 52, 60.
Desiderius, 197.
Dicomano, 72.
Dielai, works by, 18.
Dietisalvi, works by, 177, 178.
Dionysius of Syracuse, 171.
Doceno, works by, 135, 140.
Dogs of Bologna, 64.
Dolabella, 198.
Dolci, Carlo, works by, 58.
Dolciano, 159, 206.
Domenichino, works by, 30, 56, 58, 108, 109, 153, 154, 211, 244, 245.
Domenico, San, tomb of, 41.
Donatello, works by, 180, 181, 204.
Doni, Adone, works by, 240, 249, 250.
Donnini, Girolamo, works by, 48.
Dossi, Dosso, works by, 16, 19, 241.
Dotti, Carlo Francesco, works by, 49.
Dow, Gerard, works by, 90.
Drove, torrent, 204.
Ducci, Virgilio, works by, 137.
Duccio, works by, 178, 179, 181.
Dupré, works by, 182.
Dürer, Albert, works by, 90, 194.

E.

EARTHQUAKES at Foligno and the neighbourhood, 252.
"Ecasu," "Ecasuthineal," 199.

FAENZA.

Ecclesiastical establishment, xii.
Echo, a famous, at Ferrara, 15.
Education in the Papal States, xiii.
Elias, Fra, 246.
Elsa, 173, 175; valley of the, 205.
Elvella torrent, 190.
Emissarii, 266.
Emo river, 204.
Emperors of Germany, list of, xxxiii.
—— of Italy, xxxii.
—— of Rome, xxx.
Empoli, 173, 230.
Enzius, king of Sardinia, 27. His tomb, 42. His prison, 54.
Era, valley of the, 207.
Esino, the, 112.
Esse river, 205, 226.
Este, house of, 11. Their patronage of art, 11.
—— tombs of, 15, 18.
Etruscan remains at Ansedonia, 167.
—— at Campiglia, 164.
—— at Chiusi, 156-159.
—— at Civita Castellana, 262.
—— at Nepi, 265.
—— of Populonia, 163.
—— at Rusellæ, 165.
—— at Todi, 148.
—— at Vetulonia, 167.
—— at Volterra, 208.
Etruscan plain, 193.
Etruscans, probable descent of the, xx. Arts, xxi. Language, xxi. Alphabet, xxii. Inscriptions, xxii. Bas-reliefs, illustrating their costumes and manners, 210.
Eugubian tables, 146. Inscriptions on, 146. Opinions concerning, 146.
Exarchs of Ravenna, 79.
—— —— list of, xxxii.
—— of the Pentapolis, 102.

F.

FABRIANO, 129.
Fabriano, Gentile da, works by, 153, 182, 239.
Fabricius, birthplace of, 190.
Facini, works by, 42.
Faenza :—Inns, 97. History, 97. Manufactures, 97. Liceo, 97. Cathedral, 98. Hospital, 98. Lunatic asylum, 98. Palazzo Comunale, 98.
—— to Florence, 71.
—— to Ravenna, 73.
Faenza, Pace da, works by, 249.

FAIR.

Fair of St. Mary Magdalen at Sinigallia, 111.
—— at Città di Castello, 141.
Falerii Novi, Roman city, site of, 263. Wall, towers, gates, tombs, 263. Necropolis, theatre, statues, 264.
Falerium Vetus, Etruscan city, site of, 262. Ancient wall, 262. Bridge, 263. Tombs, 263.
Falls of Terni : — Conveyance to, expense, 257. Guides, 257. Points of view, 257, 258. Lord Byron's opinion, 258. Historical notice of, 258. Height, 259.
Fano :—Inns, 108. Triumphal arch, 108. Cathedral, 108. Churches, 109. College, 109. Theatre, port, 110.
—— to Foligno, 126.
—— to Urbino, 130.
Fanum Voltumnæ, 194.
Farma, river, 207.
Farmanuova, valley of the, 233.
Farnesi, 192, 201.
Fava, Niccolò, monument of, 46.
Faventia, site of, 97.
Federighi, Antonio, works by, 180, 183.
Federigo, duke of Urbino, 130.
Felsina, 26.
Ferentinum, 193.
Férento, 193.
Ferguson, Mr., his Handbook of Architecture, xxix.
Ferrantini, Gabriele, works by, 44.
Ferrara :—Inns, 11. Present aspect and population, 11. Historical notice, 11. School of art, 11. Reformation at, 13. Commerce, 14. Atmosphere, 18.
　　Churches :—S. Andrea, 17; S. Benedetto, 16; Campo Santo, 18 ; Capuchins, 17; Cathedral, 14 ; Corpus Domini, 18 ; S. Domenico, 17; S. Francesco, 15 ; Gesu, 18 ; S. Giorgio, 18 ; Sta. Maria del Vado, 16 ; S. Paolo, 17; Theatines, 17.
　　Castle, 18. Gallery of Pictures, 19. Palazzo del Magistrato, 19. Studio Pubblico, 19. Public Library, 19. Casa d'Ariosto, 20. C. degli Ariosti, 20. C. Guarini, 21. Piazza di Ariosto, 21. Tasso's prison, 21. Theatre, 22. Citadel, 22.
Ferrara to Bologna, by Malalbergo, 23.
—— by Cento, 23.
—— to Mantua, 10.
—— to Modena, 10.
—— to Padua, 10.
—— list of sovereigns of, xxxvii.

FONTANA.

Ferrata, Ercole, works by, 181.
—— Raggi, works by, 181.
Ferreri, Andrea, works by, 15, 17.
Ferruzzi, Andrea, works by, 212.
Fescennium, 198.
Fiammingo, Gio., works by, 240.
Fiano, 161.
Ficulle, 154.
Fidenæ, site of, 161.
Fiesole, Andrea da, works by, 50.
—— Beato Angelico da, works by, 152, 229, 239.
—— Mino da, works by, 211, 212, 240.
Figline, 221.
Filelfo, Francesco, 125.
Filigare, 66.
Finale, 10.
Fiora, the, 168.
Fiorentino, Agnola, works by, 237.
—— Fuccio, works by, 249.
—— Rosso, works by, 137, 143, 212.
Fiorini, works by, 37, 46.
—— Gabriele, works by, 44.
Firenze, Arnolfo da, works by, 151.
Fistona valley, 71.
Fiumicello, the, 144.
Fiumicino, the, 101.
Fiamberti, Tommaso, works by, 85.
Flaminius at the Thrasimene Lake, 230.
Florence, 67.
—— to Faenza, 71.
—— to Forlì, 72.
—— to Rome, by Siena, 172.
—— to Rome, by the Val d' Arno di Sopra, Arezzo, Cortona, Perugia, Assisi, Foligno, Spoleto, and Civita Castellana, 221.
—— to Siena, by the post-road, 204.
—— to Volterra (the Lagoni, and Massa Maritima), 207.
Foci torrent, 175.
Föenna, valley of the, 206, 226.
Foglia, the, 106.
Foix, Gaston de, 80, 95.
Fojano, 226.
Foligno, 252.
—— plain of, 126.
—— to Ancona, 116.
—— to Fano, 126.
Follonico, 164.
Fontana, Prospero, works by, 29, 45, 46, 48, 52, 57, 140.
—— Giovanni, of Como, works by, 183.
—— Lavinia, works by, 29, 46, 47, 48, 50, 53.
—— Orazio, works by, 122.
Fontana Grande at Viterbo, 197.

FRESCOES.

Fonte Nuova at Siena, 185.
Fonte di Papa, 161.
Fontebuona, 67.
Fonte Gaja, 184.
—— di Fullonica, 185.
—— Branda, 185.
—— Carbonari, 201.
—— San Felice, 214.
Forlì, historical notice and associations, 98, 100. Circus and public garden, 99. Cathedral, 99. Churches : S. Filippo Neri, S. Girolamo, S. Mercuriale, 99. Spezeria Morandi, 99. Palazzo Comunale, 99. Citadel, 99. Ramparts, 100.
Forlì to Florence, 72.
—— to Ravenna, 73.
Forlimpopoli, 100.
Formone, 189.
Fortebraccio, Braccio, 234, 239.
Fortress of Pesaro, 108.
—— of Ravenna, 91.
—— of Rimini, 104.
Forum Cassii, 199.
—— Flaminii, site of, 129.
Foscherari, tomb of the, 41.
Fossa d' Acqua Sona, 172.
Fossalta, battle of, 27.
Fossato, 129.
Fossil remains, 127.
Fossombrone, 126.
Fossombroni, Count, birthplace of, 226 ; his engineering operations, 227 ; his work on the Val di Chiana, 227.
Francesca, Pietro della, notice of, 142. His MSS., 142.
—— works by, 133, 141, 143, 223, 224.
Francesca da Rimini, house of, 104.
Franceschini, works by, 37, 42, 44, 45, 48, 52, 153, 154.
—— Marcantonio, works by, 45.
Francesco, Bastiano di, works by, 180.
Francesco Maria I., duke of Urbino, 131.
—— II., 132.
Francia, Francesco, his style, 28.
—— works by, 29, 36, 39, 42, 44, 45, 46, 50, 53, 61, 101.
—— Giacomo, works by, 29, 44, 45, 47, 53.
Francis, St. foundation of his Order, 247 ; paintings representing the events of his life, 248 ; his tomb, 250.
Frankish emperors of Italy, list of, xxxii.
Fraser, Dr., his journey from Ravenna to Venice, 75.
Fratta, 144.
Frederick II., emperor, 197, 205.
Fredi, Bartolo, works by, 175.
Frescoes at Ancona, 115.
—— Assisi, 248.

FRESCOES.

Frescoes at Bologna, 33, 35, 36, 37, 40, 45, 46, 47, 49, 51, 52, 53, 55, 59, 61, 64.
—— Borgo San Sepolcro, 143.
—— Cagli, 128.
—— Caprarola, 201.
—— Certaldo, 174.
—— Città di Castello, 138, 140.
—— Città della Pieve, 155.
—— Fano, 108, 109.
—— Forlì, 99.
—— S. Giacomo, 254.
—— S. Gimignano, 175.
—— Loreto, 120, 121.
—— Sta. Maria degli Angeli, 247.
—— Monte Uliveto Maggiore, 189.
—— Narni, 260.
—— Orvieto, 150, 152, 154.
—— Osimo, 117.
—— Perugia, 241, 242.
—— near Pesaro, 107.
—— Ravenna, 86, 92.
—— Spello, 251.
—— Spoleto, 255.
—— Todi, 148.
—— Tolentino, 124.
—— Urbania, 135.
—— Viterbo, 196.
—— Volterra, 211.
Frontier stations, 3.
Fugger, Bp. Johann, 193.
Fuligno, Pietro Antonio da, works by, 251.
Fungai, Bernardino, works by, 182.
Fuochi, the, 66.
Furlo, pass of the, 127.
Fusignano, 77.
Futa, la, pass of, 66.

G.

GABBRO rosso, 215, 216.
Gaddi, Taddeo, works by, 249.
Gagliardi, Bernardino, works by, 137, 138.
—— Scaramuccia, works by, 238.
Galanino, works by, 44.
Galera, Counts of, 171.
—— river, 171.
Galiana, 196.
Galilei, the Florentine architect, works by, 229.
Galla Placidia, mausoleum of, 86.
Galleries at Ancona, 115.
—— at Bologna, 29.
—— at Ferrara, 19.
—— at Perugia, 243.
—— at Siena, 177.
Gallese, 198.
Galuzzo, 204.

GOVERNMENT.

Gambara, Card., 197.
Gandolfi, Gaetano, works by, 52.
Garbieri, Lorenzo, works by, 48, 51.
Garbo, Raffaelino del, works by, 133.
Gardens at Bologna, 35.
—— at Forlì, 99.
Garisenda tower, 59.
Garofalo, works by, 14, 15, 17, 19, 52.
Gases, natural, 69, 72.
Gasparini, works by, 121.
Gates, five, of Ravenna, 91.
—— of Falerii, 263.
—— of Spello, 251.
Gatta, Bartolommeo della, works by, 227.
Gattemalata, birthplace of, 260.
Gelagno, 125.
Genga, Girolamo, works by, 86, 134.
Gennari, Gio. Battista, works by, 53, 240.
Geological collection at Città di Castello, 141.
Gerfalco, Cornata of, 220.
German emperors of Italy, list of, xxxii.
Germany, list of emperors of, xxxiii.
Gessi, Francesco, works by, 50, 52, 55, 60, 61, 63, 83.
Ghent, Justus van, works by, 133.
Gherardi, Cristoforo, works by, 138.
Ghiberti, Lorenzo, works by, 181.
Ghirlandaio, Domenico, works by, 103, 175, 215.
Ghisilieri, Beato Buonaparte, 49.
Giacomo, Maestro, works by, 133.
Giannicola, works by, 237, 239, 241, 243.
Gieremei family, 27.
Gilio, Maestro, works by, 178.
Gimignani, Giacinto, works by, 240.
Giordani, Sig., 174.
Giordano, Luca, works by, 90.
Giorgio, Francesco di, works by, 133, 178, 185, 187.
Giottino, works by, 249, 250.
Giotto, works by, 29, 62, 83, 92, 141, 177, 182, 248.
Giovane, Palma, works by, 86, 142.
Giovanni, Giovanni da S., birthplace of, 221, 222.
—— works by, 211.
—— Matteo di, works by, 180, 183.
Giusti, works by, 178.
Gonfolina, la, 173.
Gonzaga, Elizabetta, 131.
Gothic (East) kings of Italy, list of, xxxii.
Governalo, 10.
Government of the Papal States, viii.

HENRY.

Gozzoli, Benozzo, works by, 152, 175, 212, 243, 252.
Gradara, 106.
Grecos, Ad, 226.
Grecos, 226.
Granajuolo, 173.
Grandi, Ercole, 17.
Graziani, Ercole, works by, 37, 50, 51, 52, 53, 57, 64.
Grazini, Ercole, works by, 38.
Gregory X., tomb of, 224.
Greve river, 204.
Grosseto, 165, 207.
—— to Siena, 206.
Grotta d' Orlando, 203.
Grotta de' Volunni, 235.
Grotto on Mons Soracte, 264.
—— of Pythagoras, 228.
—— Sergardi, 228.
Gruner's, Mr., arabesque engravings, xxviii.
Gualdo, Matteo da, works by, 251.
Gualdo Tadino, 129.
Gualterio, Count, 153.
Guarnacci, Monsig. Mario, 209; his tomb, 213.
Gubbio:—Inns, 145. Palaces, 145. Cathedral, churches, 145.
Eugubian tables, 146.
—— plain of, 145.
—— to Città di Castello, 144.
Gubbio, Oderigi da, works by, 185.
Guercino, birthplace and residence of, 24. His chapel, 24.
—— works by, 17, 19, 24, 37, 42, 47, 48, 51, 52, 53, 57, 58, 86, 90, 99, 101, 103, 104, 107, 109, 115, 121, 183, 237, 241, 244, 245.
Guglielmi, Sig., 170.
Guidi family, tombs of, 213.
Guido, tomb of, 42.
—— works by, 25, 31, 39, 41, 42, 44, 45, 49, 50, 52, 53, 56, 57, 58, 63, 80, 81, 90, 98, 99, 109, 115, 121, 183, 244, 245.
Guidoccio, works by, 180.
Guid' Ubaldo I., duke of Urbino, 131.
Guiduccio, works by, 177, 178.
Guittone, Fra, birthplace of, 225.
Guittone, the poet, birthplace of, 225.

H.

HANNIBAL at the Thrasimene Lake, 230.
—— his attack on Spoletium, 254.
Harvey, 190.
Hawkswood, Sir John, his capture of Faenza, 97.
Henry of England, Prince, scene of his murder by Guy de Montfort, 194.

HENRY.

Henry VII., emperor, scene of his death, 188.
Hensius, king of Sardinia, 27.
—— his tomb, 42.
Herculanus, St., 236.
Hobhouse, Sir John, his description of the local features of the country near the Thrasimene Lake, 230.
Horta, 197.
Hospitals at Ancona, 114.
—— at Bologna, 35.
—— at Faenza, 98.
—— at Imola, 96.
—— at Loreto, 122.
—— at Ravenna, 90.
Hydraulic works in the Val di Chiana, 160.

I.

IDICE, the, 96.
Iguvium, site of, 145.
Imola, 96. Public establishments and cathedral, 96. Its bishops, 97.
Imola, Innocenzio da, works by, 29, 35. 45, 50, 52, 53, 61, 62, 64, 90, 98, 99, 244.
Imposta, l', 201.
Impruneta, l', 204.
Incisa, 221.
Incontri, Abp., tomb of, 211.
—— Camillo, works by, 212.
Ingegno, l', works by, 249.
Inghirami, Gen. Jacopo, 211.
INNS, 9.
Inscriptions, 93, 102, 104, 117, 127, 128, 133, 134, 146, 154, 159, 197, 210, 235, 236, 243, 264, 265.
Irnerius, or Wernerus, 33.
Iron-works at Follonica, 164.
Isaac, the exarch, his tomb, 83.
Isola d' Ariano, 74.
—— Maggiore, 232.
—— Minore, 232.
—— Polvese, 232.
Istituto delle Belle Arte at Siena, 177.
Italy, list of emperors, xxxii.
—— kings, xxxii.
Ivory chair, 81.
—— sculptures at Volterra, 211.

J.

JACOMETTI, works by, 118, 121, 123.
Jacomone of Faenza, works by, 98.
Jacone, works by, 229.
Jescio torrent, 247.
Jesi, 112.

LIBIANO.

Jesuits' college of S. Vigilio, 185.
Jews in Ferrara, 14.
—— in Ancona, 116.
John XXI., tomb of, 194, 195.
Julius II., statue of, 40.
—— III., bronze statue of, 241.
Juno, statue of, 264.
Justice, administration of, x.

K.

KINGS of Italy, list of, xxxii.
—— of Rome, xxx.
Kügler's Handbook of Painting, xxix.

L.

LABYRINTHS at Chiusi, 157.
Lacus Cimini, 201.
Lagoni di Monte Cerboli, or Lardarello, 217.
Lajatico, 207.
Lake of Bassano, 198.
—— Bolsena, 149.
—— Bracciano, 265, 266.
—— Burano, 168.
—— Castiglione, 165.
—— Chiusi, 206.
—— Colfiorito, 126.
—— Martignano, 266.
—— Montepulciano, 206.
—— Thrasimene, 230, 232.
—— Vico, 201.
Lambertazzi family, 27.
Lamoli, 135.
Lamone, the, 71, 73, 75, 77, 97, 98.
Landi, works by, 244.
Lando, Maestro, works by, 179.
Lanfranco, works by, 123.
Lanzi, birthplace of, 124.
Lapis, Gaetano, works by, 128.
Lapo, works by, 223.
—— Jacopo di, works by, 248.
Lardarel, Count, 217.
Lardarello, 217.
" Larth Vel Arnies," 198.
Lasca, 232.
Lascia-passare, 2.
Lastra river, 173.
Laudi, Thuestro, works by, 179.
Laura, 177.
Lauretti, works by, 53, 57.
Lavino, the, 25.
Leghorn to Civita Vecchia, 163.
Lely, Sir Peter, works by, 58.
Lenzoni Medici, Marchioness, 174.
Leo X. at the battle of Ravenna, 95.
Leopoldo, S., Moje or salt-works of, 216.
Levane, 221, 222.
Libiano, castle of, 208.

LUNATIC.

Liberale, illuminated missal by, 181.
Libraries at Arezzo, 225.
—— Bologna, 34, 43, 61.
—— Cesena, 101.
—— Cortona, 229.
—— Ferrara, 17, 19.
—— Imola, 96.
—— Macerata, 123.
—— Perugia, 237, 245.
—— Pesaro, 107.
—— Ravenna, 89.
—— Rimini, 104.
—— Siena, 185.
—— Volterra, 211.
Limentra, the, 69.
Linaro, Cape, 171.
Linguessa torrent, the, 160, 161.
Lippi, Filippo, tomb of, 255.
—— works by, 212, 255.
Lojano, 65.1
Lombard kings of Italy, list of, xxxii.
Lombardelli, works by, 120, 121.
Lombardo, Alfonso, 17, 38, 39, 41, 44, 47, 48, 49, 51, 54, 55, 57.
—— Fra Aurelio, works by, 119.
—— Girolamo, works by, 118, 119, 120.
—— Pietro, works by, 85, 90, 121.
Longhi, Barbara, works by, 83, 86, 90.
—— Francesco, works by, 83, 84, 86, 92.
—— Luca, works by, 16, 83, 84, 85, 86, 90.
Lorenzetti, Ambrogio, works by, 177, 178, 184.
—— Pietro, works by, 177, 181, 184.
Lorenzini, Lorenzo, prison of, 213.
Lorenzo, Fiorenzo di, works by, 239.
Loreto:—Inns, 117. Its names, 117. Santa Casa, 117, 118. Beggars, 117. Chiesa della Santa Casa, 118 ; casing of the Santa Casa, 119 ; baptistery, 120 ; chapels, 120 ; treasury, 121 ; cupola, 121. Palazzo Apostolica, 121. Spezieria, 122. Fountains, 122. Hospitals, 122.
Loricum, 171.
Lotto, Lorenzo, works by, 115, 120.
Louis XIV., medallion portrait of, 49.
Lugano, Giroldo da, works by, 214.
Luggage, 7.
Lugo, 77.
Luigi, Andrea di, works by, 249.
Lunatic Asylum at Faenza, 98.

LUNATIC.

Lunatic Asylum at Pesaro, 107.
Lupi, Antonio, works by, 53.
Lusignano, Ecuba di, 249.

M.

MACDONALD, Marshal, his defeat of Mack, 261.
Macerata, 123.
Machiavelli, 187.
Macigno, 233, 247.
Maderno, Carlo, works by, 238.
Madonna della Perzola, 147.
Maffei, Mario, tomb of, 211.
—— Raffaello, tomb of, 212.
Magano, 144.
Maggieri, Cesare, works by, 141.
Magione, 233.
Maglianella, river, 172.
Magliano, 166.
—— river, 172.
Magnani, Antonio, 43.
Magnavacca, 74.
Mainardi, works by, 175.
Maitani, Lorenzo, architect, 150, 179.
Majano, Benedetto da, works by, 175.
——, Giuliano da, works by, 121.
Majolica, collection of, at Fratta, 145.
Malagrotta, 172.
Malalbergo, 23.
Malaria, effects of, 192.
Malatesta, family of the, 102. Tombs of, 103, 109.
—— Carlo, 234.
Malpasso, 161.
Manciano, 168.
Mancini, works by, 109, 141.
—— Domenico (guide), 261.
Manetti, works by, 182.
Manfred, 176.
Manfredi, of Bologna, 33.
—— Andrea, of Faenza, tablet to, 33.
—— Galeotto, murder of, 98.
Mannozzi, Giovanni, birthplace of, 221, 222.
Mantua to Ferrara, 10.
Manufactories of alabaster, 214.
—— of boracic acid, 217.
—— of earthenware, 97.
—— of iron, 257.
—— of paper, 97, 129.
—— of parchment, 252.
—— of pins, 134.
—— of silk, 97, 125, 126, 257.
—— of straw hats, 135.
—— of woollens, 252, 254, 257.
Manufactures of the Papal States, xiii.
Manutius, Paulus, 101.
Manzolina, Madonna, 33.
Maps of the Papal States, xxix.

MEMMO.

Maratta, Carlo, works by, 99, 181, 194, 213.
Marble quarries at San Ippolito, 127.
Marca, Lattanzio della, works by, 103.
Marchesi, Giuseppe, works by, 42.
Marchione, works by, 223.
Marcigliana Vecchia, 161.
Marcilla, works by, 223.
Marescotti, works by, 15.
Marignano, Marquis de, 177, 187.
Marot, Clement, 13.
Marotta, la, 110.
Marradi, 71.
Marseilles, Guillaume de, works by, 223.
Marsigli, Count, 33, 42.
Marta, river, 169, 192.
Martana, 192.
Martinello, works by, 251.
Mardini, works by, 182, 185.
Masaccio, birthplace of, 221, 222.
Mascagni, the anatomist, 186; his birthplace, 217.
—— Donato, works by, 215.
Maschere, le, 66.
Massa, 165.
Massa Lombarda, 76.
Massadi, 125.
Massari, Lucio, works by, 44, 45, 48, 50, 51, 52, 56, 61, 63.
Mastelletta, works by, 39, 41, 50, 51, 52, 53.
Mastio, Il, Torre, 213.
Matera, Fra Benedetto da, works of, 181.
Matilda, Countess, 194.
Mausoleum of Galla Placidia, 86.
—— of Theodoric, 91.
—— of Barbara Ordelaffi, 99.
—— of Porsena, 157.
Mazza, Giuseppe, works by, 45, 48.
Mazzuola, Giuseppe, works by, 186.
Measures, 4.
Mecænas, birthplace of, 222.
Medals, collections of, at Ravenna, 90.
—— at San Marino, 106.
—— of Cav. Mancini at Città di Castello, 141.
Medici, Card. de', 191.
——, Cosmo de', 177.
Medicis, Lorenzo de, 220.
Melano, Giovanni da, works by, 249.
Melone, Il, 228.
Melozzo da Forlì, works by, 99.
Memmi, Lippo, works by, 177, 178.
——, Simone, works by, 153, 177, 184, 249.
Memmo, Lippo di, works by, 175, 182.

MONTE.

Menganti, Alessandro, works by, 54.
Menicatore, 197.
Mentana, la, 161.
Mercanti, Gabriele, works by, 152.
Mercatello, 135.
Meridian line at Bologna, 40.
Mesola, 74.
Meta, the, 135.
Metastasio, birthplace of, 251.
Metauro, river and valley, 126, 135.
Mezzofanti, Cardinal, 35.
Michael Angelo, works by, 39, 40, 41, 83, 90, 181, 182, 196, 244, 269.
Michele, S., cupola by, 191.
Mignone, river, 169.
Milani, Aureliano, works by, 49.
Milano, Bramantino da, works by, 56.
Miles, various, 8.
Mileto, 173.
—— Agricultural School at, 173.
Mines:—copper, of La Cava, 215.
—— valley of the Pavone, 220.
—— Miemo, 216.
—— Castellina, 216.
—— Monte Vaso, 216.
—— coal (lignite) of Monte Bamboli, 220.
Miracle of Sta. Maria at Ferrara, 16.
Mirandola, Domenico, works by, 51.
Mitelli, Agostino, works by, 42.
—— Giuseppe, works by, 52.
Mochi, Francesco, works by, 151, 152, 269.
Modena to Ferrara, 10.
—— to Bologna, 25.
Mogdigliana, 73.
Molli, Clemente, works by, 90.
Moje, or salt-works of S. Leopoldo, 216.
Mona, works by, 15.
Monache, Deposito delle, 158.
Monastery of Monte Luco, 256.
Mondavio, 127.
MONEY, 3.
Money, Table of, 4.
Montagnuola, 207.
Montalcino, 189.
Montalto, 168.
Monte Acuto, 144.
—— Amiata, 150, 189.
—— S. Antonio, 215.
—— Aperto, 176.
—— Argentaro, 167.
—— d' Asdrubale, 127.
—— Bamboli, 220.
—— S. Bartolo, 107.
—— di Belvedere, 141.
—— Beni, 66.
—— Buoni, 204.

MONTE.

Monte Calvo, 145.
—— Cardo, 69.
—— Carelli, 66.
—— Carlo, 221.
—— Carpignano, 160.
—— Cassiano, 123.
—— Castelli, 208, 220.
—— Catini, 208, 215.
—— Catria, 135.
—— Cerboli, Count of, 217, 218.
—————— Lagoni di, 217.
—— Cimino, 194, 201.
—— Coronaro, 246.
—— Cucco, 135.
—— di Fo, 66.
—— Genaro, 161.
—— Gualandro, 230.
—— Guardia, 25.
—— di Lucchetti, 265.
—— Luce, la Fiera di, 246.
—— Luco, 256.
—— Massi, 215, 216.
—— Nero, 163.
—— Nerone, 135.
—— Petrano, 128.
—— Pincio, 269.
—— Poggio alle Croce, 215.
—— Radicofani, 189.
—— Razzano, 266.
—— Riggione, 205.
—— Rinaldi, 71.
—— Rotondo, 161.
—— San Savino, 205.
—— Senario, convent of, 67.
—— Somma, 256.
—— Subasio, 251.
—— Trebbio, 73.
—— Uliveto Maggiore, 189.
—— Vaso, 208.
Montecchio, 228.
Montefalco, 252.
Montefeltro, house of, 130.
——, Federigo di, 208.
——, Guido di, 250.
Montefiascone, 193. Cathedral, 193 ; Drei Mohren, 193.
Monteleone, 154.
Montelupo, 173.
——, Raffaele da, works by, 119, 152.
Montemerano, 168.
Montepulciano, 159.
—— Chiaro di, 159.
—— wines of, 159.
——, Benedetto of, works by, 180.
Monterone, 171, 188.
Monterosi, 265.
Montes Cortonenses, 231.
Montevarchi, 221, 222.
Montfort, Guy de, 194.
Montmorenci, Anne de, at the battle of Ravenna, 95.
Montone, Braccio da, 234.
Montorsoli, Fra Angelo, works by, 212.
Monuments at Ancona, 115.
—— Assisi, 249.

MUZIANI.

Monuments at Bologna, 39, 41, 42, 43, 46, 50, 53, 60, 64.
—— Camuscia, 228.
—— Cerialdo, 174.
—— Chiusi, 156.
—— Fano, 108, 109.
—— Ferrara, 15, 16, 17, 18.
—— Forli, 99.
—— Montefiascone, 193.
—— Orvieto, 153.
—— Perugia, 238.
—— Ravenna, 83, 85.
—— Siena, 81.
—— Spoleto, 255.
Morano, the, 106.
Morata, Fulvio, 14.
—— Olympia, 14.
Morcia, 145.
Morgagni, tomb of, 99.
Mortadella, the, 64.
Mosaics at Civita Castellana, 262.
—— Loreto, 120, 121.
—— Orvieto, 150, 151.
—— Populonia, 164.
—— Ravenna, 81, 82, 84, 85, 89, 91.
—— Siena, 180.
—— Spoleto, 255.
—— Volterra, 209, 211.
Mosca, Francesco, works by, 151.
—— Simone, works by, 119, 120, 152, 153, 245.
Moschino, works by, 152.
Moscona, 207.
—— hill of, 165.
Mosso, the, 161.
MSS. at Bologna, 35.
—— Cesena, 101.
—— Ferrara, 19.
—— Imola, 96.
—— Perugia, 245.
—— Pesaro, 107.
—— Ravenna, 89.
—— Rimini, 104.
—— Siena, 185.
Muccia, la, 125.
Mugello, the, 71.
Mugnone, the, 71.
Murano, Antonio da, works by, 107.
Murat, execution of, 124.
Muratori, Teresa, works by, 36, 48.
Museums at Arezzo, 225.
—— Bologna, 34.
—— Chiusi, 156.
—— Cortona, 229.
—— Macerata, 123.
—— Montevarchi, 222.
—— Osimo, 117.
—— Perugia, 243.
—— Pesaro, 107.
—— Ravenna, 90.
—— Sarteano, 159.
—— Siena, 177.
—— Viterbo, 197.
—— Volterra, 209.
Muziani, works by, 109, 153.

OSIMO.

N.

NALDINI, Giobattista, works by, 212, 213.
Nanni, Fra Giovanni, 197.
Nar, valley and river, 257, 258, 260.
Narni, 259. Bridge of Augustus, 260. Cathedral, 260.
Nasini, works by, 183.
Navarra, Pietro, 186.
Navy, Papal, xiii.
Nepi, 265.
Neptune, figure of, 53.
Nera, valley and river, 148.
—— plain of the, 257.
Neroccio, works by, 180.
Nerola, 160.
Neroni, Bartolommeo, works by, 177.
Nestore, valley, 148.
Nicolo, Lorenzo di, works by, 230.
Nocera, 129.
Nomentum, site of, 161.
Norchia, necropolis of, 199.
Norcia, the goddess, 191, 210.
Notte, Gherardo della, works by, 121, 154.
Nottula, 206.
Novella, 190.
Nucci, Allegretto, works by, 123.

O.

OAKS, groves of, 256, 265.
Obelisk of Rhamses I., 269.
Oderigi, missal-painter, 146.
Olmo, l', 205, 227.
Ombrone, valley and river, 70, 165, 166, 173, 188.
Onofri, Antonio, 105.
Onofrio, Vincenzo, works by, 50.
Orbetello, 167.
Orcagna, works by, 204, 211.
—— Jacopo, works by, 213.
Orcia, river, 189.
Orcle, 200.
Ordelaffi, family of the, 98.
Orioli, Professor, 198, 200.
Orley, Bernhard von, works by, 185.
Orsini, 171.
Orte, 197.
Ortolano, 15, 19.
Orvieto :—Historical notice, 150. Cathedral, 150. Chapels, 152. Church, 153. St. Patrick's well, 153. Palaces, 153.
Orvieto, plateau of, 150.
Orvieto to Montefiascone, 149.
Osa, the, 166.
Osimo, 116.

OSSAJA.

Ossaja, 230.
Osservanza, l', Franciscan convent of, 187.
Otho, emperor, birthplace of, 191.
Otricoli, 261.
Overbeck, works by, 247.

P.

PACCHIAROTTO, Jacopo, works by, 177, 183.
Pacetti, works by, 137.
Padua to Ferrara, 10.
Pagani, Gregorio, works by, 138.
Paganico, 165, 207.
Paglia, valley and river, 149, 150, 154, 190.
Painters at Arezzo, 223.
—— Assisi, 248.
—— Bologna, 28.
—— Ferrara, 12.
—— Perugia, 236.
—— Siena, 177.
—— Urbino, 133.
—— Viterbo, 194.
—— Volterra, 211.
Painting, schools of, xxvi.
Paintings at Ancona, 115.
—— S. Angelo in Vado, 135.
—— Arezzo, 223.
—— Assisi, 248.
—— Bologna, 29-64.
—— Borgo San Sepolcro, 142.
—— Cagli, 128.
—— CastiglioneFiorentino, 227.
—— Città di Castello, 137-141.
—— Cortona, 229.
—— Faenza, 98.
—— Fano, 108.
—— Ferrara, 14-19.
—— Forlì, 99.
—— Gubbio, 145.
—— Loreto, 118.
—— Macerata, 123.
—— Orvieto, 152.
—— Perugia, 236.
—— Pesaro, 107.
—— Ravenna, 80-86.
—— Rimini, 103.
—— Siena, 177.
—— Tolentino, 125.
—— Urbania, 135.
—— Urbino, 133.
—— Volterra, 211.
Palace of Theodoric, 87.
Palaces at Ancona, 115.
—— Bologna, 55.
—— Ferrara, 19.
—— S. Gimignano, 175.
—— Loreto, 121.
—— Orvieto, 153.
—— Perugia, 233, 244.
—— Pomarance, 217.
—— Ravenna, 89.
—— Recanati, 123.

PELLICCIAJO.

Palaces at Siena, 183.
—— Urbino, 132.
Palazzuolo, 205, 206.
Pale, 126.
Palimpsests at Ferrara, 19.
Palladio, works by, 56.
Palma Giovane, works by, 178, 230.
Palmegiani, Marco, works by, 99.
Palo, 171.
Palombara, 161.
Palus Clusina, 222.
Panaro, the, 10, 25.
Panchina, 208.
Panetti, works by, 16, 17.
Panfilio canal, 11, 23.
Pania, la, peaks of, 208.
Paola, Francesco di, works by, 133.
Paolo, Giovanni di, works by, 182.
—— Jacopo, works by, 29.
Paolozzi, Signor, his collection of antiquities at Chiusi, 156.
PAPAL STATES:—General topography, vii. Government, viii. Justice, x. Revenue, xi. Ecclesiastical establishment, xii. Army and Navy, xii. Education, xiii. Commerce and manufactures, xiii. Agriculture, xv. Characteristics of the country, xvi. Pelasgic architecture, xviii. Cyclopean architecture, xx. The Etruscans, xx. The Romans, xxii. Christian architecture, xxiii. Christian sculpture, xxv. Schools of painting, xxvi. Books, xxviii. Maps, xxix. Chronological tables, xxx.
Paper manufacture, 97, 129.
Parisina, story of, 18.
Parmegiano, works by, 32, 39, 241.
Parolini, works by, 15, 18.
Paschal calendar at Ravenna, 81.
Pasinelli, Lorenzo, works by, 39, 54, 63, 64.
Pasquali, Filippo, works by, 84.
Pasquinelli, Signor, excavation of Vetulonia by, 166.
Passaggeri, Rolandino, tomb of, 41.
Passerotti, Bartolommeo, works by, 45, 48, 49, 50, 55, 61, 64.
—— Tiburzio, works by, 46, 49.
Passignano, 231, 233.
Passignano, Domenico, works by, 143.
Passports, 2.
Patrizi, 171.
Pears of Monte Rotondo, 161.
Pelasgic architecture, xviii.
Pellicciajo, Mino del, works by, 178.

PERUZZI.

Pepoli, Taddeo, 27. His tomb, 42.
Pereta torrent, 189.
Pergola, 110.
Perugia :— Inns, 233. Diligences, 246.
Historical notice, 233. Walls and gates, 234. Necropolis, 235, 246. Fountain, 241. House of Perugino, 244. Citadel, 245. Casino letterario, 245. Fairs, 246. Roads from Perugia, 246. Excursion to Assisi, 247.
School of Umbria, 236.
Cathedral, 237.
Churches :— S. Agostino, 237. S. Angelo, 238. S. Antonio da Padoa, 238. S. Domenico, 238. S. Ercolano, 239. S. Florenzo, 239. S. Francesco dei Conventuali, 239. S. Francesco del Monte, 240. Sta. Giuliana, 240. Madonna della Luce, 240. Sta. Maria Nuova, 240. S. Pietro de' Casinensi, 240. S. Severo, 241. S. Tommaso, 241.
Monastic Establishments :— St. Agnese, 237; S. Agostino, 238 ; S. Bernardino, 238 ; La Giustizia, 238 ; S. Pietro Martire, 240.
Public buildings :— Exchange, 242. Library, 245. Lunatic Asylum, 245. Museum, 243. Palazzo Comunale, 242. P. Governativo, 242. Piazza del Papa, 241. P. del Soprammuro, 241. Pinacoteca, 243. Sala del Cambio, 242. University, 243.
Private Galleries :— Palazzo Baglioni, 244. P. Baldeschi, 244. P. Bracceschi, 244. P. Camilletti, 244. P. Cenci, 244. P. Cesarei, 244. P. Connestabili, 244. P. Donini, 244. P. Monaldi, 245. P. degli Oddi, 244. P. Penna, 245. P. di Porta Sole, 244. P. Sorbello, 245.
Perugia, delegation of, 129.
Perugia to Città di Castello, 147.
—— to Città della Pieve, 148.
—— to Rome, 147.
Perugino, Pietro, works by, 50, 53, 109, 111, 142, 155, 182, 237, 238, 239, 240, 242, 243, 244, 245, 246, 251, 253.
—— his birthplace, 155.
—— his own portrait, 242.
—— his death by the plague, 234.
Perusia, 233.
Peruzzi, Baldassare, works by, 55, 177, 180, 182, 183, 185, 187.

PERUZZI.

Peruzzi, Baldassare, his port-folio, 186.
Peruzzini, works by, 52.
Pesa, river, 173.
Pesaro :—Historical notice, 106. Cathedral, 107. Biblioteca Olivieri, museum, 107. Palace, 107.
  Environs : — Villa Imperiale, 107. Church of the Gerolamita, 107. La Vittoria, 108. Fortress, port, promenade, 108.
Pesaro, Niccolò da, works by, 107.
—— Simone da, works by, 32.
Peter Chrysologus, St. 96.
Peter, St., patrimony of, 194.
Petrarch, birthplace of, 222; town where the family had its origin, 221.
Petrazzi, works by, 184.
Petriano, 134.
Petriolo, 207.
Petrucci, Celia, tomb of, 187.
—— Pandolfo, 177, 185, 187.
Pianoro, 65.
Piazzano, Il, 191.
Piccioli, 207.
Piccione, 145.
Piccolomini, Card., 181.
Piegaro, 148.
Pienza, 189.
Pietralata, hill of, 127.
Pietramala, 66, 232.
Pietra serena, 233, 247.
Pietro, Lorenzo di, works by, 180, 181, 186.
—— Sano di, works by, 178, 186.
Pieve Bovigliano, 125.
—— di Cento, 25.
—— Favera, 125.
—— al Intoppo, 205.
—— Torrina, 125.
Pin manufacture, 134.
Pinelli, Antonio, works by, 61.
Pineta, the, near Ravenna, 94.
Pinturicchio, works by, 175, 178, 181, 243, 244, 251.
Pio, Angelo, works by, 33, 42, 49.
Piombino, 164.
Piombo, Sebastiano del, works by, 196, 240.
Pisa, Arnolfo da, works by, 180.
—— Niccolò di, works by, 41, 179, 180, 211, 230, 241.
—— Giovanni da, works by, 151, 180, 223, 230, 238, 241.
—— Giunta da, works by, 183, 248, 250.
Pisanello, Vittore, works by, 239.
Pisciatello, the, 101.
Pistoja, Gerino da, works by, 143.
—— Leonardo da, works by, 212.
Pitigliano, 168.

PORT.

Pius II., birthplace of, 189.
—— III., birthplace of, 189.
—— VI., his treaty with the French, 125.
Pizzoli, Gioacchini, works by, 49, 54.
Po, the, 10.
—— port of the, 10.
Pò di Goro, 74.
—— Grande, 74.
—— di Primaro, 23, 75, 98.
—— di Volàno, 23, 74.
Poderina, la, 189.
Podesti, works by, 115.
Poggibonsi, 175, 204.
Poggio Bagnuoli, 222.
—— Gojella, Deposito del, 157.
—— San Lorenzo, 160.
—— de Sette Bagni, 162.
—— di San Cornelio, 225.
Polenta, Ostasio, monument of, 85.
Polenta, village of, 100.
Polesina, plain of the, 11.
Pollajuolo, Pietro, works by, 181.
Pomarance, 217.
Pomerancie, works by, 217.
Pomposa, 74.
Ponsacco, 207.
Ponte dell' Adunata, 154.
—— S. Ambrogio, 25.
—— dell' Asse, 73.
—— della Badia, 71, 168.
—— a Botte, 128.
—— della Branca, 147.
—— Busco, 147.
—— della Castellina, 73.
—— Centesimo, 129.
—— Centino, 190.
—— a Elsa, 173.
—— Felcino, 147.
—— Felice, 261.
—— S. Giovanni, 246.
—— Gregoriano, 190.
—— Grosso, 128.
—— Lagoscuro, 10.
—— a Macereto, 207.
—— Manlio, 128.
—— Molle, 267.
—— Novo, 147.
—— Nuovo (Pesa), 204.
—— (Ronco and Montone), 92.
—— Patoli, 147.
—— della Rocca, 200.
—— Rotto, 204.
—— Salaro, 162.
—— Sanguinetto, 230.
—— de Tassi, 145.
—— del Terreno, 263.
—— della Trave, 125.
Pontedera, 207.
Popes, list of, xxxiii.
Populonia, ruins of, 163.
Porretta, la, 69.
—— waters of, 69.
Port of Ancona, 113.
—— Ercole, 167.
—— Fano, 110.

RAFFAELO.

Port of Pesaro, 108.
—— Ravenna, 91.
—— Recanati, 123.
—— Rimini, 104.
—— Sinigallia, 110.
Porta all' Arco, 209.
Porta, Guglielmo della, works by, 119, 120.
Portico, 72.
Porto, diocese of, 170.
Porto della Rosa, 261.
—— del Popolo, 268.
—— San Clementino, 169.
Portoferrajo, 164.
Portraits at Ferrara, 20.
Portus Trajani, 170.
Possera, valley of the, 218.
Post, Roman, 8.
Posting, 6.
—— tariff, 8.
Potassa, la, 165.
Potenza, la, 123, 125.
Pozzi, Padre, 224.
Pozzo di San Patrizio, 152.
Prat'antico, 222.
Prato, 173.
Prato, Card. di, 238.
Pratolino, 67.
Prefoglio, 125.
Prenner's ' Illustri Fatti Farnesiani,' 202.
Presciutti, works by, 107, 109.
Primo torrent, 145, 147.
Procaccini, Camillo, works by, 32, 46.
——, Ercole, works by, 45, 46, 47, 49.
Pronti, Cesare, works by, 86, 103.
Propertius, birthplace of, 252.
Provaglia, Alessandro, works by, 52.
Punicium, 171.
Puntone del Ponte, 198.
Pyrgos, 171.

Q.

Quaini, Francesco, works by, 54.
——, Luigi, works by, 45, 48.
Quatrelle, 10.
Quercia, Jacopo dalla, works by, 38, 179, 180, 181, 183, 184.
——, Madonna della, sanctuary and Domenican couvent of, 197.

R.

Radicofani, 189.
Raffaelo del Colle, works by, 135, 137, 139, 141, 142, 143, 144.

RAGONE.

Ragone torrent, 207.
Railroads, 5.
—— Florence to Siena, 172.
—— Leopolda, 173, 207.
Rambaldi, Carlo Antonio, works by, 47.
Ranuccio, Giacomo, works by, 53.
Raphael, birthplace of, 132. His connexion with the court of Urbino, 132. House of, 134. His residence at the court of Vitellozzo Vitelli, 136. Dispersion of his works, 136.
—— works by, 32, 47, 139, 141, 181, 187, 191, 241, 242, 243, 244, 245.
Rapinium, 169.
Rapolano, 206.
Ravenna:—Inns, 77. Historical notice, 78. The modern city, 80.
Churches:—Sta. Agata, 85; S. Apollinare Nuovo, 84; Baptistery, 81; Cathedral, 80; Sta. Croce, 85; S. Domenico, 84; S. Francesco, 85; S. Giovanni Battista, 83; S. Giovanni Evangelista, 83; Sta. Maria in Cosmedin, 85; Sta. Maria in Porto, 86; S. Michele in Affricisco, 85; S. Niccolò, 86; S. Romualdo, 86; Santo Spirito, 85; S. Vitale, 81; S. Vittore, 84.
Convent of Sta. Chiara, 86. Mausoleum of Galla Placidia, 86. Palace of Theodoric, 87. Tomb of Dante, 87. Palaces, 89. Library, 89. Museum, 90. Academy of the Fine Arts, 90. Hospital, 90. Theatre, 90. Piazza, 90. Torre del Pubblico, 91. Gates, 91. Fortress, 91. Port, 91.
Environs:—Mausoleum of Theodoric, 91. Sta. Maria in Porto Fuori, 92. S. Apollinare in Classe, 92. Pineta, 94. Colonna de' Francesi, 94.
Ravenna to Faenza, 73.
—— to Forlì, 73.
—— to Venice, 73.
—— to Bologna, 76, 95.
—— to Rimini, 95.
—— list of exarchs of, xxxii.
Razotta torrent, 71.
Razzali, Sebastiano, works by, 52.
Recanati, 122.
Reformation, the, at Ferrara, 13.
Redi, tomb of, 224.
Relics at Assisi, 251.
—— Bolsena, 191, 192.
—— Volterra, 212.
Reliquiary, silver, at Città di Castello, 137.

ROMAN.

Reliquiary, silver, of the Corporale of Bolsena, 152.
Renée, the Duchess, 13, 15, 19.
Reno, the, 23, 25, 68, 70.
—— valley, 69.
Republic, Roman, xxx.
Revenue of the Papal States, xi.
Reynolds, Sir J., 29.
Riario, Cardinal, 197.
—— Girolamo, murder of, 100.
Ricci, works by, 181.
Ricciarelli, Leonardo, works by, 211, 212.
Riccio, works by, 177, 180, 182, 185.
Ricorsi, 189.
Ridolfi, Claudio, works by, 109.
—— Marquis, Agricultural School founded by, at Mileto, 173.
Rieti to Rome, 160.
Rignano, 265.
Rigo, valley of the, 190.
Rigomagno, 206.
Rigossa, the, 101.
Rimane, 161.
Rimini:—Historical notice, 102. Arch of Augustus, 102. Cathedral, churches, 103. Palaces, 103. Port, fortress, library, 104. House of Francesca da Rimini, 104.
Rimini to Ravenna, 95.
Rio Maggiore, 163, 262.
Roads, 5.
Robbia, Agostino della, works by, 238.
—— Andrea della, works by, 224.
—— Luca della, works by, 107, 121, 141, 187, 197, 212, 223.
Robert of Geneva, Cardinal, his massacre of the inhabitants of Cesena, 101.
Rocca Romana, 265.
—— San Casciano, 72.
—— Silana, castle of, 208, 219.
—— di Varano, 125.
Romagna, la, 95.
Roman art, xxii.
Roman bishops and popes, list of, xxxiii.
—— emperors, xxx.
—— kings, xxx.
—— republic, xxx.
Roman remains at Ancona, 115.
—— at Arezzo, 225.
—— at Bolsena, 191.
—— near Cagli, 128.
—— at Campeglia, 164.
—— at Cortona, 228.
—— near Fossombrone, 126.
—— at Sta. Maria di Falleri, 263.
—— on Monte Razzano, 266.
—— near Musignano, 168.
—— at Nepi, 265.
—— near Orvieto, 154.
—— at Palmolara, 141.
—— at Populonia, 164.

SABBATINI.

Roman remains near Sambuchetto, 123.
—— at Spello, 252.
—— at Spoleto, 256.
—— at Terni, 257.
—— at Volterra, 209.
Romanelli, Gio. Francesco, works by, 194. 197.
—— Urbano, works by, 194.
Romano, Giulio, works by, 32, 58, 60, 106, 255.
Rome:—Passports, lascia passare, luggage, 268. Porto del Popolo, 268. Piazza del Popolo, 269. Obelisk, 269. Churches, Corso, Via Ripetta, Via Babuino, Piazza di Spagna, 269.
—— approach to, 267.
—— view of the country near, 266.
—— to Civita Vecchia, 170.
—— to Florence, by Siena, 172.
—— to Florence, by Civita Castellana, Spoleto, Foligno, Assisi, Perugia, Cortona, Arezzo, and the Val d' Arno di Sopra, 221.
—— to Perugia, 147.
—— to Rieti, 160.
Roncalli, works by, 115, 117, 118, 121, 217.
Ronciglione, 198, 202, 265.
Ronco, the, 73, 98, 100.
Rondinello, Niccolò, works by, 84.
Rosa, Salvator, works by, 58, 196, 245.
Rosaro, Constantino da, works by, 237.
Roselle, 207.
Rosselli, Matteo, works 1 y, 211.
—— Niccolò, works by, 18.
Rossetti, Gio. Paolo, works by, 215.
Rossi, Antonio, works by, 42.
—— Giacomo, works by, 49.
—— Properzia de', works by, 39, 40, 48, 56.
—— her death, 40.
Rosso, Maestro, works by, 241.
Rovere, 73.
—— la, house of, 131.
Rubens, works by, 90.
Rubicon, the, 96, 101. Its identity disputed, 101. Streams supposed to be the Rubicon, 102.
Ruffolo, 205.
Rufinus, St., 250.
Rupibus, Peter de, 197.
Rusellæ, ruins of, 165.

S.

SABATELLI, works by, 224.
Sabbatini, Lorenzo, works by, 29, 36, 44, 46, 57, 59, 64.

SACCA.

Sacca, Paolo, works by, 47.
Sacristies at Bologna, 37, 40, 43.
—— Borgo San Sepolcro, 143.
—— Città di Castello, 137.
—— Loreto, 120.
—— Perugia, 237.
—— Pesaro, 105.
—— Ravenna, 81, 83, 86.
—— Siena, 181.
—— Urbino, 133.
—— Viterbo, 194.
—— Volterra, 212.
Salica torrent, 207.
Salimbeni, works by, 177, 182, 183, 240.
Salsernus, works by, 255.
Salt-lake near Monte Argentaro, 167.
Salt-works of the Albegna, 166.
—— at Cervia, 95.
—— of S. Leopoldo, 216.
Salutati, Colluccio, 174.
Samacchini, Orazio, works by, 29, 37, 46, 49, 57, 59, 64.
Sambuca, 204.
Sambuchetto, 123.
Samoggia, 25.
San Andrea, 130.
—— Angelo, 161.
—— Angelo in Vado, 135.
—— Benedetto, 72.
—— Casciano, 204.
—— Clementino, 169.
—— Cristoforo, 145.
—— Dalmazzo, 176.
—— Donato, Pass of, 221.
—— Donino, 173.
—— Facondino, 129.
—— Fiorenzo, 144.
—— Flaviano, 193 ; church of, 149.
—— Gaggio, 204.
—— Galgano, 207.
—— Gemini, 148.
—— Giacomo, 254.
—— Gimignano, 173, 174. Palaces, 175. Frescoes, 175. Torri degl. Ardinghelli, 175. Churches, 175. Penitentiary, 175.
—— Giorgio, Count di, 200.
—— Giovanni (Val d'Arno), 221.
—— Giovanni on the Cecina, 163.
—— Giovanni pro Fiamma, 129.
—— Giovanni in Pietro, 135.
—— Giustino, 135.
—— —— to Borgo Sepolcro and Arezzo, 142.
—— Godenzo, 72.
—— Ippolito, 127.
—— Leo, 222.
—— Lorenzo, 154.
—— —— Nuovo, 191.
—— —— Vecchio, 191.
—— Manno, Tempio di, 236.
—— Marcello, 125.
—— Marco, 125.
—— Marino, republic of, 104.

SASSO.

Its constitution, 105. Hamlet of Borgo, 105. Origin and history of the republic, 105. Cavern, 106. Collection of the Cavaliere Borghese, 106.
San Martino, 265.
—— in Colle, 148.
—— al Piano, 126.
—— Miniato dei Tedeschi, 173.
—— Niccolò, 96.
—— Oreste, 264.
—— Paolo, 129.
—— Piero, 71.
—— Pietro, church, 160.
—— Prospero, 71.
—— Quirico, 189, 205.
—— Salvatore, Badia di, 215.
—— Sisto, 148.
—— Stefano, 167.
—— —— farms belonging to the Order of, 226.
—— Vincenzio, 163.
Sanctuary of Loreto, 117.
Sangallo, works by, 119, 121, 153, 204, 235, 245.
—— his portfolio, 186.
Sanguinara torrent, 171.
Sanseverino, Domenico di, works by, 248.
—— Jacopo da, works by, 124, 133.
—— Lorenzo, works by, 124, 133.
Sansovino, Andrea, works by, 18, 39, 119, 212.
Santa Casa of Loreto, 117, 118.
—— Chiara, tomb of, 250.
—— Colomba, 161.
—— Eufemia, 71.
—— Margherita, tomb of, 230.
—— Maria, 76.
—— —— degli Angeli, 247.
—— —— di Colonnata, 145.
—— —— di Falieri, 263.
—— Marinella, 171.
—— Rufina, diocese of, 170.
—— Severa, 171.
Santerno, the, 76, 97.
Santi, Domenico, works by, 57.
—— Giovanni, works by, 106, 107, 109, 128, 133, 134.
Sarcophagi at Ancona, 114, 115.
—— at Bieda, 200.
—— at Bologna, 37, 42.
—— at Chiusi, 156.
—— at Cortona, 229.
—— at Fano, 109.
—— at Ferrara, 109.
—— at Ravenna, 84, 86, 87, 88, 92, 93.
—— at Rimini, 103.
—— near Rome, 267.
—— at Viterbo, 197.
—— at Volterra, 209.
Sarteano, 159.
Sarto, Andrea del, works by, 121, 244, 245.
Sasso di Castro, 66.
—— Il, pass of, 68.
—— di Pale, 126.

SIENA.

Sassoferrato, works by, 90, 109, 115, 240, 244.
Saturnia, ruins of, 168.
Savena valley, 65.
—— river, 96.
Savignano, 101.
—— castle, ruins of, 69.
Savio, the, 95, 100.
Scala, la, 189.
Scalza, Ippolito, works by, 151, 152, 153, 237, 245.
Scaminossi, Raffaelo, works by, 143.
Scarabelli, works by, 54.
Scaramuccia, works by, 54.
Scarsellino, works by, 15, 16, 17.
Schidone, works by, 121.
Schiegggia, la, 128.
Schools of painting, xxvi.
Scimia, Deposito della, 158.
Scritto, 145.
Sculpture, Christian, xxv.
—— , Grecian, at Siena, 181 ; fine altar by Marzini, 182 ; early Christian sculptures at Capranica, 201 ; at Volterra, illustrating ancient mythology, 210.
Scuole Pie at Bologna, 59.
—— Fathers of the, 186, 213.
Seccadenari, Ercole, works by, 38.
Segna, Nicolo di, works by, 178.
Sejanus, birthplace of, 191.
Sementi, works by, 50.
Semonte, 145.
Senatus-Consultum, 101.
Senio, the, 77, 97.
Sentina, 129.
Seriate torrent, 189.
Sermei, Cesare, works by, 249.
Sermide, 10.
Serodine, Giovanni, works by, 137.
Serra di Genga, 134.
Serravalle, 105, 125.
Serre, 206.
Serri, works by, 183.
Servius Tullius, birthplace of, 161.
Setta valley, 68.
Sette Vene, 265.
Settignano, Balsimelli da, works by, 212.
—— Desiderio da, bust by, 99.
Sforza, rival of Fortebraccio, 234, 239.
—— Attendolo, 77.
—— Battista, 131.
—— Catherine, 100.
Sicciolante, Girolamo, works by, 50.
Siciliano, Giacomo, works by, 255.
Siele torrent, 190.
Siena :—Inns, 176. Diligences, 176, 188. Railroad, 176, Roads from Siena, 188. Historical notice, 176. School of Siena, 177. Istituto delle

SIENA.

Belle Arte, 177. Tolomei College, 182; Gates, 186. Citadel, 186. Lizza, 186. Festival of St. Catherine, 186. Franciscan convent, 187. Castle of Belcaro, 187. Manners and language of the Sienese, 187. Climate, 187. Duomo, 178-181. Baptistery, 181.
Churches: — S. Agostino, 182; Carmine, 182; la Concessione, 182; S. Domenico, 182; S. Francesco, 182; Fonte Giusta, 182; S. Giorgio, 183; S. Martino, 183; S. Quirico, 183; dei Servi, 182; S. Spirito, 183; La Trinità, 183.
Oratories: — House of St. Catherine of Siena, the Fullonica, 183.
Public buildings: — Accademia degli Intronati (the library), 185. Casino de' Nobili, 183. Collegio Tolomei, 186. Hospital, 186. Loggia di S. Paolo, 183. Palazzo Buonsignori, 185; P. del Governo, 185; P. del Magnifico, 185; P. Pannilini, 185; P. Piccolomineo, 185; P. Piccolomini, 185; P. Pollini, 185; P. Pubblico, 183; P. Saracini, 185; P. Tolomei, 185. Piazza del Campo, 183. University, 185.
Siena to Arezzo, 205.
—— to Chiusi, 205.
—— to Florence, 204.
—— to Grosseto, 206.
Siena, Agnolo da, works by, 179, 181, 182, 184, 186, 224.
—— Agostino da, works by, 179, 181, 182, 184, 186, 224.
—— Bartolino of, works by, 180.
—— Benvenuto da, works by, 212.
—— Berna da, works by, 177.
—— Bernardino da, works by, 212.
—— Fra Gabriele Mattei of, works by, 181.
—— Giovanni da, works by, 179.
—— Goro di Gregorio da, works by, 185.
—— Guido da, works by, 177, 182.
—— Marco da, works by, 177.
—— Matteo di, works by, 178, 182.
—— Michaelangelo da, works by, 177.
—— Pastorino of, works by, 179.
Sieve valley, 66, 71, 72.
Sigillo, 129.
Signa, 173.
Signorelli, Luca, works by, 118,

STATUES.

120, 138, 139, 141, 143, 150, 152, 153, 154, 178, 182, 185, 189, 212, 213, 224, 229, 230, 237, 245.
Silaro, the, 96.
Silk manufacture, 97, 125, 126, 257.
Silos, 227.
Simone, Sermino di, works by, 184.
Singerna, valley of the, 144.
Sinigallia, 110. Port, 110. History, 110. Convent, 111. Fair, 111.
Sirani, Andrea, works by, 44, 48, 63.
—— Elisabetta, works by, 32, 48, 53, 63.
Sixtus V., statue of, 118.
Sodoma, works by, 177, 178, 182, 183, 184, 185, 186, 189, 212, 213.
Sole, Giuseppe dal, works by, 36.
Solimene, works by, 250.
Soracte, Mons, 264.
Sorbolungo, 127.
Sorore, Fra, 186.
Soubise, Madame de, 13.
Sovana, ruins of, 168.
Sovara, valley of the, 143, 144.
Sovrano, Deposito del, 158.
Spada, Lionello, works by, 42, 43, 48, 56.
Spagna, Lo, works by, 240, 247, 248, 249, 255, 260.
Spagnoletto, works by, 182.
Spello: — Gate, cathedral, churches, 251. Roman remains, 252. View from, 252.
Spelunca, la, 230.
Spina, 75.
Spoleto: — Inns, manufacture, 254. Historical notice, 254. Cathedral, 254. Churches, 255. Palace, piazza, 255. Citadel, 255. Aqueduct, 255. Antiquities, 256.
Spoleto, duchy of, 254.
Springs, hot, at Talamonaccio, 166.
—— mineral, at Bagnarea, 149.
—— —— Bagni, 154.
—— —— Chianciano, 159.
—— —— Civita Vecchia, 170.
—— —— Nocera, 129.
—— —— Rapolano, 206.
—— salt, of S. Leopoldo, 216.
—— sulphur, at Rusellæ, 165.
Squazzino, works by, 137, 138.
Staffa, Count, 244.
Staggia, 175, 176; valley of the, 205.
Stagio, works by, 212.
Statilius Taurus, amphitheatre of, 203.
Statues at Ancona, 115.
—— Bologna, 33, 34, 40, 41, 43, 48, 49, 51, 54, 55.
—— Bolsena, 191.
—— Cesena, 100.

TEMPLE.

Statues at Fano, 108.
—— Ferrara, 14, 17, 18.
—— Loreto, 118, 119.
—— Sta. Maria di Falleri, 264.
—— Nepi, 265.
—— Orvieto, 151, 152, 153.
—— Osimo, 117.
—— Perugia, 241.
—— Rimini, 104.
—— Rome, 269.
—— Siena, 180, 183, 186.
Steam-packets at Ancona, 116.
—— Civita Vecchia, 169.
Stellata, 10.
Sterza river, 207.
Storta, la, 267.
St. Peter's, piazza of, 172.
Strada Anconitana, 143.
—— del Littorale, 163.
Straw-hat manufacture, 135.
Straw-plait manufacture, 173.
Stretta, 135.
Strettura, la, 256.
Subterranean church, 137.
Succinium, 201.
Sulphur-mines near Cesena, 101.
Sutri, 198, 202.
Sutrium, 202.

T.

TABULA Cibellaria, 197.
Tacco, Ghino di, 189.
Tacitus, birthplace of, 257.
Tadolini, Francesco, works by, 39, 54.
—— Petronio, works by, 39, 49.
Taglio del Pò, 74.
Talamonaccio, 166.
Talamone, 166.
Tambroni, Matilda, 33.
Tamburini, works by, 49, 60.
Tapestries at Loreto, 122.
Tarlati, Guido, of Pietramala, tomb of, 223.
Tarquinian lake, 192.
Tarsia-work at Siena, 180.
Tartagni, Alessandro, tomb of, 42.
Tarugi, Cardinal, 179.
Tasso, MSS. of, 19, 107.
—— prison of, 21.
—— house of, 107.
—— his offering at Loreto, 122.
Tavernelle, 148.
Taverne d' Arbia, 205.
Tavollo, the, 106.
Tedaldi, Lattanzio, 174.
Tedesco, Jacopo, works by, 248.
—— Marco, works by, 61.
Tempesta, works by, 201, 202.
Temple of Clitumnus, 253.
—— of Jupiter Apenninus, ruins of, 128.
—— of Lucina, 171.
—— of Minerva at Assisi, portico of the ancient, 250.

TENERANI.

Tenerani, works by, 181, 247.
Teniers, works by, 90.
Teodosio, works by, 53.
Terni :— Inns, manufactures, 257. Cathedral, 257. Antiquities, 257.
—— plain of, 256.
—— falls of, 257.
—— valley of, 259.
Terra del Sole, 73.
Terranova, 222.
Terranova, Fra Francesco di, works by, 248.
Terribilia, works by, 41, 47, 53, 54, 59, 60.
Tesi, Mauro, works by, 50.
Theatres at Bologna, 60.
—— Fano, 110.
—— Férento, ruins of, 193.
—— Ferrara, 22.
—— Grosseto, 165.
—— Imola, 96.
—— Orvieto, 154.
—— Ravenna, 90.
—— Urbino, 134.
Theodoric, palace of, 87.
—— mausoleum of, 91.
Thorwaldsen, bust by, 89.
Thrasimene, lake of, 230.
Tiarini, Alessandro, works by, 30, 37, 39, 41, 44, 46, 49, 50, 52, 53, 60.
Tibaldi, Domenico, works by, 37.
—— Pellegrino, works by, 29, 33, 46, 57, 115, 120.
Tiber, valley and river, 135, 143, 144, 147, 148, 150, 161, 172, 246.
—— source of, 246.
Timia, the, 252.
Tintoretto, works by, 32, 50, 58, 90.
Titian, works by, 17, 58, 115, 121, 133, 178, 241, 244.
Tito, Santi di, works by, 138, 139, 142, 211.
Todi, 148.
Tolentino :— Gateway, Cathedral, 124. Historical notice, 125.
Tolfa, 170, 171.
Tolomei College, 182, 186.
Tomb of Dante, 87.
—— of Nero, 267.
Tombs, Etruscan, at Chiusi, 157.
—— —— near Sarteano, 159.
—— —— at Civita Castellano, 262.
—— Roman, at Sta. Maria di Falleri, 263.
Tombolo, il, 164.
Tommasi, Giambattista, tomb of, 229.
Tommasini, 33.
Tonghi, Francesco, works by, 180.
Topina, valley and river, 129, 252.

URBANO.

Topography of the Papal States, vii.
Torre, village, 231.
—— degli Auguri, 214.
—— Chiarruccia, 171.
—— Giuliana, 262.
—— della Mangia, 183, 184.
—— del Mastio, 214.
—— di Monte, 150.
—— del Vescovo, 139.
Torrenieri, 189.
Torretta, 112.
Torri degl. Ardinghelli, 175.
Torricella, 190, 233.
Torricelli, 227.
Torricelli, mathematician, birthplace of, 98.
Torrita, 206, 226.
Toscanella, 168.
Toti, Fabiano, works by, 151, 152.
Totila, defeat and death of, 129.
Tower of Bertaldo, or Sant' Agostino, 169.
" Tower of Hannibal the Carthaginian," 231.
Towers at Bologna, 58.
—— at San Gimigniano, 175.
—— at Sta. Maria di Falleri, 263.
—— at Ravenna, 91.
Tozzo, Il, works by, 185.
Trajan, arch of, 113.
Treaty of Tolentino, 125.
Trèja, the, 262.
Trevi, 253.
Treviso, Girolamo da, works by, 39, 52.
Triachini, Bartolommeo, works by, 33.
Tribolo, works by, 38, 39, 119.
Triglia, the, 266.
Troppola, 147.
Tuoma river, 189.
Turamini, Crescentius, 187.
Turano, the, 160.
Tuscan agriculture, 173.
Tuscany, list of grand dukes of, xxxvii.
Tusci, Pliny's villa, 141.

U.

UBERTI, Farinata degli, 176.
Udine, Lodovico da, works by, 248.
Ugoni, Filippio, 27.
Ulma, Giacomo da, works by, 50.
Umbria, the ancient, 246.
——, school of, 236.
University of Bologna, 32.
—— of Camerino, 125.
—— of Perugia, 243.
Urbania, 135.
Urbano, Forte, 25.

VENTUROLI.

Urbino, delegation of, 129.
—— historical notice of the dukedom of, 130.
—— city of, 130. Inns, 130. Historical notice, 130. Eminent natives, 132. Ducal palace, 132. Fortifications, 133. Cathedral, churches, 133. Convent, 134. House of Raphael, 134. Theatre, manufactures, college, diligence, 134.
Urbino to Città di Castello, 134.
—— to Fano, 130.
——, list of dukes of, xxxvii.

V.

VACCINIA, 171.
Vadimon, Lake, 198.
Vaga, Pierino del, works by, 179, 244.
Val d'Arno, 173, 207, 221.
—— Cecina, 207.
—— di Chiana, 154, 159, 222, 226.
—— d' Era, 207.
—— Possera, 218.
Valcimara, 125.
Valdemone, lake, 198.
Valesio, works by, 52.
Valiano, locks of, 227.
Vallata Romana, 232.
Valle di Comacchio, 74.
Vandervelde, works by, 90.
Vandyke, works by, 141.
Vanni, the elder, works by, 230.
—— Andrea di, works by, 177.
—— Francesco, works by, 177, 182, 183 ; his tomb, 183.
—— Onofrio, works by, 175.
—— Raffaele, works by, 183.
Vanvitelli, works by, 182.
Varignano, works by, 119.
Vasari, birthplace of, 222.
——, works by, 32, 90, 138, 141, 178, 211, 223, 224, 227, 240.
—— his Lives of the Painters, xxix.
Vases, Etruscan, 156.
Vassalva, anatomist, 97.
Vatican, bastions of, 172.
Vecchi, Giovanni de', works by, 143.
Vecchietta, works by, 180, 181.
Vecchio, Palma, works by, 16, 109.
Velathri, 208.
Velimnas, Arnth and Larth, 235.
Velino, the, 257.
—— plain of, 258.
Vene, le, 253.
Venice to Ravenna, 73.
Venturoli, Angelo, works by, 49.

VENUSTI.

Venusti, Marcello, works by, 196.
Venuti, Ridolfino, 229.
Vergatello torrent, 69.
Vergato, 69.
Vergil, Polydore, birthplace of, 132.
Veri, Ugolino, reliquary by, 152.
Vermiglioli, Cav., 235, 244.
Verona, Fra Giovanni da, works by, 180.
Veronese, Paolo, works by, 103.
Verzelli, Tiburzio, works by, 118, 120.
Vetralla, 198, 199.
Vetturini, 8.
Vetulonia, site of, 166, 167.
Via Æmilia, 96, 100, 102.
—— Amerina, 194, 265, 266.
—— Aurelia, 166, 171, 172.
—— Babuino, 269.
—— Cassia, 194, 226, 227, 265, 266.
—— Claudia, 200.
—— del Crocifisso, 214.
—— Flaminia, 102, 126, 127, 129, 147, 253, 260, 269.
—— Leopolda, 70.
—— Nomentana, 160.
—— Ripetta, 269.
—— Salaria, 160.
Viani, Giovanni, works by, 52.
Viarini, Alessandro, works by, 109.
Vicano torrent, 262.
Vicentini, Alessandro, works by, 17.
Vicenza, Antonio, architect, 38.
Vicus Matrini, 198, 201.
Vigilio, S., Jesuits' College of, at Siena, 185.
Vignola, works by, 39, 55, 57, 197, 201, 202, 247, 268.
Vitro, destruction of, 69.
Vigri, Santa Caterina, works by, 29.
Villa, village of, 143.
—— of Antoninus Pius, 171.
—— Bacciocchi, 207.
—— Baglioni, 235.
—— Imperiale, 107.
—— Inghirami, 214.
—— Lante, 197.

VOLTERRA.

Villa Machiavelli, 204.
—— Pamfili Doria, 172.
—— Poggio Imperiale, 204.
—— of Pompey, 171.
—— Savorelli, 203.
—— Spada, 161.
—— di Torre à Cona, 221.
—— Vittoria, 108.
—— Zollio, 104.
Villani, Giovanni, 195.
Vinci, Leonardo da, works by, 90, 196.
Vitali, Giobattista, works by, 120.
Vite, Timoteo delle, works by, 32, 128, 133.
Vitelli, house of the, 136.
Viterbo:—Inns, 194. Cathedral, 194. Episcopal palace, 195. Churches, 196. Museum, 197. Fountains, 197. Domenican convent, 197. Palazzo San Martino, 197. P. Pubblico, 196. Fairs, 197.
Viterbo, Lorenzo di Giacomo da, works by, 196.
Vitorchiano, 193.
Viviani the mathematician, 227.
Viviani, works by, 109.
Volaterræ, 208.
Volsinii, 191.
Volta, 66.
Volterra:—Inns, 208. Walls, 208. Gates, 209. Necropolis, 209. Piscina and baths, 209. Palazzo Pubblico, 209. Library, 211. Cathedral, 211. Churches, 212. Citadel, 213. Prison (Il Mastio), 213. Casa Guarnacci, 214. C. Ducci, 214. C. Ricciarelli, 214. C. Masselli, 214. Alabaster manufactories, 214.— *Environs:* Villa Inghirami, 214. Balze, 214. Camaldolese monastery of S. Salvatore, 215. — *Excursions:* Copper-mines of La Cava, 215. Monte Massi, 216. Salt-works of S. Leopoldo, 216. Boracic Acid Works of Lardarello, 217. Castle of Rocca Silana, 219. Volterra to Florence (the La-

ZUCCARI.

goni, and Massa Maritima), 207.
Volterra, Daniele da, works by, 90, 214.
Volterrano, Il, works by, 212, 213, 215.
—— Antonio, 212.
Volumnii, tomb of the, 235.
Vouet, Simon, works by, 121.
Vulci, ruins of, 168.

W.

WEIGHTS and measures, 4.
Welden, General, 27.
Whiteside, Mr., xxix.
Wicar, Cav., works by, 237, 240.
Wines of Arezzo, 226.
—— of Montalcino; 189.
—— of Montepulciano, 159.
Wiseman, Cardinal, on the Christian monuments of Ravenna, 78. On the fair of Sinigallia, 111.
Women of Ancona, 116.
Woollen manufacture, 252, 254, 257.

X.

XAVIER, S. Francis, letter of, 47. His chamber, 48.

Z.

ZANOTTI, works by, 37, 50.
Zeneroli, the Canonico, his portico at Bologna, 62.
Zeppoloni, Giambattista, guide, 155.
Zocchi, Giuseppe, works by, 213.
Zuccari, Federigo, works by, 120, 135, 201.
—— Ottaviano, works by, 201.
—— Taddeo, works by, 153, 201, 268.

LONDON: PRINTED BY W. CLOWES AND SONS, STAMFORD STREET.

www.ingramcontent.com/pod-product-compliance
Ingram Content Group UK Ltd.
Pitfield, Milton Keynes, MK11 3LW, UK
UKHW020817161225
9594UKWH00048B/1100

9 781023 896894